DocBook XSL:
The Complete Guide

Fourth Edition

Bob Stayton

Sagehill Enterprises

DocBook XSL: The Complete Guide

Bob Stayton
Copyright © 2002-2007 Sagehill Enterprises

Fourth Edition
Published September, 2007
ISBN: 978-0-9741521-3-4

Warning and Disclaimer

Trademarks

Sagehill Enterprises

PO Box 2911
Santa Cruz CA
95063-2911
Website:
http://www.sagehill.net
<info@sagehill.net>

Contents

Part III. Customizing DocBook XSL

Part IV. Special DocBook features

Preface

The nature of publishing has changed so much over the last twenty years that anybody can be a publisher these days. Now you can reach a world-wide audience by putting a few HTML pages up on your website. Or you can use desktop publishing software to produce beautifully typeset material that can be printed on demand or downloaded to a printer anywhere in the world. With DocBook, you can publish both ways from the same source material.

What is DocBook?

DocBook is a collection of standards and tools for technical publishing. DocBook was originally created by a consortium of software companies as a standard for computer documentation. But the basic "book" features of DocBook can be used for other kinds of content, so it has been adapted to many purposes.

The core DocBook standard is the *DocBook Document Type Definition (DTD)* maintained by the DocBook Technical Committee in *OASIS*[1]. The DTD defines the vocabulary of content elements that an author can use and how they relate to each other. For example, a `book` element can contain a `title` element, any number of `para` elements for paragraphs, and any number of `chapter` elements. Using the DTD and XML syntax, authors mark up their text content with tag names enclosed in angle brackets like `<chapter>`. The markup is similar to HTML, but with more tags and tighter rules.

Text that is marked up in this standard way can be processed by any number of software tools. A major advantage of DocBook is the availability of DocBook tools from many sources, not just from a single vendor of a proprietary file format. You can mix and match components for editing, typesetting, version control, and HTML conversion. You can assemble a custom system that is well suited to your needs, and many of the components are available for free.

The other major advantage of DocBook is the set of free stylesheets that are available for it. Written by Norman Walsh in the Extensible Stylesheet Language (XSL), these stylesheets enable anyone to publish their DocBook content in print and HTML. The stylesheets are now developed and maintained as an open-source project on *SourceForge*[2]. An active community of users and contributors keeps up the development of the stylesheets and answers questions.

As a publishing system, DocBook is best suited for any of these situations:

- Large quantities of content.

- Highly structured content.

- Content that needs to be interchanged among otherwise incompatible systems.

- Content that needs automated batch processing.

---

[1] http://www.oasis-open.org/docbook/
[2] http://sourceforge.net/projects/docbook/

- Content to be rendered in multiple output forms and versions.

DocBook is not a WYSIWYG word processor (although graphical editors are available for DocBook). DocBook is hardly worth the trouble for short or one-off documents. And since the formatting is strictly by batch process with stylesheets, DocBook is not well matched to highly designed layout-driven content like magazines.

DocBook is well suited to any collection of technical documentation that is regularly maintained and published. Because you are not locked into a single vendor, you have flexibility in your choice of processes and tools, both now and in the future. Multiple authors can contribute, and their content can easily be merged because all the authors are using a standard markup language. The files are plain text, not binary, so they also work well with most version control systems.

Setting up a DocBook system will take some time and effort. But the payoff will be an efficient, flexible, and inexpensive publishing system that can grow with your needs.

Audience

This book is for people who want to publish DocBook XML files using the DocBook XSL stylesheets. It is a "how to" guide that gets you up and running quickly, and then provides the details you need to gain access to the full power of DocBook. The book covers:

- Obtaining and setting up XSL tools and the DocBook XSL stylesheets.

- Using the built-in options to control the XSL stylesheets.

- Customizing the XSL stylesheets to match your design needs.

(This book does not cover the SGML version of DocBook, nor the DocBook DSSSL stylesheets.)

You do not need to be an XML expert to use DocBook XSL. You will need to know about XML elements and attributes, since you will be working with DocBook XML files. And you will need to know how to execute commands by typing them on a command line rather than through a point-and-click interface. If you know nothing about XSL, you can still use the stylesheets to generate high-quality output. You can also customize to a degree using the built-in stylesheet parameters. Learning some XSL will enable you to more fully customize the output. This book can teach you basic XSL, and provides dozens of examples that you can use and learn from.

This book will not show you how to write DocBook documents. The best reference for writing in DocBook is *DocBook: The Definitive Guide* by Norman Walsh. That book has been made available by O'Reilly Books for reading from the web at *http://docbook.org/tdg/en/html/docbook.html*. Keep that link bookmarked for future reference. A printed and bound version of the book is also available from O'Reilly Books, but it is a bit out of date now. The online book documents the most recent version of the DTD.

Changes in the Fourth Edition

Here is a list of the major changes since the Third Edition of *DocBook XSL: The Complete Guide*. The Fourth Edition covers version 1.73 of the DocBook XSL stylesheets and versions 4.5 and 5.0 of the DocBook XML schema. Links to websites are up-to-date as of August 2007.

- Updated Java product names and version numbers in Table 3.2, "Java versions" (page 19).
- Describe control of FO root messages in the section called "Using FOP" (page 27).
- Add Chapter 4, *DocBook 5 tools* (page 33).
- Info on prefer="public" not working as expected in the section called "Example DocBook catalog file" (page 52).
- Add the section called "Filename prefix" (page 64).
- Use chunkfast.xsl stylesheet rather than chunk.fast parameter in the section called "Fast chunking" (page 66).

- Add Table 7.1, "Number formats for autolabel parameters" (page 75).
- Add SVG callout icons in the section called "Callout icons" (page 93).
- Add the section called "Crop marks" (page 94).
- Add the section called "Utility templates and modes" (page 109).
- New section on adding new templates in the section called "Adding new templates" (page 111).
- Add the section called "Customizing DocBook 5 XSL" (page 116).
- Add the section called "Set TOC" (page 129).
- Add the section called "Adding elements to a TOC" (page 133).
- Add the section called "Formal title numbering" (page 136).
- Add the section called "Formal title customization" (page 137).
- Add the section called "Generate custom class values" (page 147).
- Add the section called "Bread crumbs" (page 150).
- Add the section called "Changing the <h> levels" (page 159).
- Add the section called "How chunking works" (page 162).
- Add the section called "Footer link to legalnotice" (page 165).
- Add Return To Top links in the section called "Return to top" (page 166).
- Add the section called "Head links for legalnotice" (page 166).
- Add the section called "Customized hrefs" (page 167).
- Add the section called "Hyphenation" (page 170).
- Add the section called "Run-in section titles" (page 178).
- Add the section called "Additional front or back matter" (page 193).
- Add the section called "Book covers" (page 194).
- Add the section called "Landscape page sequence" (page 199).
- Add the section called "Custom page sequences" (page 204).
- Add controlling TOC margins in the section called "TOC Page margins" (page 206).
- Add the section called "Part TOC on part titlepage" (page 210).
- Add customizing head.sep.rule in the section called "Changing header or footer styles" (page 218).
- Add the section called "Page x of y numbering" (page 222).
- Describe Arabic-Indic numbering in the section called "Page number format" (page 222).
- Underline and strikethrough text in the section called "Underline and strike-through" (page 228).
- Add the section called "Side-by-side formatting" (page 230).
- Add the section called "Clearing a side float" (page 237).
- Add the section called "Multi-columns and spans" (page 238).
- Updated FOP font configuration in the section called "Configuring a font in FOP" (page 241).
- Add numbering paragraphs customization in the section called "Numbering paragraphs" (page 244).
- Add line break processing instruction in the section called "Adding line breaks" (page 245).
- Added the section called "ISO 690 bibliography standard" (page 254).
- Add the section called "RefDB bibliographic database" (page 255).
- Add the section called "Breaking long URLs" (page 261).
- Add the section called "DocBook 5 cross references" (page 262).
- Add `insert.link.page.number` parameter in the section called "Using "select:"" (page 263).
- Add the section called "Customizing page citations" (page 266).
- Add the section called "Customizing cross reference behavior" (page 269).
- Glossary sorting was added in the section called "Glossary sorting" (page 284).
- Add the section called "Graphic size extension" (page 291).
- Add the section called "Landscape images" (page 292).
- Add the section called "Inline graphics" (page 296).
- Add the section called "SVG DTD" (page 301).
- Add the section called "Imagemaps" (page 303).
- Add the section called "EPS to SVG" (page 303).
- Add the section called "XSL-FO processor indexing extensions" (page 322).
- Add the section called "Index punctuation" (page 322).
- Add the section called "Space characters" (page 330).

- Add font family list and Unicode font information to the section called "FO font-family list" (page 331).
- Add the section called "Text direction" (page 335).
- Add the section called "Print properties for itemizedlist" (page 344) and the section called "Print properties for orderedlist" (page 347).
- Add the section called "Multiple term elements" (page 347).
- Add the section called "simplelist options" (page 349).
- Add mathphrase to the section called "Plain text math" (page 353).
- Add the section called "Equation numbering" (page 356).
- Clarify xpointer() scheme in Note (page 362).
- Add the section called "Putting customized entities in the DTD" (page 373).
- Changed Java XIncluder to use XOM jar file in the section called "Using XIncluder in XOM to resolve XIncludes" (page 377).
- Add the section called "Using an XSL-FO processor with XIncludes" (page 378).
- Add the section called "Using modified id values" (page 380).
- Tip on using document id for targetdoc for olinking, in the section called "How to link between documents" (page 383).
- Clarify that olink filename parameters can include directory names in the section called "Target database location" (page 391).
- Add the section called "Target database location" (page 391).
- Add the section called "Open target in new window" (page 394).
- Describe nodocname xrefstyle value for olinks in the section called "Using xrefstyle attributes" (page 396).
- Add the section called "Customizing the olink template" (page 397).
- Add the section called "Microsoft Word" (page 425).
- Add xsl:output with doctype in the section called "Validation and profiling" (page 432).
- Add the section called "Adding new profiling attributes" (page 434).
- Add the section called "Adding attributes to RelaxNG" (page 435).
- Add the section called "Formatting listings" (page 440).
- Add the section called "Tab expansion" (page 440).
- Show template that handles callout number sequencing in the section called "Callouts" (page 447).
- Add the section called "Q and A cross references" (page 458).
- Add the section called "Q and A in table of contents" (page 460).
- Add Chapter 29, *Revision control* (page 461).
- Add table centering in the section called "Table alignment" (page 473).
- Add the section called "Full-width tables" (page 474).
- Add the section called "table.row.properties template" (page 489).
- Add the section called "tabstyle template" (page 489).
- Add SilkPage to Website in the section called "SilkPage: enhanced Website" (page 520).
- Remove the section on dbtexmath since PassiveTex no longer supported.

Acknowledgements

DocBook is an open source standard with a large number of contributors. The author would like to thank Norman Walsh in particular for writing most of the DocBook XSL stylesheets and freely giving them to the world. His depth of technical knowledge and quality of programming skills are the main reasons the stylesheets work so well. I learned most of my XSL from reading his stylesheets. I also owe thanks to the other members of the DocBook community, especially Jirka Kosek, Dave Pawson, Robert P. J. Day, Jeff Beal, and Michael Smith, who contributed suggestions and valuable feedback on early drafts. Thanks also go to the members of the docbook-apps mailing list that sent me corrections and suggestions. Finally, I want to thank Mary (the "DocBook widow") for supporting me and cheering me on during this long effort.

Part I. Setting up the tools

Contents

1

Introduction

The *Extensible Stylesheet Language (XSL)*[1] is a formal Recommendation put forward by the *World Wide Web Consortium (W3C)*[2] as a language for expressing stylesheets. It complements the *Extensible Markup Language (XML)*[3] by providing the methods for formatting content written in XML. One of the major goals of XML was keeping content and its semantic markup separate from its formatting, so that formatting could be applied independently. An XSL stylesheet describes the formatting that can be applied to XML files using an XSL processor. The XSL standard and XSL processors are described more fully in Chapter 2, *XSL processors* (page 7).

The DocBook XSL stylesheets were written by Norman Walsh to help people publish their DocBook content with XSL. The stylesheets are now an open-source project maintained on *SourceForge*[4]. The stylesheet distribution consists of a collection of modular XSL files that are assembled into several complete XSL stylesheets. There is a stylesheet for generating a single HTML file, and one for generating multiple smaller HTML files from a single DocBook document. There are stylesheets for print output, XHTML output, HTML Help output, and JavaHelp output. The stylesheet collection is freely available for download. Since there are XSL processors for all major computer types, you can use DocBook on Unix, Linux, Windows, and Macintosh computers.

This book shows you how to use and customize the DocBook XSL stylesheets. It unlocks the power of these stylesheets by documenting all of their features and making them easy to use.

How this book is organized

Applying an XSL stylesheet to an XML file is a very straightforward process, once you get the tools working. **Part I** of this book tells you how to obtain and set up the XSL tools. It covers several XSL processors, and provides essential details for each one. It also covers XML Catalogs, which are used to map file references to actual directory locations on your system. XML Catalogs make the tools more versatile and portable.

Once you have the tools working, you can generate formatted print and HTML output from your DocBook XML documents. As you use the stylesheets, you will probably want to change certain aspects about the format or processing. The DocBook stylesheets provide a large number of options. The options are in the form of stylesheet parameters, which let you assign a value to a named variable that is used in the stylesheet. You can do quite a bit

---

[1] http://www.w3.org/Style/XSL/
[2] http://www.w3.org
[3] http://www.w3.org/XML/
[4] http://sourceforge.net/projects/docbook/

of customization of your output using just the parameters. **Part II** of this book describes the various stylesheet parameters and how to use them.

You will turn to **Part III** when you want to change something but you cannot find a parameter to do it. At that point you will need to do some stylesheet customization, which is done using the XSL language. You'll need to learn the syntax and methods of XSL, so that you can write a customization file with it. The chapters in Part III describe the methods of customization, as well as many applications for HTML and print output. You can use Appendix A, *A brief introduction to XSL* (page 521) to get started with XSL, but it is beyond the scope of this book to teach you all about XSL. You will need a good XSL reference book to create extensive customization. You can also use Appendix B, *Debugging XSL stylesheets* (page 531) for help with debugging your customizations.

Part IV of this book covers all of the special features of DocBook that require extra attention. That part is an encyclopedia of special topics, from bibliographies to websites. Use it as a reference when you need to process a certain feature, or browse it for new possibilities that you did not know DocBook could do.

Note on examples:

Some examples of commands and code in this book are too long to fit on one line. Where a long line is broken to fit, the line will end with a backslash character "\". If you are using Microsoft Windows, you should omit the backslash character and join such a line to the following line. If you are using a Unix shell, you can use the example "as is".

Online resources for finding solutions to problems

If you run into problems with the DocBook XSL stylesheets that are not addressed anywhere in this guide, you can use a number of online resources to find solutions.

- First try searching the archives of the docbook-apps mailing list for keywords related to the problem. There is a good chance that someone else has run into something similar. Archives of the list are available at two different sites: an *archive at OASIS*[5] (which also hosts the actual mailing list) and an *archive at Red Hat*[6].

  If, for example, you are seeing a specific error message, trying cutting and pasting the error message (or some part of it) into the search form for the mailing list archives.

- You can get help in real time on the #docbook channel on `irc.openprojects.net`. If your browser supports IRC URLs (or, like Mozilla, has a built-in IRC client), you can access the channel by entering the following URL in your browser:

      irc://irc.openprojects.net#docbook

- If you cannot find a solution in the docbook-apps or on the #docbook, you should try posting a question to docbook-apps. To subscribe to the list, send a "subscribe" message to:

      `<docbook-apps-request@lists.oasis-open.org>`

  To post a message to the list, send it to:

      `<docbook-apps@lists.oasis-open.org>`

  Please read the *list guidelines*[7] first, and to include examples of your DocBook source document and your output (for example, HTML or FO output) along with details about the tools you're using (including version numbers of the tools).

---

[5] http://lists.oasis-open.org/archives/docbook-apps/
[6] http://sources.redhat.com/ml/docbook-apps/
[7] http://www.oasis-open.org/docbook/mailinglist/guidelines.html

Note:

Do not include attachments when you post to docbook-apps—the mailing list management software automatically strips out attachments. If you have a long example or an output format that you cannot paste into your message, post it to a Web site, and then include the URL in your message to the list.

- The *DocBook Wiki*[8] website collects contributions from DocBook users and makes them available to the world.

- If you find something that seems to be a legitimate bug in the DocBook XSL stylesheets, you can file a bug report from the *Tracker page*[9] at the *DocBook Open Repository*[10] site at SourceForge. If instead you want to request an enhancement to the stylesheets, file a *feature request* from the same Tracker page at the SourceForge site.

Note:

You will need to have a SourceForge user account to file a bug report or feature request. This requirement makes it easier follow up on bug reports. If the DocBook XSL stylesheet developers need to get more details about a specific bug report, it's difficult to follow up on it if it was submitted anonymously.

You can *register for an account*[11] at the SourceForge site.

---

[8] http://wiki.docbook.org
[9] http://sourceforge.net/tracker/?group_id=21935
[10] https://sourceforge.net/projects/docbook/
[11] https://sourceforge.net/account/register.php

2

XSL processors

An *XSL processor* is the software that transforms an XML file into formatted output. There is a growing list of XSL processors to choose from. Each tool implements parts or all of the XSL standard, which actually has several components:

The XSL Standards

Extensible Stylesheet Language (XSL)	A language for expressing stylesheets written in XML. It includes the XSL formatting objects (XSL-FO) language, but refers to separate documents for the transformation language and the path language.
XSL Transformation (XSLT)	The part of XSL for transforming XML documents into other XML documents, HTML, or text. It can be used to rearrange the content and generate new content.
XML Path Language (XPath)	A language for addressing parts of an XML document. It is used to find the parts of your document to apply different styles to. All XSL processors use this component.

To publish HTML from your XML documents, you just need an *XSLT processor*. It will include the XPath language since that is used extensively in XSLT. To get to print, you need an XSLT processor to produce an intermediate formatting objects (FO) file, and then you need an *XSL-FO processor* to produce PostScript or PDF output from the FO file. A diagram of the *DocBook Publishing Model*[1] is available if you want to see how all the components flow together.

XSLT processors

Currently there are three processors that are widely used for XSLT processing because they most closely conform to the XSLT specification:

Saxon	Saxon (*http://saxon.sourceforge.net/*) was written by Michael Kay, the author of *XSLT Reference*, one of the best books on XSLT. Saxon is a free processor written in Java, so it can be run on any operating system with a modern Java interpreter. Saxon now comes in two flavors: Saxon 6 which handles the

---

[1] http://nwalsh.com/docbook/procdiagram/index.html

XSLT 1.0 standard, and Saxon 8 which handles the newly emerging XSLT 2.0 and other new XML standards.

Xalan   Xalan (*http://xml.apache.org/xalan-j/index.html*) is part of the Apache XML Project. It has versions written in both Java and C++, both of them free. The Java version is described in this book because it is highly portable and easier to set up. Generally Xalan is used with the Xerces XML parser, also available from the Apache XML Project.

xsltproc   The xsltproc (*http://xmlsoft.org/XSLT/*) processor is written in C by Daniel Veillard. It is free, as part of the open source libxml2 library from the Gnome development project. It is considered the fastest of the processors, and is highly conformant to the specification. It is much faster than either of the Java processors. It also processes XIncludes.

There are a few other XSLT processors that should also be mentioned:

XT   James Clark's XT (*http://www.blnz.com/xt/index.html*) was the first useful XSLT engine, and it is still in use. It is written in Java, so it runs on many platforms, and it is free. XT comes with James Clark's nonvalidating parser XP, but you can substitute a different Java parser.

MSXML   Microsoft's MSXML (*http://msdn.microsoft.com/xml/*) engine includes an XSLT processor. It is reported to be fast, but only runs on Windows.

Sablotron   Sablotron (*http://www.gingerall.com/charlie/ga/xml/p_sab.xml*), written in C++, from Ginger Alliance.

4XSLT   4XSLT (*http://sourceforge.net/projects/foursuite/*), written in Python, now an open project on SourceForge.

XSL-FO processors

XSL-FO processors are really typesetting engines. An XSL-FO file is a mixture of text from your XML source document and XSL-FO tags that suggest how the text should be formatted. It is the XSL-FO processor that actually creates the typeset lines of text and lays them out on pages. An XSL-FO processor typically generates a PDF or PostScript file which can be fed to a printer to produce hardcopy output.

Currently there are many XSL-FO processors, but few of them have completely implemented the standard. There are at least three reasons for this:

• The XSL-FO standard was finalized almost two years after the XSLT standard.

• The XSL-FO standard is big and complicated.

• Typesetting is hard.

The authors of the XSL-FO standard recognized how difficult it would be to implement, and so divided it into three levels of conformance: basic, extended, and complete. That way a processor can claim conformance to the lower conformance levels and produce useful output, while still be under development for the higher conformance levels.

Here are some of the currently available XSL-FO processors, listed in alphabetical order. FOP, PassiveTeX, and xmlroff are the free processors, but the commercial products implement more of the XSL-FO standard.

E3   High end publishing server from Arbortext, Inc. (*http://www.arbortext.com*). It runs on Windows and Unix.

FOP   FOP is a Java-based processor available free from the Apache XML Project (*http://xml.apache.org/fop/*). FOP can produce usable output, but it is still under development and has some limitations.

PassiveTeX	PassiveTeX from Sebastian Rahtz (*http://www.tei-c.org.uk/Software/passivetex/*) is a free XSL-FO processor based on TeX. It has fallen behind in its implementation of the XSL-FO specification, and many features of DocBook XSL do not work in PassiveTeX. Not recommended.
Unicorn Formatting Objects	A commercial product from Unicorn Enterprises SA (*http://www.unicorn-enterprises.com*). Implements only a subset of the XSL-FO standard. For Windows only.
XEP	A commercial product from RenderX (*http://www.renderx.com*). It is a Java-based product that runs on most platforms.
Xinc	A commercial product from Lunasil LTD (*http://www.lunasil.com/*). It is a Java-based product that runs on Linux and Windows.
XML2PDF	A commercial product from Altsoft (*http://www.alt-soft.com/*). For Windows only.
XML Professional Publisher (XPP)	A high-end XML publishing environment from XyEnterprise (*http://www.xyenterprise.com/*). It runs on Windows and Unix.
xmlroff	xmlroff (*http://xmlroff.sourceforge.net/*) is a free open source project based on libxml2 and other GNOME libraries. It is written in C.
XSL Formatter	A commercial product from Antenna House (*http://www.antennahouse.com*). It runs on Windows, Unix, and Linux.
other	Other XSL-FO processors are listed on the *W3C's XSL information page*[2].

A useful method for evaluating an XSL-FO processor is to review its compliance to the XSL-FO standard. Most processor vendors can provide a summary of which XSL-FO elements and properties their processor supports. Scan the list for features you need to see if they are supported. Such summaries are also useful in comparing different processors.

Portability considerations

If you need to be able to process XML files on more than one operating system, you need to consider how portable the XSL processors are.

- Java-based processors are highly portable, as long as each platform has a modern Java interpreter. (How modern depends on the individual processor and version. Check the processor's requirements list.) With Saxon, Xalan-Java, FOP, and other Java-based processors, you can install a few Java archives without any compiling and produce identical results on Linux, Unix, Windows, and Macintosh.

- Processors written in C such as xsltproc and Sablotron are less portable. You need a version compiled for each platform you want to run it on. Many are available in precompiled packages, such as RPMs for Linux or Zip files for Windows. But the packaged versions can lag behind the latest version, so you may need to compile it yourself for a given platform. The C code is written to be portable, but there are always issues that come up when you have to compile.

- The PassiveTeX FO processor is unique in that it is written in TeX, a typesetting language. TeX is also very portable, but it is currently difficult to get PassiveTeX to work properly with the DocBook XSL stylesheets

---

[2] http://www.w3.org/Style/XSL/

Another portability consideration is file permissions. Some packages may try to install files into areas of a filesystem controlled by a system administrator. If you do not have the necessary permissions, you may not be able to install a given package. All of the processors can be installed elsewhere, but you may need to spend time figuring out how to do so.

3

Getting the tools working

The first step to using the DocBook XSL stylesheets is to get the processing tools installed, configured, and tested to make sure they are working. There are several components that need to be installed:

- DocBook DTD

- DocBook XSL stylesheets

- XSLT processor

- XSL-FO processor

This chapter provides the details for obtaining, installing, and executing the individual tools to process DocBook files.

You can avoid most of those details by installing one of the already-assembled packages of DocBook tools that are available for download. A good number of them are inventoried at the DocBook Wiki site at *http://wiki.docbook.org/topic/DocBookPackages*. There are RPM and Debian packages for Linux systems, Fink packages for Mac systems, and Cygwin and other packages for Windows systems. The packages include most or all of the components listed above, and usually a convenience script to help you get started. If one of those packages meets your needs, then go for it.

The disadvantage of such packages is that they may not keep up with the latest releases of all of the components. Each of the components follows its own development schedule, and it is hard for all of the package developers to quickly integrate each new release into a new package. Installing your own components lets you update the components individually whenever they become available. Even if you install one of the packages, the information in this chapter can help you update individual components when you need to.

Note on Windows pathnames:

For most XSL tools, pathnames on a Microsoft Windows system should be specified using the standard URI syntax. For example, a Windows pathname such as `c:\xml\docbook-xsl` should be entered as `file:///C:/xml/docbook-xsl`. If you have spaces in part of the path, they must be escaped as %20. So a pathname such as `c:\xml\docbook xsl` would be entered as `file:///C:/xml/docbook%20xsl`. Generally spaces in pathnames should be avoided where possible.

Installing the DocBook DTD

You can download the DocBook XML DTD from the OASIS website where it is maintained. Go to *http://www.oasis-open.org/docbook/xml/* and select the current version of the DocBook XML DTD. As of this writing the current version is 4.5. From there you should be able to download the zip archive of the XML DTD. You do not want the SGML DTD. If you are considering using DTD version 5.0, then see Chapter 4, *DocBook 5 tools* (page 33).

If you prefer to use the package installation software on your operating system, the DocBook DTD is also available in some package formats. Check the *DocBook Wiki*[1] packages page to see if there is a DTD package for your system. If you install from a package, you might want to note where the files install so you can refer to that path later.

The DocBook XML DTD consists of a main file docbookx.dtd and several module files. You only need to reference the main file, and it will pull in the other module files to make up the complete DTD.

Finding the DTD during processing

In general, your XML documents must identify the DTD they are written against by means of a DOCTYPE declaration at the top of the file. The information in the DOCTYPE provides the processor with clues for finding the DTD files. It might contain a PUBLIC identifier, and either a local file reference, or a URL reference (that may still be resolved to a local file).

Local DTD

DocBook documents written to version 4.5 of the DocBook XML DTD might look like the following:

Linux example:
```
<!DOCTYPE book SYSTEM "/usr/share/docbook-4.5/docbookx.dtd">
```

Windows example:
```
<!DOCTYPE book SYSTEM "file:///C:/xml/docbook45/docbookx.dtd">
```

This is a simple direct reference to a specific file location on your machine. It will work if the main DTD file is at that location. The problem with a specific reference like this is that it is not flexible. If you move your XML file to another machine where the DTD is installed somewhere else, or if you move the DTD on your machine, then the connection is lost. Fixing it is not a big problem if you have just a few files, but if you have hundreds of XML files, it is a tedious chore. It's also unnecessary if you use catalog files.

Network DTD

It is possible to fetch the DocBook DTD over the web. The XML standard supports using URLs for DTD references. The advantage is that the DTD is always available, as long as a web connection is available. That makes the document very portable.

The DOCTYPE declaration for network DTD access looks like the following:

```
<!DOCTYPE book PUBLIC "-//OASIS//DTD DocBook XML V4.5//EN"
                "http://www.oasis-open.org/docbook/xml/4.5/docbookx.dtd">
```

Most XSL processors know how to fetch the DTD over the web, including all the DTD file modules that it references. This is not recommended for a slow network or flaky network connection. Even with a fast connection, it is slower than a local filesystem access. The next section shows you how to use a catalog to combine local and network access.

---

[1] http://wiki.docbook.org/topic/DocBookPackages

XML catalog to locate the DTD

With an XML catalog, you can have the best of both local and network access. The catalog lets you map the standard network URL to a local file. If the catalog processor finds the local file during processing, it will use it. Otherwise, it falls back to using the network URL. With this arrangement, you get the speed of local access with the reliability and portability of network access.

An XML catalog entry looks like the following:

```
<catalog xmlns="urn:oasis:names:tc:entity:xmlns:xml:catalog">
  <group id="DocbookDTD" prefer="public">
    <system
        systemId="http://www.oasis-open.org/docbook/xml/4.5/docbookx.dtd"
        uri="file:///usr/share/xml/docbook45/docbookx.dtd"/>
  </group>
</catalog>
```

When processed with a catalog-aware XSL processor, a DOCTYPE reference to the URL `http://www.oasis-open.org/docbook/xml/4.5/docbookx.dtd` will be replaced with the uri attribute value `/usr/share/xml/doc-book45/docbookx.dtd` if that file exists on the local system. If not, then the URL is used through network access.

See Chapter 5, *XML catalogs* (page 47) for complete information on XML catalogs.

SGML catalog to locate the DTD

You can achieve a similar mapping with an SGML catalog, which is an older technology using a simpler syntax. The following is an example of an SGML catalog that maps both the PUBLIC and SYSTEM identifiers to a local file:

```
PUBLIC  "-//OASIS//DTD DocBook XML V4.5//EN"  \
                "/usr/share/xml/docbook45/docbookx.dtd"
SYSTEM  "http://www.oasis-open.org/docbook/xml/4.5/docbookx.dtd"  \
                "/usr/share/xml/docbook45/docbookx.dtd"
```

Character entities

The DocBook DTD defines the character entities that make it easy to add special characters to your XML files. To enter a copyright symbol, for example, it is easier to remember a name like © than the equivalent © Unicode entity.

Depending on the source for your DTD download, the files that define the character entity names may not be included. They are on the OASIS website under *http://www.oasis-open.org/docbook/xmlcharent/index.shtml*. Create a directory named ent in the directory where the DocBook DTD files are, and extract the entity files into ent. The DTD will find them in that location because it has references that look like "ent/iso-amsa.ent".

Validation

Validation is the act of checking your document against the element names and rules in the DTD. Most XSL processors will not automatically take the time to validate your document while it is converting it to HTML or XSL-FO. The processor will read a DOCTYPE declaration in your file and try to find the DTD, and will likely report an error if it cannot. If it does find the DTD, it will read and use an entity declarations in it. If you use any DocBook character entities, the processor must be able to find the DTD to resolve those entity references.

Since the XSL processor does not automatically validate your document, it is possible to process invalid but well-formed DocBook documents. But you do so at your own risk, because the DocBook stylesheets expect to be processing a valid document. Your output may not be what you expect if you do not follow the rules. You will have fewer mysterious problems if you validate your documents before processing them.

Some of the XSLT processors described in later sections include validation utilities. For example, the libxml2 package that is required for xsltproc also includes a program called xmllint that can validate an XML document using a command like the following:

```
xmllint  --valid  --noout  document.xml
```

If you are looking for a Java-based validation tool, there is a XML validation tool hidden in the distribution of Xalan 2.4 or newer. The xalansamples.jar file that is located with the other Xalan jar files has a Validate utility. If you include the xalansamples.jar file in your Java CLASSPATH along with the other Xalan jar files, then you should be able to use this command:

```
java  Validate  document.xml
```

Installing the DocBook stylesheets

The DocBook XSL stylesheets are a fairly large collection of files that can be downloaded as a collection from the DocBook SourceForge website where they are maintained. Go to *http://docbook.sourceforge.net* to reach the main project page. From there, select Files, and then scroll down to list of file archives. You'll generally want the latest stable version. Then download the archive and unpack it anywhere that's convenient.

If you prefer to use the package installation software on your operating system, the DocBook XSL stylesheets are also available in many package formats such as Debian and RPM. Check the *DocBook Wiki*[2] packages page to see if there is an XSL package for your system. If you install from a package, you might want to note where the files install so you can refer to that path later.

If you are on a Linux system or Windows with Cygwin, and install from a package (not the zip file), then the package installation should run the included shell script named install.sh to create a file named /etc/xml/catalog that indicates where the stylesheet files were installed. This file is an XML catalog file that maps generic identifiers to specific locations on your system. By default, xsltproc will use that catalog file. See Chapter 5, *XML catalogs* (page 47) for more information on catalogs. The file named INSTALL that is included in the stylesheet distribution provides more information about installation.

Once you install the stylesheet distribution, you'll see these core subdirectories.

Table 3.1. Stylesheet subdirectories

Subdirectory	Description
common	Shared stylesheet modules, including languages.
doc	Documentation for the stylesheets in browsable HTML.
extensions	Program files that extend XSL for particular processors.
fo	Stylesheet modules that produce XSL-FO output.
html	Stylesheet modules that produce HTML output.
images	Icons and other images used in the output.
lib	Stylesheet modules shared among many outputs.

There will be other directories containing documentation source in XML, stylesheet customizations for specialized output such as HTML Help, and other tool files. But if you ever need to copy just the basic set of files for running

---

[2] http://wiki.docbook.org/topic/DocBookPackages

the stylesheets in their standard HTML or XSL-FO outputs, then these are the directories you will need (plus the VERSION file in the top-level directory).

The stylesheet distribution includes an INSTALL file. This is a Bash shell script that builds an XML catalog file using the xmlcatalog utility. It only works on systems with a Bash shell (not Windows unless it is under Cygwin), and it is not required for using the stylesheets. See Chapter 5, *XML catalogs* (page 47) for more on setting up your own XML catalog file.

Note:

You do not actually have to download the stylesheet files to use them. Most XSL processors, if given a URL instead of a file-name, will fetch the stylesheet over the Internet. However, because the DocBook stylesheets are big and use many file modules, this process uses a lot of network bandwidth and greatly slows down the processing of your documents. But it can be used in a pinch when you are on a machine that does not have the stylesheets installed. For example:

```
xsltproc \
    http://docbook.sourceforge.net/release/xsl/current/html/docbook.xsl \
    myfile.xml
```

Installing an XSLT processor

This section describes how to install the free processors. The commercial processors are assumed to provide instructions and support. You should check the details with each product that is described here, as the steps may change over time.

Installing xsltproc

The installation of xsltproc is platform dependent since it is a compiled C program. You will need a C compiler and associated Make tools unless you are using Windows. Macintosh users can download binaries from *http://www.zveno.com/open_source/libxml2xslt.html*.

Installing xsltproc on Windows

You can download precompiled versions for Windows from Igor Zlatkovic's website: *http://www.zlatkovic.com/libxml.en.html*

That page also describes how to install the files and use xsltproc on Windows. You need to download the packages for libxml2, libxslt, zlib, and iconv. They arrive as .zip files which can be unpacked with any of the zip utilities on Windows.

Once you have unpacked them, your environment's PATH variable must include the locations of the command files like xsltproc.exe and the set of library files named with the .dll suffix. Since they install into separate directories, you may need to add several PATH entries. So it is perhaps simplest to just copy all the files into a single location already in the PATH. For example, find and copy thefollowing files into C:\Windows\System32:

```
libxslt.dll          iconv.dll          xmllint.exe
libxml2.dll          zlib.dll
libexslt.dll         xsltproc.exe
```

You will know it is working if you can execute the following command in a Command shell to list the version information:

```
xsltproc -version
```

Installing xsltproc on Cygwin

Cygwin is a Linux-like environment that runs on Windows. It gives you the same command shells and utilities that are available on Linux systems. If you are comfortable with Linux, then you can have it on Windows too. There is a version of xsltproc for Cygwin.

If your Windows machine is connected to the Internet, then go to this website:

```
http://www.cygwin.com/
```

You will see information for installing Cygwin over the Internet. The complete Cygwin collection of packages is big, so it might take a long time over a slow connection. You can select only the packages you need. Read the directions for understanding the GUI interface used by the Cygwin setup. The two packages you must have are libxml2 and libxslt, both available under the Libs category. You should also install one of the shells such as bash.

Once you have installed the packages, you should be able to start a Cygwin shell and execute this command to see the version installed:

```
xsltproc -version
```

Installing xsltproc on Linux

If you are running a recent vintage of Linux, there is a good chance you will already have xsltproc installed on your system. Try the following command to see if you do:

```
xsltproc -version
```

If that command fails, or if it reports an old version, you can install the files you need using the RPM packages. The RPM packages can be found using the following URLs:

```
http://rpmfind.net/linux/rpm2html/search.php?query=libxml2
http://rpmfind.net/linux/rpm2html/search.php?query=libxslt
```

You need system administration privileges (root) to install packages. Then commands such as these should work:

```
rpm -Uv libxml2-2.6.27-1.i386.rpm
rpm -Uv libxslt-1.1.20-1.i386.rpm
```

Then try xsltproc -version to see if it reports the new version number.

Compiling xsltproc

If you cannot find a precompiled version of xsltproc for your platform, or if you want the very latest version, then you can compile it yourself from source. It is pretty easy to compile xsltproc if you use the GNU compiler. That compiler is generally available on all Linux distributions, and is also available for many Unix systems. It is even available for Cygwin (a Linux environment that runs on Windows). You might need to search the Internet to find one for your system if it does not already have one.

Once you have gcc set up, download and unpack the latest xsltproc source archives from http://xmlsoft.org/XSLT/ (unless you are compiling under Cygwin, in which case you should download the source from the Cygwin archive). To run the xsltproc processor, you need the libxml2 and libxslt packages, the ones with the highest version numbers. Then do the following:

1. Unpack the distribution archives (the version numbers will be different from this example):

    ```
    tar zxvf libxml2-2.6.27.tar.gz
    tar zxvf libxslt-1.1.20.tar.gz
    ```

2. Compile libxml2:

    ```
    cd libxml2-2.6.27
    ./configure
    make
    make install
    ```

    You will need to have root permission to run the install step.

3. Compile libxslt:

    ```
    cd libxslt-1.1.20
    ./configure
    make
    make install
    ```

    You will need to have root permission to run the install step. If these steps proceed without error, you should be able to run this command to test it:

    ```
    xsltproc -version
    ```

If you get a Command Not Found error message, then you need to find where xsltproc is installed and add that location to your PATH environment variable.

Using xsltproc

To use xsltproc, you specify the location of the main stylesheet file and your DocBook document, as well as any options and parameters:

General usage:
```
xsltproc \
    [options] \
    [--stringparam name value] \
    stylesheet-path \
    xml-document
```

HTML example:
```
xsltproc \
    --output myfile.html \
    --stringparam use.extensions 0 \
    docbook-xsl/html/docbook.xsl \
    myfile.xml
```

FO example:
```
xsltproc \
    --output myfile.fo \
    --stringparam use.extensions 0 \
    docbook-xsl/fo/docbook.xsl \
    myfile.xml
```

You can place any options such as --output after xsltproc. The options are listed at *http://xmlsoft.org/XSLT/xsltproc2.html*. You can use any number of --stringparam options to pass stylesheet parameter values on the command line, in this case setting the parameter named use.extensions to a value of 0 (because xsltproc cannot use the Java stylesheet extensions). If a parameter value includes spaces or special characters, put it in quotes.

Note:

Two xsltproc options you do *not* want to use with DocBook are `--html` which is for HTML *input*, and `--docbook` which is for DocBook *SGML* input, not XML input.

If you do not like using a command line interface, you can download the free tkxsltproc from *http://tclxml.sourceforge.net/tkxsltproc.html*. It is a graphical interface to xsltproc that lets you browse for filenames and set options and parameters.

Installing Saxon

Saxon is a Java-based XSLT processor that is well respected for its adherence to the XSLT standard. Currently Saxon is available in four packages:

Saxon 6.5.5	This is the full version of Saxon that implements the XSLT 1.0 standard. It runs on any Java-capable system, and provides opportunities for adding extensions. It is probably the most commonly used Saxon package, and is the version used in the examples in this book.
Instant Saxon 6.5.3	The Instant Saxon processor is a precompiled version of Saxon 6.5.3 that runs only on Microsoft Windows. Instant Saxon relies on the Microsoft Java VM, which is no longer shipped with Windows XP but can be separately downloaded from Microsoft.
Saxon-B 8	This is the open source version of Saxon 8 that supports the emerging XSLT 2.0 standard, as well as several other new XML standards. It is under active development, as are several of the standards that it implements.
Saxon-SA 8	This is the commercial version of Saxon 8. The SA stands for "schema aware", because it implements the W3C XML Schema standard.

Some people choose to replace the XML parser that is included with Saxon with the Xerces XML parser, which provides additional features. That optional step is included here too.

1. **Update your Java**

   Saxon is a Java-based XSLT processor. So your system must have a Java processing environment for it to work. Java version 1.3 and higher is recommended for processing speed, which is a significant consideration for DocBook XSL because the stylesheets are big.

   You can find out which Java is on your system by executing **java -version**. If you get Command not found then you may not have Java installed on the system, or it may not be in your PATH environment variable. Java version numbering has evolved over the years. The following table lists past and current Java versions:

Table 3.2. Java versions

Product name	Java Versions
Java	`1.0` `1.1`

Java 2	`1.2`
	`1.3`
	`1.4`

Java 2 Platform, Standard Edition 5.0 (J2SE 5.0)	`1.5`
Java Platform, Standard Edition 6 (Java SE 6)	`1.6`

The Java runtime system is available for download from *Sun Microsystems, Inc.*[3] for Windows, Linux, and Sun Solaris. If you have a different platform (UNIX or Mac, for instance), then you need to contact your OS vendor to see if they make available an up-to-date Java runtime environment. You are looking for the Java 2 Platform Standard Edition (J2SE).

2. **Download full Saxon 6.5.5**

    To download Saxon, go to *http://saxon.sourceforge.net/* and locate the full (not Instant) 6.5.5 version for download.

3. **Unpack the archive**

    Saxon is distributed as a zip file, so you need to unzip it into some suitable location. It can be a temporary location because you can move the few files you really need to a new location.

4. **Locate the Saxon .jar files**

    To run Saxon, you only need to tell your Java processor where the Saxon .jar files are. There are three files in the directory you unpacked Saxon into:

    `saxon.jar`   The Saxon XSLT processor.

    `saxon-fop.jar`   Classes for integrating Saxon with FOP within a Java application.

    `saxon-jdom.jar`   Classes for integrating Saxon with *JDOM*[4].

    You will not need `saxon-fop.jar` or `saxon-jdom.jar` for use with the DocBook XSL stylesheets.

5. **Locate the DocBook Saxon extensions file**

    The DocBook stylesheets have some custom extension functions written specifically for the Saxon processor. These functions are contained in a `saxon653.jar` file that is included with the DocBook distribution in its **exten-sions** subdirectory. There may be several saxon jar files there, labeled by the version number of Saxon. Use the one closest to your Saxon version number. See the section called "DocBook Saxon and Xalan extensions" (page 21) for a more complete description of the DocBook Saxon extensions.

6. **(Optional) Download Xerces XML parser**

    If you want to use the Xerces XML parser in place of the default Saxon parser, download the Xerces parser from *http://xml.apache.org/xerces2-j/*. You want the Xerces2 Java parser. The web page has a link to where you can

---

[3] http://java.sun.com/j2se/
[4] http://www.jdom.org/

download just the latest jar file, xercesImpl.jar. Put the file in a convenient location. See the section called "Using the Xerces parser with Saxon" (page 21) to get it working.

7. **Update your CLASSPATH**

You need to include the full path to the necessary .jar files (described above) in your CLASSPATH environment variable. That environment variable is used by the Java processor to locate compiled code used by Java programs. You can copy the .jar files to a convenient location (perhaps where other jar files are stored) before specifying that location in your CLASSPATH.

To update your CLASSPATH on Linux, put these lines in your .profile file, changing the pathnames to match the locations on your system:

```
CLASSPATH=$CLASSPATH:/usr/saxon/saxon.jar:\
/usr/docbook-xsl/extensions/saxon653.jar
export CLASSPATH
```

If you want to use the Xerces XML parser, then include the path to xercesImpl.jar:

```
CLASSPATH=$CLASSPATH:/usr/saxon/saxon.jar:\
/usr/docbook-xsl/extensions/saxon653.jar:/usr/share/xercesImpl.jar
export CLASSPATH
```

To update your CLASSPATH on Windows, do the following:

a. Use the Windows Control Panel to open the System icon.

b. Select the Advanced tab, and then the Environment Variables button.

c. In the System Variables list, scroll to the CLASSPATH variable if it exists and select Edit. If it does not already exist in the list, then select New.

d. The Variable name is CLASSPATH. The Variable value for CLASSPATH is a single string containing a sequence of directory paths separated by semicolons. Each path should be a full path to one of the required .jar files. For example:

```
c:\saxon\saxon.jar;c:\docbook-xsl\extensions\saxon653.jar
```

e. Choose OK to close the dialog boxes and exit the System utility.

f. If you are already in a DOS window, you will need to exit and restart it for the new environment variable to take effect.

You can tell if your Saxon processor is working by exectuting the following command:

```
java  com.icl.saxon.StyleSheet -t
```

This should report the version of Saxon that you have installed, as well as usage and command options. If instead you get an error message about NoClassDefFoundError, then your CLASSPATH is not set correctly.

Using Saxon

Saxon is a Java application that is executed from a command line. In order for the command to find all the Java code it needs, you must add the Java .jar files described above to your CLASSPATH environment variable. Once you have done that, then you execute the **java** command as follows. The backslashes mean the line continues without break, but is shown here on separate lines for clarity.

General syntax:
```
java  com.icl.saxon.StyleSheet \
    options  \
    xml-document  \
    stylesheet-path  \
    param=value
```

HTML example:
```
java  com.icl.saxon.StyleSheet  \
    -o myfile.html  \
    myfile.xml  \
    docbook-xsl/html/docbook.xsl  \
    use.extensions=1
```

FO example:
```
java  com.icl.saxon.StyleSheet   \
    -o myfile.fo   \
    myfile.xml   \
    docbook-xsl/fo/docbook.xsl   \
    use.extensions=1
```

Note that the XML document name precedes the stylesheet path in a Saxon command line. You can put any Saxon options such as -o before the document filename. The possible options are listed at *http://saxon.sourceforge.net/saxon6.5.2/using-xsl.html*. You can also set any number of stylesheet parameters such as use.extensions=1 after the stylesheet path. See Chapter 6, *Using stylesheet parameters* (page 59) for details on using parameters.

Using the Xerces parser with Saxon

The XML parser that comes with Saxon has limited features, so many people choose to substitute the Xerces XML parser when using Saxon. The section on installing Saxon included an optional step for downloading the Xerces parser. Once you have added the path to xercesImpl.jar to your CLASSPATH, you just need to add a couple of options to the Saxon command line:

Saxon with Xerces parser:
```
java \
  -Djavax.xml.parsers.DocumentBuilderFactory=\
    org.apache.xerces.jaxp.DocumentBuilderFactoryImpl \
  -Djavax.xml.parsers.SAXParserFactory=\
    org.apache.xerces.jaxp.SAXParserFactoryImpl \
  com.icl.saxon.StyleSheet  \
  -o myfile.html  \
  myfile.xml  \
  docbook-xsl/html/docbook.xsl
```

These -D options must appear before the com.icl.saxon.StyleSheet class name. The options will fail if the xercesImpl.jar file is not included in the CLASSPATH.

DocBook Saxon and Xalan extensions

The DocBook XSL distribution comes with a set of extensions to the Saxon or Xalan XSLT processors. These extensions are Java programs that provide functions that are not part of the XSLT standard. The DocBook Saxon extensions are contained in the file `extensions/saxon65.jar`, and the Xalan extensions are in `extensions/xalan.27` (or the latest version). To make the extensions available to the stylesheets, you have to include this file in your Java CLASSPATH, as described in the section called "Installing Saxon" (page 18).

The DocBook Saxon and Xalan extensions are not enabled by default. They are enabled by setting various stylesheet parameters. See Chapter 6, *Using stylesheet parameters* (page 59) to learn how to set stylesheet parameters. Each extension has its own stylesheet parameter, and they are all set to 1 (on) by default. However, they are not actually turned on by default because the overall `use.extensions` parameter that enables all of them is set to zero (off) by default. To use any of the extensions, set the `use.extensions` parameter to 1. The following is a list of the functions and their enabling parameters.

Stylesheet parameter	Function	More information
`use.extensions`	When set to zero, disables all of these extensions. Set it to 1 to use any of these extensions. Default value is zero.	
`callouts.extension`	Positions callout markers in `programlistingco` and `screenco` based on the area coordinates. The default value is 1.	See the section called "Callouts on imported text" (page 448).
`textinsert.extension`	Imports a text file into an example and escapes any characters that would otherwise be interpreted as markup. The default value is 1.	See the section called "External code files" (page 443).
`tablecolumns.extension`	Adjusts the widths of table columns to better match the CALS table specifications. The default value is 1.	See the section called "Column widths" (page 475).
`linenumbering.extension`	Displays line numbers at the beginning of line in a `programlisting`, when it has a `linenumbering="numbered"` attribute. The default value is 1.	See the section called "Line numbering" (page 445).
`graphicsize.extension`	Computes the intrisic size of images to help size the image for HTML output. Not used for print output. The default value is 1.	See the section called " Image sizing" (page 290).

If you are not using any of these features in your documents, then you have no need to turn on the extensions. However, there is no harm in turning them on.

Installing Xalan

Xalan's installation process depends on which version of the Java runtime you will be using to run it. In Java 1.4, a version of Xalan was bundled into the runtime. Unfortunately, the version that was bundled was superceded by improved versions from Apache.org. Most people preferred the newer versions, but they required taking some extra steps to make sure the bundled version was not being used instead. In the following procedure, any extra steps needed for Java 1.4 are called out.

Xalan is very easy to install because it is a Java program and requires no compiling. It will run on any Java platform, including Linux, Windows, and UNIX.

1. **Update your Java**

    Since Xalan-J requires a Java runtime environment, you might need to obtain or update your Java setup before Xalan will work. See the step on updating Java in the section called "Installing Saxon" (page 18).

2. **Download Xalan**

   Be sure to get the Xalan Java version, not the Xalan C++ version. To download Xalan-J, go to *http://xml.apache.org* and locate the latest stable binary version for download. You probably will not want the latest experimental version. They provide .zip files with everything you need. That site will also provide you with detailed instructions for getting started with Xalan. As of version 2.5.1 of Xalan, it is available in two binary distributions. In one, the Xalan Compiled processor (XSLTC) is included in xalan.jar, and in the other, it is not. Either one will work for DocBook processing. If you want to take advantage of XSLTC, see *http://xml.apache.org/xalan-j/xsltc_usage.html*.

3. **Unpack the archive**

   Xalan is distributed as a zip file, so you need to unzip it into some suitable location. It can be a temporary location because you can move the few files you really need to a new location.

4. **Locate the Xalan .jar files**

   To run Xalan, you only need to tell your Java processor where the Xalan .jar files are. The bin directory in the directory you unpacked Xalan into will contain the three files you need:

   ```
   xalan.jar
   xml-apis.jar
   xercesImpl.jar
   ```

   Here is what all the files are for:

xalan.jar	The main Xalan XSLT processor.
xercesImpl.jar	The XML parser used to parse the XML file.
xml-apis.jar	Provides the SAX, DOM, and JAVAX interfaces used by Xalan.
xalansamples.jar	A set of sample Java applications using Xalan. This file is not needed for DocBook processing.
xalanservlet.jar	Sample application using Xalan in a Java servlet. This file is not needed for DocBook processing.
xsltc.jar	Bundled set of XSLTC functions for compiling XSL stylesheets into a set of Java classes. This file is not needed for DocBook processing. It may not be present, depending on which package of Xalan you downloaded.

   The following additional .jar files may be included with your Xalan distribution. Most are the unbundled XSLTC functions that are now available as a bundle in xsltc.jar. They are not needed for DocBook processing.

   ```
   BCEL.jar
   JLex.jar
   bsf.jar
   java_cup.jar
   regexp.jar
   runtime.jar
   ```

5. **Locate the Xalan DocBook extensions file**

   The DocBook stylesheets have some custom extension functions written specifically for the Xalan processor. See the section called "DocBook Saxon and Xalan extensions" (page 21) for details. These functions are contained in a file named `xalan27.jar` (or the latest version) that is included with the DocBook distribution in its `extensions` subdirectory. If your version of Xalan is earlier that 2.7, then use the `xalan2.jar` file instead.

6. **Install the .jar files**

Your version of Java determines where the main `xalan.jar` file is installed.

- If you have Java version 1.4, you need to put the Xalan jar files in the `lib/endorsed` directory under your Java distribution. For example, if your Java is installed under `/usr/jre2`, then copy the Xalan files into `/usr/jre2/lib/endorsed`. Then the new Xalan will be used in place of the built-in Xalan that comes with Java 1.4. If you do not have write permission to the Java installation directory, you can use a different method as described in the section called "Bypassing the old Xalan installed with Java" (page 25).

    Important:

    If you do not register the newer Xalan as the "endorsed" version, then your processing will use the older version of Xalan and you may not get the results you expected.

- If your Java is not version 1.4 (version 1.3 or below or 5.0 or later), then you can put the jar files in any convenient location for creating a CLASSPATH. You do not have to worry about the Java endorsing process.

7. **Update your CLASSPATH**

You need to include the full path to .jar files in your CLASSPATH environment variable.

To update your CLASSPATH on Linux, put these lines in your `.profile` file:

```
CLASSPATH=$CLASSPATH:/usr/Xalan/xalan.jar:/usr/Xalan/xml-apis.jar:\
/usr/Xalan/xercesImpl.jar:/usr/docbook-xsl/extensions/xalan25.jar
export CLASSPATH
```

On Windows, use the Control Panel to open the System icon, where you can set environment variables for Windows. Use semicolons instead of colons to separate items in the CLASSPATH.

The `bsf.jar` file (Bean Scripting Framework) is used to support XSLT extensions written in languages other than Java. Since Norm Walsh wrote the DocBook extensions for Xalan in Java, you do not need to include `bsf.jar` in your CLASSPATH for DocBook. But you may want it for other stylesheets.

You can tell the Xalan processor is working by running this command:

```
java  org.apache.xalan.xslt.EnvironmentCheck
```

It reports on the Java environment and the version of Xalan. If you get a message about a class not found, then your CLASSPATH is not set up right to use Xalan.

Using Xalan

Like Saxon, Xalan is a Java application, so you need to set the CLASSPATH environment variable as described in the section called "Installing Xalan" (page 22). Then you can execute the Xalan **java** command that includes a stylesheet, an input filename, and any number of Xalan options.

General syntax:
```
java  org.apache.xalan.xslt.Process    \
    -out outputfile  \
    -in xml-document  \
    -xsl stylesheet-path  \
    -param name value
```

HTML example:
```
java org.apache.xalan.xslt.Process  \
    -out myfile.html  \
    -in myfile.xml  \
    -xsl docbook-xsl/html/docbook.xsl  \
    -param use.extensions 1
```

FO example:
```
java  org.apache.xalan.xslt.Process  \
    -out myfile.fo  \
    -in myfile.xml  \
    -xsl docbook-xsl/fo/docbook.xsl  \
    -param use.extensions 1
```

With Xalan, all the arguments to the command are entered as options, and the order of the options does not matter. The Xalan options are listed at *http://xml.apache.org/xalan-j/commandline.html*. You can set any number of *stylesheet parameters* with multiple -param options. In this example, the parameter named use.extensions is set to a value of 1. If a parameter value includes spaces or special characters, put it in quotes.

If for some reason Xalan does not work, you may need to know what version of Xalan and Java you are running to track down the problem. The following command will provide that information:

```
java  org.apache.xalan.xslt.EnvironmentCheck
```

Bypassing the old Xalan installed with Java

If you are running Java 1.4, an older version of Xalan is bundled with Java. You will want to download and install a newer version of Xalan. Unfortunately, just setting your CLASSPATH to the new jar files is not sufficient. You also need to supply a Java option to force it to use the newer versions.

```
CLASSPATH=$CLASSPATH:/usr/Xalan/xalan.jar:/usr/Xalan/xml-apis.jar:\
/usr/Xalan/xercesImpl.jar:/usr/docbook-xsl/extensions/xalan25.jar
export CLASSPATH
java -Djava.endorsed.dirs=/usr/Xalan  \
    org.apache.xalan.xslt.Process  \
    -out myfile.html  \
    -in myfile.xml  \
    -xsl /docbook-xsl/html/docbook.xsl
```

The java.endorsed.dirs option tells Java it is ok to use the jar files contained in the specified directory. You could also install the Xalan jar files into */javahome/*lib/endorsed directory, in which case you do not need to supply the command line option. Here *javahome* is the directory where the runtime software is installed (which is the top-level directory of the Java 2 Runtime Environment or the jre directory in the Java 2 SDK).

See *http://java.sun.com/j2se/1.4.1/docs/guide/standards/* for more information on the endorsed override mechanism in Java.

DocBook Xalan extensions

The DocBook XSL distribution comes with a set of extensions to the Xalan XSLT processor. These extensions are Java programs that provide functions that are not part of the XSLT standard. The DocBook Xalan extensions are contained in the file extensions/xalan25.jar. To make the extensions available to the stylesheets, you have to include this file in your Java CLASSPATH, as described in the section called "Installing Xalan" (page 22).

For a description of the available functions and how you enable them, see the section called "DocBook Saxon and Xalan extensions" (page 21), which describes the equivalent extensions for Saxon.

Installing an XSL-FO processor

This section describes how to install and use the free XSL-FO processor, FOP. The commercial processors are assumed to provide their own documentation and support, so installation instructions for commercial processors are not provided in this book.

Note:

For a long time, version 0.20.5 of FOP was the only stable version while the code was being refactored. Now the refactored version has been released, with the first stable version 0.93. It is highly recommended that you not use version 0.20.5 anymore because of its limitations.

Installing FOP

FOP is also a Java program, so it is easy to install, especially if you already are using Java programs such as Saxon or Xalan.

1. **Update your Java**

   Since FOP requires a Java runtime environment, you might need to obtain or update your Java setup before FOP will work. See the step on updating Java in the section called "Installing Saxon" (page 18).

2. **Download FOP**

   To download FOP, go to *http://xml.apache.org* and locate the latest stable version for download (currently version 0.93). You probably want the binary version rather than the source version. The distribution comes as a compressed zip file with everything you need. That site will also provide you with detailed instructions for getting started with FOP.

3. **Unpack the archive**

   FOP is distributed as a zip file, which can be opened on almost all systems. Linux users can also download a gzipped tar file (.tar.gz suffix).

4. **Locate the FOP .jar files**

   Although most people will run FOP using its included convenience scripts, it is useful to know where the files are. The main file is build/fop.jar in the directory you unpacked FOP into. The lib directory has other .jar files that may be used by the FOP convenience scripts. The version numbers shown here may differ from the ones in your distribution.

   avalon-framework-4.2.0.jar   A software framework that allows software components to work together. It is used internally by FOP.

   batik-all-1.6.jar   Provides the support library for SVG graphics.

`xalan-2.7.0.jar`	The Xalan XSLT processor that may be used by the FOP convenience scripts. The scripts have an option to convert your XML to XSL-FO using Xalan, and then process the XSL-FO, all with one command.
`xercesImpl-2.7.1.jar`	The XML parser used to parse the XSL-FO file.
`xml-apis-1.3.02.jar`	Provides the SAX, DOM, and JAVAX interfaces used by Xalan.

5. **Download the graphics library files**

   You will most likely want to process bitmap graphics in your document. FOP has built-in support for some graphics formats, but some popular formats such as PNG are not supported natively. To process other graphics formats, FOP supports the use of Sun's Java Advanced Imaging (JAI) library, although it does not include the files. You can download the JAI files from *http://java.sun.com/products/java-media/jai/current.html* (you do not need the Image IO Tools download). If you do the CLASSPATH installation, you can put the files wherever you like. The easiest way to get JAI included is to copy the `jai_core.jar` and the `jai_codec.jar` files from the JAI installation area to the `lib` subdirectory of the FOP installation. Then they will automatically be included in the CLASSPATH for FOP processing.

6. **Download the hyphenation .jar file**

   If you are processing languages other than English, then you need to download an additional file named `fop-hyph.jar` from *http://offo.sourceforge.net/hyphenation/index.html*. Copy it to the `lib` subdirectory of the FOP install-ation. Then it will automatically be included in the CLASSPATH for FOP processing.

Using FOP

FOP will convert a `.fo` file generated by one of the above processors into a `.pdf` file. FOP is a Java application, so to use the FOP Java command line, you need to set the CLASSPATH environment variable as described in the section called "FOP Java command" (page 28). However, if you use one of the FOP convenience scripts, they will set the CLASSPATH for the duration of the script.

Before you run the FOP command, you need to process your DocBook file with the fo/docbook.xsl stylesheet to generate a `.fo` file. The `.fo` file is the input to the FOP processor. The stylesheet will tune the XSL-FO output for FOP when you set the stylesheet parameter `fop1.extensions` to 1.

Note:

Use the stylesheet parameter `fop1.extensions` with FOP version 0.93 and later. The old `fop.extensions` parameter should only be used with FOP version 0.20.5 and earlier.

The following is an example command line using xsltproc to generate an XSL-FO file suitable for input to FOP:

```
xsltproc  \
    --output myfile.fo
    --stringparam fop1.extensions 1  \
    docbook-xsl/fo/docbook.xsl  \
    myfile.xml
```

See Chapter 6, *Using stylesheet parameters* (page 59) for more information on using stylesheet parameters.

You will know that it is working if you see a message like "Making portrait pages on US letter paper". That message comes from a template named `root.messages` in the stylesheet file fo/docbook.xsl. You can change what the message says in a customization layer, or you could define it as an empty template there to turn off the message entirely. Once you have generated to XSL-FO file, you are ready to use FOP.

Fop convenience scripts

The FOP distribution includes some convenience scripts that set the CLASSPATH for you and run the Java command. Which script you use depends on the operating system: fop is a shell scripts for Linux or Unix, or fop.bat for Windows. The scripts can optionally run the XSLT process on your XML source file to produce the XSL-FO file before generating PDF. That may save you a step, but you will not be able to examine the XSL-FO output when you do that. The following are some examples of using the scripts:

Convert a .fo file on Unix or Linux:
```
fop.sh -fo myfile.fo -pdf myfile.pdf
```

Convert an XML source file Unix or Linux:
```
fop.sh -xsl /docbook-xsl/fo/docbook.xsl -xml myfile.xml -pdf myfile.pdf
```

Convert a .fo file on Windows:
```
fop.bat -fo myfile.fo -pdf myfile.pdf
```

Convert an XML source file on Windows:
```
fop.bat -xsl /docbook-xsl/fo/docbook.xsl -xml myfile.xml -pdf myfile.pdf
```

All of the arguments to the command are in the form of options, and they can be presented in any order. The options for FOP are listed at *http://xml.apache.org/fop/running.html*. One option you will not find is the ability to set DocBook stylesheet parameters on the command line when you use the -xsl option that processes the stylesheet. If you need to use parameters, you should use a separate XSLT processor first to generate the XSL-FO file for FOP to process.

FOP Java command

You may want to set your CLASSPATH yourself to run the FOP Java command. See the section called "Installing FOP" (page 26) for information on what files need to included in the CLASSPATH. The safest approach is to include everything in the lib directory of the FOP distribution as well as build/fop.jar. The following example assumes the FOP .jar files are installed into /usr/java. Replace any *version* strings in the example below with the actual version numbers on the files in your FOP distribution.

Setting CLASSPATH:
```
CLASSPATH="/usr/java/fop-0.93/build/fop.jar:\
/usr/java/fop-0.93/lib/avalon-framework-version.jar"
/usr/java/fop-0.93/lib/batik-version.jar:\
/usr/java/fop-0.93/lib/commons-io-version.jar:\
/usr/java/fop-0.93/lib/commons-logging-version.jar:\
/usr/java/fop-0.93/lib/fop-hyph.jar:\
/usr/java/fop-0.93/lib/jai_core.jar:\
/usr/java/fop-0.93/lib/jai_codec.jar:\
/usr/java/fop-0.93/lib/serializer-version.jar:\
/usr/java/fop-0.93/lib/xalan-version.jar:\
/usr/java/fop-0.93/lib/xercesImpl-version.jar:\
/usr/java/fop-0.93/lib/xml-apis-version.jar:\
/usr/java/fop-0.93/lib/xmlgraphics-commons-version.jar:\
export CLASSPATH
```

General syntax:
```
java  org.apache.fop.cli.Main  [options]  \
    [-fo|-xml] infile \
    [-xsl stylesheet-path]  \
    -pdf  outfile.pdf
```

Convert a .fo file to pdf:
```
 java  org.apache.fop.cli.Main  \
    -fo  myfile.fo  \
    -pdf myfile.pdf
```

Convert an XML source file directly to pdf:
```
 java  org.apache.fop.cli.Main  \
    -xml myfile.xml  \
    -xsl docbook-xsl/fo/docbook.xsl  \
    -pdf myfile.pdf
```

This form of the command takes the same set of options as the FOP convenience scripts.

FOP java.lang.OutOfMemoryError

Depending on the memory configuration of your machine, your FOP process may fail on large documents with a java.lang.OutOfMemoryError. It may be that your system is not allocating enough memory to the Java Virtual Machine. You can increase the memory allocation by adding a -Xmx option to any Java command. You can make the change permanent by adding it in the FOP convenience script, such as fop.bat:

```
java -Xmx256m -cp "%LOCALCLASSPATH%" ...
```

In this example, the memory allocation is 256 MB. The value you use should be less than the installed memory on the system, and should leave enough memory for other processes that may be running.

Using other XSL-FO processors

The number of XSL-FO processors is growing. Most of them are commercial products, but they are in serious competition on price and features, which benefits the user community. They also differ in the features they offer. Here is a quick description of some of the features:

- Some products like Antenna House's XSL Formatter provide a graphical interface that previews the formatted output.

- Some products provide a command line interface or convenience script. These are useful for automated batch processing of many documents, so you do not have to open them one at a time in a graphical interface.

- Some provide a programming API, so that you can incorporate the XSL-FO processing into larger applications.

- Some provide extension elements and processing instructions to enable features that are not covered in the XSL-FO 1.0 standard. Many of those extensions were incorporated into the recently finalized XSL-FO 1.1 standard.

- Some products can generate multiple output types, such as PDF and PostScript.

Because these products are undergoing rapid development, and because they provide their own documentation and support, this book will not provide general instructions on how to use them. But the DocBook XSL stylesheets include support for some of the extensions provided by a few of the processors, and those will be described in this book.

Processor extensions

As of the current writing, the DocBook stylesheets support extensions in PTC's Arbortext, RenderX's XEP, and Antenna House's XSL Formatter products. When the extensions for one of these processors is turned on, extra code is written by the stylesheet into the XSL-FO file. That extra code is understood only by a specific processor, so this feature is controlled by stylesheet parameters.

If you are using XEP, then set the `xep.extensions` parameter to 1. If you are using Antenna House's product, then set the `axf.extensions` parameter to 1. If you are using the Arbortext processor, then set the `arbortext.extensions` parameter to 1. You should never turn on the extensions for a processor you are not using, or you will likely get a lot of error messages from the XSL-FO processor that does not understand the extra code.

Not all extension functions in each product are used by the DocBook stylesheets. If you find in their documentation an extension you want to use, you can write a customization layer that implements an extension.

Here are the XSL-FO processor extensions that the stylesheets currently implement:

- PDF bookmarks. When you open a PDF file in a PDF reader, the left window pane may show a table of contents. Those links are PDF bookmarks inserted into the PDF file by the stylesheet using the processor's extension elements. In XEP, the extension element is `rx:bookmark`. In Antenna House, an extension attribute named `axf:outline-level` is used. In Arbortext, the element is `fo:bookmark`, which is part of the XSL 1.1 standard that is recognized by the Arbortext processor.

- PDF document information. When you view a PDF file's document properties in the reader, it may show title, author, subject, and keywords information. That information is inserted by the stylesheet as extension elements in the XSL-FO file. In XEP, the extension element is `rx:meta-info`. In Antenna House, the extension element is `axf:document-info`.

- Index cleanup. The XSL-FO 1.0 standard has no way of specifying how page numbers in a book's index should be cleaned up. The cleanup process entails removing duplicate page numbers on an entry, and converting a sequence of consecutive numbers to a page range. This produces a more usable index. In XEP, the extension element is `rx:page-index`. In Antenna House, the extension is an attribute named `axf:suppress-duplicate-page-number`.

Makefiles

You may have noticed that processing DocBook with the XSL stylesheets may require several steps and options. If you have to run the commands often, you can save typing by using a **make** utility to execute the commands for you. If you are familiar with the Java Ant utility, you can use it instead for similar purposes.

A `Makefile` is like a script or batch file, but it can have several make "targets" to run different command sequences from the same file. It can also track which files are dependent on others and process them in the right order. To use **make** effectively, you will need to read its documentation. The **make** utility is generally available on Linux and UNIX systems. It can be installed in Cygwin on Windows as well.

A very basic `Makefile` for automating the use of xsltproc and FOP might look like the following:

```
html:
        xsltproc  \
          --output  myfile.html  \
          ../docbook-xsl-1.73.1/html/docbook.xsl  \
          myfile.xml

pdf:
        xsltproc  \
          --output  myfile.fo  \
          ../docbook-xsl-1.73.1/fo/docbook.xsl  \
          myfile.xml

        fop.sh  -fo  myfile.fo  -pdf  myfile.pdf
```

The words `html` and `pdf` are **make** targets, while the indented lines are the commands that are executed if that target is selected. There are tab characters indenting the commands, and you must use tabs, not spaces. Once this file is set up, you can generate your HTML output by just typing `make html`, and your PDF output by typing `make pdf`.

A more complete example uses make variables and dependencies:

```
XSLSTYLE=../docbook-xsl/html/docbook.xsl
%.html:  %.xml
        xsltproc  --output  $@  $(XSLSTYLE)  $<

html:  myfile.html
```

This example has these features:

- It puts the stylesheet path in a variable that it references on the command line.

- It uses a suffix rule `%.html` to provide a command that works for many xml files.

- It uses `$@` to refer to the target file and `$<` to refer to the dependency file. This results in a command that looks like the following:

```
xsltproc --output myfile.html ../docbook-xsl/html/docbook.xsl myfile.xml
```

- It creates dependencies for the html target on the output file, and for the output file on the xml input file. With those dependencies, the process is not run unless the XML file modification date is newer than the HTML file.

An alternative to Makefiles is Apache Ant, which is written in Java so it runs on all platforms. It is described at *http://ant.apache.org/*. For help in using Ant with DocBook, see Dave Pawson's article *Docbook and Ant*[5].

XSL servers

Once you have learned how to process DocBook documents into HTML and PDF output, you may want to take the automation a step further. You can set up an HTTP server environment in which DocBook documents are processed on demand when they are requested by a user from their web browser. The server selects and applies a stylesheet, and may even run an XSL-FO processor to deliver fully formatted PDF documents. This permits you to keep an active repository of documents in source form, and they are rendered for delivery only when requested.

Here are two XSLT server packages. Configuring and using these packages is beyond the scope of this book.

Apache AxKit[6]   AxKit is an open source XSLT server written in C and Perl. It integrates into an Apache server and includes an embedded Perl interpreter.

Apache Cocoon[7]   Cocoon is an open source XSLT server written in Java. It uses a pipeline approach to process in multiple stages. It integrates into an Apache server, and supports Java Server Pages and database connections.

---

[5] http://www.dpawson.co.uk/docbook/ant.html
[6] http://axkit.org/
[7] http://cocoon.apache.org/

4

DocBook 5 tools

DocBook 5 is the next generation of DocBook. While it is not a radical change in terms of element names and structures, it signficantly changes the foundation on which DocBook is based. The changes allow DocBook 5 to interact with other modern XML standards and practices.

DocBook 5 differences

These are the major changes included in DocBook 5. They are each described in more detail in the following sections.

- **DocBook namespace**. The biggest change for DocBook 5 is that its elements are all defined in a DocBook namespace `http://docbook.org/ns/docbook`. This allows elements from other namespaces to be mixed into DocBook documents without creating element name conflicts. For example, MathML can be embedded using the MathML namespace. Likewise, DocBook fragments can more easily be embedded in other compound document types.

- **RelaxNG schema**. For the first time, the DocBook standard is defined using the RelaxNG schema language. RelaxNG is more powerful than DTDs, and easier to customize than XML Schemas. RelaxNG permits an element in different contexts to have different content models. For convenience (or necessity in some cases), versions of DocBook 5 are also available in DTD and XML Schema form, but those are considered non-normative and do not match all the features of the RelaxNG version.

- **Universal linking**. In DocBook 4, only a few elements like `link` and `xref` were used to form links. In DocBook 5, most elements that generate some output can be made into a link. The link can go to an internal or external destination. Also, the `id` attribute in DocBook 4 is replaced with the `xml:id` attribute.

- **Unform metadata elements**. In DocBook 5, elements from DocBook 4 such as `bookinfo`, `chapterinfo`, `sectioninfo`, etc. are all replaced by a single `info` element. The element may have different content models in different contexts, to manage titled and non-titled elements, for example.

- **Annotations**. DocBook 5 introduces a general purpose annotation mechanism that allows you to associate information with any element.

DocBook 5 namespace

A DocBook 5 XML file will look a lot like a DocBook 4 XML file. The main difference is that the document's root element must have the DocBook namespace attribute and a schema `version` attribute. For example:

```
<?xml version="1.0"?>
<book xmlns="http://docbook.org/ns/docbook" version="5.0">
...
```

A namespace attribute is the special XML attribute `xmlns` that identifies a unique URI that is the *namespace name*. In this case, the URI is `http://docbook.org/ns/docbook`, which was defined by the OASIS DocBook Technical Committee as the official namespace name for DocBook.

A namespace attribute may optionally define a *namespace prefix*, and then the elements in that namespace must use the prefix on the element name. In the following example, the prefix is d:

```
<?xml version="1.0"?>
<d:book xmlns:d="http://docbook.org/ns/docbook">
...
```

Note that the root element is now `d:book`, and all other DocBook elements in the document must also have the `d:` prefix on their names (in both opening tags and closing tags of elements). When a namespace attribute has no prefix, the namespace becomes the *default* namespace.

A namespace attribute on an element means that the namespace is *in scope* for that element and all of its descendants. That does not necessarily mean those elements are in the namespace, just that the namespace is recognized. An element within that scope is actually in the namespace only if the element's prefix matches the namespace attribute's prefix. That includes the special case of the default namespace when the attribute does not define a prefix, in which case any element that is in scope and without a prefix is in that namespace.

Setting the namespace as the default namespace is usually more convenient when creating an entire document in a single namespace, as is typically done with DocBook. If you put a default namespace attribute on the root element, then the namespace is in scope for all elements, and all elements without a prefix are in the namespace. Compare these two equivalent documents, one using the default namespace and the other using a prefix:

Default namespace:
```
<?xml version="1.0"?>
<book xmlns="http://docbook.org/ns/docbook" version="5.0">
  <info>
    <title>My book title</title>
    <subtitle>My subtitle</subtitle>
  </info>
  ...
```

Namespace prefix:
```
<?xml version="1.0"?>
<d:book xmlns:d="http://docbook.org/ns/docbook" version="5.0">
  <d:info>
    <d:title>My book title</d:title>
    <d:subtitle>My subtitle</d:subtitle>
  </d:info>
  ...
```

If a file does not have the DocBook namespace declaration on its root element, then the DocBook XSL stylesheets will try to process it as a DocBook 4 document.

Of course, just adding a namespace declaration may not make a DocBook 4 into a *valid* DocBook 5 document. There are differences in elements and content models between the two versions, so some fixup may be required.

Fortunately, a guide and conversion stylesheet exist to help transition DocBook 4 documents to DocBook5. First consult *DocBook V5.0: The Transition Guide*[1]. It provides guidelines for conversion and describes the db4-upgrade.xsl stylesheet that can upgrade a version 4 document to version 5.

Included files

If you are assembling modular DocBook files into larger documents as described in Chapter 23, *Modular DocBook files* (page 359), then each of the included files must also have the DocBook namespace declaration on its root element. If not, then the stylesheet will report that the module's root element has no matching template.

DocBook 5 schemas

Another major difference between DocBook 4 and DocBook 5 is the schema language. An XML schema defines the element and attribute names, and the rules for how they are combined into documents. DocBook 4 was created when the only XML schema language was the Document Type Definition (DTD) so the official DocBook 4 schemas are all DTDs. But DTDs predate namespaces, so a DTD is not suitable as a namespace-aware schema.

The DocBook 5 reference schema is written in RelaxNG, a relatively new XML schema language. Its major advantages for use as the official DocBook schema include:

- It handles namespaces.

- It allows the content model of an element to be different when that element is in different contexts.

- It is relatively easy to read in its compact form.

- It is quite easy to customize in order to extend or subset the DocBook schema. See the section called "Adding attributes to RelaxNG" (page 435) for an example of customizing DocBook's RelaxNG schema to add attributes.

Although the normative version of the DocBook 5 schema is written in RelaxNG, there are non-normative versions generated from it in DTD form and in the W3C XML Schema language. These other versions contain the same element and attribute names. However, in each of these other versions, certain features of the schema are lost. For example, the DTD version does not permit an element to have different content when the element appears in different contexts.

The disadvantages of using RelaxNG include the following:

- No support for entity declarations.

- Fewer tools for validation.

Universal linking in DocBook 5

In DocBook 4, only specialized elements are used for creating links within and between documents. In DocBook 4, you can use xref or link with linkend attributes to form links within a DocBook document, you can use olink to form links between DocBook documents, and you can use ulink to form an arbitrary URL link.

In DocBook 5, almost all elements can be used as the basis for a link. That's because almost all elements have a set of attributes that are defined in the XLink namespace, such as xlink:href. For example, you can turn a command element into a link that targets the reference page for the command.

---

[1] http://www.docbook.org/docs/howto/

```
<para>Use the
<command xlink:href="#ref-preview">Preview</command>
command to generate a preview.</para>
```

The *XML Linking Language (XLink)*[2] has been a W3C standard since 2001. That standard says that any XML element can become the source or target of a link if it has the universal XLink attributes on it. These attributes are in their own namespace named `http://www.w3.org/1999/xlink`. Because these attributes are in their own namespace, they do not interfere with any native attributes declared for an element.

An `xlink:href` attribute value can have several different forms:

- An attribute such as `xlink:href="#intro"` refers to an `xml:id` attribute that exists in the current document. This is similar to the DocBook 4 `link` and `xref` elements. The `link` and `xref` elements were retained in DocBook 5.

- An attribute such as `xlink:href="http://docbook.org"` refers to an arbitrary URL. This is similar to the DocBook 4 `ulink` element, which was removed in DocBook 5. Instead of `ulink`, use a `link` element with a URL in its `xlink:href` attribute.

- An olink-style link from any element can be formed using two attributes. If there is a `xlink:role="http://docbook.org/xlink/role/olink` attribute present, then a link attribute of the form `xlink:href="`*targetdoc#targetptr* is interpreted as the two parts of an `olink`. The `olink` element itself is retained in DocBook 5. See Chapter 24, *Olinking between documents* (page 383) to learn more about DocBook olinks.

At the same time, the familiar DocBook linking attribute `linkend` has also been added anywhere an XLink can be used. The `linkend` attribute is limited to linking to an `xml:id` target within the same document.

The universal linking mechanism enables you to create logical links between any two DocBook elements. However, such logical links may or may not be expressible in formatted output. For example, if you put an `xlink:href` on an inline element, then the text of the inline element can become clickable link text in the output. However, if you put an `xlink:href` attribute on a block element such as `section`, then it is doubtful that making all the text in the section into a clickable link will be useful. The DocBook stylesheets currently only handle `xlink:href` on inline elements for this reason. If you want to express linking from a block element, you will have to customize the stylesheet to do so, perhaps by putting a clickable icon in the margin.

Table 4.1, "DocBook 5 linking examples" (page 37) shows the range of linking syntax in DocBook 5. The middle column shows DocBook 4 syntax, and the right columns shows DocBook 5 syntax. In DocBook 5, many links can be done in more than one way.

---

[2] http://www.w3.org/TR/xlink/

Table 4.1. DocBook 5 linking examples

Type	DocBook 4 example	DocBook 5 examples
Internal link with generated text	`<xref linkend="preview"/>`	`<xref linkend="preview"/>`
		`<xref xlink:href="#preview"/>`
Internal link with literal text	`<link linkend="preview">` `previewing</link>`	`<link linkend="preview">previewing</link>`
		`<link xlink:href="#preview">previewing</link>`
Element as internal link	`<link linkend="preview"><command>` `Preview</command></link>`	`<command linkend="preview">Preview</command>`
		`<command xlink:href="#preview">Preview</command>`
URL link with generated text.	`<ulink url="http://docbook.org"/>`	`<link xlink:href="http://docbook.org"/>`
URL link with literal text	`<ulink url="http://docbook.org">` `DocBook</ulink>`	`<link xlink:href="http://docbook.org">` `DocBook</link>`

Element as URL link	`<ulink url="http://docbook.org">`
	`<sgmltag>simplelist</sgmltag>`
	`</ulink>`
		`<tag xlink:href="http://docbook.org">`
		`simplelist</tag>`

Olink with generated text	`<olink targetdoc="reference"` `targetptr="more.1"/>`	`<olink targetdoc="reference" targetptr="more.1"/>`
		`<olink xlink:href="reference#more.1"` `xlink:role="http://docbook.org/xlink/role/olink"/>`
Olink with literal text	`<olink targetdoc="reference"` `targetptr="more.1">more(1)</olink>`	`<olink targetdoc="reference" targetptr="more.1">` `more(1)</olink>`

		`<olink xlink:href="reference#more.1"`
		`xlink:role="http://docbook.org/xlink/role/olink">`
		`more</olink>`

Element as olink	`<olink targetdoc="reference"`
	`targetptr="more.1">`
	`<command>more</command></olink>`
		`<command xlink:href="reference#more.1"`
		`xlink:role="http://docbook.org/xlink/role/olink">`
		`more</command>`

Uniform metadata elements

DocBook 5 introduces two major changes to the handling of metadata:

- All hierarchical elements and many block elements can have a metadata container.

- A single `info` element name is used as the metadata container for all elements.

In DocBook 4, only elements that defined the document hierarchy had a container element for metadata, and each hierarchical element had its own name for its metadata element. For example, book had bookinfo, chapter had chapterinfo, etc. Using separate element names permitted each of them to have a different content model in the DTD, if it was needed.

In DocBook 5, only a single metadata element is needed because it uses RelaxNG as the schema language. RelaxNG permits an element to have a different content model when the element appears in a different context. For example, the DocBook 5 info element in book can contain a title, but the info element in para cannot.

RelaxNG also solves some other problems that DTDs had for managing titles. In DocBook 4, a title element is permitted as a child of chapter, but also as a child of chapterinfo. It was never intended that title elements be used in both locations, because it is not clear which title should be used in the output. But in DTD syntax there was no way to write a content model to prevent that combination. In RelaxNG there is, so you can have only one title on a chapter if you validate with RelaxNG. The title can be in either location, but not both.

DocBook 5 also has consistent placement of the info element relative to a separate title element. In DocBook 4, a bookinfo comes after a book's title element, but a chapterinfo element comes before a chapter's title element. In DocBook 5, the info element always comes after any separate title element and before any other content. Of course, you can always put the title inside the info element so you do not have to remember the order at all.

Annotations

DocBook 5 has a new system for associating annotations with elements. It adds the following two new elements and defines the semantics of associating an annotation with an element.

- The alt element for a short text description.

- The annotation element for an arbitrarily complex description.

These are described in more detail in the following sections.

The alt element

The alt element lets you attach a short text description to an element. In HTML, an alt attribute lets you describe an IMG with text. In DocBook 5, the alt element serves a similar function except that it is an element and it can be applied to many elements, not just images. It permits as content only text and inlinemediaobject (which is only included to support characters not in the current font).

An alt element is placed as a child of the element it is describing. So an alt element is always describing its parent element. The following are some examples:

Alt text for a mediaobject
```
<mediaobject>
  <alt>mouse buttons</alt>
  <imageobject>
    <imagedata fileref="mouse.png"/>
  </imageobject>
</mediaobject>
```

An equation
```
<equation>
  <title>Computing energy use</title>
  <alt>Integral of power over time</alt>
  <mediaobject>
    <imageobject>
      <imagedata fileref="power-time.svg"/>
    </imageobject>
  </mediaobject>
</equation>
```

The text in an `alt` element may not appear in the output, depending on the application. For example, in HTML output an `alt` element in a `mediaobject` will become an `alt` attribute on an IMG element. But it is not be used at all in PDF output, unless a customization does so.

The annotation element

The `annotation` element takes over when the `alt` element is too limited. It is a general purpose element that can be used for a wide variety of annotation semantics. It has these features:

- An `annotation` element's content can be any mix of DocBook block elements. Its content model is like `section` but without any nested sections. So it can contain any number of paragraphs, lists, admonitions, etc. Plain text without a container element is not permitted (use `alt` for such cases).

- An `annotation` is associated with an element using attributes, not by placement, and the association can go in either or both directions. Specifically:

  — An `annotates` attribute on an `annotation` element matches the value of the `xml:id` of the element it is annotating.

  — An `annotations` attribute on any element matches the value of the `xml:id` of an `annotation` element associated with it.

- The `annotation` element's `annotates` attribute accepts multiple space-separated values, so any `annotation` can be associated with more than one annotated element.

- An element's `annotations` attribute accepts multiple space-separated values, so any element can be associated with more than one `annotation`.

- Because the association is by attributes, an `annotation` element can be located close to or far from the element it is annotating. In fact, there is no implied association based on element position, proximity, or lineage, such as parent-child.

- You can assign a `role` attribute to an `annotation` to identify it as a certain kind of annotation. There are no pre-defined role values.

An example is probably easier to understand than the explanations. The following is an example of an annotation element associated with a chapter element:

```
<chapter xml:id="setup" annotations="setup-background">
  <title>Setting up the system</title>
  <info>
    <annotation xml:id="setup-background" annotates="setup">
      <title>Background information for setup</title>
      <para>...</para>
    </annotation>
  </info>
  ...
```

This example shows how the association of an annotation and its target element can be formed in both directions. The chapter's xml:id value is referenced in the annotation's annotates attribute. Likewise, the annotation's xml:id value is referenced in the chapter's annotations attribute. Either direction is sufficient to establish the association. Using both directions makes it easier to find and maintain your annotations.

Placing this annotation element in the chapter's info element is simply a convenience. It could just as well have been placed in the book element's info element, in an appendix element, or anywhere else in the document, and it would have the same association.

To make them more flexible for modular documents, the annotates and annotations attributes are declared as attribute type CDATA. This means they are plain text, and not of attribute type IDREF. If they were of type IDREF, then the elements would have to be in the same file as the associated xml:id attributes to be validated. As CDATA, the annotations can be stored off in a separate file and used as needed. The disadvantage is that they will not be validated by the parser, but then they will also not generate validation errors if they are not stored in the same file. If your application requires annotations to work, then be sure your stylesheets check the integrity of the associations.

The DocBook XSL stylesheets do not output the content of annotation elements by default. That is because the semantics of a particular annotation are defined by the application, not the DocBook schema. You will need to develop a stylesheet customization if you want to include annotation information in your output. See the section called "Annotations customization" (page 118) for an example.

Entities with DocBook 5

When you switch from DTDs to RelaxNG (or to W3C XML Schema, for that matter), you lose the ability to define XML entities in the schema. Neither RelaxNG nor the XML Schema language provide a mechanism for declaring entities. Although there were probably good reasons for these decisions, it comes as a surprise to those who find entities to be a very useful feature of XML.

You can still use entities in DocBook 5, but you cannot declare them in the RelaxNG schema. Instead, you must reference your entity declarations in the DOCTYPE declaration of each document that needs them.

An XML DOCTYPE declaration can have two parts. The *external DTD subset* is the part that is referenced by the PUBLIC and SYSTEM identifiers of document's DTD. The *internal DTD subset* consists of any DTD declarations inside the document itself, enclosed within a set of square brackets within the DOCTYPE. When using RelaxNG as your DocBook schema, you can skip the external subset because you are not using a DTD, and just declare an internal subset. See the following example.

```
<?xml version="1.0"?>
<!DOCTYPE book [
<!ENTITY company "Acme Widgets, Inc.">
<!ENTITY product "Top Widget">
...
]>
<book xmlns="http://docbook.org/ns/docbook" version="5.0">
...
```

With these declarations in place, you can use entity references in your document and they will be valid. See the next section for a method of storing these declarations in a separate file.

Separate DocBook 5 entities file

Maintaining a consistent set of entities in all your documents' DOCTYPEs will be a maintenance headache if you have many documents. So instead, you should put all your entity declarations in a separate file and reference it using a *parameter entity*. A parameter entity is an entity that is used only within DTD declarations. In this case, you will use a parameter SYSTEM entity to reference your external file of entity declarations. The following describes how it is done:

1. Create a file such as myentities.ent containing your entity declarations:

   ```
   <!ENTITY company "Acme Widgets, Inc.">
   <!ENTITY product "Top Widget">
   <!ENTITY productversion "11.3">
   ...
   ```

2. In each document's DOCTYPE, declare a parameter system entity and then immediately reference it :

   ```
   <?xml version="1.0"?>
   <!DOCTYPE book [
   <!ENTITY % myent SYSTEM "/path/to/myentities.ent">
   %myent;
   ]>
   <book xmlns="http://docbook.org/ns/docbook" version="5.0">
   ...
   ```

If the path to the entities file resolves properly, then the entities in it are available to be used in the document. When you update the entity declarations in myentities.ent, the changes will apply to all documents that reference the file.

If you want to swap in a different entities file, you can use an XML catalog to map the system identifier in the parameter entity declaration to another filename. This can be useful if you maintain several parallel entity sets that you use for different products, for example. You can choose an entity set at runtime by selecting a different catalog file. See Chapter 5, *XML catalogs* (page 47) for more information.

DocBook character entities

Even if you do not define your own entities, you may want to make use of the predefined entities in DocBook for the various special characters. The named character entities described in the section called "Special characters" (page 328) are normally included in the DocBook DTD that is referenced by a document. If you are using RelaxNG instead of a DTD, those entities are not automatically available.

To use the DocBook character entities, you need to locate a set of files that include entity declarations such as the following:

```
<!ENTITY bull            "&#x02022;" ><!--BULLET -->
<!ENTITY caret           "&#x02041;" ><!--CARET INSERTION POINT -->
<!ENTITY check           "&#x02713;" ><!--CHECK MARK -->
<!ENTITY cir             "&#x025CB;" ><!--WHITE CIRCLE -->
...
```

The official source for these entity declarations is the W3C website *http://www.w3.org/2003/entities/*. The entities commonly used in DocBook are under the heading "ISO 8879" on the website. Rrecent versions of the DocBook version 4 DTD included copies of those entity declarations for convenience. They are no longer included, starting with DocBook 5.

To use the W3C entities, you can download the declaration files and reference them with parameter entities as described in the previous section. Or you can directly reference them over the Internet by putting a URL in the system identifier of the parameter system entity. Internet access may slow your processing down, though.

A more convenient way to get these entity declarations for DocBook 5 is to install version 4.5 of the DocBook DTD, which includes the entities. Then you can reference a single file named dbcentx.mod that in turn references all the entity declarations. For example, if you install the DocBook 4.5 DTD in /usr/local/docbook, then your document can reference all the entity declarations this way:

```
<?xml version="1.0"?>
<!DOCTYPE book [
<!ENTITY % sgml.features "IGNORE">
<!ENTITY % xml.features "INCLUDE">
<!ENTITY % dbcent PUBLIC "-//OASIS//ENTITIES DocBook Character Entities V4.5//EN"
    "/usr/local/docbook/dbcentx.mod">
%dbcent;
]>
<book xmlns="http://docbook.org/ns/docbook" version="5.0">
...
```

This is how the DocBook 4.5 DTD references the same entities. First the DOCTYPE declares two entities to turn off the SGML features of the DTD and turn on the XML features (these are needed to access the entity declarations). Then the DOCTYPE declares a parameter system entity with PUBLIC and SYSTEM identifiers for the dbcentx.mod file. Then it references that parameter entity using %dbcent; to load all the entity declarations. All you need to do is change the system identifier to match the path to the dbcentx.mod module as it is installed on your system. Or use an XML catalog file as described in Chapter 5, *XML catalogs* (page 47).

To avoid putting all this syntax in each document, move it all to a separate entities declaration file as described in the the section called "Separate DocBook 5 entities file" (page 41). Then a single reference in each file's DOCTYPE gets everything.

Processing DocBook 5

Processing DocBook 5 files typically has two phases:

- Validating DocBook 5 documents.

- Processing DocBook 5 with XSL to produce HTML or XSL-FO.

Each of these is described in the following sections.

DocBook 5 validation

With the proliferation of XML schema languages, validation of a document has gotten more complicated. Validation used to be simple when there was only a DTD to validate a document against. Each document identified its DTD in its DOCTYPE declaration, and there were many tools available to validate it.

You can still use those same tools if you choose to use the DTD version of the DocBook 5 schema instead of RelaxNG. However, the DocBook 5 DTD is different from the RelaxNG DocBook 5 standard in several ways, and you should not expect all documents that validate against the DTD version to also validate against the RelaxNG schema, and vice versa.

All of the DocBook 5 schemas can be downloaded from *DocBook.org*[3]. The different schema types are in different subdirectories of the distribution. The RelaxNG schema comes in two versions: one with support for XIncludes and one without. If you plan to use XIncludes (as described in Chapter 23, *Modular DocBook files* (page 359)), then use the filename starting with `docbookxi` instead of `docbook`. Also, each version comes in the two RelaxNG syntax types: the full XML syntax version with a `.rng` filename extension, and the compact syntax version with a `.rnc` extension.

If you want to validate against the DocBook 5 RelaxNG schema, then you have to find the right validation tool. The DocBook 5 RelaxNG schema includes embedded Schematron rules to express certain constraints on some content models. For example, a Schematron rule is added to prevent a `sidebar` element from containing another `sidebar`. For complete validation, a validator needs to check both the RelaxNG content models and the Schematron rules.

Many people use `xmllint` from the libxml2 toolkit to validate their DocBook 4 documents. Although `xmllint` has a `--relaxng` option to validate against a RelaxNG schema (XML syntax only), it does not process Schematron rules. So you will not be able to fully validate a DocBook 5 document with `xmllint` currently.

The following sections describe three tools that handle complete DocBook 5 validation, including Schematron rules.

Sun MSV

Sun Microsystem's Multi-Schema Validator is a free tool that can be used to validate a document against more than one schema at a time. This is useful if your document has components from more than one namespace, each of which has its own schema.

To use MSV with the DocBook 5 RelaxNG schema, you need to get the *relames* version which has support for embedded Schematron rules, which are used in DocBook 5.0.

Download the latest version of `relames` from Sun's *MSV website*[4]. Unpack the zip file and note the location of the `relames.jar` file. To validate a file, use a command like the following:

```
java -Xss512K -jar relames.jar rng/docbook.rng mydocument.xml
```

The `-Xss512K` option raises the Java stack size to avoid stack overflow errors.

More details on using Sun's Multi-Schema Validator are available in *DocBook 5.0: The Transition Guide*[5].

Topologi validator

Topologi Pty. Ltd. makes a number of commercial XML tools, but it also makes available a free validation tool for RelaxNG schemas with embedded Schematron rules. Their `Schematron.zip` implementation is available for download

---

[3] http://docbook.org/schemas/5x
[4] http://msv.dev.java.net
[5] http://www.docbook.org/docs/howto/

at *http://www.topologi.com/resources/Schematron.zip*. The download includes a Windows batch file for running the validator:

The batch file syntax:
`EmbRNG_java.bat document RNG-schema`

Example batch command:
`EmbRNG_java.bat  mybook5.xml  docbook50/rng/docbook.rng`

You have to execute the batch file from within its own directory because it depends on relative paths to its jar files and XSL stylesheets. The document and schema can be elsewhere. The validator will check the RelaxNG content rules, as well as any embedded Schematron rules. You can only use this validator with the full XML syntax version of RelaxNG (`docbook.rng`), not the compact syntax version (`docbook.rnc`).

Oxygen XML editor

The commercial product Oxygen XML editor can validate a DocBook 5 document. It handles both the RelaxNG content models and the embedded Schematron rules. It can also validate while you are editing the document.

To associate the DocBook 5 RelaxNG schema with DocBook 5 documents, you can associate the DocBook 5 namespace with the schema pathname. Use this menu sequence:

Options+Preferences+Editor+Default Schema Associations

More details on using Oxygen are available in *DocBook 5.0: The Transition Guide*[6].

DocBook 5 XSLT processing

To process your DocBook 5 documents, you can use the same XSLT and XSL-FO processors that you use for DocBook 4 documents. You do have a choice of two sets of stylesheets:

- The original *docbook-xsl* stylesheet distribution can process DocBook 5 documents, but it first strips the DocBook namespace from the document elements so they match the patterns in the stylesheet.

- The *docbook-xsl-ns* stylesheet distribution operates directly in the DocBook 5 namespace for pattern matching on elements.

The two approaches are discussed in the following sections.

Using DocBook 4 stylesheets with DocBook 5

The original DocBook XSL stylesheets written for Docbook 4 documents would not normally work with DocBook 5 documents. That's because a pattern match in an XSL template must match on any namespace as well as the local name of an element. When you process a DocBook 5 document with the original stylesheets, none of the pattern matching templates include the DocBook 5 namespace, so none of the templates will match any elements in the document.

The stylesheets work around this problem with a simple mechanism. If the stylesheet detects a document whose root element is in the DocBook 5 namespace, it first copies the entire document into a variable while stripping out the namespace from all the elements. The stylesheet then converts the variable into a node set, and applies templates to the node set normally. Because the elements in the node set are no longer in the DocBook 5 namespace, its elements will match the patterns in the original stylesheets. All this takes place automatically before the actual processing starts.

---

[6] http://www.docbook.org/docs/howto/

The result is that you can process DocBook 5 documents with the same commands as for DocBook 4 documents. You will see these messages indicating what is going on:

```
Stripping namespace from DocBook 5 document.
Processing stripped document.
```

The advantages of processing DocBook 5 documents with the original DocBook 4 stylesheets are:

- You can use your existing customizations.

- You can process both DocBook 4 and DocBook 5 documents with the same tool chain.

The disadvantages of these stylesheets for DocBook 5 are:

- The act of copying the content into a node set loses the base URI of the document. This can create problems with relative path references for images and for finding the olink database (if you use olinks).

- You do not learn anything about namespaces.

Using DocBook 5 stylesheets

The stylesheets included in the docbook-xsl-ns distribution are copies of the original stylesheets, but with the DocBook namespace prefix added to element names in pattern matches and expressions. For example:

```
<xsl:template match="d:para">
...
```

You can process DocBook 5 documents using the same commands as for DocBook 4 documents, just substituting the path to the equivalent docbook-xsl-ns stylesheet instead. The behavior of the stylesheets should be identical to the originals.

If you happen to process a DocBook document whose element is without the namespace declaration, the stylesheet does not fail. Rather, it detects that the document does not have the namespace, and preprocesses it to add the namespace to all elements in the document. It uses the same node set trick that the original stylesheets use to strip the namespace from DocBook 5 documents. Generally it will be better to use the original DocBook 4 stylesheets for DocBook 4 documents.

The advantages of processing DocBook 5 documents with the DocBook 5 stylesheets are:

- You can write customization layers using the DocBook namespace.

- There is no temporary node set that loses the document URI, which can mess up resolving relative paths in some cases.

The disadvantages of these stylesheets for DocBook 5 are:

- You cannot use an existing customization layer until you add the DocBook namespace prefix to all element names used in patterns and expressions in the stylesheet.

- You have to learn something about namespaces.

See the section called "Customizing DocBook 5 XSL" (page 116) for more information about creating customizations for the DocBook 5 stylesheets.

Using XIncludes with DocBook 5

XInclude is an XML inclusion mechanism that is described in Chapter 23, *Modular DocBook files* (page 359). An XInclude uses an href attribute to reference another file that is to be included in the main file. The XInclude may also have a fragment reference to a specific id attribute (DocBook 4) or xml:id (DocBook 5) in the included file in order to include just that specific element from the file.

If you use this mechanism with DocBook 4 files, a fragment reference will fail if the processor cannot load the included file's DTD to confirm that an attribute named id is of attribute type ID, and therefore subject to being referenced. ID is a specific attribute type defined in the XML specification, to be declared in the DTD or schema. If the DTD is not readable for some reason, the processor cannot assume that an attribute named id is of type ID, and the XInclude will fail. Often the error message is not very helpful for determining the cause of the problem.

With DocBook 5, you must use xml:id instead of id to identify each element. This has the advantage that xml:id is predefined by a separate W3C Recommendation to have attribute type ID. Therefore you do not have to worry about fragment references failing due to lack of schema.

What about XSLT 2 and Saxon 8?

You may have heard about XSLT version 2 and the implementation of it in Saxon 8, and you might be wondering how it applies to DocBook 5? The short answer is that it does not yet apply very much, any more than it applies to DocBook 4. But it will in the future, big time.

XSLT 2.0 became a full W3C Recommendation on 23 January 2007. It is the next generation of XSLT processing, with a simpler processing model and a greatly enhanced XPath 2.0 selection language associated with it. Version 8 of the Saxon XSLT processor has long been the only implementation of XSLT 2, since it was essentially used as a test bed by Michael Kay, the editor of the XSLT 2 specification. Now that XSLT 2 is an official Recommendation, many more XSLT 2 processors are expected to become available.

More importantly for DocBook users, Norman Walsh was an active member of the working group that created XSLT 2. Norman Walsh was the original creator of the DocBook XSL stylesheets, and he is working on an XSLT 2 set of DocBook stylesheets. They are not finished, but available as alpha releases for those who want to experiment with XSLT 2. To customize the XSLT 2 stylesheets, you will need to learn XSLT 2 and XPath 2.

But you do not need XSLT 2 to process DocBook 5 documents. The current set of docbook-xsl-ns stylesheet files are written in XSLT 1 and work with existing XSLT 1 processors such as Saxon 6, Xalan, and xsltproc.

The Saxon 8 processor can be used with some XSLT 1 stylesheets, because the XSLT 2 standard defines a backwards compatibility mode. When an XSLT 2 processor such as Saxon 8 sees a version="1.0" attribute in the stylesheet's root element, it switches into that mode. But the backwards compatibility is not complete, so there is no guarantee that the existing DocBook XSL stylesheets will work with Saxon 8. Unless a stylesheet is written in XSLT 2, there is no advantage to using Saxon 8 over Saxon 6.

5

XML catalogs

A catalog in XML provides a mapping from generic addresses to specific local directories on a given machine. A catalog can be used to locate the DocBook DTD, system entity files, and stylesheet files during processing. Catalog files add a degree of flexibility to your setup. Once you have set up your scripts and Makefiles to use catalog files, if you rearrange things or transfer to a different system, you can just edit the catalog file to remap all the old paths to new locations.

There are two kinds of catalogs that can be used with DocBook: SGML catalogs and XML catalogs. They use different syntax, and different tools may support one kind or the other. SGML catalogs are older and simpler. XML catalogs do everything that SGML catalogs do and much more. For that reason, only XML catalogs are discussed here. If you want to read the original standards documents, see *XML Catalogs: Committee Specification 06 Aug 2001*[1] for XML catalogs, or *Entity Management -- OASIS Technical Resolution 9401:1997*[2] for SGML catalogs. The web article *XML Entity and URI Resolvers*[3] by Norman Walsh provides further information about both kinds of catalogs.

Why use XML catalogs

People use catalogs to make their XML setup more portable and more flexible. With catalogs, you can:

- Use stable PUBLIC identifiers in your DOCTYPE declarations in your files, and not worry about using the SYSTEM identifier to find the DTD file or system entity files. The PUBLIC identifier can be mapped to a specific location on a given machine with a catalog. If you move your files to a new machine, you do not have to edit them all to change the SYSTEM reference, you just edit the catalog's mapping of the PUBLIC identifier.

- Write Makefiles with generic pathnames to your stylesheet, and let the catalog remap the pathname to a location on the machine. When you move your setup and files to a different machine or to different locations, you do not have to fix internal references in your documents, stylesheets, and Makefiles. You can just use a catalog file to map the generic paths to the new locations.

- Use stable Internet URL addresses for your DTD system identifier or stylesheet pathname, but let the catalog resolve them to pathnames on the local machine. That way you get efficient processing if they are available locally, and it falls back to network access only if it has to.

---

[1] http://www.oasis-open.org/committees/entity/spec-2001-08-06.html
[2] http://www.oasis-open.org/committees/entity/background/9401.html
[3] http://xml.apache.org/commons/components/resolver/resolver-article.html

- Select a different stylesheet for the same command by selecting a different catalog file that maps the pathname to a different location. For example, you could put `docbook.xsl` on all your command lines in your Makefiles, then have the Makefile map that to, say, `chunk.xsl` stylesheet if a variable is set.

- Test new releases of the stylesheets or DTD by temporarily changing your catalog to point to them.

How to write an XML catalog file

An XML catalog is made up of entries from one or more *catalog entry files*. A catalog entry file is an XML file whose document element is `catalog` and whose content follows the XML catalog DTD defined by OASIS at *http://www.oasis-open.org/committees/entity/spec.html*. Most of the elements are *catalog entries*, each of which serves to map an identifier or URL to another location. Following are some useful examples.

Resolve the DTD location

The `DOCTYPE` declaration at the top of an XML document gives the processor information to identify the DTD. Here is a declaration suggested by the DTD itself:

```
<!DOCTYPE book PUBLIC "-//OASIS//DTD DocBook XML V4.5//EN"
          "http://www.oasis-open.org/docbook/xml/4.5/docbookx.dtd">
```

The first quoted string after `PUBLIC` is the DTD's `PUBLIC` identifier, and the second quoted string is the `SYSTEM` identifier. In this case, the `SYSTEM` identifier is a full URL to the OASIS website.

You can use a `public` catalog entry to resolve a DTD's `PUBLIC` identifier, or you can use a `system` catalog entry to resolve a DTD's `SYSTEM` identifier. These two kinds of catalog entries are used only to resolve DTD identifiers and system entity identifiers (external files), not stylesheet references. Here is a simple XML catalog file that shows how to resolve a DTD identifier:

Example 5.1. Catalog entry to resolve DTD location

```
<?xml version="1.0"?>
<!DOCTYPE catalog
    PUBLIC "-//OASIS/DTD Entity Resolution XML Catalog V1.0//EN"
    "http://www.oasis-open.org/committees/entity/release/1.0/catalog.dtd"> ❶
<catalog  xmlns="urn:oasis:names:tc:entity:xmlns:xml:catalog">  ❷
  <group  prefer="public"  xml:base="file:///usr/share/xml/" >  ❸

    <public
        publicId="-//OASIS//DTD DocBook XML V4.5//EN"  ❹
        uri="docbook45/docbookx.dtd"/>

    <system
        systemId="http://www.oasis-open.org/docbook/xml/4.5/docbookx.dtd"  ❺
        uri="docbook45/docbookx.dtd"/>

    <system
        systemId="docbook4.5.dtd"  ❻
        uri="docbook45/docbookx.dtd"/>
  </group>
</catalog>
```

Note these features of this catalog:

❶ The catalog file's DOCTYPE identifies the file as an OASIS XML catalog file. If you do not have an Internet connection, you should remove or comment out the entire DOCTYPE declaration. If you do not, the catalog processor will try to load the `catalog.dtd` file over the network and fail. You cannot use the catalog to resolve its own DTD location.

❷ The `catalog` element contains the catalog content, and it includes a catalog namespace identifier.

❸ The `group` element is a wrapper element that sets attributes that apply to all the catalog entries contained in the group. The `prefer="public"` attribute means the catalog resolver should try to use the PUBLIC identifier before resorting to the SYSTEM identifier. The `xml:base` attribute is the location that all URIs are resolved relative to.

❹ The `public` element maps the given `publicId` string to the given `uri` location (with the `xml:base` value prepended).

❺ The `system` element maps the given `systemId` string to the same location.

❻ An abbreviated system identifier that maps to a full path location.

Why have multiple entries? So different documents that specify their DOCTYPE differently can resolve to the same location. So when a DocBook document that has this DOCTYPE declaration is processed with this catalog and a catalog resolver:

```
<?xml version="1.0"?>
<!DOCTYPE  book  PUBLIC  "-//OASIS//DTD DocBook XML V4.5//EN"
     "http://www.oasis-open.org/docbook/xml/4.5/docbookx.dtd">
```

The catalog resolver loads the catalog, and as it reads the files to be processed, it looks for items to resolve. In this case we have a DOCTYPE with both a PUBLIC identifier (`-//OASIS//DTD DocBook XML V4.5//EN`) and a SYSTEM identifier (`http://www.oasis-open.org/docbook/xml/4.5/docbookx.dtd`). It finds a match on the public identifier in the catalog, and since that entry's group wrapper element prefers using the public identifier, it uses that entry. It uses the `uri` attribute value for that entry, and then prepends the `xml:base` value from its group wrapper. The result is a full pathname `/usr/share/xml/docbook45/docbookx.dtd`.

If it turns out that such a file is not at that location, then the catalog resolver looks for other catalog entries to resolve the item. It then tries the first `system` entry, which in this case matches the `www.oasis-open.org` URL to the same local file. If no catalog entry works, then the resolver gives up. Then the XML processor falls back to using the literal DOCTYPE's SYSTEM identifier `http://www.oasis-open.org/docbook/xml/4.5/docbookx.dtd` without catalog resolution, and tries to retrieve the DTD over the web.

> **Note:**
>
> The XML catalog file that ships with version 4.3 of the DocBook XML DTD is missing an entry for the `htmltblx.mod` file. If your resolver reports it as missing, then add an entry like the following to your catalog file:
>
> ```
> <public publicId="-//OASIS//ELEMENTS DocBook XML HTML Tables V4.3//EN"
> uri="htmltblx.mod"/>
> ```
>
> This problem was fixed in version 4.4.

Windows pathnames

When you are specifying an `xml:base` or `uri` attribute for use on a Microsoft Windows system, you must include the drive letter in the full URI syntax if you want it to work across processors. A Windows URI has this form:

```
file:///c:/xml/docbook/
```

Note the use of forward slashes, which is standard URI syntax.

Relative SYSTEM identifiers may not work

Another document might have a much simpler DOCTYPE declaration:

```
<!DOCTYPE book SYSTEM "docbook4.5.dtd">
```

If processed with the same catalog, there is no PUBLIC identifier to match on. So despite the prefer="public" attribute, it is forced to try to match the DOCTYPE's SYSTEM identifier with a system catalog entry. It finds a match in the systemId attribute and the uri value maps it to the same location.

Unfortunately, XML catalog entries that try to use relative system identifiers like systemId="docbook4.5.dtd" do not work with the Java resolver software currently available. The problem is that when a document with the example DOCTYPE is processed, the SAX interface in the XML parser resolves such references relative to the current document's location before the resolver gets to see it. So the resolver never has a chance to match on the original string. If you are going to use catalog files, you should probably stick with the recommended value of http://www.oasis-open.org/docbook/xml/4.5/docbookx.dtd for the SYSTEM identifier. Or you could use a phony full path, such as file:///docbookx.dtd, which will prevent the SAX interface from changing it before the catalog resolver sees it.

Locate an XSL stylesheet

You use the uri element in an XML catalog to locate stylesheets and other files. It can be used for everything that is not a declared PUBLIC or SYSTEM identifier for a DTD or system entity file. The following is an example of mapping a relative stylesheet reference to an absolute path:

Example 5.2. Catalog entry to locate a stylesheet

```
<?xml version="1.0"?>
<!DOCTYPE catalog
    PUBLIC "-//OASIS/DTD Entity Resolution XML Catalog V1.0//EN"
    "http://www.oasis-open.org/committees/entity/release/1.0/catalog.dtd">

<catalog xmlns="urn:oasis:names:tc:entity:xmlns:xml:catalog">
    <uri
        name="docbook.xsl"
        uri="file:///usr/share/xml/docbook-xsl-1.73.1/html/docbook.xsl"/>
</catalog>
```

With a catalog entry like this, your scripts and Makefiles can refer to the stylesheet file simply as docbook.xsl and let the catalog find its location on the system. By using a different catalog, you can map the name to a different stylesheet file without changing the script or Makefile command line.

Map a web address to a local file

As mentioned above, you can specify an web URL for the DTD or stylesheet to fetch it over the Internet. For efficiency, though, it's better to map the URLs to local files if they are available. The following catalog will do that.

Example 5.3. Catalog entry to map web address to local file

```
<?xml version="1.0"?>
<!DOCTYPE catalog
    PUBLIC "-//OASIS/DTD Entity Resolution XML Catalog V1.0//EN"
    "http://www.oasis-open.org/committees/entity/release/1.0/catalog.dtd">

<catalog xmlns="urn:oasis:names:tc:entity:xmlns:xml:catalog">

<system
  systemId="http://www.oasis-open.org/docbook/xml/4.5/"
  uri="file:///usr/share/xml/docbook45/" />
<uri
  name="http://docbook.sourceforge.net/release/xsl/current/html/docbook.xsl"
  uri="file:///usr/share/xml/docbook-xsl-1.73.1/html/docbook.xsl" />
<uri
  name="http://docbook.sourceforge.net/release/xsl/current/html/chunk.xsl"
  uri="file:///usr/share/xml/docbook-xsl-1.73.1/html/chunk.xsl" />
</catalog>
```

There are two uri entries here, to handle both the regular and the chunking stylesheets.

Map many references with rewrite entries

To reduce the number of catalog entries, you can map a prefix instead of a bunch of similar names. Two catalog entry elements named rewriteSystem and rewriteURI let you map the first part of a reference to a different prefix. That lets you map many files in the same location with a single catalog entry. Use rewriteSystem to remap a DOCTYPE system identifier, and use rewriteURI to remap other URLs like stylesheet references.

Here is the previous example done with rewrite entries:

```
<?xml version="1.0"?>
<!DOCTYPE catalog
    PUBLIC "-//OASIS/DTD Entity Resolution XML Catalog V1.0//EN"
    "http://www.oasis-open.org/committees/entity/release/1.0/catalog.dtd">
<catalog xmlns="urn:oasis:names:tc:entity:xmlns:xml:catalog">
    <rewriteSystem
        systemIdStartString="http://www.oasis-open.org/docbook/xml/4.5/"
        rewritePrefix="file:///usr/share/xml/docbook45/" />
    <rewriteURI
        uriStartString="http://docbook.sourceforge.net/release/xsl/current/"
        rewritePrefix="file:///usr/share/xml/docbook-xsl-1.73.1/" />
</catalog>
```

The two stylesheet `uri` entries are replaced with a single `rewriteURI` entry. Whatever directory structure below that point that matches on both ends can be mapped. For example:

This URL:
`http://docbook.sourceforge.net/release/xsl/current/html/docbook.xsl`
is mapped to:
`file:///usr/share/xml/docbook-xsl-1.73.1/html/docbook.xsl`

This URL:
`http://docbook.sourceforge.net/release/xsl/current/fo/custom.xsl`
is mapped to:
`file:///usr/share/xml/docbook-xsl-1.73.1/fo/custom.xsl`

Using multiple catalog files

You can use the `nextCatalog` element to include other catalog entry files in the process. If a reference cannot be resolved in the current catalog entry file, then the processor moves on to the next catalog specified by such an element. You can put `nextCatalog` elements anywhere in a catalog entry file, since they are not looked at until all catalog entries in the current file have been tried. Each new catalog file can also contain `nextCatalog` entries.

Using this feature lets you organize your catalog entries into modular files which can be combined in various ways. For example, you could separate your DTD lookups from your stylesheet lookups. Since the DocBook DTD comes with a catalog file, you can just point to that catalog to resolve DTD PUBLIC identifiers.

For DocBook 4.5:
`<nextCatalog  catalog="/usr/share/xml/docbook45/catalog.xml" />`

For DocBook 4.1.2:
`<nextCatalog  catalog="/usr/share/xml/docbook412/docbook.cat" />`

In the latter example, it is pointing to the SGML catalog that was included with an older version of the DTD. The references in either of those catalog files are all relative to the catalog file location, so the resolver should be able to find any of the DTD files by its PUBLIC identifier. do not try to move the DocBook catalog file out of the directory that contains the DTD files or the relative references will not work.

Example DocBook catalog file

Here is a complete example of an XML catalog file that can resolve PUBLIC and SYSTEM identifiers for the DocBook DTD, and references to stylesheets. It assumes all the DocBook files are stored under `/usr/share/xml` so the `group` `xml:base="/usr/share/xml/"` element provides the main pathname prefix. You would need to replace that path with your own. If your system puts the stylesheet under a different location from the DTD, then you would need two `group` elements to specify the two `xml:base` values.

Example 5.4. Example XML catalog file

```
<?xml version="1.0"?>
<!DOCTYPE catalog
    PUBLIC "-//OASIS/DTD Entity Resolution XML Catalog V1.0//EN"
    "http://www.oasis-open.org/committees/entity/release/1.0/catalog.dtd">

<catalog xmlns="urn:oasis:names:tc:entity:xmlns:xml:catalog">

  <!-- DTD and stylesheet files installed under /usr/share/xml -->
  <group  xml:base="file:///usr/share/xml/">

    <!-- Resolve DTD URL system ID to local file -->
    <rewriteSystem
        systemIdStartString="http://www.oasis-open.org/docbook/xml/4.5/"
        rewritePrefix="docbook45/" />
    <!-- Resolve stylesheet URL to local file -->
    <rewriteURI
        uriStartString="http://docbook.sourceforge.net/release/xsl/current/"
        rewritePrefix="docbook-xsl-1.73.1/" />

    <!-- Resolve DTD PUBLIC identifiers -->
    <nextCatalog  catalog="docbook45/catalog.xml" />

    <!-- To resolve simple DTD SYSTEM identifiers. -->
    <!-- Note: this does not work with Java resolver -->
    <!--    classes in Saxon or Xalan -->
    <system
        systemId="docbook.dtd"
        uri="docbook45/docbookx.dtd" />

    <!-- To resolve short stylesheet references -->
    <uri
        name="docbook.xsl"
        uri="docbook-xsl-1.73.1/html/docbook.xsl" />
    <uri
        name="chunk.xsl"
        uri="docbook-xsl-1.73.1/html/chunk.xsl" />
    <uri
        name="fo-docbook.xsl"
        uri="docbook-xsl-1.73.1/fo/docbook.xsl" />

  </group>

</catalog>
```

It is sometimes useful to include DTD catalog entries for both the system and public identifiers. Oddly enough, that may negate the use of a prefer="public" attribute in the catalog for that DTD. The rules for catalog resolution say that the given DOCTYPE system identifier is first checked against the catalog system entries, regardless of the prefer setting. If the given system identifier is matched in the catalog, then that match is always used. If there is no match on the system identifier in the catalog, then the prefer="public" setting comes into play and means the catalog should first check for a match on the public identifier of the DTD. If that is not matched in the catalog, then the given system identifier is used. If prefer="system", then the public identifier is ignored entirely.

How to use a catalog file

Once you have your catalog file, you have to tell the processor to use it. How you do that depends on which processor you are using.

All of the Java XSL processors can use the Java resolver classes written by Norm Walsh and made available through the Apache XML Project. Download the latest version of `resolver.jar` from *http://xml.apache.org/commons/dist/* (it may have a version number in the name) and copy it to a convenient location. The `resolver.jar` file is also included in distribution of the Xerces parser starting with version 2.6.2.

To use the resolver, you add the file's pathname to your CLASSPATH environment variable, create a `CatalogManager.properties` file, and add several resolver options to your command line as described below.

Using catalogs with Saxon

Here is how you get catalogs working with Saxon:

1. Download the `resolver.jar` file from *http://xml.apache.org/commons/dist/* (it may have a version number in the filename).

2. Add the pathname of the `resolver.jar` file to your CLASSPATH. See the section called "Installing Saxon" (page 18) for information on setting CLASSPATH.

3. Create a file named `CatalogManager.properties`, as described below.

4. Add the directory containing the `CatalogManager.properties` file to your CLASSPATH.

The `CatalogManager.properties` file tells the resolver where to look for catalog files and sets configuration options. That file is placed in a directory that is included in your Java CLASSPATH. The content of the file looks something like the following:

```
catalogs=catalog.xml;../../dtd/docbook45/docbook.cat
relative-catalogs=false
static-catalog=yes
catalog-class-name=org.apache.xml.resolver.Resolver
verbosity=1
```

The first line is the most important, as it indicates the pathnames of catalog files to use, in a semicolon-separated list. The filenames can be absolute paths, or relative to the `CatalogManager.properties` file. If you want relative pathnames to be interpreted relative to your document's location, then set `relative-catalogs=true`. In this example, the path `../../dtd/docbook45/docbook.cat` is taken to be relative to the directory containing the `CatalogManager.properties` file. The list of catalogs can include SGML catalogs, such as that included with the DocBook XML DTD.

If the catalog setup is not working, try setting the `verbosity` value to a higher number, up to 4 for maximum debug information.

A Saxon command line that uses the catalog resolver looks like the following:

For Saxon:
```
java  -cp "/usr/java/saxon.jar:/docbook-xsl/extensions/saxon653.jar:\
/usr/share/resolver.jar;/usr/share" \
  com.icl.saxon.StyleSheet \
  -x org.apache.xml.resolver.tools.ResolvingXMLReader \
  -y org.apache.xml.resolver.tools.ResolvingXMLReader \
  -r org.apache.xml.resolver.tools.CatalogResolver \
  -u \
  -o myfile.html \
  myfile.xml  docbook.xsl
```

In this example, the `resolver.jar` and `CatalogManager.properties` files are placed in `/usr/share`. The example includes the -cp Java command option to temporarily add to the CLASSPATH for that command. If you instead add them to your CLASSPATH environment variable, you do not need that option in each command. The -u Saxon option tells Saxon to treat pathnames specified on the command line as URIs, so that the catalog can use URI lookups. The -x, -y, and -r options configure Saxon to use the resolver code.

Note:

Resolving short references like docbook.xsl on the command line requires Java version 1.4 or later. If you are using Java version 1.3 or earlier, the name must use URI syntax such as `file:///docbook.xsl`. Such URIs are mapped to the real location by the catalog.

Using catalogs with Xalan

Note:

XML catalogs do not work with Xalan 2.4 1 in Java 1.4. See the section called "Bypassing the old Xalan installed with Java" (page 25) for information on updating your Xalan on Java 1.4.

To use catalogs with Xalan, you must first set up the `resolver.jar` and `CatalogManager.properties` files as described in the section called "Using catalogs with Saxon" (page 54). Then you can use a command line such as:

For Xalan:
```
java  -cp "/usr/java/xerces.jar:/usr/java/xalan.jar:\
/docbook-xsl/extensions/xalan25.jar:\
/usr/share/resolver.jar:/usr/share" \
  org.apache.xalan.xslt.Process  \
  -ENTITYRESOLVER  org.apache.xml.resolver.tools.CatalogResolver \
  -URIRESOLVER  org.apache.xml.resolver.tools.CatalogResolver \
  -out  myfile.html  \
  -in  myfile.xml  \
  -xsl  http://docbook.sourceforge.net/release/xsl/current/html/docbook.xsl
```

Note:

The current version of Xalan (2.7.0) does not resolve URIs from the command line using the catalog file. However, if the same URI is used in a stylesheet processing instruction inside the document (instead of using the -xsl option), then the catalog is consulted and the URI remapped.

As with the Saxon example, the `resolver.jar` and `CatalogManager.properties` files are assumed to be located in `/usr/share`, but you can locate them wherever it is convenient.

Using catalogs with xsltproc

The **xsltproc** processor is not Java based so it uses its own mechanism for catalogs. It does not use `resolver.jar` or `CatalogManager.properties`. By default, xsltproc looks for an XML catalog file named `/etc/xml/catalog` (except on Windows, for which there is no default location). You can specify a different file by setting an `XML_CATALOG_FILES` environment variable. It should contain URIs to one or more catalog files. A local URL can be a relative pathname such as `catalog.xml` in the current directory, or an absolute pathname if it uses the `file:///path/to/file` URI syntax (even on Windows). If you have more than one catalog file, then separate the URIs with spaces in the environment variable. (Earlier versions of xsltproc supported only one catalog file.) The `XML_DEBUG_CATALOG` environment variable is optional and turns on catalog debugging if its value is nonzero. The following is an example of their usage.

For xsltproc:
```
XML_CATALOG_FILES="catalog.xml  file:///usr/share/xml/catalog.xml" \
   XML_DEBUG_CATALOG=1 \
   xsltproc  docbook.xsl  myfile.xml
```

This example set the environment variables on for this command. Normally you would set the environment variables using the regular mechanism for your operating system so you do not have to add them to every command.

Alternately, you can name your catalog file with the default pathname `/etc/xml/catalog`, and xsltproc will just use it (except on Windows).

The catalog processing mechanism in xsltproc will properly handle short references such as `fo/docbook.xsl` for the stylesheet name on the command line.

Part II. Stylesheet options

Contents

6

Using stylesheet parameters

The DocBook XSL stylesheets have many *parameters* that can be used to control various aspects of the output that the stylesheets generate. A parameter is simply a named variable that you give a value to. For example, with parameters you can control what level of headings appear in the tables of contents, whether you want a CSS stylesheet attached to your HTML output, and what body type size you want for your print output.

The great thing about parameters is that they are very easy to use. They are the easiest way to customize the behavior of the stylesheets. You can specify parameter values on the command line, or you can create a file full of them to use with each processing job. The only downside to parameters is when there is no parameter for some particular change you would like to see. You can certainly request additional parameters of the DocBook stylesheet maintainers at *http://docbook.sourceforge.net*, but that would not solve your immediate problem.

In order to use parameters, you have to know the names of available parameters, what they do, and what values to assign them. An up-to-date set of HTML reference pages is included in each DocBook XSL distribution in the doc/html and doc/fo directories. You can also bookmark these online reference links that provide the information for the latest distribution:

- *HTML Parameter Reference*[1]

- *FO Parameter Reference*[2]

If you are not using the latest version, you should probably consult the reference pages that came with your distribution.

Parameters on the command line

Each of the XSL processors use slightly different syntax to specify parameters on the command line. Here are some examples that set two parameters: html.stylesheet to specify the name of a CSS stylesheet to associate with your HTML files, and admon.graphics to turn on the icon graphics for admonition elements such as note.

---

[1] http://docbook.sourceforge.net/release/xsl/current/doc/html/
[2] http://docbook.sourceforge.net/release/xsl/current/doc/fo/

Using parameters with xsltproc:

```
xsltproc  --output myfile.html  \
  --stringparam  html.stylesheet "corpstyle.css"  \
  --stringparam  admon.graphics 1 \
  docbook.xsl  myfile.xml
```

Put parameters at end of line with Saxon:

```
java  com.icl.saxon.StyleSheet  -o myfile.html  myfile.xml  docbook.xsl \
  html.stylesheet="corpstyle.css" \
  admon.graphics=1
```

Options including -param can be in any order with Xalan:

```
java  org.apache.xalan.xslt.Process  -out myfile.html  -in myfile.xml \
  -xsl docbook.xsl \
  -param  html.stylesheet "corpstyle.css" \
  -param  admon.graphics 1
```

If a parameter value includes spaces or special characters, put it in quotes.

Parameters in a file

If you find yourself using lots of parameters and they are always the same values, then you might want to shorten your commands by putting all the parameter settings into one file. Unfortunately, the XSL processors do not have an option to read all the parameter settings from a file. Instead, you need to create a stylesheet customization layer that includes all of your parameter settings using XSL syntax. Customization layers are described in the section called "Customization layer" (page 100), but here is a short example:

```
<?xml version='1.0'?>
<xsl:stylesheet xmlns:xsl="http://www.w3.org/1999/XSL/Transform" version="1.0">
<xsl:import href="/usr/share/xsl/docbook/html/docbook.xsl"/>
<xsl:param name="html.stylesheet" select="'corpstyle.css'"/>
<xsl:param name="admon.graphics" select="1"/>
</xsl:stylesheet>
```

You would use this file instead of the regular docbook.xsl stylesheet file in your command line. If you decide to add additional customizations, they can go in this file as well.

7
HTML output options

This chapter describes some common options for HTML output. These options can all be specified on the command line and do not require a customization file for the XSL stylesheets. A much larger set of options that include stylesheet customizations is described in Chapter 12, *HTML customizations* (page 147)

Single HTML file

The DocBook stylesheet html/docbook.xsl produces a single HTML file from your DocBook XML input file. The stylesheet itself does not name the file, so you have to supply the output filename. You can do this with the specific output option of your XSL processor, or you can simply redirect the output of the processor to a file.

```
xsltproc  --output  myfile.html  docbook.xsl  myfile.xml
```
or
```
xsltproc  docbook.xsl  myfile.xml  >  myfile.html
```

If you want the output to appear in another directory, then use a relative or absolute pathname instead of just the filename. For example

```
xsltproc  --output  /usr/apache/htdocs/myfile.html  docbook.xsl  myfile.xml
```

Several other options for single-file output are described in the section called "Single file options with onechunk" (page 69).

Processing part of a document

You may want to generate output for only part of large DocBook document. For example, you might need just one book from a set document, one chapter from a book document, or one refentry page from a reference document. When you are developing a back-of-book index, it helps to periodically generate only the index output so you can check it. The DocBook XSL stylesheets have a parameter that lets you output part of a document.

There are two conditions to use this feature:

- The content you want to output is contained in a single element. You cannot use this feature to output an arbitrary selection of elements.

- The selected element must have an id attribute on it.

If these two conditions are met, then generating output for one element is easy. You process the document as you normally would, but you set the stylesheet parameter rootid to the id attribute value of the element you want to process. For example, if you have a book with three chapters:

```
<book>
<chapter id="intro">
  ...
</chapter>
<chapter id="using">
  ..
</chapter>
<chapter id="administering">
  ...
</chapter>
</book>
```

You can generate an HTML file for the second chapter with a command like the following:

```
xsltproc \
    --stringparam rootid "using" \
    --output chap2.html \
    html/docbook.xsl myfile.xml
```

The chap2.html output file will contain just the second chapter. Note these features:

- The entire document is still parsed, so there will not be signficant savings of processing time.

- The content is still processed within the context of the entire document, so it will still be labeled "Chapter 2".

- Any cross references to other chapters will be properly formed, but the links will not actually go anywhere because the targets are not included in the output.

Chunking into multiple HTML files

You may want to split the output for a large document into several HTML files. That process is known in DocBook as *chunking*, and the individual output files are called *chunks*. The results are a coherent set of linked files, with a title page containing a table of contents as the starting point for browsing the set.

You get chunked output by processing your XML input file with html/chunk.xsl stylesheet file instead of the standard html/docbook.xsl file. For example:

```
xsltproc /usr/share/docbook-xsl/html/chunk.xsl myfile.xml
```

The default behavior in chunking includes:

- The name of the main titlepage/table of contents file is index.html.

- Each of the following elements start a new chunk:

```
appendix
article
bibliography    in article or book
book
chapter
colophon
glossary        in article or book
index           in article or book
part
preface
refentry
reference
sect1           except first
section         if equivalent to sect1
set
setindex
```

- Each chunk filename is generated with an algorithm. It can instead be named after the id attribute value of its starting element, if it has one (see the section called "Generated filename" (page 64)).

- A message is displayed for each chunk filename that is generated. If you prefer not to see those messages, then set the chunk.quietly parameter to 1.

Chunk filenames

Each chunk has to have a filename. The filename (before adding .html) can come from three sources, selected in this order:

- A dbhtml filename processing instruction embedded in the element.

- If it is the root element of the document, then the chunk is named using the value of the parameter root.filename, which is index by default.

- The chunk element's id attribute value (but only if the use.id.as.filename parameter is set).

- A unique name generated by the stylesheet.

dbhtml filenames

You can embed processing instructions (PI) in your DocBook XML files that instruct the XSL stylesheets what filename to use for a chunk. The following is an example:

```
<chapter><?dbhtml filename="intro.html" ?>
<title>Introduction</title>
...
```

The dbhtml name indicates that this processing instruction is intended for DocBook HTML processing. This dbhtml filename processing instruction says that the HTML chunk file for this chapter should be named intro.html. The stylesheet does not add a filename extension when dbhtml filename is used. The processing instruction needs to be an immediate child of the element you are naming, not inside one of its children. For example, it will not work if you put it inside the title element of a chapter. If there is more than one such PI in an element then the first one is used.

id attribute filenames

If the element that starts a new chunk has an id attribute, then that value can be used as the start of the chunk filename. The stylesheet parameter use.id.as.filename controls that behavior. If that parameter is set to a non-zero value, then your chunk filenames will use the element's id attribute. By default, the parameter is set to zero, so you have to turn that behavior on if you want it. For example:

```
<chapter id="intro">
<title>Introduction</title>
...
```

This will work for all elements that have an id value and that start a chunk, *except* for the main index file. By default, that file is named using the value of the root.filename parameter, whose value is index by default. To use your document root element's id as that filename, set the root.filename parameter to blank.

When the id value is used, then the .html filename extension is automatically added. You can change the default extension by setting the html.ext parameter to some other extension, including the dot.

Filename prefix

There may be situations where you need to add a prefix to all the chunk filenames. For example, if you are putting the output for several chunked books into one directory, you could use a different prefix for each book to avoid filename duplication (and subsequent overwritten files).

If you need all of your chunk filenames to include some sort of prefix string, then you can use the base.dir stylesheet parameter. Normally the base.dir parameter is used specify a directory to contain the chunked files, as described in the section called "base.dir parameter" (page 65). When defining just an output directory with base.dir, you must end the parameter value with a literal / character. If you omit the trailing slash, then the chunk filename is appended to the value without a slash separator, effectively adding it as a prefix to each chunk filename. You can also combine a prefix and a directory name, as shown in the third example below.

base.dir parameter value	Description	Example chunk filename
base.dir="htmlout/"	Output directory only.	htmlout/chap1.html
base.dir="refbook-"	Filename prefix only.	refbook-chap1.html
base.dir="htmlout/refbook-"	Output directory and filename prefix.	htmlout/refbook-chap1.html

Generated filename

If not specified by a PI or id attribute, then the XSL stylesheet will generate a filename. The names are abbreviations of the element name and a count. For example, the first chapter element would be ch01.html, the second chapter would be ch02.html, and so on. The first sect1 in a chapter might be s01.html. But that filename would not be unique if each chapter had a sect1. To make each sect1 name unique, the stylesheet prepends the chapter part. So the first sect1 in the second chapter would be chunked into ch02s01.html. In general, the stylesheet keeps adding parent prefixes to make sure each name is unique. If a document is a set with multiple books, then the stylesheet would also add a book prefix to make a name like bk01ch02s01.html.

The names are not pretty, but they do have a recognizable logic. They are also somewhat stable, as opposed to random number names that might have been used instead. But the filenames may change if the document is edited, because when you insert a chapter, subsequent chapters are bumped up in number. If you are creating a website in which other files refer to these chunk filenames, then they are moving targets unless the document never changes. If you want to point to your generated files, it's best not to use generated filenames, and instead to use one of the other methods to name them. Using the id attribute is the easiest.

Chunked files output directory

The first thing you will notice when you chunk a document is that it can produce a lot of HTML files! Suddenly your directory is very crowded with new HTML files. When chunking, most people choose to place the chunked files into a separate directory.

One method that does *not* work is to use the processor's --output option. That option is used to redirect the standard output of the processor to a file. During chunking, the stylesheet creates the filenames and files, and also needs to handle the directory location.

base.dir parameter

You inform the stylesheet of the desired directory location using the base.dir parameter. For example, to output the chunked files to the /usr/apache/htdocs directory::

```
xsltproc --stringparam base.dir /usr/apache/htdocs/ chunk.xsl myfile.xml
```

Things to watch out for:

- Be sure to include that trailing / because the stylesheet simply appends the filename to this string. If you forget the trailing slash, you'll end up with all your filenames beginning with that name. If you need such a filename prefix, then see the section called "Filename prefix" (page 64) for details.

- The stylesheets can create files, but some processors will not create directories. Saxon and Xalan will create directories, but xsltproc will not. So create any directories before running xsltproc.

- Be aware that the base.dir parameter only works with the chunk stylesheet, not the regular docbook.xsl stylesheet. It does work with the onechunk.xsl stylesheet, though.

dbhtml dir processing instruction

You can also use a dbhtml dir processing instructions to modify where the chunked output goes. For example:

```
<book><?dbhtml dir="UserGuide" ?>
<title>User Guide</title>
...
<chapter id="intro">
...
```

This sets the output directory to be UserGuide for the root element chunk and all of its children and descendants (unless otherwise specified). Since this is a relative pathname, the output will be relative to the current directory. So in this example the root element chunk will be UserGuide/index.html, and the first chapter chunk will be in UserGuide/intro.html since it is a child of the book element. Note that the dbhtml dir value does *not* have a trailing slash because the stylesheet inserts one.

If the base.dir parameter is set, then that value is prepended to the dir value. For example, you could process the above file using:

```
xsltproc --stringparam base.dir /usr/apache/htdocs/ chunk.xsl myfile.xml
```

Then the root element chunk will be in /usr/apache/htdocs/UserGuide/index.html. Remember that base.dir does need a trailing slash.

If any of the descendants of the root element also have a dbhtml dir processing instruction, then that value is appended to ancestor value. That means it is relative to its ancestor element's directory. This allows you to build up a longer pathname to divide the output into several subdirectories of the main directory. For example:

```
<book><?dbhtml dir="UserGuide" ?>
<title>User Guide</title>
...
<chapter id="intro"><?dbhtml dir="FrontMatter" ?>
...
<chapter id="installing">
...
<appendix id="reference"><?dbhtml dir="BackMatter" ?>
...
```

Now the output chunks will be:

```
UserGuide/index.html
UserGuide/FrontMatter/intro.html
UserGuide/installing.html
UserGuide/BackMatter/reference.html
```

Note that the second chapter is not a child of the first chapter, so its directory reverts to that of the book-level PI. Again, if the `base.dir` parameter is set, then all of these become relative to that value. Remember that you need to create any directories you specify, because the stylesheets will not.

The dbhtml `dir` processing instruction can be used to specify a full pathname if you do not use a `base.dir` parameter, but that's not a good idea. That hard codes the path into your file, which means you have to edit the file to put the output elsewhere. Generally this PI is used to create directories relative to some base output directory that you specify on the command line with a parameter. That gives you the flexibility to put the output where you want, yet maintains the relative structure of the subdirectories specified by the PIs.

In all cases, cross references between your chunked files should still resolve, regardless what the relative locations are.

Fast chunking

If you are chunking large documents, then there is a stylesheet variation you can use that will speed up the processing. The caveat is that the XSL processor you are using must support the *EXSLT* `node-set()` function. That includes Saxon, Xalan, and xsltproc. It does not include MSXSL, however.

To speed up chunking, use the `chunkfast.xsl` stylesheet instead of the regular `chunk.xsl` stylesheet. The `chunkfast.xsl` stylesheet is a customization of `chunk.xsl` and is included with the distribution in the `html` (or `xhtml`) directory. It handles chunks in a more efficient manner. In the regular `chunk.xsl` stylesheet, the calculation of the Next and Previous elements for each chunk is performed each time a chunk is output. That calculation requires searching the document using XPath, which can take some time for large documents. When `chunkfast.xsl` is used instead, those calculations are all done once ahead of time, so that output can proceed without delay.

You may notice that there is a `chunk.fast` parameter included in the stylesheets. Setting that parameter is not sufficient for getting the correct fast chunking behavior. You have to use the `chunkfast.xsl` stylesheet in order for the headers and footers to be correct. That stylesheet sets the parameter and customizes some templates.

Table of contents chunking

When chunking a book, the DocBook XSL stylesheets normally put the table of contents (TOC) in the same chunk as the book's title page. The stylesheets provide options for generating separate chunks for the table of contents, and for any lists of titles such as List of Tables.

If you set the stylesheet parameter `chunk.tocs.and.lots` to 1, then the stylesheet will generate a separate chunk that contains the table of contents and all the lists of titles. The title page chunk will then contain a link to the new chunk. If you also set the parameter chunk.separate.lots to 1, then each of the lists of titles will get a separate chunk as well. If you set only chunk.separate.lots to 1, then your table of contents will appear in the title page chunk, and only the lists of titles will get separate chunks. The chunk.separate.lots parameter was added in version 1.66.1 of the stylesheets.

Note:

The chunk.toc parameter does not generate a separate table of contents chunk. Rather, it is used to manually designate chunking boundaries. See the section called "Manually control chunking" (page 67) for more information.

Controlling what gets chunked

There are three options in the DocBook XSL stylesheets for controlling what gets chunked:

- Set the parameters chunk.section.depth and/or chunk.first.sections.

- Chunk based on a manually edited table of contents file.

- Modify the chunk template.

If you only want to control what section levels get put into separate HTML files, then you should set the chunk.section.depth parameter. By default it is set to 1. So if you want sect1 and sect2 elements to be chunked into individual files, set the parameter to 2.

The chunk stylesheet by default includes the first sect1 of a chapter (or article) with the content that precedes it in the chapter. If you want those also to be chunked to separate files, then set the chunk.first.sections parameter to 1.

Manually control chunking

If the standard chunking process does not meet your needs, and you are willing to manually intervene, then you can completely control how content gets chunked. This might be useful if some sections are very short and you would rather keep them together. But since it requires hand editing of a generated table of contents file, it is only useful if done infrequently or with documents that have stable structure.

Here are the steps for manually chunking HTML output:

1. Make sure all the elements you want to become chunks have an id attribute on them.

2. Process your document with the special maketoc.xsl stylesheet, which generates an XML table of contents file. Using xsltproc for example:

    ```
    xsltproc  -o mytoc.xml \
      --stringparam chunk.section.depth 8 \
      --stringparam chunk.first.sections 1 \
      html/maketoc.xsl  myfile.xml
    ```

    The two parameters ensure that all sections are included in the generated TOC file.

3. Edit the generated mytoc.xml file to remove any tocentry elements that you do not want chunked, or add entries that you do want chunked.

4. Process your document with the special chunktoc.xsl stylesheet instead of the regular chunk.xsl stylesheet, and pass it the generated TOC filename in the chunk.toc parameter. For example:

```
xsltproc
   --output  output/  \
   --stringparam chunk.toc  mytoc.xml  \
   html/chunktoc.xsl  myfile.xml
```

This will chunk your document based on the entries in the generated TOC file. You can still use any of the chunking parameters to modify the chunking behavior.

If you also want the HTML TOC that is produced during chunking to match your XML TOC file, then set the parameter manual.toc to that same filename.

Note:

When you use this process, you must have an id attribute on every element that you want to start a new chunk. This includes the document element, which generates the title page and table of contents. You can see which elements do not have an id by examining the generated TOC file and looking for empty id attributes in the tocentrys. Any such entries will be merged with their parent elements during chunking.

Modify chunking templates

If you want to control what elements produce chunks, beyond just the section level choice, then you must modify the templates that do chunk processing. See the section called "Chunking customization" (page 161) for more information.

Output encoding for chunk HTML

You may need to change the output encoding for your chunked HTML files. The chunker.output.encoding parameter lets you change the default value of the HTML character encoding from the default value of ISO-8859-1. For example, if you want your HTML files to use UTF-8 encoding instead, you could process your document with the following:

```
xsltproc
  --output  output/  \
  --stringparam chunker.output.encoding UTF-8  \
  html/chunk.xsl  myfile.xml
```

This will produce the following line in each chunked HTML file:

```
<meta content="text/html; charset=utf-8" http-equiv="Content-Type">
```

It will also encode the HTML content itself using UTF-8 encoding. When a browser opens the file, the meta tag informs it that the file is encoded in UTF-8 so it will use a UTF-8 font to display the text. This feature is only available with Saxon and XSL processors that support EXSLT extensions (such as xsltproc). It does not work in Xalan, however.

Note:

By default, chunked HTML output from Saxon will not contain any non-ASCII characters, regardless of the encoding your specify. Any non-ASCII characters will be represented as named entities or numerical character references. This behavior is controlled by the saxon.character.representation stylesheet parameter. See the section called "Saxon output character representation" (page 327) for more information.

The default output encoding for XHTML is UTF-8, as described in the section called "XHTML" (page 407).

Specifying the output DOCTYPE

You may want to specify a particular DOCTYPE at the top of your chunked HTML files. This is most useful for XHTML output where you may want to validate the chunked files against the DTD.

There are two stylesheet parameters for the chunking stylesheet that affect the DOCTYPE:

`chunker.output.doctype-public`   Specifies the PUBLIC identifier of the DTD in the DOCTYPE.

`chunker.output.doctype-system`   Specifies the SYSTEM identifier of the DTD in the DOCTYPE.

See the section called "Generating XHTML" (page 408) for an example of using these parameters. Note that they do not work with the Xalan processor because it uses a different way of writing chunk files.

Unfortunately, there is no way to add an internal subset to the output DTD using XSLT. If you do not know what an internal DTD subset is, then you probably do not need it. See a good XML reference for more information.

Indenting HTML elements

If you use a text editor to open an HTML file produced by DocBook XSL, you will notice that by default it produces long text lines that contain many elements. If you would prefer your HTML elements to start on a new line and have nested indents to show the HTML element structure, you can do that by setting the `chunker.output.indent` parameter to `yes`. Note that this feature is only available with XSL processors that support *EXSLT*[1] extensions, but that includes most of the major ones. Xalan does not support this indenting option.

There are limits to which HTML elements can start an indented line. In general, any element that permits #PCDATA (plain text) as part of its content model will not allow the extra line breaks inside it. That is because white space must be respected inside such elements, and that respect includes not adding extra white space.

To add indentation with the non-chunking `docbook.xsl` stylesheet, you need to use a customization layer with an `xsl:output` element similar to the example in the section called "Output encoding" (page 326). Use the `indent="yes"` attribute value to turn on indentation. The other approach for single-file output is to use the `onechunk.xsl` stylesheet and its extra parameters, as described in the section called "Single file options with onechunk" (page 69).

Single file options with onechunk

The chunking stylesheet gives you several options you do not have with the nonchunking `docbook.xsl` stylesheet that generates a single HTML output file. These extra features come from the XSLT extension functions used to generate multiple output files from a single DocBook document. This is not a standard feature of the XSLT 1.0 standard, but each XSLT processor provides such an extension because it is so useful.

The DocBook XSL distribution includes a special stylesheet named `onechunk.xsl` that uses the same extension function to generate a single HTML file. This is most useful when you want your output in a single file, but you want to set one or more of these options:

- Specify the output filename. See the section called "Name the file using an id" (page 70).

- Specify the output directory. See the section called "Putting the file elsewhere" (page 70).

- Specify the output encoding. See the section called "Output encoding for chunk HTML" (page 68).

- Specify the output document type (DTD). See the section called "Specifying the output DOCTYPE" (page 69).

---

[1] http://www.exslt.org

Name the file using an id

You can name the output file after the `id` value of the main document element in your XML input file. That way you do not have to specify the output filename on the command line, and you get a consistent output filename for that input file. The trick is to use the onechunk.xsl stylesheet instead of docbook.xsl. It uses the chunking stylesheet mechanism but only outputs one chunk. That lets you use the chunking options, which include naming the output file. Here is how you do it:

1. Add an id value to your document root element:

   ```
   <?xml version="1.0"?>
   <!DOCTYPE chapter SYSTEM "docbook.dtd">
   <chapter  id="intro">
   ...
   ```

2. Process the document with the `html/onechunk.xsl` stylesheet file instead of the standard `html/docbook.xsl` stylesheet. Use the following stylesheet parameters with it:

   ```
   xsltproc \
       --stringparam  use.id.as.filename 1 \
       --stringparam  root.filename  '' \
       onechunk.xsl  myfile.xml
   ```

The output filename in this case will be `intro.html`. The `use.id.as.filename` parameter tells the stylesheet to use the element's `id` value in the filename. Setting the `root.filename` parameter to blank tells the stylesheet to not use the default root filename of `index.html`. The `html.ext` parameter could also be used to specify a different filename extension, such as `.htm` instead of the default `.html`.

Putting the file elsewhere

The `base.dir` parameter can specify an output directory for the file produced by `html/onechunk.xsl`. This is useful since an `id` value cannot include '/' characters. For example:

```
xsltproc \
    --stringparam  base.dir  /usr/apache/htdocs  \
    --stringparam  use.id.as.filename 1 \
    --stringparam  root.filename  '' \
    onechunk.xsl  myfile.xml
```

Using the example above, the output file would be `/usr/apache/htdocs/intro.html`. This parameter has no effect when using the standard `html/docbook.xsl` stylesheet, which has no knowledge of the output filename.

Specify the output encoding and DOCTYPE

If you want to specify the *output encoding* of your onechunk output file, see `chunker.output.encoding` parameter described in the section called "Output encoding for chunk HTML" (page 68).

If you want to specify the *DOCTYPE* of your onechunk output file, see `chunker.output.doctype-public` and `chunker.output.doctype-system` parameters described in the section called "Generating XHTML" (page 408)

Using CSS to style HTML

You may want to change the way the generated HTML output looks. The best way to do that is with a Cascading Style Sheet (CSS), which modern browsers support. Font family, type size, colors, and other styles can be controlled with CSS for each kind of element.

You use a text editor to create a separate CSS stylesheet file that contains all the style information, and then associate that stylesheet with all of your HTML files. If you look at the HTML output from DocBook, you'll see a lot of <div class="*element*"> tags, where *element* is the DocBook element that produced that <div>. You write your css stylesheet to associate CSS styles with specific combinations of HTML element names and DocBook class attributes (see a good CSS reference to learn how to do that). Here is a short sample that styles DocBook note output:

```
P.note {
  font-family: Helvetica,Arial,sans-serif;
}
H3.note {
  font-family: Helvetica,Arial,sans-serif;
  font-weight: bold;
  font-size: 12;
}
```

To connect the CSS stylesheet with your HTML files, you set the html.stylesheet parameter to the name of your stylesheet file. That parameter causes an HTML <LINK> element to be inserted into each generated HTML file that associates your CSS stylesheet with that HTML file. Then just make sure the stylesheet file gets copied to each HTML output directory.

For example, this command sets the parameter as it chunks the file:

```
xsltproc --stringparam html.stylesheet  corpstyle.css  chunk.xsl  myfile.xml
```

Then each HTML file has this in its <HEAD> element:

```
<link rel="stylesheet" href="corpstyle.css"
      type="text/css">
```

Using CSS to style your HTML is a nice system because you can control all the formatting for all of your output from a single CSS file. And you do not have to customize the DocBook XSL stylesheets to do it.

If you need to specify more than one CSS stylesheet for your HTML files, you can put all the pathnames in the html.stylesheet parameter separated by spaces. When processed, each pathname will be output in its own HTML link element, in the order they appear in the parameter. That order is significant since it determines style precedence in CSS.

Styling section headings with CSS

By default, the HTML stylesheets generate H2 headings for both chapter and sect1 titles. That's because H1 is reserved for book titles. The basic problem is that there are too few HTML heading levels to map uniformly to the deeper structure that DocBook provides. But if you are willing to use CSS, then you can style the HTML headings as you like. Take a look at the HTML output, and you will see that each title is wrapped in HTML div elements with class attributes:

```
<div class="chapter" lang="en">
  <div class="titlepage">
    <div>
      <div>
        <h2 class="title">
          <a name="Catalogs"></a>Chapter 3. XML catalogs
        </h2>
      </div>
    </div>
  ...
```

Here is a CSS specification that increases the font size for chapter title H2 headings and adds other style properties:

```
div.chapter div.titlepage h2 {
    font-size: 180%;
    font-family: Helvetica;
    font-weight: Bold;
    color: #444444
}
```

If you examine the HTML output, there are additional div wrappers around the h2. Those are artifacts of the way the titlepage templates are handled. They are not needed in the CSS selector syntax to establish the ancestry of the h2 as a chapter title.

You can write similar specifications for section heading levels, using different class values. The nice thing about this feature is that you do not have to customize the XSL stylesheets at all. You just need to put the styles in a CSS file and reference that from your HTML output by setting the html.stylesheet parameter.

Styling displays with CSS

You may want to apply styles to block displays such as programlisting and other elements. For example, you might want to set a background color and draw a border around each program listing. You could use the shade.verbatim stylesheet parameter to turn on the background color, but that parameter also affects screen and literallayout elements. The preferred method is to use CSS.

The HTML output for a programlisting looks like the following:

```
<div class="programlisting">
<pre class="programlisting">Text of the program
...
</pre>
</div>
```

You could create a selector and set styles in your CSS stylesheet like the following:

```
pre.programlisting {
  background-color: #FFFF99 ;
  border: 1px solid #006600 ;
}
```

Adding custom class attributes

The default class attributes in the HTML output may not provide you with sufficient control of your formatting. You may want to treat some element instances differently, for example, or you may need to use predefined class names from an existing CSS stylesheet. The HTML stylesheets provide two methods for defining your own class names for HTML output:

- Using `role` attribute as class name. Use this method when individual elements need a different class name.

- Custom template in `mode="class.value"`. Use this method when tailoring class names to specific types of elements.

Each of these methods is described in more detail in the following sections.

Using role as class name

You may need to designate certain element instances as needing special formatting in your HTML output. The XSL stylesheets automatically generate `class` attributes on HTML `DIV` and `SPAN` elements that identify the DocBook element they came from. But those are applied uniformly, so they do not give you control over particular instances that need different handling.

The HTML stylesheets have a feature that let you control the `class` attribute value that is output for certain DocBook elements. If the right parameter is turned on, then the value of the element's `role` attribute is copied as the HTML `class` attribute value. The DocBook elements are `emphasis`, `entry` (table cell), `para`, and `phrase`. Each of them has a corresponding stylesheet parameter that controls the feature for that element.

> **Note:**
>
> If the element whose class you want to change is not `emphasis`, `entry`, `para`, or `phrase`, then you can still use the other method described in the section called "Generate custom class values" (page 147).

For example, if you set the `para.propagates.style` parameter to a nonzero value, then you get this behavior.

DocBook XML:
```
<para role="primary">This feature of the product ...</para>
```

HTML output:
```
<p class="primary">This feature of the product ...</p>
```

Then you can write a CSS selector like `P.primary` that styles such paragraphs differently from ordinary paragraphs.

In a similar manner, you can set any of the `entry.propagates.style`, `emphasis.propagates.style`, and `phrase.propagates.style` parameters to get similar behavior for `role` values on those DocBook elements.

The following is an example of generating an emphasis style using small capital letters. Process this file with the `emphasis.propagates.style` parameter set to 1.

DocBook XML:
```
Using an SQL <emphasis role="sqlsyntax">select</emphasis> statement
```

HTML output:
```
Using an SQL <span class="sqlsyntax">select</span> statement
```

CSS stylesheet entry:
```
.sqlsyntax {font-variant: small-caps;}
```

For print output, however, this parameter will have no effect because there is no downstream CSS stylesheet. If you also want small caps in your print output, you will need to add something like the following to your fo stylesheet customization layer:

```
<xsl:template match="emphasis[@role = 'sqlsyntax']">
  <fo:inline font-variant="small-caps">
    <xsl:apply-templates/>
  </fo:inline>
</xsl:template>
```

For general use, the phrase.propagates.style permits you to add custom class values to just about any part of your output. You may want certain titles to be distinguished, for example. You can wrap the text in the DocBook title element in a phrase with a role attribute. The HTML will have an HTML SPAN element with

DocBook XML:
```
<title><phrase role="primary">Using a Mouse</phrase><title>
```

HTML output:
```
...<span class="primary">Using a Mouse</span>...
```

Then you can write an appropriate CSS selector to style such titles differently from other titles.

If you need further customization of HTML class names, then see the section called "Generate custom class values" (page 147)

Generating id attributes

Modern browsers also support CSS selectors on the id attribute of HTML elements. An id attribute differs from the class attribute in that it is unique in the HTML file.

By default, the stylesheets do not output id attributes because some older browsers could not locate cross references by id attribute. They only worked with named anchors like <a name="foo">. Modern browsers can locate content by id, so the stylesheets provide an option to output the id value from the DocBook XML to the corresponding HTML element. Set the stylesheet parameter generate.id.attributes to 1 to turn on this feature.

Even when this parameter is used, not all id attributes in the source document are passed through to the HTML output. Only the major components get an id:

appendix	colophon	preface
article	glossary	set
bibliography	index	setindex
book	part	
chapter	partintro	

Chapter and section numbering

There are several parameters that control numbering of chapter and section titles. By default, part and chapter titles are numbered but section titles are not. Appendix titles are numbered with uppercase letters. In the DocBook XSL stylesheets, the number part of a title is called a *label*.

If you prefer to turn off chapter numbering, then set the chapter.autolabel parameter to zero. If you also want to turn off appendix numbering (A, B, C, etc.), then also set the appendix.autolabel parameter to zero.

```
xsltproc  --output myfile.html  \
   --stringparam  chapter.autolabel 0 \
   --stringparam  appendix.autolabel 0 \
   html/docbook.xsl  myfile.xml
```

To turn on basic section numbering, set the section.autolabel parameter to 1. Then your titles will be numbered as follows:

```
Chapter 3. Using a mouse
1.  Basic mouse actions    sect1
1.1  Left button           sect2
1.2  Right button          sect2
1.2.1 Context menus        sect3
2.  Selecting              sect1
2.1  Click and drag
2.2  Double click
```

Notice that the section numbers do not include the chapter number by default, so section numbering starts over with each new chapter. If you prefer the section numbers to include the chapter number, then set the `section.label.includes.component.label` parameter to 1. This assumes that you leave chapter numbering turned on. For example:

```
xsltproc  --output myfile.html  \
  --stringparam  section.autolabel 1 \
  --stringparam  section.label.includes.component.label 1 \
  html/docbook.xsl  myfile.xml
```

This results in the following numbering style:

```
Chapter 3. Using a mouse
3.1.  Basic mouse actions    sect1
3.1.1  Left button           sect2
3.1.2  Right button          sect2
3.1.2.1 Context menus        sect3
3.2.  Selecting              sect1
3.2.1  Click and drag
3.2.2  Double click
```

Section titles in an appendix will prepend the appendix letter instead of a chapter number.

Starting with version 1.69.1 of the stylesheets, you can change the numbering style of any of these elements using its parameter. For example, you could use uppercase letters instead of numbers for chapters. You specify the format by using one of the following characters as the autolabel parameter value.

Table 7.1. Number formats for autolabel parameters

Parameter value	Numbering style	Example
1	Arabic numerals	1, 2, 3, 4, ...
A	Uppercase letters.	A, B, C, D, ...
a	Lowercase letters.	a, b, c, d, ...
I	Uppercase roman numerals.	I, II, III, IV, ...
i	Lowercase roman numerals.	i, ii, iii, iv, ...
&#x661;	Arabic-Indic numerals	١, ٢, ٣, ٤, ...

Here are the default settings for the autolabel parameters:

```
<xsl:param name="appendix.autolabel" select="'A'"/>
<xsl:param name="chapter.autolabel" select="1"/>
<xsl:param name="part.autolabel" select="'I'"/>
<xsl:param name="reference.autolabel" select="'I'"/>
<xsl:param name="section.autolabel" select="0"/>
```

Depth of section numbering

You may want to limit the depth of sections that get a section number. If you have deeply nested sections, then the string of numbers in the section label can get quite long. Or perhaps you just want sections at levels 1 and 2 to be numbered, since any lower level sections are not important enough to have a number label.

You can use the `section.autolabel.max.depth` parameter to control which section levels get a number label. If you set the parameter to 2, then only sections at levels 1 and 2 will have the label. The default value is 8, meaning all section levels have numbering (if it is turned on).

Docbook icon graphics

The DocBook stylesheets can use icon graphics for these purposes in the HTML output:

- Icons to indicate the different types of admonitions (note, tip, warning, caution, and important).

- Icons to indicate Next, Previous, Up, and Home for navigating among chunked output.

- Numbered icons for callouts.

Admonition graphics

By default, when you process an admonition element such as `note`, the output displays the label `Note` in the appropriate language, followed by the text of the note. You can add a distinctive admonition graphic before the label by setting the `admon.graphics` parameter to non-zero:

```
xsltproc  --stringparam admon.graphics 1 docbook.xsl myfile.xml
```

This will generate an HTML element `<img src="images/note.png>`. This references a `note.png` graphics file that is expected to be available in a `images` subdirectory relative to the HTML file.

Other options include:

- If you want to display just the icon alone without the text label, then set the `admon.textlabel` stylesheet parameter to zero.

- Use the `admon.graphics.path` and `admon.graphics.extension` parameters to change the generated pathname to the image file. The pathname written to the HTML file is built up from three components, two of which can be changed with parameters. Here is how the default `images/note.png` pathname is generated:

Path component	Example	Comes from
Directory	`images/`	`admon.graphics.path` parameter. Include the trailing slash.
Filename prefix	`note`	Admonition element name.
Filename suffix	`.png`	`admon.graphics.extension` parameter. Include the dot.

These parameters change the path written into the HTML file. The directory could be a single website location, so you do not have to copy them to each of your HTML output directories. Being able to change the filename extension is useful when you have created your own admonition graphics and they are in a different format. They all have to use the same extension, however.

Note:

> The HTML stylesheet does not create or copy the actual image files to the specified location. It just creates references to the images in the HTML files. If you turn on admonition graphics, you will need to put the image files in the appropriate place in the output. If you do not, then your HTML files will have unresolved image references. Using a Makefile makes it easier to not forget this chore each time you generate your output.

Custom admonition graphics

You may want to replace the stock DocBook admonition graphics with those of your own design. That's easy to do. When you create your image files, just name them after the admonition element they represent, such as `note.png`. Then you just copy your graphics files to the HTML output directory and they will be used. If your graphics use a different filename extension such as `.jpg`, then set the stylesheet parameter `admon.graphics.extension` parameter to `.jpg` to indicate that. If your graphics are larger or smaller than the stock graphics, then you can customize the template named `admon.graphic.width`. See the section called "Customizing admonitions" (page 229) for more information.

Navigational icons

When you chunk your output into multiple HTML files, each file is given a header and footer that helps readers navigate among the multiple files. The header and footer indicate the Next and Previous files, in document order, as well as Up and Home to move up in the hierarchy of content. The default output uses words (in the appropriate language) to indicate these options, but you can use icons like these instead:

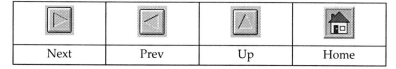

Next	Prev	Up	Home

To enable these navigational icons, you set the `navig.graphics` parameter to nonzero when you process with the chunk stylesheet:

```
xsltproc --stringparam  navig.graphics 1  chunk.xsl  myfile.xml
```

This will replace the word Next, for example, with an HTML tag `<img src="images/next.png">` in the header and footer.

Note:

> The stylesheet does not create or copy the actual image files to the specified location. It just creates references to the images in the HTML files. If you turn on navigational graphics, you will need to put the image files in the appropriate place in the output. If you do not, then your HTML files will have unresolved image references. Using a Makefile makes it easier to not forget this chore each time you generate your output.

You can change the directory path by resetting the `navig.graphics.path` parameter to a new directory, but be sure to include the trailing slash. And you can use a different graphics extension by specifying the `navig.graphics.extension` parameter. Include the period if the extension is like `.gif`.

The header and footer also shows the titles of the other files by default. If you want a very clean presentation with just the icons and not the titles, then you can set the `navig.showtitles` parameter to zero (it is one by default).

Callout icons

Callouts are used to connect annotation comments to points in a program listing or literallayout. They are like numbered footnotes, in that a user follows a given number label in the display to a specific comment by matching the numbers. See the section called "Callouts" (page 447) for more information on using callouts.

By default the HTML stylesheets use small graphical icons for the numbers (such as ❶). The stylesheets insert HTML tags like `<img src="images/callouts/1.png">` in the display and next to the callout annotation. The icon graphics are included with the stylesheet distribution in the `images/callouts` directory.

As with the other icons in the output, the stylesheets do not create or copy the actual image files to the output location. If you use callouts but do not copy the provided image files, then you will have unresolved graphics references in your HTML output. You may choose to replace the icons with ordinary numbers to avoid having to deal with the icon graphics. Another reason to switch is when you have more than ten callouts in a single list. The distribution only includes icons for the numbers 1 through 10.

To replace the icon graphics with text numbers like (1), set the `callout.graphics` parameter to zero (it is one by default).

Another option is to replace the icons with special Unicode characters that are similar. To do that, set the `callout.unicode` parameter to 1 and the `callout.graphics` parameter to zero. Then the HTML output looks like `&#10102;`. This entity is rendered by the browser as the callout number. These numbers also only go up to ten, however.

If you use callout graphics, then there are three parameters that give you more control over the generated `img` tag.

`callout.graphics.extension`   Use this parameter to change the icon file extension from `.png` to something else. Of course, you must have the graphics that match that extension.

`callout.graphics.path`   Use this parameter to change the generated directory name from the default `images/callouts/`. Be sure to include the trailing slash.

`callout.graphics.number.limit`   Use this parameter to set the highest number for which you have a callout graphic. The stylesheets are distributed with callout graphics files with numbers up to 15, but you could create graphics with additional numbers if you need them. If you have more numbers but you do not reset this parameter, then any numbers over 15 will still format like (16).

Date and time

The stylesheets have a feature to generate date and time strings. These can be used to insert the processing date for display or for meta data. These features make use of the $EXSLT^2$ `date-time()` function. That function is supported by the Saxon, Xalan, and xsltproc processors, but not MSXSL.

There is no DocBook element that represents the current date, so the stylesheets use a processing instruction to insert a timestamp. The following is an example:

```
<para>This document was generated
<?dbtimestamp format="Y-m-d H:M:S"?>.</para>
```

When processed, this input will result in the following output in either HTML or print:

```
This document was generated 2007-07-23 12:13:00.
```

---

[2] http://www.exslt.org

The `dbtimestamp` processing instruction name triggers the date functions, and the `format` string is used to select and format the components of date and time. The component letters are as follows:

Date-time format letter	Example	Description
a	Thu	Day abbreviation
A	Thursday	Day name
b	Jul	Month abbreviation
c	2007-07-10-07:00 12:20:33-07:00	Complete ISO date and time, including offset from UTC.
B	July	Month name
d	10	Day in month
H	11	Hour in day
j	191	Day in year
m	07	Month in year
M	20	Minute in hour
S	14	Second in minute
U	28	Week in year
w	5	Day in week (Sunday = 1)
x	2007-07-10-07:00	ISO date
X	12:20:33-07:00	ISO time
Y	2007	Year.

Any other characters in the format string are passed through, allowing you to add punctuation as needed. If no format string is supplied in the processing instruction, then the stylesheet uses the gentext template named `format` in the context named `datetime` for the current language, as in the following example for English. See the section called "Generated text" (page 105) for more on gentext templates.

```
<l:context name="datetime">
    <l:template name="format" text="m/d/Y"/>
</l:context>
```

The `dbtimestamp` processing instruction supports an option to omit the leading zero for single digit dates and times. That is, if the date value is 5, the stylesheet will output 05 by default. You can turn off the zero padding by setting a pseudo-attribute `padding="0"` in the processing instruction:

```
<?dbtimestamp format="Y-m-d"  padding="0" ?>
```

The change in zero padding applies to hour, minute, and date values used in the processing instruction. If you want it to apply only to date and not minute (you get the odd looking 3:5 for time instead of 3:05), then create two separate `dbtimestamp` processing instructions for the date and time, and set the `padding="0"` value only for the date.

You can also use the date functions more directly in a customization layer. See the section called "Adding a date timestamp" (page 157) for an example.

8

Printed output options

This section describes some common options for printed output. These options can all be specified on the command line and do not require a customization file for the XSL stylesheets. A much larger set of options that include stylesheet customizations is described in Chapter 13, *Print customizations* (page 169).

Printed output is generated by processing your DocBook XML files with the DocBook XSL stylesheets (fo version), and then processing the resulting .fo file with an XSL-FO processor such as FOP or XEP. Most of the options that affect output are applied in the first step using DocBook stylesheet parameters. See Chapter 6, *Using stylesheet parameters* (page 59) to learn how to set parameters. See *FO Parameter Reference*[1] for the standard documentation of the parameters.

Units of measure:

When specifying a page dimension or font size in a parameter, you need to supply a number and a unit of measure. The syntax for such expressions is a number followed by a unit abbreviation, without any space between. The number can be an integer or decimal number, and the unit is one of these:

cm	*centimeters*
mm	*millimeters*
in	*inches*
pt	*points*
pc	*picas*
px	*pixels*
em	*relative to font size*

Examples include 8.5in, 12pt, and 0.35cm.

Page layout

You can control the basic page size and layout using stylesheet parameters. You can set the paper size as well as the margins on all sides. You can also turn on landscape, double-sided, and two-column printing.

---

[1] http://docbook.sourceforge.net/release/xsl/current/doc/fo/

Paper size

The default paper size is US letter size (8.5 x 11 inches). You can select a different standard paper size by setting the `paper.type` parameter to one of the designated values. Some of the common values include `USletter` (the default), A3, A4, and A5. The complete list of paper codes is listed on the reference page for the *page.width.portrait*[2] parameter. For example:

```
xsltproc  --output myfile.fo  \
  --stringparam  paper.type  A4 \
  fo/docbook.xsl  myfile.xml
```

Finished page size

What if you are preparing page masters for a publication that is not a standard paper size, such as for a 7 x 9 inch book? You can set your own custom page size with the `page.width` and `page.height` parameters. These override whatever the `paper.type` parameter is set to. You can still print your page masters on larger paper, with the expectation that you will be trimming it down to the finished page size. If you are submitting PDF files to a publisher, then you need to arrange this process, because the PDF viewer will show the page size as what you specified.

See the Units of measure (page 81) note about units of measurement.

For example:

```
xsltproc  --output myfile.fo  \
  --stringparam  page.height 9in \
  --stringparam  page.width 7in \
  fo/docbook.xsl  myfile.xml
```

If you plan to use your stylesheet for both portrait and landscape books, you should use the `page.width.portrait` and `page.height.portrait` parameters instead. Those set the values for page width and height, respectively, when the parameter `page.orientation` is set to `portrait`. If the parameter `page.orientation` is set to `landscape`, then the values are switched. If you set the page dimensions using the `page.width` and `page.height` parameters, then the `page.orientation` parameter will have no effect.

Left and right margins

The side margins are set using the `page.margin.inner` and `page.margin.outer` parameters. They are named this way for double sided and bound output, where the margins alternate for left and right pages of a spread. For single-sided output, the `page.margin.inner` value corresponds to the left margin on all the pages. The margins are measured inward from the boundaries set by the page size. When you shrink the page size, the margins stay the same but the printed text area shrinks. For example:

```
xsltproc  --output myfile.fo  \
  --stringparam  page.height 9in \
  --stringparam  page.width 7in \
  --stringparam  page.margin.inner 2in \
  --stringparam  page.margin.outer 1in \
  fo/docbook.xsl  myfile.xml
```

The remaining width for the text area is 7 minus 2 minus 1, or 4 inches.

---

[2] http://docbook.sourceforge.net/release/xsl/current/doc/fo/page.width.portrait.html

You can also indent body text relative to section titles, or add global indents on the right or left to provide space for margin notes. See the section called "Indenting body text" (page 84) for more information.

Top and bottom margins

The top and bottom margins are a bit more complicated because they include the space reserved for any headers and footers. In the DocBook XSL stylesheets, the following figure shows the parameters that control those spaces.

Figure 8.1. Top and bottom margin parameters

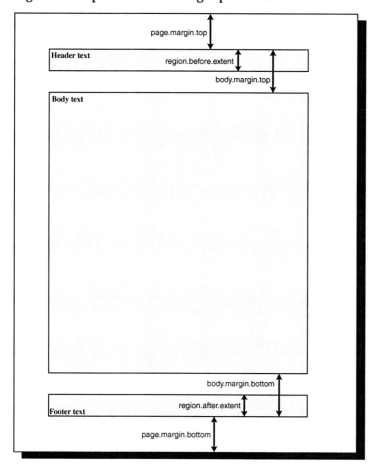

Parameter name	What it specifies
page.margin.top	Top of page edge to top of header area.
region.before.extent	Height of header area, from top of the header text to the bottom of the header area.
body.margin.top	Top of header area to top of main text area.
body.margin.bottom	Bottom of main text area to bottom of footer area.
region.after.extent	Height of footer area, from the top of the footer area to the bottom of the footer text.
page.margin.bottom	Bottom of footer area to bottom of page edge.

Note that both the `region.before.extent` and `body.margin.top` are measured from the `page.margin.top`, with a similar arrangement at the bottom of the page. An example should make it easier to set your own values. The following could be the FO stylesheet parameter settings for a 7in by 9in page with headers and footers.

Example 8.1. Page margins

```
<xsl:param name="page.height.portrait">9in</xsl:param>  ❶
<xsl:param name="page.width.portrait">7in</xsl:param>
<xsl:param name="page.margin.inner">0.75in</xsl:param>
<xsl:param name="page.margin.outer">0.50in</xsl:param>
<xsl:param name= "page.margin.top">0.17in</xsl:param>  ❷
<xsl:param name="region.before.extent">0.17in</xsl:param>  ❸
<xsl:param name="body.margin.top">0.33in</xsl:param>  ❹
<xsl:param name="region.after.extent">0.35in</xsl:param>
<xsl:param name="page.margin.bottom">0.50in</xsl:param>
<xsl:param name="body.margin.bottom">0.65in</xsl:param>
<xsl:param name="double.sided">1</xsl:param>
```

❶ Specifies the finished page size to be 9 inches tall. That means the paper size after it has been trimmed. It can be printed on a larger sheet before being trimmed.
❷ Top of page edge to top of header text area. If the header text is vertically aligned to top, then this will also be to the top of the header text itself.
❸ Height of the header area.
❹ Top of header text to top of body text.

So in this example, the total distance from the top page edge to the top of the body text is `0.17in` (`page.margin.top`) plus `0.33in` (`body.margin.top`), or 0.50 inches total. The bottom distance is `0.50in` (`page.margin.bottom`) plus `0.65in` (`body.margin.bottom`), or 1.15in total. The larger `region.after.extent` allows for two lines of text in the footer.

Indenting body text

By default, the DocBook XSL stylesheets indent the body text relative to the section titles in print output. Starting with stylesheet version 1.68, the indent is controlled by the `body.start.indent` parameter. The default value is 4pc (four picas). This parameter is used by the template named `set.flow.properties` to add a `start-indent="4pc"` attribute to certain `fo:flow` elements. There is a similar `body.end.indent` parameter to add an indent on the right side. That parameter can be used to create space on the right for margin notes, but its default value is 0pt.

If you want to turn off the indenting of body text, then set the `body.start.indent` parameter to 0pt. You cannot just use zero, because a `start-indent` property requires a unit of measure.

These parameters are used by the template named `set.flow.properties`, which lets you add properties that apply to an entire `fo:flow` in a page sequence. By default, these parameters are used only for page-sequences using the body page-master, such as chapters, and for `preface` and `appendix` pages. You can customize the `set.flow.properties` template to change which flows use these indent parameters.

Chapter titles and section titles are not indented by default. That's because they have their own `start-indent` property that is set to zero in their titlepage specifications. If you do want your chapter or section titles to be indented as well, then add your own `start-indent` property and set its value to `$body.start.indent`. See the section called "Title fonts and sizes" (page 172) to learn how to set properties on titles.

Prior to version 1.68, the body indent was implemented differently, using the `title.margin.left` parameter. The `title.margin.left` parameter was set to -4pc, a negative four picas that moves the titles left (a pica is about 0.166 inches). The body area's margin was increased by the same amount to provide the body indent. If your stylesheet version is prior to 1.68 and you want to remove the body indent, set this parameter to `0pc`. Be sure to keep units on the value, or the stylesheet will generate an error message.

So the use of the `body.start.indent` parameter has the same effect as the `title.margin.left` parameter, except `body.start.indent` is specified with a positive value. The `title.margin.left` parameter was retained for backwards compatibility, but you should not try to use both parameters at the same time.

Landscape documents

The default page orientation for the standard paper sizes is portrait (long edge vertical). You can change your document to landscape (long edge horizontal) by using the `page.orientation` parameter, whose values can be either `portrait` (the default) or `landscape`. For example:

```
xsltproc  --output myfile.fo \
  --stringparam  page.orientation  landscape \
  fo/docbook.xsl  myfile.xml
```

See the section called "Finished page size" (page 82) for a discussion of setting page dimensions if you use one stylesheet for both portrait and landscape output.

Double sided

You can choose single-sided or double-sided output. Double-sided means pages are to be printed on both sides of the paper, and the margins, headers, and footers should be mirrored on the two sides. The default is single sided. Set the `double.sided` parameter to 1 to change it. For example:

```
xsltproc  --output myfile.fo \
  --stringparam  double.sided 1 \
  fo/docbook.xsl  myfile.xml
```

Multi-column

The default formatting uses one wide column for the whole page, except in the index which has two columns by default. You can specify two or more columns for different page types of your document using the set of `column.count.*` parameters. The following is a list of these parameters and their default values:

```
<xsl:param name="column.count.titlepage" select="1"/>
<xsl:param name="column.count.lot" select="1"/>
<xsl:param name="column.count.front" select="1"/>
<xsl:param name="column.count.body" select="1"/>
<xsl:param name="column.count.back" select="1"/>
<xsl:param name="column.count.index" select="2"/>
```

For example, to change your output for chapters (a body page type) and appendixes (a back matter page type) to two column:

```
xsltproc  --output myfile.fo \
  --stringparam  column.count.body  2 \
  --stringparam  column.count.back  2 \
  fo/docbook.xsl  myfile.xml
```

The title pages and table of contents remain single column.

To see which DocBook elements are processed with each page type, see Table 13.4, "DocBook XSL-FO page master names" (page 195)

Double spacing

If your format calls for double spacing lines of text, which is often needed for editing review, then set the `line-height` stylesheet parameter to a value of 2 or more. That value is multiplied by the font size to set the line spacing. Since the normal line height is 1.2, you might try a value of 2.4 to double the spacing. The `line-height` parameter is set at the root element level for the entire document. This will only work if your XSL-FO processor supports the line height property.

Typography

A few of the typographical specs used by the DocBook XSL stylesheets can be changed with individual parameters on the command line. Because there are so many possible specs, however, most are contained in XSL `attribute-set` elements that bundle together many specs. Changing such specs requires a customization layer.

The following is an example of several typography changes using parameters:

```
xsltproc  --output myfile.fo  \
  --stringparam  body.font.family  Helvetica \
  --stringparam  body.font.master  11 \
  --stringparam  title.font.family  "Times Roman" \
  --stringparam  footnote.font.size 9 \
  fo/docbook.xsl  myfile.xml
```

Body and title font families

To change the font family for the body text, use the `body.font.family` parameter. The default value is `serif`, which most FO processors render as Times Roman. Although you can specify any font name in the parameter, there is no guarantee that the XSL-FO processor can produce that font. You need to consult the documentation of the current version of the processor to see what fonts it supports. As installed, FOP supports only Times Roman, Helvetica, and Courier. These are the fonts supported by the Adobe PDF files. To configure a new font into your FO processor, see the section called "Adding a font" (page 240).

The font used for the title page and chapter and section titles can be changed with the `title.font.family` parameter. It is set to `sans-serif` by default, which maps to Helvetica in most FO processors.

For elements such as `literal` and `programlisting` that require a monospace font, the `monospace.font.family` parameter provides the font family name. By default it is `monospace`, which maps to Courier in most FO processors.

Font sizes

To change the body font size, use the `body.font.master` parameter. That parameter is a pure number representing point size, but specified without units. That parameter is then used to compute the actual font size values relative to the master size. So you need *not* set the `body.font.size` parameter, because it is computed from the `body.font.master` value.

You can also change the footnote font size using the `footnote.font.size` parameter. By default, the footnote size is 80% of the size of the body master size. You could set it to `8pt` for example.

The title font sizes cannot be set with parameter values, and must be set using a customization file. See the section called "Title fonts and sizes" (page 172).

Using renderas to style section titles

The DocBook DTD defines a strict hierarchy of section elements. Unlike HTML, you cannot put a level 3 heading directly under a level 1 heading. However, sometimes the content does not fit well into this strict hierarchy when being formatted. For example, you may have a level 1 section that has a great many short level 2 sections. When formatted, the level 2 section titles may appear too large relative to their small section content. If you were writing in HTML, you might just break the hierarchy and resort to `h3` titles to reduce their size.

The creators of DocBook recognized this problem, and provided a solution in the `renderas` ("render as") attribute. Its value can be `sect1`, `sect2`, etc. You can use the `renderas` attribute to tell the stylesheet to render a particular section title as if it were a different section level.

For example:

```
<sect1>
  <title>Options</title>
  <para>This section describes a lot of options</para>
  <sect2 renderas="sect3">
    <title>The A option</title
    ...
```

The section level 2 element has a `renderas="sect3"` attribute. The stylesheet will then format the title "The A option" in the type size and style of a level 3 section. If you have several such `sect2` sections, you have to add the attribute to each to keep the headings consistent. The attribute has no other effect on how the section in handled. It is still numbered as a level 2 section, and it appears as a level 2 section in the table of contents.

Chapter and section numbering

There are several parameters that control numbering of part, chapter and section titles. By default in printed output, part and chapter titles are numbered but section titles are not. Appendix titles are numbered (with letters) when in a book, but not numbered by default when in an article. In the DocBook XSL stylesheets, the number used in a title is called a *label*.

The print stylesheet provides an identical set of parameters with `autolabel` in the name as in the HTML stylesheets. For a description of how to use such parameters for turning off numbering or changing the numbering style, see the section called "Chapter and section numbering" (page 74) in Chapter 7, *HTML output options*.

Depth of section numbering

You may want to limit the depth of sections that get a section number. If you have deeply nested sections, then the string of numbers in the section label can get quite long. Or perhaps you just want sections at levels 1 and 2 to be numbered, since any lower level sections are not important enough to have a number label.

You can use the `section.autolabel.max.depth` parameter to control which section levels get a number label. If you set the parameter to 2, then only sections at levels 1 and 2 will have the label. The default value is 8, meaning all section levels have numbering (if it is turned on).

Numbering book parts

When producing a book, it is sometimes appropriate to group related chapters into book parts. To do that, you use `part` elements in your `book` element, and then put your `chapter` elements inside your `part` elements. Each part has a title, and may have a title page to indicate a new grouping of chapters.

Numbering of book parts is turned on by default, using uppercase roman numerals. You can turn off part numbering by setting the `part.autolabel` parameter to zero.

Regardless of whether parts are numbered, you can restart chapter numbering at the beginning of each part. If you want that type of chapter numbering, set the `label.from.part` parameter to 1. If you use that option, you will probably also want to set the `component.label.includes.part.label` parameter to 1. That changes the chapter numbering so the chapters in the first part are numbered I.1, I.2, I.3, etc., and the chapters in the second part are numbered II.1, II.2, II.3, etc. If you do not set the second parameter, then your output will have more than one "Chapter 1" and citations and cross references will be ambiguous. The parameter similarly modifies appendix numbers.

If you would rather number your parts using arabic numerals instead of uppercase roman numerals, you can put the number format in the parameter value.

```
<xsl:param name="part.autolabel">1</xsl:param>
```

This works for the other autolabel parameters as well.

Page breaking

When generating print output, you may find that some pages break in awkward places in your text flow. Because DocBook XSL is a batch processing system, you cannot just visually adjust page breaks by adding blank lines in your file as you can with a word processor. Even if you were to insert empty paragraphs to add space, those empty lines might be out of place if you edit your content and repaginate.

The DocBook DTD does not contain any elements or attributes that control page breaking. Most people mistakenly assume the `pagebreak` element would create a page break. But it was created to record where there was a page break in a legacy document before it was converted to DocBook XML, and it does not generate a page break.

The DocBook XSL stylesheet tries hard to prevent bad page breaks in print output. It assigns `keep-together` properties to some output blocks, which prevents insertion of a page break within the block. For example, a table with this property will be pushed to the next page if the whole table does not fit at the bottom of a page. For other blocks the stylesheet adds a `keep-with-next` property to keep the block with the following block. This is useful for section titles so they do not appear at the bottom of a page with nothing after them.

Note:

The previous version of FOP (0.20.5) did not support these keep properties. Be sure to use FOP 0.93 or higher.

Automatic page breaking is great when it works, but it does not always produce aestheically pleasing pages. There are times when the author needs to assist the formatter in page breaking. Since page breaking applies only to print output, the stylesheet supports several dbfo processing instructions to let the author provide help in page breaking.

Keep-together processing instruction

The dbfo keep-together processing instruction can be used with tables, examples, figures, and equations (and their informal versions too). By default, each of those elements is automatically kept together, by means of the following attribute in the formal.object.properties attribute-set in fo/param.xsl:

```
<xsl:attribute-set name="formal.object.properties">
    <xsl:attribute name="keep-together.within-column">always</xsl:attribute>
    ...
</xsl:attribute-set>
```

For more information on attribute sets, see the section called "Attribute sets" (page 103). The full name of this XSL-FO property is keep-together.within-column. The within-column part means the block will be kept together across column breaks in a multi-column page, as well as across page breaks. The value of always means to always keep the block together. If it were set to auto instead, then breaks would be permitted.

If you do not change the formal.object.properties attribute set, then none of your tables, examples, figures, or equations will be broken across page boundaries. That's good, except when you do not want that behavior. Consider a long table that starts fairly high on the page. If the whole table does not fit on the page, then it breaks the page and leaves a lot of blank space behind. In such cases it would be better to start the table on the current page, and permit it to break and continue on the next page. But you do not want to change the attribute-set, because that would change it for all tables, including short ones that should be kept together.

So to permit a single table to break, add the dbfo keep-together processing instruction to your DocBook XML table element as follows:

```
<table>
  <title>My long table</title>
  <?dbfo keep-together="auto" ?>
  ...
```

When this processing instruction is a child of the DocBook table element, the stylesheet will add a keep-together.within-column="auto" property to the output table. That value will override the attribute set value of always and permit a page break within the table.

This processing instruction can also be used for figures, examples, and equations (and their informal counterparts) when they contain content that can be broken across pages (this does not include graphics). For example, if you put a long programlisting in an example or informalexample, you could add the same PI to permit it to break across pages.

The dbfo keep-together PI can also be used to turn on a keep for a single table if you turn it off globally in the formal.object.properties attribute set. The same is true if you turn it off for all your tables in the table.table.properties attribute set. See the section called "table.table.properties attribute-set" (page 488) for more information on attribute sets for tables.

Soft page breaks

The one thing you *do not* want to do is insert a hard page break in your XML document. A hard page break always forces a page break at that point. While this may be useful for solving an immediate problem, the next time you edit your document and reformat you may find that your hard page break is positioned higher up on the page and breaks it inappropriately. Maintaining a document with hard page breaks is a pain. For that reason there is no processing instruction in DocBook XSL to insert a hard page break.

The stylesheet does provide a processing instruction for *soft page breaks*. A soft page break is a conditional page break. If the conditions on the page are not met, then the page does not break. The idea is borrowed from the troff typesetting system, which uses the term "need". You put a processing instruction in your document that effectively says "I need at least 2 vertical inches left on the current page to fit the following material. If that much space is not available on the page, then break to the next page at this point. If there is enough space, do not break."

This kind of conditional page break is handy when the normal "keeps" used in the stylesheet are not sufficient, either for technical reasons or for aesthetic reasons. For example, you may want to make sure a short introductory paragraph that precedes a code listing has at least a few lines of code with it on the page. The para and the programlisting are separate elements that normally would not have a "keep". The following is an example.

```
<para>Some text in a paragraph</para>
<?dbfo-need height="2in" ?>
<para>The following code snippet illustrates
the technique.</para>
<programlisting># Some sample code
</programlisting>
```

Here is what happens when this page is being typeset by the XSL-FO processor. If at the point on the page where the second paragraph in the above example would start there is less than 2 inches of vertical space left , then the rest of the page is left blank and the second paragraph is pushed to the next page. How does it work? The stylesheet outputs an empty fo:block-container with a 2 inch height, followed by an empty fo:block with a negative 2 inch space-before property. If there is 2 inches of space left on the page, then it backspaces up to the start of the block container and starts the next text output without breaking the page. If there is not 2 inches of space left, then the block-container will force a page break and the text will start at the top of the next page.

Note:

The current version of FOP (0.93) does not support this soft page break mechanism.

Because the mechanism uses blocks, you cannot put the processing instruction inline. It must be *between* elements that generate blocks of text, otherwise you may get invalid XSL-FO. Also note that the processing instruction name is dbfo-need, not dbfo like other DocBook PIs.

If you are managing breaks between items in a list, then you might have to put the processing instruction just inside the listitem element to get it to work. This is especially true for varlistentry.

This kind of page breaking is not perfect, because you need to estimate how much physical space is needed for the content you want to keep together. You would typically use it after the first printout so can measure vertical sizes of typeset elements. But since it is not wrapping elements, it can create keeps of arbitrary size.

The dbfo-need PI also accepts a second optional pseudo attribute named space-before. This is useful to manually adjust the spacing when the stylesheet cannot quite resolve the spacing the way it was without the PI. For example:

```
<?dbfo-need  height="0.5in"  space-before="3em" ?>
```

The space-before pseudo attribute also could be used to add extra vertical space wherever you need it. If you leave out the height pseudo attribute, then you will just get the extra spacing.

Hard page breaks

Although the DocBook XSL stylesheets do not provide direct support for hard (unconditional) page breaks, you can implement your own as a customization. Hard page breaks are not recommended for the reasons described in the section called "Soft page breaks" (page 89). But there may be times when it is useful. Although customizations are discussed later, this short one is included here to make it easier to find. To enable hard page breaks, you add the following template to your customization layer:

```
<xsl:template match="processing-instruction('hard-pagebreak')">
   <fo:block break-after='page'/>
 </xsl:template>
```

Then you put the following processing instruction in your document where you want an unconditional page break:

```
<para>Some text in a paragraph</para>
<?hard-pagebreak?>
<para>The following code snippet illustrates
the technique.</para>
<programlisting># Some sample code
</programlisting>
```

When the stylesheet processes this PI, it inserts an empty block with the `break-after='page'` property, which forces a page break. As with soft page breaks, this PI cannot appear inline; it must be placed between elements that generate blocks of text.

PDF bookmarks

PDF files can optionally include an active table of contents that is displayed alongside the pages in the PDF viewer. These references are called *bookmarks*.

PDF bookmarks are generated using special functions in each XSL-FO processor because XSL cannot produce them directly. So if you are using Apache FOP, for example, you need to turn on the FOP extension functions by setting the `fop.extensions` parameter to 1. For example:

```
xsltproc  --output myfile.fo \
  --stringparam  fop.extensions  1 \
  fo/docbook.xsl  myfile.xml
```

If you are instead using Antenna House's XSL Formatter, you should set the `axf.extensions` parameter to 1, or if you are using RenderX's XEP you should set the `xep.extensions` parameter to 1. When you turn on one of these extensions, special FO elements and/or attributes are written by the DocBook XSL stylesheets to the FO file. These elements and attributes belong to processor-specific namespaces. By convention, the following namespace prefixes are used: `fox` for FOP, `axf` for Antenna House, and `rx` for XEP. Those special FO elements are only recognized by the specific processor being used. If you turn on the wrong extensions, you probably will not be successful.

Note:

These FO extensions are not controlled by the `use.extensions` parameter. That parameter controls the use of XSLT extension functions used by some XSLT processors, not the extensions in the FO processors.

Extra blank lines

You may have a need to create extra vertical space at certain places in your output. For example, a workbook could allow extra space for writing in answers to questions or exercises. The easiest way to create extra white space is to insert a literallayout element and add as many blank lines as you need to it. When formatted, the blank lines inside a literallayout are preserved, so you will get as much extra space as you need.

Cross reference page numbers

If your document contains xref elements, then you can turn on page number references to enable the reader to find the reference more easily in print. Set the insert.xref.page.number parameter to yes. Note that link elements do not get a page number reference.

The default format of the page reference is set by the page.citation gentext template. You can control the style of an individual xref by adding an xrefstyle attribute to it. See the section called "Customizing cross references" (page 262) for more information.

Docbook icon graphics

The DocBook stylesheets can use icon graphics for these purposes in the print output:

- Icons to indicate the different types of admonitions (note, tip, warning, caution, and important).

- Numbered icons for callouts.

Admonition graphics

By default, when you process an admonition element such as note, the output displays the label Note in the appropriate language, followed by the text of the note. You can add a distinctive admonition graphic before the label by setting the admon.graphics parameter to non-zero:

```
xsltproc  --stringparam admon.graphics 1 fo/docbook.xsl myfile.xml
```

This will put an image reference before the word "Note" in the FO output file:

```
<fo:external-graphic src="url(images/note.png)"/>
```

When this is subsequently processed with the XSL-FO processor, it will look for that image file in that location to include it in the PDF. The admonition icon graphics are included with the stylesheet distribution in the images directory.

Other options include:

- If you want to display just the icon alone without the text label, then set the admon.textlabel stylesheet parameter to zero.

- Use the admon.graphics.path and admon.graphics.extension parameters to change the generated pathname to the image file. The pathname written to the FO file is built up from three components, two of which can be changed with parameters. Here is how the default images/note.png pathname is generated:

Path component	Example	Comes from
Directory	images/	admon.graphics.path parameter. Include the trailing slash.
Filename prefix	note	Admonition element name.
Filename suffix	.png	admon.graphics.extension parameter. Include the dot.

These parameters change the path written into the FO file. The directory could be a single location, so you do not have to copy them to each of your source directories. Being able to change the filename extension is useful when you have created your own admonition graphics and they are in a different format. They all have to use the same extension, however.

Callout icons

Callouts are used to connect annotation comments to points in a program listing or literallayout. They are like numbered footnotes, in that a user follows a given number label in the display to a specific comment by matching the numbers. See the section called "Callouts" (page 447) for more information on using callouts.

By default the FO stylesheets use small graphical icons for the numbers (such as ❶). The stylesheets insert references like the following into the FO output:

```
<fo:external-graphic src="url(images/callouts/1.svg)"
  content-width="7pt" width="7pt"/>
```

When this is subsequently processed with the XSL-FO processor, it will look for that image file in that location to include it in the PDF. The callout icon graphics are included with the stylesheet distribution in the `images/callouts` directory.

The SVG callout icons have been available starting with version 1.73 of the stylesheets. They provide a sharp rendering of the circle and number at any resolution. The SVG icons go up to the number 30. Prior to version 1.73, the callout image files were bitmap PNG graphics, and they do not look good in print because they are not high resolution graphics.

For print, you could also replace the icon graphics with special Unicode characters that are a similar white number on a black disk. To do that, set the `callout.unicode` parameter to 1 and the `callout.graphics` parameter to zero. Then the FO output uses character entities like `&#10102;`. This entity is rendered by the XSL-FO processor as the callout number. These Unicode numbers also only go up to ten, however.

To replace the callout icons with plain text numbers in parentheses like (1), set the `callout.graphics` parameter to zero (it is one by default) and the `callout.unicode` parameter to zero (the default).

If you use callout graphics, then there are four parameters that give you more control over the generated graphics tag.

`callout.graphics.extension`	Use this parameter to change the icon file extension from `.svg` to some other extension for which you have icon graphics.
`callout.graphics.path`	Use this parameter to change the location where the XSL-FO processor should look for the image files. The default value is `images/callouts/`, which may not work for you unless you copy the `images` directory from the stylesheet distribution to where your XML files are located. Be sure to include a trailing slash.
`callout.graphics.number.limit`	Use this parameter to set the highest number for which you have a callout graphic. The stylesheets are distributed with SVG callout graphics files with numbers up to 30, but you could create graphics with additional numbers if you need them. If you have more numbers but you do not reset this parameter, then any callout numbers over 30 will still format like (31).
`callout.icon.size`	The size to render the callout icons. The default value is 7pt.

Printing one chapter

By setting the `rootid` parameter, you can tell the processor to select one chapter of a book for printing. More precisely, you tell the processor to select one element of your document to use as the root element. For printed output, the selected element must be of a type that generates a page-sequence in FO output, so it could be an appendix, reference, or preface. It must also have an `id` attribute, because that is the value used in the `rootid` parameter.

When you print a single chapter from a book, it will always be numbered 1. So you cannot assemble a book from individual chapter outputs. But printing a single chapter is useful for checking formatting and page breaking.

If you want a table of contents with the chapter, you need one more parameter. By default, chapters do not have a TOC. But the `generate.toc` parameter can turn one on for your single chapter.

```
xsltproc  --output myfile.fo \
  --stringparam  rootid  mychapterid \
  --stringparam  generate.toc  "chapter  title,toc" \
  fo/docbook.xsl  myfile.xml
```

The first parameter selects the element whose `id` attribute is `mychapterid`. The second parameter turns on the TOC for chapters, and prints the `Table of Contents` title at the top of the TOC. If you do not want that title on the TOC, you can remove the word `title` (and the comma) from the parameter value.

Crop marks

Crop marks are marks printed in the corners of the paper to indicate where a physical page is to be trimmed to final size. Sometimes it is necessary to add these when preparing a PDF for rendering on a printing press instead of a desktop printer. There is no standard means for specifying crop marks in the XSL-FO 1.0 specification, but it is a feature that some XSL-FO processors offer as an extension.

If you are using an XSL-FO processor from Antenna House or RenderX, then there are several stylesheet parameters you can use to control crop marks.

Parameter	Example	Description
`crop.marks`	`<xsl:param name="crop.marks" select="1"/>`	Turn on crop marks. The default value is zero (off).
`crop.mark.width`	`<xsl:param name="crop.mark.width">1pt </xsl:param>`	The thickness of the crop mark lines. The default is 0.5pt.
`crop.mark.offset`	`<xsl:param name="crop.mark.offset">0.5in </xsl:param>`	The distance from the trimmed page edge to the outer end of a crop mark. The default value is 24pt.
`crop.mark.bleed`	`<xsl:param name="crop.mark.bleed">0.25in </xsl:param>`	The distance from the trimmed page edge to the inner end of a crop mark. The default value is 6pt. This is the amount of the crop mark line to hide, in order that it not show by accident.

The trimmed page edge is the page size specified by the stylesheet parameters `page.height` and `page.width`. The crop marks are drawn outward from those corners. If you specify a `crop.mark.bleed` of 0pt, then the two crop marks will meet at each page corner, extending outward from the corner to a distance equal to the `crop.mark.offset`. However, it is not a good idea for the crop marks to meet at the corner, because if a sheet is positioned slightly off at trim time, part of the crop mark will show. If you specify a `crop.mark.bleed` distance, then that much of the line will be hidden, so the crop marks will no longer meet at the corner. It shortens the displayed crop mark line by that amount, without moving its outer end.

Keep in mind that if you want to the crop marks to show on a desktop printer, you have to print onto a sheet of paper large enough to accomodate both your page size and the crop marks. If you want an accurate printing, then turn off the page scaling that the PDF browser might apply in the print dialog box.

Note that the Document Properties dialog box in a PDF viewer will show the page size including the crop marks. That is, if you specify `page.width="6in"`, `page.height="8in"`, and `crop.mark.offset=".5in"`, the the document properties will show the page size as 7 in by 9 in.

Part III. Customizing DocBook XSL

Contents

9
Customization methods

When you find that you need to change something that does not seem to have a parameter, then you will have to customize the DocBook XSL stylesheets. Fortunately, the stylesheets were designed to make them easy to customize (thanks to Norm Walsh). The basic idea is to create a *customization layer* in which you put all your changes, and then rely on the standard DocBook stylesheets for everything else. The following sections describe the various methods you can use:

- Creating a customization layer.

- Setting parameter values.

- Modifying attribute-sets.

- Filling in placeholder templates.

- Customizing generated text.

- Replacing stylesheet templates.

- Adding new templates.

- Creating custom processing instructions.

- Generating customized titlepage templates. This method is covered in Chapter 11, *Title page customization* (page 141).

   Note:

   You do not need a customization layer to customize how your HTML output looks. You can control your HTML presentation by simply adding your own CSS stylesheet to the standard DocBook HTML output. See the section called "Using CSS to style HTML" (page 71) for more information.

Customization layer

A customization layer is a new XSL stylesheet that layers your changes on top of the existing DocBook XSL templates. It permits you to customize your processing without actually editing the original DocBook stylesheet files. Your changes are a thin layer on top of the extensive collection of DocBook code.

Keeping your changes separate has a lot of advantages:

- You can generally upgrade to a new release of the DocBook stylesheets without having to reintegrate your changes into a lot of separate DocBook files. You may have to tweak your customization layer a bit, depending on the changes introduced in the new version. But you will not have to repeat typing a lot of code into the new version's files.

- It makes it easy to distribute a customization to other users, because you only have to distribute one file and not a large collection of modified DocBook files.

- Getting help with problems is easier because your changes are completely isolated. You can attach just your customization layer to an email, and others can apply it to their own standard DocBook files for testing.

Writing a customization layer

Writing a customization layer requires knowledge of XSLT syntax. You can read Appendix A, *A brief introduction to XSL* (page 521) and the examples here to get started, but you will probably need to obtain a good XSLT reference book, such as Michael Kay's *XSLT Programmer's Reference*. For help in debugging a customization, see Appendix B, *Debugging XSL stylesheets* (page 531)

The basic features of a customization layer are:

- It is an XSLT stylesheet file, using standard XSLT syntax.

- It imports one of the DocBook XSL stylesheet files, which acts as the starting point.

- It adds whatever modifications are needed.

- It is used in place of the standard DocBook stylesheet when you process your DocBook XML files.

The file can be named whatever you like, and you can create more than one customization layer with different customizations. The following is a very short example of a customization layer with each line explained. It just sets a few parameters for HTML processing:

Example 9.1. Customization layer

```
<?xml version='1.0'?> ❶
<xsl:stylesheet
    xmlns:xsl="http://www.w3.org/1999/XSL/Transform" version="1.0"> ❷

<xsl:import href="html/docbook.xsl"/> ❸

<xsl:param name="html.stylesheet" select="'corpstyle.css'"/> ❹
<xsl:param name="admon.graphics" select="1"/>

</xsl:stylesheet> ❺
```

❶ The standard XML file marker.
❷ Standard root element for XSL stylesheets.
❸ Import the standard DocBook HTML stylesheet file using `xsl:import`.
❹ Set a couple of parameters, using XSL syntax.
❺ Close the root element to end the stylesheet.

If you use chunking for HTML, then replace docbook.xsl with chunk.xsl in the xsl:import statement. To customize print output, put a reference to the FO docbook.xsl file in the import statement.

If you write a customization layer for print output that includes FO elements such as fo:inline, then the stylesheet top element has to include the FO namespace declaration:

```
<?xml version='1.0'?>
<xsl:stylesheet
    xmlns:xsl="http://www.w3.org/1999/XSL/Transform"
    xmlns:fo="http://www.w3.org/1999/XSL/Format"
    version="1.0">

<xsl:import href="fo/docbook.xsl"/>

<xsl:template match="lineannotation">
  <fo:inline font-style="italic">
    <xsl:call-template name="inline.charseq"/>
  </fo:inline>
</xsl:template>
</xsl:stylesheet>
```

Using a customization layer

To process your XML files with the customization layer, you simply use your customization layer file in place of the standard DocBook file that it imports. For example, if the above example was saved to a file named mystyles.xsl, then you could use it as follows:

```
xsltproc  --output myfile.html  mystyles.xsl  myfile.xml
```

Here you have replaced the standard docbook.xsl stylesheet file with mystyles.xsl. Because your file imports the standard docbook.xsl file, the effect is the same as processing with the standard file but with your customizations added.

Customizing both HTML and FO

If you do customizations for both HTML and FO output, you need to start with separate customization layers. You might be tempted to write one customization layer that conditionally imports either the HTML or FO DocBook stylesheet. Unfortunately, it does not work, because the xsl:import statement cannot be placed inside an XSL conditional statement like xsl:if or xsl:choose. So you must have separate customization files for each. If you also do chunk and nonchunk HTML processing, then you will need a third customization layer.

Maintaining multiple customization layers can lead to inconsistencies as they change over time. Many of the parameters apply to both chunk and nonchunk HTML output, or to both HTML and FO output. If you set the admon.graphics parameter in one, you will probably want to set it in all. You can do that easily if you separate the common parts of your customization layer into a separate file. Then you can use xsl:include in all of your customization layers to include the same file with the same parameter settings. Here are two customizations that share a common-customizations.xsl file that contains shared parameters:

HTML customization:
```
<?xml version='1.0'?>
<xsl:stylesheet
       xmlns:xsl="http://www.w3.org/1999/XSL/Transform"  version="1.0">
  <xsl:import href="html/docbook.xsl"/>
  <xsl:include href="common-customizations.xsl" />
  <xsl:param name="html.stylesheet" select="'corpstyle.css'"/>
</xsl:stylesheet>
```

FO customization:
```
<?xml version='1.0'?>
<xsl:stylesheet
       xmlns:xsl="http://www.w3.org/1999/XSL/Transform"  version="1.0">
  <xsl:import href="fo/docbook.xsl"/>
  <xsl:include href="common-customizations.xsl" />
  <xsl:param name="paper.type" select="'A4'"/>
</xsl:stylesheet>
```

Any parameters that are specific to one output type are defined in that customization layer only.

If you use a relative path in the href of the xsl:include statement, then that is taken as relative to the location of your customization layer file. That's probably ok if you keep them all in one place.

Using catalogs with customizations

A customization layer imports the standard DocBook stylesheet file as its starting point. This means you must supply some URI in the href attribute of xsl:import.

That URI can be:

- A relative pathname, which is taken to be relative to the location of the customization layer file.

- An absolute pathname.

- A web address.

Relative and absolute pathnames are not very portable. That means if you give someone else a copy of your customization layer, it may not work because the processor cannot find the original DocBook stylesheet file at the specified location.

Using a web address is generally more portable because most systems have web access today. But having to fetch a large number of stylesheet files over the web will greatly slow down your processing.

A good compromise is to use a web address for the URI but apply an XML catalog to map it to a local file location. See the section called "Map a web address to a local file" (page 50).

Setting parameters

The most common use of a customization layer is to consistently set parameter values without having to enter them on the command line. Notice in the previous example how simple the command line is, even though two parameters are being set. If you have more than a couple of parameters you regularly use, you might be better off putting them into a customization layer. It simplifies the typing, and ensures you will not forget one.

The XSL syntax for setting parameter values within the stylesheet comes in two forms:

```
<xsl:param name="parametername" select="'parametervalue'"/>
    or
<xsl:param name="parametername">parametervalue</xsl:param>
```

In the first form, the `xsl:param` element is empty and you enter the parameter value as the attribute value of the `select` attribute. As with all XML attribute values, it is enclosed in quotes (double quotes here). But it also has a second set of inner single quotes. That's to indicate that the parameter value is a string. This is necessary because an XSL parameter can also contain XML elements (called nodes in this context), and an unquoted string is treated as an element name that is expected to have some element content.

> **Note:**
>
> The most common mistake when specifying parameter values as `select` attribute values in a customization layer is to omit the inner quotes for a string value. You will not necessarily see any error message, and you'll be wondering why your parameter did not work. The second form avoids that mistake.

In the second form, the `select` attribute is not used. Instead, the content of the `xsl:param` element is the parameter value. It does not need to be enclosed in single quotes because content text is already treated as a string value.

Attribute sets

XSL supports the definition of named sets of attributes. An attribute-set is like a complex parameter that lets you define a collection of attribute names and values that can be referenced by a single attribute-set name. That permits you to "define once, use globally" any groups of attributes that apply in more than one place. The DocBook FO stylesheet defines many attribute-sets in the `fo/param.xsl` stylesheet file. The DocBook attribute-sets are documented in the *FO Parameter Reference*[1].

The DocBook attribute-sets can be customized like parameters in your customization layer. The following is an example of the original definition of an attribute-set named `section.title.properties` in `fo/param.xsl`:

---

[1] http://docbook.sourceforge.net/release/xsl/current/doc/fo/index.html

```
<xsl:attribute-set name="section.title.properties">
  <xsl:attribute name="font-family">
    <xsl:value-of select="$title.font.family"/>
  </xsl:attribute>
  <xsl:attribute name="font-weight">bold</xsl:attribute>
  <!-- font size is added dynamically by section.heading template -->
  <xsl:attribute name="keep-with-next.within-column">always</xsl:attribute>
  <xsl:attribute name="space-before.minimum">0.8em</xsl:attribute>
  <xsl:attribute name="space-before.optimum">1.0em</xsl:attribute>
  <xsl:attribute name="space-before.maximum">1.2em</xsl:attribute>
  <xsl:attribute name="text-align">left</xsl:attribute>
  <xsl:attribute name="start-indent">0pt</xsl:attribute>
</xsl:attribute-set>
```

It consists of a set of `xsl:attribute` elements enclosed in a `xsl:attribute-set` wrapper. The name of the set is assigned to the wrapper. This attribute-set is used for all section titles, on the assumption that they share many formatting properties.

These attributes are to be inserted into the `fo:block` start tag for the section title. That is accomplished in a DocBook XSL template with a `xsl:use-attribute-sets` attribute. The following is an example from the `fo/sections.xsl` stylesheet file:

```
<xsl:template name="section.heading">
  <xsl:param name="level" select="1"/>
  <xsl:param name="title"/>

  <fo:block  xsl:use-attribute-sets="section.title.properties">
  ...
```

Note that this attribute-set contains all the properties except the font-size. The `section.heading` template also determines what level of heading is currently being processed and adds a font-size property using another attribute-set specific to each level. For example, the attribute-set named `section.title.level1.properties` is used for level 1 section headings. With this design, you can specify common properties for all section headings by customizing the general `section.title.properties` attribute set, and customize individual heading levels with the more specific attribute-sets.

To customize an attribute-set, you do not have to copy the whole thing to your customization layer. It is a feature of attribute-sets that if more than one set has the same name, then they are effectively merged. That means you can add or modify just a few attributes and leave the rest as they are in the DocBook stylesheet. For example, if you want to left-align all your section headings and turn off boldface, you could add this to your customization layer:

```
<xsl:attribute-set name="section.title.properties">
  <xsl:attribute name="font-weight">normal</xsl:attribute>
  <xsl:attribute name="text-align">left</xsl:attribute>
</xsl:attribute-set>
```

The `font-weight` attribute overrides the value in the original attribute-set, and the `text-align` attribute adds a new property to the set. These attributes are merged with the other attributes at processing time. If two attributes have the same name within an attribute set, then the rules of import precedence apply. Basically this means your customization's value will override the default value in that attribute set in the stylesheet.

Completing placeholder templates

One of the customization features of the DocBook XSL stylesheets is a set of empty XSL templates. These are placeholder templates that can be filled in by you. They are automatically called at particular points during processing, but by default they are empty and have no effect. If you fill them in, then they will have the effect you define.

For example, there is an empty template named user.header.content in the HTML stylesheet. It is called at the top of each HTML page generated during chunking. If you put some content in such a named template in your customization layer, then that content will appear at the top of every HTML output file. A trivial example is:

```
<xsl:template name="user.header.content">
  <p><b>Hi Mom!</b></p>
</xsl:template>
```

The template body can be any valid XSL coding that can generate whatever content you want. A more complete example of HTML headers and footers is in the section called "HTML headers and footers" (page 148).

Generating new templates

The DocBook XSL distribution includes some tools for generating new versions of certain templates. Title pages are one feature that are hard to standardize, because everyone seems to want to do them differently. So the distribution includes a special stylesheet template/titlepage.xsl that generates a titlepage stylesheet module from a titlepage specification file. The titlepage specification file is written in XML (although not DocBook XML). See Chapter 11, *Title page customization* (page 141) for a complete example.

Generated text

Generated text is any text that appears in the output that was not in the original XML input file. Examples include "Chapter 5", "Example 7.2", "Table of Contents", as well as the text generated for xref cross references. The customization features for generated text, or *gentext*, are quite powerful. You can customize each type of generated text separately, and you can do it for any of the languages supported by DocBook.

Default generated text

If you want to see where the default generated text comes from, start by looking in the file common/en.xml included with the DocBook distribution. That file has all the text strings generated for English text. You'll notice that the common directory also has similar files for many other languages.

In the common/en.xml file, you'll see several groups of elements. The first group looks like the following:

```
<l:gentext key="Abstract" text="Abstract"/>
<l:gentext key="abstract" text="Abstract"/>
<l:gentext key="Answer" text="A:"/>
<l:gentext key="answer" text="A:"/>
<l:gentext key="Appendix" text="Appendix"/>
<l:gentext key="appendix" text="appendix"/>
```

These l:gentext elements associate a printable string (the text attribute) with each element name (the key attribute). These gentext elements are in the l: namespace (localization) to keep them separate. The equivalent lines in the German file common/de.xml look like the following:

```
<l:gentext key="Abstract" text="Zusammenfassung"/>
<l:gentext key="abstract" text="Zusammenfassung"/>
<l:gentext key="Answer" text="A:"/>
<l:gentext key="answer" text="A:"/>
<l:gentext key="Appendix" text="Anhang"/>
<l:gentext key="appendix" text="Anhang"/>
```

Other groups of elements are contained within a `l:context` element which indicates in what context those strings will be used. Here is a sample from the English `title` context:

```
<l:context name="title">
   <l:template name="abstract" text="%t"/>
   <l:template name="answer" text="%t"/>
   <l:template name="appendix" text="Appendix %n. %t"/>
```

Here the `text` attribute value is taken to be a text template that is filled in at run time. Any `%t` mark in the attribute value is a placeholder for the element's title, and `%n` is a placeholder for its number (if it is numbered).

Customizing generated text

To customize one or more generated text strings, you create local versions of the generated text elements in your customization layer. Your collection of new generated text elements is put into a DocBook parameter named `local.l10n.xml`. During processing that requires generated text, that parameter is always checked before using the default values.

Following is a short customization for changing the generated text for a chapter cross reference from the default `Chapter 3, Using a Mouse` to something like `Chapter 3: "Using a mouse"` (replaces comma with colon and adds quotes around title).

Example 9.2. Customized generated text

```
<xsl:param name="local.l10n.xml" select="document('')"/> ❶
<l:i18n xmlns:l="http://docbook.sourceforge.net/xmlns/l10n/1.0"> ❷
   <l:l10n language="en"> ❸
      <l:context name="xref-number-and-title"> ❹
         <l:template name="chapter" text="Chapter %n: &#8220;%t&#8221;"/> ❺
      </l:context>
   </l:l10n>
</l:i18n>
```

❶ Defines an XSL parameter named `local.l10n.xml`. The `select` attribute that provides the content of the parameter performs a neat trick. The XSL `document()` function normally opens and reads another file. But the blank function argument is a special case, which means to read the *current* document, that is, the current XSL file. This loads your entire customization layer file into the parameter. Once loaded, specific instances of generated text can be extracted as needed.

❷ The root element for a set of generated text elements. The name `i18n` is short for *internationalization*.

❸ Wrapper element for a set of generated text elements for a given language, in this case English. The name `l10n` is short for *localization*.

❹ Identifies which context the contained generated text strings will be applied to. The `xref-number-and-title` context is used when generating text for `xref` cross reference elements, assuming the `xref.with.number.and.title` parameter has not been changed from its default value of one.

❺ Defines a new generated text string for a given element, in this case `chapter`. The numerical character references are left and right double quotes.

See the section called "Customizing cross references" (page 262) for a longer example.

Replacing templates

At some point in your customization efforts you may find that none of the above methods will achieve the result you want. The most powerful customization method is to replace specific XSL templates in the DocBook collection with your own customized templates. The general technique is:

1. Find the DocBook XSL template that handles the text you want to change.

2. Copy that template to your customization layer.

3. Modify the copy to do what you want. Your version will override the behavior of the standard template because yours has a higher import precedence.

This method is very powerful, but it is not easy. It requires extensive knowledge of XSLT programming, and familiarity with the internals of the DocBook XSL stylesheet collection. This customization method is possible because the DocBook stylesheets are written in a highly modular fashion.

Here is a simple example of a template replacement. The default formatting for the `command` element is boldface. Perhaps you prefer your commands to appear in a monospaced font. In the collection of files for the DocBook XSL distribution, you will find `html/inline.xsl` that contains this `xsl:template`:

```
<xsl:template match="command">
  <xsl:call-template name="inline.boldseq"/>
</xsl:template>
```

Also in that file you will notice a template named `inline.monoseq` that does what you want. So you can add the following template to your customization layer to change how `command` is formatted:

```
<xsl:template match="command">
  <xsl:call-template name="inline.monoseq"/>
</xsl:template>
```

You can see a longer example of rewriting a template in the section called "Customizing TOC presentation" (page 134).

Finding the right template

Most DocBook templates perform a very specific and limited function. The trick is to find the template that is handling the behavior you want to change. Typically many templates are called during the processing of a given element. Depending on what you are trying to change, you may have to trace through several templates to find the one you need to replace.

There are two basic kinds of XSLT template:

- Templates that have a `match` attribute, which are called during `xsl:apply-templates` when the processor encounters an element satisfying the match pattern.

- Templates that have a `name` attribute and are called by name like a subroutine using `xsl:call-template`.

If you are trying to change how a particular element is handled, you can usually start by scanning for `match` attributes that include the name of your element. Sometimes there will be more than one template whose `match` attribute could apply. Then the processor generally selects the one with the best match, that is, the most specific match. For example, a match pattern of `chapter/para` is more specific than `para`. The more specific the match, the higher the priority in selecting that template.

Once you have found the starting point, you can trace through the template body to see what other templates it uses. Named templates are explicitly called by name using `xsl:call-template`. Those templates are easy to find because there is only one for each name.

If a template uses `xsl:apply-templates`, then you need to consider several factors that affect which template might be applied:

- If `xsl:apply-templates` includes a `select` attribute, then those elements matched by the select expression are going to be processed. So you need to find templates with `match` attributes that apply to those elements.

- If `xsl:apply-templates` does not include a `select` attribute, then the children of the current element will be processed. So you need to look for templates with `match` attributes that apply to the children.

- If `xsl:apply-templates` includes a `mode` attribute, then you can narrow your search to those matching templates that have the same mode value.

You may need to look in several directories to find the right template. Most of the templates for HTML processing are in the `html` subdirectory of the stylesheet distribution, and most of the templates for generating FO output are in the `fo` subdirectory. But they share templates in the `common` and `lib` directories, so you may need to look there as well. Here is a handy Linux command for searching three directories at once, showing how to find all references to `href.target`:

```
find html lib common -name '*.xsl' | xargs grep 'href.target'
```

This command is run in the directory above `html`. It uses **find** to search the `html`, `lib`, and `common` directories for files named `*.xsl`. It uses the **xargs** command to feed that list to the **grep** command that scans each file for the given regular expression. If you are a Windows user, this command is available if you install Cygwin.

Hopefully at some point you will find the specific template that does the processing you want to change. That's the template you want to duplicate and modify in your customization layer.

Import precedence

When you add overriding templates to your customization layer, you have to pay attention to XSLT *import precedence*. This says that the importing stylesheet's templates take precedence over the imported stylesheet's templates. In general, that is what you want, since that is how you override the behavior of the stock templates. Also, when your customization has several import statements, one that occurs later in the file has precedence over those that precede it in the file. That is useful for managing modular stylesheet files.

But what is not obvious is that import precedence is stronger than priority selection. Within a stylesheet, a match pattern that is more specific has a higher priority than a less specific pattern. So a template with `match="formalpara/para"` has a higher priority than a template with `match="para"`. That's how you get templates to apply in certain contexts but not others. But import precedence can override this priority selection.

A detailed example will make this easier to understand. In the DocBook stylesheet file `html/block.xsl`, there is a `<xsl:template match="para">` template for general `para` elements that outputs HTML `<p></p>` tags around its content. There is another `<xsl:template match="formalpara/para">` template for a `para` within a `formalpara` element. It does not output `<p></p>` tags, because the wrapper element's template `match="formalpara"` does that, so that the title and the para are in one set of `<p></p>` tags. The more specific template has a higher priority in the DocBook stylesheet.

Now copy the `<xsl:template match="para">` template to your customization layer. Now your `formalpara` elements will start generating invalid HTML, because there will be nested `<p></p>` tags, which is not permitted in HTML. The reason you get this error is because your `match="para"` template now has higher import precedence than the `match="formalpara/para"` template in `block.xsl`, even though your template is less specific. The import precedence is stronger than the match priority.

The solution is to provide another template in your customization layer:

```
<xsl:template match="formalpara/para">
  <xsl:apply-imports/>
</xsl:template>
```

Now this template has equal import precedence to your `match="para"` template, because they are both in the importing stylesheet. It also has a higher priority since it is more specific. So it will be used for any `para` elements inside `formalpara`. Its effect is to just apply the original such template in `block.xsl`, which avoids the nested `<p></p>` tags.

Passing parameters

When rewriting a template, pay careful attention to any parameters the original template is being passed. These are always declared at the top of the template. For example:

```
<xsl:template name="href.target">
  <xsl:param name="context" select="."/>
  <xsl:param name="object" select="."/>
  ...
```

Such a template may be called with one or more of the parameters set. For example:

```
<xsl:call-template name="href.target">
  <xsl:with-param name="context" select="some-context"/>
  <xsl:with-param name="object" select="some-object"/>
  ...
</xsl:call-template>
```

You want your new template to fit in as a direct replacement for the original, so it should handle the same parameters as the original. Since it is not required that all parameters be passed when a template is called, it should also handle missing parameter values. This requires you to understand when parameters are passed, what might be passed as a parameter value, and how it is expected to be handled. So if you are modifying a named template, check all the templates that call the template you are modifying to see what they do with the parameters.

You may extend a modified template by passing it new parameters. Be sure to declare your new parameters with a default value at the top of your new template. Of course, you'll also have to replace one or more of the calling templates so they can pass the parameter to your new template. You do not have to replace all of the calling templates, since parameters are optional. But you do need to make sure your default value works in case they do not pass a value.

Utility templates and modes

The DocBook XSL stylesheets include many templates that would be considered general purpose subroutines in other programming languages. Such utility templates handle common tasks in a consistent manner and reduce code duplication. You can call these same utility templates in your own templates for the same reasons.

The following table shows some of the more commonly used utility templates. The table includes a link to an example in this book of how the template is used, but there are many more examples in the DocBook stylesheets themselves.

Table 9.1. Commonly used utility templates and modes

Template or mode name	Purpose	See usage example in:
mode="object.title.markup"	Returns the full numbered title of an element, such as "Chapter 5, Using a Mouse". It finds the appropriate gentext template and fills it in.	"Customizing admonitions" (page 229)
mode="title.markup"	Returns the title only of an element, possibly looking in an info element to find it.	"Styling print TOC entries" (page 208)
mode="label.markup"	Returns the number only of an element, if it has one. For example, when applied to the fifth chapter element, it returns 5.	"Styling print TOC entries" (page 208)
name="gentext"	Returns the gentext string matching a given key passed as a parameter, in the current language.	"Customizing TOC presentation" (page 134)
name="l10n.language"	Returns the current language code, normalized to lowercase, with dash replaced by underscore.	"Sorting a bibliography" (page 251)
name="gentext.template"	Selects a gentext template from the locale file for the current language, based on a name, context, and optional style passed as parameters.	"Controlling page citations by element" (page 267)
name="substitute.markup"	Fills in the placeholders in a gentext template passed as a parameter. It replaces %t with the title, %n with the number, etc.	"Controlling page citations by element" (page 267)
mode="object.xref.markup"	Returns the generated cross reference text for the current element as a target of a cross reference. It finds the appropriate gentext template and fills it in.	"Customizing cross reference behavior" (page 269)
name="section.level"	Computes the section level of the context node.	"Return to top" (page 166)
name="object.id"	Returns the value of the id or xml:id attribute of the context element. May generate a value using the generate-id() function if no id attribute.	"Sorting a bibliography" (page 251)
name="href.target"	Returns the link URL for a cross reference, for either HTML or FO output.	"Bread crumbs" (page 150)
name="dbfo-attribute" name="dbhtml-attribute"	Returns the value of a DocBook processing instruction that uses the pseudo attribute syntax.	"Processing instructions" (page 115)
mode="xref-to"	Returns the text that is generated for an xref to the context node. Usually applies templates in mode object.xref.markup to fetch a gentext template and fill it in.	"Customizing cross reference behavior" (page 269)
name="gentext.startquote" name="gentext.endquote"	These two templates can be used to generate the start and end double-quote characters, respectively, in the current locale.	"Q and A cross references" (page 458)
name="string.lower" name="string.upper"	Converts a text string to lowercase or uppercase, respectively. Takes a string template parameter, and converts it using the gentext templates named uppercase.alpha and lowercase.alpha in the current locale.	

As the usage examples show, those templates with a `name` attribute are called using `xsl:call-template`, with the current node as the context node. Such templates may also have parameters passed to them.

Those templates with a `mode` attribute are called using `xsl:apply-templates` with the mode attribute. The apply-templates may also include a `select` attribute to specify an element other than the current one to apply the template to. There must be a template with a `match` for each element it is being applied to. Usually there is a `match="*"` to handle any elements that do not have their own template in that mode.

Adding new templates

One of the beauties of a template-driven language like XSLT is that you can add to the collection of templates. Your new templates follow the same rules of selection as the stock templates, so your templates participate on an equal footing with the originals.

A new template is an `xsl:template` element with a `match` attribute that you add to your customization layer. The `match` attribute specifies an XSL *pattern* that selects which elements it should be applied to. See the section called "Template selection rules" (page 114) if your template is not getting used as expected.

Here are some reasons why you might want to add new templates:

- You want to specify different behavior for an element based on different values of an attribute such as `role`.

- You have extended the DocBook schema to add elements or attributes that need to be formatted.

- You want to add extra steps to the processing of a given element.

The following sections provide guidelines and examples.

Formatting determined by attribute value

The DocBook `role` attribute is often used to distinguish one use of an element from another. If you want the difference expressed in formatting, you can add a template that responds to an attribute value. The following is an example of a template that draws a border around a `para` that has `role="intro"`.

```
<xsl:template match="para[@role = 'intro']">
  <fo:block border="0.5pt solid blue"
            padding="3pt"
            xsl:use-attribute-sets="normal.para.spacing">
    <xsl:call-template name="anchor"/>
    <xsl:apply-templates/>
  </fo:block>
</xsl:template>
```

In this example, the original template matching on `para` was copied from `fo/block.xsl` to the customization layer and then changed. The match attribute with `@role='intro'` means that this template is applied only to `para` elements with that `role` attribute value. The template adds `border` and `padding` properties for format such paragraphs.

This process is similar to replacing a template, but in this case the original template matching on plain `para` was not changed. This template is new, and applies only to the special paragraphs.

This second example applies different formatting for different values of `role`:

```
<xsl:template match="para[@role]">
  <fo:block padding="3pt"
            xsl:use-attribute-sets="normal.para.spacing">
    <xsl:choose>
      <xsl:when test="@role = 'intro'">
        <xsl:attribute name="border">0.5pt solid blue</xsl:attribute>
      </xsl:when>
      <xsl:when test="@role = 'concept'">
        <xsl:attribute name="border">1pt solid black</xsl:attribute>
        <xsl:attribute name="margin-left">14pt</xsl:attribute>
        <xsl:attribute name="background-color">#EFEFEF</xsl:attribute>
      </xsl:when>
      ...
    </xsl:choose>
    <xsl:call-template name="anchor"/>
    <xsl:apply-templates/>
  </fo:block>
</xsl:template>
```

Now the match is on any para that has any role attribute. The xsl:choose statement tests the role value and applies attributes for each value. You can use xsl:attribute to add an attribute to the parent block, as long as no output has been generated for the block yet. Unfortunately, XSL does not permit applying an attribute-set within an xsl:choose statement.

Adding processing steps

If you want to add some steps to an existing template, you may be able to avoid copying and editing the whole template. Instead, you can use xsl:apply-imports to call the original template, and put that in a new template that adds new steps.

For example, if you wanted to add an icon in the margin for each figure element, you can create a new template that matches on figure, generates the icon, and then applies the original figure template.

```
<xsl:template match="figure">
  <xsl:call-template name="floater">
    <xsl:with-param name="content">
      <fo:external-graphic src="url(figure-icon.png)"/>
    </xsl:with-param>
    <xsl:with-param name="position">left</xsl:with-param>
    <xsl:with-param name="width">4pc</xsl:with-param>
  </xsl:call-template>
  <xsl:apply-imports/>
</xsl:template>
```

The template match attribute matches on all figure elements. Because it is in a customization layer that imports the DocBook XSL stylesheet, it has higher import precedence than the original template that matches on figure. So this template will be used instead of the original. It calls a utility template in the DocBook stylesheet named floater that generates an fo:float in the output. After that, xsl:apply-imports is used to apply the original figure template to output the figure title and graphic.

Handling new elements

If you customize the DocBook schema to add new elements, then you must customize the stylesheet to handle the new element names. If that is not done, then you will see error messages like the following when you process a document with such elements:

element encountered in *parent* but no template matches

If a new element is to be formatted the same as an existing element, you can probably copy and change the original template for the existing element so it handles the new element too. For example, if you add an element named concept whose content model is just like para, then you can copy the template with match="para" to your customization layer and change the match attribute:

```
<xsl:template match="para | concept">
  <fo:block xsl:use-attribute-sets="normal.para.spacing">
    <xsl:call-template name="anchor"/>
    <xsl:apply-templates/>
  </fo:block>
</xsl:template>
```

The only change here is to match on either para or concept. Both are handled like paragraphs.

If a new element is similar to but not the same format as an existing element, then you have a decision to make. You could share a customized version of the existing template as in the previous example, and use xsl:choose to handle any differences within the template. Or you could copy the original template, change it to match on only the new element name, and customize it as needed. Which method you choose depends on how different they need to be, and how hard they will be to maintain. If you want to apply a new attribute-set, it is usually easier to dedicate a new template to the element, like the following:

```
<xsl:template match="concept">
  <fo:block xsl:use-attribute-sets="concept.properties">
    <xsl:call-template name="anchor"/>
    <xsl:apply-templates/>
  </fo:block>
</xsl:template>
```

If a new element is not similar to any existing DocBook element, you will need to write an entirely new template to handle it. In that case, it is best to study some of the existing DocBook templates to discover the numerous named utility templates, gentext features, and general methods used for handling DocBook content. A good XSLT reference is a must.

Triggering processing

Once you have created a template matching on your new element, you have to make sure it gets used. Generally that is not a problem, because most (but not all) templates in DocBook XSL use a general <xsl:apply-templates/> to process all their children. If the *parent* element of your new element includes such, then your new template will get used because it is the only one that matches on the new element.

But some parent elements are selective in what elements they process. For example, the following template for simplelist selects only member elements to process:

```
<xsl:template match="simplelist[@type='inline']">
  ...
  <fo:inline>
    <xsl:for-each select="member">
      ...
    </xsl:for-each>
  </fo:inline>
</xsl:template>
```

If you were to create a new element that is a child of `simplelist`, this its matching template would never be called in this context, because the new element name does not match `member`. You would need to customize this template to process your new element.

The worst case in the stylesheets of this kind of selective processing is the handling of Next and Previous in chunked HTML. See for example the template named `chunk-all-sections` in `html/chunk-code.xsl`. Those templates use long lists of element names in `select` attributes to figure out the next chunk.

Mode processing

Many elements are processed in more than one XSL mode, so you'll need to also add templates for those modes if appropriate. For example, if you want an element to appear in the table of contents, you may need a `mode="toc"` template, and check the parent element that would call your new template too. If you want to cross reference to an element, then you need a `mode="xref-to"` template. An element with title might need a `mode="title.markup"` template.

New gentext elements

If any of your new elements is to generate text labels or titles, then you will want to add gentext elements to the `local.l10n.xml` parameter (it is a parameter, not an XML file). You might need to add a general `l:gentext` element, as well as `l:template` elements in the contexts of `title` and `xref`. See the section called "Generated text" (page 105) for more information.

Template selection rules

In order for your new templates to be used, it helps to understand the rules by which a template is selected to handle a given element. The rules are summarized here, from lowest to highest importance.

- **Assigned priority.** Every template has an implicit priority number assigned to it based on how specifically it matches. For example, a `match="para[@role]"` is more specific than `match="para"`, and so the first has a higher assigned priority. Assigned priorities are always in the range -0.5 to +0.5. If more than one template in a stylesheet file matches on the same element, the template with the highest priority is used. It is possible that two templates with different `match` attributes resolve to the same assigned priority value, so you may need to add an explicit `priority` attribute to resolve the conflict.

- **Explicit priority attribute.** You can add a `priority` attribute to any template to override the implicit priority assigned to it. Setting `priority="1"`, for example, will establish a higher priority than any assigned priority, since the latter are limited to the range -0.5 to +0.5.

- **Import precedence.** If two templates match on the same element and one is imported, then the template in the importing stylesheet takes precedence, regardless of the relative priority values (assigned or explicit). The local template is said to have a higher *import precedence* than the imported template. This it the key feature that makes customization layers work. When you import the DocBook stylesheet, you only have to change the templates you need to change, and your templates always have higher import precedence than the originals.

Keep in mind that import precedence always wins over priority values. That can sometimes lead to surprising results. For example, if a template with a `priority="10"` attribute is imported, and the importing stylesheet has a match on that element but no `priority` attribute, then the high priority value on the imported template counts for nothing, because the higher import precedence of the local template wins. Likewise with assigned priorities. An imported template with a very specific match will not be used if any template in the importing stylesheet matches on the same element, even if it is a looser match.

See the section called "Import precedence" (page 108) for more information and examples of import precedence.

Processing instructions

A processing instruction is a means of passing hints to the XSLT processor about how to handle something. XML permits the placement of processing instructions just about anywhere in a document. A processing instruction (sometimes referred to as a PI) uses a special syntax, `<?name content ?>`, to indicate that it is not an element, comment, or text. For example:

```
<?dbfo bgcolor="#EEEEEE" ?>
```

The first word in a PI is the name. In this example, the name of the processing instruction is `dbfo` and the content is `bgcolor="#EEEEEE"`. This style of PI content could be called a "pseudo attribute", because it provides a name-value pair similar to a real attribute (which only elements can have). You can put several such pseudo attributes in one PI, or you can put each of them in their own PI.

The DocBook stylesheets accept certain predefined processing instructions to specify information for which no DocBook element or attribute exists. In this example, it specifies the background color for a table cell, as described in the section called "Cell background color" (page 484). DocBook processing instructions use the naming convention `dbhtml` to mean processing instructions intended for the HTML stylesheets, and `dbfo` for those PIs intended for the FO stylesheets. See the index for a list of predefined PIs of each type.

You can add your own processing instructions as part of your customization. If you use the DocBook PI name (`dbhtml` or `dbfo`) and the pseudo attribute style of content, then you can use some of the stylesheet machinery to parse the content. The following is an example of how the DocBook stylesheet gets the value of the above example:

Example 9.3. Custom processing instruction

```
<xsl:variable name="bgcolor">  ❶
  <xsl:call-template name="dbfo-attribute">  ❷
    <xsl:with-param name="pis"
         select="ancestor-or-self::entry/processing-instruction('dbfo')"/>  ❸
    <xsl:with-param name="attribute" select="'bgcolor'"/>  ❹
  </xsl:call-template>
</xsl:variable>
```

❶ Put the selected value into a stylesheet variable named bgcolor for use later in the template.
❷ Call the template named dbfo-attribute, which is used to process dbfo PIs. There is a similar template named dbhtml-attribute for processing dbhtml PIs. Each requires two parameters that are specified on the next two lines.
❸ The pis parameter should select the candidate processing instructions in a given location. The syntax for specifying a PI in an XSL select statement is processing-instruction('*name*'). This looks like a function, but it is really a way of specifying this special kind of node in the document. In this case, it is looking for all PIs whose names are dbfo that are contained in the current entry element.
❹ The above selection step could get several PIs, each of which could have several pseudo attributes. The attribute parameter specifies which of those pseudo attribute values is needed here. The dbfo-attribute template searches through all the selected PIs for the given pseudo attribute and returns its value, which gets stored in the variable for use by the stylesheet.

To create processing instructions of your own, you need to do the following:

• Decide on the names and possible values for your pseudo attributes.

• Decide where you might place your processing instructions in your document.

• For the elements that will contains such PIs, you will want to customize that element's template to make use of the PI.

• Add XSL code similar to the above example to the customized template, changing the select statement in the pis parameter, and changing the value of the attribute parameter to match your usage.

Customizing DocBook 5 XSL

Customizing the DocBook 5 stylesheets is almost identical to customizing the original DocBook 4 stylesheets. The main difference is the namespace.

A DocBook 5 customization must:

• Declare the DocBook namespace, including a namespace prefix.

• Import the appropriate base stylesheet from the DocBook 5 XSL distribution.

• Add the namespace prefix to any DocBook element names in patterns and expressions in the customization.

Example 9.4 is a short customization example.

Example 9.4. DocBook 5 customization

```
<?xml version="1.0"?>
<xsl:stylesheet
    xmlns:xsl="http://www.w3.org/1999/XSL/Transform"
    xmlns:fo="http://www.w3.org/1999/XSL/Format"
    xmlns:d="http://docbook.org/ns/docbook" ❶
    exclude-result-prefixes="d" ❷
    version="1.0">

<xsl:import href="docbook-xsl-ns/fo/docbook.xsl"/>  ❸

<xsl:param name="double.sided">1</xsl:param>
...
<xsl:template mode="vl.as.list" match="d:varlistentry"> ❹
  <xsl:variable name="id"><xsl:call-template name="object.id"/></xsl:variable>
  <fo:list-item id="{$id}" xsl:use-attribute-sets="list.item.spacing">
    <fo:list-item-label end-indent="label-end()" text-align="start">
      <fo:block>
        <xsl:apply-templates select="d:term"/>  ❺
      </fo:block>
    </fo:list-item-label>
    <fo:list-item-body start-indent="body-start()">
      <fo:block>
        <xsl:apply-templates select="d:listitem"/> ❺
      </fo:block>
    </fo:list-item-body>
  </fo:list-item>
</xsl:template>
```

❶ Declare the DocBook namespace and include a prefix, which here is d:. You can use any prefix in your stylesheet as long as you declare it like this.
❷ Tell the processor to not add the DocBook namespace declaration in the output. This has no effect except to omit a namespace declaration that is never used in the output content, keeping it a bit cleaner. If you accidentally write a DocBook element to the output (using, say, xsl:copy), then the processor will override this instruction and add the namespace declaration anyway.
❸ Import the base stylesheet from the DocBook 5 XSL stylesheet distribution.
❹ Add the prefix to any DocBook element names in match attributes.
❺ Add the prefix to any DocBook element names in XPath expressions.

A more useful DocBook 5 customization is described in the section called "Annotations customization" (page 118).

DocBook 5 customization details

There are a few differences you will need to remember of when customizing DocBook 5 instead of DocBook 4 stylesheets. These include:

- Be sure to add the namespace prefix to all DocBook element names in your stylesheet. They can be found in any of the following XSL attributes:

```
match      select
test       count
from       use
elements
```

If you have element names in any general entities that you declare and use in your stylesheet, then those must also get a prefix.

- In DocBook 5, the id attribute is replaced with the xml:id attribute. Although it has a namespace prefix, you do not need to declare it because it is a standard prefix in XML.

- In DocBook 5, the lang attribute is replaced with the xml:lang attribute.

- In DocBook 4, you could use the XSL name() function to test an element's name. That only worked because DocBook 4 did not use a namespace. The name() function normally returns the namespace prefix *and* local name for an element. In a DocBook 5 stylesheet, you should use the local-name() function if you just want the element name without its prefix.

- In DocBook 5, the metadata container for all elements is named info. If you want to match on perhaps a title of an element, you may need to look in its info element.

- If your stylesheet is divided into several modular files that are combined with xsl:import or xsl:include, be sure that all modules follow these guidelines.

Annotations customization

This section shows how to write a stylesheet customization for DocBook 5. It also shows how the new annotation element might be put to use.

The customization decribed below puts annotations of a certain type into the side margin as floats. The example is kept simple for clarity, so it is not a very robust implementation of annotations. For example, it handles annotations associated only with para elements that are children of chapter or section. This is to avoid conflicting with para elements in footnote and other locations incompatible with side float.

Example 9.5 shows how an annotation element can be entered in a document.

Example 9.5. Annotation usage

```
<chapter xmlns="http://docbook.org/ns/docbook" version="5.0">
  <title>My chapter title</title>
  <info>
    <annotation annotates="intro" role="instructor.note">
      <para>Show intro slides and wait for questions.</para>
    </annotation>
  </info>
  <para xml:id="intro">This chapter introduces ...
```

Note these features of the usage example:

- The annotation element is placed in any convenient location, in this case the chapter's info element.

- The annotation is associated with an element by matching its annotates attribute to an xml:id elsewhere in the document. In this case, the xml:id is on a para element.

- This annotation has a role attribute that will be used to select it for output.

Example 9.6 shows a stylesheet customization to output this type of annotation.

Example 9.6. Annotation stylesheet customization

```
<xsl:param name="body.start.indent">40mm</xsl:param> ❶
<xsl:param name="show.instructor.notes" select="1"/>

<xsl:template match="d:para[parent::d:section or parent::d:chapter]"> ❷
  <fo:block xsl:use-attribute-sets="normal.para.spacing">
    <xsl:call-template name="anchor"/>
    <xsl:call-template name="apply.annotations"/>
    <xsl:apply-templates/>
  </fo:block>
</xsl:template>

<xsl:template name="apply.annotations">
  <xsl:variable name="id" select="@xml:id"/> ❸

  <xsl:for-each select="//d:annotation[@role='instructor.note']"> ❹
    <xsl:if test="@annotates = $id"> ❺
      <xsl:apply-templates mode="show.annotation" select="."/>
    </xsl:if>
  </xsl:for-each>
</xsl:template>

<xsl:template match="d:annotation[@role = 'instructor.note']"
              mode="show.annotation"> ❻
  <xsl:if test="$show.instructor.notes != 0">
    <xsl:call-template name="floater"> ❼
      <xsl:with-param name="position">left</xsl:with-param>
      <xsl:with-param name="width">35mm</xsl:with-param>
      <xsl:with-param name="content"> ❽
        <fo:block xsl:use-attribute-sets="instructornote">
          <fo:block font-weight="bold">
            <xsl:text>Instructor Note</xsl:text>
          </fo:block>
          <xsl:apply-templates/>
        </fo:block>
      </xsl:with-param>
    </xsl:call-template>
  </xsl:if>
</xsl:template>

<xsl:attribute-set name="instructornote"> ❾
  <xsl:attribute name="font-size">8pt</xsl:attribute>
  <xsl:attribute name="line-height">9.5pt</xsl:attribute>
  <xsl:attribute name="text-align">left</xsl:attribute>
  <xsl:attribute name="end-indent">2mm</xsl:attribute>
  <xsl:attribute name="padding">1mm</xsl:attribute>
  <xsl:attribute name="border">0.2pt solid blue</xsl:attribute>
</xsl:attribute-set>
```

❶   Set the body.start.indent parameter to leave sufficient room for the side notes. Add a new parameter that
controls whether or not the instructor notes are output.

❷   Annotations are not output by default, so in this example the template for para is customized to trigger annotation
processing. Note that all DocBook element references have the namespace prefix. The call to the apply.annota-
tions templates is made inside the fo:block for the paragraph so the float is positioned with that block.

❸ The context node for `apply.annotations` is the `para` element that called it. Save the `xml:id` value of the current `para` element in a variable to use for comparison.

❹ Look at each `annotation` element in the entire document that has the right role value. This XPath is not very efficient, so creating and using an `xsl:key` would speed up such lookups for large documents.

❺ Select only those `annotation` elements whose `annotates` attribute matches the `para` ID. This comparison with equals is not robust because an `annotates` attribute can contain a space-separated list of values.

❻ For each selected annotation, process the element in a special mode. If you do not use a mode, then the annotations may accidentally be processed when the elements of the document are processed in document order. In this case the annotation is safe inside the `info` element, but it could be anywhere.

❼ If the parameter to control instructor notes is turn on, create a float by calling the DocBook utility template named `floater`. That template takes parameters to specify position, width, and content of the float.

❽ Into the template's `content` parameter, process the annotation into a block with an attribute-set to apply properties. You can add a title as shown here as well.

❾ The attribute-set is used for these special annotation floats. This example formats the text into a blue border with sufficient spacing around it, and in a smaller font size.

10
General customizations

Many customizations can be applied to both HTML and FO (print) output because the stylesheets share some code and processing styles. See the section called "Customizing both HTML and FO" (page 102) for a technique of sharing such customizations.

Custom section numbering

As described in the section called "Chapter and section numbering" (page 74), you can turn on standard section numbering with stylesheet parameters. But you may want to further refine the numbering style.

The number label for an element is generated using the `label.markup` mode. That is, the element needing the number is processed with:

```
<xsl:apply-templates select="." mode="label.markup"/>
```

The XSL processor finds the template with `mode="label.markup"` that best matches the current element. The templates with this mode are in the stylesheet file `common/labels.xsl` for all the elements that might get numbered. They are in `common` so the same templates can be used for both HTML and FO output. Templates with mode `label.markup` return just the number. The same templates are used to generate the numbers that appear in any tables of contents and cross references.

Section labeling such as `2.1.4` uses several of the `label.markup` mode templates, because the number is assembled from ancestor elements as well as the current element. Those templates apply templates on their parent element, selected as `".."` in the template. The following example is how a `sect1` label is generated:

Example 10.1. Applying label.markup mode to sect1

```
<xsl:template match="sect1" mode="label.markup">  ❶
  <!-- if the parent is a component, maybe label that too -->
  <xsl:variable name="parent.is.component">
    <xsl:call-template name="is.component">  ❷
      <xsl:with-param name="node" select=".."/>
    </xsl:call-template>
  </xsl:variable>

  <xsl:variable name="component.label">
    <xsl:if test="$section.label.includes.component.label != 0  ❸
                  and $parent.is.component != 0">
      <xsl:variable name="parent.label">
        <xsl:apply-templates select=".." mode="label.markup"/>
      </xsl:variable>
      <xsl:if test="$parent.label != ''">
        <xsl:apply-templates select=".." mode="label.markup"/>  ❹
        <xsl:apply-templates select=".." mode="intralabel.punctuation"/>
      </xsl:if>
    </xsl:if>
  </xsl:variable>

  <xsl:variable name="is.numbered">
    <xsl:call-template name="label.this.section"/>  ❺
  </xsl:variable>

  <xsl:choose>
    <xsl:when test="@label">
      <xsl:value-of select="@label"/>  ❻
    </xsl:when>
    <xsl:when test="$is.numbered != 0">
      <xsl:copy-of select="$component.label"/>
      <xsl:number count="sect1"/>  ❼
    </xsl:when>
  </xsl:choose>
</xsl:template>
```

❶   Applying a template using mode="label.markup" just returns the number of an element, if it has one.
❷   It calls the template named parent.is.component, which returns true if the parent element is a DocBook component (chapter, appendix, etc.).
❸   Then if the parameter section.label.includes.component.label is turned on, and the parent is a component, it generates the parent element's label and inserts the separator punctuation.
❹   Get the parent label by using label.markup mode on "..", which selects the parent element.
❺   It checks to see if the current section level is numbered by calling the template named label.this.section. A section may not be numbered if its level is greater than the value set by the section.autolabel.max.depth parameter (see the section called "Depth of section numbering" (page 88)).
❻   Before using the section number, though, it checks to see if the current section element has a literal label attribute, which manually overrides the automatic label.
❼   The automatic number for this sect1 is generated using the XSLT xsl:number element, set to count sibling sect1 elements.

Label punctuation

When a label has several components, such as 2.1.4, each of the components is separated by some punctuation. Since the label is generated by the stylesheet, the punctuation also must be generated. You might think the character used for punctuation is controlled by a stylesheet parameter, but it is not. Rather, the punctuation is generated by templates in a special mode, the intralabel.punctuation mode. Here is the default template included with the stylesheets (from common/labels.xsl):

```
<xsl:template match="*" mode="intralabel.punctuation">
  <xsl:text>.</xsl:text>
</xsl:template>
```

So the default label separator is the period within the `<xsl:text>` element in the template.

Why use a mode? Because the stylesheet can provide different punctuation for different elements, depending on your style. As a label is built up from its components, the stylesheet applies templates in this mode to generate the punctuation. For example, a number label for a figure such as 3.2 is made up of the chapter number and punctuation prepended to the figure count within the chapter. These two lines generate the prefix:

```
<xsl:apply-templates select="$pchap" mode="label.markup"/>
 <xsl:apply-templates select="$pchap" mode="intralabel.punctuation"/>
```

The first line applies templates in mode="label.markup", which generates the number for the chapter node contained in the $pchap variable. The second line applies templates to the chapter node in mode="intralabel.punctuation. In the stock stylesheets, the chapter node is matched by the "*" pattern and the period is generated.

If you want the chapter number to be followed by a dash instead of a period, you could add this template to your customization layer:

```
<xsl:template match="chapter|appendix" mode="intralabel.punctuation">
  <xsl:text>-</xsl:text>
</xsl:template>
```

Now your figure labels will look like 3-2 if that is your style.

Tables of contents (TOC)

The DocBook stylesheets have several features for generating tables of contents. In addition to the traditional list of chapters and sections at the beginning of a book or article, you can optionally generate lists of figures, tables, examples, equations, and procedures. You can also generate mini tables of contents for each chapter or even each section, down to a section level of your choice.

Some aspects of customizing tables of contents can be controlled with parameters, and others require a customization layer.

Which components have a TOC

The DocBook XSL stylesheets use the generate.toc parameter to determine which elements have a TOC generated at the beginning of the element in the output. For print output or non-chunked HTML output, a single TOC at the beginning may suffice. But when you are generating chunked HTML files, you may want certain sublevels to provide TOCs to help orient the reader.

Although generate.toc is a parameter that can be set on the command line, it is a bit awkward to use that way because it can contain a lot of information. The default value of generate.toc (HTML version) is:

```
<xsl:param name="generate.toc">
appendix  toc,title
article/appendix  nop
article   toc,title
book      toc,title,figure,table,example,equation
chapter   toc,title
part      toc,title
preface   toc,title
qandadiv  toc
qandaset  toc
reference toc,title
sect1     toc
sect2     toc
sect3     toc
sect4     toc
sect5     toc
section   toc
set       toc,title
</xsl:param>
```

The parameter value is read as white-space separated pairs (leading whitespace is trimmed off). The first word of each pair is an element name, and the second word is a comma-separated list that specifies what kind of TOCs it should have. Most of them just use `toc`, which is a list of section titles. But the entry for the book element will also generate tables of figures, tables, examples, and equations. The word `title` triggers printing a title for the list, such as "Table of Contents". Use a value of `nop` to turn off all TOCs for an element. You can also turn off a TOC by removing the element entirely from the parameter.

You can change which elements have TOCs by putting a new version of this parameter in your customization layer. For example, to remove the TOC from the elements `preface`, `part`, `qandadiv`, `qandaset`, `appendix`, and `sections`, and remove the TOC title from `chapter`, use this parameter value:

```
<xsl:param name="generate.toc">
 appendix  nop
 article   toc,title
 book      toc,title,figure,table,example,equation
 chapter   toc
 part      nop
 preface   nop
 qandadiv  nop
 qandaset  nop
 reference toc,title
 section   nop
 set       toc
 </xsl:param>
```

If your document is a book and you only want a book-level TOC and no others, then you can use a very simple value:

```
<xsl:param name="generate.toc" select="'book toc'"/>
```

That is a space between book and `toc`, and do not forget the single quotes to make it a string. You can even set this simple value on the command line:

```
xsltproc  --stringparam generate.toc "book toc" ...
```

Because the list uses white space to separate items in the list, and then counts through the list to establish pairs of items, you have to follow a few rules with this parameter:

- A "white space" includes any sequence of blanks spaces, tabs, and carriage returns. So you could put all the information on one line with single blanks between items. In fact, that is what the processor does using the normalize-space XSL function.

- do not leave a value blank, because that messes up the pairing. Either remove the element name or enter nop to turn off an element you leave in the list.

- do not insert spaces in a comma separated list like toc,figure,table. The spaces will mess up the pairing.

You can get even finer control of when TOCs are used by adding context information. For example, an article in a book can be treated differently from an article as a whole document. See the reference page for the *generate.toc*[1] parameter for more information.

> **Note:**
>
> Section TOCs are also controlled by the generate.section.toc.level parameter, which is by default set to zero. See the section called "Turning on section TOCs" (page 130).

Levels in book and chapter TOCs

You can control how many nested levels of headings a TOC list should have. A book TOC always lists the titles for part and chapter elements, as well as any other components at the chapter level such as preface, appendix, glossary and index. A book TOC may also contain titles of sections within the chapters, depending on the value of the toc.section.depth parameter. If chapter TOCs are turned on by the generate.toc parameter, then what appears in the chapter TOC is completely controlled by the toc.section.depth parameter. The following table summarizes its effect on book and chapter TOCs.

Use the toc.section.depth parameter to indicate how many levels of section titles should appear in the TOCs. If you set it to a value of 3, for example, then TOCs will include up to sect3 titles. The default value is 2. The following table summarizes the effect of the parameter.

Table 10.1. How toc.section.depth affects book and chapter TOCs

toc.section.depth	Book TOC includes:	Chapter TOC includes:
0	chapter	No TOC
1	chapter 　sect1	sect1
2 (default)	chapter 　sect1 　　sect2	sect1 　sect2
3	chapter 　sect1 　　sect2 　　　sect3	sect1 　sect2 　　sect3

---

[1] http://docbook.sourceforge.net/release/xsl/current/doc/html/generate.toc.html

If you use `bridgehead` titles in your document, you also have the option of including those titles in your TOCs. To do so, set the `bridgehead.in.toc` parameter to 1. Then all `bridgehead` titles will be included at the appropriate level in the TOC.

There is a different style of hierarchy for TOCs that the `toc.max.depth` parameter controls. In this style, each TOC regardless of where it is located has the same number of levels (if the content is there and the TOC is enabled with the `generate.toc` parameter). The `toc.max.depth` parameter controls the maximum number of levels in any TOC. This parameter first appeared in version 1.61 of the stylesheets, and only applies to HTML output. The following table summarizes the effect of the parameter.

Table 10.2. How toc.max.depth affects book and chapter TOCs (HTML output only)

toc.max.depth	Book TOC includes:	Chapter TOC includes:
0	No TOC	No TOC
1	chapter	sect1

2	chapter
	  sect1
		sect1
		  sect2

3	chapter
	  sect1
	    sect2
		sect1
		  sect2
		    sect3

You will notice that both the book and chapter TOCs contain the same number of levels for each value of the parameter. The table assumes that the `toc.section.depth` parameter has been increased to at least 3. If not, then the default value of 2 would limit the chapter TOC in the last row to `sect1` and `sect2` entries. The default value of `toc.max.depth` is 7, so normally the `toc.section.depth` parameter is the limiting factor in a given TOC's depth.

Customized TOC levels

The stylesheet parameters described in the section called "Levels in book and chapter TOCs" (page 127) give you some control of what levels of headings appear in a book, chapter, and section TOCs. There are some combinations that cannot be achieved with just parameters and require template customization.

For example, you might want your book TOC in HTML to just list the chapter titles, and then rely on complete TOCs in each chapter to provide section titles. The following short customization does that.

```
<xsl:template match="preface|chapter|appendix|article" mode="toc">
  <xsl:param name="toc-context" select="."/>

  <xsl:choose>
    <xsl:when test="local-name($toc-context) = 'book'">
      <xsl:call-template name="subtoc">
        <xsl:with-param name="toc-context" select="$toc-context"/>
        <xsl:with-param name="nodes" select="foo"/>
      </xsl:call-template>
    </xsl:when>
    <xsl:otherwise>
      <xsl:call-template name="subtoc">
        <xsl:with-param name="toc-context" select="$toc-context"/>
        <xsl:with-param name="nodes"
              select="section|sect1|glossary|bibliography|index
                      |bridgehead[$bridgehead.in.toc != 0]"/>
      </xsl:call-template>
    </xsl:otherwise>
  </xsl:choose>
</xsl:template>
```

It is a copy of a template in `html/autotoc.xsl`, modified to add a choose statement. It processes the chapter element (and other elements) in `mode="toc"` to generate lines in your TOC. The `$toc-context` template parameter contains the element in which the TOC is appearing. So if you take the `local-name()` of that element and compare it to 'book', the template can take a different action. In this case, you tell it to select `foo` children of the chapter element, which will be an empty node set since there is no such element. Then the depth of the chapter toc can be controlled by the `toc.section.depth` parameter.

Set TOC

If you process a group of books inside a `set` element, then the set can have a table of contents too. Normally it would be a complete table of contents, listing the books, chapters, and sections to whatever level was specified for books.

You might not need such detail in a set TOC, since each book TOC has those details. If you want your set TOC to list just the book titles, then you can customize a template. The template is different if you are doing print or HTML output.

For print output, you would customize the template with `match="book|setindex" mode="toc"` from the stylesheet module `fo/autotoc.xsl`. After calling the template named `toc.line` to format the book title, the template selects the child nodes to process under it. Since this template is only called by the `set.toc` template, you can reduce it to formatting just its own title.

```
<xsl:template match="book|setindex" mode="toc">
  <xsl:param name="toc-context" select="."/>
  <xsl:call-template name="toc.line"/>
</xsl:template>
```

For HTML output, the `set.toc` template processes each book element in `mode="toc"`. Normally that template calls the `subtoc` template with a parameter named `nodes` that selects the book's child elements. Instead, select an empty node set by selecting a non-element name, such as `EMPTY` (since DocBook has no element of that name).

```
<xsl:template match="book" mode="toc">
  <xsl:param name="toc-context" select="."/>

  <xsl:call-template name="subtoc">
    <xsl:with-param name="toc-context" select="$toc-context"/>
    <xsl:with-param name="nodes" select="EMPTY"/>
  </xsl:call-template>
</xsl:template>
```

The subtoc template generates the book title, and then stops because it has no child nodes to process. This change will not affect the book's own TOC because it does not use this template, instead calling division.toc.

Turning on section TOCs

By default, sections do not have their own TOCs. But you can use parameters to turn on TOCs for sections and control what levels are listed. Section TOCs are particularly useful with chunked HTML output for which the user might need some context for complex documents.

Two parameters control which section levels have a TOC: generate.toc and generate.section.toc.level. You will notice that the default value of the generate.toc parameter described in the section called "Which components have a TOC" (page 125) includes entries for all the section levels, yet the default output does not have section TOCs. That is because a second parameter generate.section.toc.level also controls which section levels have a TOC. For example, if you set generate.section.toc.level to a value of 2, then you will get a TOC for all sect1 and sect2 elements, or their equivalents in nested section elements. Why two parameters? This arrangement lets you establish a style for which TOCs could appear at various section levels by modifying the complex generate.toc parameter in your customization layer. Then you can select the actual output level at runtime with the simple generate.section.toc.level parameter. Both parameters must enable a section level for its TOC to appear.

The depth of section levels that appear in a given section TOC is usually controlled by the toc.section.depth parameter. This parameter indicates the deepest section level that can appear in any TOC. It's default value of 2 means only sections up to sect2 will appear in any TOC. For HTML output, a second parameter toc.max.depth can be used to produce a different style of TOC hierarchy. This parameter indicates the maximum number of levels that appear in any TOC. A value of 2 means only up to two levels of titles will appear in any TOC, regardless of where the TOC appears.

The following two tables show how these two parameters affect section TOCs for various values of the generate.section.toc.level parameter.

Table 10.3. Section TOCs with toc.section.depth

generate.section.toc.level	toc.section.depth	sect1 TOC includes:	sect2 TOC includes:	sect3 TOC includes:	sect4 TOC includes:
1	2	sect2	No TOC	No TOC	No TOC
	3	sect2 sect3	No TOC	No TOC	No TOC

	4	sect2
		    sect3
		        sect4
			No TOC	No TOC	No TOC

2	2	sect2	No TOC	No TOC	No TOC
	3	sect2 sect3	sect3	No TOC	No TOC

	4	sect2
		    sect3
		        sect4
			sect3
			    sect4
				No TOC	No TOC

3	2	sect2	No TOC	No TOC	No TOC
	3	sect2 sect3	sect3	No TOC	No TOC

	4	sect2
		    sect3
		        sect4
			sect3
			    sect4
				sect4	No TOC

In some cases, there is no TOC because the TOC would be in a section level outside the range of the generate.section.toc.level parameter. In other cases, there is no TOC because the toc.section.depth parameter prevents it from having any entries. This table assumes the other parameter, toc.max.depth, has a value high enough to not interfere with the selection of levels.

Table 10.4. Section TOCs with toc.max.depth (HTML only)

generate.section.toc.level	toc.max.depth	sect1 TOC includes:	sect2 TOC includes:	sect3 TOC includes:	sect4 TOC includes:
1	1	sect2	No TOC	No TOC	No TOC
	2	sect2 sect3	No TOC	No TOC	No TOC

	3	sect2
		  sect3
		    sect4
			No TOC	No TOC	No TOC

2	1	sect2	sect3	No TOC	No TOC

	2	sect2
		  sect3
			sect3
			  sect4
				No TOC	No TOC

	3	sect2
		  sect3
		    sect4
			sect3
			  sect4
			    sect5
				No TOC	No TOC

3	1	sect2	sect3	sect4	No TOC

	2	sect2
		  sect3
			sect3
			  sect4
				sect4
				  sect5
					No TOC

	3	sect2
		  sect3
		    sect4
			sect3
			  sect4
			    sect5
				sect4
				  sect5
				    [sect6]
					No TOC

Using `toc.max.depth`, you will notice that if a TOC exists, then it has the same number of levels as every other TOC (if the content is there). This table assumes that the other parameter, `toc.section.depth`, has a high enough value to not interfere with the selection of levels. If it is not changed from its default value of 2, then none of these examples would show titles beyond `sect2`.

Keeping selected titles out of the TOC

There may be situations where you want to exclude certain titles from the table of contents. This may be because they are of minor importance, or perhaps they are meant to be only accessed using an online help system. You can assign a `role` attribute to such elements, and then add a small template to your customization layer. For example, you might use the attribute value `NotInToc` to designate elements that should not be in the TOC. The following template would work.

```
<xsl:template match="sect1[@role = 'NotInToc']" mode="toc" />
```

Normally an element's title appears in the toc because the element is processed with a template in `mode="toc"` to generate the title. In this customization, the template is empty, which means it does nothing. So any element matching it will not appear in the TOC. In this case, it is matching on any `sect1` element with the `role="NotInToc"` attribute. Create similar templates for other elements you might want to exclude.

Caution:

If you use profiling using the role attribute, you must include NotInToc in your selected values. If you do not, then those elements with that attribute value will not appear in your output at all because they will be excluded in the profiling step. This is another reason why it is not a good idea to use the role attribute for profiling.

Adding elements to a TOC

Some document designs require that certain extra elements be added to the document's table of contents. Some candidate elements include refentry, article (mixed in with chapters), procedure (those with titles), block elements like sidebar or titled lists, or certain of the formal elements like table, figure, or example. For instance, you might customize example elements to contain formal exercises, and want to list those along with section titles in the TOC.

Adding an element to a TOC is generally a two-step process in DocBook XSL:

- Add the new element to the templates that select TOC elements.

- Add a template for the new element in mode="toc" to generate its entry.

To understand how to customize, it helps to know the sequence of processing for a table of contents. All of the these templates that generate a TOC are in the stylesheet files named autotoc.xsl (for both HTML and FO).

Template sequence for a TOC

1. Before a TOC is started, the stylesheet parameter generate.toc is checked to see if it has an entry for the current element. If not, then there will be no TOC started at that element level. See the section called "Which components have a TOC" (page 125) for information on that parameter.

2. If the generate.toc parameter also has a title entry for the current element, then a template is called to generate the title in the current language.

3. A TOC list starts with a call to one of the top-level templates such as set.toc, division.toc (for book or part), component.toc (for chapter, appendix, article), or section.toc.

4. The top-level TOC template selects the child elements that should be included in the TOC. Note that a book TOC does not include the title of the book itself, only the child elements of book. Likewise for the other top-level templates. It is this selection process that must be customized to include a new element.

5. The top-level template then processes the set of child nodes. In FO, the selected nodes have templates applied in mode="toc". In HTML, the selected nodes are passed as a parameter to a template named make.toc to process them in mode="toc".

6. The mode="toc" template for the selected child calls toc.line to format its title. It then selects its children in turn, and processes them in mode="toc" to produce nested entries. In this way the stylesheet descends through the entire document hierarchy. Note that in HTML, the subtoc template is called to apply templates in mode="toc" in order to add the proper HTML wrapper elements to indent the sub entries.

For instance, if you want to add sidebar elements to a book TOC, you first have to customize where to select them for the TOC. Since a sidebar cannot appear as a direct child of book, you do not need to customize the division.toc template that starts the TOC. But you will need to customize these two templates to include sidebar, as shown in these two code snippets. Since a title element is optional in sidebar, these select only those sidebar elements that contain a title.

Add sidebar under chapter:

```
<xsl:template match="preface|chapter|appendix|article" mode="toc">

  ...
  <xsl:call-template name="toc.line"/>

  <xsl:variable name="nodes" select="section|sect1|sidebar[title]
                                     |simplesect[$simplesect.in.toc != 0]
                                     |refentry|appendix"/>
```

Add sidbar under section:

```
<xsl:template match="section" mode="toc">

  ...
  <xsl:if test="$toc.section.depth &gt;= $depth">
    <xsl:call-template name="toc.line"/>

    <xsl:if test="$toc.section.depth > $depth
                  and $toc.max.depth > $depth.from.context
                  and (section or sidebar)">
      <fo:block id="toc.{$cid}.{$id}">
        <xsl:attribute name="margin-left">
          <xsl:call-template name="set.toc.indent">
            <xsl:with-param name="reldepth" select="$reldepth"/>
          </xsl:call-template>
        </xsl:attribute>
        <xsl:apply-templates select="section|sidebar[title]" mode="toc">
          <xsl:with-param name="toc-context" select="$toc-context"/>
        </xsl:apply-templates>
```

The second step is to add a template matching on `sidebar` in `mode="toc"`, since one does not already exist in the stylesheet.

```
<xsl:template match="sidebar" mode="toc">
  <xsl:call-template name="toc.line"/>
</xsl:template>
```

This template just calls the `toc.line` template to process the title, and does not try to add any children of `sidebar` to the TOC.

Customizing TOC presentation

If you need to further customize how TOCs are presented, you may need to modify some of the XSL templates. The following is an example of adding the word "Appendix" to `appendix` entries in the print table of contents (which by default just shows the appendix letter).

```
<xsl:template name="toc.line">
  <xsl:param name="toc-context" select="NOTANODE"/>

  <xsl:variable name="id">
    <xsl:call-template name="object.id"/>
  </xsl:variable>

  <xsl:variable name="label">
    <xsl:choose>
      <xsl:when test="self::appendix">
        <xsl:call-template name="gentext">
          <xsl:with-param name="key">appendix</xsl:with-param>
        </xsl:call-template>
        <xsl:text> </xsl:text>
        <xsl:apply-templates select="." mode="label.markup"/>
      </xsl:when>
      <xsl:otherwise>
        <xsl:apply-templates select="." mode="label.markup"/>
      </xsl:otherwise>
    </xsl:choose>
  </xsl:variable>
  ...
```
rest of toc.line template

For print output, you can customize this template named `toc.line` which can be found in `fo/autotoc.xsl`. See the section called "Styling print TOC entries" (page 208) for a detailed example. For HTML output, the stylesheets also implement a `toc.line` template in `html/autotoc.xsl` that can be customized in a manner similar to that for print output.

Customizing by TOC context

Both versions of the `toc.line` template include a passed-in template parameter named `toc-context`. That parameter references the element that contains the TOC list. So if a book TOC is being generated, for example, that parameter references the `book` element. You can change the TOC presentation based on the `toc-context` parameter. In this example, the label number is printed in bold when the TOC is not at the book level:

```
<xsl:template name="toc.line">
  <xsl:param name="toc-context" select="NOTANODE"/>

  <xsl:variable name="id">
    <xsl:call-template name="object.id"/>
  </xsl:variable>

  <xsl:variable name="label">
    <xsl:choose>
      <xsl:when test="$toc-context/self::book">
        <xsl:apply-templates select="." mode="label.markup"/>
      </xsl:when>
      <xsl:otherwise>
        <fo:inline font-weight="bold">
          <xsl:apply-templates select="." mode="label.markup"/>
        </fo:inline>
      </xsl:otherwise>
    </xsl:choose>
  </xsl:variable>
...
```

Since the `toc-context` template parameter contains a node, not a string, it can be used in an XPath statement that tests if it is a book element. If it is, then it just generates the label number, otherwise it wraps the label number in an `fo:inline` to add the bold property.

Figure, table, and other titles

The following elements all share the designation of *formal* objects in DocBook because they include a `title` element and are assigned a number label:

```
figure
table
example
equation
procedure     if the formal.procedures parameter is set to 1
```

When processed, these elements have a labeled title that is generated from gentext templates for each locale. To customize the generated title text, see the section called "Customizing generated text" (page 106).

Formal title placement

By default, the generated title is placed before the object itself. You can move the title to appear after the object by altering the `formal.title.placement` parameter. The default value of that parameter in `fo/param.xsl` or `html/param.xsl` looks like the following:

```
<xsl:param name="formal.title.placement">
figure before
example before
equation before
table before
procedure before
</xsl:param>
```

The parameter is pairs of strings, each pair matching an element name to a location string. They are all `before` by default. In your customization layer, you can modify this parameter to place titles after the object. The following example moves figure and equation titles to appear below their respective content:

```
<xsl:param name="formal.title.placement">
figure after
example before
equation after
table before
procedure before
</xsl:param>
```

Be sure to keep the values paired up, or the stylesheet will not parse the parameter properly. The string does not have to be `after`; it just has to be anything except `before` to work.

If you output both print and HTML, then you can put different values of this parameter in the respective stylesheet customization files.

Formal title numbering

Formal elements like `table`, `figure`, and `example` are all automatically numbered by the stylesheets. In general, these titles are generated by processing the formal element in `mode="object.title.markup"`. In that mode, the element's gentext template is taken from the locale file such as `common/en.xml` using the `context="title"` section of the file. The following example shows the gentext template for figure, except the non-breaking space characters are replaced by ordinary spaces for clarity:

```
<l:context name="title">
  <l:template name="figure" text="Figure %n. %t"/>
```

The `%n` code is replaced by the number during processing, and the `%t` by the title. The number itself is generated by processing the element in `mode="label.markup"`, and the title using `mode="title.markup"`.

If you want to display just titles for your formal elements, you must customize its gentext templates and the `label.markup` mode for each element. See the section called "Table titles without number labels" (page 494) to see how it is done for tables.

If you want to remove just the chapter number prefix and number the elements continuously through a book, then you need to customize the template in `mode="label.markup"`. That template is found in `common/labels.xsl`. Much of that template deals with generating the prefix, so if you eliminate the prefix, the template is much shorter. The key line is highlighted in this example customization:

```
<xsl:template match="figure|table|example" mode="label.markup">
  <xsl:choose>
    <xsl:when test="@label">
      <xsl:value-of select="@label"/>
    </xsl:when>
    <xsl:otherwise>
      <xsl:number format="1" from="book|article" level="any"/>
    </xsl:otherwise>
  </xsl:choose>
</xsl:template>
```

Note that the choice of using a `label` attribute is retained. If you want to override the number for a given formal element, you can add a `label` attribute to the element in your XML document. That value (any text string) will be used instead of the regular generated number for that instance.

Formal title customization

You can change some format features for titles of tables, figures, and examples in print output using the attribute-set named `formal.title.properties`. See the section called "Formal title properties" (page 181) for examples. For HTML output, similar formatting properties can be applied using CSS.

Any such properties are applied to both the number label and the title. If you want to separately format the number and the title, or change the layout of your formal element titles, then consider customizing the template named `formal.object.heading` from either `fo/formal.xsl` or `html/formal.xsl`. That template uses `mode="object.title.markup"` to generate the number and title. To separate them, you should replace that mode with separate modes for label and title. The following example customization for print output applies different attribute-sets to label and title.

```
<xsl:template name="formal.object.heading">
  <xsl:param name="object" select="."/>
  <xsl:param name="placement" select="'before'"/>

  <fo:block>
    <xsl:choose>
      <xsl:when test="$placement = 'before'">
        <xsl:attribute
              name="keep-with-next.within-column">always</xsl:attribute>
      </xsl:when>
      <xsl:otherwise>
        <xsl:attribute
              name="keep-with-previous.within-column">always</xsl:attribute>
      </xsl:otherwise>
    </xsl:choose>
    <fo:inline xsl:use-attribute-sets="formal.label.properties">
      <xsl:call-template name="gentext">
        <xsl:with-param name="key" select="local-name($object)"/>
      </xsl:call-template>
      <xsl:text> </xsl:text>
      <xsl:apply-templates select="$object" mode="label.markup">
      <xsl:text>: </xsl:text>
    </fo:inline>
    <fo:inline xsl:use-attribute-sets="formal.title.properties"
      <xsl:apply-templates select="$object" mode="title.markup"/>
    </fo:inline>
  </fo:block>
</xsl:template>
```

This customization generates the localized element name by calling the gentext template with the key parameter set to the element's name. It adds a space and then it generates the number using mode="label.markup", then adds a colon and space, and then wrapping it all in an fo:inline to apply an attribute-set. Then it generates the title using mode="title.markup" and applies a different attribute-set.

For HTML output, a similar customization can be used, except using HTML span elements with class attributes, which can then be formatted using a CSS stylesheet.

Person names

The stylesheets support three different styles for rendering a person's name from a personname element. You select the style for a given instance by adding a role attribute to the personname element. The styles are:

personname role attribute	Example output
none or role="first-last"	Bob Stayton
role="last-first"	Stayton, Bob
role="family-given"	Stayton Bob [FAMILY Given]

The family-given style commonly used in Asia adds a text label to identify the style so it will not be confused with the first-name last-name order. If you want to change the way that style is handled, you can customize the template named person.name.family-given in common/common.xsl as follows:

```
<xsl:template name="person.name.family-given">
  <xsl:param name="node" select="."/>

  <!-- The family-given style applies a convention for identifying given -->
  <!-- and family names in locales where it may be ambiguous -->
  <xsl:apply-templates select="$node//surname[1]"/>

  <xsl:if test="$node//surname and $node//firstname">
    <xsl:text> </xsl:text>
  </xsl:if>

  <xsl:apply-templates select="$node//firstname[1]"/>

  <xsl:text> [FAMILY Given]</xsl:text>
</xsl:template>
```

The style of person names can also be globally changed for each language using the gentext locale files. For example, the English gentext file common/en.xml has this entry which sets the English style to first-last:

```
<l:context name="styles">
    <l:template name="person-name" text="first-last"/>
 </l:context>
```

See the section called "Generated text" (page 105) for more information on customizing gentext.

If you want to change the handling of a named style or add additional person name styles, you can customize the template named person.name in the stylesheet module common/common.xsl.

11

Title page customization

The design of title pages is one area where customization is often needed. You may want to customize both the content and the format of your book, article, chapter, or section title pages. DocBook provides a wide range of metadata elements that can be entered in *info elements such as bookinfo or chapterinfo. You may want to output some metadata elements such as author, but not display others such as revhistory. Also, a title page for a book would likely contain different information from the title page for an article.

> **Note:**
>
> A "title page" in DocBook may not be a separate page. The stylesheets use the term "titlepage" to mean the presentation of an element's title and other info element content, such as author and copyright. The "titlepage" mechanism in the stylesheets is designed to be very general, so that it handles many different output styles. Page breaking after the title and info is just one possible feature. Sometimes it generates separate title pages, as in the FO output for a book, and sometimes it just prints the title and info elements without a page break, as in HTML output.

The DocBook XSL stylesheets provide a complete subsystem for customizing title pages. This chapter describes the overall process. Specific details for HTML or FO titlepages are covered in subsequent chapters. Also covered later are certain attribute-sets that can override the properties for some titles.

With the titlepage mechanism described here, you can:

- Add or remove information elements on a titlepage.

- Change the order that elements appear on a titlepage.

- Add formatting attributes to titlepage elements.

- Assign a custom template for processing a titlepage element.

The steps for customizing titlepages are listed here, and are further described in the sections that follow.

1. Create or modify a title page specification file, which is written in XML with its own special element names.

2. Run a special XSL stylesheet on the spec file to generate your customized title page XSL templates. That's right, you use XSL to generate XSL.

3. Include the generated templates in your stylesheet customization layer.

4. Modify templates in mode="titlepage.mode" and more specific modes to customize how individual elements are handled.

Create a titlepage spec file

To create your title page spec file for FO output, you can copy fo/titlepage.templates.xml from the XSL stylesheet distribution. An annotated version of the top of that file follows. To modify title pages for HTML output, you would copy the html/titlepage.templates.xml instead.

Example 11.1. Title page specification file for FO output

```
<!DOCTYPE t:templates [
<!ENTITY hsize0 "10pt">        ❶
<!ENTITY hsize1 "12pt">
<!ENTITY hsize2 "14.4pt">
<!ENTITY hsize3 "17.28pt">
<!ENTITY hsize4 "20.736pt">
<!ENTITY hsize5 "24.8832pt">
<!ENTITY hsize0space "7.5pt"> <!-- 0.75 * hsize0 -->
<!ENTITY hsize1space "9pt"> <!-- 0.75 * hsize1 -->
<!ENTITY hsize2space "10.8pt"> <!-- 0.75 * hsize2 -->
<!ENTITY hsize3space "12.96pt"> <!-- 0.75 * hsize3 -->
<!ENTITY hsize4space "15.552pt"> <!-- 0.75 * hsize4 -->
<!ENTITY hsize5space "18.6624pt"> <!-- 0.75 * hsize5 -->
]>
<t:templates xmlns:t="http://nwalsh.com/docbook/xsl/template/1.0"   ❷
             xmlns:param="http://nwalsh.com/docbook/xsl/template/1.0/param"
             xmlns:fo="http://www.w3.org/1999/XSL/Format"
             xmlns:xsl="http://www.w3.org/1999/XSL/Transform">
<!-- ============================================================ -->

<t:titlepage t:element="article"❸ t:wrapper="fo:block"❹
             font-family="{$title.fontset}"❺ >

  <t:titlepage-content t:side="recto"❻
             text-align="center">

    <title ❼
           t:named-template="component.title" ❽
           param:node="ancestor-or-self::article[1]" ❾
           font-size="&hsize5;" ❿
           font-weight="bold"
           keep-with-next="always" />

    <subtitle/>

    <corpauthor space-before="0.5em"
                font-size="&hsize2;"/>
    <authorgroup space-before="0.5em"
                 font-size="&hsize2;"/>
    <author space-before="0.5em"
            font-size="&hsize2;"/>
    ...
  </t:titlepage-content>
```

```
<t:titlepage-content t:side="verso">  ⓫
</t:titlepage-content>

<t:titlepage-before t:side="recto">  ⓬
</t:titlepage-before>

<t:titlepage-before t:side="verso">
</t:titlepage-before>

<t:titlepage-separator>  ⓭
</t:titlepage-separator>
</t:titlepage>
```

❶   The DOCTYPE is used to declare a set of XML entities. These entities are used in the spec file to set font-sizes and such. They let you use the same number for more than one element for consistency. Then if you need to change them all, you just change the entity declaration.

❷   The specification's root element is `t:templates`, which declares the name spaces and contains all the other elements. All elements and attributes that control the processing are in the `t:` (template) namespace. Intermixed are DocBook element names that not in the template namespace. That enables the spec file to clearly designate which are controlling elements and which are actual DocBook content elements.

❸   A `t:titlepage` element contains the specs for one element type, in this example `article`. There is one of these for each of `book`, `chapter`, `appendix`, and any other *division* and *component* element.

❹   A `t:wrapper` attribute indicates the output element to wrap the whole title page in. In this case, it is an `fo:block` element.

❺   This `font-family` attribute is not in the `t:` namespace and so will be passed through. It will add a `font-family` attribute to the `fo:block` wrapper. The attribute value comes from the `title.fontset` parameter (an internal parameter that includes the title font and symbol fonts).

❻   A `t:titlepage-content` element lists the actual content for one side of the title page, in this case `recto` (front side).

❼   Inside the `t:titlepage-content` element you see a list of DocBook element names, posed as empty elements. These are placeholders, for the content that comes from your DocBook documents. The order in which DocBook element names appear in the spec file is the order they will appear in the output title page. In this example, the `title` element is first on the page. You can add, move, or remove elements as needed to meet your title page requirements. If instead you want to force the output order to match the order of those elements in your documents, add a `order="document"` attribute to the `t:titlepage-content` element.

❽   You can assign a named template to process an element. The `component.title` template exists in the stylesheet and is used for chapter, appendix, glossary, and other component-level titles. You can also write your own customized templates and assign them with this mechanism.

❾   You can pass parameters to the named template you assigned to the element in the previous spec. In this case, the parameter name is `node`, and the value is an XPath expression for the ancestor element of the title element being processed.

❿   You can also set properties to format the element. In this case, it is setting the `font-size` of the article title to the value of the `&hsize5;` entity, which was declared to be `24.8832pt` at the top of the spec file. This is the nominal size, and can be overridden by a named template such as `component.title`. For HTML output, formatting properties are usually applied from a separate CSS stylesheet instead of the titlepage spec file.

⓫   Another `t:titlepage-content` element, this time with `t:side="verso"`, is used to list the content for the `verso` (back) side of the title page. By default, only a `book` element has a two-page titlepage. For all other elements, the `verso` titlepage is empty because there is no second titlepage. See the specs for `book` if you want to create a two-page titlepage.

⓬   Three other elements inside a `t:titlepage` can be used to declare templates for the transitions before and after each title page side. A `<t:titlepage-before t:side="recto">` element lets you define processing to take place just before the recto side. In print, this could be used to generate a page break. Any empty elements have no effect, as in this example.

Here is a list of all three transition elements, shown in the order in which they are presented in the output:

t:titlepage-before   t:side="recto"
t:titlepage-content   t:side="recto"
t:titlepage-before   t:side="verso"
t:titlepage-content   t:side="verso"
t:titlepage-separator

For a book, the t:titlepage-before element for verso is used to specify a page break, to ensure that the verso content is on its own page.

⑬ A t:titlepage-separator element defines what happens between the title pages and the rest of the element's content. In print, this could be a page break if you want your table of contents on its own page. In HTML it could output a rule line separator.

HTML titlepage specs

The titlepage specifcation file for HTML output is similar to the one for FO output. It uses the same element names in the t: namespace, and you can add, remove, or move information elements for any of the titlepages.

These are some of the main differences for the HTML spec file:

- Formatting properties are generally left out of the HTML spec file. That's because an external CSS stylesheet is the preferred method for formatting HTML.

- To assist in applying CSS styles, each element's titlepage gets a class attribute so that CSS class selectors can be used. The value is titlepage by default, but can be changed to be more specific.

- The terms recto and verso are meaningless in a pageless presentation like HTML. So all content is specified on the recto titlepage.

Special titlepages

The titlepage spec files include a few special titlepage elements that do not correspond to actual DocBook elements. For example:

```
<t:titlepage t:element="table.of.contents" t:wrapper="fo:block">
```

This set of specs handles the formatting for the title in the table of contents. Since that title is generated by the stylesheets, it does not actually come from a DocBook element. But the stylesheet lets you add properties to control its formatting.

Generate custom XSL templates

Once you have your complete spec file modified, you process it with an XSLT processor such as Saxon or xsltproc. The stylesheet you use is template/titlepage.xsl in the DocBook XSL distribution. If your customized copy of html/titlepage.templates.xml was named mytitlepage.spec.xml, then you could process it with this command:

```
xsltproc  \
    --output  html/mytitlepages.xsl  \
    template/titlepage.xsl  \
    html/mytitlepage.spec.xml
```

The result should be html/mytitlepages.xsl. You'll find in that file a large collection of XSL templates for generating title pages.

Add to customization layer

The last step is to add your new file of templates to your customization layer. You can do that most easily with an xsl:include statement:

```
<?xml version='1.0'?>
<xsl:stylesheet  xmlns:xsl="http://www.w3.org/1999/XSL/Transform"
      version="1.0">
<xsl:import href="docbook.xsl"/>
<xsl:import href="mytitlepages.xsl"/>
</xsl:stylesheet>
```

This href example assumes you put your customization layer and new title page template file with the DocBook distribution files. You may have to adjust the paths. Since your title page template file is imported after the main stylesheet is imported, your new title page templates will override the default templates in DocBook XSL.

Note that if you have customization layers for both chunked and non-chunked HTML output, you will need to add the import statement to both customization layers. But by keeping the new templates in a separate common file, you can easily regenerate it without needing to re-edit other files.

Modify individual element templates

Your new title page templates handle the format and sequence of elements on title pages, but do not alter the handling of the individual elements that are included. For example, an author element can have many child elements that need arrangement. The way to change an individual element on title pages is to modify a template which uses a title page mode on that element. There are two levels of such templates:

- A mode such as book.titlepage.recto.mode is applied only to an element being output to a destination specified in the mode name, which in this case is a recto (front side) titlepage of a book.

- The titlepage.mode is applied to the element on all types of title pages, except when it is overridden by a more specific mode such as book.titlepage.recto.mode.

If you want a customization to be applied to a given element when it appears on any type of title page, then customize its template in mode="titlepage.mode". Such templates can be copied from the stylesheet module fo/titlepage.xsl or html/titlepage.xsl, depending on your output type, and modified in your customization layer as needed.

If you want a customization only applied to a specific title page destination, then use a more specific mode such as that shown in the first list item above. You follow a similar process, in that you copy the template for that element with mode="titlepage.mode" from fo/titlepage.xsl or html/titlepage.xsl, and then change the name of the mode to the more specific name, such as book.titlepage.recto.mode, before making your customization changes. That custom template will be used in place of the mode="titlepage.mode" template.

The original templates are in html/titlepage.xsl or fo/titlepage.xsl, depending on your output type. For example, here is the HTML template for affiliation in that mode:

```
<xsl:template match="affiliation" mode="titlepage.mode">
  <div>
    <xsl:apply-templates select="." mode="class.attribute"/>
    <xsl:apply-templates mode="titlepage.mode"/>
  </div>
</xsl:template>
```

The template for handle author and editor elements in HTML calls a template named credits.div, a template that is also shared by othercredit elements.

```
<xsl:template match="author|editor" mode="titlepage.mode">
  <xsl:call-template name="credits.div"/>
</xsl:template>

<xsl:template name="credits.div">
  <div>
    <xsl:apply-templates select="." mode="class.attribute"/>
    <xsl:if test="self::editor[position()=1] and not($editedby.enabled = 0)">
      <h4 class="editedby"><xsl:call-template name="gentext.edited.by"/></h4>
    </xsl:if>
    <h3>
      <xsl:apply-templates select="." mode="class.attribute"/>
      <xsl:call-template name="person.name"/>
    </h3>
    <xsl:if test="not($contrib.inline.enabled = 0)">
      <xsl:apply-templates mode="titlepage.mode" select="contrib"/>
    </xsl:if>
    <xsl:apply-templates mode="titlepage.mode" select="affiliation"/>
    <xsl:apply-templates mode="titlepage.mode" select="email"/>
    <xsl:if test="not($blurb.on.titlepage.enabled = 0)">
      <xsl:choose>
        <xsl:when test="$contrib.inline.enabled = 0">
          <xsl:apply-templates mode="titlepage.mode"
                               select="contrib|authorblurb|personblurb"/>
        </xsl:when>
        <xsl:otherwise>
          <xsl:apply-templates mode="titlepage.mode"
                               select="authorblurb|personblurb"/>
        </xsl:otherwise>
      </xsl:choose>
    </xsl:if>
  </div>
</xsl:template>
```

If you do not want your author and editor names output as H3 headings, then copy this template to your customization layer and modify it as needed. If you want your author elements handled differently from your editor elements, then create a new template in mode="titlepage.mode" instead of using the shared credits.div named template.

At another level, perhaps you want author names on article title pages to be different from author names on book title pages. The DocBook XSL stylesheets are set up to use a more specific mode first. So instead of the above template, you would create two new templates, one using mode article.titlepage.recto.mode and the other using book.titlepage.recto.mode. Modify each according to your needs. If your author names are on the verso side (as specified in your title page spec file), you need to specify verso in the mode name instead. See the section called "Title page element templates" (page 188) for an example.

Following is the sequence of modes that are tried for each element on an article recto title page. This arrangement provides control of each element in any context on each side of each kind of title page. You cannot ask for more control than that.

article.titlepage.recto.auto.mode	*Defined in the generated stylesheet*
article.titlepage.recto.mode	*Generic template just applies titlepage.mode, but can be customized.*
titlepage.mode	*Defined in titlepage.xsl*
[no mode]	*Default handling of the element*

12

HTML customizations

This chapter describes some of the more commonly used customizations for HTML output. They use the techniques described in Chapter 9, *Customization methods* (page 99). Before you start writing a customization layer for HTML, consider whether you really need one.

- If you just want to customize how your HTML looks, then you can use a CSS stylesheet. See the section called "Using CSS to style HTML" (page 71) and the section called "Generate custom class values" (page 147) for more information.

- Some features of HTML processing can be controlled by stylesheet parameters without having to write a customization. See Chapter 7, *HTML output options* (page 61) for more information.

Use the methods described in this chapter if neither of the above can meet your needs.

Generate custom class values

The standard method for styling HTML output is with a Cascading Stylesheet (CSS). The Docbook HTML stylesheets help by automatically including a `class` attribute on many elements in the output. By default, the class name is the same as the name of the element that generated the output, for example `<div class="chapter">`. Such class names can be used in CSS selectors such as `div.chapter`.

You might need need to customize the class names themselves, possibly for one of the following reasons:

- Your `class` values must match an existing CSS stylesheet with different names.

- You need to tailor class values based on attribute values or element ancestry in your XML.

- If the element whose `class` you want to customize is not covered by the method in the section called "Using role as class name" (page 73).

Prior to version 1.72 of the stylesheets, changing the default `class` attribute values required copying the entire template for each element you wanted to change, just to change the `class` value. Starting with version 1.72, each `class` attribute is instead generated by processing the current element with a template in `mode="class.value"`. That makes it easier to customize for specific elements.

The `mode="class.value"` template in the stylesheet that generates the default class values is the following:

```
<xsl:template match="*" mode="class.value">
  <xsl:param name="class" select="local-name(.)"/>
  <!-- permit customization of class value -->
  <!-- Use element name by default -->
  <xsl:value-of select="$class"/>
</xsl:template>
```

The default behavior for all elements (`match="*"`) is to use the `local-name()` XSL function, which generates the name of the element. Because this feature uses a mode, you can create new templates in that mode that match on only the elements you want to change. The selection can be by element name, or by any other XSL pattern that includes attribute qualifiers or ancestry.

For example, if you wanted to add a style for chapters that have a `status="draft"` attribute, you could add this template to your customization layer:

```
<xsl:template match="chapter[@status = 'draft']" mode="class.value">
  <xsl:value-of select="'draft-chapter'"/>
</xsl:template>
```

This template outputs a string (note the extra quotes) `draft-chapter`, which is used to generate `div class="draft-chapter"` for any such chapters in the HTML output. Then you can add a class selector and styles to your CSS stylesheet.

```
div.draft-chapter {
  color: blue;
}
```

When viewed in a browser, such chapters will display in blue.

This mode is a very powerful tool for customizing the formatting of HTML output generated by DocBook XSL. Since you can define a template for any pattern that you can apply-templates to, you can create any number of `class` values to completely customize the presentation of the HTML in a browser.

There is also a similar template mode named `class.attribute`. While the `class.value` mode generates a string value, the `class.attribute` mode generates the entire `class` attribute including the name and value (which it gets using the `class.value` mode). The `class.attribute` mode makes it easy to add a `class` attribute to any custom output element you generate using one line:

```
...
<div>
  <xsl:apply-templates select="." mode="class.attribute"/>
  Content of the div
  ...
```

This mode will first use the `class.value` mode to get the class value, and then generate an `xsl:attribute` element with that value. Since it appears right after the opening tag for `div`, the `class` attribute is added to the `div` output. If you decide to customize the class value, then also add a template in the `class.value` mode as described above.

HTML headers and footers

The DocBook XSL stylesheets provide options for controlling HTML headers and footers. First, let's distinguish the two kinds of headers in HTML:

• Generated content to be displayed at the top of chunked HTML output.

- HTML elements that should appear in the HEAD of the HTML file. See the section called "HTML HEAD elements" (page 154) for more information on this kind of header.

This section covers just the first kind of header. By default, chunked HTML output gets a couple of lines of navigational links at the top and bottom of each output file. That permits the user to move from file to file to see all the content. If you do not chunk your HTML output, then there is no displayed header or footer in the file.

Adding extra lines

If you want to leave the navigational headers and footers in place, and just add something of your own, such as a copyright line, then you can fill in some no-op templates that are already called by the stylesheets. These are the header and footer templates in the order in which they are called on the page, including four that can be user defined:

Table 12.1. Templates for HTML headers and footers

Template name	When it is called
user.header.navigation	Called before standard navigational header.
header.navigation	The standard navigational header.
user.header.content	Called after standard navigational header but before any other content.
user.footer.content	Called after the chunk content but before the standard navigational footer.
footer.navigation	The standard navigational footer.
user.footer.navigation	Called after the standard navigational footer.

Inserting a copyright

The following is an example of adding a copyright string to the bottom of each chunked file, above the standard navigational footer. It processes the first copyright element it finds in the document, using the titlepage.mode which adds the copyright symbol:

```
<xsl:template name="user.footer.content">
  <HR/>
  <xsl:apply-templates select="//copyright[1]" mode="titlepage.mode"/>
</xsl:template>
```

If you would rather have the copyright appear below the navigational footer, then use the user.footer.navigational template instead. The content of the template can include IMG elements to reference a graphical logo, and any other HTML content that makes sense. If you add class attributes, then you can control the formatting with your CSS stylesheet.

See the section called "Footer link to legalnotice" (page 165) if you want the copyright string to link to a separate legalnotice chunk.

Inserting a CVS identifier

If your DocBook XML file is kept under a content management system such as CVS, you might want to insert the CVS version information on the HTML pages generated from the file. That informs the reader of when the content of the page was last changed.

The XSLT processor cannot directly request the version identifier from the CVS system. But that information can be stored in the XML document itself, where the stylesheet can access it. The trick is to put the CVS identifier string

Id in a releaseinfo element in your document. It can go in the bookinfo element of a book, or the articleinfo element of an article. Each time the file is checked into the CVS system, the identifier string is updated by CVS with the latest information. For example:

```
<releaseinfo>
  $Id: dbxsl.xml,v 1.131 2007/10/06 05:56:46 bobs Exp $
</releaseinfo>
```

Once this information is in the XML file, it is easy to insert it into the HTML footer:

```
<xsl:template name="user.footer.content">
  <P class="CVSinfo">
    <xsl:value-of select="//releaseinfo[1]"/>
  </P>
</xsl:template>
```

The select attribute has an XPath expression that finds the first releaseinfo element in the document, and the xsl:value-of element takes its string value.

Navigational labels or graphics

The standard navigational headers and footers in chunked output use words such as Next, Prev, Up, and Home.

You can replace those words with different words by customizing the generated text. See the section called "Customizing generated text" (page 106) for a description of this method of customization. The following is an example that changes the word Home with Table of Contents for English output:

```
<xsl:param name="local.l10n.xml" select="document('')" />
<l:i18n xmlns:l="http://docbook.sourceforge.net/xmlns/l10n/1.0">
 <l:l10n language="en">
  <l:gentext key="nav-home" text="Table of Contents"/>
 </l:l10n>
</l:i18n>
```

See the stylesheet file common/en.xml to see all the l:gentext elements with key names that begin with nav- that specify the navigational labels.

You can also replace the navigational words with graphical icons. See the section called "Navigational icons" (page 77) for the parameters to turn that feature on. You can also supply your own graphics.

Brief headers and footers

The standard navigational headers and footers also show the titles of the other files by default. If you want a very clean presentation without the titles, then you can set the navig.showtitles parameter to zero (it is 1 by default). Then you will see only Next and Prev or their icon equivalents.

Bread crumbs

Bread crumbs are a common navigational aid that displays the sequence of nested elements that generated the currently displayed chunk. Each of the items in the sequence is a link to an ancestor element, which provides a higher context than the current node. So if you chunk at section level 2, then the breadcrumbs for such a section might display the titles for its book, chapter, and section level 1 as links.

The following example shows a custom template that generates the links, and how it can be called.

Template to generate breadcrumbs:
```
<xsl:template name="breadcrumbs">
  <xsl:param name="this.node" select="."/>
  <div class="breadcrumbs">
    <xsl:for-each select="$this.node/ancestor::*">
      <span class="breadcrumb-link">
        <a>
          <xsl:attribute name="href">
            <xsl:call-template name="href.target">
              <xsl:with-param name="object" select="."/>
              <xsl:with-param name="context" select="$this.node"/>
            </xsl:call-template>
          </xsl:attribute>
          <xsl:apply-templates select="." mode="title.markup"/>
        </a>
      </span>
      <xsl:text> &gt; </xsl:text>
    </xsl:for-each>
    <!-- And display the current node, but not as a link -->
    <span class="breadcrumb-node">
      <xsl:apply-templates select="$this.node" mode="title.markup"/>
    </span>
  </div>
</xsl:template>
```

Call the template:
```
<xsl:template name="user.header.content">
  <xsl:call-template name="breadcrumbs"/>
</xsl:template>
```

The `breadcrumbs` template selects the ancestors using `ancestor::*`, and then generates a link for each. The `select` in an `xsl:for-each` presents the nodes in document order, with the current context node designated as `"."` within the `xsl:for-each`. The href is generated using the template named `href.target`, which will generate an appropriate link between any two chunks. The `context` param should contain the starting point for the link, whose value was saved before the `xsl:for-each` changed the context node, and the target chunk is designated by the `object` param. The template then generates the title using `mode="title.markup"`. A separator string is added after each, which can be customized for your style. Then the title of the current node is added, but not as a link. Each title is contained in a `span` element with a `class` attribute so it can be styled using CSS.

You call your new template using the placeholder template named `user.header.content`, which is automatically called at the top of each chunked output file.

Replace headers and footers

If you decide you need to completely replace the navigational headers and footers, then you can either create replacement templates, or you can turn them off and apply the user-defined templates instead.

If you want to retain the navigational features such as Next and Previous, then it is probably easiest to modify the existing templates. Copy the templates named `header.navigation` and `footer.navigation` from the `html/chunk-common.xsl` file to your customization layer for modification. You'll find they are substantial templates that create small tables to format the header and footer. They are passed two parameters named `prev` and `next`, which are the XML nodes for those pointers.

If your goal is to completely replace the standard headers and footers, then set the `suppress.navigation` parameter to 1 to turn them off. You can then define your own in templates named `user.header.navigation` and `user.footer.navigation`. If you do not define any new templates, then you will completely suppress headers and footers.

Server-side includes

A server-side include (SSI) is a feature provided by HTTP servers to automatically insert content into an HTML file as it is being sent out. When that feature is turned on in the HTTP server, then each HTML file that is being sent is scanned by the server. The server looks for special markup that provides instructions for inserting content. The instructions can insert static content files, or can initiate scripts to generate dynamic content.

The syntax used for SSI instructions varies with the server setup. The examples here show the syntax for a standard Apache SSI and for a Java ServerPages (JSP) inclusion. To produce output at the top of an HTML page generated by DocBook XSL, the examples are added to a `user.header.content` customization, which is described in the section called "HTML headers and footers" (page 148).

```
<xsl:template name="user.header.content">
  <div>
    <!-- Apache SSI -->
    <xsl:comment>#include virtual="/cgi-bin/counter.pl"</xsl:comment>
    <!-- JSP inclusion -->
    <xsl:text disable-output-escaping="yes">
       &lt;%@ include file="/header.html" %>
    </xsl:text>
  </div>
</xsl:template>
```

Here is the output generated by this template:

```
<!--#include virtual="/cgi-bin/counter.pl"-->
<%@ include file="/header.html" %>
```

The Apache SSI instruction is output in a standard HTML comment. When a comment starts with `#include`, then server in which SSI is turned on will act to execute the specified CGI script and insert the output of the script.

The JSP instruction is output between the character sequences <% and %>. Since this syntax is not an HTML element, comment, or processing instruction, the left angle bracket has to be escaped to be output. That's why the example uses the `disable-output-escaping="yes"` attribute on the `xsl:text` element that contains the instruction.

When this HTML file is requested by a browser, a properly configured HTTP server will execute these instructions and fill in the content before sending out the file.

Inserting external HTML code

The server-side includes described in the previous section require you to configure an HTTP server to execute the includes when the file is accessed. What if you want to insert static HTML code from an external source into the HTML files that DocBook builds? For example, many website pages are based on templates that use boilerplate HTML code or Javascript libraries that already exist in external files. How do you insert such content verbatim into DocBook-generated HTML files?

The basic method is to use the XSLT `document()` function to open the code file, and then use `xsl:copy-of` to copy its content to your output. However, the `document()` function can only open well-formed XML files, not just any text file. But you can turn a text file into a well-formed XML document by wrapping its content in some element's start and end tags. Then the code text will be taken as the content of the wrapper element. As you will see in the examples below, you do not have to include the wrapper element in your output, so you can use any element name. The examples use `htmlcode`.

If your external code file includes HTML markup, be sure that any HTML elements are well-formed. The easiest way to do that is to convert it to XHTML. You can use the *HTML Tidy*[1] tool to do that.

In the page header

If you want to insert the external code into the header on your HTML pages, you can use the `user.header.content` template as described in the section called "HTML headers and footers" (page 148). The following is an example:

```
<xsl:template name="user.header.content">
   <xsl:variable name="codefile" select="document('mycode.html',/)"/>
   <xsl:copy-of select="$codefile/htmlcode/node()"/>
</xsl:template>
```

The first line of the template opens the code file and puts its well-formed content into a variable named `codefile`. This example assumes the code is contained in a file named `mycode.html` located in the current directory. You may want to make that a parameter reference so you can change the pathname more easily. You could also use a URI and have your XML catalog map that URI to the actual code file on your system. See Chapter 5, *XML catalogs* (page 47) for more information about using catalogs.

The example also assumes the code file uses a wrapper element named `htmlcode` to make it well-formed XML. The second line of the template copies the content of the wrapper element to your output, without including the wrapper element itself. It selects using `node()`, which matches everything, including elements, text, comments, and processing instructions. If you do not want to hard code the wrapper element name in your template, then use this selection instead:

```
<xsl:copy-of select="$codefile/*/node()"/>
```

This will copy the content of whatever the root element is in the code file.

In the HEAD element

If you want to insert boilerplate HTML code into your HTML head element, then you can use the `user.head.content` template instead. See the section called "HTML HEAD elements" (page 154) for further information on that template. The following is an example that is similar to the one in the previous section:

```
<xsl:template name="user.head.content">
   <xsl:variable name="codefile" select="document('mycode.html',/)"/>
   <xsl:copy-of select="$codefile/htmlcode/node()"/>
</xsl:template>
```

In the page content

If you want to insert boilerplate HTML code mixed in with the content of your pages, then you can use the same technique as the previous sections to customize any of the element templates that generate output.

If you want the authors of your documents to be able to insert their own HTML code in arbitrary places, then they can use a `dbhtml-include` processing instruction to indicate the location and filename. At the point where you want the HTML code inserted, add a processing instruction like the following to your DocBook XML document:

---

[1] http://tidy.sourceforge.net/

```
...
</para>
<?dbhtml-include href="mycode.html"?>
<para>
...
```

The DocBook HTML stylesheet will open the file referenced by the `href` pseudo-attribute and attempt to copy it into the output.

- To be read by an XSL stylesheet, any external HTML code file must be well-formed XML. Well-formed means:

    —It must have a single root element.

    —All non-empty elements must have an end tag as well as a start tag.

    —Empty elements must include a closing slash, such as `<br/>`.

    —Attribute values must be in quotes.

    Loose HTML coding will not be recognized as XML by the parser.

- If the HTML code has a single root element, then the stylesheet will just copy it all into the output.

- If the HTML code is not a single root element, then you must make it a single root element by wrapping all the content in an `html` wrapper element. That is, put an `<html>` tag at the start of the file and an `</html>` tag at the end of the file. The DocBook stylesheet will recognize that wrapper tag and copy everthing inside the element, not including the `<html>` wrapper. This only happens with that element name.

HTML HEAD elements

The HTML `HEAD` element is used to pass additional information to the browser that is not displayed. There are several DocBook XSL parameters that can add specific items to the `HEAD` output. There are also three emtpy placeholder templates that you can use in your customization layer. These are described at the end of the section.

The parameters that affect the `HEAD` content include:

`html.base`	If this parameter is set to a URL string, the output will include:
	`<base href="url">`
	This value establishes the base URL for all relative URLs in the document.
	Note that it is not possible to add a `target` attribute to the `base` element to set an output window name for the browser.
`html.stylesheet`	If this parameter is set to the pathname of your CSS stylesheet, then the output will include:
	`<link rel="stylesheet" href="mystyle.css" type="text/css">`
	Remember that you must copy the CSS stylesheet to where it is expected to be found relative to the HTML output.
`link.mailto.url`	If this parameter is set to a mail URI such as `mailto:bobs@sagehill.net`, then the output will include:

```
<link rev="made" href="mailto:bobs@sagehill.net">
```

inherit.keywords	This parameter controls whether a keyword meta element is created in chunked section files. If your document contains a DocBook keywordset element, then the output will automatically include something like the following:

```
<meta name="keywords" content="word1, word2, word3">
```

Normally the keywords in a chunked file would only include the ones that appear within its content. If inherit.keywords is set to 1, then the list of keywords in each chunked file will include those from its ancestor elements.

generate.meta.abstract — If this parameter is set to 1, and if your document contains an abstract element, then the output will include something like the following:

```
<meta name="description" content="text of abstract">
```

Since content is an attribute, it cannot contain markup, so only the plain text of the abstract is included.

If you need to add other items to the HTML HEAD, there are three user-defined templates you can fill in.

Table 12.2. Templates for HTML HEAD additions

system.head.content	Called first in the head element.
user.head.content	Called last in the head element.
user.preroot	Template called prior to output of html root element. Lets you output processing-instructions or comments, but not elements.

The template named system.head.content is called at the beginning of the HEAD element, before the standard head content is output. That lets you define style attributes that can be overridden by the CSS stylesheet. The user.head.content template is called at the end of the HEAD element, after the standard head content. The following is an example that would add a copyright inside of an HTML comment, and a base element with a target attribute that can be passed as a parameter value:

```
<xsl:param name="target.window" select="'_self'"/>
<xsl:template name="user.head.content">
  <xsl:comment> (c) 2007 Copyright Megacorp, Inc. </xsl:comment>
  <base  target="{$target.window}"/>
</xsl:template>
```

If this document is processed with the custom parameter target.window set to 'main', then this customization adds this output to the HEAD:

```
<!-- (c) 2007 Copyright Megacorp, Inc. -->
<base target="main">
```

There is also a special empty placeholder template named user.preroot. This template is called *before* the html root element is output. Since it placed outside the root element, it cannot contain any elements or plain text. But the XML standard permits comments or processing instructions to be output before the root element. The most common processing instruction is the one that identifies a stylesheet to associate with the file.

Adding CSS style rules

Although you can specify a CSS stylesheet by using the `html.stylesheet` parameter, you may want to supplement it with additional CSS style rules in the `head` element. To do so, you can output an HTML `style` element using either the `user.head.content` template or the `system.head.content` template. The following example shows how to do it.

```
<xsl:template name="user.head.content">
  <style type="text/css">
    <xsl:comment>
      @import "stylesheets/override.css"
      body {background: url(graphics/bluesea.png);}
    </xsl:comment>
  </style>
</xsl:template>
```

This results in the following output in the HTML `head` element:

```
<style type="text/css">
  <!--
    @import "stylesheets/override.css"
    body {background: url(graphics/bluesea.png);}
  -->
</style>
```

Using the `user.head.content` template means these style rules will appear *after* the CSS stylesheet specified in `html.stylesheet`, so they will have higher CSS precedence. Using `system.head.content` instead means these style rules will appear *before* any other content in `head`, and so will have lower CSS precendence and can be overriden by rules in the file specified by `html.stylesheet`.

Embedding CSS styles

Instead of referring to an external CSS stylesheet, you may want to embed the CSS styles in your HTML output. That makes the HTML files more portable, since they no longer are dependent on a separate CSS file. You can make use of the placeholder template `user.head.content` as described in the following steps:

1. Add a DOCTYPE declaration to your customization layer so you can declare a *system entity* that references your CSS stylesheet. For example:

    ```
    <?xml version="1.0"?>
    <!DOCTYPE xsl:stylesheet [
    <!ENTITY css SYSTEM "mystyle.css">
    ]>
    <xsl:stylesheet
      xmlns:xsl="http://www.w3.org/1999/XSL/Transform">
    ```

    A system entity is a way of identifying an external file. Adjust the path to the CSS file if it is not in the current directory. The path is taken to be relative to your customization file.

2. Now you will use that system entity in the user.head.content in your customization:

```
<xsl:template name="user.head.content">
<style type="text/css">
&css;
</style>
</xsl:template>
```

This creates a style element in the HTML output and puts the content of the system entity into it. If the CSS file cannot be found or opened, the XSLT processor should report it as an error. do not forget to turn off the html.stylesheet parameter if you were using that to insert a reference the stylesheet.

Adding a date timestamp

You can add a date-of-processing timestamp in a META tag in your HTML HEAD output. This example uses an EXSLT extension function named date-time() that reads the system clock and generates a date timestamp at the moment the process is run. Not all XSLT processors support EXSLT functions, but Saxon, Xalan, and xsltproc do.

To add a date timestamp to your output, add a call to the extension function to the user.head.content template in your customization layer. You will also have to add a couple of attributes to the xsl:stylesheet element itself in order to identify the namespace used by the extension function. The following annotated example shows what needs to be done.

Example 12.1. Timestamp in meta element

```
<?xml version="1.0"?>
<xsl:stylesheet xmlns:xsl="http://www.w3.org/1999/XSL/Transform"
                xmlns:date="http://exslt.org/dates-and-times"   ❶
                exclude-result-prefixes="date"   ❷
                version='1.0'>

<xsl:import href="../docbook-xsl-1.73.1/html/docbook.xsl"/>

<xsl:template name="user.head.content">   ❸
  <meta name="date">   ❹
    <xsl:attribute name="content">   ❺
      <xsl:call-template name="datetime.format">   ❻
        <xsl:with-param name="date" select="date:date-time()"/>   ❼
        <xsl:with-param name="format" select="'m/d/Y'"/>   ❽
      </xsl:call-template>
    </xsl:attribute>
  </meta>
</xsl:template>
```

...

❶   You have to add the `xmlns:date` namespace declaration to the customization layer's `xsl:stylesheet` element.
❷   Also add an `exclude-result-prefixes` attribute so the namespace does not appear in the HTML output.
❸   The `user.head.content` template is an empty placeholder template in the stylesheets to be filled in by the customizer.
❹   Start an HTML META element and give it a `name="date"` attribute.
❺   Start the addition of a `content` attribute on the META element.
❻   Call the stylesheet template `datetime.format` to generate the `content` attribute's value. That template is located in `common/pi.xsl`.
❼   Pass the template a `date` parameter whose value is generated by the EXSLT `date-time()` function. The `date:` prefix ensures that this function call is not confused with the built-in XSLT functions.
❽   Pass the template a `format` parameter whose value is a string of date and time component letters. The string must be enclosed in single quotes, or it will be misinterpreted as a document node resulting in a blank date output. These component letters are listed in the section called "Date and time" (page 78). You can use whatever format you desire.

This example customization results in the following HTML output:

```
<meta name="date" content="03/10/2007">
```

This customization uses the `datetime` extension feature that is described in more detail in the section called "Date and time" (page 78).

Removing the HEAD element

In some website setups, such as those that use Java ServerPages, HTML content is stored in modular pieces without HTML HEAD elements. The HTTP server is responsible for assembling a complete HTML file by dynamically adding a HEAD element. That makes it possible for the server to customize the output for each request. In other setups, the content files also have the HTML and BODY tags removed. Such content can be combined from several files by the server, which also dynamically adds the HTML, HEAD, and BODY tags.

If you want to generate such modular output, you will need to customize the template that generates the HTML wrapper elements. If you are using the nonchunking stylesheet, you want to customize the template with mode="process.root" in html/docbook.xsl. If you are using the chunking stylesheet, you need customize the chunk-element-content template in html/chunk-common.xsl.

In both cases, you want to eliminate all those parts of the template that output the HTML elements you do not want. If you want to eliminate just the HEAD, then remove the literal <head> and </head> tags and their content. If you want completely bare content, then remove the <html>, <head>, and <body> tags, as well as the template calls that fill the <head> element and generate the header and footer. There will not be much left. For example, process.root could end up looking like the following:

```
<xsl:template match="*" mode="process.root">
  <xsl:call-template name="root.messages"/>
  <xsl:apply-templates select="."/>
</xsl:template>
```

BODY attributes

By default, the HTML stylesheets add several attributes to the generated HTML BODY element. These attributes are added with the following named template in html/docbook.xsl:

```
<xsl:template name="body.attributes">
  <xsl:attribute name="bgcolor">white</xsl:attribute>
  <xsl:attribute name="text">black</xsl:attribute>
  <xsl:attribute name="link">#0000FF</xsl:attribute>
  <xsl:attribute name="vlink">#840084</xsl:attribute>
  <xsl:attribute name="alink">#0000FF</xsl:attribute>
</xsl:template>
```

This results in a body element in the HTML output like the following:

```
<body bgcolor="white" text="black" link="#0000FF"
vlink="#840084" alink="#0000FF">
```

If you want to add, change or remove any of these attributes, you should copy this template to your customization layer and make your changes there. For example, you could remove all of the default attributes to allow your CSS stylesheet to handle the styling, and you could add an event handler attribute as in this example.

```
<xsl:template name="body.attributes">
  <xsl:attribute name="onLoad">alert('Thanks for visiting')</xsl:attribute>
</xsl:template>
```

This will result in the following HTML body element, which triggers a Javascript alert message each time the document is opened:

```
<body onLoad="alert('Thanks for visiting')">
```

Changing the <h> levels

The DocBook stylesheets generate HTML heading elements H1, H2, H3, etc. according to the hierarchy of elements in the document. However, you may want to alter which HTML heading level gets assigned to a particular element. Keep in mind that you need not customize the XSL just to change the styling, because an external CSS stylesheet can handle that. But if you need to change the heading level elements, the following are some guidelines.

- Unless otherwise specified, the title of the document's root element, such as book, is handled by the template that starts with this line in `html/titlepage.xsl`:

```
<xsl:template match="title" mode="titlepage.mode">
```

This template outputs an H1 element. You could add a customized template to match on book/title in that mode to change just book titles.

- A part title is handled by the template named `division.title` in the stylesheet module `html/division.xsl`. That template was specified in the titlepage spec file. You could customize that template, or customize the titlepage spec file to use a new named template instead for part title elements.

- A chapter or appendix title is handled by a template named `component.title` in the stylesheet module `html/component.xsl`. That template is used for other component-level elements such as bibliography that might appear inside a section. So it first computes a level variable based on its ancestry, and then adds 1 to that to use in an HTML heading element. Since chapter cannot appear inside a section, the level value is 1, and so an H2 heading is produced.

- A section title is handled by a template named `section.heading` in the stylesheet module `html/sections.xsl`. That template is called from a template named `section.title` with a template parameter named level computed by using the template named `section.level`.

HTML frameset

There may be situations where an HTML frameset is appropriate for the presentation of your documents. A typical frameset arrangement puts a table of contents list in the left frame, and the main text in the right frame. When a user clicks on any title in the left frame, the content is displayed in the right frame.

A simple two-frame setup like this can be easily done with the DocBook chunk stylesheet, provided you write the frameset file by hand. The following is an example frameset file:

```
<html>
<head>
  <title>My Document Title</title>
</head>
<frameset cols="30%,*">
 <frame src="index.html" name="list">
 <frame src="intro.html" name="body">
</frameset>
</html>
```

This creates two frames, the left one named list and the right one named body. You need to put the table of contents file in the left frame. In a typical chunked output, that file is named `index.html`. You can put an introductory file into the right frame so it is not empty when the frameset starts up.

In order for links in the left frame list to show up in the right frame, you need to add `<base target="body">` to the HEAD element of the `index.html` file. Without further customization, there is no way to put that base element into just one of the chunked files. But it still works if you put it in all of them. That just means any hot links from the body files to also appear in the body window, which is the behavior you expect.

The following customization will add the base element to all the HTML files:

```
<xsl:param name="target.window" select="'body'"/>
<xsl:template name="user.head.content">
  <base  target="{$target.window}"/>
</xsl:template>
```

Then when you open up the frameset file, you will find that all the links on the left show up on the right. But one problem with this setup is the Home link in the footer of the HTML files. That link takes you to the index.html table of contents file, but it will show up in the right frame. You will need to do an additional customization to remove that link. It is not needed, since the index.html file remains visible in the left frame. See the section called "HTML headers and footers" (page 148).

Chunking customization

Although the chunk stylesheet provides many parameters that control the chunking of your document into multiple HTML files, you may have a need for further customization. If you need to customize how elements are chunked, as opposed to how they look, then you should use version 1.73 or later of the stylesheets. Those templates are cleanly separated, so customization is easier.

If you examine the html/chunk.xsl file from version 1.73 or above, you will see that all it does is load other stylesheet modules.

```
<xsl:import href="docbook.xsl"/>
<xsl:import href="chunk-common.xsl"/>
<xsl:include href="chunk-code.xsl"/>
```

The use of both xsl:import and xsl:include, and the order in which they are used, are important for allowing clean customization. It also allows you to create a customized version of the single-page stylesheet as well as the chunking stylesheet using modular files.

Here are the steps for creating customizations of both chunking and single-page stylesheets.

1. Create a customization file for single-page output as described in the section called "Customization layer" (page 100). Let's say you name that file mydocbook.xsl. It should contain:

    - An xsl:import of the stock html/docbook.xsl non-chunking stylesheet.

    - Any parameter settings and customizations of how elements should be styled. You can include any parameters that appear in the html/param.xsl stylesheet module, even if they control chunking.

2. Copy the html/chunk.xsl file to another customization file, such as mychunk.xsl. Edit that file as follows:

    Import your single-page customization file, which imports docbook.xsl:
    ```
    <xsl:import href="mydocbook.xsl"/>
    <xsl:import href="chunk-common.xsl"/>
    <xsl:include href="chunk-code.xsl"/>
    ```
    Add your parameter settings and customizations that affect chunking behavior here.

    Note that chunk-code.xsl is included, not imported.

3. If you customize any chunking templates with a match attribute (as opposed to a name attribute), then add a priority="1" attribute to the xsl:template element in your customization layer. The next section explains why.

How chunking works

The chunking stylesheet has to process any chunked element in two different ways. A chapter, for example, is always a chunk, and so there must be a template for chapter that generates a new file and adds the correct navigational header and footer. A chapter also has content to be formatted, and so there is another template for chapter that converts its content into HTML elements within the chunk file.

In most situations, processing an element in two different ways is done using a template mode. This does not work for chunking, because of the nature of nested chunks. If you were to create a template for chapter with mode="chunk", then you could use that to create the chunk file and navigational header/footer. Inside that template you just process the chapter in normal mode to format it for HTML. When that normal processing hits a section, it just processes the section as part of the chapter, and does not chunk the section. Somehow the normal mode has to apply-templates to sections in mode="chunk", but the normal mode template has no knowledge of chunking.

So the chunking stylesheet takes a different approach. It operates the two different processes at two different import levels. The chunking stylesheet imports the regular stylesheet, and so the chunking templates have a higher import precedence. There is a chunking template with match="chapter" (in chunk-code.xsl), but it is in normal mode. It is applied first because it has a higher import precedence than the match="chapter" template in the non-chunking stylesheet. It opens a new chunk file and writes the navigational header. Then it uses xsl:apply-imports to format the elements in the chapter. The xsl:apply-imports element ignores matches in the current import level and reaches back to find a match in lower import levels. It finds the match="chapter" template in component.xsl, and uses that to generate HTML for the chapter.

When a section element within a chapter is encountered, the non-chunking template is using an xsl:apply-templates instruction. The processor looks for a match="section" template, and it looks for the match *with the highest import precedence*. The chunking version of match="section" in chunk-code.xsl has the highest import precedence. This is the case even when the chapter is being processed with a template found via xsl:apply-imports. The import level is not inherited when templates are applied. So the section chunking template starts a new chunk file (while the chapter file is still open for writing), and adds the section navigational header. Then the chunking section template does xsl:apply-imports, and the section is processed with the non-chunking section template to format it. Repeat as needed. When all the section chunks are completed, the non-chunking chapter template runs out of content and finishes. Control returns to the chunking version of the chapter template, which writes the navigational footer and closes the chapter chunk file.

The advantage of this approach is that there is no mode to keep track of, and the original non-chunking templates can be reused without being duplicated (which is a maintenance headache). This approach does require care when customizing, because customization introduces more import levels. The following list describes how the templates are arranged in import levels in a customization, starting with the lowest import precedence. This description applies to version 1.73 and later of the stylesheets.

1. The original non-chunking templates are at the bottom of the import ladder. If there is no match on an element in the higher import levels, then these are the templates of last resort. In fact, most elements are handled at this level. Only chunked elements and elements you customize are affected by higher import levels.

2. The next import level up consists of customizations of templates from the non-chunking stylesheet. These are the templates in a non-chunking customization layer such as mydocbook.xsl that imports the base stylesheet. You can use mydocbook.xsl to generate single-file HTML output.

3. The next import level up consists of the stock chunking templates.

   - All of the chunking templates with a name attribute are in chunk-common.xsl. These are utility templates that are not matched to specific elements.

- All of the chunking templates with a `match` attribute are in `chunk-code.xsl`. These are the templates that initiate chunking for specific elements.

4. The final import level consists of your customizations of chunking templates. These are in a customization layer such as `mychunk.xsl` that looks like the following:

```
<xsl:import href="mydocbook.xsl"/>
<xsl:import href="chunk-common.xsl"/>
<xsl:include href="chunk-code.xsl"/>
```
Add your template customizations that affect chunking behavior here.

- The `chunk-common.xsl` templates are imported. If you customize a named template from `chunk-common.xsl`, then your template will have higher import precedence than the original imported template.

- Note that `chunk-code.xsl` is included, not imported. Because it is included, if you customize a template from `chunk-code.xsl`, then your customization has the same import precedence as the original chunking template. That's why you must add a `priority="1"` attribute to your customized match template. If you do not, then the XSL processor will complain that there are two templates that match on one element. Adding the `priority` attribute resolves the conflict.

Why use `xsl:include` instead of `xsl:import` for `chunk-code.xsl`? The reason is the use of `xsl:apply-imports` in those templates. It must maintain a single level of import level difference in order to reach the non-chunking template when `xsl:apply-imports` is used.

If you were to use `xsl:import` on `chunk-code.xsl`, and then customize one of those templates, here is what would happen:

1. Your customized chunking template initiates a chunk file for an element such as chapter.

2. Then your customized chunking template uses `xsl:apply-imports` to format the content of the chapter.

3. The processor looks for a template with `match="chapter"` below the current import level.

4. It finds the template with `match="chapter"` in `chunk-code.xsl`, which is imported. But that is the original *chunking* chapter template, not the non-chunking version that you need.

5. The original chunking chapter template starts a chunk file of the same name, and then it also does `xsl:apply-imports`. This time the non-chunking chapter template is found, and it formats the chapter content into the file.

6. The original chunking chapter template closes the file and returns control to the customized chunking chapter template.

7. The customized chunking chapter template then writes the footer and then writes the file. Because it is the same filename, it overwrites the previous file. You are left with a chunk that has the correct filename and the correct header and footer, but no content. Its content was separately chunked into a file of the same name that was just overwritten.

When `xsl:include` is used for `chunk-code.xsl`, then no new import level is introduced for those templates. When `xsl:apply-imports` is used, in either the original or a customized version, then it finds the non-chunking template to fill in the content.

Chunking templates

Even with this arrangement, customization of the chunking behavior will require you to understand the templates that perform the chunking process. The behavior is further complicated by options such as fast chunking (when using `chunkfast.xsl` instead of `chunk.xsl`) and the `onechunk.xsl` variation. The following table summarizes the important chunking templates (as of version 1.73 and later).

Table 12.3. Chunking templates

Template	Location	Function
`<xsl:template match="/">`	chunk-code.xsl	Matches document root to start processing.
`<xsl:template match="set|book|part|...`	chunk-code.xsl	Matches elements that are always chunks and calls the `process-chunk-element` template.
`<xsl:template match="sect1|sect2|...`	chunk-code.xsl	Matches section elements, calls the chunk template to determine if it is to be chunked, and then calls the `process-chunk-element` if it is.
`<xsl:template name="chunk">`	chunk-common.xsl	Determines if the current element is a chunk. It returns 1 if the element is a chunk, or 0 otherwise.
`<xsl:template name="process-chunk-element">`	chunk-common.xsl	Applies templates to style the element content and saves the styled result in a variable. Routes the content to the appropriate template based on chunking options that are set.
`<xsl:template name="chunk-all-sections">` and others	chunk-common.xsl	Determines the Next and Previous links for the given chunk element and calls the `process-chunk` template.
`<xsl:template name="process-chunk">`	chunk-common.xsl	Determines the filename of the chunk and calls the `write-chunk` template.
`<xsl:template name="write.chunk">`	chunker.xsl	Calls the appropriate extension function for the current processor to write the styled content to a chunk file.

When customizing any of these templates, be sure to set up your chunking customization using the guidelines in the section called "Chunking customization" (page 161).

Separate legalnotice

The default title pages in HTML include the `legalnotice` element in its entirety. Sometimes this element can be quite long, and it becomes intrusive when it appears between the document title and the table of contents in HTML output.

You can still include your `legalnotice` but put it in a separate HTML file, with a link to it from the title page. You can do that by simply setting the `generate.legalnotice.link` parameter to 1 instead of the default zero. This works for both the chunking and nonchunking HTML stylesheets.

In your customization layer, set this parameter:

```
<xsl:param name="generate.legalnotice.link" select="1"/>
```

When processed, the `title` of the `legalnotice` element will appear on the HTML title page, and it will link to a separate HTML file. If the legalnotice has no title, then the text `Legal Notice` is used instead. This default link text is generated using the gentext machinery, so it will be in the appropriate language.

Filename of the legalnotice chunk

The name of the legalnotice chunk file is generated from a combination of the prefix `ln-`, plus the `id` attribute value of the `legalnotice` element, plus the `.html` filename extension. If the element has no `id` attribute, then a unique id is generated for it. A generated id is different each time the document is processed. If you want a stable filename so you can cross reference to it, say from a copyright notice you add to your footer, be sure to add an id attribute to the legalnotice element.

If you want to customize the chunk filename for legalnotice, then customize the template that matches the element in `mode="chunk-filename"` as follows. The example also adds a new stylesheet parameter so you could set the filename from the command line if necessary.

```
<xsl:param name="legalnotice.filename">legalnotice.html</xsl:param>

<xsl:template match="legalnotice" mode="chunk-filename">
  <xsl:value-of select="$legalnotice.filename"/>
</xsl:template>
```

This mode is used to create legalnotice chunk file, as well as any references to it, such as from the titlepage.

Footer link to legalnotice

In chunked HTML output, putting a copyright string in each page's footer is a common practice, as described in the section called "Inserting a copyright" (page 149). With further customization, you could also turn the copyright string into an active link that connects to the separate legalnotice page:

```
<xsl:template name="user.footer.content">
  <HR/>
  <a>
    <xsl:attribute name="href">
      <xsl:apply-templates select="//legalnotice[1]" mode="chunk-filename"/>
    </xsl:attribute>

    <xsl:apply-templates select="//copyright[1]" mode="titlepage.mode"/>
  </a>
</xsl:template>
```

Processing the legalnotice element in `mode="chunk-filename"` will generate its filename, which is used in the `href` attribute of the link.

More than one legalnotice

It is perfectly legal to have more than one `legalnotice` in your document. You will find that they are processed in sequence, each generating a separate chunk file with its own link on the title page. You will probably want to give each one a different `title` element so the reader knows from the link text what the different legal notices are for.

Head links for legalnotice

An HTML file's HEAD element can contain one or more link elements to identify relationships of the current file to other files. You can form a relationship to your separate legalnotice chunk file using the stylesheet parameter html.head.legalnotice.link.types. For example:

A stylesheet parameter setting like this:
```
<xsl:param name="html.head.legalnotice.link.types">copyright</xsl:param>
```

will generate the following in each HTML HEAD element:
```
<link rel="copyright" href="ln-id234232.html" title="Legal Notice">
```

If you have more than one key word separated by spaces in the parameter, then a similar link will be generated for each key word. If you have more than one legalnotice element in your document, only the first one is referenced by a link.

Separate revhistory

A revision history as recorded in a revhistory element often contains information that might be useful to a reader, but you may not want it presented on the title page where it can take up a lot of space.

You can still include your revhistory but put it in a separate HTML chunk, with a link to it from the title page. You can do that by simply setting the generate.revhistory.link parameter to 1 instead of the default zero. This works for both the chunking and nonchunking HTML stylesheets.

See Chapter 29, *Revision control* (page 461) for more information about the revhistory element.

Return to top

A formatting feature that is commonly used in longer HTML output is a link at each section title that enables the reader to return to the top of the page. If you are using section elements, then the following customization will do it. Versions are provided for both chunked and non-chunked HTML. Put the appropriate version in your customization stylesheet.

Use this version for section in chunked output:
```
<xsl:template name="section.titlepage.before.recto">
  <xsl:variable name="level">
    <xsl:call-template name="section.level"/>
  </xsl:variable>
  <xsl:variable name="chunkfn">
    <xsl:apply-templates mode="chunk-filename" select="."/>
  </xsl:variable>

  <xsl:if test="$level &gt; $chunk.section.depth">
    <p class="returntotop">
      <a href="{$chunkfn}">
        <xsl:text>Return to top</xsl:text>
      </a>
    </p>
  </xsl:if>
</xsl:template>
```

Use this version for section in non-chunked output:
```
<xsl:template name="section.titlepage.before.recto">
  <xsl:variable name="top-anchor">
    <xsl:call-template name="object.id">
      <xsl:with-param name="object" select="/*[1]"/>
    </xsl:call-template>
  </xsl:variable>

  <p class="returntotop">
    <a href="#{$top-anchor}">
      <xsl:text>Return to top</xsl:text>
    </a>
  </p>
</xsl:template>
```

They both make use of the placeholder template named `section.titlepage.before.recto`. This template is called just before the template that generates a section title, so it will put the link to the top just before each section title. You can customize the look with CSS applied to the `class="returntotop"` selector.

If you are using sect1, sect2, etc. instead of `section`, you will need to create customized templates for `sect1.titlepage.before.recto`, and the same for sect2, sect3, etc.

Customized hrefs

You may need to customize the `href` attributes generated in the HTML output beyond what you can do with stylesheet parameters. For example, your hrefs may require a different form for a help system, or for an HTTP server that remaps hrefs.

If you need complete control of generated hrefs, then consider customizing the template named `href.target`. That template has two input parameters: `context` is the element containing the link source, and `target` is the element that is the destination of the link. The output of the template depends on whether or not you are using the chunking stylesheet.

There are two versions of the `href.target` template:

- For non-chunked output, the href.target template in html/html.xsl simply adds the # character in front to the id of the target of the link. If the target element does not have an id attribute, then the stylesheet uses the generate-id() function to create one.

- For chunked output, the href.target template in html/chunk-common.xsl has to do quite a bit more, including the following:

  —It must determine if the target is a chunked element. If so, it must get the chunk filename.

  —If the target is inside a chunked element, it must add the # and id of the target.

  —It must compute the relative path from the file containing the link to the target file. They may be in different directories because the dbhtml dir processing instruction was used. See the section called "dbhtml dir processing instruction" (page 65) for more details.

Customizing the non-chunked version is relatively easy. Customing the chunking version requires more care because it does so much more, and because it uses several other templates. Depending on what kind of changes you need to make to hrefs, you might need to trace through the sequence of templates to see where best to apply your changes.

> **Note:**
>
> When you customize templates from the chunking stylesheet modules, be sure to put them in the customization layer that handles chunking behavior, as described in the section called "Chunking customization" (page 161).

13

Print customizations

Getting your printed output to look the way you want may require more DocBook customization than for HTML output. HTML output can be styled using a separate CSS stylesheet applied to the generated HTML files. For print output, you need to specify style properties in the DocBook XSL stylesheet for FO output. In Chapter 8, *Printed output options* (page 81) you saw how to set parameters on the command line to change some formatting features. Given the number and type of parameters that need to be set, a customization layer makes more sense for print customization.

The basic framework for a print customization is an XSL stylesheet that imports the standard DocBook FO stylesheet and then adds your changes. Here is a simple example that just sets some page parameters.

```
<?xml version="1.0" encoding="UTF-8"?>
<xsl:stylesheet xmlns:xsl="http://www.w3.org/1999/XSL/Transform"
                xmlns:fo="http://www.w3.org/1999/XSL/Format"
                version="1.0">

<xsl:import href="../../docbook-xsl-1.73.1/fo/docbook.xsl"/>

<xsl:param name="page.height.portrait">9in</xsl:param>
<xsl:param name="page.width.portrait">7in</xsl:param>
<xsl:param name="page.margin.inner">0.75in</xsl:param>
<xsl:param name="page.margin.outer">0.50in</xsl:param>
<xsl:param name="page.margin.top">0.17in</xsl:param>
<xsl:param name="page.margin.bottom">0.50in</xsl:param>

</xsl:stylesheet>
```

In addition to letting you set parameters, such a customization layer lets you add properties to attribute sets and customize individual stylesheet templates.

Document level properties

The root.properties attribute-set lets you assign XSL-FO properties that apply to the whole document. For example, you might want to globally turn off hyphenation, or print everything in blue type. By default, the stylesheet puts several important properties in this attribute set. Most of the property values can be changed with stylesheet parameters.

Table 13.1. root.properties attribute-set

FO property	From stylesheet parameter	Default value
`font-family`	`body.font.family`	`serif`
`font-size`	`body.font.size`	`10pt`
`text-align`	`alignment`	`justify`
`line-height`	`line-height`	`normal`
`font-selection-strategy`	No parameter	`character-by-character`

Generally you should use the appropriate parameter to reset any of these properties. But if you want to add new properties, you can do that by putting an attribute-set of the same name in your customization layer. Since attribute-sets of the same name are merged, your new properties will be added to the default properties. The following is an example that sets the font color to blue:

```
<xsl:attribute-set name="root.properties">
  <xsl:attribute name="color">blue</xsl:attribute>
</xsl:attribute-set>
```

When processed, the attributes in this attribute-set are placed in the `fo:root` element in the XSL-FO output:

```
<fo:root xmlns:fo="http://www.w3.org/1999/XSL/Format" font-family="serif"
font-size="10pt" text-align="justify" line-height="normal"
color="blue" font-selection-strategy="character-by-character"
language="en">
```

The resulting PDF file will have all blue type. Keep in mind that only properties that are inheritable can be set this way. For example, the `widows` and `orphans` properties are inheritable and can be changed from their default values of 2. See a good XSL-FO reference to see which properties are inheritable. The `root.properties` attribute-set first appeared in version 1.61 of the stylesheets.

Hyphenation

The DocBook print stylesheet lets you set the overall hyphenation policy with a stylesheet parameter named `hyphenate`, whose value is either `true` or `false`. The print stylesheet uses that parameter to set the XSL-FO property of the same name in each `fo:page-sequence`. From there, it is inherited by all elements contained in the page sequence, unless it is overridden by a descendant element.

The print stylesheet enables hyphenation but does not actually hyphenate words. That job is handled by your XSL-FO processor, so you need to check your processor's documentation for more information about how it handles hyphenation. If you are using FOP and processing languages other than English, then you need to download an additional file named `fop-hyph.jar` from *http://offo.sourceforge.net/hyphenation/index.html*. This file needs to be included in the Java CLASSPATH used for FOP processing. You can just add this file to the FOP distribution's `lib` subdirectory, and then the `fop.bat` and `fop.sh` convenience scripts will use it automatically.

Hyphenation is helpful when lines are short and justification is turned on, because it helps avoid large gaps between words in justified lines. However, you may need to turn off hyphenation if your XSL-FO processor does not have a hyphenation algorithm or dictionary for the language you are processing, or if it does a poor job of hyphenating.

You may want to use hyphenation for the body of your document, but turn it off for the title pages and index, for example. You can override the main hyphenation setting for specific page types by customizing the template named `set.flow.properties` from `fo/pagesetup.xsl`. That template adds attributes to each `fo:flow` element, which is nested inside the `fo:page-sequence`. You can select different hyphenation values for different parts of the document as the following example shows:

```
<xsl:template name="set.flow.properties">
  <xsl:param name="element" select="local-name(.)"/>
  <xsl:param name="master-reference" select="''"/>

  <xsl:choose>
    <xsl:when test="starts-with($master-reference, 'index') or
                    starts-with($master-reference, 'titlepage') or
                    starts-with($master-reference, 'lot') or
                    starts-with($master-reference, 'front')">
      <xsl:attribute name="hyphenate">false</xsl:attribute>
    </xsl:when>
    <xsl:otherwise>
      <xsl:attribute name="hyphenate">
        <xsl:value-of select="$hyphenate"/>
      </xsl:attribute>
    </xsl:otherwise>
  </xsl:choose>
  ...

</xsl:template>
```

This customization turns hyphenation off for titlepages, front matter, TOCs, and indexes. For other page types it uses the value of the global `hyphenate` parameter.

The `hyphenate` property can also be controlled for certain elements using the attribute-set used to format that element. For example, to turn off hyphenation in tables, you could use this attribute-set customization:

```
<xsl:attribute-set name="table.table.properties">
  <xsl:attribute name="hyphenate">false</xsl:attribute>
</xsl:attribute-set>
```

See the section called "Attribute sets" (page 103) for more information on customizing attribute-sets. The stylesheets provide separate support for hyphenation in `programlisting` and other verbatim elements, as described in the section called "Breaking long lines" (page 442). The stylesheets also support special hyphenation in `ulink` URLs, as described in the section called "Breaking long URLs" (page 261).

You can use a short customization to control hyphenation of certain inline elements. The following is an example that turns hyphenation off for **code** elements. It simply wraps the original template body in an `fo:inline`, so the hyphenation property will be inherited by the content. However, not all processors may support putting the hyphenation property on an inline, since normally it goes on a block element.

```
<xsl:template match="code">
  <fo:inline hyphenate="false">
    <xsl:call-template name="inline.monoseq"/>
  </fo:inline>
</xsl:template>
```

The print stylesheet includes three gentext templates that are used to control hyphenation behavior in different languages. See the section called "Generated text" (page 105) for general information on gentext. The gentext templates listed in the following table correspond in name to three XSL-FO properties:

Table 13.2. Hyphenation gentext templates

Gentext template name	English value	Description
`hyphenation-character`	-	The hyphenation character output by the XSL-FO processor when a word is hyphenated.
`hyphenation-push-character-count`	2	The minimum length of the word fragment after a hyphen when a word is hyphenated.
`hyphenation-remain-character-count`	2	The minimum length of the word fragment before a hyphen when a word is hyphenated.

These properties are set using the gentext mechanism rather than a parameter because they may need to be different for different languages. For example, the hyphenation character for Arabic is the Unicode character ‐ rather than dash. Most of the DocBook gentext files use the ordinary dash character rather than the default XSL-FO value of Unicode ‐ because some fonts do not have a glyph for the latter character.

The process of actually hyphenating words is handled entirely by the XSL-FO processor, not the XSL stylesheet. The XSL-FO processor lays out the words in text lines and makes the decisions about how to fit text when hyphenation is turned on. In general, the hyphenation rules used to insert hyphens are language dependent, so you may need to consult the documentation of the XSL-FO processor if words are not breaking where you expect them to.

In some cases, an XSL-FO processor will hyphenate a word where you do not want it to break. There are three special characters that can help you control breaking of individual words.

- You can insert soft hyphen characters at potential hyphenation points in a word. A soft hyphen does not normally print unless the word has to be hyphenated. You can use the Unicode character ­ or the DocBook character entity ­ as in print­able. If your XSL-FO processor supports soft hyphens, it should break at that point if it has to break at all.

- You can prevent an already hyphenated word (such as a person's name or product name) from breaking by replacing the ordinary hyphen with a non-breaking hyphen character ‑.

- If your XSL-FO processor does not support that character, then you can try following the ordinary hyphen with a zero-width no-break space character . That should prevent the word from breaking at that point if your XSL-FO processor supports that character. It may, however, still hyphenate the word in other places.

Most XSL-FO processors let you add specific problem words or additional languages to the hyphenation configuration of the processor. For example, the XEP processor uses TeX hyphenation files, while Antenna House uses XML files, and both support adding specific words as exceptions. The FOP processor has hyphenation patterns in a file named fop-hyph.jar that must be in the Java CLASSPATH for FOP. That jar file can be downloaded from *http://offo.sourceforge.net/hyphenation/index.html*.

Title fonts and sizes

The font families and sizes used for most titles are defined as part of the titlepage setup. See Chapter 11, *Title page customization* (page 141) for the general process of customizing titlepages. The titlepage specs also include other elements such as author and publisher. Customizing titlepages for print output is covered more completely in the section called "Print title pages" (page 182)

Some titles also have attribute-sets that can override the titlepage specs. This makes customization a bit easier since you do not have to regenerate XSL templates, but then you have to be careful to not try to change a title through both methods. Some titles also have their own templates, which can be customized to any degree you need.

Your choice of font names depends on those available in the back end XSL-FO processor that converts your FO file to a print format. The processors usually have some built-in font families, and can be configured to add other fonts. Consult your processor documentation for details. Two font names that can reliably be used with any of the XSL-FO processors are Helvetica and Times Roman.

You can also choose to make a title font bold or italic. You can choose bold by specifying font-weight="bold" in the titlepage spec file. You can specify italic by adding font-style="italic". If you specify both properties, you will get bold-italic.

Book titles

A book title's format is specified by the titlepage spec file. If you copied the original fo/titlepage.templates.xml titlepage spec file to create your customized version, it includes a set of entities declared at the top of the file.

```
<!DOCTYPE t:templates [
<!ENTITY hsize0 "10pt">
<!ENTITY hsize1 "12pt">
<!ENTITY hsize2 "14.4pt">
<!ENTITY hsize3 "17.28pt">
<!ENTITY hsize4 "20.736pt">
<!ENTITY hsize5 "24.8832pt">
<!ENTITY hsize0space "7.5pt"> <!-- 0.75 * hsize0 -->
<!ENTITY hsize1space "9pt"> <!-- 0.75 * hsize1 -->
<!ENTITY hsize2space "10.8pt"> <!-- 0.75 * hsize2 -->
<!ENTITY hsize3space "12.96pt"> <!-- 0.75 * hsize3 -->
<!ENTITY hsize4space "15.552pt"> <!-- 0.75 * hsize4 -->
<!ENTITY hsize5space "18.6624pt"> <!-- 0.75 * hsize5 -->
]>
```

The set of hsize entities are candidates for use in the titlepage templates. The hsize*space entities are used to set space-before (space above) a heading. These entities are used further down in the spec file where the titlepages for individual elements are defined. The entities let you define a set of sizes that can be used by titles more several elements, giving your document a consistent look. Using an entity lets you change all of them at once by just changing the entity value. In your custom titlepage spec file, you can add and use your own entities as needed, or you can enter specific values in any font-size specification. Regardless of how the values are specified, they are converted to the numbers when the spec file is processed into the titlepage template file that becomes part of your customization layer.

Here are the specs for a book title:

```
<t:titlepage element="book" wrapper="fo:block">
    <t:titlepage-content side="recto">
      <title
             named-template="division.title"
             param:node="ancestor-or-self::book[1]"
             text-align="center"
             font-size="&hsize5;"
             space-before="&hsize5space;"
             font-weight="bold"
             font-family="{$title.fontset}"/>
    ...
```

The font-size and space-before specs use entities that were declared at the top of the file. In your customization, you can change the value of the entities, add your own entities, or put your values directly in the spec file, such as `font-size="36pt"`. You can also change or add other properties for the title, and they will be used after you regenerate the titlepage templates from the spec file.

The `font-family` property is set to the value of the `title.fontset` parameter. That is an internal parameter that uses the `title.font.family` parameter that you can specify in your customization layer. That parameter value will be resolved when the generated template is used to process XML files to produce FO output. The actual font family name can be set at runtime on the command line, or in a customization layer. A parameter is used to permit global changes in all titles by simply setting the parameter value. Of course, you do not have to use the parameter in your specification. You can specify individual font names in each spec, or declare some font-family entities as was done for font sizes and use those entity references in your specs. Once you do that, the parameter will not have any effect on those titles. Your XSL-FO processor must be configured for any font you specify, though.

The book's title is finally processed by calling the template named `division.title`. That template is called within the block that has already set the properties according to the spec file. So you could override the spec file properties by customizing that template. If you do so, be sure to copy the original from the `fo/divsion.xsl` stylesheet file to add your customizations, because it performs other functions such as adding the `id` attribute and PDF bookmark.

Chapter titles

Chapter titles can be customized in three ways, listed here from lowest to highest precedence:

* Customize the titlepage spec file.

* Customize the attribute-set named `component.title.properties`.

* Customize the template named `component.title`.

Here is the titlepage specification for chapter title, `recto` side.

```
<t:titlepage element="chapter" wrapper="fo:block">
    <t:titlepage-content side="recto">
      <title
            named-template="component.title"
            param:node="ancestor-or-self::chapter[1]"
            margin-left="{$title.margin.left}"
            font-size="&hsize5;"
            font-weight="bold"
            font-family="{$title.font.family}"/>
      ...
```

This example specifies several FO properties for the `title` element of the chapter. Notice that `font-size="&hsize5;"` references one of the entities declared at the top of the file.

The following is the XSL template generated from the above spec (indented for clarity):

```
<xsl:template match="title" mode="chapter.titlepage.recto.auto.mode">
  <fo:block xmlns:fo="http://www.w3.org/1999/XSL/Format"
            xsl:use-attribute-sets="chapter.titlepage.recto.style"
            margin-left="{$title.margin.left}"
            font-size="24.8832pt"
            font-weight="bold"
            font-family="{$title.font.family}">
    <xsl:call-template name="component.title">
      <xsl:with-param name="node" select="ancestor-or-self::chapter[1]"/>
    </xsl:call-template>
  </fo:block>
</xsl:template>
```

You can see that the properties defined in the titlepage spec file are applied to the outer block, which then calls the template named `component.title`. That template is located in `fo/component.xsl` and can be copied and customized to any degree to format a chapter title. Inside that template is a block that applies the attribute-set named `component.title.properties`. Because the attribute-set is used on an inner block, it will override properties that are also specified in the titlepage spec file.

You can customize the `component.title` template and `component.title.properties` attribute-set. That template and attribute-set are shared by other component titles, including those of appendix, `article`, glossary, `bibliography`, `preface`, `index`, `dedication`, and `colophon`. So any customizations of that template and attribute-set will change the title style for all of those elements. That may be what you want for consistency of design.

If you want to change just the handling of one element's title, then you should create another template by a different name. For example, you might want to customize titles only for chapter and appendix. Here is how do so:

1. Copy the `component.title` named template from `fo/component.xsl` to your customization file and give it a different name, such as `chapappendix.title`.

2. Customize how the label and number are formatted in your new template. The following example formats the label and title on separate lines with different attribute-sets:

    ```
    <xsl:template name="chapappendix.title">
      <xsl:param name="node" select="."/>

      <fo:block xsl:use-attribute-sets="chap.label.properties">
        <xsl:call-template name="gentext">
          <xsl:with-param name="key">
            <xsl:choose>
              <xsl:when test="$node/self::chapter">chapter</xsl:when>
              <xsl:when test="$node/self::appendix">appendix</xsl:when>
            </xsl:choose>
          </xsl:with-param>
        </xsl:call-template>
        <xsl:text> </xsl:text>
        <xsl:apply-templates select="$node" mode="label.markup"/>
      </fo:block>
      <fo:block xsl:use-attribute-sets="chap.title.properties">
        <xsl:apply-templates select="$node" mode="title.markup"/>
      </fo:block>
    </xsl:template>
    ```

    The `gentext` templates generate the appropriate Chapter or Appendix text (in the right language). The `mode="label.markup"` generates just the label number, and the `mode="title.markup"` generates the title.

3. Add your new template to the titlepage spec file in place of `component.title` where appropriate. For example:

```
<t:titlepage t:element="chapter" t:wrapper="fo:block"
             font-family="{$title.fontset}">
  <t:titlepage-content t:side="recto" margin-left="{$title.margin.left}">
    <title t:named-template="chappendix.title"
           param:node="ancestor-or-self::chapter[1]"/>
...
```

Make a similar change for the appendix title in the spec file since it is to share the same customized template.

4. Create your own attribute-sets named `chap.label.properties` and `chap.title.properties` to apply formatting attributes.

Other component titles

The titles of all of the following component elements are processed like chapter titles:

```
appendix            preface
article             index
glossary            dedication
bibliography        colophon
```

By default, they all share the use of the `component.title` template and the `component.title.properties` attribute-set. They can have their own specs in the titlepage spec file, but such specs can be overriden by the template and attribute-set.

You can customize the title of any of these components in a manner similar to the way chapter titles are customized. See the section called "Chapter titles" (page 174) for examples.

Section titles

Section titles can be customized in three ways, listed from lowest to highest precedence:

- Customize properties in the `section.title.properties` attribute-set, which apply to titles in all section levels.

- Customize properties in one of the `section.levelX.title.properties` attribute-sets, where X is the section level (1 to 6) that the properties are applied to.

- Customize the template named `section.heading`.

You may notice that the titlepage spec file is *not* included in this list. Although some section title specs are in the titlepage spec file, those specifications are overridden by these attribute-sets. In the case of section titles, attribute-sets are used because there is no way to specify the multiple font sizes for the `section` element in the titlepage spec syntax, since `section` can nest to form different section levels.

The formatting properties for section titles are primarily controlled by the attribute-sets, which are defined in the `fo/param.xsl` stylesheet file, and can be customized in your customization layer.

The style properties for a given section title level are controlled by two attribute sets. The first is `section.title.properties` which defines properties for all levels of section titles. That is where you put the common properties that give your section titles a consistent look, such as `font-family`.

There is another attribute-set for each section level, such as `section.title.level2.properties`, which adds properties only for level 2 sections. A level 2 section uses either the `sect2` element, or a `section` element nested inside another `section` element. These attribute-sets are where you put properties specific to each section level, such as `font-size`. These properties can also override any of the same name in `section.title.properties`.

The following example shows the default `section.title.properties` attribute set from the `fo/param.xsl` stylesheet file:

```
<xsl:attribute-set name="section.title.properties">
  <xsl:attribute name="font-family">
    <xsl:value-of select="$title.font.family"/>
  </xsl:attribute>
  <xsl:attribute name="font-weight">bold</xsl:attribute>
  <!-- font size is calculated dynamically by section.heading template -->
  <xsl:attribute name="keep-with-next.within-column">always</xsl:attribute>
  <xsl:attribute name="text-align">left</xsl:attribute>
  <xsl:attribute name="space-before.minimum">0.8em</xsl:attribute>
  <xsl:attribute name="space-before.optimum">1.0em</xsl:attribute>
  <xsl:attribute name="space-before.maximum">1.2em</xsl:attribute>
</xsl:attribute-set>
```

It defines the font family using a parameter value, sets all headings to bold, and adds a `keep-with-next` property so there is no page break right after the title. This example also makes the titles left-aligned, so that if you have line justification turned on for your document you do not get large gaps when section titles are justified. Then it assigns several vertical spacing values, using the em unit so they scale relative to each title's font size.

Here is the default `section.title.level2.properties` attribute-set:

```
<xsl:attribute-set name="section.title.level2.properties">
  <xsl:attribute name="font-size">
    <xsl:value-of select="$body.font.master * 1.728"/>
    <xsl:text>pt</xsl:text>
  </xsl:attribute>
</xsl:attribute-set>
```

This attribute set has only the font size for this section level.

Changing section title sizes

As you can see from the above examples, one attribute-set defines all the shared properties for section titles. Then there are individual attribute-sets for each section level for properties specific to each level. Since font size is usually specific to each level, you need to customize the attribute-sets named like `section.title.level1.properties`. Here are two examples:

```
<xsl:attribute-set name="section.title.level1.properties">
  <xsl:attribute name="font-size">
    <xsl:value-of select="$body.font.master * 1.8"/>
    <xsl:text>pt</xsl:text>
  </xsl:attribute>
</xsl:attribute-set>

<xsl:attribute-set name="section.title.level2.properties">
  <xsl:attribute name="font-size">16pt</xsl:attribute>
</xsl:attribute-set>
```

The first example alters the calculation for computing the size of the level 1 headings relative to the body font size. The second example just sets a hard-coded font-size that does not change with the body size. You can use either method in your customization.

Generally the `line-height` property will adjust appropriately to the new font size to provide adequate vertical spacing of text lines. But you can also add your own `line-height` property in the attribute-set.

Changing section title styles

During processing, the stylesheet first applies the common attributes and then the level-specific attributes. So if you wanted your level 1 section titles to be italic instead of bold, and blue instead of black, you could add this to your customization layer:

```
<xsl:attribute-set name="section.title.level1.properties">
  <xsl:attribute name="font-weight">normal</xsl:attribute>
  <xsl:attribute name="font-style">italic</xsl:attribute>
  <xsl:attribute name="color">blue</xsl:attribute>
</xsl:attribute-set>
```

Since attribute-sets of the same name are merged, you do not need to repeat the font size value. In addition to setting the font-style to italic, you also need to set the font-weight to normal or you will get bold-italic because the bold font-weight will be inherited. This attribute-set does not affect the font-style or weight of the other section levels.

These attribute-sets let you add or modify many other style properties for section headings, such as text alignment, line height, color, background, or borders. See a good XSL-FO reference for full details.

Section rule lines

If your page design calls for drawing rule lines above or below section titles at some levels, you can accomplish that with the section title attribute-sets. That is because the attribute-set is applied to the `fo:block` containing the title, and such blocks can take border properties that you specify.

A horizontal rule line can be drawn using the `border-top` property to draw a line above, or the `border-bottom` property to draw a line below. The line will extend the length of the block. That is usually from where the title starts to the right margin. You may also want to use a padding property to add some space between the rule and the title text.

The following example draws solid rule lines above and below the level 1 section titles:

```
<xsl:attribute-set name="section.title.level1.properties">
  <xsl:attribute name="border-top">0.5pt solid black</xsl:attribute>
  <xsl:attribute name="border-bottom">0.5pt solid black</xsl:attribute>
  <xsl:attribute name="padding-top">6pt</xsl:attribute>
  <xsl:attribute name="padding-bottom">3pt</xsl:attribute>
</xsl:attribute-set>
```

If you want to put your titles inside a box, then just use the `border` property, which will draw lines on all sides of the block.

Run-in section titles

Run-in titles. A *run-in title* is one that appears as the first part of a paragraph, like this paragraph. A `formalpara` element is formatted like this in DocBook. You might want to use this for section titles below a certain level, such as for `sect3`.

This effect can be accomplished for section titles using a customization. You have to put the title and first paragraph inside a single `fo:block` to prevent a line break after the title. It is a bit more complicated than for `formalpara`, because a section can start with many elements that are not `para`. For sections that do not start with a `para`, a run-in title should be avoided, and instead the title should be stacked above the first element in the section.

```
<xsl:template name="sect3.titlepage">   ❶
  <fo:block xsl:use-attribute-sets="normal.para.spacing">   ❷
    <xsl:apply-templates select="title" mode="inline.title"/>   ❸
    <xsl:if test="para[preceding-sibling::*[1][self::title]]">   ❹
      <xsl:text>: </xsl:text>   ❺
      <xsl:apply-templates select="para[preceding-sibling::*[1][self::title]]"   ❻
                           mode="inline.para"/>
    </xsl:if>
  </fo:block>
</xsl:template>

<xsl:template match="sect3/title" mode="inline.title">   ❼
  <fo:inline xsl:use-attribute-sets="inline.sect3.title.properties">
    <xsl:apply-templates/>
  </fo:inline>
</xsl:template>

<xsl:attribute-set name="inline.sect3.title.properties">   ❽
  <xsl:attribute name="font-weight">bold</xsl:attribute>
</xsl:attribute-set>

<xsl:template match="sect3/para[preceding-sibling::*[1][self::title]]"   ❾
             mode="inline.para">
  <xsl:apply-templates/>
</xsl:template>

<xsl:template match="sect3/para[preceding-sibling::*[1][self::title]]">   ❿
</xsl:template>
```

❶ Replace the original template named sect3.titlepage with a customization. If you are using nested section instead of sect3, you will instead need to copy the original section.titlepage template from fo/titlepage.templates.xsl, test for the section level, and use an xsl:choose to act differently based on the section level.

❷ Start a block to contain the run-in title and paragraph, and use this standard attribute-set or create a custom one.

❸ Select and process the section title in a new mode that does not generate its own block.

❹ Test that a para immediately follows the title. This test looks for a para child element whose first preceding sibling element is a title. If the first element after the title is not a para, then this test will fail and the block will only contain the title. This test as written will not work if you put the title inside an info element.

❺ Add a colon and space to separate the title from the paragraph text.

❻ Select and process the para after the title in a new mode that prevents it from starting its own fo:block, which would break the line.

❼ Process the title in its new mode as an fo:inline that applies the font properties.

❽ Define whatever inline formatting properties you want for the title.

❾ Process the para that follows the title by processing all of its children, which prevents it from forming its own fo:block as a normal para does.

❿ Turn off normal mode processing of this para so its content does not repeat.

Section page breaks

You can use attribute-sets to generate page breaks on a given section level. These are attribute-sets that apply to the whole section, not just the title. For example, if you wanted to start each new section level 1 on a new page, you could add this to your customization layer:

```
<xsl:attribute-set name="section.level1.properties">
  <xsl:attribute name="break-before">page</xsl:attribute>
</xsl:attribute-set>
```

When the level 1 section (either a `sect1` or equivalent `section`) is processed into an `fo:block`, this attribute value will force the block to a new page.

If you want your DocBook `refentry` elements to each start on a new page, that will be done automatically by the print stylesheet. The breaking behavior is controlled by a stylesheet parameter named `refentry.pagebreak`, whose default value is 1. If you do not want your `refentry` elements to force a page break, then set this parameter to zero.

Simplesects

A `simplesect` element is like a `section` element, but it cannot contain any other sections. For that reason, they always appear at the end of their container element, after any other sections.

By default, simplesects do not appear in the table of contents because they are usually not considered part of the document's structural hierarchy. But if you set the stylesheet parameter named `simplesect.in.toc` to a nonzero value, then all simplesects will be added to the table of contents.

Simplesect titles are normally formatted like the titles of `section` elements, whose format depends on the level of section nesting. Their formatting is controlled by the same mechanisms, as described in the section called "Section titles" (page 176). If you want to differentiate `simplesect` titles, you can customize the template named `simplesect.titlepage`. That template normally would handle all aspects of the elements on a `simplesect` title page, but in most cases only the title is output. If you do create your own template of that name, you may need to add a `priority` attribute with a value greater than zero. That's because you need to override the template of the same name in `titlepage.templates.xsl`, which may be at the same import precedence as your new template.

Bridgeheads

A `bridgehead` element is considered a "free-floating heading". Unlike section titles, bridgeheads are not part of the regular section hierarchy. They can be placed between block elements in the normal text flow, and they are not connected to their surrounding text. They can be used to indicate a change of subject in a text flow, or as simply a label for the text the follows.

By default, bridgeheads do not appear in the table of contents because they are usually not considered part of the document's structural hierarchy. But if you set the stylesheet parameter named `bridgehead.in.toc` to a nonzero value, then all bridgeheads will be added to the table of contents.

Bridgeheads are normally formatted like section titles. Since they are treated as being contained within a section, a bridgehead's format duplicates that of a section title one below the current section level. That is, if a bridgehead appears within a `sect2` element (or an equivalent level `section` element), then the bridgehead formats like a `sect3` title.

You can change the style of an individual bridgehead to match that of a different section level by adding a `renderas` attribute with a value of `sect1`, `sect2`, etc. The following example shows how it done in the document file:

```
<sect2>
  <title>Level 2 section<title>
  <para>Some interesting text.</para>
  <bridgehead renderas="sect4">New features</bridgehead>
  ...
</sect2>
```

In this example, the bridgehead element appears inside a sect2, and would normally be formatted like a sect3. But the renderas="sect4" attribute forces the style to match that of a sect4 element instead.

If you want to control bridgehead formatting beyond just the renderas attribute, then you will have to customize the bridgehead template. There are no bridgehead specifications in the titlepage.templates.xml spec file described in the section called "Title page spec file" (page 184), because bridgeheads are not given real title pages. The template to copy to your customization layer is in fo/sections.xsl and starts with <xsl:template match="bridgehead">. Most of that template is used to determine the proper section level to imitate, and then it calls the template named section.heading. If you want to divorce bridgeheads completely from section titles, then do not call the section.heading template. Instead, call your own template, add your own attribute-set, or just add the formatting properties you want directly in the template.

Figure, table, and other titles

The following elements all share the designation of *formal* objects in DocBook because they include a title element and are assigned a number label:

figure
table
example
equation
procedure   *if the formal.procedures parameter is set to 1*

When processed, these elements have a labeled title that is generated from gentext templates for each locale. To customize the generated title text, see the section called "Customizing generated text" (page 106).

You can choose to place formal titles above or below their element's content. See the section called "Formal title placement" (page 136) for a description of how to do that.

Formal title properties

You can adjust the font family, size, weight, and style, and the title vertical spacing using the formal.title.properties attribute set. The default list of attributes from fo/param.xsl looks like the following:

```
<xsl:attribute-set name="formal.title.properties"
                   use-attribute-sets="normal.para.spacing">
  <xsl:attribute name="font-weight">bold</xsl:attribute>
  <xsl:attribute name="font-size">12pt</xsl:attribute>
  <xsl:attribute name="hyphenate">false</xsl:attribute>
  <xsl:attribute name="space-after.minimum">0.4em</xsl:attribute>
  <xsl:attribute name="space-after.optimum">0.6em</xsl:attribute>
  <xsl:attribute name="space-after.maximum">0.8em</xsl:attribute>
</xsl:attribute-set>
```

By default the font-family attribute is not included, which means the formal title font is inherited from the body font. You could change the formal titles to use, for example, 10pt Helvetica by adding the following to your customization layer:

```
<xsl:attribute-set name="formal.title.properties">
  <xsl:attribute name="font-size">10pt</xsl:attribute>
  <xsl:attribute name="font-family">Helvetica</xsl:attribute>
</xsl:attribute-set>
```

Your new attributes will be merged with those in the default attribute-set.

All of the formally titled objects use the same properties because they all share this attribute-set. If you wanted different title properties for different formal elements, you would have to create a separate attribute-set in your customization and add some xsl:choose logic to a customized formal.object.heading template (the original is in fo/formal.xsl). See the section called "Formal title customization" (page 137) for an example.

If you just want to change a single property for one formal element, you can add an xsl:choose logic to its attribute definition. For example, if you only want table titles to use Helvetica, you could do it this way:

```
<xsl:attribute-set name="formal.title.properties">
  <xsl:attribute name="font-family">
    <xsl:choose>
      <xsl:when test="self::table">Helvetica</xsl:when>
      <xsl:otherwise>inherit</xsl:otherwise>
    </xsl:choose>
  </xsl:attribute>
</xsl:attribute-set>
```

But sure to include the xsl:otherwise clause so you do not end up with an empty property in your XSL-FO output. In this case, the other formal elements will inherit the body font family.

Print title pages

The customization of titles was covered in the previous sections. But title pages include more than just titles. They can include information about authors, publishers, copyright, legal notice, and even a revision history. Title pages are one part of printed output that often demands customization, for example, to match a corporate style.

The overall process for customizing title page specifications is covered in Chapter 11, *Title page customization* (page 141). For print output, some additional options are available. There are four approaches to customizing the title pages produced by DocBook XSL. They are listed here from lowest to highest precedence:

- Customize existing attribute-sets that apply to whole title pages of a given element type (book, chapter, etc.).

- Use a title page spec file to generate a customized title page stylesheet file. Use this method if you want to add or remove elements to the title page and do not need fine control over page layout. You can also add formatting properties or specify a custom template for processing an element. The general process is described in Chapter 11, *Title page customization* (page 141).

- Customize attribute-sets that are available for some elements, such as titles in chapter and sections. These attribute-sets are described in the section called "Title fonts and sizes" (page 172).

- Add a new template for a particular element in the proper title page mode. Use this to customize how one element is processed on a title page, assuming it is included on the title page.

Which method you use depends on what you are trying to accomplish with your customization. The following table should help guide you.

Table 13.3. Title page customization guide

To accomplish this:	You need to do this:
Change page margins for title pages only.	Create a custom page-master for title pages. See the section called "Custom page design" (page 195).
Set common properties on title pages.	Customize parameters and attribute-set values. See the section called "Title page attribute-sets" (page 183).
Add or rearrange elements to a title page.	Customize titlepage spec file and generate custom stylesheet module. See the section called "Title page spec file" (page 184).
Customize an element on a title page	Add a new element template. See the section called "Title page element templates" (page 188).
Add sub elements to a title page.	Customize an element template. See the section called "Title page element templates" (page 188).
Customize layout of title page.	Create your own titlepage templates. See the section called "Custom title page layout" (page 189).

Title page processing in DocBook XSL involves a large number of templates and many opportunities for intervention for customization purposes. At some point you may want to better understand the inner workings. See the section called "Template sequence for book title pages" (page 191) for a description of the sequence of templates executed for a book's title pages. Title pages for other elements are handled in a similar manner.

Title page attribute-sets

The stylesheets are set up to use attribute-sets to specify many characteristics of title pages. To the degree that properties are parameterized with attribute-sets, you can customize them without having to modify any XSL templates. Attribute-sets of the same name are merged, so you do not have to repeat all properties in your customization. See the section called "Attribute sets" (page 103) for general information on how attribute-sets work.

The main feature for controlling the overall title page style is a collection of attribute-sets. These are defined and used for each kind of title page, as for example the `book.titlepage.recto.style` attribute set, which would be used for the front (recto) side of book title pages. Dozens of these attribute sets are defined in `fo/titlepage.xsl` and can be overridden in your customization layer. The following example shows the default properties for a book's front title page:

Example 13.1. Title page attribute set (default)

```
<xsl:attribute-set name="book.titlepage.recto.style">
  <xsl:attribute name="font-family">
    <xsl:value-of select="$title.font.family"/>
  </xsl:attribute>
  <xsl:attribute name="font-weight">bold</xsl:attribute>
  <xsl:attribute name="font-size">12pt</xsl:attribute>
  <xsl:attribute name="text-align">center</xsl:attribute>
</xsl:attribute-set>
```

These attributes form the base properties for the title page. Unless otherwise specified by one of the other customization methods, each element that appears on the title page will have these properties. The following is an example.

Example 13.2. Customized title page attribute set

```
<xsl:attribute-set name="book.titlepage.recto.style">
  <xsl:attribute name="font-family">Garamond</xsl:attribute>
  <xsl:attribute name="text-align">right</xsl:attribute>
  <xsl:attribute name="color">#E0E0E0</xsl:attribute>
</xsl:attribute-set>
```

This customized version overrides the `font-family` and `text-align` values from the original attribute-set in `fo/titlepage.xsl`, and adds a `color` attribute. The `font-weight` and `font-size` properties remain as originally defined.

You can override these base properties for specific elements on the title page by customizing the title page spec file, or by adding title page element templates, as described in the next sections.

Title page spec file

The title page spec file provides a means to add FO properties to each element you list for the title page sides (recto and verso). Those properties might include font family and size, or color, spacing, or alignment.

The general process for customizing title pages is described in Chapter 11, *Title page customization* (page 141), summarized in these steps:

1. Create a customized title page specification file.

2. Process the spec file with the special stylesheet `template/titlepage.xsl` that generates a title page stylesheet file.

3. Include the generated title page stylesheet file in your customization layer.

In HTML, title pages are a single virtual page without specific boundaries. In print, title pages have recto and verso pages, or front side and back side of double-sided output. So some thought must be given to which information appears on which printed page. You can also apply specific style properties to any elements on the title pages. The following is the book element's default title page spec, from `fo/titlepage.templates.xml`.

Example 13.3. Print title page spec file

```
<t:titlepage t:element="book" t:wrapper="fo:block">  ❶
    <t:titlepage-content t:side="recto">  ❷
      <title  ❸
            t:named-template="division.title"  ❹
            param:node="ancestor-or-self::book[1]"  ❺
            text-align="center"  ❻
            font-size="&hsize5;"  ❼
            space-before="&hsize5space;"
            font-weight="bold"
            font-family="{$title.font.family}"/>
      <subtitle
            text-align="center"
            font-size="&hsize4;"
            space-before="&hsize4space;"
            font-family="{$title.font.family}"/>
      <corpauthor
            font-size="&hsize3;"
            keep-with-next="always"
            space-before="2in"/>
      <authorgroup space-before="2in"/>
      <author font-size="&hsize3;"
              space-before="&hsize2space;"
              keep-with-next="always"/>
    </t:titlepage-content>
```

❶ Start of title page specs for book element. Note that all elements and attributes used to control the templates use the `t:` name space, such as `t:titlepage` and `t:element`. The `t:wrapper` attribute indicates that the whole title page is to be wrapped in an `fo:block` element.

❷ Start the content for the recto (front) side of the title page.

❸ First element on page should be the book `title`. DocBook elements do *not* use the `t:` namespace.

❹ Use the named template `division.title` to process the title within the wrapper `fo:block`.

❺ Call the named template with a parameter named `node` and value `ancestor-or-self::book[1]`. In the `division.title` template, the `node` parameter is expected to contain the node of the element containing the title. This is an XPath expression that selects the book element itself.

❻ Add a `text-align` property to the block containing the title. Attributes not in a namespace are copied through to the wrapper element.

❼ Add a `font-size` property to the block containing the title. This uses as its value an entity reference to one of the entities declared in the spec file itself. Following this are several other properties for title, and other elements in the order in which they should appear on the title page.

This default title page spec results in the generated title page stylesheet template that looks like the following:

Example 13.4. Generated template for title on book title page

```
<xsl:template match="title" mode="book.titlepage.recto.auto.mode">
  <fo:block xmlns:fo="http://www.w3.org/1999/XSL/Format"
            xsl:use-attribute-sets="book.titlepage.recto.style"
            text-align="center"
            font-size="24.8832pt"
            space-before="18.6624pt"
            font-weight="bold"
            font-family="{$title.font.family}">
    <xsl:call-template name="division.title">
      <xsl:with-param name="node" select="ancestor-or-self::book[1]"/>
    </xsl:call-template>
  </fo:block>
</xsl:template>
```

You can see that most of the property attributes in the fo:block element come from the spec file. But an additional set comes from xsl:use-attribute-sets="book.titlepage.recto.style", which is automatically inserted by the template-generating stylesheet. This attribute-set is defined in fo/titlepage.xsl to declare default characteristics for all elements on this title page. See Example 13.1, "Title page attribute set (default)" (page 183) for a listing of the attributes.

Notice that the attribute-set includes attributes such as font-size that are also specified in the spec file (and hence the book.titlepage.recto.auto.mode template). It is a feature of attribute sets that an explicit instance of an attribute will override the same attribute from the attribute-set. That allows the attribute-set to supply a default set of values that apply to all elements on the title page, yet gives you the freedom to specify values for particular elements. That lets you specify most of the attributes once, and then add only the changes for specific elements.

The resulting FO output includes properties from the attribute set (default or customized), from explicit properties on each element as listed in the spec file, and from the template used to format the title, which is division.title in this case. Any parameter or entity variables are resolved as well. The following shows the resulting FO output:

Example 13.5. FO output for title on book title page

```
<fo:block font-family="sans-serif"
          color="#E0E0E0"
          font-weight="bold"
          font-size="24.8832pt"
          text-align="center"
          space-before="18.6624pt">
  <fo:block keep-with-next.within-column="always"
            hyphenate="false">
    Using the DocBook XSL Stylesheets
  </fo:block>
</fo:block>
```

In this case, all of the properties in the attribute set except color were explicitly overridden by the spec file. The inner fo:block with its keep and hyphenate properties come from the division.title template.

Adding title page elements

You can add elements to your title pages by expanding the list of elements declared in the title page spec file. With print output you generally have two pages to work with, recto and verso. You need to decide which page to put new elements on, and in what order. Then you need to decide what properties you want to apply to each element. For example, if you want to add revhistory to a book's verso title page, then add a line to the spec file as follows:

Example 13.6. Adding an element to a title page

```
<t:titlepage-content t:side="verso">
    <title
            t:named-template="book.verso.title"
            font-size="&hsize2;"
            font-weight="bold"
            font-family="{$title.font.family}"/>
    <corpauthor/>
    <authorgroup t:named-template="verso.authorgroup"/>
    <author/>
    <othercredit/>
    <pubdate space-before="1em"/>
    <revhistory/>          Add this line
    <copyright/>
    <abstract/>
    <legalnotice font-size="8pt"/>
</t:titlepage-content>
```

When this spec file is processed into the titlepage templates module, it adds a template in the right mode for outputting the revision text at that point on the title page.

Styling title page elements

The spec file can include any FO properties you want to apply to a given element on a given title page. For example, if the added revhistory element in the preceding example needs some styling:

```
<revhistory
    font-weight="normal"
    font-style="italic"
    color="green"/>
```

The revhistory element has revision children, each of which has child elements. In this example, all those descendant elements would have those properties. For structured elements such as this, you might want to supply your own custom XSL template for formatting all the descendants. That can simplify the spec file considerably. For example:

```
<revhistory
    t:named-template="book.verso.revhistory"/>
```

You could write the book.verso.revhistory XSL template to create a fo:table to format all of its ancestors in an orderly fashion. The template could also apply properties to specific elements as needed.

Adding title page graphics

Many companies want to put a logo graphic on each title page. This is easily done with the spec file:

```
<t:titlepage-content t:side="recto">
    <mediaobject/>
    <title
            t:named-template="book.verso.title"
            font-size="&hsize2;"
            font-weight="bold"
            font-family="{$title.font.family}"/>
    <corpauthor/>
    ...
</t:titlepage-content>
```

The `<mediaobject/>` entry in the spec file will generate a template on `bookinfo/mediaobject` in your custom titlepage XSL module. You then just need to put a `mediaobject` element in your `bookinfo` element to specify the actual graphic file, and that template will process it onto the titlepage, located above the title in this case.

Title page element templates

The title page machinery provides a means to insert XSL templates to customize how individual elements are handled.

You can do this in two ways. You can list in the spec file a `named-template` attribute on an element, as was done for the `title` element in Example 13.3, "Print title page spec file" (page 185). Then you add the named template to your customization layer. Or if you do not want to modify the titlepage spec file and generate a new titlepage stylesheet module, then you can use the built-in mechanism. If the template has a match on the element name and uses the proper mode name, it will be automatically applied by the stylesheets.

You can use the built-in mechanism if all of the following are true:

- An element is already included in the title page spec file.

- The spec file does not specify a `named-template` attribute for that element.

- You do not want to bother generating your own custom title page stylesheet module.

An example best illustrates how to declare such a template in your customization layer:

Example 13.7. Custom title page element template

```
<xsl:template match="corpauthor" mode="book.titlepage.recto.mode">
  <fo:external-graphic>
    <xsl:attribute name="src" select="$my.corporate.logo"/>
  </fo:external-graphic>
  <fo:inline color="blue">
    <xsl:apply-templates mode="titlepage.mode"/>
  </fo:inline>
</xsl:template>
```

This template is automatically applied to any `corpauthor` elements that appear on the recto title page of a book (if it is so specified in the title page spec file). If you want to apply it on a verso title page of a `set` element, then you would change the mode to `mode="set.titlepage.verso.mode"` instead.

The action of this example template is to insert a corporate logo graphic (defined with a parameter) before the corporate author name, and then wrap that name in a `fo:inline` element to apply a blue color.

In this example, any children of `corpauthor` are then processed using templates with `mode="titlepage.mode"`. These are defined in the stylesheet module `fo/titlepage.xsl`. This is the fallback mode when a specific titlepage mode is not defined for an element. If you wanted to apply the `mode="titlepage.mode"` templates to the `corpauthor` element itself, then you need to add a `select` attribute:

```
<xsl:apply-templates  select="."  mode="titlepage.mode"/>
```

The template processing takes place within the `fo:block` that holds the properties from the spec file. That means you do not have to specify those properties in your custom template. But it also means those property values will be inherited by any output generated by your template. Also, before using `mode="titlepage.mode"` this way, you should check in `fo/titlepage.xsl` for the template that uses this mode for your customized element to make sure it is compatible. For example, some of them output their own fo:block element, which would not be permitted inside an fo:inline as in this example.

Custom title page layout

If you need to customize the layout of a title page, then you will find that difficult to do using the title page spec file and generated stylesheet module. The spec file is best at adding, sequencing, and formatting elements that are included on a title page, but not any layout relationships they have have with each other.

You can completely control the layout of a title page by using a fo:table element to locate content on the page in table cells. This is similar to the process used to lay out HTML pages. Within a given table cell you apply templates to the elements you want to appear in that cell. This is usually done in a mode such as titlepage.mode to ensure proper handling in the title page context.

Your custom page layout is activated by giving it the appropriate template name to override the default title page processing. For example, if your customization layer includes a template named book.titlepage.recto, then it will be used instead of the template generated from the title page spec file. The following example uses a layout table to position content on the page:

Example 13.8. Table-based title page layout

```
<xsl:template name="book.titlepage.recto">
  <fo:block>
    <fo:table inline-progression-dimension="100%" table-layout="fixed">
      <fo:table-column column-width="50%"/>
      <fo:table-column column-width="50%"/>
      <fo:table-body>
        <fo:table-row >
          <fo:table-cell number-columns-spanned="2">
            <fo:block text-align="center">
              <xsl:choose>
                <xsl:when test="bookinfo/title">
                  <xsl:apply-templates
                        mode="book.titlepage.recto.auto.mode"
                        select="bookinfo/title"/>
                </xsl:when>
                <xsl:when test="title">
                  <xsl:apply-templates
                        mode="book.titlepage.recto.auto.mode"
                        select="title"/>
                </xsl:when>
              </xsl:choose>
            </fo:block>
          </fo:table-cell>
        </fo:table-row>
        <fo:table-row>
          <fo:table-cell>
            <fo:block>
              <xsl:apply-templates
                    mode="book.titlepage.recto.mode"
                    select="bookinfo/corpauthor"/>
            </fo:block>
          </fo:table-cell>
          <fo:table-cell>
            <fo:block>
              <xsl:apply-templates
                    mode="book.titlepage.recto.mode"
                    select="bookinfo/edition"/>
            </fo:block>
          </fo:table-cell>
        </fo:table-row >
      </fo:table-body>
    </fo:table>
  </fo:block>
</xsl:template>
```

This rather trivial example outputs the book title, the corpauthor, and the edition. The layout is a two-column table. The title spans both columns and is centered in them. In the second row, the corpauthor appears in the left table cell and the edition in the right table cell. A real example would include more properties on the fo:table-cell elements to control how each element is placed in its cell.

Template sequence for book title pages

This section summarizes the sequence of templates used to generate title pages for a book. A similar sequence is used for other elements that might have title pages, including article, chapter, reference, etc. Use this as a guide for figuring out where to intervene for customization.

1. Template with `match="book"` in `fo/division.xsl` starts the book processing.

2. That template calls the named template `book.titlepage` in `fo/titlepage.templates.xsl` (the stylesheet module generated from `titlepage.templates.xml`). It passes it the book element to process.

3. That template calls these named templates on the book element in sequence:

   ```
   book.titlepage.before.recto (null)
   book.titlepage.recto
   book.titlepage.before.verso
   book.titlepage.verso
   book.titlepage.separator
   ```

   By default, the first template does nothing, but could be customized to do something. The `book.titlepage.separator` and `book.titlepage.before.verso` templates just output a page break. That leaves the two main templates to process the recto and verso sides of the title page.

4. The `book.titlepage.recto` template is in `fo/titlepage.templates.xsl` (the generated file). It processes the title page elements in the order in which they appear in the spec file (`fo/titlepage.templates.xml`).

5. It does an `apply-templates mode="book.titlepage.recto.auto.mode"` on the first element in the list, which is `title`. Since the title could reside inside or outside the `bookinfo` container, it first tries to select `bookinfo/title`. If that fails, then it tries `title`.

6. There is a template with `match="title"` `mode="book.titlepage.recto.auto.mode"` in the generated file `fo/titlepage.templates.xsl`. It does the following:

   a. It starts an `fo:block`.

   b. It adds a `use-attribute-set name="book.titlepage.recto.style"`. This provides the properties that are common to all elements on that page.

   c. It adds the property attributes assigned to book title (recto) from the spec file.

   d. It calls the template named `division.title` on the title element to output the title text. It calls that template because the spec file assigned it to the title element on book recto title pages. That template resides in `fo/division.xsl`, and it does the following:

      i. If `passivetex.extensions` is turned on, it outputs a `fotex:bookmark` element, which is used to generate PDF bookmarks.

      ii. It starts a nested `fo:block` with a couple more properties.

      iii. Then it outputs the title text.

      iv. Then it closes the inner `fo:block`.

   e. It closes the outer `fo:block` element to complete the title element.

7. Then the `book.titlepage.recto` template processes the next element in the sequence, which is `subtitle`. Its processing is similar, but not the same. It does an `apply-templates mode="book.titlepage.recto.auto.mode"` on the `subtitle` element.

8. There is a template with `match="subtitle" mode="book.titlepage.recto.auto.mode"` in the generated file `fo/titlepage.templates.xsl`. It does the following:

   a. It starts an `fo:block`.

   b. It adds the property attributes assigned to book subtitle (recto) from the spec file.

   c. It adds a `use-attribute-set name="book.titlepage.recto.style"`. This the properties that are common to all elements on that page.

   d. Since subtitle does not have a `call-template` attribute in the spec file to assign it a special template, it uses the default behavior. It executes an `apply-templates mode="book.titlepage.recto.mode"` on the subtitle element. Any element that does not have a specific template assigned to it in the spec file gets the same treatment.

      i. In the stock stylesheets, there is no template with `match="subtitle" mode="book.titlepage.recto.mode"`. This is an opportunity for a customization layer to intercept processing by supplying a template with those attributes.

      ii. If no such custom template exists, then instead the template with `match="*" mode="book.title-page.recto.mode"` in `fo/titlepage.templates.xsl` is used.

      iii. This default template does `apply-templates mode="titlepage.mode"` on the matching element, which is subtitle in this case.

      iv. There is a template with `match="subtitle" mode="titlepage.mode"` in `fo/titlepage.xsl`. This stylesheet module is *not* generated. It contains templates for each element to handle its default processing on title pages. That template processes its children in the same mode to ensure the generated text is appropriate for title page output.

   e. It closes the `fo:block` element to complete the title element.

9. The `book.titlepage.recto` template processes the rest of the elements listed in the spec file for the recto page in a similar manner.

10. Then the `book.titlepage` template calls the `book.titlepage.verso` template, which processes all the elements listed in the spec file for the verso title page.

11. Then the `book.titlepage` template calls the `book.titlepage.separator` template, which just outputs a page break. That completes the book title page processing.

If a given element that you want to appear on a title page does not have any titlepage template, then it will not appear. An element can be output with any of these:

• A call to a specific template named in the spec file. See the section called "Chapter titles" (page 174) for an example.

• A match on the element with a template in `book.titlepage.recto.mode` (or whichever title page you need).

• A match on the element with a template in `titlepage.mode`.

Additional front or back matter

If your book calls for additional front or back matter beyond the normal sequence of elements, you can customize the template with match="book" in fo/division.xsl to process additional content. Starting with version 1.73 of the stylesheets, the book template was modularized to make it easier to customize. The following example adds a contributors section at the front and an end notes list before the index.

Example 13.9. Customizing the book template

```
<xsl:template match="book">
  <xsl:variable name="id">
    <xsl:call-template name="object.id"/>
  </xsl:variable>
  <xsl:variable name="preamble"
                select="title|subtitle|titleabbrev|bookinfo|info"/>
  <xsl:variable name="content"
                select="node()[not(self::title or self::subtitle
                            or self::titleabbrev
                            or self::info
                            or self::bookinfo
                            or self::index)]"/> ❶

  <xsl:variable name="titlepage-master-reference">
    <xsl:call-template name="select.pagemaster">
      <xsl:with-param name="pageclass" select="'titlepage'"/>
    </xsl:call-template>
  </xsl:variable>

  <xsl:call-template name="front.cover"/>

  <xsl:if test="$preamble">
    <xsl:call-template name="page.sequence">
      <xsl:with-param name="master-reference"
                      select="$titlepage-master-reference"/>
      <xsl:with-param name="content">
        <fo:block id="{$id}">
          <xsl:call-template name="book.titlepage"/>
        </fo:block>
      </xsl:with-param>
    </xsl:call-template>
  </xsl:if>

  <xsl:apply-templates select="dedication" mode="dedication"/>
  <xsl:call-template name="make.contributors.list"/> ❷
  <xsl:call-template name="make.book.tocs"/>
  <xsl:apply-templates select="$content"/> ❸
  <xsl:call-template name="make.endnotes.list"/> ❹
  <xsl:apply-templates select="index"/> ❺
  <xsl:call-template name="back.cover"/>
</xsl:template>

<xsl:template name="make.contributors.list"> ❻
  Make contributors page-sequence
</xsl:template>
```

```
<xsl:template name="make.endnotes.list"> ❼
```
  Make end notes page-sequence
```
</xsl:template>
```

❶   Remove the index from the `content` variable so it can be processed after the end notes.

❷   Call the template to generate a page-sequence for a contributors list (not included here). It will appear after any dedication and before the table of contents.

❸   Process the main book content, minus the index.

❹   After the main content and before the index, call the template to generate a page-sequence for the end notes list.

❺   Now process the index after the end notes.

❻   Write a template to generate a page-sequence for a contributors list. That is most easily done by calling the template named `page.sequence` in `fo/component.xsl` and pass the formatted content in its `content` template parameter.

❼   Write a template to generate a page-sequence for a list of end notes. See the section called "End notes" (page 276) for an example.

Notice that any new content generated by the book template must generate its own `fo:page-sequence`. If you want it to be included in the table of contents, you will have to customize the template that generates a book table of contents, which is `division.toc` in `fo/autotoc.xsl`.

Book covers

The DocBook XSL stylesheets currently do not provide direct support for covers, only front title pages. Covers can come in a variety of configurations, such as single-sheet for front and back, wrap-around with spine, or wrap-around without spine for saddle stitch. Text placement and graphics are highly individual, so it is hard to write a general-purpose stylesheet for all possible designs. Also, cover PDFs are often produced separately because their production process (color, heavier paper) may differ from the process for the book block.

If you have a simple page-size cover design that can be executed in XSL-FO and you want it to be part of your book, then the DocBook print stylesheet provides hooks to include it. Starting with version 1.73 of the stylesheets, the book template includes the following empty placeholder templates:

```
<!-- Placeholder templates -->
<xsl:template name="front.cover"/>
<xsl:template name="back.cover"/>
```

The `front.cover` template is called first in the book template, and the `back.cover` template is called last. By default, they do nothing, but you can customize either or both of these templates to produce cover pages.

Each template must wrap any content in an `fo:page-sequence` that it generates. There is a utility template named `page.sequence` in `fo/component.xsl` that you can use to do that. It takes a template parameter named `master-reference` to specify the name of the page sequence master, and another parameter named `content` in which you put the formatted content.

Starting with DocBook 5.0, the `cover` element was added to DocBook as part of the collection of metadata in the `info` element. The `cover` element is simply a container of information that can be presented on a cover. By default, the `cover` element is not processed, so you can add whatever information you need and create custom templates to format it.

Custom page design

If you find that the stylesheet parameters used in the DocBook stylesheets are not sufficient for meeting your page design needs, you can create your own custom page masters and use them in your documents.

Default page masters

Before creating custom page masters, it helps to understand the set up of the default page masters so you can see how to fit your customizations in.

In DocBook XSL-FO, a standard set of FO `simple-page-master` elements are declared and used. The page masters are grouped into *page classes*, one for each specialized type of page such as title page or body. The six page classes are listed in the following table. Within each class, there are different page masters to handle the sequence of pages of that type, such as first, left, and right pages. There is a `page-sequence-master` element for each page class to set the conditions for sequencing the group of page masters. The following is a list of the built-in page masters.

Table 13.4. DocBook XSL-FO page master names

Page Class	Used by	simple-page-master name	Description
titlepage	Title pages for `set`, `part` and `book` elements.	titlepage-first	First title page
		titlepage-odd	Right-hand title pages
		titlepage-even	Left-hand title pages
lot	Lists of titles, including table of contents and lists of figures, tables, examples, or procedures.	lot-first	First page of table of contents or list of titles such as figures, tables, examples or procedures that appear at front of book.
		lot-odd	Right-hand list of titles
		lot-even	Left-hand list of titles

front	Used by these elements:
	
	`dedication`
	`preface`
		front-first	First page of new page sequence in book front matter, used for dedication and preface.

		front-odd	Right-hand front matter page.
		front-even	Left-hand front matter page.

body	Used by these elements:
	
	`chapter`
	`article`
	`reference`
	`refentry`
	`section` (*if root element*)
	`sect1` (*if root element*)
		body-first	First page of new page sequence in body of document, such as chapters.

		body-odd	Right-hand body page.
		body-even	Left-hand body page.

back	Used by these elements:
	
	`appendix`
	`bibliography`
	`colophon`
	`glossary`
		back-first	First page of new page sequence in book back matter, which includes appendix, glossary, bibliography, and colophon (but not index).

		back-odd	Right-hand back matter page.
		back-even	Left-hand back matter page.

Page Class	Used by	simple-page-master name	Description
index	Book or set index	index-first	First page of index.
		index-odd	Right-hand index page.
		index-even	Left-hand index page.
		blank	Blank page that may be automatically inserted at the end of a page sequence to even out the page count. It can be used in all page-sequence-masters.

Note:

In each page class, there is a second set of page masters with the same names except the names all end in -draft, such as titlepage-first-draft. These are used when a document is processed in draft mode, which happens when you set the draft.mode parameter to a value other than no.

Each of the page-master-sequence and simple-page-master elements is defined in the fo/pagesetup.xsl stylesheet file. The page-master-sequence elements are used to set the conditions under which different page masters are selected, such as the first page or even page number. The simple-page-master elements define the margins of the page, using the stylesheet parameters. The following example shows a complete page master declaration:

Example 13.10. Page master declaration

```
<fo:simple-page-master master-name="titlepage-even" ❶
                       page-width="{$page.width}" ❷
                       page-height="{$page.height}"
                       margin-top="{$page.margin.top}"
                       margin-bottom="{$page.margin.bottom}"
                       margin-left="{$page.margin.inner}"
                       margin-right="{$page.margin.outer}">
    <fo:region-body margin-bottom="{$body.margin.bottom}" ❸
                    margin-top="{$body.margin.top}"
                    column-count="{$column.count.titlepage}">
    </fo:region-body>
    <fo:region-before region-name="xsl-region-before-even" ❹
                      extent="{$region.before.extent}"
                      display-align="before"/>
    <fo:region-after region-name="xsl-region-after-even" ❺
                     extent="{$region.after.extent}"
                     display-align="after"/>
</fo:simple-page-master>
```

❶ The master-name attribute indicates that this page master is for even-numbered title pages.
❷ The attributes set the page size and margins using stylesheet parameter values.
❸ The region-body child sets the margins for the body area on the page.
❹ The region-before child element sets the height of the header area. The display-align attribute puts the header text at the top of the header area.
❺ The region-after child element sets the height of the footer area, with the text aligned at the bottom of the footer area.

The DocBook FO stylesheets do not call the page masters directly, but instead call the page sequence masters, which then call the appropriate page masters as needed. The following is an example of a complete page sequence declaration:

Example 13.11. Page sequence declaration

```
<fo:page-sequence-master master-name="titlepage">    ❶
    <fo:repeatable-page-master-alternatives>    ❷
        <fo:conditional-page-master-reference
                master-reference="blank"    ❸
                blank-or-not-blank="blank"/>    ❹
        <fo:conditional-page-master-reference
                master-reference="titlepage-first"    ❺
                page-position="first"/>    ❻
        <fo:conditional-page-master-reference
                master-reference="titlepage-odd"
                odd-or-even="odd"/>
        <fo:conditional-page-master-reference
                master-reference="titlepage-even"
                odd-or-even="even"/>
    </fo:repeatable-page-master-alternatives>
</fo:page-sequence-master>
```

❶   The stylesheet calls this master-name when setting up a page sequence for title pages.
❷   Wrapper element for a set of conditions that select a particular page master when its conditions are met.
❸   Calls the page master named `blank` when its conditions are met.
❹   The value of `blank` for this property indicates that this page master is to be used if a page must be generated but there is no content from the flow to put on it. This occurs when the page sequence properties are set to end on an even page number, but the last of content happens to be on an odd page number.
❺   Calls the page master named `titlepage-first` when its conditions are met.
❻   The value of `first` for the `page-position` property indicates that this page master is to be used for the first page of a new titlepage sequence. The other conditions follow a similar pattern for odd-numbered and even-numbered pages.

Declaring custom page masters

The FO stylesheets let you set up your own page masters while leaving the original default page masters in place. To do so, you create an XSL template named `user.pagemasters` in your customization layer. In it, you add as many `fo:simple-page-master` and `fo:page-sequence-master` elements as you need. The names must be different from the default names, which means each `master-name` attribute must be unique and different from those already declared. Then you add any page properties you need as attributes to the `simple-page-master` element. The `user.pagemasters` template is automatically called by the template that sets up the default page masters. So all you have to do is define it and your page masters will become part of your FO output files, ready to be used in page sequences.

The easiest way to make your own page masters is to cut and paste from the original `fo/pagesetup.xsl` stylesheet file to your customization, and then change the name and property attributes. You will most likely want to copy a `page-sequence-master` and its related `simple-page-master` elements so you can have proper handling of first, left, and right pages.

In your property attributes for your custom page masters, you can refer to any of the existing stylesheet parameter values, or define your own parameters in your customization layer. You can also use any of them in expressions, so you can adjust the regular value by increments. There are many `simple-page-master` property attributes that you can add as well. You will need a good FO reference or the XSL-FO specification to know what attribute names and values can be used. Keep in mind that not all property attributes are supported by all XSL-FO processors.

Using custom page masters

Declaring custom page masters just makes them available to be used, but does not employ them in page sequences. To do that, you have to add some logic to the stylesheets so your custom page masters are selected instead of the default page masters. That logic is put into a template named `select.user.pagemaster` that you add to your customization layer. The way this works is as follows:

1. The DocBook elements that start a page sequence call the template named `select.pagemaster`. It is supposed to return a master-name for a `page-sequence-master` such as `titlepage` or body. That template's first step is to select the appropriate default page master name for that element.

2. Then the `select.pagemaster` template automatically calls the `select.user.pagemaster` template, passing the selected default master name as a parameter.

3. The default version of the `select.user.pagemaster` template simply returns the default page master. But if you customize that template, then it can return the master name of one of your customized `page-sequence-masters` in place of the default.

The following is an example of a customized template that selects a new name if for titlepage, otherwise returns the default:

```
<xsl:template name="select.user.pagemaster">
  <xsl:param name="element"/>
  <xsl:param name="pageclass"/>
  <xsl:param name="default-pagemaster"/>

  <!-- Return my customized title page master name if for titlepage,
       otherwise return the default -->

  <xsl:choose>
    <xsl:when test="$default-pagemaster = 'titlepage'">
      <xsl:value-of select="'my-new-titlepage'" />
    </xsl:when>
    <xsl:otherwise>
      <xsl:value-of select="$default-pagemaster"/>
    </xsl:otherwise>
  </xsl:choose>
</xsl:template>
```

You could also use the element name or the pageclass parameter value in the conditions for choosing a page master.

Landscape pages

There are three levels at which landscape (horizontally oriented) pages can be used:

- The entire document is to be rendered on landscape pages. Use the `page.orientation` parameter as described in the section called "Landscape documents" (page 85).

- Some chapters or appendixes are to be landscape, in a document that is otherwise portrait. See the section called "Landscape page sequence" (page 199).

- Tables, figures, or other block elements are to be displayed in landscape. See the section called "Landscape elements" (page 204).

Landscape page sequence

If you want an individual chapter or appendix to be presented in landscape mode, then you can accomplish that with a new page master. In fact, this can be done for any element that generates a page-sequence in XSL-FO:

```
appendix
article
bibliography*
chapter
colophon
dedication
glossary*
index
preface
refentry*
reference
```

* Except when it is contained inside an element that generates a page-sequence.

To put an element into a landscape page-sequence, you have to do two things:

1. Set up a new XSL-FO page-sequence-master with landscape specifications.

2. Apply the page-sequence-master to your selected element.

To set up a new page-sequence-master, you define it in your customization layer inside a template named `user.pagemasters`. Then you customize the template named `select.user.pagemaster` to apply it.

There are two methods to handle landscape in a page sequence:

- Add a `reference-orientation="90"` attribute to the `fo:region-body` of custom page-masters. This option works best for printed output.

- Swap the vertical and horizontal page dimensions in custom page-masters. This option works best for viewing output in a PDF viewer.

See the following sections for details of each method.

Rotated body-region

This method of rotating the content of a page-sequence is the easiest. It works best for printed out. That's because it leaves the headers and footers in their portait positions and rotates only the body content on the page. When printed, page numbers and running header and footer titles are in consistent positions on all pages. But when viewed in a PDF browser, the body content will be rotated, and the user will have to select an option in the PDF viewer to unrotate the pages for reading.

In XSL-FO, a page has five primary regions that can hold content. These are the top and bottom margin areas, the left and right margin areas, and the center body area. See the following table.

Location	Region name
Top margin area	fo:region-before
Bottom margin area	fo:region-after
Left margin area	fo:region-start
Right margin area	fo:region-end
Center body area	fo:region-body

Note:

If your document is set up for text that reads right-to-left as in Hebrew or Arabic, the left area is fo:region-end and the right area is fo:region-start.

To use this method, you add a reference-orientation="90" attribute to the fo:region-body element in a custom page-master declaration. That rotates only the center body area, leaving the headers and footers in their original locations.

1. Create a template named user.pagemasters in your customization layer.

2. Locate the set of fo:simple-page-master elements for body in fo/pagesetup.xsl. You will need those with master-name of body-first, body-odd, and body-even. Copy these elements into your user.pagemasters template.

3. Change the master-name values in your copies so they do not conflict with the originals. For example, use landscape-first instead of body-first, etc.

4. In each fo:region-body element, add the reference-orientation="90" attribute.

```
<fo:simple-page-master master-name="landscape-odd"
                       page-width="{$page.width}"
                       page-height="{$page.height}"
                       margin-top="{$page.margin.top}"
                       margin-bottom="{$page.margin.bottom}"
                       margin-left="{$margin.left.inner}"
                       margin-right="{$page.margin.outer}">
    <fo:region-body margin-bottom="{$body.margin.bottom}"
                    margin-top="{$body.margin.top}"
                    reference-orientation="90"
                    column-gap="{$column.gap.body}"
                    column-count="{$column.count.body}">
    </fo:region-body>
    ...
</fo:simple-page-master>
```

5. Also in your user.pagemasters template, copy the fo:page-sequence-master for body, and edit it to change the master-name and to use your new simple page-master names, as follows:

```
<fo:page-sequence-master master-name="landscape">
  <fo:repeatable-page-master-alternatives>
    <fo:conditional-page-master-reference master-reference="blank"
                                          blank-or-not-blank="blank"/>
    <fo:conditional-page-master-reference master-reference="landscape-first"
                                          page-position="first"/>
    <fo:conditional-page-master-reference master-reference="landscape-odd"
                                          odd-or-even="odd"/>
    <fo:conditional-page-master-reference
                                          odd-or-even="even">
      <xsl:attribute name="master-reference">
        <xsl:choose>
          <xsl:when test="$double.sided != 0">landscape-even</xsl:when>
          <xsl:otherwise>landscape-odd</xsl:otherwise>
        </xsl:choose>
      </xsl:attribute>
    </fo:conditional-page-master-reference>
  </fo:repeatable-page-master-alternatives>
</fo:page-sequence-master>
```

6. Once the page-sequence-master has been set up this way, you customize the template named `select.user.page-master` to employ it for certain elements. For example, if you intend to use `role="landscape"` on a chapter or appendix element to rotate it, then you would use the following:

```
<xsl:template name="select.user.pagemaster">
  <xsl:param name="element"/>
  <xsl:param name="pageclass"/>
  <xsl:param name="default-pagemaster"/>

  <xsl:choose>
    <xsl:when test="@role = 'landscape'">landscape</xsl:when>
    <xsl:otherwise>
      <xsl:value-of select="$default-pagemaster"/>
    </xsl:otherwise>
  </xsl:choose>
</xsl:template>
```

The `select.user.pagemaster` template is automatically called when the stylesheet is selecting a page-master for an element. Normally it just selects the default, but in this case it will select your custom page-master and rotate the content in the body region.

Landscape page dimensions

A different approach to landscape output is to change the page dimensions to landscape, without rotating any content. Of course, you can change an entire document to landscape by setting the stylesheet parameter `page.ori-entation="landscape"`. But if you only want a chapter or appendix in landscape, you have to do it with a custom page-master.

When you use this method, none of the content is rotated. When you view the output in a PDF browser, the pages will simply switch from tall to wide, with all the content remaining upright. The headers and footers will still be at the top and bottom, but they will be longer. That output style makes this method the most convenient for users consuming the output using a PDF reader instead of through printed output.

If you print such a PDF document, most (perhaps not all) PDF browsers know to rotate the landscape pages to fit a portrait-oriented printed page. But the headers and footers will also rotate. When the printed pages are assembled into a portrait document, the headers and footers on the landscape pages will be on the sides instead of top and bottom.

To use this method, copy the declaration for body pages into a template named user.pagemasters in your customization layer and swap the horizontal and vertical dimensions. The following example highlights the changes necessary.

```
<xsl:template name="user.pagemasters">
  <!-- landscape body pages -->
  <fo:simple-page-master master-name="body-first-landscape"
                         page-width="{$page.height}"
                         page-height="{$page.width}"
                         margin-top="{$margin.left.inner}"
                         margin-bottom="{$page.margin.outer}"
                         margin-left="{$page.margin.bottom}"
                         margin-right="{$page.margin.top}">
    <fo:region-body margin-bottom="{$body.margin.bottom}"
                margin-top="{$body.margin.top}"
                column-gap="{$column.gap.body}"
                column-count="{$column.count.body}">
    </fo:region-body>
    <fo:region-before region-name="xsl-region-before-first"
                    extent="{$region.before.extent}"
                    display-align="before"/>
    <fo:region-after region-name="xsl-region-after-first"
                    extent="{$region.after.extent}"
                    display-align="after"/>
  </fo:simple-page-master>
  <fo:simple-page-master master-name="body-odd-landscape"
                         page-width="{$page.height}"
                         page-height="{$page.width}"
                         margin-top="{$margin.left.inner}"
                         margin-bottom="{$page.margin.outer}"
                         margin-left="{$page.margin.bottom}"
                         margin-right="{$page.margin.top}">
    <fo:region-body margin-bottom="{$body.margin.bottom}"
                margin-top="{$body.margin.top}"
                column-gap="{$column.gap.body}"
                column-count="{$column.count.body}">
    </fo:region-body>
    <fo:region-before region-name="xsl-region-before-odd"
                    extent="{$region.before.extent}"
                    display-align="before"/>
    <fo:region-after region-name="xsl-region-after-odd"
                    extent="{$region.after.extent}"
                    display-align="after"/>
  </fo:simple-page-master>
  <fo:simple-page-master master-name="body-even-landscape"
                         page-width="{$page.height}"
                         page-height="{$page.width}"
                         margin-top="{$page.margin.outer}"
```

```
                         margin-bottom="{$margin.left.inner}"
                         margin-left="$page.margin.bottom}"
                         margin-right="{$page.margin.top}">
  <fo:region-body margin-bottom="{$body.margin.bottom}"
                  margin-top="{$body.margin.top}"
                  column-gap="{$column.gap.body}"
                  column-count="{$column.count.body}">
  </fo:region-body>
  <fo:region-before region-name="xsl-region-before-even"
                    extent="{$region.before.extent}"
                    display-align="before"/>
  <fo:region-after region-name="xsl-region-after-even"
                   extent="{$region.after.extent}"
                   display-align="after"/>
</fo:simple-page-master>
<!-- blank pages -->
<fo:simple-page-master master-name="blank-landscape"
                       page-width="{$page.height}"
                       page-height="{$page.width}"
                       margin-top="{$page.margin.outer}"
                       margin-bottom="{$margin.left.inner}"
                       margin-left="{$page.margin.bottom}"
                       margin-right="{$page.margin.top}">
  <fo:region-body display-align="center"
                  margin-bottom="{$body.margin.bottom}"
                  margin-top="{$body.margin.top}">
    <xsl:if test="$fop.extensions = 0 and $fop1.extensions = 0">
      <xsl:attribute name="region-name">blank-body</xsl:attribute>
    </xsl:if>
  </fo:region-body>
  <fo:region-before region-name="xsl-region-before-blank"
                    extent="{$region.before.extent}"
                    display-align="before"/>
  <fo:region-after region-name="xsl-region-after-blank"
                   extent="{$region.after.extent}"
                   display-align="after"/>
</fo:simple-page-master>

<fo:page-sequence-master master-name="body-landscape">
  <fo:repeatable-page-master-alternatives>
    <fo:conditional-page-master-reference master-reference="blank-landscape"
                                          blank-or-not-blank="blank"/
    <fo:conditional-page-master-reference master-reference="body-first-landscape"
                                          page-position="first"
    <fo:conditional-page-master-reference master-reference="body-odd-landscape"
                                          odd-or-even="odd"/>
    <fo:conditional-page-master-reference
                                          odd-or-even="even">
      <xsl:attribute name="master-reference">
        <xsl:choose>
          <xsl:when test="$double.sided != 0">body-even-landscape</xsl:when>
          <xsl:otherwise>body-odd-landscape</xsl:otherwise>
        </xsl:choose>
      </xsl:attribute>
```

```
        </fo:conditional-page-master-reference>
      </fo:repeatable-page-master-alternatives>
    </fo:page-sequence-master>
</xsl:template>
```

To apply the new `body-landscape` master-name, you customize the template named `select.user.pagemaster` as described in the section called "Rotated body-region" (page 199).

Then when you add `role="landscape"` to a chapter or appendix element, it will be output in landscape mode to the PDF file. A PDF viewer should display all the pages upright, with the landscape pages shown more wide than tall.

Landscape elements

The XSL-FO method of rotating a given element in an otherwise portrait page-sequence is to use the `fo:block-container` element. That element accepts a `reference-orientation="90"` property to rotate the content relative to the page. This method is used for the following:

- A table with an `orient="land"` attribute, as described in the section called "Landscape tables" (page 493).

- A table cell with a `<?dbfo orientation="90"?>` processing instruction, as described in the section called "Cell rotation" (page 478).

- An image with a custom processing instruction, as described in the section called "Landscape images" (page 292).

Sometimes the result may not be quite what you expected. When a block-container with rotated content is placed on a portrait page, it is the width rather than the height of the content that determines how much vertical space it takes up. You may need to manually set the width on the DocBook element to get correct formatting.

Long landscape tables are a special problem in XSL-FO. The standard does not support flowing the content of a block-container from one page to the next. It is likely that a table longer than a page will simply be truncated. There is a workaround for this problem, though. G. Ken Holman of *Crane Softwrights Ltd.*[1] has published a method for creating multipage landscape tables in XSL-FO. His Page Sequence Master Interleave (PSMI) method uses two passes to rearrange the pages in an FO file. PSMI is described at *http://www.cranesoftwrights.com/resources/psmi/index.htm*.

Custom page sequences

The top-level elements in DocBook generate one or more page sequences that contain their content. For example, the book template creates page sequences for the titlepage information, the table of contents, and then lets its chapter and appendix elements generate their own page sequences.

You may want to change how a top-level element creates page sequences. For example, an `article` element by default creates a single page sequence for all of its content, but you may want to divide that into more than one sequence. You could create a landscape sequence, or a multicolumn sequence for part of the output.

You can use a utility template named `page.sequence` to create your own page sequences. You can specify the page master name, the content, and the page numbering style as parameters passed to the template. The following example customizes the template for `article` to output the article body in a two-column layout while the titlepage and bibliography are in single column full page width. It uses the existing page master names `titlepage`, `body`, and `back`, but you could substitute your own custom page masters.

---

[1] http://www.cranesoftwrights.com

Example 13.12. Custom page sequences

```
<xsl:param name="column.count.titlepage" select="1" />
<xsl:param name="column.count.body" select="2" />
<xsl:param name="column.count.back" select="1" />

<xsl:template match="article">
  <xsl:variable name="id">
    <xsl:call-template name="object.id"/>
  </xsl:variable>

  <xsl:call-template name="page.sequence">
    <xsl:with-param name="master-reference">titlepage</xsl:with-param>
    <xsl:with-param name="content">
      <fo:block id="{$id}"
                xsl:use-attribute-sets="component.titlepage.properties">
        <xsl:call-template name="article.titlepage"/>
      </fo:block>

      <xsl:variable name="toc.params">
        <xsl:call-template name="find.path.params">
          <xsl:with-param name="table" select="normalize-space($generate.toc)"/>
        </xsl:call-template>
      </xsl:variable>

      <xsl:if test="contains($toc.params, 'toc')">
        <xsl:call-template name="component.toc">
          <xsl:with-param name="toc.title.p"
                          select="contains($toc.params, 'title')"/>
        </xsl:call-template>
        <xsl:call-template name="component.toc.separator"/>
      </xsl:if>
    </xsl:with-param>
  </xsl:call-template>

  <xsl:call-template name="page.sequence">
    <xsl:with-param name="master-reference">body</xsl:with-param>
    <xsl:with-param name="content">
      <xsl:apply-templates select="*[not(self::bibliography)]"/>
    </xsl:with-param>
  </xsl:call-template>
  <xsl:if test="bibliography">
    <xsl:call-template name="page.sequence">
      <xsl:with-param name="master-reference">back</xsl:with-param>
      <xsl:with-param name="content">
        <xsl:apply-templates select="bibliography"/>
      </xsl:with-param>
    </xsl:call-template>
  </xsl:if>
</xsl:template>
```

Print TOC control

The main features for controlling tables of contents are described in the section called "Tables of contents (TOC)" (page 125). This section describes features specific to print output.

TOC Page margins

You can adjust the page margins for a table of contents by customizing the `toc.margin.properties` attribute set. The following shows the default settings:

```
<xsl:attribute-set name="toc.margin.properties">
  <xsl:attribute name="space-before.minimum">0.5em</xsl:attribute>
  <xsl:attribute name="space-before.optimum">1em</xsl:attribute>
  <xsl:attribute name="space-before.maximum">2em</xsl:attribute>
  <xsl:attribute name="space-after.minimum">0.5em</xsl:attribute>
  <xsl:attribute name="space-after.optimum">1em</xsl:attribute>
  <xsl:attribute name="space-after.maximum">2em</xsl:attribute>
</xsl:attribute-set>
```

These properties do not change the margins for the page-master, but for the `fo:block` that contains the table of contents on the page. The `space-before` values add space above the TOC and `space-after` add space below the toc. You would use `start-indent` to indent from left, but `end-indent` will not work to indent from the right. The right (end) indent is set in the template named `toc.line.properties`, which is applied to the block containing each line in a TOC. A customization to indent both sides by 1 inch might look like the following:

```
<xsl:attribute-set name="toc.margin.properties">
  <xsl:attribute name="start-indent">0.5in</xsl:attribute>
</xsl:attribute-set>

<xsl:attribute-set name="toc.line.properties">
  <xsl:attribute name="text-align-last">justify</xsl:attribute>
  <xsl:attribute name="text-align">start</xsl:attribute>
  <xsl:attribute name="end-indent">1.25in</xsl:attribute>
  <xsl:attribute name="last-line-end-indent">-0.25in</xsl:attribute>
</xsl:attribute-set>
```

In `toc.line.properties`, the end-indent property sets the block value, then the `last-line-end-indent` adds a negative value for the last line of the block. The result is that single lines get both properties, and hence a net indent of `1in`. Any long lines that roll over to a second line have the first line indented by `1.25in`. Note that the overall block alignment is `start` (left), and only the last line is justified. This combination of properties keeps long lines out of the space reserved for the page numbers, making it more readable. These properties work in the attribute-set starting with version 1.72 of the stylesheets.

As with all attribute-sets, your customized properties are merged with the default set. You could add other properties that would apply to the whole TOC block. For example, a TOC in an `article` does not have a page break after it by default. The following example would add that page break.

```
<xsl:attribute-set name="toc.margin.properties">
  <xsl:attribute name="break-after">page</xsl:attribute>
  </xsl:attribute-set>
```

If you want to change the page layout beyond these properties, you will need to add a customized page-master, in this case for the `lot` (list of titles) page class. See the section called "Custom page design" (page 195) for a description of how to do that. In addition to a new page master, you will need to customize the `select.user.pagemaster` template to select your new page master file during processing.

TOC title

The `Table of Contents` title that appears at the top of a TOC is turned on or off with the `generate.toc` parameter. See the section called "Which components have a TOC" (page 125) to see how to change that parameter.

The title text in a table of contents is generated text, using the `TableofContents` key word. For English, the text comes from the gentext file `common/en.xml`, where the text associated with the key word is "Table of Contents". You can change it for a given language in a customization layer with something like the following:

```
<xsl:param name="local.l10n.xml" select="document('')"/>
<l:i18n xmlns:l="http://docbook.sourceforge.net/xmlns/l10n/1.0">
  <l:l10n language="en">
    <l:gentext key="TableofContents" text="Contents"/>
  </l:l10n>
</l:i18n>
```

The formatting of the title is controlled by the same machinery that controls title pages. While a TOC could have a complete title page, the default behavior is just to start a page and put the title at the top. If you want to change how the title is formatted, then you will need to customize the titlepage spec file and generate a new titlepage stylesheet module. See the section called "Title page spec file" (page 184) information on how to do that. Specifically, you will want to change the following entry in the spec file:

```
<t:titlepage element="table.of.contents" wrapper="fo:block">
  <t:titlepage-content side="recto">
    <title
          force="1"
          named-template="gentext"
          param:key="'TableofContents'"
          fo:space-before.minimum="1em"
          fo:space-before.optimum="1.5em"
          fo:space-before.maximum="2em"
          fo:space-after="0.5em"
          fo:margin-left="{$title.margin.left}"
          fo:font-size="&hsize3;"
          fo:font-weight="bold"
          fo:font-family="{$title.font.family}"/>
  </t:titlepage-content>
```

The spec file needs to be processed into a stylesheet module that gets included in your customization layer.

If you do not want to generate a new titlepage spec file just to modify the table of contents title, you can instead replace the template named `table.of.contents.titlepage`. If your customization has a template of this name, then it will override the processing done by the regular title page machinery. You may need to give your version a `priority` attribute with a value of greater than zero, in case there is a problem with import precedence. The template must get the title using the `gentext` template, and then generate an `fo:block` with the appropriate properties. After outputting the title, it must close the `fo:block`. For example:

```
<xsl:template name="table.of.contents.titlepage" priority="1">
  <fo:block xsl:use-attribute-sets="section.title.level1.properties"
            space-before="1in"
            space-before.conditionality="retain"
            space-after="12pt"
            border-bottom="0.5pt solid black">
    <xsl:call-template name="gentext">
      <xsl:with-param name="key" select="'TableofContents'"/>
    </xsl:call-template>
  </fo:block>
</xsl:template>
```

The space-before.conditionality="retain" property forces the formatter to use the specified space-before value, even though it is at the top of the page where it would normally be ignored.

Styling print TOC entries

An entry in a table of contents is produced by applying templates that have mode="toc" and that match the element associated with that entry. So the template that formats an entry for a sect1 title would start with:

```
<xsl:template match="sect1" mode="toc">
```

These templates are located in the fo/autotoc.xsl stylesheet file. They are not good candidates for customization because they are pretty complex. The complexity comes from the recursive nature of processing all the elements in the document in the toc mode. Each mode="toc" template generates the entry for its element, and then checks to see if the element has children that should appear in the TOC. If so, then it increments the indent by the amount of the parameter toc.indent.width and applies templates in toc mode to process the children.

To change to overall left indent, or the right indent in a table of contents, see the section called "TOC Page margins" (page 206). To change the indent increment, set the toc.indent.width parameter to a pure number which is interpreted as points by the stylesheet (do not add the pt unit to the parameter). To further customize the incremental indents, you can customize the template named set.toc.indent from fo/autotoc.xsl which applies that parameter.

Some styles can be set using the toc.line.properties attribute-set that is applied to the block containing each line. You can use it to set overall properties for all entries, or you can make an attribute value conditional on the current element. For example, if you want to set the font size for all entries to 10pt, and display chapter-level entries in bold:

```
<xsl:attribute-set name="toc.line.properties">
  <xsl:attribute name="font-size">10pt</xsl:attribute>
  <xsl:attribute name="font-weight">
    <xsl:when test="self::chapter | self::preface | self::appendix">bold</xsl:when>
    <xsl:otherwise>normal</xsl:otherwise>
  </xsl:attribute>
</xsl:attribute-set>
```

If you need further control, the template that can be customized more easily is named toc.line, because it formats a single entry of a TOC. By default, it formats all TOC lines the same, since the left indent has been set by the template that called toc.line. If you want to customize certain TOC entries, then your customization would need to test for the name of the context node (the element whose TOC entry is being generated) and act accordingly. The template also has a toc-context parameter, which is set to the element containing the TOC. That way you can style an entry in a book TOC differently from one in a chapter or article TOC.

In the following example customization, chapter and appendix entries add the label Chapter or Appendix preceding the number label:

```
<xsl:template name="toc.line">
  <xsl:param name="toc-context" select="NOTANODE"/>
  <xsl:variable name="id">
    <xsl:call-template name="object.id"/>
  </xsl:variable>

  <xsl:variable name="label">
    <xsl:apply-templates select="." mode="label.markup"/>
  </xsl:variable>

  <fo:block xsl:use-attribute-sets="toc.line.properties">
    <fo:inline keep-with-next.within-line="always">

      <fo:basic-link internal-destination="{$id}">

        <xsl:if test="self::appendix or self::chapter">
          <xsl:call-template name="gentext">
            <xsl:with-param name="key" select="local-name()"/>
          </xsl:call-template>
          <xsl:text> </xsl:text>
        </xsl:if>

        <xsl:if test="$label != ''">
          <xsl:copy-of select="$label"/>
          <xsl:value-of select="$autotoc.label.separator"/>
        </xsl:if>
        <xsl:apply-templates select="." mode="title.markup"/>
      </fo:basic-link>
    </fo:inline>
    <fo:inline keep-together.within-line="always">
      <xsl:text> </xsl:text>
      <fo:leader leader-pattern="dots"
                 leader-pattern-width="3pt"
                 leader-alignment="reference-area"
                 keep-with-next.within-line="always"/>
      <xsl:text> </xsl:text>
      <fo:basic-link internal-destination="{$id}">
        <fo:page-number-citation ref-id="{$id}"/>
      </fo:basic-link>
    </fo:inline>
  </fo:block>
</xsl:template>
```

Note:

For best results in your TOC, be sure to omit any leading or trailing white space in your `title` elements. In XML, white space includes linefeeds, tabs, and space characters. Any white space at the end of a title may cause its dot leaders in the TOC to start on the next line instead of staying with the last word in the title. Any white space at the beginning of a title will show as a single blank space when the title is quoted in cross references.

TOC page numbering

When a TOC page is started, it is assigned a format for its own page numbers. It gets the format by calling the template named `page.number.format`. That is a simple template that can be customized in a customization layer. The following is an example that changes the page numbering style of the TOC to 1, 2, 3 etc.

```
<xsl:template name="page.number.format">
  <xsl:param name="element" select="local-name(.)"/>
  <xsl:choose>
    <xsl:when test="$element = 'toc'">1</xsl:when>
    <xsl:when test="$element = 'preface'">i</xsl:when>
    <xsl:when test="$element = 'dedication'">i</xsl:when>
    <xsl:otherwise>1</xsl:otherwise>
  </xsl:choose>
</xsl:template>
```

Part TOC on part titlepage

If you include part in the generate.toc parameter in order to generate a table of contents for each part element, you may want to customize the output. By default, the part titlepage is a page-sequence (2 pages in double-sided output), and the part TOC is another page-sequence (two more pages). A typical customization merges the TOC onto the titlepage, and reduces the TOC to just the chapter and appendix listings.

The following customization will add a TOC to the part title page:

```
<xsl:template name="part.titlepage.before.verso" priority="1">
  <xsl:variable name="toc.params">
    <xsl:call-template name="find.path.params">
      <xsl:with-param name="table"
            select="normalize-space($generate.toc)"/>
    </xsl:call-template>
  </xsl:variable>
  <xsl:if test="contains($toc.params, 'toc')">
    <xsl:call-template name="division.toc">
      <xsl:with-param name="toc.context" select="."/>
    </xsl:call-template>
  </xsl:if>
</xsl:template>
```

Turn off the original part toc page-sequence template
```
<xsl:template name="generate.part.toc">
</xsl:template>
```

The part.titlepage.before.verso template is one of those generated by the titlepage spec file, and you can see it in fo/titlepage.templates.xsl. Normally it is empty, so you can override it to do something else, like put the TOC before the verso titlepage (which means on the recto titlepage after the title information).

It first checks to see if you have a part toc or part toc,title string in your generate.toc parameter (it is there by default). If so, it calls division.toc to generate the part TOC, without generating a page-sequence.

The last template nulls out the template that generates a page sequence for the part TOC. The generate.part.toc template is what generates the extra pages, because it is in its own page sequence.

If you want to reduce the part TOC to just chapters and appendixes and not include sections, then one further customization is needed. An element is processed for a TOC in mode="toc". Normally each element processed in that mode also processes its children in that mode, down to the level of the toc.section.depth parameter. If you turn off processing sections in that mode completely, you also lose them in a book's TOC. Instead, use the toc-context local parameter in a conditional statement to process sections only when the context is not a part TOC. The following customization of the template from fo/autotoc.xsl does that.

```
<xsl:template match="preface|chapter|appendix|article"
              mode="toc">
  <xsl:param name="toc-context" select="."/>
  ...
  <xsl:if test="local-name($toc-context) != 'part'
                and $toc.section.depth > 0
                and $toc.max.depth > $depth.from.context
                and $nodes">
  ...
```

Editable table of contents

You may need more control over a table of contents than is provided with the customization features in the stylesheets. In those situations, you may need to create a table of contents as an XML file that you can edit and process as part of your document. You can do this for the main table of contents in HTML processing, but not currently for FO output. Fortunately, you do not have write the TOC from scratch.

The extra stylesheet file `html/maketoc.xsl` will output a TOC document that has a main `toc` element that contains a set of nested `tocentry` elements. If you output that to a file, you can edit it and feed it back into the processing of your document. Here are steps to do that.

Using an editable table of contents

1. Generate a table of contents XML file from your document. For example:

    ```
    xsltproc  -o customtoc.xml \
      --stringparam chunk.section.depth 8 \
      --stringparam chunk.first.sections 1 \
      html/maketoc.xsl  mybook.xml
    ```

    Use the two parameters `chunk.section.depth` and `chunk.first.sections` to ensure the generated TOC includes all the sections you want.

2. Edit the TOC file `customtoc.xml` as needed.

3. Generate your document output by processing your document with the `manual.toc` parameter:

    ```
    xsltproc  -o mybook.html  \
        --stringparam manual.toc  customtoc.xml  \
        html/docbook.xsl  mybook.xml
    ```

The stylesheet parameter `manual.toc` identifies the filename of your editable XML TOC file. If you pass this parameter to the stylesheet during processing, it will use that file in place of the automatically generated TOC.

Note:

If you regenerate your document, you may also have to re-edit the table of contents. Unless you can automate the changes with a script, using an editable TOC is efficient only for documents that rarely change.

Running headers and footers

Running headers and footers are to the text that appears in the top and bottom margins of each page to help with navigation through the paginated document. They typically include information such as page numbers, chapter title, and such. The running headers and footers are formatted using tables. Each table is a single row with three cells, for left, center, and right aligned text.

Default headers and footers

The default content for running headers is as follows:

- For double-sided output in a book, the center header is the current section name.

- For single-sided output, or double-sided not in a book, the center header is the title of the element that starts the page sequence, which could be article, chapter or appendix title.

- Title page headers are blank.

- Headers on the first page of a page sequence are blank.

- If the `draft.mode` parameter is set to `yes`, then the left and right headers show the word "Draft" in the appropriate language.

The default content for footers is as follows:

- For double-sided output, the page number appears in the outside corner (right footer on right-hand pages, left footer on left-hand pages).

- For single-sided output, the page number appears in the center footer.

- Title page footers are blank.

Changing the header or footer text

The content for running headers is defined in a stylesheet template named `header.content`. Likewise, the footers are defined in a template named `footer.content`. You see the default versions in `fo/pagesetup.xsl`. To customize the headers and footers, you redefine these templates in your customization layer.

The `header.content` template is called three times for each page-sequence, once each for left, center, and right header cells. It should select and return the appropriate text to fill each cell. The same is true for the `footer.content` template.

The header and footer content is considered `static-content` in FO, which means it is repeated in the same place on each page in a page sequence. However, the text itself can vary to show the current section title or page number. The static content is declared at the beginning of each different page sequence that is started during the processing of the document. Within a page sequence, FO supports variations for where a given page-master appears in the sequence, such as for odd- or even-numbered pages.

Table 13.5. Header/footer content examples

XSL-FO	Description
`<fo:page-number/>`	Inserts the current page number.
`<xsl:apply-templates select="."` `mode="title.markup"/>`	Inserts the title of the current chapter, appendix, or other component.
`<xsl:apply-templates select="."` `mode="titleabbrev.markup"/>`	Inserts the titleabbrev of the current chapter, appendix, or other component, if it is available. Otherwise it inserts the regular title.
`<xsl:apply-templates select="."` `mode="object.title.markup"/>`	Inserts the chapter title with chapter number label. Likewise for appendices.
`<fo:retrieve-marker ... />`	Used to retrieve the current section name.
`<xsl:apply-templates select="//corpauthor[1]"/>`	Inserts the value of the first `corpauthor` element found anywhere in the document.
`<xsl:call-template name="datetime.format">` `<xsl:with-param ...`	Inserts a date timestamp. Seethe section called "Adding a date timestamp" (page 157).
`<xsl:call-template name="draft.text"/>`	Inserts the `Draft` message if `draft.mode` is currently on.
`<fo:external-graphic ... />`	Inserts a graphical image. See the section called "Graphic in header or footer" (page 217) for details.

The `header.content` or `footer.content` template is called with the element that starts the page sequence as the context node. This means you can select elements to appear in the content using XPaths relative to that element. An example below adds `corpauthor` to a header.

The `header.content` or `footer.content` template is also called with several parameters that you can use in your logic for deciding what should appear in each position. There are also global parameters that can be included in the decision making. The parameters each template is called with include the following:

pageclass   There is a specific `pageclass` value for each type of page design that might be needed. For example, an index might be two-column layout while the rest of the book is single column. Each pageclass has a set of FO simple-page-masters defined for it. The following pageclass values are available by default, but this list could be extended by adding custom page masters.

`titlepage`	*Division title page, including set, book, part.*
`lot`	*Page with a list of titles, including book table of contents, list of figures, etc.*
`front`	*Front matter pages, including preface, dedication*
`body`	*Main content pages*
`back`	*Back matter pages, including appendix, glossary, etc.*
`index`	*Alphabetical book-style index*

sequence   Within a pageclass, the sequence of pages can have different page designs. For example, the first page of sequence might omit the running header so it will not detract from the main title. The enumerated sequence values are:

first	First page of a page class.
odd	Odd-numbered pages in the page class.
even	Even-numbered pages.
blank	Blank page at end of sequence, to even out page count.

If the output format is single-sided, then odd and even pages should have the same design, and the blank page is not called upon.

position   The location of text cell within the header or footer. The values are:

```
left
center
right
```

gentext-key   Some pages need to have a title generated for them, such as Table of Contents or Index. Since these titles need to appear in the language of the document, they are designated using a gentext-key, such as TableofContents. These keys appear in the localization files such as common/en.xml to identify a particular generated text string.

```
<l:gentext key="TableofContents"
           text="Table of Contents"/>
```

In addition to these passed parameters, you can use these global parameters to select header/footer content.

double.sided   Selects single- or double-sided page layout. Typically a double-sided layout uses mirrored page designs for odd- and even-numbered pages, while a single-sided layout has a single page design.

draft.mode   This parameter indicates whether the formatted document is to be marked as Draft. This condition might be marked in the header or footer. See the section called "Draft mode" (page 464) for a description of how draft mode is turned on.

A customized version of the header.content template is typically a big xsl:choose structure where each xsl:when states its conditions for choosing the text for a particular header or footer cell. It only has to cover the cells that might have content. Here is a complete example.

Example 13.13. Customized header.content template

```
<xsl:template name="header.content">
  <xsl:param name="pageclass" select="''"/>
  <xsl:param name="sequence" select="''"/>
  <xsl:param name="position" select="''"/>
  <xsl:param name="gentext-key" select="''"/>

  <fo:block>  ❶
    <!-- sequence can be odd, even, first, blank -->
    <!-- position can be left, center, right -->
    <xsl:choose>

      <xsl:when test="$sequence = 'odd' and $position = 'left'">  ❷
        <fo:retrieve-marker retrieve-class-name="section.head.marker"  ❸
                      retrieve-position="first-including-carryover"
                      retrieve-boundary="page-sequence"/>
      </xsl:when>

      <xsl:when test="$sequence = 'odd' and $position = 'center'">
```

```
      <xsl:call-template name="draft.text"/>   ❹
    </xsl:when>

    <xsl:when test="$sequence = 'odd' and $position = 'right'">
      <fo:page-number/>   ❺
    </xsl:when>

    <xsl:when test="$sequence = 'even' and $position = 'left'">
      <fo:page-number/>
    </xsl:when>

    <xsl:when test="$sequence = 'even' and $position = 'center'">
      <xsl:call-template name="draft.text"/>
    </xsl:when>

    <xsl:when test="$sequence = 'even' and $position = 'right'">
      <xsl:apply-templates select="." mode="titleabbrev.markup"/>   ❻
    </xsl:when>

    <xsl:when test="$sequence = 'first' and $position = 'left'">   ❼
    </xsl:when>

    <xsl:when test="$sequence = 'first' and $position = 'right'">
    </xsl:when>

    <xsl:when test="$sequence = 'first' and $position = 'center'">
      <xsl:value-of
            select="ancestor-or-self::book/bookinfo/corpauthor"/>   ❽
    </xsl:when>

    <xsl:when test="$sequence = 'blank' and $position = 'left'">
      <fo:page-number/>
    </xsl:when>

    <xsl:when test="$sequence = 'blank' and $position = 'center'">
      <xsl:text>This page intentionally left blank</xsl:text>   ❾
    </xsl:when>

    <xsl:when test="$sequence = 'blank' and $position = 'right'">
    </xsl:when>

  </xsl:choose>
 </fo:block>
</xsl:template>
```

❶ Make sure any content is enclosed in an `fo:block` so it is valid XSL-FO output.

❷ Each `xsl:when` statement sets conditions for a particular header cell location's content.

❸ Sets an `fo:retrieve-marker` to retrieve the text of the first section title on the page. See the section called "Running section titles" (page 216) for more information.

❹ This built-in template returns the appropriately translated "Draft" label, but only if the conditions for printing it have been met. See the section called "Draft mode" (page 464) for a description of how draft mode is turned on.

❺ Prints the current page number in that header cell.

❻ This applies templates to the current element using `mode="titleabbrev.markup"`. The current element is the one that starts the page-sequence, which might be a chapter, appendix, or TOC. This mode generates a title from the element's `titleabbrev` if available, otherwise from its `title`. This feature lets the running header track the current chapter or appendix name. You can add a `titleabbrev` when a `title` is too long to comfortably fit in the running header. If you want the full title including its label such as `Chapter 3`, then use `mode="object.title.markup"` instead.

❼ You can include empty clauses in case you want to add something later.

❽ If this page sequence is part of a book that has a `corpauthor` element, then that element's text is printed.

❾ This entry generates the phrase "This page intentionally left blank" for generated blank pages. These occur when a double-sided chapter ends on an odd page, which generates a blank even page after it. This phrase is in English only, however, so adding a gentext template for multiple languages would probably be more flexible. See the `draft.text` template in `fo/pagesetup.xsl` for an example of using a gentext template.

As you can see from the example, there is quite a bit of flexibility in what can appear in a given header or footer location. You can use static text, or dynamic content. You can also include graphics.

Keep in mind that the sequence name `odd` does not include the sequence `first`, even though the first page may be an odd page. If you specify something for odd pages, you may also want to specify it for the first page too, as for example:

```
<xsl:when test="$double.sided != 0
                and ($sequence = 'odd' or $sequence = 'first')
                and $position='right'">
```

Running section titles

It is a common feature to put the current section title in the running header or footer. This is possible with XSL-FO, using the `fo:marker` and `fo:retrieve-marker` elements. The stylesheet automatically inserts the `fo:marker` elements, and you specify the `fo:retrieve-marker` element in your header or footer content.

You can control which levels of sections are included in the running section titles. Often only the first or second levels are important enough to warrant inclusion. The stylesheet parameter `marker.section.level` sets the maximum section level to be used. The default value is 2, so only sections at levels 1 and 2 are considered for the running titles. Set the parameter to 1 if you only want top-level sections, or set it to a higher number to include more levels. When the stylesheet processes your document, it inserts the following hidden marker for each section that meets the parameter condition:

```
<fo:marker marker-class-name="section.head.marker">
  My section title
</fo:marker>
```

The content of the element is the title to be displayed, if it is selected. The marker name `section.head.marker` is the same for all section levels by default. If you want to display both the first and second section levels on the same page, you would need to customize the stylesheet to output different marker names for the different levels.

When the pages are being laid out by the FO processor, each hidden marker is placed on the page within its section block. A section's block starts with the section title and extends as far as the section's content goes. That may be over more than one page. Then when the header or footer includes a `fo:retrieve-marker`, the processor looks for markers with the matching name. Which one it selects depends on the attributes on the `fo:retrieve-marker` element. The following example shows the typical attributes for running section titles:

```
<fo:retrieve-marker
     retrieve-class-name="section.head.marker"
     retrieve-position="first-including-carryover"
     retrieve-boundary="page-sequence"/>
```

The `retrieve-class-name` attribute identifies the group of markers to select from. The `retrieve-position="first-including-carryover"` attribute picks up the first matching marker on the current page, or from a section carried over from a previous page if there is no marker on the current page. The `retrieve-boundary="page-sequence"` attribute sets the boundary for selecting a previous marker as the current page-sequence, as opposed to the whole document. That prevents carryover from the previous chapter.

Graphic in header or footer

Your page design may call for putting a graphical image in headers or footers. The overall process is the same as for other header or footer content. You just add the appropriate XSL-FO markup in the right place in your customized `header.content` or `footer.content` template, which are described in the section called "Changing the header or footer text" (page 212).

The following is an example of the XSL-FO markup as it might appear in the template:

```
...
<xsl:when test="$position = 'center'">
  <fo:external-graphic content-height="1.2cm">
    <xsl:attribute name="src">
      <xsl:call-template name="fo-external-image">
        <xsl:with-param name="filename" select="$header.image.filename"/>
      </xsl:call-template>
    </xsl:attribute>
  </fo:external-graphic>
</xsl:when>
...
```

The `fo:external-graphic` element is used in XSL-FO to specify a graphical file to include in your output. The `content-height` attribute sets the height, to make sure it will fit within the allocated height for the header or footer. See the section called "Allocating height for headers and footers" (page 220) for details on adjusting the height to fit the graphic.

The image filename itself is specified here using a parameter value `$header.image.filename`. This is not a DocBook XSL parameter, but one that you could add to your stylesheet. A parameter that is specified at the top of the stylesheet makes it easier to change the filename without searching through code in your customization. But why does it call a template named `fo-external-image` instead of just adding a literal `src` attribute? Because different XSL-FO processors handle slightly different syntax for the file reference. That template handles generating the right syntax for each processor.

Multi-line header or footer

Some page designs cram more information into the headers or footers by stacking it onto multiple lines. For example, you could have the chapter title on the first line and the running section title on the second. There are two approaches to achieving this effect, using multiple blocks or customizing the layout table.

If you just need to stack two pieces of information into one location in the header or footer, then using two blocks is the easiest customization. In the appropriate `xsl:when` clause in your customization of the `header.content` or `footer.content` template, use two `fo:block` elements. The following example uses two stacked blocks:

```
...
<xsl:when test="$sequence = 'odd' and $position = 'left'">
  <fo:block>
    <xsl:apply-templates select="." mode="titleabbrev.markup"/>
  </fo:block>
  <fo:block>
    <fo:retrieve-marker retrieve-class-name="section.head.marker"
                        retrieve-position="first-including-carryover"
                        retrieve-boundary="page-sequence"/>
  </fo:block>
</xsl:when>
...
```

In this example, the first block would contain the chapter title, and the second block would contain the section title.

If your header or footer design uses stacked information in more than one position, then you may want to use the second method, which is customizing the layout table. Using multiple rows in a layout table ensures that the different information will align vertically.

The `header.table` template in `fo/pagesetup.xsl` lays out the table rows and cells in the page header. Likewise the `footer.table` lays out the footer area. You can customize either template to write a table to display whatever combination of rows and cells and spans you want, expressed in XSL-FO table elements.

As you will see in the original template, each `fo:table-cell` must have a call to the `header.content` template, and it must communicate that cell's location in the table using the `position` param. The original `left`, `center`, and `right` values are just strings that are matched in the default `header.content` template. You can add your own position values like `row1col2`, as long as you match it with a selection in your customized `header.content` template.

Changing header or footer styles

You can change the font family, size, style, and other attributes of the headers or footers such as borders and background color by customizing the default attribute-sets. You can put FO properties into the `header.content.properties` attribute set to change the running header style, or into the `footer.content.properties` attribute-set to change the running footer style. For example:

```
<xsl:attribute-set name="header.content.properties">
  <xsl:attribute name="font-family">Helvetica</xsl:attribute>
  <xsl:attribute name="font-size">9pt</xsl:attribute>
</xsl:attribute-set>
```

The rule lines in the headers and footers can be changed or turned off. If you want to change the style of the header rule line, you can customize the following template that is found in `fo/pagesetup.xsl`:

```
<xsl:template name="head.sep.rule">
  <xsl:param name="pageclass"/>
  <xsl:param name="sequence"/>
  <xsl:param name="gentext-key"/>

  <xsl:if test="$header.rule != 0">
    <xsl:attribute name="border-bottom-width">0.5pt</xsl:attribute>
    <xsl:attribute name="border-bottom-style">solid</xsl:attribute>
    <xsl:attribute name="border-bottom-color">black</xsl:attribute>
  </xsl:if>
</xsl:template>
```

An identical template named `foot.sep.rule` lets you control footer rules. The template parameters let you customize which pages have rules or have different rule styles. These parameters are described in the section called "Changing the header or footer text" (page 212). For example, if you wanted to turn off the header rule line for book title pages and the first page of chapters, you could use the following customization:

Example 13.14. Customizing header rule lines

```
<xsl:template name="head.sep.rule">
  <xsl:param name="pageclass"/>
  <xsl:param name="sequence"/>
  <xsl:param name="gentext-key"/>

  <xsl:if test="$header.rule != 0">
    <xsl:choose>
      <xsl:when test="$pageclass = 'titlepage'">
        <!-- off -->
      </xsl:when>
      <xsl:when test="$pageclass = 'body' and $sequence = 'first'">
        <!-- off -->
      </xsl:when>
      <xsl:otherwise>
        <xsl:attribute name="border-bottom-width">0.5pt</xsl:attribute>
        <xsl:attribute name="border-bottom-style">solid</xsl:attribute>
        <xsl:attribute name="border-bottom-color">black</xsl:attribute>
      </xsl:choose>
    </xsl:choose>
  </xsl:if>
</xsl:template>
```

If you want to turn off the header rule entirely, set the stylesheet parameter `header.rule` to zero. To turn off the footer rule, set `footer.rule` to zero.

You can use the `header.table.properties` attribute-set to apply properties to the table used to lay out the header content. Likewise there is a `footer.table.properties` attribute-set for footers (both becoming available in version 1.72 of the stylesheets). You can use these attribute-sets to draw a border or apply a background color. The following example does both:

```
<xsl:attribute-set name="header.table.properties">
  <xsl:attribute name="background-color">#DDDDDD</xsl:attribute>
  <xsl:attribute name="border">0.5pt solid black</xsl:attribute>
  <xsl:attribute name="padding-left">5pt</xsl:attribute>
  <xsl:attribute name="padding-right">5pt</xsl:attribute>
</xsl:attribute-set>

<xsl:param name="header.rule">0</xsl:param>
```

To improve the appearance, this example adds some padding to separate the text from the border, and turns off the normal header rule so it does not override the new border.

If you need more control, then you will need to customize the template files that create the tables that format the headers or footers. These templates are named `header.table` and `footer.table`, respectively, and they are located in `fo/pagesetup.xsl`. Customizing these templates gives you complete control over the handling of content in the headers and footers.

Allocating widths in the headers and footers

The header or footer is laid out using a single row three-cell table for the left, center, and right positions. Text in the left cell is left-aligned, text in the middle cell is centered, and text in the right cell is right-aligned. By default, all three cell positions are assigned the same width. But you may need to adjust the relative widths to fit your pattern of text. A page number requires very little space, while a long chapter title may need more than a third of the page width.

You can use the `header.column.widths` and `footer.column.widths` parameters to adjust the relative widths. Each parameter takes three numbers separated by white space. Each number represents its proportion of the sum of the three numbers. For example:

```
<xsl:param name="header.column.widths">1 2 1</xsl:param>
```

The first number represents the relative width of the left position, the second number the relative width of the middle position, and the third number the relative width of the right position. That is for single-sided output. For double-sided output, a mirrored design is assumed, so the first number represents the inside position, and the third number represents the outside position. So in this example, the middle position is twice as wide as either of the other two positions.

Here are some guidelines for setting these width values:

- The numbers do not have to be integers, but there must be three of them, and they must not be negative.

- Each column's relative width is taken as its value divided by the sum of the three numbers. So the left position in the above example is 1 divided by 4, or 25% of the available width.

- If you use the middle position and want to keep it centered, then the first and third numbers must be equal to each other. Otherwise the middle position will not be centered (which may be ok in your design).

- You can set any of the numbers to zero, and the stylesheet will then allocate the space among the remaining numbers. For example, using `1 0 3` means the left postion is 25% and the right position is 75%. Using `0 0 1` means the right position is 100%. Just be sure your `header.content` template does not attempt to put content into a zero-width position, or you will likely generate errors.

- If some content is longer than the allocated width, then the text will try to wrap to a second line within the cell. If the cell height is not tall enough, you may lose part of your text. See the section called "Allocating height for headers and footers" (page 220) to fix that.

If you find the table layout used in headers and footer to be too restrictive, you can always replace the header or footer table with your own XSL-FO layout. You'll need to customize the template named `header.table` or `footer.table` from `fo/pagesetup.xsl`. You can keep the same template name and template parameters, but you can customize how the information is used within the header or footer space.

Allocating height for headers and footers

If you plan to put more in the headers or footers than just short bits of text, then you need to provide sufficient space. The header text is positioned within the top margin using three parameters, as described in the section called "Top and bottom margins" (page 83), with similar parameters for the footer text in the bottom margin.

The parameter that sets the height of the header area is `region.before.extent`. It gets that name from the XSL-FO standard (enough said). The default height is 0.4 inches, which is about 29 points. Since the default line-height is 12 points, there is room for two lines of text. That's helpful when you carry running titles in the header, because some titles may be long enough to wrap to a second line.

If you increase the header font size and line height by setting attributes in the `header.content.properties` attribute-set, you may also need to increase the `region.before.extent` parameter. Remember that the header area has to fit within the top margin area, though, so you may also need to increase those two margin parameters as well, to give it more space and to adjust its position. If you are changing the footer size, then it is the `region.after.extent` and the bottom margin parameters that would need adjustment.

If you add a graphic to the header or footer content, be sure its `content-height` property fits within the appropriate region extent.

Page numbering style

The DocBook XSL print stylesheet provides a pair of named templates, `initial.page.number` and `format.page.number`, that give you complete control over the page numbering style in your document. The default numbering style for a book uses lowercase roman numerals (i, ii, iii, etc.) for the front matter, and then restarts with arabic numeral 1 on the first chapter. But you may want a style that numbers consecutively in arabic numerals without restarting, or that starts with page 1 in the table of contents. instead of the title page.

Initial page number

Customize the `initial.page.number` template to change which parts of your document restart the numbering sequence. That template is called at the start of each page-sequence, which is the only place in XSL-FO where you can change the starting page number. The template works through several `xsl:choose` statements and returns a single value for the `initial-page-number` property that is added to the `fo:page-sequence` output element. If the template returns a literal number such as 1, then the calling page sequence will restart page numbering with that number. If the template returns `auto`, then the calling page sequence continues the page numbering from the previous page-sequence. If the template returns `auto-odd`, then the calling page sequence continues the page numbering but forces the new page-sequence to start on an odd numbered page (the processor will generate a blank page if needed).

Here is the first part of the original template, which resides in `fo/pagesetup.xsl`:

```
<xsl:template name="initial.page.number">
  <xsl:param name="element" select="local-name(.)"/>    ❶
  <xsl:param name="master-reference" select="''"/>    ❷

  <xsl:choose>
    <!-- double-sided output -->
    <xsl:when test="$double.sided != 0">    ❸
      <xsl:choose>
        <xsl:when test="$element = 'toc'">auto-odd</xsl:when>    ❹
        <xsl:when test="$element = 'book'">1</xsl:when>    ❺
        <xsl:when test="$element = 'part' and not(preceding::chapter)
                        and not(preceding::part)">1</xsl:when>    ❻
        ...
```

❶   The `$element` parameter that is passed to the template has the name of the element that starts this page sequence, such as book, chapter, appendix, etc.
❷   The `$master-reference` parameter that is passed to the template has the name of the page-master, such as `titlepage`, `lot`, `front`, `body`, `back`, or `index`.
❸   The first `xsl:choose` statement determines whether the document is being formatted for double-sided or single-sided output. Generally a value of `auto` is used for single-sided output, which gets the next consecutive page number (odd or even). A value of `auto-odd` is used for double-sided output to force each page-sequence to start on a right-hand (odd) page.

❹   The table of contents (toc) continues the current page numbering without restarting. The auto-odd value forces it to start on an odd-numbered page. Although you may not have a literal toc element in your book, the stylesheet calls the template with that as the element name for table of contents page sequence.

❺   When the element is a book, the starting page number is set to 1.

❻   When the element is a part, the stylesheet has to determine if this is the first part element in the book. If so, the starting page number is 1. If it is not the first part, then the selection falls through to the xsl:otherwise statement that selects a value of auto-odd. The selection process for chapters has a similar set of conditions, so that only the first chapter restarts page numbering.

As you can see, the template provides complete control over when page numbering restarts. You can copy the template to your customization layer and change whatever parts you like.

Page number format

If you change the page numbering sequence, you may also want to change the page number format used for different page sequences. Customize the page.number.format template from fo/pagesetup.xsl to do that. It returns a value, either i or 1 that is used in the format property of the page-sequence element. Here is the original template:

```
<xsl:template name="page.number.format">
  <xsl:param name="element" select="local-name(.)"/>
  <xsl:param name="master-reference" select="''"/>

  <xsl:choose>
    <xsl:when test="$element = 'toc' and self::book">i</xsl:when>
    <xsl:when test="$element = 'preface'">i</xsl:when>
    <xsl:when test="$element = 'dedication'">i</xsl:when>
    <xsl:otherwise>1</xsl:otherwise>
  </xsl:choose>
</xsl:template>
```

As you can see, the front matter page sequences use the lowercase roman numeral by default, while all other page sequences use arabic numerals.

If you need Arabic-Indic page numbering, then use ١, which is the number 1 in Arabic-Indic numbers. That tells the XSLT processor to use that sequence of Unicode numbers instead of the sequence starting with "1".

Consecutive page numbering

Most documents use consecutive page numbering from start to finish. However, a book document numbers the front matter with lowercase roman numerals, and then restarts numbering at 1 with arabic numerals in the first chapter. If you want a consecutive page numbering style throughout a book, then the customizations of the two page numbering templates are amazingly simple. Just add these two one-line templates to your customization layer. Then all your pages will be numbered consecutively with arabic numerals:

```
<xsl:template name="initial.page.number">auto-odd</xsl:template>
<xsl:template name="page.number.format">1</xsl:template>
```

These templates always return the same value, regardless of which page-sequence calls them. The first page sequence will start with 1 even when the value is auto-odd because the default value for the first page sequence is 1.

Page *x* of *y* numbering

Some document styles call for page numbering that indicates the total number of pages in the document, such as Page 3 of 38. If you are using the XEP XSL-FO processor, you can use its extension element to achieve this effect (see the section called "XEP last page extension" (page 224)). Otherwise, use the information in this section.

This numbering style works best when the pages are numbered consecutively through the document. If you use roman numerals in your front matter, for example, you would see a page number like iii of 38, which looks a bit odd. If you restart page numbering after the roman numerals, then you will also have a page 3 of 38. See the section called "Consecutive page numbering" (page 222) to avoid these problems.

There is no stylesheet parameter for this page numbering style, but you can implement it with a customization that has two parts.

- Output an empty fo:block with an id at the end of your document.

- In your page footer or header, create a reference to this empty block and then the regular page number.

The first part is the hardest. It requires customizing the template for the last page sequence in the document. But several elements can appear last, so this solution works best when all the documents using the stylesheet end with the same element, such as index. If that is the case, then copy the template that matches on book/index to your customization and make the following customization:

```
<xsl:template match="book/index|part/index">
  ...
      <fo:block id="END-OF-DOCUMENT"/>
    </fo:flow>
  </fo:page-sequence>
 </xsl:if>
</xsl:template>
```

This will output the empty block marker at the end of the index page sequence. Depending on the location of your page numbers, you then customize the template named footer.content or header.content as described further in the section called "Changing the header or footer text" (page 212). Make the following changes:

```
...
<xsl:when test="$double.sided = 0 and $position='center'">
  <xsl:text>Page </xsl:text>
  <fo:page-number/>
  <xsl:text> of </xsl:text>
  <fo:page-number-citation ref-id="END-OF-DOCUMENT"/>
</xsl:when>
...
```

This outputs the word Page followed by the current page number, followed by the word of followed by the page number reference to the empty block.

> **Note:**
>
> This page numbering style does not work as well for double-sided output. In double-sided output, if the last page ends on an odd page, then a blank page is automatically generated to end on an even page. Unfortunately, there is no way to get the empty marker block onto that even-numbered blank page. So the last page reference is to the last page that has content, rather than the last page in the document. You might want to turn off the footer for generated blank pages by setting the stylesheet parameter footers.on.blank.pages to zero. Likewise for headers if your page numbers are in your header.

With some documents you could add a processing instruction at the end of the document and add a stylesheet customization to plant the empty block marker. You would put the processing instruction just before the closing tag of the last element that creates an fo:page-sequence. For example, if you have a book comprised of chapters, then you would place the processing instruction just before the closing tag of the last chapter. Putting it before the closing tag of the book element will not work, because that will place an fo:block outside of any fo:page-sequence, which will cause the XSL-FO processor to fail. This method also will not work if the last element's content is generated (such as `index`), or if the last element's template selects only certain children to process (such as `glossary`) instead of doing a general `xsl:apply-templates`.

XEP last page extension

The XEP XSL-FO processor has an extension to enable a reference to the last page number. With this extension, you do not have to force a marker block at the end of the content, and it will print the last page's number even when it is a generated blank page in double-sided output.

You put the extension element `rx:page-number-citation-last` where you want the last page number to be displayed in the header or footer. Like the `fo:page-number-citation` element, it requires a `ref-id` attribute, in this case to point to the `fo:root` element in the FO output. However, the DocBook stylesheet does not add an `id` to that element by default. So here are the steps to using this extension:

1. Add the RenderX extension namespace to your customization layer's root element:

```
<xsl:stylesheet xmlns:xsl="http://www.w3.org/1999/XSL/Transform"
                xmlns:rx="http://www.renderx.com/XSL/Extensions"
```

2. Add an `id` attribute of your choosing to the attribute-set named `root.properties`. The following example will add `id="fo_root_element_id"` to the `fo:root` element in the output.

```
<xsl:attribute-set name="root.properties">
  <xsl:attribute name="id">fo_root_element_id</xsl:attribute>
</xsl:attribute-set>
```

3. Place the XEP extension element in your customization of the `header.content` or `footer.content` template where your page numbers appear, and use the `ref-id` attribute to reference the root `id` value you just specified.

```
...
<xsl:when test="$double.sided = 0 and $position='center'">
  <xsl:text>Page </xsl:text>
  <fo:page-number/>
  <xsl:text> of </xsl:text>
  <rx:last-page-number-citation ref-id="fo_root_element_id"/>
</xsl:when>
...
```

Page number prefix

Some styles call for putting a chapter number prefix on page numbers and restarting the page count in each chapter. So pages in chapter one would be numbered 1-1, 1-2, 1-3, etc., and those in chapter two would be numbered 2-1, 2-2, 2-3, etc.

Currently there is no parameter in the stylesheets that turns on this style of page numbering. However, Jeff Beal has kindly made available a stylesheet customization for *Page Number Prefixes*[2] that you can download from the DocBook Wiki site. His customization lets you add a chapter prefix to page numbers that print on the pages as well as in the TOC, index, and cross references.

Index entries may present problems for chapter-page numbering style. If you are using XEP and its index page numbering extensions to create page ranges, you will find that the chapter prefix is lost in the index (which renders

---

[2] http://wiki.docbook.org/topic/PageNumberPrefixes

the index useless). That's because the XEP index extensions handle the page number references after the stylesheet has completed its work, and the XEP processor is not aware of the page number prefix.

XSL Formatter from Antenna House has an extension attribute for page number prefixes. If you set the `axf:page-number-prefix` attribute to a string value, that string is appended to all instances of generated page numbers, including index page references. You generally add this property to each `fo:page-sequence`, with a string value appropriate to that page sequence. There is no stylesheet parameter that turns this feature on, so a customization is required. One way is to customize the template for `mode="running.head.mode"`. That template is called at the beginning of each page sequence before any there is any output in the page sequence. You can customize the template to output this attribute, with a value created by a custom template mode that generates the prefix text for each chapter, appendix, etc.

Add extension property to each fo:page-sequence element:
```
<xsl:template match="*" mode="running.head.mode">
  <xsl:param name="master-reference" select="'unknown'"/>
  <xsl:param name="gentext-key" select="name(.)"/>

  <xsl:if test="$axf.extensions != 0">
    <xsl:attribute name="axf:page-number-prefix">
      <xsl:apply-templates select="." mode="page-number-prefix"/>
    </xsl:attribute>
  </xsl:if>
  ...
</xsl:template>
```

Example custom template to generate the prefix text:
```
<!-- Also match on elements inside a chapter for index and xref targets -->
<xsl:template match="chapter|chapter//*" mode="page-number-prefix">
  <xsl:if test="$page.number.prefixes != 0">
    <xsl:number count="chapter" from="book" level="any"/>
    <xsl:value-of select="$page.number.prefix.separator"/>
  </xsl:if>
</xsl:template>
```

Restart page numbering in each page-sequence:
```
<xsl:template name="initial.page.number">1</xsl:template>
```

Ending page number

If you use double-sided output, you have the choice of whether to end the document on an even-numbered page. That is, if the last bit of content lands on an odd-numbered page, should a blank even page be generated? If you are primarily interested in preparing a document to hand to a print vendor, then you probably want to end on an even page. But if you are primarily interested in generating a PDF file, you may not want to. That's because many people print their PDF on a single-sided printer, and a blank last page would just be a waste.

The default for double-sided output is to end on an even page. You can customize the `force.page.count` template to change that behavior. Here is the original template:

```
<xsl:template name="force.page.count">
  <xsl:param name="element" select="local-name(.)"/>
  <xsl:param name="master-reference" select="''"/>

  <xsl:choose>
    <!-- double-sided output -->
    <xsl:when test="$double.sided != 0">end-on-even</xsl:when>
    <!-- single-sided output -->
    <xsl:otherwise>no-force</xsl:otherwise>
  </xsl:choose>
</xsl:template>
```

The two choices are:

end-on-even   This will force a blank even-numbered page if the document content ends on an odd page.

no-force   No blank page is generated at the end.

Borders and background shading

In HTML output, you can use CSS styles to add borders and background shading to your already generated HTML. But for print, the XSL templates have to supply the border and background properties.

If the element you want to style has its own attribute-set defined in the stylesheet, then adding borders and shading is done by simply adding attributes to the set. All of these elements have such attribute-sets:

admonitions (note, caution, etc.)   qanda titles
blockquotes   refentry titles
component titles (chapter, etc.)   section titles
equations   sections
examples   sidebars
figures   tables
formal object titles   verbatims (programlisting, literallayout)
procedures

In this example, borders and shading are added to all admonitions (note, caution, warning, tip, and important).

```
<xsl:attribute-set name="admonition.properties">
  <xsl:attribute name="border">0.5pt solid blue</xsl:attribute>
  <xsl:attribute name="background-color">#E0E0E0</xsl:attribute>
  <xsl:attribute name="padding">0.1in</xsl:attribute>
</xsl:attribute-set>
```

Likewise, this example adds a shaded background band behind each level 1 section title. The band extends across the page because the title's generated block area extends across the page, even if the text does not.

```
<xsl:attribute-set name="section.title.level1.properties">
  <xsl:attribute name="background-color">#E0E0E0</xsl:attribute>
  <xsl:attribute name="padding">8pt</xsl:attribute>
</xsl:attribute-set>
```

If the element you want to style does not have its own attribute-set, you will need to customize the template that formats the element. You may also want customize a template for an element that has such an attribute-set. For example, the admonition.properties attribute set applies to the body of a note, and does not include its title.

In your customization, you will want to find where the outer fo:block is output and add a border or background-color attribute. The following example adds them for formalpara elements:

```
<xsl:template match="formalpara">
  <fo:block xsl:use-attribute-sets="normal.para.spacing"
        background-color="#E0E0E0"
        border="0.5pt solid blue"
        padding="3pt">
    <xsl:apply-templates/>
  </fo:block>
</xsl:template>
```

The padding attribute adds a bit of shaded space around the text so the border is not almost touching the text.

Customizing inline text

Inline elements such as emphasis can be customized by replacing their templates in a customization layer. See the section called "Replacing templates" (page 107) for a description of the general method. The templates to be customized can be found in fo/inline.xsl for FO output.

Many of the templates for inline elements call one of the following named templates to change font. These template names are also used in the HTML stylesheets.

`<xsl:call-template name="inline.charseq"/>`	Format with normal font.
`<xsl:call-template name="inline.boldseq"/>`	Format with boldface.
`<xsl:call-template name="inline.italicseq"/>`	Format with italics.
`<xsl:call-template name="inline.monoseq"/>`	Format with monospace font.
`<xsl:call-template name="inline.italicmonoseq"/>`	Format with italic monospace font.
`<xsl:call-template name="inline.boldmonoseq"/>`	Format with bold monospace font.
`<xsl:call-template name="inline.superscriptseq"/>`	Format with superscript.
`<xsl:call-template name="inline.subscriptseq"/>`	Format with subscript.

Customizing inline elements that use these templates may mean just calling a different one of these templates. For example, this customization changes the font for the filename element from the default monospace to italic:

```
<xsl:template match="filename">
  <xsl:call-template name="inline.italicseq"/>
</xsl:template>
```

You can also add templates with more specific match attributes to further customize elements. For example, the filename element can also be used for directory names. You might use the class attribute to distinguish directory names, and then add a custom template to format them in boldface:

```
<xsl:template  match="filename[@class='directory']">
  <xsl:call-template  name="inline.boldseq"/>
</xsl:template>
```

The @class='directory' predicate means this template will only be considered for use on filename elements that have a class="directory" attribute. Its match attribute is more specific than the regular filename template, so it has precedence when that role value is used.

A similar template lets you customize formatting of phrase elements based on its role attribute value. A phrase with role attribute is an easy way to add specialized elements to your content, without having to customize the DTD. Here is a customization that handles genus and species names:

```
<xsl:template match="phrase[@role='genus']">
  <xsl:call-template name="inline.boldseq"/>
</xsl:template>
<xsl:template match="phrase[@role='species']">
  <xsl:call-template name="inline.italicseq"/>
</xsl:template>
```

This customization will output <phrase role="genus"> in bold, and <phrase role="species"> in italic.

If you want to select a font family that is different from the body font, then you need to customize such templates a bit further. See the section called "Line annotations" (page 445) for an example of customizing the font used for the lineannotation element.

Subscripts and superscripts

The DocBook XSL stylesheets provide separate attribute-sets for subscripts and superscripts. Some designers are quite picky about how those should be formatted, so these attribute-sets let you fine tune their styles.

Use the subscript.properties attribute-set to style subscripts, and the superscript.properties attribute-set to style superscripts. The default attribute-sets just reduce the font-size to 75%. You can adjust the font size, or change other font properties as in the example below. However, the shift in vertical position of sub- and superscripts is currently not handled by these attribute-sets. That's because the current FOP does not support the preferred baseline-shift property, so a different property must be used for that processor.

```
<xsl:attribute-set name="superscript.properties">
  <xsl:attribute name="font-size">60%</xsl:attribute>
  <xsl:attribute name="font-family">serif</xsl:attribute>
</xsl:attribute-set>
```

Underline and strike-through

Underlining can be added to inline text using the XSL-FO property text-decoration="underline". Likewise, text with a horizontal line through it can be generated using text-decoration="line-through". Although there is no enumerated value of role for these properties in the DocBook schema, the DocBook print stylesheet has support for these properties on any emphasis element with a role="underline" or role="strikethrough" attribute, respectively.

This template fragment shows how the properties are applied in the template with match="emphasis" in fo/inline.xsl:

```
    <xsl:when test="@role='underline'">
      <fo:inline text-decoration="underline">
        <xsl:call-template name="inline.charseq"/>
      </fo:inline>
    </xsl:when>
    <xsl:when test="@role='strikethrough'">
      <fo:inline text-decoration="line-through">
        <xsl:call-template name="inline.charseq"/>
      </fo:inline>
    </xsl:when>
```

The template wraps the element's content in an `fo:inline` element with the appropriate property added. You can use a similar technique in a customization layer to add underlining or strikethrough to other elements.

For HTML output, you can use CSS to supply the underline or strikethrough formatting. If you set the stylesheet parameter `emphasis.propagates.style` to 1, then the value of a `role` attribute on an `emphasis` element will be passed through as a `class` attribute in the HTML output. You can add the following two lines to your cascading stylesheet:

```
span.underline {text-decoration: underline;}
span.strikethrough {text-decoration: line-through;}
```

These CSS selectors use the output element name and class name to apply the CSS `text-decoration` property to the text.

Customizing admonitions

Admonitions in DocBook include the `note`, `caution`, `warning`, `tip`, and `important` elements. They share the same DocBook templates so that their output styles are similar. You can do some customization using just stylesheet parameters, as described in the section called "Admonition graphics" (page 92). But if you want to do more extensive changes, you will need to customize some templates.

If all you are doing is customizing the admonition graphics, that is easily done. When you create your admonition image files, just name them after the corresponding DocBook element, for example `note.png`. If you are using a different file format, then use the `admon.graphics.extension` parameter to indicate the new filename extension. You may also need to use the `admon.graphics.path` parameter to indicate the location of your graphics files so the XSL-FO processor can find them and merge them into the PDF output.

If your image files are larger or smaller than the stock image files, then you can customize the template in `admon.graphic.width` mode that sets the graphic width. This is a *template mode*, not a parameter, and the templates should return a width value. Because it is a mode, you can have a different template for each admonition element to support different image widths. For example:

```
<xsl:template match="note" mode="admon.graphic.width">
  <xsl:text>24pt</xsl:text>
</xsl:template>

<xsl:template match="*" mode="admon.graphic.width">
  <xsl:text>32pt</xsl:text>
</xsl:template>
```

With this customization, the image for a `note` element gets a 24pt width, and all the other admonition elements get a 32pt width (the default is 36pt). For HTML output, there is a similar template mode for adjusting image widths.

If you want to change the typography for admonitions, there are several attribute-sets you can customize. The outermost `fo:block` containing the entire admonition (title, graphic, text) can be customized using either the `graphical.admonition.properties` or `nongraphical.admonition.properties` attribute-set, whichever style you are using (selected by the `admon.graphics` parameter). Use either of these attribute-sets to establish spacing, indents, font changes, borders, or background color for the entire admonition.

The `admonition.properties` attribute-set is applied to the text content, not including any title or graphic. Any attributes declared in it are added to the block containing the content of the admonition element, but not the title.

If you want to customize the title typography, you can use the `admonition.title.properties` attribute-set. These attribute sets can also be used to change the indents and spacing around the title.

If these methods are not sufficient for your needs, then you can customize the template that formats the admonition. If you have the `admon.graphics` parameter set to 1, then you need to customize the template named `graphical.admonition` in `fo/admon.xsl`. If you are not using graphical admonitions, then customize the template named `nongraphical.admonition` instead. For example, the following customization draws rule lines above and below each admonition:

```
<xsl:template name="nongraphical.admonition">
  <xsl:variable name="id">
    <xsl:call-template name="object.id"/>
  </xsl:variable>

  <fo:block space-before.minimum="0.8em"
            space-before.optimum="1em"
            space-before.maximum="1.2em"
            start-indent="0.25in"
            end-indent="0.25in"
            border-top="0.5pt solid black"
            border-bottom="0.5pt solid black"
            padding-top="4pt"
            padding-bottom="4pt"
            id="{$id}">
    <xsl:if test="$admon.textlabel != 0 or title">
      <fo:block keep-with-next='always'
                xsl:use-attribute-sets="admonition.title.properties">
        <xsl:apply-templates select="." mode="object.title.markup"/>
      </fo:block>
    </xsl:if>

    <fo:block xsl:use-attribute-sets="admonition.properties">
      <xsl:apply-templates/>
    </fo:block>
  </fo:block>
</xsl:template>
```

Side-by-side formatting

Displaying text items side by side with a *hanging indent* is a common format that has many applications. Here are some example design ideas:

- Display a section number next to an indented section title.

- Display a section title next to the indented body text of a section.

- Display an admonition icon next to the indented text of the admonition in a `note` or `caution`, for example.

- Display a caption next to an figure.

All of these designs can be achieved using the XSL-FO `fo:list-block` element. It formats like a two-column table. One example of its current use is for `variablelist`, where it displays each `term` element in a `varlistentry` next to its `listitem` body content. The same kind of side-by-side formatting can be done for a single pair rather than a sequence of pairs. The only restriction is that there be only two items side-by-side. Any more than that and you will need to use a table.

The following is an example customization that puts a section number at the left margin next to its indented section title.

Example 13.15. Format section titles with fo:list-block

```
<xsl:param name="body.start.indent">30mm</xsl:param> ❶

<xsl:template name="section.heading"> ❷
  <xsl:param name="level" select="1"/>
  <xsl:param name="marker" select="1"/>
  <xsl:param name="title"/>
  <xsl:param name="marker.title"/>

  <xsl:variable name="title.block"> ❸
    <fo:list-block start-indent="0mm"
            provisional-distance-between-starts="{$body.start.indent}" ❹
            provisional-label-separation="5mm">
      <fo:list-item> ❺
        <fo:list-item-label end-indent="label-end()" text-align="start"> ❻
          <fo:block>
            <xsl:apply-templates select="parent::*" mode="label.markup"/> ❼
          </fo:block>
        </fo:list-item-label>
        <fo:list-item-body start-indent="body-start()" text-align="start"> ❽
          <fo:block>
            <xsl:apply-templates select="parent::*" mode="title.markup"/> ❾
          </fo:block>
        </fo:list-item-body>
      </fo:list-item>
    </fo:list-block>
  </xsl:variable>

  <fo:block xsl:use-attribute-sets="section.title.properties">
    <xsl:if test="$marker != 0">
      <fo:marker marker-class-name="section.head.marker">
        <xsl:copy-of select="$marker.title"/>
      </fo:marker>
    </xsl:if>

    <xsl:choose>
      <xsl:when test="$level=1">
        <fo:block xsl:use-attribute-sets="section.title.level1.properties">
          <xsl:copy-of select="$title.block"/> ❿
        </fo:block>
      </xsl:when>
      ...
    </xsl:choose>
  </fo:block>
</xsl:template>
```

❶ Sets a body.start.indent to indent all body text from the left margin. In this design, the section number will be out to the left margin.

❷ Customize the template named section.heading, which formats the title with correct properties for each section level. It works for both section and the sect1, sect2 type of elements. It usually formats the value of its title parameter, but this customization will generate the title in a formatted block.

❸ Define a variable named title.block that will be used in place of the $title parameter passed into this template. The local variable will hold the fo:list-block until it is output at a given section level.

❹ The fo:list-block element has three properties:

- The `start-indent` is set to zero so the left edge of the `fo:list-block` starts at the left margin, so the section number can appear there.

- The `provisional-distance-between-starts` is set to the width of the indent of the list-block. In this case, it indents to a value equal to the body indent. Then the title will line up with the body text. You can set the indent to any value you want.

- The `provisional-label-separation` establishes the minimum space between the end of the left text and the beginning of the right text.

❺ This list block contains a single `fo:list-item` element, which contains the list item label and list item body.

❻ The `fo:list-item-label` element contains the left text. Its `end-indent` property uses a special XSL-FO `label-end()` function to compute the indent of the right side of the block that it contains. If you do not set this property, then the left block will overlap the right block.

❼ The content of the left side is generated by processing the element in `mode="label.markup"`, which generates the section number alone. Note that in this case it actually processes the parent section element, because `section.heading` is called by the template that matches the section `title` element, not by the section itself.

❽ The `fo:list-item-body` contains the right text. Its `start-indent` property uses a special XSL-FO `body-start()` function to compute the indent the left side of the block that it contains.

❾ The content of the right side is generated by processing the element in `mode="title.markup"`, which generates the section title alone.

❿ Replace the use of `$title` with `$title.block` in each of the `xsl:when` clauses that follow.

Any number of variations can be used. For example, if you use `text-align="end"` on the `fo:list-item-label`, then the section number will be right-aligned in its space, separated from the left-aligned title by the `provisional-label-separation` distance. Other elements can be formatted using similar techniques.

Side floats

A *side float* is used to position a block of content to the side of a page. The body text will wrap around the side float if it does not take up the whole width of the page, or the side float can be positioned in a side indent so it does not intrude on the text area.

The DocBook XSL print stylesheet added support for side floats starting in version 1.68 of the stylesheet. For print output, side floats only work with those XSL-FO processors that support them. Two that are known to work are RenderX's XEP and Antenna House's XSL Formatter.

The DocBook FO stylesheet provides support for several kinds of side floats:

- The `sidebar` element rendered as a side float.

- A `sidebar` element with a processing instruction that identifies it as a margin note.

- A `figure`, `table`, or `example` element with a `floatstyle` attribute. See the section called "Figure floats" (page 295) for details.

- Custom side floats.

A sidebar as side float

One common use of side floats is for the `sidebar` element. By default, a `sidebar` prints as a full-width block on the page instead of a side float. The following example shows some text in a sidebar to demonstrate how it can appear in a left side float.

Sidebar example A sidebar can be used to emphasize certain content. It can intrude into the body area, or it can appear in side indents as a margin note.	``` <sidebar> <title>Sidebar example</title> <?dbfo sidebar-width="1.5in"?><?dbfo float-type="left"?> <para>A <sgmltag class="element">sidebar</sgmltag> can be used to emphasize certain content. It can intrude into the body area, or it can appear in side indents as a margin note.</para> </sidebar> ```

The formatting of a `sidebar` is controlled by these features:

* `sidebar.float.type` parameter
* `sidebar.float.width` parameter
* `sidebar.properties` attribute-set
* `sidebar.title.properties` attribute-set
* Processing instructions for individual instances.

The overall behavior is controlled by the `sidebar.float.type` stylesheet parameter. That parameter contains one of the values of the `float` property as defined in the XSL-FO specification:

`none`	No float is used. The sidebar appears in sequence with other text blocks. This is the default value.
`left`	The float appears on the left side of the page.
`start`	The float appears on the `start` side of the page. For languages that read left-to-right, that is the left side of the page.
`right`	The float appears on the right side of the page.
`end`	The float appears on the `end` side of the page. For languages that read left-to-right, that is the right side of the page.
`inside` `outside`	Some XSL-FO processors such as Antenna House's XSL Formatter and XEP support an extension to the spec that can position the float to the inside or outside of pages using double-sided output. Here `outside` means to the left on left-hand pages, and to the right on right-hand pages.
`before`	The float appears at the top of the page, using the full width of the page. This is not a side float, but is included here for completeness.

The `sidebar.float.type` sets the default location for all sidebars, but you can change the location for an individual `sidebar` element using a `float-type` processing instruction. The following is an example that will create a float on the right side of the page:

```
<sidebar>
<?dbfo float-type="right"?>
<title>My floating sidebar</title>
...
```

The width of the sidebar float is controlled by `sidebar.float.width` parameter, which is set to 1 inch by default. You may need to set a different width for individual `sidebar` elements. You can change the width for one sidebar using a `sidebar-width` processing instruction, such as this example:

```
<sidebar>
<?dbfo sidebar-width="3.5in"?>
<title>My floating sidebar</title>
...
```

In addition to the above properties being applied to the float container, the `sidebar.properties` attribute set is applied to the block of content within the container. Use that property set to change the font size, text alignment, background, or border for the content. The following example shows the default values:

```
<xsl:attribute-set name="sidebar.properties"
        use-attribute-sets="formal.object.properties">
  <xsl:attribute name="border-style">solid</xsl:attribute>
  <xsl:attribute name="border-width">1pt</xsl:attribute>
  <xsl:attribute name="border-color">black</xsl:attribute>
  <xsl:attribute name="background-color">#DDDDDD</xsl:attribute>
  <xsl:attribute name="padding-left">12pt</xsl:attribute>
  <xsl:attribute name="padding-right">12pt</xsl:attribute>
  <xsl:attribute name="padding-top">6pt</xsl:attribute>
  <xsl:attribute name="padding-bottom">6pt</xsl:attribute>
  <xsl:attribute name="margin-left">0pt</xsl:attribute>
  <xsl:attribute name="margin-right">0pt</xsl:attribute>
  <!--
  <xsl:attribute name="margin-top">6pt</xsl:attribute>
  <xsl:attribute name="margin-bottom">6pt</xsl:attribute>
  -->
</xsl:attribute-set>
```

These properties draw a border around the sidebar content and add a background color. The padding properties add some space between the sidebar text and the border. The margin properties can be used to provide some space between the border and the body text that wraps around the sidebar. To learn how to customize an attribute-set, see the section called "Attribute sets" (page 103).

In addition, the separate `sidebar.title.properties` attribute-set is applied to the sidebar's `title` element. Here are its default values:

```
<xsl:attribute-set name="sidebar.title.properties">
  <xsl:attribute name="font-weight">bold</xsl:attribute>
  <xsl:attribute name="hyphenate">false</xsl:attribute>
  <xsl:attribute name="text-align">start</xsl:attribute>
  <xsl:attribute name="keep-with-next.within-column">always</xsl:attribute>
</xsl:attribute-set>
```

Margin notes

Margin notes are blocks of content that are meant to appear in the empty margin area, rather than having text wrap around them like with a sidebar. By putting them in the margin area, they do not interrupt the flow of paragraphs.

The DocBook DTD does not provide a standard way of specifying margin notes. However, the FO stylesheet supports a special sidebar as a margin note. You can also implement margin notes as a customization, as described in the section called "Custom margin notes" (page 236).

You can turn a `sidebar` element into a margin note by adding the following processing instruction:

```
<sidebar>
<?dbfo float-type="margin.note"?>
...
</sidebar>
```

When a sidebar is designated was a margin note in this way, the stylesheet applies a different set of properties to create the side float. This lets you create one style for regular sidebars, and another for margin notes.

To enable margin notes, you have to give them some open space so they do not intrude on your paragraphs. Increasing the side page margins will not work because the XSL float mechanism puts text within the body region, not outside of it in the margins. So you need to create an additional indent for all body text on the page, and the margin note floats can appear within the indent.

You can create such an indent on the left (or start side) of the page by using the `body.start.indent` parameter. If you want the indent on the right (or end side) of the page, then use the `body.end.indent` parameter. If you do not set the extra body indent, then your margin notes will intrude into the body text area. See the section called "Indenting body text" (page 84) for more information on these parameters. The following example indents the body text an extra 25mm on the left

```
<xsl:param name="body.start.indent">25mm</xsl:param>
```

After you have set up the indent area, you need to specify the formatting properties for margin notes. The `margin.note.float.type` determines the position of the margin note, using the same selection of values as for `sidebar.float.type`. See the section called "A sidebar as side float" (page 232). Note that you cannot use the `dbfo float-type` processing instruction to change the position of an individual margin note. That's because that PI is already being used to indicate that a sidebar is to be handled like a margin note.

You can set the standard width for all your margin notes by using the `margin.note.width` parameter. To change the width for a single instance, you can use the `dbfo sidebar-width` processing instruction within its `sidebar` element. If you make a margin note wider than the enlarged margin, then the margin note will intrude into the body text, which will wrap around it.

And to give your margin notes a distinctive look, add attributes to the `margin.note.properties` attribute-set. That attribute-set is applied to the block that contains the content of the `sidebar` element. For the `title` element in a margin note sidebar, use the `margin.note.title.properties` attribute-set.

Here is a complete example of setting the parameters and attribute-sets for margin notes:

```
<xsl:param name="body.start.indent">30mm</xsl:param>
<xsl:param name="margin.note.float.type">start</xsl:param>
<xsl:param name="margin.note.width">27mm</xsl:param>
<xsl:attribute-set name="margin.note.properties">
  <xsl:attribute name="font-size">8pt</xsl:attribute>
  <xsl:attribute name="font-family"><xsl:value-of
                  select="$title.fontset"/></xsl:attribute>
  <xsl:attribute name="border">0.5pt solid green</xsl:attribute>
  <xsl:attribute name="padding">3pt</xsl:attribute>
</xsl:attribute-set>
<xsl:attribute-set name="margin.note.title.properties">
  <xsl:attribute name="font-size">9pt</xsl:attribute>
</xsl:attribute-set>
```

To learn how to customize an attribute-set, see the section called "Attribute sets" (page 103).

Custom margin notes

You may want to turn other elements in your DocBook content into margin notes. For example, you might want to put a short phrase with a cross reference in the margin, or put a caution element in the margin. The FO stylesheet uses two templates to create margin notes, the margin.note template and the floater template.

The template named margin.note in fo/block.xsl is called by the sidebar template when the dbfo float-type="margin.note" processing instruction is used. The margin.note template applies all the margin note properties described in the section called "Margin notes" (page 234) to the context element that calls the template. So you would use the margin.note template when you want your customization to look like other margin notes.

Here are customizations that put a phrase or a caution element with a role="margin.note" attribute into a margin note:

```
<xsl:template match="phrase[@role='margin.note']">
  <xsl:call-template name="margin.note"/>
</xsl:template>

<xsl:template match="caution[@role='margin.note']">
  <xsl:call-template name="margin.note">
    <xsl:with-param name="content">
      <xsl:apply-imports/>
    </xsl:with-param>
  </xsl:call-template>
</xsl:template>
```

Both of these customizations call the margin.note template. They differ in the use of the content parameter when the template is called. The margin.note template just does an xsl:apply-templates to the context element that calls it. That means it processes the element's children, which is appropriate for a phrase element. But if you did that with caution, then it would process the para within the caution, but not the caution element itself. So that template fills in the content parameter by doing apply-imports on the caution element, which formats the caution using the admonition templates.

Custom side float

If you need more control than is provided by the margin.note template, then you can call the template named floater, which is also in fo/block.xsl. This is the template that actually creates a side float in the FO output, and it is called by the sidebar and margin.note templates. The floater template takes several parameters to define the float, and does not apply any formatting properties to the content. Thus you can use it to create custom side floats from any element.

The following is an example of using floater to put an admonition icon into the side margin:

Example 13.16. Custom side float

```
<xsl:param name="body.start.indent">1.5in</xsl:param>  ❶
<xsl:param name="title.margin.left">0pc</xsl:param>  ❷
<xsl:param name="admon.textlabel" select="0"/>  ❸

<xsl:template match="note|caution|warning|tip|important">  ❹
  <xsl:call-template name="floater">  ❺
    <xsl:with-param name="position">left</xsl:with-param>  ❻
    <xsl:with-param name="width">0.5in</xsl:with-param>  ❼
    <xsl:with-param name="start.indent">0.5in</xsl:with-param>  ❽
    <xsl:with-param name="content">  ❾
      <fo:block margin-top="1em"
                padding="3pt"
                text-align="center"
                border="1pt solid grey">
        <fo:external-graphic width="auto" height="auto">
          <xsl:attribute name="src">
            <xsl:call-template name="admon.graphic"/>
          </xsl:attribute>
        </fo:external-graphic>
      </fo:block>
    </xsl:with-param>
  </xsl:call-template>
  <xsl:apply-imports/>  ❿
</xsl:template>
```

❶ Establish a side margin area by indenting the body text 1.5 inches.
❷ Set `title.margin.left` to zero so it does not conflict with the `body.start.indent`.
❸ Turn off the admonition text label such as Note so only the icon is used to identify the admonition. You can leave the label if you like.
❹ Customized template to match on all admonition elements.
❺ Call the template named `floater` to create a side float.
❻ Indicate the position of the float. The default value is none, so pick one of the values listed in the section called "A sidebar as side float" (page 232) to put it in the margin.
❼ You can specify the width of the side float container.
❽ You can specify an indent for the side float container.
❾ Fill the `content` parameter with whatever you want to appear in the side float. In this case, it is an admonition graphic, selected using the `admon.graphic` template. It is wrapped in an `fo:block`, which is used to format the content.
❿ Now actually process the admonition element by using `xsl:apply-imports`. This uses the admonition templates imported from the DocBook stylesheet.

Clearing a side float

The formatting for a side float includes wrapping the content that follows the float in the source document around the side of the float. However, there may be times when this wrapping is not appropriate. For example, if a float is followed by a short paragraph and then the start of a new section, then the section title may be wrapped next to the float.

Any elements that you want to force below any side floats should have an XSL-FO `clear="both"` property added to its `fo:block`. For sections, this can be done with the attribute-set named `section.title.properties`:

```
<xsl:attribute-set name="section.title.properties">
  <xsl:attribute name="clear">both</xsl:attribute>
</xsl:attribute-set>
```

You could instead create a processing instruction and matching template to output an empty block with the `clear` property. Any elements that follow the processing instruction will start below the side float. Here is a template to add to your customization layer:

```
<xsl:template match="processing-instruction('float-clear')">
    <fo:block clear="both"/>
</xsl:template>
```

Then insert `<?float-clear?>` in your content where you want the break to occur.

Multi-columns and spans

The DocBook XSL stylesheets are capable of generating pages with two or more columns of text. By default, only the index uses two columns. Other XSL-FO page masters can be changed to multiple columns using stylesheet parameters, as described in the section called "Multi-column" (page 85).

When XSL-FO creates multiple columns on a page, the columns are called *snaking* columns. That's because the text flows down the first column to the bottom of the page, loops back up to the top of the second column, flows down the second column, and so on. In XSL-FO 1.0, all of the columns are the same width and evenly spaced apart.

Normally all of the content that flows onto such pages is fit into the width of the column. This includes chapter and section titles, figures, tables, code samples, lists, and other content. A narrow column can sometimes produce unwanted results. Here are some potential problem elements for narrow columns.

- Code samples with long lines may not fit into a narrow column.

- Long URLs displayed from `ulink` elements may need to be hyphenated. See the section called "Breaking long URLs" (page 261) for more information.

- If `imagedata` elements used for graphics specify a fixed width that is greater than the column width, then the image will simply exceed the column boundary. If it appears in the first column, then text in the second column will overwrite it. If it appears in the second column, then it will intrude into the margin.

- Likewise, if your tables specify fixed column widths that total more than the page column width, text will spill out of the column. In general, tables in a narrow page column must have few table columns, or fitting text into table columns becomes a problem.

- If full justification is turned on, be sure that hyphenation is also turned on, or you may get wide gaps between some words.

- Be sure to set the `body.start.indent` parameter to `0pt`, because each column will be indented by that amount.

Page column spans

When using multiple columns, the narrow column width often makes it hard to fit some figures, tables, and examples. It would be nice if you could tell the processor to span all columns for particular elements. You can, but there are limitations in the DocBook schema and stylesheets.

The DocBook 4.5 DTD provides a `pgwide` attribute on `figure`, `informalfigure`, `table`, and `informaltable`. The DocBook 5 schema adds `example` and `equation`. The `pgwide` attribute in the schema indicates the element is wide and may need special handling. There are two ways to handle a wider element:

- In a one-column layout that uses a `body.start.indent` to indent the body text relative to the headings, a wide element could intrude into the body indent space. That would be accomplished by setting the XSL-FO property `start-indent="0pt"` on just that element. The DocBook attribute-set named `pgwide.properties` is the place to do that:

```
<xsl:attribute-set name="pgwide.properties">
  <xsl:attribute name="start-indent">0pt</xsl:attribute>
</xsl:attribute-set>
```

- In a multi-column layout, a wide element could span all the columns. That would be accomplished by setting the XSL-FO property `span="all"` on just that element. Use the same attribute-set with a different attribute:

```
<xsl:attribute-set name="pgwide.properties">
  <xsl:attribute name="span">all</xsl:attribute>
</xsl:attribute-set>
```

The problem with `span="all"` is that the XSL-FO 1.0 standard says that `span="all"` can only appear on an `fo:block` that is a child of the `fo:flow` used for a page sequence. This is an unfortunate limitation for DocBook XSL, because it uses a lot of nested blocks that correspond to nested elements. That means if you have a figure inside a section, the `fo:block` for the figure will not meet that requirement because a `section` element wraps its content in its own `fo:block` to set properties that apply to all sections. A figure inside a chapter but before the first `section` element will work.

If you are using the Antenna House XSL-FO processor, you have it easy. That processor supports spans on nested blocks, so a figure with a `pgwide` attribute will work anywhere if you set the `span` property in `pgwide.properties` as shown above.

If you are using another XSL-FO processor, you can try setting the stylesheet parameter `section.container.element` to `wrapper`. This causes each section's output to use an `fo:wrapper` instead of `fo:block` as the outer element. This avoids the nesting of `fo:block` and allows a `pgwide` span to work when inside a section. This method is known to work with the XEP XSL-FO processor, but not the Antenna House processor (for which it is not needed), nor with FOP. The `fo:wrapper` element can accept the section `id` and the section attribute-set. However, the attribute-set only supports properties that are inheritable. That's because there is no block to apply them to. Properties such as `font-family` are inheritable, but properties such as `border` are not. The `section.container.element` parameter was added in version 1.73 of the stylesheets.

A span in XSL-FO alters the text layout on a page as follows:

- Content preceding a spanned element in the XML file is flowed in balanced columns above the spanned element. The content does not flow past the span to the bottom of the page and then back up to the top of the page. It stops at the span and restarts at the top of the page (or the bottom of a preceding span if it is on the same page).

- Content following a span is flowed in the columns below the span.

- Effectively, the top edge of a span acts as the bottom of a page for the content that precedes it.

- The bottom of a span acts as the top of a page for the content that follows it.

Because a span acts like a page boundary, any `space-before` or `space-after` properties are ignored. The effect is to push the text above and below a span right next to it. You can relieve such crowding by adding `padding` attributes as follows:

```
<xsl:attribute-set name="pgwide.properties">
  <xsl:attribute name="span">all</xsl:attribute>
  <xsl:attribute name="padding-top">12pt</xsl:attribute>
  <xsl:attribute name="padding-bottom">12pt</xsl:attribute>
</xsl:attribute-set>
```

Titles in chapters can also span a multiple column layout. Titles are handled as part of the titlepage specification system, described in Chapter 11, *Title page customization* (page 141). The titlepage system includes many nested `fo:block` elements, which normally would cause spans to be suppressed. But the stylesheet lets you add a span to the outer `fo:block` that handles all the title page information for a chapter. This means `subtitle`, `author` (if used), and any other title page information will be spanned.

The stylesheets support a global span feature using the attribute-set named `component.titlepage.properties` that applies to all chapters. In fact, it applies to all *component* elements including `appendix`, `preface`, `dedication`, and `colophon` in addition to `chapter`. Here is how it is used:

```
<xsl:attribute-set name="component.titlepage.properties">
  <xsl:attribute name="span">all</xsl:attribute>
</xsl:attribute-set>
```

With this property set, the title and any other titlepage information output for chapters will span across all columns. If you want the title page information centered, then specify that property in the titlepage spec file as described in Chapter 11, *Title page customization* (page 141). This attribute-set was added in the 1.73 version of the stylesheets.

Adding a font

There are three basic font families built into all the tools: Times Roman, Helvetica, and Courier. These correspond to the `serif`, `sans-serif`, and `monospace` generic families, respectively, that FO processors recognize. You can specify these font names or generic names in stylesheet parameters such as `body.font.family` and they will just work. But what if your print design calls for other fonts, or you just want to try something a little different?

Using other fonts requires three steps:

* You have to locate the font file in a format your XSL-FO processor will accept.

* You have to configure your XSL-FO processor to work with the new font.

* You have to include the new font name in the FO output.

Most of the XSL-FO processors can handle other fonts. What kind of fonts they can handle and how they are configured depend entirely on the processor, so you should consult the documentation for your XSL-FO processor. Included here are examples for FOP and XEP.

Locate the font file

Before you can use a new font, you must locate a font file that contains the diagrams of the font's characters. Font files come in various formats, not all of which will work with a given XSL-FO processor. Typical font file formats include TrueType and PostScript Type 1. If you have a Windows system, you can find several TrueType fonts under `\WINDOWS\FONTS` with a `.ttf` filename extension.

It is generally best to embed extra fonts in the generated PDF file, since the new fonts are unlikely to be resident and available on a given printer. With embedded fonts, the character diagrams are included in your PDF file, which makes your document portable. But the font file you use must permit the font to be embedded.

Configuring fonts in XSL-FO

Each of the XSL_FO processors has their own configuration process for fonts. For the latest information on your processor, see the processor's documentation.

Configuring a font in FOP

FOP will accept PostScript Type 1 and TrueType fonts. There are some restrictions and several options for using fonts in FOP. See *http://xmlgraphics.apache.org/fop/0.93/fonts.html* for more details about configuring fonts in FOP. The following procedure configures a Garamond TrueType font, including its bold and italic variations.

1. Generate a FOP font metrics file from the TrueType font file. FOP provides a Java command for doing so. The following example reads the Windows GARA.TTF file and generates a garamond.xml font metrics file in a fonts subdirectory of the current directory. Replace the *version* strings with the actual version numbers for the files in your FOP distribution.

    ```
    java -cp "../fop-0.93/build/fop.jar;../fop-0.93/lib/serializer-version.jar;\
    ../fop-0.93/lib/commons-logging-version.jar;../fop-0.93/lib/commons-io-version.jar" \
    org.apache.fop.fonts.apps.TTFReader \
    /WINDOWS/FONTS/GARA.TTF  fonts/garamond.xml
    ```

    Your Java CLASSPATH must include the fop.jar and the other jar files shown in the example. These files are included with the FOP distribution.

2. Do the same for the bold and italic variations of the font.

    ```
    java -cp "../fop-0.93/build/fop.jar;../fop-0.93/lib/serializer-version.jar;\
    ../fop-0.93/lib/commons-logging-version.jar;../fop-0.93/lib/commons-io-version.jar" \
    org.apache.fop.fonts.apps.TTFReader \
    /WINDOWS/FONTS/GARABD.TTF  fonts/garamond-bold.xml
    ```

    ```
    java -cp "../fop-0.93/build/fop.jar;../fop-0.93/lib/serializer-version.jar;\
    ../fop-0.93/lib/commons-logging-version.jar;../fop-0.93/lib/commons-io-version.jar" \
    org.apache.fop.fonts.apps.TTFReader \
    /WINDOWS/FONTS/GARAIT.TTF  fonts/garamond-italic.xml
    ```

3. Register the font with a FOP configuration file, which can have any filename such as userconfig.xml. The following example is for FOP 0.93:

```
<fop version="1.0">
  <renderers>
    <renderer mime="application/pdf">
      <fonts>
        <font  metrics-url="file:///c:/xml/fonts/garamond.xml"
               kerning="yes"
               embed-url="file://c:/Windows/fonts/GARA.TTF">
          <font-triplet name="Garamond" style="normal" weight="normal"/>
        </font>
        <font  metrics-url="file:///c:/xml/fonts/garamond-bold.xml"
               kerning="yes"
               embed-url="file://c:/Windows/fonts/GARABD.TTF">
          <font-triplet name="Garamond" style="normal" weight="bold"/>
        </font>
        <font  metrics-url="file:///c:/xml/fonts/garamond-italic.xml"
               kerning="yes"
               embed-url="file://c:/Windows/fonts/GARAIT.TTF">
          <font-triplet name="Garamond" style="italic" weight="normal"/>
        </font>
      </fonts>
    </fonts>
  ...
```

You specify the font metrics file and the path to the `.TTF` font file using attributes. You can enter the paths as absolute paths, or as relative to a path specified in a `base` element in the file. You specify the name by which you will reference the font in the `font-triplet` element. The *triplet* refers to the unique combination of name, weight, and style for each variation of the font. Those triplets are used by FOP to switch fonts for inline font changes. See the example configuration file `conf/fop.xconf` included with the FOP distribution.

4. Process your FO file with FOP using the `-c userconfig.xml` option:

```
../fop-0.93/fop.bat  \
  -c  userconfig.xml \
   booktest.fo \
   booktest.pdf
```

Configuring a font in XEP

The XEP documentation provides details for configuring XEP to use other fonts. The simplest case is to install the font directly in the `afm` directory in the XEP installation area on your system. Then you can just edit the `xep.xml` file that is in the XEP installation (or `etc/fonts.xml` prior to version 4). For example, these lines add the TrueType Palatino fonts to a version 4 installation.

```
<font-group xml:base="file:/C:/Windows/Fonts/">
  <font-family name="Palatino" embed="true"
               ligatures="&#xFB00; &#xFB01; &#xFB02; &#xFB03; &#xFB04;">
    <font>
      <font-data ttf="pala.ttf"/>
    </font>

    <font style="italic">
      <font-data ttf="palai.ttf"/>
    </font>

    <font weight="bold">
      <font-data ttf="palab.ttf"/>
    </font>

    <font weight="bold" style="italic">
      <font-data ttf="palabi.ttf"/>
    </font>

  </font-family>
</font-group>
```

The pathname to the `.ttf` file is taken to be relative to the `xml:base` path in the `font-group` container. Or place the fonts in the `fonts` subdirectory in the XEP installation, where they will be found automatically without an `xml:base`.

XEP uses the `style` and `weight` attributes in `font` elements to switch to bold and italic for inline font changes.

Configuring a font in Antenna House

If you are using Antenna House's XSL Formatter on Windows, then you can automatically use all the fonts that are registered in the Windows Fonts utility. If you are on another platform, then you add fonts to the Font Configuration file as described in the Antenna House documentation.

Adding a new font to FO output

To add a new font to your stylesheet, you may be able to do so with a stylesheet parameter. Otherwise, you will need to write a customization. The FO stylesheet provides a few parameters to specify font family names. These include:

Parameter name	Description
`body.font.family`	Used for ordinary text in paragraphs and such.
`title.font.family`	Used for book, chapter, and section titles.
`monospace.font.family`	Used for `programlisting`, `literal`, and other elements where a monospace font is called for.

If you want to change any of these, then you just need to set the corresponding parameter in a customization layer or on the command line. The value must match the name in the font configuration file for the FO processor. For example, to set the body font to Garamond, add this line to your customization layer:

```
<xsl:param name="body.font.family">Garamond</xsl:param>
```

When processed with the stylesheet, the FO output includes the following:

```
<fo:root  font-family="Garamond" ... >
```

If you then process the FO output with FOP or XEP as configured above, your PDF output should use Garamond for the body font. If you also configured the bold and italic font files, then those should automatically be used when needed.

The three stylesheet font parameters may not meet your needs if you need finer control. For example, the `title.font.family` applies to all titles, but you may want your book and chapter titles in one font, and your section titles in a different font. The section title font is controlled by a couple of attribute-sets. See the section called "Section titles" (page 176) for a description of those attribute sets. In a customization layer, you only need to specify the new font in the appropriate attribute-set. The following example sets the font for all levels of section titles:

```
<xsl:attribute-set name="section.title.properties">
  <xsl:attribute name="font-family">Garamond</xsl:attribute>
  <xsl:attribute name="font-weight">bold</xsl:attribute>
</xsl:attribute-set>
```

These properties will be merged with the attribute-set of the same name in the stylesheet, overriding the default font settings while leaving the other properties in effect.

If the element for which you want to change the font does not have an attribute-set in the stylesheet, you will have to customize the template that formats the element. For an example of customizing an element's font, see the section called "Line annotations" (page 445).

Numbering paragraphs

If your document design requires the numbering of paragraphs, such as for statutes or rules, you can use the `xsl:number` element to do that. You need to customize the template that matches `para`, but you will need to be careful how you do so. The `para` element is used in many contexts, not just for body text paragraphs. You might not want to number a `para` in a table or admonition, for example.

To be more selective, you could add a `role="statute"` attribute (or any value you choose) to those `para` elements you want to display a number. Then add this template to your customization layer:

```
<xsl:template match="para[@role = 'statute']">
  <fo:block xsl:use-attribute-sets="normal.para.spacing">
    <xsl:call-template name="anchor"/>
    <xsl:number count="para[@role = 'statute']" level="any"/>
    <xsl:text>. </xsl:text>
    <xsl:apply-templates/>
  </fo:block>
</xsl:template>
```

Or you could use an XPath qualifier to select `para` based on its lineage (its ancestor elements), in which case you do not need to add `role` attributes to the document. In this example, only `para` elements that are direct children of a `section` or `chapter` element would be numbered.

```
<xsl:template match="para[parent::section or parent::chapter]">
  <fo:block xsl:use-attribute-sets="normal.para.spacing">
    <xsl:call-template name="anchor"/>
    <xsl:number count="para[parent::section or parent::chapter]" level="any"/>
    <xsl:text>. </xsl:text>
    <xsl:apply-templates/>
  </fo:block>
</xsl:template>
```

Note that you need to change both the match attribute on xsl:template and the count attribute on xsl:number to keep them in sync.

In either case, if you want to restart the numbering in each chapter and perhaps prepend the chapter number, you can use the from attribute of xsl:number that indicates the element to start counting from. The following example restarts numbering in each chapter or appendix and adds the chapter or appendix number.

```
<xsl:template match="para[parent::section or parent::chapter]">
  <fo:block xsl:use-attribute-sets="normal.para.spacing">
    <xsl:call-template name="anchor"/>
    <xsl:if test="ancestor::chapter">
      <xsl:apply-templates select="ancestor::chapter" mode="label.markup"/>
      <xsl:text>.</xsl:text>
    </xsl:if>
    <xsl:number from="chapter" count="para[parent::section or parent::chapter]" level="any"/>
    <xsl:text>. </xsl:text>
    <xsl:apply-templates/>
  </fo:block>
</xsl:template>
```

The from="chapter" attributes restarts numbering at the start of each chapter. The label.markup mode generates the number for whatever numbered item is processed, in this case the ancestor chapter of the current para.

Adding line breaks

If you need to control where lines are breaking in certain text, you will find that DocBook does not provide much support. There is no line break element or attribute in the DocBook schemas, because line breaking is considered a formatting feature that should be kept separate from the XML source. In most cases, wrapping the text in literal-layout will allow you to control line breaking, because line breaks in that element are preserved in the output.

But there may be situations where you need to force a line break and literallayout is not suitable. You can create an XML processing instruction to indicate a line break, and add a stylesheet customization to enact it. A template like the following can be added to a customization layer:

```
<xsl:template match="processing-instruction('linebreak')">
  <fo:block/>
</xsl:template>
```

With this template in place, you can add a processing instruction <?linebreak?> in your text where you want to break a line. For example:

```
<para>This line should break right here <?linebreak?>if the template works.
```

The template will insert an empty fo:block element at that point, which will cause the line to break there. If you want the line break to appear in HTML output as well, then add a similar template to your HTML customization layer but replace fo:block with <br/> to insert the HTML line break element. If you do not add such a template to your HTML stylesheet, then be sure to include a space between the words in addition to the processing instruction, so that the words do not run together in HTML output.

If you need to insert one or more blank lines, then see the section called "Extra blank lines" (page 91).

Part IV. Special DocBook features

Contents

14

Bibliographies

DocBook has a complete set of features for supporting bibliographies.

- You can create a bibliography section in your document and populate it with bibliographic entries.

- Your bibliographic entries can be of two types: raw or cooked. See the next section for more information.

- Your set of entries can be numbered, or can use an abbreviation such as [brody98].

- You can cite (cross reference to) your bibliographic entries. In HTML output, these become hot links.

- You can create a central datafile of bibliographic entries that a document can select entries from.

- You can use the open source RefDB tool to manage and format bibliographic entries and references.

Bibliography entries

DocBook provides two approaches to entering bibliographic information, using two different elements.

biblioentry   Contains a set of bibliographic elements in random order that the stylesheet selects, orders, and renders. It does not permit PCDATA (ordinary text) except in its child elements.

bibliomixed   Contains the mix of elements, text, and punctuation as you want it presented. The stylesheet formats elements but does not rearrange them. The term *mixed* is used here because this is *mixed content* of elements and text (PCDATA).

For consistency in your bibliography, it is usually best if you use one type or the other.

Each element can contain a wide variety of bibliographic elements, such as author, publisher, etc. See *DocBook: The Definitive Guide*[1] for complete documentation of the bibliographic elements.

You can number entries in your bibliography, or you can mark each with an abbreviation such as [brody98]. You turn on numbering by setting the stylesheet parameter bibliography.numbered to a nonzero value. To get abbreviations, add an abbrev element as the first child of biblioentry or bibliomixed. It must be the *first* child element, to

---

[1] http://docbook.org/tdg/en/html/docbook.html

indicate that the text is to be presented first as a label to the bibliography entry. If numbering is not turned on, and there is not an `abbrev` element, then an entry's `xreflabel` attribute or `id` attribute is used as the label.

Bibliography database

If you find yourself needing the same bibliographic elements in more than one document, you can maintain a separate bibliographic database. Keeping the entries in one place ensures consistency between publications and makes it easier to maintain.

The database is simply a separate DocBook document with root element `bibliography` that contains a collection of bibliography entries (it can contain a mix of `biblioentry` and `bibliomixed` elements). Each entry in the database document must have a unique `id` attribute value.

To include entries from your bibliographic database in a particular document's `bibliography`, you do two things:

1. For each entry you want to pull in, put an empty `bibliomixed` element in the document's `bibliography`. The selection is made by setting its `id` attribute value to match the entry in the database that you want. Use `bibliomixed` even if you are pointing to a `biblioentry` in the database. Your bibliography can mix full bibliography entries with empty entries drawn from the database.

2. Process your document with the stylesheet parameter `bibliography.collection` set to the name of your database document.

When the stylesheets encounter an empty `bibliomixed` element, they open the database document, look up the `id` value, and copy the entry to the current document. It is equivalent to having the entry in your document.

Bibliography database catalog entry

If you need to share a bibliography database among several books, you might consider using an XML catalog entry to locate the database file. Once you set it up, all of your documents will be able to use the same collection, and you can move the collection when you need to, and then you just need to change the single catalog entry. See Chapter 5, *XML catalogs* (page 47) for general information on catalogs.

First set the `bibliography.collection` parameter to any generic path:

```
<xsl:param name="bibliography.collection">file:///foo/biblio.xml</xsl:param>
```

Then add an entry to your XML catalog that maps the generic path to the real path:

```
<uri
    name="file:///foo/biblio.xml"
    uri="file:///c:/usr/share/xml/bibliography-database.xml"/>
```

When you process your stylesheet with a catalog-aware processor (and tell it where to find the catalog), then the generic path will be mapped to the specific path.

Citing bibliographic entries

Use an `xref` or `link` element in your text to form an active link to one of the entries in your document's `bibliography`. If you are using version 4.4 or later of the DocBook DTD, you can also use `biblioref`. Each of these requires putting an `id` attribute value on the `biblioentry` or `bibliomixed` element in the bibliography, and using that value as the `linkend` attribute value in the `xref`, `link`, or `biblioref` element.

The citation element can also be used, in either of two modes;

- If the citation element's text exactly matches an abbrev element in a biblioentry or bibliomixed element, then a link will be automatically formed to the entry.

- If the citation contains any other text, then it does not form an active link to the bibliography. The element's text content is just displayed inside square brackets. You can use citation when you do not want an active link, or if the reference is not in your current bibliography.

If you use an xref or biblioref element, then text will be generated for the citation. The generated text depends on several factors, shown here in the order in which they are considered.

- If the stylesheet parameter bibliography.numbered is set to a nonzero value, then bibliographic entries are automatically numbered in the bibliography, and the matching number is used in the citation.

- If the entry element's first child is an abbrev element, then that element's text is used in the citation.

- If the entry element has an xreflabel attribute value, then that value is used in the citation.

- If none of the above applies, then the entry's id value is used.

For example:

This citation:
```
<xref linkend="BrodyArticle"/>
```

to this entry:
```
<biblioentry id="BrodyArticle">
  <abbrev>brody98</abbrev>
  <author>...
</biblioentry>
```

will generate this citation text:
```
[brody98]
```

If there were no abbrev child, then the id value would be used, so in this case it would produce [BrodyArticle].

Numbered bibliography entries

The stylesheets support numbering of bibliographic entries, and using those numbers for cross references. If you set the stylesheet parameter bibliography.numbered to nonzero, then the stylesheet will automatically number the entries in your bibliography. The numbering includes any entries pulled in from a bibliography database.

Sorting a bibliography

It is possible to present a sorted bibliography, even if the biblioentry elements are not in sorted order in the source document. One of the great things about XSLT is that it can rearrange the content before it formats it. You have to customize the template that handles the bibliodiv to add an xsl:sort instruction. You could also customize the bibliography element in the same way, but that is a much longer template so it will not be shown here. It might just be easier to put a bibliodiv inside your bibliography.

The trick to sorting the bibliography is to not process the biblioentry elements in document order, but in the order you specify. The original template for bibliodiv has an empty xsl:apply-templates instruction, which processes the entries in document order. So you will want to insert an xsl:sort instruction inside it. The following example sorts on the first author's surname.

```
<xsl:template match="bibliodiv">
  <xsl:variable name="lang">
    <xsl:call-template name="l10n.language"/>
  </xsl:variable>
  <fo:block>
    <xsl:attribute name="id">
      <xsl:call-template name="object.id"/>
    </xsl:attribute>
    <xsl:call-template name="bibliodiv.titlepage"/>
    <xsl:apply-templates
      select="*[not(self::biblioentry) and not(self::bibliomixed)]"/>
    <xsl:apply-templates select="biblioentry|bibliomixed">
      <xsl:sort select="author[1]//surname"
                lang="$lang"
                data-type="text" order="ascending"/>
    </xsl:apply-templates>
  </fo:block>
</xsl:template>
```

The original xsl:apply-templates was split into two. The first one processes all of the child elements of the bibliodiv that are not entries (i.e., optional introductory text elements). The second one processes all of the biblioentry and bibliomixed children, and it contains the sort clause. The sort's select attribute chooses what text to sort on, in this case the author's surname.

> **Note:**
>
> This customization to sort a bibliography will not work when you use an external bibliography collection. That's because the placeholder bibliomixed elements do not have any data to sort on. The data is not filled in until each entry is processed, which is after the sort process. You could fake the data, though, by putting a sort string in an attribute in each dummy bibliomixed element, and then sorting on that attribute.

Customizing bibliography output

If you want a two-column bibliography in print output, you need to create a custom page-master and use it for bibliography in place of the original back page-master, which is also used by appendix, glossary, and colophon elements. See the section called "Custom page design" (page 195) to learn how to do that.

To customize entries in the bibliography for print output, you can use the biblioentry.properties attribute-set. That attribute-set is applied to the overall fo:block containing each entry. You can set spacing, indents, and font properties for your entries. By default, it sets start-indent and end-indent properties and uses the normal.para.spacing attribute-set.

To customize entries in the bibliography for HTML output, use CSS. Each entry is contained in a div class="biblioentry" for which you can write a CSS selector such as div.biblioentry and apply properties.

The label in square brackets at the start of each entry can be customized using the biblioentry.label template. For example, you may have turned off numbering of entries, but some of your entries have an abbrev element that you do not want to show. You can turn them off with the following customization:

```
<xsl:template name="biblioentry.label">
 <!--do nothing -->
</xsl:template>
```

This template normally generates the label with a number or abbreviation. This customization turns off all labels for entries in a bibliography by redefining the template to do nothing.

If you do not like the way a particular bibliographic element such as author is formatted, then you can customize its template. Elements in a biblioentry are processed with templates in mode="bibliography.mode" Elements in a bibliomixed are processed with templates in mode="bibliomixed.mode". Look for the appropriate template in biblio.xsl (either html or fo), and then copy it to your customization layer to change it. For example:

```
<xsl:template match="author" mode="bibliography.mode">
  <span class="{name(.)}">
    <xsl:call-template name="person.name"/>
    <xsl:value-of select="$biblioentry.item.separator"/>
  </span>
</xsl:template>
```

This template formats an author within a biblioentry for HTML output. It puts the output within an HTML span element so it can add a class="author" attribute, which makes it possible to apply styles with a CSS stylesheet. Then it calls the person.name template to output the author's name. Then it adds the $biblioentry.item.separator, which is just a period by default. The template for bibliomixed using mode="bibliomixed.mode" is similar except it omits the trailing period. It assumes you are adding any necessary punctuation literally.

If you want the order of elements in the output to differ from how they appear in biblioentry element, then you will have to do a larger customization. There is no easy way to do this now, but you can expect this feature to become available in a future version of the DocBook stylesheets. To do it now, you must copy the template from biblio.xsl with match="biblioentry" to your customization layer. Within that template, locate these lines (HTML version):

```
<div class="{name(.)}">
    <xsl:call-template name="anchor"/>
    <p>
      <xsl:call-template  name="biblioentry.label"/>
      <xsl:apply-templates  mode="bibliography.mode"/>
    </p>
  </div>
```

The line <xsl:apply-templates mode="bibliography.mode"/> acts on each child of the biblioentry in the order in which they appear in the document. You need to replace that line with a sequence of similar lines, each of which selects a particular element. The order is then determined by those lines. For example:

```
<xsl:apply-templates  select="author"  mode="bibliography.mode"/>
<xsl:apply-templates  select="title"  mode="bibliography.mode"/>
<xsl:apply-templates  select="publisher"  mode="bibliography.mode"/>
```

Now the output for each entry will have the order author, title, publisher, regardless of the order of those elements in the source document.

If you do not like the square brackets used in citation cross references, you can change them with a stylesheet customization. These two templates control the prefix and suffix characters:

```
<xsl:template match="biblioentry|bibliomixed" mode="xref-to-prefix">
  <xsl:text>[</xsl:text>
</xsl:template>

<xsl:template match="biblioentry|bibliomixed" mode="xref-to-suffix">
  <xsl:text>]</xsl:text>
</xsl:template>
```

Copy these templates to your customization layer and change the text that they generate.

ISO 690 bibliography standard

If you want or need to use an established international standard for bibliographic entries, then consider ISO 690. The standard itself says it best:

> This International Standard specifies the elements to be included in bibliographic references to published monographs and serials, to chapters, articles, etc. in such publications and to patent documents. It sets out a prescribed order for the elements of the reference and establishes conventions for the transcription and presentation of information derived from the source publication.
> —International Standard ISO 690:1987

The standard specifies for each type of document what information should be included in the bibliographic citation. It also specifies the order and the punctuation.

Starting with version 1.72, the DocBook XSL stylesheets provide support for ISO 690 style bibliographic output. In order to use this feature, you need to do two things:

- Mark up your `biblioentry` elements using the recommended DocBook elements that the stylesheet recognizes for each type of referenced document.

- Set the stylesheet parameter `bibliography.style` to `iso690` when you process your bibliography.

The markup requirements for your entries are documented on the DocBook Wiki site *http://wiki.docbook.org/topic/ISO690Bibliography*. The documentation shows the DocBook XML elements and attributes to use for each type of referenced document, and provides examples of each. In general:

- The list of referenced document types includes monographs (books), serials, articles, patent documents, electronic documents, and parts of each.

- Each document type must be identified by a specific `role` attribute on its `biblioentry` element.

- Each `biblioentry` has required and optional elements according to its document type.

- The order of elements must be followed.

Any text (such as `ISBN`) and punctuation that is generated by the stylesheet comes from the standard DocBook gentext files, such as `common/en.xml` for English. See the section called "Generated text" (page 105) for more information on DocBook's gentext system. These gentext entries are contained in a `context name="iso690"` element. They may not be translated for all languages, but they can be customized using the method described in the section called "Customizing generated text" (page 106).

There are two stylesheet parameters that control the formatting of ISO 690 entries.

- The `biblioentry.primary.count` parameter identifies how many authors in an entry should be included in the output. If there are three or fewer authors, then they are all output. If there are more than three, then the output can include one, two, or three authors from the list. Set this parameter to a value of 1 to get one author, to 2 for two authors, or 3 for three authors. The default value is 1.

- The `biblioentry.alt.primary.seps` parameter controls the use of alternative punctuation and connector text between authors in the output. When this parameter is set to zero (the default), then the separators come from gentext entries in the `context name="authorgroup"` element. When set to 1, then the separators come from gentext entries in the `context name="iso690"` element.

Bibliography title

The title Bibliography that appears at the beginning of a bibliography is generated by the stylesheet if you do not include a title element. If your document uses a lang other than English, then the generated title is in the appropriate language. If you need to change the title text, just add a title element to your document, as in the following example:

```
<bibliography>
  <title>Further Reading</title>
  ...
```

The formatting of the bibliography title is handled as part of the general titlepage mechanism in DocBook XSL. That means the specifications original in the title page spec file titlepage.templates.xml (that's .xml) in the html or fo stylesheet subdirectory.

For HTML output, it is easiest to format the title using a CSS stylesheet. You can create a CSS selector like the following:

```
div.bibliography div.titlepage h2.title {
    put your CSS styles here
}
```

For print output, the bibliography title, like other component elements, is processed using the component.title template. See the section called "Other component titles" (page 176) for a description of how to customize such titles.

RefDB bibliographic database

RefDB is an open source bibliographic reference database that works with DocBook. Here are some of its features:

- It stores bibliographic information in an external SQL database.

- It can import bibliographic information from a variety of sources, including DocBook biblioentry elements, Medline (tagged and XML), BibTeX, and MARC.

- It can retrieve and format the data in a variety of formats for citations.

- It can assemble a bibliography that follows a consistent style.

The tool works particularly well with DocBook. You create citation elements with role="REFDB" and whose content is a key identifier of a bibliographic entry in the database. For example:

```
<para>This is a citation <citation role="REFDB">Nakane2002</citation>.</para>
```

Then you process your document with the RefDB tool, which collects the citations and builds a DocBook bibliography element into a separate file that you can include through an entity reference or XInclude. The kit also includes DocBook XSL stylesheet customizations to handle formatting of the bibliographic elements in specific styles.

You can get more information about RefDB from *http://refdb.sourceforge.net*.

15

Cross references

DocBook supports a rich set of elements and features for creating cross references. Here are the basic kinds of cross references you can create:

- Within a document.

- Between documents.

- To websites.

- Specialized cross references.

    Note:

    DocBook 5 introduces to DocBook the idea of universal linking between elements. In DocBook 5, you can form links between any two elements. See the section called "Universal linking in DocBook 5" (page 35) for more information.

The following sections describe how to create each kind of cross reference and what extra features are available for it.

Cross references within a document

DocBook 4 employs the built-in feature of XML for cross referencing within a document, in which attributes are used to identify starting and ending points for cross references. In an XML DTD, an attribute can be assigned an attribute type of ID. That type of attribute is used to label an element as a potential target (end point) of a cross reference. The attribute name does not have be ID, it just needs to be declared as that type. In DocBook 4, the name of the attribute assigned this purpose just happens to be named id as well. In the DocBook DTD, almost every element can have an id attribute, with attribute type ID. That means any element in your document could be the target of a cross reference.

In DocBook 5, you use xml:id instead of id. The xml:id attribute is predefined to have attribute type ID, whether or not a schema is available to confirm it.

According to the XML standard, every value of an attribute with type ID must be unique. In DocBook, this means every instance of an id (DocBook 4) or xml:id (DocBook 5) attribute in a document must be unique within that document. When you validate your document, the validator will tell you if you have any duplicate id attributes.

Other attributes can have a type of IDREF, which is used to point to an ID on another element to form a cross reference. There are a handful of elements in the DocBook DTD that have attributes of type IDREF, of various names. There are two main elements that are used to create cross references to targets within the same document:

xref   An automatic cross reference that generates the text of the reference. For that purpose, it is an empty element that takes no content of its own. The stylesheets control what output is generated. The generated text can be the target element's titleabbrev (if it has one) or title, number label (if it has one), or both.

link   A cross reference where you supply the text of the reference as the content of the link element. So it must not be an empty element.

Both of these elements require a linkend attribute whose value must match some id or xml:id value in the document. Here are two examples in DocBook 4:

Example 15.1. Internal cross references

```
...
<chapter  id="intro"> ❶
<title>Introduction</title>
<para>Welcome to our new product. One of its
new features is a <link  linkend="WidgetIntro">widget</link>.   ❷
Other new features include ...
</para>
</chapter>
<chapter  id="WidgetIntro">   ❸
<title>Introducing the Widget</title>
<para>Widgets are just one of our new features.
For a complete list of new features, see <xref  linkend="intro"/>.   ❹
</para>
</chapter>
...
```

❶   Chapter element has an id attribute.
❷   A link element has a linkend attribute that matches the second chapter, and some text content.
❸   The second chapter also has an id attribute.
❹   An xref element also has a linkend attribute, but it has no text content.

When this document is processed, the link and xref elements are converted to cross references. In HTML, they become A anchor tags, with the text of link becoming the link text and an appropriate HREF attribute being generated by the stylesheet. The HTML hot spot text for an xref is generated by the stylesheet from the chapter information. In PDF output, the links will also be active, and a page reference might also be generated.

Here is some guidance for using these cross reference elements:

• Use xref when you want to reference another element's title or number. It will automatically get the current information so you do not have to maintain such references.

• Use link when you want to create a less formal reference that does not include the title or number. You can use whatever words you want.

• When adding an id or xml:id attribute, put it on the element itself, not the title. The stylesheets know how to find the title for each element being referenced.

- Not all elements are appropriate as targets of an xref, because they do not have a title or number. For example, you may want to cross reference to a para, but you wouldn't want the whole paragraph to be copied as the reference text. See the next section for options you can add to use xref anyway.

Linking from other elements

In DocBook 5, you can use many other elements beside xref and link as the starting point for a link. DocBook 5 supports the use of XLink attributes on many elements. Those attributes effectively let you link from any element to any other element, almost. See the section called "Universal linking in DocBook 5" (page 35) for complete information.

Options for generated xref text

The stylesheets provide several options for generating the text for an xref element when it is processed.

Exclude title from chapter and section references

The generated text for chapters and appendixes is by default both the number and the title, such as Chapter 3, Using a Mouse. When section numbering is turned on, references to sections also get both. If you set the stylesheet parameter xref.with.number.and.title to zero (it's one by default), then only a number label like Chapter 3 is generated.

Attach an xreflabel to a target element

For elements like para or note that do not have a title or number, you can add an xreflabel attribute to the element. That attribute should contain the text you want to appear when an xref points to that element. The following is an example:

```
<para  id="ChooseSCSIid"  xreflabel="choosing a SCSI id">The methods
for choosing a <acronym>SCSI</acronym> id are ...
</para>
...
<para>
See the paragraph on <xref  linkend="ChooseSCSIid"/>.
</para>
```

The xref in the second paragraph points to the first paragraph. When processed, the second paragraph will read "See the paragraph on choosing a SCSI id." and an HTML hot link will take the reader to the beginning of the paragraph.

The advantage of xreflabel over using a link element is to provide consistent reference text to that element. If you decide to change the wording, you only have to change the xreflabel, and all xref references to it will change. If you had used link instead, then you would have to find and edit each instance to change the text.

> **Note:**
>
> If you put an xreflabel on an element that normally does have generated text, the attribute will override the default generated text.

Use another element's text for an xref

DocBook has another trick for generating text for an xref. You can actually grab the text from another element. Here is how it works.

You can add an `endterm` attribute to the `xref` element. The value of `endterm` must match an `id` value of an element in the document. The children of the element pointed to by `endterm` are used as the cross reference text. But the cross reference destination is still the `linkend` element.

The following is an example that matches the previous one but uses `endterm` instead:

```
<para  id="ChooseSCSIid"  >The methods
for <phrase  id="SCSIxref">choosing a <acronym>SCSI</acronym> id</phrase>
are ...
</para>
...
<para>
See the paragraph on <xref  linkend="ChooseSCSIid"  endterm="SCSIxref"/>.
</para>
```

Note that the `endterm` attribute goes in the `xref` element, not the target element. In this case it points to a `phrase` element in the paragraph that has the text you want in the reference text. When processed, the second paragraph will read "See the paragraph on choosing a SCSI id." and an HTML hot link will take the reader to the beginning of the paragraph.

There is one difference with the previous example, however. Here, the `<acronym>SCSI</acronym>` element will be processed by the stylesheet as an acronym. You could not put the acronym markup in the `xref label`, because attributes cannot contain elements. So this feature is most useful when the generated text needs to contain elements.

You also need to be careful what element you point the `endterm` to. All the children of the selected element will be processed by the stylesheet as the reference text. If you point to a list, for example, then all the `listitem` elements in the list become the reference text.

A more likely example is forming a cross reference to the question in a `qandaentry`. By default, an `xref` to a `question` element displays just the label for the question, such as `Q:1`. If you want the reference text to be the question text, then you might try pointing both the `endterm` and the `linkend` attributes to the `id` on the `question` element. But the child elements of `question` will likely include `para`, which will be processed into `<P>` tags in HTML and introduce paragraph breaks where you just wanted some inline reference text. The solution is to add an `id` attribute to the `para` and point the `endterm` to that instead. Here are both the good and bad examples for comparison:

Example 15.2. Xref to a question in qandaentry

```
<qandaentry>
  <question  id="myQuestion">
    <para  id="QuestionText">What is the circumference of the Earth?</para>
  </question>
  <answer>
    ...
  </answer>
</qandaentry>
```

Bad example: introduces paragraphs breaks in reference text
```
<xref  linkend="myQuestion"  endterm="myQuestion" />
```

Good example: selects only the text children of para
```
<xref  linkend="myQuestion"  endterm="QuestionText" />
```

Customize the generated text

You may want to change the way `xref` text is generated for a particular kind of element, such as chapter or appendix. See the section called "Customizing cross references" (page 262) for the methods of doing that.

Cross references between documents

If you want to cross reference to another DocBook document, then you cannot use `xref` and `link`, because they require the target `id` to be in the same document. In DocBook, a document could be a collection of books contained in a `set` element. If you can put all your content in one set, and you are willing to work with such a large document, then you can use the regular cross reference elements within the set.

The more flexible solution for linking to other documents is to use `olink` (outside link). See Chapter 24, *Olinking between documents* (page 383) for a complete description of how to use olinks.

Linking to websites

Creating a link from your DocBook document to a website is easy. You use the `ulink` element, putting the target URL in the ulink's `url` attribute. For example:

```
For more information on DocBook, go to the
<ulink  url="https://sourceforge.net/projects/docbook/">DocBook
SourceForge website</ulink>
or to <ulink  url="http://docbook.org"/>.
```

The first `ulink` example is not empty, so its text content becomes the hot text in HTML output. The second `ulink` is empty, so the stylesheet will automatically copy its URL to use as the hot text.

In HTML output, you can have the target document appear in a separate window if you set the `ulink.target` parameter to a different window name. That adds a `target` attribute to the HTML anchor tag. By default, the parameter's value is `_top`, which loads the content into the topmost frame, which is likely the same window.

For FO output, you can choose whether the `url` attribute value for the `ulink` is printed. If you just set the parameter `ulink.show` to nonzero, then the URL appears in square brackets after the ulink text. If you also set the parameter `ulink.footnotes` to nonzero, then the URL becomes a footnote to the ulink text. Regardless of the parameter settings, if the URL exactly matches the ulink text string (or the ulink element is empty, which produces the same result), then the stylesheet does not repeat the same URL in brackets or a footnote.

Breaking long URLs

In print output, long URLs that start near the end of a line may need to be broken to format nicely. The problem is that URLs have no spaces, and so will not be line broken on a space. If you try to insert zero-width spaces in the `ulink url` attribute to allow breaks in the printed form, you will find that the URL no longer works as a link. If you copy the `url` to the `ulink` element content and add the zero-width spaces there, you will find that the stylesheet no longer treats them as the same and repeats the URL after the text.

You can solve this problem by using a feature of the print stylesheet to enable hyphenation of ulink URLs, with a hyphenation character that you specify. The way it works is you set the stylesheet parameter `ulink.hyphenate` to contain some character. When that parameter is not empty, then that character is inserted by the stylesheet into the printed version of the URL after every character that is included in the stylesheet parameter `ulink.hyphenate.chars` (which is set to / by default). Generally you should set `ulink.hyphenate` to either Unicode soft hyphen (­) or Unicode zero-width space (). The former will generate a hyphen if the URL breaks, and the latter will not. However, not all processors support both characters, so you should test. If you want more opportunities for breaking in a URL than just after / characters, then you can expand the set of characters in `ulink.hyphenate.chars`.

The following example allows breaks after slash, ampersand, and question mark in a URL, and does not display a hyphen at the break:

```
<xsl:param name="ulink.hyphenate.chars">/&amp;?</xsl:param>
<xsl:param name="ulink.hyphenate">&#x200B;</xsl:param>
```

DocBook 5 cross references

Cross references in DocBook 5 documents are very similar to those in DocBook 4 documents, but there are some differences.

- The `xref` and `link` elements can be used the same as in DocBook 4. The only difference is that in DocBook 5 the `linkend` value must match an `xml:id` attribute on another element instead of an `id` attribute.

- The `olink` element can be used the same as in DocBook 4. The `targetptr` attribute can match on an `xml:id` value from a DocBook 5 document, or an `id` value from a DocBook 4 document. An olink database could contain documents from both versions, and olinks will work between them.

- In DocBook 5, there is no `ulink` element. Its function is handled instead by an `xlink:href` attribute on another element such as `link`.

- In DocBook 5, you can use many other elements beside `xref` and `link` as the starting point for a link. DocBook 5 supports the use of `xlink` attributes on many elements. Those attributes effectively let you link from any element to any other element, almost. See the section called "Universal linking in DocBook 5" (page 35) for complete information.

Customizing cross references

DocBook has two kinds of cross references: those that are empty and those that provide their own text. The empty cross reference elements (`xref` and empty `olink`) have their text generated by the stylesheets. The generated text can be customized.

There are three levels of customizing the generated text for empty cross references:

- Using an `xrefstyle` attribute on an `xref` element to change a single instance. See the next section.

- Modifying the stylesheet gentext templates to change punctuation and support text for all cross references for a particular type of element. See the section called "Modifying gentext templates" (page 267).

- Customizing a template in `mode="xref-to"` to change the cross reference behavior. See the section called "Customizing cross reference behavior" (page 269).

The `xrefstyle` attribute became available in version 4.3 of the DocBook DTD. If you are using an earlier version of the DTD, then you could use the `role` attribute instead (see the section called "Using role instead of xrefstyle" (page 267)).

Customizing with an xrefstyle attribute

Version 4.3 of the DocBook DTD made available an `xrefstyle` attribute to the `xref`, `link`, and `olink` elements to allow an author to indicate special handling for a single cross reference. Note that for a `link` element, an `xrefstyle` attribute is limited to controlling the generated page reference, if any. For an `olink` with text content, then `xrefstyle` currently has no effect at all on the output.

The DTD does not specify standard values for the `xrefstyle` attribute, so stylesheets are free to implement whatever scheme they want. The DocBook XSL stylesheets provide three ways to use the `xrefstyle` attribute:

- If the attribute value begins with `template:` then the rest of the text after the colon is taken to be a gentext template to use for that reference.

- If the attribute value begins with `select:` then the author can specify components to make up the generated text using key words defined by the stylesheet.

- Otherwise the attribute value is taken to be a named cross reference style that is defined in the stylesheet's collection of gentext templates.

Each of these methods is described in more detail in the following sections.

Using "template:"

Text that is generated for cross references comes from gentext templates, in which some of the text is fixed and some is filled in from the title or number of the item being referenced. The stock gentext templates reside in the locale files found in the common subdirectory of the stylesheet distribution, such as `common/en.xml` for English text. Those templates are described in the section called "Modifying gentext templates" (page 267).

If an `xrefstyle` attribute starts with the literal string `template:` then whatever text appears after the colon is taken to be the gentext template for that reference. This option lets you mix any text with a number label and/or title for the cross reference. The following is an example.

Input:
```
See <xref linkend="UsingMouse"
     xrefstyle="template:the chapter numbered %n"/>
for more information.
```

HTML output:
```
See <a href="#UsingMouse">the chapter numbered 3</a>
for more information.
```

The highlighted text is used as the gentext template. The `%n` is replaced by the chapter number during processing. You could use `%t` if you want to include the chapter title in a gentext template. Since the text is entered as an attribute value, you cannot include DocBook tags with it. You can include text entities, though. Keep in mind that if the document is translated to other languages, then any regular words in the attribute will have be translated too. Normally translators would not look in attribute values for words to translate.

Using "select:"

A somewhat more structured customization is available when you start an `xrefstyle` attribute with the literal string `select:`. This option lets you choose the components that make up the generated text. You specify one or more keywords that are defined in the stylesheet, and the stylesheet then assembles a temporary gentext template for that reference. For example:

Input:
```
<xref linkend="MouseButtons"
     xrefstyle="select: labelnumber quotedtitle"/>
```

HTML output:
```
<a href="#MouseButtons">2.1: "Using Mouse Buttons"</a>
```

The stylesheet constructs a gentext template based on the keywords `labelnumber` and `quotedtitle`. In this scheme, there are three possible components to the generated text, and each has several possible keywords. This table summarizes the keywords.

Table 15.1. Keywords for xrefstyle select:

Component	Keyword	Example	Description
number label	`label`	Table 3	Complete label name and number
	`labelname`	Table	Just the label name
	`labelnumber`	3	Just the label number
title	`title`	Using a Mouse	Title without quotes
	`quotedtitle`	"Using a Mouse"	Title in quotes
page number	*unspecified*	[12]	Stock page citation for all `xref` elements when the `insert.xref.page.number` parameter is set to yes, and for all `link` elements when the `insert.link.page.number` parameter is set to yes.
	`page`	(page 12)	Page number in parentheses
	`Page`	Page 12	Capitalized page label
	`pageabbrev`	(p. 12)	Abbreviated label in parentheses
	`pagenumber`	12	Just the page number
	`nopage`		Turn off the page number for this `xref` element when the `insert.xref.page.number` parameter is set to yes, or for this `link` element when the `insert.link.page.number` parameter is set to yes.
document name	`docname`	in *Reference Manual*	(Olinks only). Adds the title of the other document being referenced by an olink.
	`docnamelong`	in the document named *Reference Manual*	(Olinks only). Adds a longer version of a title referenced by an olink.
	`nodocname`		(Olinks only). Turn off the document name when the `olink.doctitle` parameter is set to yes.

Note these features:

- You can specify zero or one keyword for each component type. If a component does not have a keyword, then it is omitted from the output.

- Although the keywords can be specified in any order, the presentation order in the output is always label, title, and page.

- Page numbers are generated only for print output, not HTML output.

- The overall control of page references in print output is set by the `insert.xref.page.number` stylesheet parameter for `xref` elements, and by `insert.link.page.number` for `link` elements. Each has three possible values:

`no`	Page number references are not included in the output. This is the default value, so you must reset this parameter to get any page cross references in your print output.
`yes`	Page number references are included for each `xref` or `link` instance. If the style is not specified with an `xrefstyle` attribute, then the stock page citation style is used (see the table above).
`maybe`	A page number reference is output only for each `xref` of `link` with a page component in its `xrefstyle` attribute.

- If you want page references on most of your xref elements, then set insert.xref.page.number to yes and turn off individual instances with a nopage keyword in its xrefstyle attribute. If you want page references on only a few xref elements, then set insert.xref.page.number to maybe and add an xrefstyle attribute with a page component to those few instances. Likewise you can control page references on link elements by using the insert.link.page.number parameter in a similar fashion.

- If you want to globally change the default page citation style from [12] to something else, then customize the page.citation gentext entry (see the section called "Customizing generated text" (page 106) for details on customizing gentext entries). The following example changes the default style to (p. 12):

```
<xsl:param name="local.l10n.xml" select="document('')"/>
<l:i18n xmlns:l="http://docbook.sourceforge.net/xmlns/l10n/1.0">
  <l:l10n language="en">
    <l:context name="xref">
      <l:template name="page.citation" text=" (p. %p)"/>
    </l:context>
  </l:l10n>
</l:i18n>
```

The %p is the placeholder for the generated page number. If you are translating your documents to other languages, you may need to add similar customizations to the gentext for those languages.

- The whitespace and punctuation that is inserted between components in the output is specified by these stylesheet parameters:

xref.label-title.separator	Used between label and title, if both are specified. Default value is a colon and blank space.
xref.title-page.separator	Used between title and page number, if both are specified. Default value is a blank space.
xref.label-page.separator	Used between label and page number, if both are specified and a title is not. Default value is a blank space.

- The label name and quoting characters are taken from the locale files in the common subdirectory of the distribution, so they are appropriate for each language that DocBook supports.

This method is useful when you need a small variation on the standard generated text for a cross reference. It is less raw and more consistent than the ad hoc gentext template used in the template: method for xrefstyle.

Using a named xrefstyle

The two previous methods do not require a stylesheet customization to use them. If you are willing to create and use a stylesheet customization layer, then you can add any number of named gentext templates for cross references to particular target elements. Then you can call such gentext templates by specifying one of the names in an xrefstyle attribute value.

The following example adds a style named num-qt (number and quoted title) for sect1 references.

Customization layer:
```
<xsl:param name="local.l10n.xml" select="document('')"/>
<l:i18n xmlns:l="http://docbook.sourceforge.net/xmlns/l10n/1.0">
  <l:l10n language="en">
    <l:context name="xref-number-and-title">
      <l:template name="sect1" style="num-qt" text="%n-&#8220;%t&#8221;"/>
    </l:context>
  </l:l10n>
</l:i18n>
```

Input:
```
<xref linkend="MouseButtons" xrefstyle="num-qt"/>
```

HTML output:
```
<a href="#MouseButtons">2.1-"Using Mouse Buttons"</a>
```

Note these features:

- The customization layer uses the method described in the section called "Customizing generated text" (page 106) to add a new gentext template.

- The new gentext template is similar to the others, but it adds a `style="num-qt"` attribute to identify the named style.

- This gentext template applies only to the element identified by the `name` attribute, which is `sect1` in this case. To use this style on other elements you must add a similar gentext template for each element. They can share the same style name.

- Each gentext template is contained within a language and a context. It will only be used if called on that target element in the same language and context. Keep in mind that there are several possible contexts for xref gentext templates (see the section called "Modifying gentext templates" (page 267)). In this case, if section numbering is not turned on by the `section.autolabel` stylesheet parameter, then the `xref-number-and-title` context is not in effect and this template will not be used. You may need to add more gentext templates for a named style in other xref contexts.

This method of customizing `xref` generated text is most useful when you want a set of standardized styles, and you are willing to invest the time to create the new templates in a customization layer.

Customizing page citations

The print stylesheet provides several options for customizing page references generated by `xref` elements.

- You can enable or disable `xref` page references for the whole document using the `insert.xref.page.number` parameter, as described in the section called "Using "select:"" (page 263).

- If you want to change the default page reference style that uses square brackets, you can customize the gentext template named `page.citation`, which is in the `xref` context in the collection of gentext templates. See the section called "Modifying gentext templates" (page 267) for a description of the general process.

- You can select a particular page reference style for an individual `xref` in your document by adding an `xrefstyle` attribute to it, as described in the section called "Using "select:"" (page 263).

- If you want to customize the page reference styles that are selected by `xrefstyle`, then you can customize the gentext templates named `page`, `Page`, and `pageabbrev`. They are also in the `xref` context in the collection of gentext templates. See the section called "Modifying gentext templates" (page 267) for a description of the general process.

Controlling page citations by element

If you want to style (or turn off) page references for particular elements, you can add custom templates using mode="page.citation" to your customization layer. If you look in fo/xref.xsl, you will find that in the template with match="xref", each page citation is generated using this line:

```
<xsl:apply-templates select="$target" mode="page.citation">
```

By default, there is one match="*" template in that mode:

```
<xsl:template match="*" mode="page.citation">
  <xsl:param name="id" select="'???'"/>

  <fo:basic-link internal-destination="{$id}"
                 xsl:use-attribute-sets="xref.properties">
    <fo:inline keep-together.within-line="always">
      <xsl:call-template name="substitute-markup">
        <xsl:with-param name="template">
          <xsl:call-template name="gentext.template">
            <xsl:with-param name="name" select="'page.citation'"/>
            <xsl:with-param name="context" select="'xref'"/>
          </xsl:call-template>
        </xsl:with-param>
      </xsl:call-template>
    </fo:inline>
  </fo:basic-link>
</xsl:template>
```

This template generates the page reference using the name="page.citation" gentext element from the current language's locale file. Since this mechanism uses a mode, you can add templates using that mode that match on particular elements to change the behavior for those elements. For example, you might want to turn off page references to chapters or appendixes, since they are easy to find because they are numbered.

```
<xsl:apply-templates select="chapter|appendix" mode="page.citation"/>
```

This empty template will turn off page references for chapters and appendixes, and leave the default template to handle all other target elements.

Using role instead of xrefstyle

The xrefstyle attribute was introduced in version 4.3 of the DocBook DTD. If you are using an earlier version of the DTD, then you can use the role attribute instead. When the stylesheet parameter use.role.as.xrefstyle parameter is set to 1 (the default value), then a role attribute on an xref element is treated as if it were an xrefstyle attribute. This means you do not have to upgrade your documents to use DocBook 4.3 or later to use the stylesheet features for customizing cross reference text.

Modifying gentext templates

You customize cross reference text by modifying gentext strings for your locale in your customization layer. See the section called "Generated text" (page 105) for a general description of customizing generated text. For cross references, you want to look for gentext templates in one of the xref contexts in the language file you are working with, such as common/en.xml. These are the xref contexts (as of version 1.62 of the stylesheets) and when they apply:

Context	Generates:	Applies to:
context="xref"	The element's title.	Cross references to elements that are not numbered. Includes chapters when the parameter chapter.autolabel is set to zero. Same with appendix, part, preface, and section elements and their respective parameters.
context="xref-number"	The element's number label, such as Chapter 3.	Cross references to elements that are numbered, such as chapter, appendix, figure, table. Also applies to sections when they are numbered. Used when the stylesheet parameter xref.with.number.and.title is set to zero.
context="xref-number-and-title"	The element's number label and title.	Cross references to elements that are numbered, such as chapter, appendix, figure, table. Also applies to sections when they are numbered. Used when the stylesheet parameter xref.with.number.and.title is set to 1 (default).

For example, the common/en.xml file includes the following gentext templates. The text for chapter is highlighted in each context.

```
<l:context name="xref">
    <l:template name="abstract" text="%t"/>
    <l:template name="appendix" text="%t"/>
    <l:template name="chapter" text="%t"/>
    ...
</l:context>
<l:context name="xref-number">
    <l:template name="appendix" text="Appendix %n"/>
    <l:template name="chapter" text="Chapter %n"/>   (  is a non-breaking space)
    ...
</l:context>
<l:context name="xref-number-and-title">
    <l:template name="appendix" text="Appendix %n, %t"/>
    <l:template name="chapter" text="Chapter %n, %t"/>
    ...
</l:context>
    ...
```

Each DocBook element that can generate text has a l:template element within each context that can apply. The text attribute value is used to generate the output for a cross reference to that element. The %t placeholder resolves to the target element's title, and %n resolves to its number (if it is numbered).

For example, an xref that points to a chapter would normally generate text like Chapter 3, Using a Mouse (the non-breaking space was replaced for clarity). The context="xref-number-and-title" template is used because chapters are numbered and the stylesheet parameter xref.with.number.and.title is set to 1 by default. If you set xref.with.number.and.title to zero, then the context="xref-number" template is used instead. If you set chapter.autolabel to zero to turn off chapter numbering, then the context="xref" template is used.

To customize cross references, you add new gentext templates to your customization layer that override the stock templates. You have to make sure you cover all the targets elements you reference, and in all the contexts that you use.

For example, if you prefer to use a colon and quotes in cross references to chapters and appendixes, you can add the following to your customization layer:

```
<xsl:param name="local.l10n.xml" select="document('')"/>
<l:i18n xmlns:l="http://docbook.sourceforge.net/xmlns/l10n/1.0">
  <l:l10n language="en">
    <l:context name="xref-number-and-title">
      <l:template name="appendix" text="Appendix %n: &#8220;%t&#8221;"/>
      <l:template name="chapter" text="Chapter %n: &#8220;%t&#8221;"/>
    </l:context>
  </l:l10n>
</l:i18n>
```

If you want to do this for French as well as English, you'll need the following:

```
<xsl:param name="local.l10n.xml" select="document('')"/>
<l:i18n xmlns:l="http://docbook.sourceforge.net/xmlns/l10n/1.0">
  <l:l10n language="en">
    <l:context name="xref-number-and-title">
      <l:template name="appendix" text="Appendix %n: &#8220;%t&#8221;"/>
      <l:template name="chapter" text="Chapter %n: &#8220;%t&#8221;"/>
    </l:context>
  </l:l10n>
  <l:l10n language="fr">
    <l:context name="xref-number-and-title">
      <l:template name="appendix" text="Annexe %n: &#171;%t&#187;"/>
      <l:template name="chapter" text="Chapitre %n: &#171;%t&#187;"/>
    </l:context>
  </l:l10n>
</l:i18n>
```

The gentext templates are shared by the HTML and FO stylesheets. If you are satisfied that your changes work in both output formats, you can put all of your gentext changes in a separate file and bring them into each of your stylesheet customization layers using:

```
<xsl:param name="local.l10n.xml" select="document('mygentextmods.xml')"/>
```

Or if you find you need different cross reference styles for the different output formats, you can keep them as separate modification files.

Customizing cross reference behavior

The mechanism of using gentext templates to generate cross references has one big limitation. The generated text is specified using an attribute in a `l:template` element in a localization file. An attribute value cannot contain element markup, nor can it alter the cross reference behavior under different contexts. If you need more control over how a cross reference is generated, you can create or customize a template in `mode="xref-to"`.

If you look in the DocBook XSL stylesheet file `xref.xsl` (for either HTML or FO), you will see that the cross reference text is generated with this line:

```
<xsl:apply-templates select="$target" mode="xref-to">
```

The `$target` variable contains the element being referenced. Since this is a mode, there can be separate templates matching on each element type. You can customize the behavior for individual elements by creating or customizing a template that matches on that element in this mode.

If you examine the templates with `mode="xref-to"` in `xref.xsl`, you will see that most of them use `xsl:apply-templates` in `mode="object.xref.markup"`. That mode is the DocBook mechanism that selects the appropriate gentext template from the localization files, and fills in the title and number for a cross reference. For example, here is the gentext template for sections when section numbering is not turned on:

```
<l:context name="xref">
  ...
  <l:template name="section" text="the section called &#8220;%t&#8221;"/>
  ...
```

Some templates using mode="xref-to" do not use the gentext template mechanism. For example:

```
<xsl:template match="author|editor|othercredit|personname" mode="xref-to">
  <xsl:param name="referrer"/>
  <xsl:param name="xrefstyle"/>

  <xsl:call-template name="person.name"/>
</xsl:template>
```

If you want to customize the behavior or generate additional markup for a cross reference for a particular element, then add a template that matches on that element and uses that mode. For example, you could customize how an author is referenced so that their affiliation is added:

```
<xsl:template match="author" mode="xref-to">
  <xsl:param name="referrer"/>
  <xsl:param name="xrefstyle"/>

  <xsl:call-template name="person.name"/>
  <xsl:if test="child::affiliation">
    <xsl:text> (</xsl:text>
    <xsl:apply-templates select="affiliation"/>
    </xsl:text>)</xsl:text>
  </xsl:if>
</xsl:template>
```

This template for author elements checks to see if it contains an affiliation element, and if so, outputs it within parentheses after the name. This template does not affect cross references to editor or other name elements.

Customizing cross reference typography

Perhaps you want to change the typographical style for the generated text of a cross reference. For example, you might notice that xrefs to chapters italicize the chapter title, but xrefs to sections do not. You might think the gentext templates would let you customize the style, but they do not. The gentext templates specify text in attributes, and attributes are not permitted to have elements in XML. So you cannot wrap the gentext in HTML or FO elements for formatting.

You can italicize section titles with a stylesheet customization using the insert.title.markup mode. That mode is used to generate the title to replace the %t placeholder in a gentext template. For FO output, you need to create a template like the following in your customization layer:

```
<xsl:template  match="sect1|sect2|sect3|sect4|sect5|section"
               mode="insert.title.markup">
  <xsl:param name="purpose"/>
  <xsl:param name="xrefstyle"/>
  <xsl:param name="title"/>

  <xsl:choose>
    <xsl:when test="$purpose = 'xref'">
      <fo:inline font-style="italic">
        <xsl:copy-of select="$title"/>
      </fo:inline>
    </xsl:when>
    <xsl:otherwise>
      <xsl:copy-of select="$title"/>
    </xsl:otherwise>
  </xsl:choose>
</xsl:template>
```

The mode named insert.title.markup is designed to handle adding markup to titles in a given context. The template parameter named purpose indicates the context. In this case, you want to wrap an inline font-style tag around a section title, but only if the purpose of the title is an xref. That way you do not also italicize these titles in their original location or the table of contents.

If you want something similar for HTML output, just copy this template to your HTML customization layer and replace the fo:inline start and end tags with the equivalent HTML I start and end tags.

If you want to style *all* cross references in FO output, for xref, link, and ulink references, then a simpler mechanism is available. The xref.properties attribute-set can be used to add FO properties to the text of all such cross references. For example, if you want the cross reference text to appear in blue for ulink elements, then use this customization:

```
<xsl:attribute-set name="xref.properties">
  <xsl:attribute name="color">
    <xsl:choose>
      <xsl:when test="self::ulink">blue</xsl:when>
      <xsl:otherwise>inherit</xsl:otherwise>
    </xsl:choose>
  </xsl:attribute>
</xsl:attribute-set>
```

This sets the color property conditionally. When the element using the xref.properties attribute set is a ulink, then the test matches and the color is blue. Otherwise the color is inherited, so there is no color change. Be sure to include the otherwise part. If you want all three cross reference elements to be blue, then you can just set the attribute value without using the choose statement.

For olink elements, the olink.properties attribute-set is available instead. It sets properties on the text generated for olink elements. See Chapter 24, *Olinking between documents* (page 383) for more information.

To style all cross references in HTML output, just create a CSS selector on the A element, which is used for all hot links in HTML.

Specialized cross references

DocBook can create some cross references automatically without reference to an id, if you set up your documents properly and turn on the right parameters.

- You can automatically form links from your text to a glossary entry if you set the `glossary.auto.link` parameter to 1. See the section called "Linking to a glossary entry" (page 280) for more information.

- When you create a back-of-the-book index, the index entries becomes links from the index to locations in the document. See Chapter 19, *Indexes* (page 309) for more information.

- When you create footnotes, a link is automatically formed from the footnote mark in the text to the footnote at the bottom of the page. In HTML output, the reverse link is also created. That is, the mark in the footnote links back to the matching mark in the text. See Chapter 16, *Footnotes* (page 273) for more details.

DocBook also permits some elements to have a `linkend`-like attribute to form a cross reference to an `id` on another element.

Callouts

You can form links between a callout marker and its associated callout text. A `co` callout marker can take a `linkends` attribute (note the plural) to point to the `callout` element that contains its text. A `callout` elements can take an `arearefs` (not `linkend`) attribute to point back to its `co` element. See the section called "Callouts" (page 447) for more information.

If you are using `area` elements in `programlistingco` to attach callout markers to imported text, then you can put a `linkends` (note the plural) attribute on each `area` element. See the section called "Callouts on imported text" (page 448) for more information.

Callout reference

When doing callouts, sometimes more than one place in your example needs to point to the same callout description. To make sure they have the same callout bug number, use a `coref` element instead of another `co` element. See the section called "Callouts" (page 447) for more information.

Synopses

If you are using a `cmdsynopsis`, you can break out parts of a complex command synopsis using `synopfragment`. You can insert a `synopfragmentref` with a `linkend` attribute to point to a `synopfragment`. See the reference page for `synopfragment` in *DocBook: The Definitive Guide*[1] for an example.

Footnote reference

Sometimes you need to make more than one reference to the same footnote. For example, you might have two places in your text where the explanation in a footnote is appropriate. Rather than create two identical `footnote` elements, one of them can be a `footnoteref` element. That is an empty element with a `linkend` attribute that points to the `id` you put in the `footnote` element.

Glossary reference

You can link from your text into a glossary. An inline `glossterm` in a paragraph can have a `linkend` attribute that points to the `id` of a `glossentry` in a glossary. See the section called "Linking to a glossary entry" (page 280) for more information.

---

[1] http://docbook.org/tdg/en/html/synopfragment.html

16
Footnotes

Footnotes in DocBook are another form of linking. A footnote reference in HTML output is an active link to the footnote text, which is located elsewhere. Likewise, the label on the footnote is also a link back to the reference symbol in the body text. In print output, the linkage is just visual since the footnote is on the same page.

In DocBook you write a footnote element at the point in a paragraph where you want the footnote reference (number or symbol) to appear. For example:

```
<para>During the installation of
the product<footnote><para>In versions 2.3 and 2.4.</para>
</footnote> you may see messages such as these.
</para>
```

When processed, the footnote reference symbol will appear where the `footnote` start tag appears. If you do not want a space before the symbol, then do not put a space or line break before the start tag. The body of the `footnote` is moved to another location, with links connecting the reference symbol and the footnote.

In HTML output, footnotes are collected and output at the appropriate opportunity. In non-chunked output, the collected footnotes are output at the end of each chapter, appendix, or other component. In chunked output, footnotes are output at the end of each chunk. The exception is footnotes in tables, which have a separate numbering sequence and appear at the bottom of their respective tables.

In printed output, footnotes are output at the bottom of each page. In addition, if the `ulink.footnotes` parameter is not zero, then the URL associated with a `ulink` element will also be treated as a footnote. Table footnotes appear at the bottom of their respective tables. There is no stylesheet parameter to generate end notes instead of footnotes, but there is a customization you can use, as described in the section called "End notes" (page 276).

If you need to reference the same footnote more than once, you can use the `footnoteref` element. This empty element is used like an `xref`, where its `linkend` attribute matches the `id` value that you put on the footnote element that it is referencing. When processed, the `footnoteref` element will have the same symbol or number as the footnote it references. This lets more than one location in your document point to the same footnote, so you do not have to repeat it.

Footnote numbers and symbols

By default, footnotes are numbered sequentially. In HTML output, the number sequence is continuous throughout the document, regardless of whether it is chunked or not. In FO output, the numbering sequence restarts at 1 at the beginning of each chapter, appendix, and other component. If the `ulink.footnotes` parameter is not zero, then the footnotes generated for `ulink` elements in FO output will be mixed in the same numbering sequence.

There is no option that lets you restart numbering on each page of FO output. Such automatic numbering is not a feature of the XSL-FO 1.0 standard. The numbers are added by the DocBook XSL stylesheet, but stylesheet does not know where the page breaks are, because the XSL-FO processor determines them.

You can alter the number format for numbered footnotes. If you set the parameter `footnote.number.format` to A, for example, then footnotes will be numbered A, B, C, etc. You can use any of the formats supported by XSLT, including A, a, I, i, and 1 (the default). There is a separate parameter `table.footnote.number.format` for table footnotes. That can be useful to distinguish table footnotes from regular footnotes.

If you want to use symbols instead of numbers to mark footnotes, then use the `footnote.number.symbols` parameter. This parameter should be set to a string of single characters without any separation. Each character will be used in turn as a footnote mark. A character can be represented by a numerical character reference as well. For example:

```
<xsl:param name="footnote.number.symbols">*&#x2020;&#x2021;</xsl:param>
```

The first character is * and will be used for the first footnote. The second character is † (dagger) and will be used for the second footnote. The third character is ‡ (double dagger) and will be used for the third footnote. Any footnote numbers that exceed the length of the string will revert back to numbers, staring with 4 in this case.

For footnotes in tables, a separate `table.footnote.number.symbols` parameter works in the same way.

Whatever symbols you use in either parameter, be sure they can be rendered by your XSL-FO processor in the font you are using. Likewise for HTML output, as not all Unicode characters are available in all browser fonts.

Any time you need to override the mark for a given footnote, you can add a `label` attribute on the footnote. Whatever you put in the attribute will be used for the footnote mark. It need not be a single character.

If you need to completely replace the footnote numbering scheme with another scheme, then you will have to customize the template that starts with the following line, in the `footnote.xsl` stylesheet module:

```
<xsl:template match="footnote" mode="footnote.number">
```

Formatting footnotes in HTML

A footnote reference and footnote text are output to HTML as follows:

Footnote reference:
```
<sup>[<a name="id394062" href="#ftn.id394062">*</a>]</sup>
```

Footnote:
```
<div class="footnote"><p>
<sup>[<a name="ftn.id394062" href="#id394062">*</a>]</sup>
Text of footnote ...
```

The footnote mark is rendered with superscript `sup` and square brackets. Each has an `href` and a `name` attribute, so they can cross link between each other. If you want to change that rendering, you will need to customize the following two templates from `html/footnote.xsl`:

Footnote reference template:
```
<xsl:template match="footnote">
...
```

Footnote:
```
<xsl:template match="footnote/para[1]|footnote/simpara[1]" priority="2">
...
```

You can change the formatting of the footnote paragraph using CSS. Use the div.footnote CSS selector, and apply whatever styles you want with it, as shown in the following example.

```
div.footnote {
    font-size: 8pt;
}
```

See the section called "Using CSS to style HTML" (page 71) for more general information about DocBook and CSS.

Formatting footnotes in print

Footnotes are rendered in XSL-FO output as follows:

```
<fo:footnote><fo:inline font-size="75%"
        baseline-shift="super">1</fo:inline>
  <fo:footnote-body font-family="serif,Symbol,ZapfDingbats"
    font-size="8pt" font-weight="normal" font-style="normal"
    text-align="justify" margin-left="0pc">
    <fo:block><fo:inline font-size="75%"
        baseline-shift="super">1</fo:inline>
      The footnote text.
    </fo:block>
  </fo:footnote-body>
</fo:footnote>
```

The fo:footnote-body element contains the text of the footnote, including its own copy of the footnote mark. The content before fo:footnote-body is the mark that is placed in the text paragraph to reference the footnote. So both the mark and the text of the footnote are contained in the fo:footnote element. The XSL-FO processor handles placing the mark and moving the text to the bottom of the page.

Most of the formatting properties you see here are added by attribute-sets that you can customize. The footnote.properties attribute-set is applied to the fo:footnote-body, and the footnote.mark.properties attribute-set is applied to the inline mark. These attribute-sets are also applied to ulink footnotes when the ulink.footnotes parameter is turned on. There is a separate attribute-set for table footnotes named table.footnote.properties. See the section called "Attribute sets" (page 103) to learn how to customize attribute-sets.

The baseline-shift property is not in the footnote.mark.properties attribute-set, because it is not supported by the previous version of FOP (0.20.5). So the footnote template has to insert a different property that the old FOP does support.

If all you want to change is the footnote font size, then that is controlled by a separate parameter, the footnote.font.size parameter. By default it is set to 75%, but for some fonts that looks too large. You can set it to a percentage or to a fixed point size.

If you need to further customize footnotes for print, you can customize the template with match="footnote" in fo/footnote.xsl. It also calls the template named format.footnote.mark to format the footnote symbol. It actually calls it twice to format the mark in both the reference and the footnote text.

There is one other feature of print footnotes that you can customize: the rule line separating the footnotes from the body text. The rule is actually a `fo:static-content` element in XSL-FO. It is defined in the stylesheet in `fo/page-setup.xsl` as the following:

```
<xsl:template name="footnote-separator">
  <fo:static-content flow-name="xsl-footnote-separator">
    <fo:block>
      <fo:leader xsl:use-attribute-sets="footnote.sep.leader.properties"/>
    </fo:block>
  </fo:static-content>
</xsl:template>
```

The content consists of a block containing an `fo:leader`, which is what draws the line. You can customize the `footnote.sep.leader.properties` attribute-set to set the line length, weight, color, and style.

If you want to change more than just the leader properties, then you can customize the template named `footnote-separtor` that is shown above, to put something else inside the `static-content`.

End notes

There is no stylesheet parameter that converts footnotes to endnotes, but it can be done with a customization. Take a look at the template with `match="footnote"` in `fo/footnote.xsl`, for example. You can customize that to generate endnotes.

First copy the template to your customization layer and remove the `fo:footnote` elements, because they generate bottom-of-page footnotes. Leave just the part that generates the footnote number, inside an `fo:inline`:

```
<xsl:template match="footnote">
  <fo:inline>
    <xsl:call-template name="format.footnote.mark">
      <xsl:with-param name="mark">
        <xsl:apply-templates select="." mode="footnote.number"/>
      </xsl:with-param>
    </xsl:call-template>
  </fo:inline>
</xsl:template>
```

Then add a template with a new `mode="endnote"` like the following to format each footnote:

```
<xsl:template match="footnote" mode="endnote">
  <fo:block xsl:use-attribute-sets="footnote.properties">
    <xsl:apply-templates/>
  </fo:block>
</xsl:template>
```

The footnote mark is included when doing `apply-templates` to a `footnote` element. Then you can generate the list of end notes by putting a template like the following in your customization layer. It is meant to be called at the end of each chapter or appendix.

```
<xsl:template name="make.endnotes.list">
    <xsl:apply-templates mode="endnote"
                         select="ancestor-or-self::chapter//footnote |
                                 ancestor-or-self::appendix//footnote"/>
</xsl:template>
```

This will select and process all the footnotes in the current chapter or appendix, in document order. If you are putting all your end notes at the end of a book, you should use `select="//footnote"` instead. You will also want to turn off the way each chapter restarts the footnote number sequence, by customizing the template that starts with the following line:

```
<xsl:template match="footnote" mode="footnote.number">
```

The only remaining item is figuring out how to call the `make.endnotes.list` template at the point where you want the list of end notes to appear. If you want them at the end of the book, you will have to customize the template with `match="book"`. You'll need to create a new page-sequence, add a title, and call the `make.endnotes` template inside the page-sequence. You can use the utility template named `page.sequence` in `fo/component.xsl` to handle most of the page-sequence setup.

If you want end notes to appear at the end of each chapter, you can customize the end of the template with `match="chapter"` from `fo/component.xsl` as follows:

```
<xsl:template match="chapter">
      [first part of the template]
      ...
      <xsl:apply-templates/>

      <xsl:if test="descendant::footnote">
        <fo:block space-before="44pt" font-weight="bold"
                  font-size="14pt" font-family="{$title.fontset}">
          <xsl:text>Endnotes</xsl:text>
        </fo:block>
        <fo:block >
          <xsl:call-template name="make.endnotes.list"/>
        </fo:block>
      </xsl:if>
    </fo:flow>
  </fo:page-sequence>
</xsl:template>
```

It tests to see if the current chapter has any `footnote` elements. If so, it outputs a title and calls `make.endnotes.list`.

If you are generating end notes instead of footnotes, you might want to turn off the `ulink.footnotes` parameter (it is zero by default).

17

Glossaries

The DocBook XSL stylesheets have some special features for glossaries. In addition to formatting glossary elements and their glossentrys, they let you form cross references from your text to glossary entries, sort glossary entries, and create a separate glossary database.

Glossary formatting

These formatting options are available for both HTML and print output.

- The title and start of a glossary is considered a glossary title page. It can be controlled by the same title page customization methods as other components, and described in Chapter 11, *Title page customization* (page 141).

- You can divide a glossary into sections using glossdiv wrappers around groups of glossentry elements. You must give each glossdiv a title.

- If your glossentry elements include an abbrev or acronym element, then you can control how it appears with the glossentry.show.acronym parameter. Its values can be:

primary   Put the abbrev or acronym first, followed by the glossterm in parentheses.

yes   Put the glossterm first, followed by the abbrev or acronym in parentheses.

no   do not show the abbrev or acronym at all.

If your entry has both abbrev and acronym, then both will appear in the output.

Glossary formatting in print

In addition to the above features, the print stylesheet supports these additional formatting features.

- You can format a glossary as a list with the terms to the left of the indented definition paragraphs, or as blocks with each term stacked above its unindented paragraph. By default, a glossary is formatted as a list. If you want to change all of your glossaries to format as blocks, set the glossary.as.blocks stylesheet parameter to a nonzero value. If you are using a glosslist instead of a glossary element, then use the glosslist.as.blocks parameter instead. You can also control how an individual glossary is presented by using a processing instruction inserted into that `glossary` element in your document. The following is an example:

```
<glossary><title>Glossary</title>
<?dbfo glossary-presentation="blocks" ?>
<glossentry>
 . . .
```

You can set the value to `list` to format one glossary as a list when the parameter formats the rest as blocks. For a `glosslist`, the processing instruction name is `glosslist-presentation`, and it takes the same values. In all cases, the processing instruction overrides the stylesheet parameter for an individual glossary.

- If your glossary is formatted as a list, you can control the indent of the definition paragraphs to allow space for the terms. The `glossterm.width` stylesheet parameter sets the indent for all `glossary` and `glosslist` elements. Its default value is `2in`. You can also set the indent width for an individual glossary using a processing instruction, as in this example.

```
<glossary><title>Glossary</title>
<?dbfo glossterm-width="3.5cm" ?>
<glossentry>
 . . .
```

- For a glossary formatted as a list, you can also control the minimum size of the space separating the term from the paragraph. That value is controlled by the `glossterm.separation` parameter, and its default value is `0.25in`. There is no processing instruction for this feature.

Linking to a glossary entry

You can form a link from your text to a glossary entry by adding an `id` or `xml:id` attribute to a `glossentry` that contains a `glossterm` in a glossary (do not put the id on the `glossterm`). Then add a matching `linkend` attribute to an inline `glossterm` in your text. Note that the element `glossterm` is used in both places, but they serve different functions.

```
<para>Set your <glossterm linkend="NetAddr">network address</glossterm>.
</para>
. . .
<glossary>
  <glossentry id="NetAddr">
    <glossterm>Network address</glossterm>
    <glossdef><para>Four numbers separated by periods</para></glossdef>
  </glossentry>
</glossary>
```

In this method of linking, the inline text can differ from the text of the term in the glossary. That's useful if you need to change capitalization or a word ending.

The other type of glossary link can be formed automatically. To turn this feature on, set the stylesheet parameter `glossterm.auto.link` to 1. Then you can skip adding the `id` and `linkend` attributes. To form the link, the stylesheet tries to match the words of the inline `glossterm` with the words in any `glossterm` child of a `glossentry`, which must appear in a glossary. What about capitalization and word ending variations? In those cases, add a `baseform` attribute to the inline `glossterm` in your text, and set its value to match the words of the `glossterm` in the glossary. It will use the `baseform` to find the match to form the link but will display the text content of the inline `glossterm` as you have entered it. Here are two examples. The matching words are highlighted.

```
<para>Set your
<glossterm baseform="Network address">network address</glossterm>.
</para>
<para><glossterm>Domain name</glossterm>
is expressed as part of the address.</para>
...
<glossary>
  <glossentry>
    <glossterm>Domain name</glossterm>
    <glossdef><para>First part of a network address.</para></glossdef>
  </glossentry>
  <glossentry>
    <glossterm>Network address</glossterm>
    <glossdef><para>Domain name plus machine name.</para></glossdef>
  </glossentry>
</glossary>
```

Caution:

If you edit the words on just one end of such automatic links, the link will be broken and the stylesheet will issue a warning message. This could easily happen if you edit a glossary entry, without realizing there are inline references to it elsewhere. The `id` and `linkend` method is more robust since it does not depend on matching text. You can also use both methods within a document, and the linkend method will take precedence in a given reference.

You can also form links in a glossary from one related glossary entry to another using `glosssee` and `glossseealso` elements. The `glosssee` element is used in place of a `glossdef` element when you want to refer the reader to another entry for the entire definition. The `glossseealso` element can be put into a `glossdef` element to supplement a definition with a reference to another.

To form active links, you put an `id` attribute on the destination `glossentry` (or its `glossterm`), and then point to that id with an `otherterm` attribute. Here are some examples:

```
<glossary>
  <glossentry id="DomainName">
    <glossterm>Domain name</glossterm>
    <glossdef><para>First part of a network address.</para>
        <glossseealso otherterm="NetAddr"/>
    </glossdef>
  </glossentry>
  <glossentry>
    <glossterm>Machine address</glossterm>
    <glosssee otherterm="NetAddr">network address</glosssee>
  </glossentry>
  <glossentry>
    <glossterm id="NetAddr">Network address</glossterm>
    <glossdef><para>Domain name plus machine name.</para>
        <glossseealso otherterm="DomainName"/>
    </glossdef>
  </glossentry>
</glossary>
```

If the matchup between `otherterm` and `id` is made, then the stylesheet will generate a link and its text, using the words of the destination `glossterm`. If the matchup fails, then it falls back to using the content of the `glosssee` or `glossseealso`.

What about link and xref?

You might wonder why you cannot use `link` or `xref` elements to link to a glossary entry. Actually, a `link` element can be used, but it will act exactly like an inline `glossterm` since you have to supply the text for the link.

Trying to use `xref` can be a problem, because the stylesheets do not know how to generate text for the link. Usually `xref` resolves to the title of the target element, but a `glossentry` does not have a title. The glossentry's `glossterm` is similar, but it can contain inline markup and graphics, so it is considered too complex to use for generated text. However, if you keep your entries simple, you can force the stylesheet to use the text of the glossentry's `glossterm`. Just add an `id` attribute to the `glossterm` and add a matching `endterm` attribute to the `xref` element. The following is an example:

```
<xref linkend="ge-xslfoprocessor" endterm="gt-xslfoprocessor"/>
...

<glossentry id="ge-xslfoprocessor">
<glossterm id="gt-xslfoprocessor">XSL-FO processor</glossterm>
<glossdef>
<para>Software component that converts an XSL-FO document into a
formatted document.</para>
</glossdef>
</glossentry>
```

The `linkend` attribute in the `xref` points to the `glossentry` element's `id`, but the `endterm` attribute points to the `glossterm` inside the entry. Using `endterm` causes the generated text to come from the children of the element whose id is referenced in the `endterm`, which is the `glossterm` in this case. This `xref` should generate a link whose hot text is `XSL-FO processor`.

You have another option if the `glossterm` is too long to use as the generated cross reference text. You could put some link text in an `xreflabel` attribute on the target `glossentry` element. Then the `xref` will copy that text to form the link. See the section called "Attach an xreflabel to a target element" (page 259) for more information.

Glossary database

If you find yourself needing the same glossary entries in more than one document, you can maintain a separate glossary entry database. Keeping the entries in one place ensures consistency between publications and makes it easier to maintain. It gets better. Your glossary can be assembled automatically from the `glossterm` and `firstterm` elements scattered throughout your document. And they can be automatically hot linked to the generated glossary.

A glossary database is simply a separate DocBook document with root element `glossary` that contains a collection of `glossentry` elements. Each entry in the database document must have a unique `glossterm` element, because that is used for matching. Put your entries in the order you want them to appear in any of your glossaries. You can use `glossdiv` elements too.

To generate a glossary automatically, you do three things:

1. Create a placeholder `glossary` element in your document, with a `role="auto"` attribute. In DocBook 4's DTD, `glossary` cannot be empty, so you must put one dummy `glossentry` in it. It does not matter what it says, because it will not be used. In DocBook 5, the dummy entry is not needed because it permits an empty glossary.

2. Add `glossterm` and `firstterm` elements anywhere in your document as needed. Either the text content or the element's `baseform` attribute value must match the `glossterm` in one of the entries in your database.

3. Process your document with the stylesheet parameter `glossary.collection` set to the filename of your database document.

When the stylesheet reaches your nearly empty `<glossary role="auto">` element in your document, it opens the glossary database document specified by the `glossary.collection` parameter. For each `glossentry` in the database, it looks at the text content of its `glossterm` child. It then checks to see if there is a `glossterm` or `firstterm` element somewhere in your document that matches it (or one with a `baseform` attribute that matches). If so, then it outputs that `glossentry` in your glossary.

You have a couple of options:

- You can restrict the glossary to generating entries only for `firstterm` elements in your document by setting the `firstterm.only.link` parameter to 1.

- You want to turn on the automatic hot links from each `glossterm` in your text to the matching `glossentry` in the glossary, then set the `glossterm.auto.link` parameter to 1.

Glossary database catalog entry

If you need to share a glossary database among several books, you might consider using an XML catalog entry to locate the database file. Once you set it up, all of your documents will be able to use the same collection, and you can move the collection when you need to, and then you just need to change the single catalog entry. See Chapter 5, *XML catalogs* (page 47) for general information on catalogs.

First set the `glossary.collection` parameter to any generic path:

`<xsl:param name="glossary.collection">`**`file:///foo/gloss.xml`**`</xsl:param>`

Then add an entry to your XML catalog that maps the generic path to the real path:

```
<uri
    name="file:///foo/gloss.xml"
    uri="file:///c:/usr/share/xml/glossary-database.xml"/>
```

When you process your stylesheet with a catalog-aware processor (and tell it where to find the catalog), then the generic path will be mapped to the specific path.

Links in a glossary collection

There are significant limitations on cross references within a glossary collection. These arise because the glossary collection is processed as a separate document in its own context, not in the context of the main document.

- A glossary entry cannot cross reference back to the body of the document. It often useful to refer from a glossary entry to a section of the document that provides more information, but that is not possible when you use a glossary collection.

- A cross reference from one `glossentry` to another in the collection using either `glossterm`, `glosssee`, or `glossseealso` may fail. However, there is a workaround that will enable them to work. See the `glossary.collection`[1] parameter reference page in the stylesheet documentation.

---

[1] http://docbook.sourceforge.net/release/xsl/current/doc/html/glossary.collection.html

- Even if your links within your glossary collection do not give an error, they can still fail in the output. That can happen when the target entry is not included in the glossary generated for that document. If there is no `glossterm` in the document body that references the target entry, then it will not be included in the generated glossary. The stylesheet thinks the entry is present in the context of the glossary collection during processing, so there is no error message. But the generated link will fail when viewed.

You can still link from your document body to entries in the glossary collection.

Glossary sorting

You can automatically sort your glossaries by setting a stylesheet parameter. Glossary sorting is particularly useful when translating a glossary, because translation in place usually puts entries out of alphabetical order. Rather than rearranging the entries in the source file, you can just specify the sort feature.

You can turn on glossary sorting by setting the stylesheet parameter `glossary.sort` to 1 (default value is zero). Then each group of `glossentry` elements is sorted alphabetically on the `glossterm` element contained within each `glossentry`. The sort feature works for regular glossaries as well as those generated from a glossary database. The glossary sort feature was added starting with version 1.73 of the stylesheets.

Entries are sorted within each `glossdiv`, `glosslist`, or `glossary` container, whichever is the parent element. There is currently no provision for generating letter titles to divide letter groups. The templates in the `glossary.xsl` stylesheet module would need to be customized to generate such groupings.

The sort sequence is determined by the current value of the `lang` attribute (which defaults to `en` if no `lang` or `xml:lang` attribute is present).

The sort attempts to fold together uppercase and lowercase, and accented and unaccented characters, for most Latin alphabet languages. It does that by using the gentext templates named `normalize.sort.input` and `normalize.sort.output`, which are defined in each of the locale files that are described in the section called "Generated text" (page 105). The `normalize.sort.input` text is a sequence of all the lowercase letters, and they are matched by the sequence of uppercase letters in `normalize.sort.output`. These are used as arguments in the XSLT `translate()` function, whose purpose is to substitute one character for another. Each glossary term is converted to uppercase for sorting purposes only, and presented in its original letter case. If the case folding for the language you are processing is not correct (leading to an incorrect sort order), then you can customize those gentext templates for each language.

18
Graphics

Graphics are a frequent cause of problems in DocBook documents. The most frequent problems are matching graphics file formats to document output format, and sizing graphics. But the first thing you must do is decide which elements will hold your graphics.

Elements for graphics

DocBook has two main graphic elements. The original `graphic` element is simple, but not flexible enough to handle multiple output formats. The preferred element for graphics is `mediaobject`. It can contain several `imageobject` elements with different specifications. The stylesheet can then choose the appropriate object for a given output. Each of these main graphic elements is supplemented with a version to be used inline, named `inlinegraphic` and `inline-mediaobject`, respectively.

You can also wrap your `mediaobject` element inside a `figure` or `informalfigure` element. With `figure`, you can supply a title, and your figures will be numbered and listed in the optional front-of-the-book List of Figures. Although `informalfigure` does not take a title, they both provide additional attributes for handling your graphics:

`pgwide`	If your print content is styled so that headings are at the left margin and body text is indented, then setting this attribute to 1 lets you indicate that the figure is wide and should be positioned starting at the left margin. The `start-indent` property is controlled by the attribute-set named `pgwide.properties` if you need to customize it.
`float` `floatstyle`	These attributes let you indicate that the figure can float to the top, left, or right. See the section called "Figure floats" (page 295) for details.

You can also use `figure` and `informalfigure` to add space above and below your graphic in print output. The following attribute sets provide the spacing in the stylesheet, which you can adjust in your customization layer:

```
<xsl:attribute-set name="figure.properties"
     use-attribute-sets="formal.object.properties"/>

<xsl:attribute-set name="formal.object.properties">
  <xsl:attribute name="space-before.minimum">0.5em</xsl:attribute>
  <xsl:attribute name="space-before.optimum">1em</xsl:attribute>
  <xsl:attribute name="space-before.maximum">2em</xsl:attribute>
  <xsl:attribute name="space-after.minimum">0.5em</xsl:attribute>
  <xsl:attribute name="space-after.optimum">1em</xsl:attribute>
  <xsl:attribute name="space-after.maximum">2em</xsl:attribute>
  <xsl:attribute name="keep-together.within-column">always</xsl:attribute>
</xsl:attribute-set>

<xsl:attribute-set name="informalfigure.properties"
     use-attribute-sets="informal.object.properties"/>

<xsl:attribute-set name="informal.object.properties">
  <xsl:attribute name="space-before.minimum">0.5em</xsl:attribute>
  <xsl:attribute name="space-before.optimum">1em</xsl:attribute>
  <xsl:attribute name="space-before.maximum">2em</xsl:attribute>
  <xsl:attribute name="space-after.minimum">0.5em</xsl:attribute>
  <xsl:attribute name="space-after.optimum">1em</xsl:attribute>
  <xsl:attribute name="space-after.maximum">2em</xsl:attribute>
</xsl:attribute-set>
```

The `formal.object.properties` attribute set is used in the attribute sets for all formal objects, including figures, tables, examples, and equations, so changing it for `figure` will also change it for those other elements. If that is not desirable, then add the changes to the `figure.properties` attribute set only. The same is true for `informal.object.properties` and `informalfigure.properties` (starting with version 1.66 of the stylesheets).

If you use `example` or `informalexample`, then you can use the `example.properties` or `informalexample.properties` instead.

Selecting file formats

Graphics files come in many different formats, such as PNG, EPS, and JPEG. Unfortunately, there is no single graphics file format that meets all needs. HTML output files require bitmap graphics such as PNG or JPEG. Some browsers are beginning to accept SVG (scalable vector graphics), but support is not universal. XSL-FO processors generally accept bitmap graphics and vector graphics, but not all of them accept all formats.

If you are publishing only HTML output, then you just need to convert your pictures to one of the common bitmap formats such as PNG, GIF, or JPEG. All graphical browsers support these formats. But if you need to produce both HTML and print output from the same DocBook documents, then you may need more than one format. The formats you choose will depend on the type of illustration and the XSL-FO processor you use.

If you are using a screenshot, then a bitmap graphic can work for both HTML and print output. That's because the original screen itself was a bitmap display, so it will look good in HTML. It also will not improve or degrade when used in print. You still may want to scale the graphic differently for the two outputs.

If you are using a drawn illustration, you probably want to generate two graphic files derived from the same source drawing. Computer drawings use vector graphics, which produce smooth lines when reproduced at high resolution, such as in print. They can also be rendered at lower resolution if needed. But most HTML browsers do not accept vector graphics at all. So a typical solution is to produce two versions of the same picture, using a vector graphic format for print, and a bitmap format for HTML. All drawing programs provide several output formats to choose from, so check your software documentation to see which formats it can export to.

You also need to check the documentation of your XSL-FO processor to see what graphics file formats it supports. The following is a list as of this writing.

Table 18.1. XSL-FO processor supported graphics formats

FO Processor	Bitmap formats	Vector formats
Antenna House	PNG JPEG GIF TIFF BMP	SVG PDF EPS EMF WMF CGM
FOP	PNG JPEG GIF TIFF BMP	SVG EPS
XEP	PNG JPEG GIF TIFF	SVG PDF EPS

Note:

An EPS graphic requires a PostScript interpreter to display its vector artwork. XSL-FO processors, PDF browsers and many printers do not contain PostScript interpreters, and will only display the low resolution bitmap image that is often embedded in an EPS file. Generally SVG gives better results with PDF and print output. If you have EPS graphics, you can convert them to SVG using Adobe Illustrator (not free) or Ghostscript (free).

Once you have determined which graphics formats are supported, you can convert your graphics to those formats and save the files with the appropriate filename extensions. Then you can create your mediaobject elements with multiple formats. See the section called "Stylesheet's selection process" (page 288) to see how a given format is chosen.

Adding graphics formats

What if you have a graphics file format that is supported in your output but is not supported by the stylesheets? For example, the Macromedia Flash Movie file format has a format of SWF. This file format is supported in browsers with the Flash plugin.

To add a graphics format to the list of supported formats in the HTML stylesheet, copy the template named is.graphic.format from html/graphics.xsl to your customization layer. Add your new format to the xml:if statement, as in the following example:

```
<xsl:template name="is.graphic.format">
  <xsl:param name="format"></xsl:param>
  <xsl:if test="$format = 'SVG'
                or $format = 'PNG'
                or $format = 'JPG'
                or $format = 'JPEG'
                or $format = 'linespecific'
                or $format = 'GIF'
                or $format = 'GIF87a'
                or $format = 'GIF89a'
                or $format = 'BMP'
                or $format = 'SWF'">1</xsl:if>
</xsl:template>
```

Now you can add a format="SWF" attribute to a videodata element in your DocBook file. You will likely have to do some further customization of the videodata template to output the correct HTML to support Flash movies, though.

You may also want to add a new graphics format when your XSL-FO processor upgrades to support a new format before the DocBook stylesheet distribution can catch up. In that case, copy the same template from the fo/graphics.xsl stylesheet file to your customization layer and add the new format name.

Stylesheet's selection process

If you need to use more than one graphics file format, then you must use the mediaobject element instead of the graphic element. You could use profiling to select from among several graphic elements, but mediaobject is designed to do it without the need for the profiling step.

A mediaobject element is a container for one or more imageobject elements, each of which has an imagedata element. Usually, the various images in a mediaobject are different formats of the same illustration, with the idea that only one of them at a time will be used by the stylesheet. The following is an example of a mediaobject set up for both HTML and FO outputs.

Example 18.1. Multiple graphics in a mediaobject

```
<mediaobject  id="MousePicture">  ❶
  <imageobject  role="html">  ❷
    <imagedata  format="PNG"  fileref="mouse.png"/>  ❸
  </imageobject>
  <imageobject  role="fo">
    <imagedata  format="PDF"  fileref="mouse.pdf"/>
  </imageobject>
</mediaobject>
```

Note these features of this example:

❶ The mediaobject element contains two graphical elements. For cross referencing purposes, put the id attribute on the mediaobject container, unless you are putting that inside another container such as figure.
❷ The first imageobject element has a role="html" attribute that designates it for HTML output. The second imageobject has a role="fo" attribute that designates it for FO output.
❸ Each imagedata element indicates its file name and format. You could also put sizing attributes there.

Select by role

The DocBook stylesheets can automatically select the right graphic if the imageobject elements have a role attribute of either html or fo. When you process this example with the html stylesheet, you get the PNG graphic, and when you process it with the FO stylesheet, you get the PDF graphic. Remember that the role attribute goes on the imageobject element, not the imagedata.

If you are using the xhtml stylesheet, then you can use role="xhtml" if you need a different format for that output. Otherwise the xhtml stylesheet falls back to the object with role="html". Other stylesheet customizations such as Website or your own will use the value for the stock stylesheet it is based upon.

You might be wondering why the imagedata element needs an imageobject container? Because imageobject can also contain an objectinfo element. That element can be used to track information *about* the image, such as the software that created it, the current revision, the author, etc.

The automatic selection behavior is controlled by the use.role.for.mediaobject parameter. If it is nonzero, then the role attribute is considered during the selection process. You can turn that behavior off if you set the parameter to zero.

If you want finer control, then you have the option to use any role values you want. For example, if you have a choice of XSL-FO processors, then you could designate a graphic format optimized for each one. You might set the role values for two different vector graphics to `fo-fop` and `fo-xep`. Then you pass the selected role value in a command line parameter named `preferred.mediaobject.role`. For example:

```
<mediaobject  id="MousePicture">
  <imageobject  role="html">
    <imagedata  format="PNG"  fileref="mouse.png"/>
  </imageobject>
  <imageobject  role="fo-fop">
    <imagedata  format="SVG"  fileref="mouse.svg"/>
  </imageobject>
  <imageobject  role="fo-xep">
    <imagedata  format="PDF"  fileref="mouse.pdf"/>
  </imageobject>
</mediaobject>
```

If you are processing with the FOP processor, then set the parameter `preferred.mediaobject.role="fo-fop"` on the command line. The DocBook stylesheet will use the SVG graphic reference into the FO output file. If you are using XEP, then set the parameter `preferred.mediaobject.role="fo-xep"` to use the PDF graphic instead.

Select by format

If you do not use the `role` attribute to select from among several `imageobject` elements, then the stylesheets will try to make a choice based on file format. The stylesheets contain several lists of file formats that are acceptable for each output type. For the various XSL-FO processors, it checks to see if any of the parameters `fop.extensions`, `passivetex.extensions`, `arbortext.extensions`, or `xep.extensions` is set.

The process of selection by format goes like this:

1. It looks at the first `imageobject` inside the `mediaobject`.

2. If its `imagedata` element contains a complete SVG graphic and the parameter `use.svg` is nonzero, then it accepts that object and does not consider any others.

3. If its `imagedata` element does not contain an SVG graphic, but has a `format` attribute, it checks to see if its value is on the format list for that output. If so, then it accepts that object and does not consider any others.

4. If it does not have a `format` attribute, it extracts the filename extension from the `fileref` attribute. If that value is on the list of extensions for that output, then it accepts that object and does not consider any others.

5. If the `fileref` does not have an extension, it checks the `graphic.default.extension` parameter to see what extension would be added to such a file reference. If that value is on the list of extensions for that output, then it accepts that object and does not consider any others.

6. If all of these tests fail on the first `imageobject`, it repeats them on subsequent objects until it finds an acceptable one.

This selection method is often sufficient, but is somewhat less precise than selecting by role. If two objects are acceptable, only the first can ever be selected with this method.

Image sizing

People who are familiar with HTML markup often try to use the `width` attribute in an `imagedata` tag to scale their graphic. And often it works. But when they try to use other image attributes, they get strange results. Image sizing can be somewhat complex because there are many `imagedata` attributes that affect it. In addition to sizing the image itself, you can specify a *viewport* area, which is the space reserved for the image. If the viewport area is larger than the final image size, then there is white space around it. If the viewport area is smaller than the final image size, then the image is supposed to be clipped (but it does not happen in HTML output, may not happen in print output).

These are the attributes available in the `imagedata` element for sizing:

Imagedata scaling attributes

`contentwidth`
`contentdepth`
Specify the horizontal width or vertical height, respectively, of the image itself. You can specify a size using any of these units (with no space between the number and the unit):

px	*Pixels (the default unit if none is specified)*
pt	*Points (1/72 of an inch)*
cm	*Centimeters*
mm	*Millimeters*
pc	*Picas (1/6 of an inch)*
in	*Inches*
em	*Ems (type size)*
%	*Percentage (of intrinsic image size)*

If one of these attributes is specified, then the image is scaled proportionally to that size. You can stretch the image by specifying values for both attributes that differ from the original ratio of width to height of the image.

`width`
`depth`
Specify the horizontal width and vertical height, respectively, of the *viewport* area, not the graphic. It uses the same units as above, except percentage is taken to be of the available area (so 50% means half the available width after the current indent is subtracted). If these attributes are not specified, then the viewport is the whole page. These attributes will not affect the size of the image itself, with one exception. For backwards compatibility, if they are used without any other scaling attributes, the stylesheets will scale the image itself to the specified sizes. Think of it as a way of specifying the viewport area with the assumption that it should be filled up.

`scale`
A percentage scaling factor, but expressed without the percent sign. A value of 75 means to scale the graphic to 75% of its intrinsic size. It scales both width and height proportionally, so the image retains its original *aspect ratio*.

`scalefit`
If set to a value of 1, then the processor will scale the graphic proportionally to fit the allowed area. The image is scaled to fit the specified `width` or `depth` viewport dimension, whichever fills up first. If neither are specified, then it will scale to the available page width.

The definitive description of how these attributes are supposed to affect the output appears in the reference page for imagedata in *DocBook: The Definitive Guide*[1]. In practice, some of the attributes are not fully supported by some processors.

---

[1] http://docbook.org/tdg/en/html/imagedata.html

Here is some guidance for using the scaling attributes.

- To scale a graphic to a given width, set the `contentwidth` in the `imagedata` element to that size, for example `contentwidth="8.5cm"`. If you specify a number without units, it is assumed to be pixels.

- To scale a graphic to fit the available width in printed output, use `width="100%"` and `scalefit="1"` attributes. For indented text as in a list, the available width is from the current indent to the right margin.

- To keep a graphic for printed output at its natural size unless it is too large to fit the available width, in which case shrink it to fit, use `scalefit="1"`, `width="100%"`, and `contentdepth="100%"` attributes.

- To set a default *viewport* width for graphics that have no scaling attributes, set the stylesheet parameter `default.image.width` parameter to the desired width. This sets only the viewport size, not the image size. For HTML output, if no other scaling attribute is used, then the image will be scaled to fit this viewport. For print output, the image is not scaled to fit this viewport.

- Using percentages in `contentwidth` to scale a graphic for HTML output can be tricky. It means a percentage of the image's intrinsic width, but the XSLT processor will not be able to figure out what is the intrinsic width of a graphic unless it uses an extension function. See the section called "Graphic size extension" (page 291).

- In HTML output, combinations of `contentwidth` and `width` are handled by putting the graphic in an HTML table. The `width` attribute sets the table width to create a reserved area, and the `contentwidth` is used to scale the image within the table.

- The following attributes are mutually exclusive: `contentwidth`, `scale`, and `scalefit`. If more than one of these attributes is used on an image, then the earliest one in this list takes precedence.

- Some XSL-FO processors do not support all of these attributes. You may need to experiment to see what works. For example, FOP version 0.20.5 treats `width` as if it were `contentwidth` and ignores any real `contentwidth` attribute.

Graphic size extension

The DocBook XSL stylesheets come with an XSL extension function written in Java that can be used to extract the intrinsic size information from an image file. Most bitmap formats include header information that identifies the width and height in pixels of the image, and sometimes intended dots per inch (dpi).

When an image is processed for print output, the stylesheet passes the image filename to the FO file. The XSL-FO processor opens the image file, reads the header information, and adjusts the size of the image based on that information as it adds the image to the PDF file. For HTML output, the stylesheet passes the image filename to the HTML file, but the image file is not opened until it is read by the web browser, so no image data can be used by the stylesheet in sizing the image.

The stylesheet needs the intrinsic image size when the `contentwidth` or `contentdepth` attributes in an `imagedata` element are expressed as percentages. For those two attributes, the percentage is of the intrinsic image size, not the page size.

The XSLT standard does not provide a function to read image data, but the DocBook XSL stylesheets provide extension functions written in Java to do so. Since they are written in Java, they are only available with the Saxon and Xalan processors. The appropriate extension jar file needs to be configured into your Java CLASSPATH to make them available, as described in the section called "Installing Saxon" (page 18).

To enable the extension function, set the `graphicsize.extension` stylesheet parameter to 1, and also set the `use.extensions` parameter to 1. Then if the stylesheet needs to perform any computation on the `contentwidth` value, the extension function will open the image file to get intrinsic width information to use in the calculation. Without that information, the stylesheet has to fall back to the fixed value in the `nominal.image.width` parameter, which has a default value of 540 pixels for HTML output. Since that is not likely the actual image size, the results will not be very satisfactory.

If you set the extensions parameters but the results are not as expected, then check to make sure your CLASSPATH is set correctly. If the stylesheet cannot find the Java graphic size extension function, it does not report an error. Instead, it falls back to a default value. That is the only extension function that does not report an error if it is not available.

One complication arises when you are using the img.src.path parameter to prepend an output path to each fileref value in the IMG element's src value. Normally the extension function just uses the fileref value to locate the image file to open and read. If it needs to include the img.src.path value to locate the file to open, then also set the stylesheet parameter graphicsize.use.img.src.path to 1.

Different sizes for HTML and FO output

You may find that you need to scale an image differently in HTML than in FO output. You can do this by creating nearly duplicate imageobject elements in a mediaobject. You can put different values for the scaling attributes in the imagedata element in each imageobject. Then you let the stylesheet select the appropriate imageobject for a given output. See the section called "Selecting file formats" (page 286) for more information.

If you just want to turn off scaling for HTML output, then that is even easier. If you set the stylesheet parameter ignore.image.scaling to a non-zero value, then all images in HTML output will appear in their intrinsic size. So you use the scaling attributes solely for FO output, and they will be ignored for HTML output.

Landscape images

Sometimes an image is too wide to fit into a regular portrait page width. Rotating a figure 90 degrees and presenting it in landscape mode is one way to handle such figures. DocBook's schema does not have an attribute for figure or mediaobject to indicate rotation the way orient="land" is available for tables.

One solution is to create a processing instruction for use inside a figure element. The DocBook stylesheet does not define one, so you have to make up your own processing instruction and write a matching template to process it. For example:

```
<figure>
  <?landscapeFigure?><title>My figure title</title>
  ...
</figure>
```

Here is a customization that will rotate a figure that has such a processing instruction.

```
<xsl:template match="figure[processing-instruction('landscapeFigure')]">
  <fo:block-container reference-orientation="90">
    <xsl:apply-imports/>
  </fo:block-container>
</xsl:template>
```

This customization matches only figure elements that contain the processing instruction. It just wraps a fo:block-container element around the normal processing of figure that is achieved with the xsl:apply-imports statement. The block container has reference-orientation="90", which means the content of the container will be rotated 90 degrees counterclockwise. Depending on the behavior of your XSL-FO processor with block containers, you may need to add other properties to achieve proper formatting of the rotated figure.

This customization will also rotate the figure title along with the figure. That is because it uses xsl:apply-imports, which calls the original figure template that handles both the title and the image.

Image alignment

In addition to image scaling you can alter the position of the graphic. The imagedata element accepts a align attribute to position the image horizontally. It takes a value of left, center, or right. The alignment is relative to the viewport area, which may be less than the whole page if you specify a width attribute. You can also use a valign attribute to position the graphic vertically within the viewport area. It takes a value of top, middle, or bottom.

If you want all your images to be centered in HTML output without having to set the align attribute, then you should add a selector to your CSS for the class="mediaobject" attribute that appears on each mediaobject's div wrapper. Then you can specify alignment and other formatting properties in your cascading stylesheet.

If you want all your images centered in XSL-FO output, there is no parameter or attribute-set that will center all mediaobject elements. However, if you put each of your mediaobject elements inside informalfigure, you can center those using:

```
<xsl:attribute-set name="informalfigure.properties">
  <xsl:attribute name="text-align">center</xsl:attribute>
</xsl:attribute-set>
```

Background color

The DocBook XSL stylesheets allow you to specify a background color for the *viewport* of a graphic. If you specify a viewport larger than the image, and center the image in the viewport, then you can create a matte border for the image.

The background color is specified using a <?dbhtml?> or <?dbfo?> processing instruction within the imageobject element. The following example includes one of each:

```
<mediaobject>
  <imageobject><?dbhtml background-color="#E8E8E8"?><?dbfo
  background-color="#F8F6A3"?>
    <imagedata  width="10cm"  contentwidth="8cm"
                depth="10cm"  contentdepth="8cm"
                align="center" valign="middle"
                fileref="graphics/hardware.png"/>
  </imageobject>
</mediaobject>
```

The processing instruction name must be background-color, and the value must be a color name or color number (expressed using the three-part hexadecimal number syntax #123456 used for HTML colors).

This example creates a viewport 10 cm square, and centers the image scaled to 8 cm square in that area. That leaves a 1 cm border in the background color around the image.

Titles and captions

If you want to add a title to a graphic, you need to wrap the graphic element in one of the *formal* display elements, such as figure or example. See the section called "Elements for graphics" (page 285) for more information.

The DocBook DTD permits a mediaobject to contain a caption element. A caption differs from a title by being longer text describing the image. It can contain paragraphs, lists, admonitions, and other text blocks. A caption does not take a title element, but if you need to supply a title you could use a formalpara which takes a title. The stylesheets process the contents of the caption element as it would any other text, and places it after the image.

If you want to customize the placement of the caption text (for example, above the image), then you would need to customize the stylesheet template that starts with `<xsl:template match="mediaobject|mediaobjectco">` in the `graphics.xsl` file in `html` or `fo` directories of the stylesheet distribution.

If you want to customize how the caption text itself is handled, then you need to customize the template that starts with `<xsl:template match="caption">`. The current template (fo version shown here) is pretty simple:

```
<xsl:template match="caption">
  <fo:block>
    <xsl:apply-templates/>
  </fo:block>
</xsl:template>
```

Alt text

For HTML output, readers appreciate when `alt` attributes are added to `IMG` tags to provide a text alternative to the graphic. This is particularly important for accessibility to vision-impaired readers. Also many browsers display the `alt` text when the mouse hovers over an image.

You can provide the `alt` text by including in each `mediaobject` element a `textobject` element containing a `phrase` element. For example:

```
<mediaobject  id="MousePicture">
  <imageobject  role="html">
    <imagedata  format="PNG"  fileref="mouse.png"/>
  </imageobject>
  <imageobject  role="fo">
    <imagedata  format="SVG"  fileref="mouse.svg"/>
  </imageobject>
  <textobject>
    <phrase>Picture of mouse</phrase>
  </textobject>
</mediaobject>
```

When processed into HTML, the output looks like:

```
<img  src="mouse.png" alt="Picture of mouse">
```

The text you provide should be plain text, since attributes like `alt` do not accept markup tags. Text entities and character entities are supported, however.

Long descriptions

DocBook XSL also provides support for the `longdesc` attribute in HTML `IMG` tags. This attribute lets you specify a URL that points to a long description of the image. That feature would be particularly helpful for complex graphics being served to vision-impaired readers.

To create a long description, you add another `textobject` element that does *not* contain a `phrase` element. Any `textobject` that does will be used as the `alt` text. The following is the previous example with both kinds of `textobject`.

```
<mediaobject  id="MousePicture">
  <imageobject  role="html">
    <imagedata  format="PNG"  fileref="mouse.png"/>
  </imageobject>
  <imageobject  role="fo">
    <imagedata  format="SVG"  fileref="mouse.svg"/>
  </imageobject>
  <textobject>
    <phrase>Picture of mouse</phrase>
  </textobject>
  <textobject id="foo">
    <formalpara>
      <title>Mouse mechanics</title>
      <para>The mouse consists of a rolling ball and two or three buttons.
      </para>
    </formalpara>
    <para>...</para>
  </textobject>
</mediaobject>
```

The HTML stylesheet does quite a bit of processing with this second `textobject`.

1. It creates a file named `ld-xxxx.html` where xxxx is some generated id.

2. It processes the content of the `textobject` using the stylesheet and writes the output to that file.

3. It adds an HTML link to the current page using the mark [D] as the text and the filename as the href URL. The link appears below the graphic and right aligned.

When the reader clicks on the [D] link, another window pops up showing the formatted content.

There are limitations on what DocBook markup you can use inside the `textobject` for a long description. No hierarchical elements like chapter or section are permitted. You can use block elements like paragraphs, lists, admonitions, and literallayout. If you want to start with a title, try using a `formalpara`. See the reference page for *textobject*[2] for complete details.

Figure floats

A *float* is a characteristic of a formatting object that lets it float to a different location on the page. This assumes that the object does not have to maintain its strict location in the sequence of text. A figure can move the top or side of a printed page, or the side of an HTML page, and the text can adjust to its new location. If it is to one side, then the text can wrap around the opposite side.

Note:

Not all XSL-FO processors support floats. The current version of FOP does not, for example. Other processors may have limitations when handling floats. Check your processor documentation.

---

[2] http://docbook.org/tdg/en/html/textobject.html

Each type of float has a name to indicate its position:

```
left
right
start
end
inside
outside
before
none
```

These are described in more detail in the section called "A sidebar as side float" (page 232).

What about floating to the bottom of a printed page? That float location is not part of the XSL-FO 1.0 specification. It could be done using the XSL-FO footnote mechanism, but the DocBook XSL stylesheets do not do that.

You can make a figure float using any of these methods:

- Add a floatstyle attribute to the figure element. The floatstyle attribute was added in version 4.3 of the DocBook DTD. Set the attribute value to the type of float.

- Add a float attribute to the figure element, and set the attribute value to the type of float. This attribute can be used for all versions of the DTD.

- Add a float attribute to the figure element, and set the attribute value to 1. This indicates that the stylesheet should use the value of the default.float.class parameter as the type of float. That parameter has a default value of before (which has no effect in HTML).

- Put the figure element inside a sidebar element and configure the sidebar as a float. See the section called "A sidebar as side float" (page 232) for more information. do not include a float or floatstyle attribute on the figure element.

Whatever value you assign to the float or floatstyle attribute is used to create the appropriate property in the HTML or print output. When you specify a float for HTML output, it will appear in the HTML as follows:

```
<div class="figure-float" style="float: left;">
...
```

FO output looks something like the following:

```
<fo:float float="left">
  <fo:block ...>Figure 1.1. My figure</fo:block>
  <fo:external-graphic src="url(images/mypicture.png)"/>
</fo:float>
```

For print output, you can also customize how side floats are handled for any element. See the section called "Custom side float" (page 236) for details.

Inline graphics

An inline graphic is one that appears within a paragraph of text, inline with the words. You use an inlinemediaobject (or the deprecated inlinegraphic in DocBook 4) to place a graphic in a line of text. These elements output the graphic without first breaking the line before or after the graphic.

Usually an inline graphic is small, such as an icon illustration, so as to not disrupt the paragraph format too much. When an inline graphic is taller than the text, however, the text line it is sitting on must be provided extra space to avoid having the graphic intrude into the line of text above it. In HTML output, this is handled automatically by the browser. In XSL-FO output, it is the default behavior as well. But in XSL-FO output, you can override the default extra space by changing the property `line-stacking-strategy` from its default value of `max-height` to `font-height`. That leads to evenly spaced lines based on the font size, regardless of any taller elements. You may have to add scaling attributes to your inline graphic elements to keep them from intruding into the line above.

An inline graphic is normally placed with the bottom of the graphic on the baseline of the text. If you prefer that your inline graphics extend below the baseline a bit, then put each one inside a `subscript` element. If you want a little extra space around an inline graphic, then add a `width` attribute, and perhaps an `align="center"` attribute to center the graphic in the extra space.

Graphic file locations

When you are including graphic images in your documents, you need to manage the locations of the graphics files. It helps to know that the handling of graphics files is quite different for HTML and FO outputs.

Note:

An XSLT processor cannot copy graphics files to an output location. Any file copying that needs to be done must be done outside of the stylesheet process, using a tool such as Make or Ant. To help identify the filenames to be copied, you can use a contributed utility stylesheet named *xmldepend.xsl*[3] available from the DocBook SourceForge SVN repository. When you process a DocBook document with this stylesheet, it lists all the image pathnames in the file.

HTML output directory

When a DocBook XML file with an `imagedata` or `image` element is processed with one of the HTML stylesheets, the graphics file is not opened and read; only the file pathname is passed through to the HTML `IMG` tag. The image file itself does not have to be present when the HTML is generated, so no error is generated during processing if the graphics file is not present. But it does need to be present at the address specified in the `IMG` tag when the HTML file is viewed.

For this reason, managing graphics files for HTML output means managing their locations in the output, relative to the HTML files that are generated. When you generate HTML and place them on a server or other accessible location, you also need to manually place the graphics files with them. The XSLT processor will not copy image files to the output location.

Where you place a graphics file in the output area depends on the pathname used to reference it in the HTML `IMG` tag. That pathname comes from the `imagedata` or `graphic` element in the XML document. Those elements let you specify an image path in two ways: with a `fileref` attribute or an `entityref` attribute.

Using fileref

A `fileref` attribute value is interpreted as a literal pathname string. It can be modified in three ways before it is output as the `src` attribute.

- If the `fileref` value does not have a filename extension that indicates the format, then one is appended to the filename. The graphic element must have `format` attribute for this to work.

- If the `img.src.path` parameter is set, its value is prepended to each `fileref` value if it is not an absolute path. This parameter lets you specify the path to the image files when you build the HTML. If its value is `images/` then a `fileref` value of `caution.png` is written to the HTML file as `src="images/caution.png`. But sure to include the trailing slash. This parameter permits you to specify just the filename in your graphics elements, without specifying

---

[3] http://docbook.svn.sourceforge.net/viewvc/docbook/trunk/contrib/xsl/xmldepend/

the details of the location. If you later move the output directory, you can just change the parameter value, and not have to edit every graphics instance in your document.

- If your document uses XIncludes, then the path may be altered by xml:base attributes inserted by the XInclude processor. See the section called "XIncludes and graphics files" (page 365) for details.

When you build your HTML, you must place the image file in the location specified by the fileref, as modified by the above points. If the result is a relative pathname, then the graphics file must be placed relative to the final output location of the HTML files. If it is an absolute pathname, then the graphics file should be placed relative to the document root of the HTTP server for the HTML files. The fileref attribute value or the img.src.path parameter can also be an absolute URI, to the same or different website.

Using entityref

If you require more flexibility in handling a graphics file, then consider using an entityref attribute with an XML catalog instead. An entityref attribute has an XML attribute type of ENTITY in its declaration. This means the attribute value is not interpreted as a literal pathname string, but as an entity name. The entity name must correspond to a system entity declared in the current document's DTD.

Typically, such system entities are declared in the *internal subset* of the DTD within the DOCTYPE declaration of the document. The following is an example.

```
<!DOCTYPE book PUBLIC "-//OASIS//DTD DocBook XML V4.5//EN"
                "http://www.oasis-open.org/docbook/xml/4.5/docbookx.dtd" [
<!ENTITY  screenshot3  SYSTEM  "/usr/local/graphics/tutorial3.png"  NDATA  PNG>
...
]>
<book>
...
<imagedata  entityref="screenshot3"/>
```

The HTML output from processing this example file will include:

```
<IMG  src="/usr/local/graphics/tutorial3.png">
```

An important difference from fileref is that an entityref is always resolved to an absolute URI. If you enter a relative path, then it is resolved relative to the absolute path of the document that declares the entity. That could be the current document or a DTD customization file. This behavior comes from the use of the unparsed-entity-uri() XSL function in the DocBook template, and the XSL standard says that function always returns an absolute URI.

Absolute paths in HTML src attributes are a problem if you put the HTML files on a webserver. It is likely the absolute path will not match the document root of the HTTP server, so such references will result in missing graphics when the HTML file is viewed. Relative paths are preferred, but there is no way to get relative paths when using entityref. For this reason, the img.src.path parameter has no effect on entityref paths, because it cannot be prepended to absolute paths.

However, if you put your entity declarations in a separate file, and use an XML catalog to find the declarations file, then you can substitute different pathnames at runtime by using a different catalog. For example, if you move the above entity declaration to a file named mygraphics.ent, you can reference it as follows:

```
<!DOCTYPE book PUBLIC "-//OASIS//DTD DocBook XML V4.5//EN"
              "http://www.oasis-open.org/docbook/xml/4.5/docbookx.dtd" [
<!ENTITY % graphicset SYSTEM "graphics/mygraphics.ent">
%graphicset;
...
]>
<book>
...
<imagedata entityref="screenshot3"/>
```

This arrangement uses a *parameter entity* to specify the location of the file containing the declarations, then it imme-diately uses a parameter entity reference `%graphicset;` to pull in the file's contents at that point in the DTD.

You can swap declarations files at runtime by using a catalog entry such as the following:

```
<system
    systemId="graphics/mygraphics.ent"
    uri="../graphics/myothergraphics.ent"/>
```

You just need to make sure that your alternate graphics declarations file declares the same set of entity names, and that they resolve to full pathnames that work for the HTML output.

You might think that since a system entity uses a SYSTEM identifier and an optional PUBLIC identifier to specify the pathname to the graphics file, that you could use a catalog entry for each graphics file. Unfortunately, this does not work for HTML output. A catalog resolver is triggered when a requested file is to be opened. During HTML processing, the graphics files themselves are never opened. Only their pathname is passed through to the HTML, so such catalog entries would not be used.

FO input directory

Generating PDF from a DocBook file is a two-step process. First the DocBook FO stylesheet is applied to the XML document to generate an intermediate XSL-FO file. Then the XSL-FO is converted to PDF by an XSL-FO processor such as FOP. In the first step, each `imagedata` and `graphic` element is handled in a manner similar to the HTML processing described above. That is, the pathname in a `fileref` or `entityref` attribute is passed through to a XSL-FO graphics element:

```
<fo:external-graphic src="url(graphics/tutorial.png)">
```

The path can be modified in two ways before output:

- If the `fileref` value does not have a filename extension that indicates the format, then one is appended to the fi-lename. The graphic element must have `format` attribute for this to work.

- If you set the stylesheet parameter `img.src.path`, then its value is prepended to any `fileref` that is not an absolute path. This allows you to store your images in a central location rather than with individual documents, for example.

- If your document uses XIncludes, then the path may be altered by `xml:base` attributes inserted by the XInclude processor. See the section called "XIncludes and graphics files" (page 365) for details.

As with HTML processing, the graphics file itself is not opened during the stylesheet processing, so the graphics file does not actually need to be present. However, in the second phase, the XSL-FO processor must open such graphics references to incorporate the graphics data into the PDF file. So it is during the XSL-FO processing phase that the file must be readable at the graphics element's address, possibly modified by the above points.

Once the second stage is completed, the PDF file contains the graphics data, so access to the graphics files is no longer needed. The PDF file can be moved as needed without losing the graphics.

SVG images

Scalable Vector Graphics (SVG)[4], a W3C Recommendation, is "a language for describing two-dimensional vector and mixed vector/raster graphics in XML". In other words, you can draw pictures with XML elements. The following is a small sample that draws three circles:

```
<?xml version="1.0"?>
<svg xmlns="http://www.w3.org/2000/svg" width="12cm" height="12cm">
   <g style="fill-opacity:0.7; stroke:black; stroke-width:0.1cm;">
     <circle cx="6cm" cy="2cm" r="100" style="fill:red;"
                     transform="translate(0,50)" />
     <circle cx="6cm" cy="2cm" r="100" style="fill:blue;"
                     transform="translate(70,150)" />
     <circle cx="6cm" cy="2cm" r="100" style="fill:green;"
                     transform="translate(-70,150)"/>
   </g>
</svg>
```

When rendered, this SVG image looks like the following:

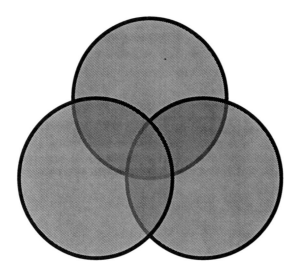

---

[4] http://www.w3.org/TR/SVG/

SVG has some nice advantages:

- SVG is a vector graphic format, which means it scales to different sizes smoothly without jagged lines.

- An SVG file is plain text, not a binary file format. You can read and edit an SVG graphic (assuming you understand SVG) using a plain text editor or XML editor.

- SVG is an open standard, so there are several commercial and free SVG graphics tools available to choose from. See the *W3C list of SVG implementations*[5].

Although you could include SVG image data directly in your DocBook file (inside an `imageobject` element, in place of an `imagedata` element), you probably will want to keep each image in a separate file. Then you can include the image as you would other graphics:

```
<mediaobject  id="MousePicture">
  <imageobject>
    <imagedata  format="SVG"  fileref="mouse.svg"/>
  </imageobject>
</mediaobject>
```

Be sure to include the `format="SVG"` attribute to ensure the file is handled properly.

Support of SVG in XSL-FO processors is not complete. The XEP FO processor from RenderX and the XSL Formatter processor from Antenna House have substantial support for SVG in their current products. But some SVG elements may not be supported, so check the processor documentation for details. Apache FOP uses the *Batik SVG Toolkit*[6] to render SVG graphics. Be sure to include the `batik.jar` file in your CLASSPATH when trying to render SVG with FOP (it is included in the FOP convenience scripts).

SVG DTD

One problem you may run into when processing SVG files with an XSL-FO processor is the DTD reference in SVG files. Most SVG files contain a DOCTYPE declaration similar to the following (the version may vary):

```
<!DOCTYPE svg PUBLIC "-//W3C//DTD SVG 1.0//EN"
      "http://www.w3.org/TR/2001/REC-SVG-20010904/DTD/svg10.dtd">
```

An XSL-FO processor that interprets the SVG file will try to load the DTD, not for validation, but for potential default attribute values or entity declarations. If the processing machine is connected to the Internet, then the DTD will be downloaded from the URL specified in the system identifier. Such downloads can slow the processing considerably. If there are connection problems, or no connection at all, then some XSL-FO processors will fail on an image if it cannot read the DTD.

A Java-based XSL-FO processor such as XEP can be configured to use an XML catalog to map the SVG DTD URL to a local file.

1. Download the SVG DTDs for the versions you need and install them in a convenient location. *Version 1.0*[7] and *version 1.1*[8] are available from the W3C website.

2. Set up a catalog file and add one or more entries for the SVG DTD references (you may need more than one version of the SVG DTD) to map the SVG identifiers to the local files. See the section called "How to write an XML catalog file" (page 48) for examples of catalog entries.

---

[5] http://www.w3.org/Graphics/SVG/SVG-Implementations
[6] http://xml.apache.org/batik/
[7] http://www.w3.org/TR/2001/REC-SVG-20010904/DTD/svg10.dtd
[8] http://www.w3.org/Graphics/SVG/1.1/DTD/

3. Download the Java `resolver.jar` file and set up a `CatalogManager.properties` file as described in the section called "Using catalogs with Saxon" (page 54).

4. Configure the Java process in the XEP batch file or shell script to use the Java catalog resolver. The following example is a modified `xep.bat` batch file:

Example 18.2. Adding XML catalog support to XEP

```
set CP=c:\xml\java\resolver.jar;C:\xml\java;C:\xml\xep.49\lib\xep.jar;\
C:\xml\xep.49\lib\saxon.jar;C:\xml\xep.49\lib\xt.jar

java -Dcom.renderx.sax.entityresolver=org.apache.xml.resolver.tools.CatalogResolver \
-Dcom.renderx.jaxp.uriresolver=org.apache.resolver.tools.CatalogResolver \
-Xmx356m -classpath "%CP%" com.renderx.xep.XSLDriver "-DCONFIG=C:\xml\xep.49\xep.xml" %*
```

When you upgrade your version of XEP, do not forget to edit the new batch file or shell script.

SVG in HTML

SVG is a relatively new graphics format, and many web browsers do not yet support it directly. Plug-in SVG viewers such as Adobe SVG Viewer are available for some browsers, but you cannot rely on them being installed by all your potential readers.

In Docbook's HTML output, if you do not specify a `format="SVG"` attribute in the `imagedata` element, then the SVG reference is put inside an HTML `img` element. If you do specify the `format="SVG"` attribute, then an `object` element is used instead:

```
<object data="circles.svg" type="image/svg+xml"/>
```

Some browsers respond better to an `embed` element, even though that is not a standard HTML element. If you set the stylesheet parameter `use.embed.for.svg` to 1 (the default is zero), then an `embed` element is added to the `object` element:

```
<object data="circles.svg" type="image/svg+xml">
  <embed src="circles.svg" type="image/svg+xml"/>
</object>
```

Since not all browsers support SVG graphics, you might consider substituting a bitmap replica of any SVG graphics when generating HTML output. Otherwise some of your readers will not see anything of the graphic. Here is how you do it in the `mediaobject` element:

```
<mediaobject  id="MousePicture">
  <imageobject  role="fo">
    <imagedata  format="SVG"  fileref="mouse.svg"/>
  </imageobject>
  <imageobject  role="html">
    <imagedata  format="PNG"  fileref="mouse.png"/>
  </imageobject>
</mediaobject>
```

In this example, the SVG graphic is selected only for XSL-FO output, and a PNG bitmap replica is substituted for HTML output.

Where do you get a PNG replica? You can use an SVG viewer on your own system and take a screenshot of the rendered image. Or you can use the free *SVG Rasterizer*[9] tool that is included in the Apache Batik SVG Toolkit. Some commercial graphics tools such as Adobe Illustrator can also render an SVG graphic as a bitmap.

EPS to SVG

Before SVG, the common file format for vector graphics was Encapsulated PostScript (EPS). While EPS was widely supported, it required a PostScript interpreter to be available to interpret the PostScript code to render the image.

If you use an EPS filename in a `mediaobject` in DocBook, the filename will be passed through to the output, but the results will probably not be satisfactory. If the output is PDF, then neither XSL-FO processors nor PDF browsers have a PostScript interpreter. If the EPS file contains a bitmap preview image, then that can be displayed in a PDF browser, but at lower resolution. If you send the PDF to a PostScript printer, then you can get good results. But if a printer does not handle PostScript, then you will only get the lower resolution preview image.

SVG, on the other hand, is an open standard and works well with XSL-FO processors and PDF output.

If you have a collection of EPS images, you can convert them to SVG, using either of these programs:

- Adobe Illustrator (not free)

- pstoedit (free), which uses ghostscript to interpret the PostScript code. You can download pstoedit from *http://www.pstoedit.net/*.

Imagemaps

An imagemap displays an image in an HTML browser that has active areas that a user can click on to jump to another location. The DocBook HTML stylesheets have some support for creating client-side imagemaps using the `mediaobjectco` element. But there are some limitations in how imagemaps are supported in the HTML stylesheets.

- A link from a DocBook `area` element must be to a destination in the current document, not to an external URL. That is because the `linkends` attribute in the DocBook `area` element is of attribute type `IDREFS`, so it must point to an `id` attribute in the current document.

- Only bitmap images are supported, not vector art such as SVG.

- The image cannot be resized in the output. Any scaling of the image breaks the conversion of areas in the current implementation.

- Only rectangular areas are supported.

- Only the `calspair` type of coordinates or an application-specific set of units named `imagemap` are supported in DocBook `area` elements. These two options are described in the section called "Using calspair coords" (page 305) and the section called "Using imagemap coords" (page 306).

- If you are using `calspair` type of units, the stylesheet parameters `graphicsize.extension` and `use.extensions` must both be set to 1. This means you must be using either Saxon or Xalan and have the appropriate DocBook Java extensions file in your processor's CLASSPATH. See the section called "DocBook Saxon and Xalan extensions" (page 21).

If you can live with these limitations, imagemaps can be quite useful for certain kinds of documentation efforts. Because the area links must land inside the current document, they are best used for providing dynamic explanation

---

[9] http://xml.apache.org/batik/svgrasterizer.html

of a diagram., or a graphical map to the rest of the documentation. Unfortunately, none of the area links will be active in a PDF version if you produce that also.

A DocBook imagemap is created using the DocBook elements mediaobjectco, imageobjectco, imagedata, areaspec and area. An optional calloutlist can be used for the link destinations. The following example shows the DocBook elements to produce an imagemap with one area specified.

Example 18.3. DocBook imagemap using calspair units

```
<mediaobjectco>   ❶
  <imageobjectco>   ❷
    <areaspec id="map1"   ❸
              units="calspair">   ❹
      <area linkends="callout1"   ❺
            coords="1000,5000 6000,8000"   ❻
            id="area1"/>   ❼
    </areaspec>
    <imageobject>
      <imagedata fileref="tablerules.png" />
    </imageobject>
    <calloutlist>
      <callout arearefs="area1"   ❽
               id="callout1">   ❾
        <para>My only callout</para>
      </callout>
    </calloutlist>
  </imageobjectco>
</mediaobjectco>
```

❶   You must use a mediaobjecto element instead of a mediaobject element. It can be contained in a figure or example element in you want to add a title.

❷   The imageobjectco element contains a required areaspec, an imageobject, and an optional calloutlist. You do not have to use a calloutlist. The area links can be to any elements inside your documents.

❸   The areaspec element is the container for one or more area elements. Its id attribute becomes the map name in the HTML output.

❹   The units attribute is used to specify what kind of units the coords attribute contains. Only a calspair value and a nonstandard imagemap value are supported currently. You can put a units attribute on each area element, or put one units attribute on areaspec and it will be inherited by all the area elements contained by it.

❺   The area element specifies one area to become a link. Its linkends attribute should contain a reference to an id somewhere in the document. In this case, it is to a callout element below it. Although the DocBook linkends attribute allows more than one id value in it, the HTML imagemap can only take one reference.

❻   The coords attribute specifies the area size and location, using calspair units in this example. See the section called "Using calspair coords" (page 305) for details.

❼   You can specify an optional id attribute on each area, which you can link to from other locations. In most browsers, such links go to the whole graphic, not the specific area in it.

❽   If you use callout as the destination for an area link, then it must have an arearefs attribute that specifies an id for the callout to link back to. Most browsers follow such links to the overall image, not the specific area within the image. A callout is also numbered, so it might be useful to include the numbers in the image if you want them to correspond. Alternatively, you could use a bullet list item or ordinary paragraph with the id as the target of an imagemap link.

❾   The id on the callout element is the destination of the area link in this example.

The following shows how the DocBook XHTML stylesheet renders this imagemap. The various id and coordinate values are shown in bold.

```
<div class="mediaobjectco">
  <img border="0" usemap="#map1" src="tablerules.png" alt="imagemap"/>
  <map name="map1">
    <area shape="rect" href="#callout1" coords="102,154,614,384"/>
  </map>
  <div class="calloutlist">
    <table border="0" summary="Callout list">
      <tr>
        <td width="5%" valign="top" align="left">
          <a id="callout1"/>
          <img src="images/callouts/1.png" alt="1" border="0"/>
        </td>
        <td valign="top" align="left">
          <p>My only callout</p>
        </td>
      </tr>
    </table>
  </div>
</div>
```

Using calspair coords

The hardest part of creating an imagemap in DocBook using calspair units is figuring out how to express the HTML coordinates in the CALS semantics. Here is the description of calspair from *DocBook: The Definitive Guide*.

> The format of the coordinates is "x1,y1 x2,y2". This identifies a rectangle with the lower-left corner at (x1,y1) and the upper-right corner at (x2,y2). The X and Y coordinates are integers in the range 0 to 10000; they express a percentage of the total distance from 0.00 to 100.00%. The lower-left corner is (0,0).

You measure the area in hundredths of percentage of whatever is the size of the graphic, measured from the lower left corner. Note the space between the two pairs of numbers. In Figure 18.1, "DocBook calspair coordinates" (page 305), the calspair values are shown as ordinary percentages on the diagram.

Figure 18.1. DocBook calspair coordinates

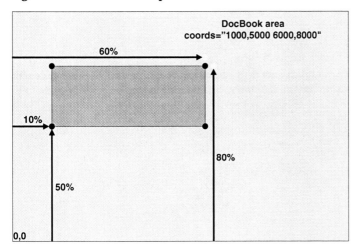

Since calspair are proportional units, the stylesheet has to determine what the intrinsic pixel size of the whole image is so it can compute the HTML imagemap area, which must be in pixels. Getting the intrinsic image size requires a stylesheet extension. This means you must use either Saxon or Xalan as your XSLT processor, and you must have the appropriate DocBook Java extensions .jar file in your processor's CLASSPATH (see the section called "DocBook Saxon and Xalan extensions" (page 21) for more information). The stylesheet parameters graphicsize.extension and use.extensions must both be set to 1. When these conditions are met, the stylesheet computes the equivalent HTML imagemap pixel units as shown in Figure 18.2, "HTML Imagemap Area Coordinates" (page 307).

Norman Walsh has written an article called *Image callouts*[10] that describes a method and provides a Perl script for creating callouts on images using calspair coordinates without having to perform hand calculations.

Using imagemap coords

If you are using mediaobjectco only to create HTML imagemaps, then the stylesheets provide an easier way to specify the area coordinates. The DocBook DTD enumerates the types of units that can be used in the units attribute, of which only calspair is supported by the stylesheet. However, the enumeration also permits specifying units="other", and then specifying the type of units in the otherunits attribute.

The DocBook stylesheets support setting units="other" and otherunits="imagemap", and then entering the imagemap pixel ranges directly in the coords attribute of a DocBook area element. An imagemap coords value is four numbers in the form x1,y1,x2,y2 (all comma separated). These specify the positions of the upper-left corner (x1,y1) and the lower-right corner (x2,y2) of the area, measured in pixels. The upper-left corner of the entire image is (0,0). The following is an example.

Example 18.4. DocBook imagemap using "imagemap" units

```
<mediaobjectco>
  <imageobjectco>
    <areaspec id="map1">
      <area linkends="callout1"
            units="other"
            otherunits="imagemap"
            coords="102,154,614,384"
            id="area1"/>
    </areaspec>
    <imageobject>
      <imagedata fileref="tablerules.png" />
    </imageobject>
  ...
```

When otherunits="imagemap", the stylesheet just copies the value of the input coords attribute to the output coords attribute. The following figure shows how the same output as the previous calspair example can be achieved by entering the pixel values directly.

---

[10] http://norman.walsh.name/2006/06/10/imageobjectco

Figure 18.2. HTML Imagemap Area Coordinates

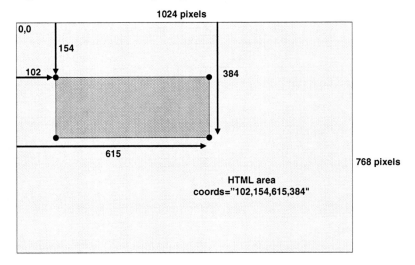

19

Indexes

The DocBook XSL stylesheets can automatically generate a back-of-the-book index while your document is being processed. You have to do two things:

- Add an empty <index/> element to your document at the location where you want the index to appear.

- Insert indexterm elements throughout your document.

Creating a good index is an iterative process. The first time you generate the index after inserting indexterm elements, you will likely notice index entries that are similar, but not quite the same. You must decide if they should be exactly the same, and then find and edit the indexterm elements to merge them. You may also notice related entries that would work better using primary, secondary, and possibly tertiary elements to group them together. You will also want to create entries for alternative wording of your entries, and you have to think creatively to anticipate what words your readers might use to find something. Keep adding and editing entries, and keep building and reviewing your index until you are satisfied with the results.

Adding indexterms

By far the hardest of these two tasks is inserting the indexterm elements in your document. You need to insert one for every entry that is to appear in your index. You place an indexterm at the location where the reference from the index is to land. The DocBook DTD permits indexterm elements to be included as content in a wide variety of elements. Certain ambiguous locations are not permitted, such as between two section elements. The DocBook DTD is the final reference. Validating your document against the DTD will confirm that you have placed your indexterms in permitted locations.

You may have noticed that entries in an index can have more than one level. That permits grouping of subtopics under a keyword. For example:

Example 19.1. Index output

```
...
start characters, changing, 12
start tags
  beginning, 11
  case sensitivity, 579
  empty element, 22, 609
  errors, 58
    misspelling, 58
    out of context, 60
  minimization, 19
step element, 36
...
```

The `indexterm` element provides sufficient structure to permit such multi-level entries to be created. Inside, you assign the highest level part to the `primary` element, any second level part to a `secondary` element, and any third level part to a `tertiary` element. The following are examples of the above entries as they appeared in their `indexterm` elements scattered through the document.

Example 19.2. Indexterms

```
<indexterm>
    <primary>start characters, changing</primary></indexterm>    ❶
<indexterm>
    <primary>start tags</primary>
    <secondary>beginning</secondary></indexterm>    ❷
<indexterm>
    <primary>start tags</primary>
    <secondary>case sensitivity</secondary></indexterm>    ❸
<indexterm>
    <primary>start tags</primary>
    <secondary>empty element</secondary></indexterm>
<indexterm>
    <primary>start tags</primary>
    <secondary>errors</secondary></indexterm>
<indexterm>
    <primary>start tags</primary>
    <secondary>errors</secondary>
    <tertiary>misspelling</tertiary></indexterm>    ❹
<indexterm>
    <primary>start tags</primary>
    <secondary>errors</secondary>
    <tertiary>out of context</tertiary></indexterm>    ❺
<indexterm>
    <primary>start tags</primary>
    <secondary>minimization</secondary></indexterm>
<indexterm>
    <primary>step element</primary></indexterm>
```

❶ Index term with only a primary level.
❷ Second-level index term with `secondary` element. Note that there is no page reference on `start tags` itself in Example 19.1, "Index output" (page 310). It would have one only if there were another `indexterm` with just a primary element containing `start tags`.

❸   For secondary values to sort together, their primary values must match exactly. The exception is when a sortas attribute is used on the primary element and it is an exact match.

❹   Third-level index term with secondary and tertiary elements. Note that in this case errors has a page number, due to the previous indexterm.

❺   For tertiary values to sort together, their primary values must match exactly and their secondary values must match exactly. The exception is when a sortas attributes provide the exact match.

If you want entries to sort together, you must make sure the text matches exactly, at all the levels that need to match. When you are working through your document to add indexterms, it helps to keep a running list of words and phrases you are using. That way you can reuse a word or phrase in another indexterm and they will sort together. Generating a thorough and consistent index requires a lot of work and care, but your readers will thank you for it.

There are several other index features you might want to use:

- If you need an entry to sort to some other location in the index, then add a sortas attribute whose value is the text to be used for sorting. For example:

```
<indexterm>
  <primary sortas="Fourthought">4Thought</primary></indexterm>
```

This entry will sort with the F's, but will appear as 4Thought.

- If you want to indicate that one destination is more significant that other destinations for the same entry, then add a significance="preferred" attribute to its indexterm element. When processed into the index, the page number for such entries will appear first and in bold. You can change the formatting by customizing the index.preferred.page.properties attribute-set.

- If an index entry should logically cover a range of pages, you can indicate the start and end of the range with just two entries:

Start of page range:
```
<indexterm class="startofrange" id="makestuff">
  <primary>Makefiles</primary></indexterm>
```
...
End of page range:
```
<indexterm class="endofrange" startref="makestuff">
  <primary>Makefiles</primary></indexterm>
```

The content of the entries must be the same. The first entry must have an id attribute that the second one points to with its startref attribute. That link establishes the pair of entries. The class attributes trigger the processing to generate the range. Not all FO processors support index ranges.

Specialized indexes

Some document designs call for creating a specialized index, possibly in addition to a general index. A specialized index contains one category of information, such as all species mentioned in a biology book, or all function names in a programming library. Such indexes make it easier for readers to locate such specialized information.

DocBook supports the creation of specialized indexes. There are three things you have to do:

1. Add a type attribute to every indexterm you want to appear in a specialized index. The value of the type attribute identifies the index category.

2. Add an empty index element that has a type attribute whose value matches the category of indexterm elements intended for it. As with the general index, you place the empty index element in your document in the location

where you want the specialized index to appear. Actually, it should not be entirely empty. You might want to add a `title` element as the only child of the `index` element, so you can give the specialized index a title that differs from the general index title.

3. Set the parameter `index.on.type` to 1. If you do not set this parameter, then the `type` attribute is not considered when processing index entries, and your specialized index will contain all index entries like the general index.

The following is an example of indexing on `type`:

Index terms:
```
<indexterm type="species">
  <primary>Espostoa lanata</primary></indexterm>
<indexterm>
  <primary>soil pH</primary></indexterm>
...
```

Index elements:
```
<index type="species">
  <title>Species Index</title>
</index>
<index/>
```

Only the first `indexterm` in this example will appear in the first index, whose title will be `Species Index`. Both entires will appear in the second index.

You can create multiple specialized indexes by using additional category names in your `indexterm` elements, and adding additional empty `index` elements for each category. However, each `indexterm` can have only one `type` value.

Note that all entries end up in the general index, the one with no `type` attribute on its `index` element. If you want to exclude the specialized entries from the general index, then you will have to add a different `type` attribute to all non-specialized `indexterm` elements, such as `type="general"`. Then you build the general index as another specialized index by adding `type="general"` to its `index` element.

> **Note:**
>
> If you are using version 4.2 or earlier of the DocBook DTD, then substitute `role` for every time you see `type` in the above instructions. That's because the `type` attribute was added in version 4.3 of the DTD, and using it in earlier versions will make the document invalid. So you would use `role="species"` as the attribute, and set the parameter `index.on.role` to 1. The stylesheets can handle either attribute.

Outputting an index

After adding your `indexterms` and an empty `<index/>` element to your document, you just have to process your document with one of the DocBook XSL stylesheets and you will get an index generated automatically. If for some reason you do not want to include an index in your output, then you can turn it off by setting the stylesheet parameter `generate.index` to zero.

> **Note:**
>
> The default indexing does not handle accented characters properly. Characters such as a, à, and ä should sort together, but they do not. However, there is a customization that can provide such sorting. See the section called "Internationalized indexes" (page 314).

When you generate an index for HTML output, you may notice these features.

• Instead of page numbers (which do not exist in HTML), each link shows the title of the section that contained the `indexterm`. That gives the reader some context for the link.

- If you have used `titleabbrev` elements to add optional short titles, you can have the stylesheets use the shorter title in the index by setting the `index.prefer.titleabbrev` parameter to 1 (it is zero by default).

- The links go to the top of the section rather than to the anchor point within the section. That's done to permit multiple identical `indexterms` in the same section to collapse to a single entry. That's done to avoid having to repeat the section title.

When you generate an index for FO output, you may notice these features.

- Identical entries on the same page will display multiple page references to the same page. It should display only one reference to that page.

- Consecutive page numbers are not collapsed into a page range.

See the next section for a possible solution to these problems.

Cleaning up an FO index

The index page number problems described in the previous section cannot be solved by the DocBook XSL stylesheets because the page number for a given `indexterm` is not known in the XSLT step. Text is placed on pages by the XSL-FO processor, which does not necessarily recognize that text is an index entry. Also, there are no properties in the XSL-FO standard to consolidate page ranges.

Some FO processors such as XEP and Antenna House have extension functions that can be used to fix up index page numbers. The DocBook XSL stylesheets output these indexing extensions if the `xep.extensions` parameter or the `axf.extensions` parameter, respectively, is set to 1. The FOP processor does not yet have such extensions.

For FOP, one solution to this problem is to extract page number information from the PDF output file, and then use that to fix up the FO file. This method is described briefly on the reference page for the *make.index.markup*[1] parameter. The following is a summary of the steps.

1. You need a utility named *pstotext*[2] to extract information from PDF files. It is available packaged in an RPM for Linux from *http://rpmfind.net*.

2. Process your document containing an empty `<index/>` element with the `fo/docbook.xsl` stylesheet with the `make.index.markup` parameter set to 1. That will generate the index but will insert it as XML markup in the FO file. For example:

```
xsltproc  -o mybook.fo  \
    --stringparam  make.index.markup  1  \
    fo/docbook.xsl  mybook.xml
```

3. Convert the FO file to PDF using your favorite XSL-FO processor.

4. Execute this Perl script on your PDF file and save the output to a file:

```
fo/pdf2index  mybook.pdf  >  myindex.xml
```

The content of that `myindex.xml` is an index marked up with DocBook index elements, with page information inserted as well.

---

[1] http://docbook.sourceforge.net/release/xsl/current/doc/fo/make.index.markup.html
[2] http://pages.cs.wisc.edu/~ghost/doc/pstotext.htm

5. Replace the empty `<index/>` element in your document with the contents of this generated file. You can do it with a system entity or XInclude.

6. Process your document again with `fo/docbook.xsl` and your favorite XSL-FO processor, this time omitting the `make.index.markup` parameter.

The result of this process is a PDF file for your document that contains an index with page numbers properly collapsed. Duplicate numbers should be removed, and sequences of consecutive pages should appear as page ranges.

Internationalized indexes

Indexes that are generated from `indexterm` elements are a challenge for the stylesheets. The index entries have to be collected from throughout the document, sorted into groups, and sorted within each group, before being formatted in the output. How index terms are sorted and grouped is highly dependent on the language and alphabet being used in the document. English is probably the simplest, with only 26 letters. Latin alphabet languages that add accented characters such as French are a bit more complex, and ideographic languages such as Chinese are even more complex. The DocBook XSL stylesheets provide the tools and methods to handle all of these languages and alphabets.

There are two processes that govern how an index is generated: sorting and grouping. Sorting means arranging the characters of an alphabet in a certain order. Grouping means treating a set of characters as the same character as far as assigning them to index sections (the A, B, C sections in an English index). For example, words starting with a, A, á and Ã should all be in an index section labelled A. Likewise, all the letters in the group should sort as if they were the same letter. For example, áb, ac, and ád should sort in that order, and not sort the two words starting with á together.

The basic steps for generating an index are to put each entry in a group based on its first letter, sort the groups, and then sort the words within each group. The DocBook XSL stylesheets provide three different methods to perform these functions (starting with version 1.71.1 of the stylesheets). The index method is chosen using the stylesheet parameter `index.method`, which can have one of three values.

Table 19.1. Index methods

index.method	Description	Grouping	Sorting
basic	• Suitable for English and many Latin-based languages. • It does not require any extensions, so it works with any XSLT processor. • Not configurable. • The default indexing method.	Index groups are defined only for the 26 English letters, and the order of the groups is fixed. A word is assigned to a group by internally mapping accented characters to their unaccented version.	The letter groups are output in fixed order. Sorting within each group is based on the language algorithm available to the XSLT processor.
kosek	• Suitable for languages that need more index groups or different group order, and for which it is feasible to assign all letters to a group. • Uses custom XSLT functions that do not work with the xsltproc processor. • Requires using a customization layer to import templates. • Employs a user-customizable index configuration that part of the DocBook gentext file that is specific to each locale. • Named for its author, Jirka Kosek.	Any number of index groups can be created in the configuration for a given locale. Each group must identify which letters are included in that group.	The groups can be output in any order based on the configuration. Sorting within a group is based on the language algorithm available to the XSLT processor.
kimber	• Suitable for all languages and alphabet types, including ideographic languages. • Uses Java extension functions that only work with Saxon. • Requires using a customization layer to import templates. • Employs a user-customizable external configuration file that has a section for each locale. • The most flexible method, but more complicated to set up. • Named for its author Eliot Kimber.	Any number of index groups can be created in the configuration for a given locale. Groups are specified by group membership lists, or by specifying break points in the sort order.	A custom Java sort algorithm can be specified. A separate Java collation configuration file can also be specified. In the current version, the order of groups is always based on the current sort order.

Each of these index methods is described in more detail in the sections that follow.

index.method = "basic"

When the stylesheet parameter index.method is set to basic, the default indexing processing is used. Since this is the default value, all you need to do is add an empty index element to your document in the location where you want an index to be generated. The stylesheet will do the rest.

If you are wondering how the basic method operates, here is a summary of the steps:

1. The stylesheet defines the mapping of characters to letter groups using the XSLT translate() function, which can substitute one character for another from the lists in its second and third arguments. The lists come from two text entities named &lowercase; and &uppercase; that are defined in the stylesheet (in the file common/entit-ies.ent). The names are misleading, because the lowercase list includes lowercase and uppercase letters in accented and unaccented form. The uppercase list is repeated copies of the corresponding uppercase, unaccented letter. For example:

   lowercase:
   AaÀàÁáÂ...Bb...

   uppercase:
   AAAAAAA...BB...

2. An xsl:key is created with name letter, which contains all the indexterm elements. The access key is the first letter of its primary child element, mapped to the uppercase, unaccented version of the letter using the translate function. Then by specifying an access key of A, the stylesheet can immediately find all indexterm elements whose primary element starts with any of these letters:

   A a À à Á á Â ...

3. The template named generate-basic-index is called, which first gathers the first instance of each indexterm with a unique access key value. Thus it gather the first A term if there is one, the first B, etc. Any letters for which there are no entries are omitted, and so no empty index letter sections will be created.

4. The select group of entries is sorted using the sort algorithm available to the XSLT processor. It uses the document lang attribute if available, otherwise it defaults to English. This puts the groups into the order they will be presented in the index.

5. Each indexterm in the select group is processed in mode="index-div-basic", which starts a new index letter group.

6. In each invocation of mode="index-div-basic", all indexterm elements matching that particular access key are gathered. Then they are sorted and formatted within that letter group. Although the selection key is the uppercase, unaccented letter, each entry is output using its original characters that include lowercase and accented letters.

index.method = "kosek"

When the stylesheet parameter index.method is set to kosek, a different indexing process is used. This method adds the ability to define indexing groups and their members, and the order of the groups within the index.

However, setting the parameter is not sufficient. You must use a customization layer in order to import a supple-mental stylesheet module that contains some additional templates that are needed by this method. For example:

```
<?xml version="1.0"?>
<xsl:stylesheet xmlns:xsl="http://www.w3.org/1999/XSL/Transform"
                xmlns:fo="http://www.w3.org/1999/XSL/Format"
                version="1.0">
<xsl:param name="index.method">kosek</xsl:param>
<xsl:import href="docbook-xsl/fo/docbook.xsl"/>
<xsl:import href="docbook-xsl/fo/autoidx-kosek.xsl"/>
...
```

For an HTML customization layer, you would import the corresponding `autoidx-kosek.xsl` file from the `html` or `xhtml` stylesheet directory.

The definitions of the groups used by this method are in the gentext locale files, such as `common/fr.xml` for French.

```
<l:letters>
      <l:l i="-1"/>
      <l:l i="0">Symboles</l:l>
      <l:l i="1">A</l:l>
      <l:l i="1">a</l:l>
      <l:l i="1">&#224;</l:l>
      <l:l i="1">&#192;</l:l>
      <l:l i="1">&#226;</l:l>
      <l:l i="1">&#194;</l:l>
      <l:l i="1">&#198;</l:l>
      <l:l i="1">&#230;</l:l>
      <l:l i="2">B</l:l>
      <l:l i="2">b</l:l>
      ...
```

Note these features of the configuration:

- All members are contained in the `l:letters` element, with each member specified by a `l:l` element.

- The groups are identified by the different values of the `i` attribute in each letter element `l:l`. In this example, group 1 has all the "A" letters, group 2 has all the B's, etc. Included in the "A" group are all the accented versions of upper- and lowercase A, entered as Unicode character values (e.g., `&#224;` which is à). In this way, you can expand each group to include new characters if necessary, and create new groups with a new number index.

- The first member of each group is used as the displayed section heading for that group in the index. So group 1 would display A as the section heading.

- Any numerical `i` values can be used, not necessarily contiguous values (e.g., 10, 20, 30, etc.).

- The order of groups in the index is based on the ascending numerical order of the `i` values that identify the groups.

- All index entries that do not fall into one of the letter groups are assigned to the group with `i="0"` for symbols.

All of the gentext files in the `common` directory of the stylesheet distribution have a set of groups defined. But many have not yet been actually prepared for the specific language, and are just a copy of the groups from the English file (which has many accented characters in its groups anyway). You can identify such groups by the `lang="en"` attribute on the `l:letters` element in the gentext file. If your language has not been properly prepared, you can create a further customization of the gentext elements. That process is described in the section called "Customizing generated text" (page 106). If you are confident that it is correct, you could submit it back to the DocBook development team for inclusion in future releases.

The sorting of entries within each group is handled in the stylesheet by an `xsl:sort` element, with a `lang` attribute whose value is taken from the document being processed. So you must have an appropriate `lang` attribute on the root element of your document.

XSLT processors hand off the actual sorting process to the operating system. So the results will depend on how well your operating system can sort the language specified. If it does not have the proper collation rules for your language, then the results will likely be unsatisfactory.

For the customization to work, the XSLT processor must be able to use *EXSLT* extension functions, and it must be able to use them in `xsl:key` elements. Saxon is known to work with the customization. But xsltproc does not support using the EXSLT extensions in `xsl:key`, and so will not work.

index.method = "kimber"

When the stylesheet parameter `index.method` is set to `kimber`, Java extension functions are used in building the index. The Java classes used in this method were written by Eliot Kimber of Innodata Isogen, Inc. and donated to the open source community. A white paper describing the package is available at:

http://www.innodata-isogen.com/resources/white_papers/back_of_book_for_xsl_fo.pdf

This index method is the most flexible and powerful, but also the most difficult to set up. Currently the Saxon 6 and 8 processors work with the extensions. Here is what you need to do.

1. Download and unpack to some convenient location the Innodata Isogen Internationalization Support Library. You may need to register (for free) before getting access.

   http://www.innodata-isogen.com/knowledge_center/tools_downloads/i18nsupport

2. Set the stylesheet parameter `index.method` to `kimber`.

3. Create a customization layer in order to import a supplemental stylesheet module that contains some additional templates that are needed by this method. For example:

```
<?xml version="1.0"?>
<xsl:stylesheet xmlns:xsl="http://www.w3.org/1999/XSL/Transform"
                xmlns:fo="http://www.w3.org/1999/XSL/Format"
                version="1.0">
<xsl:param name="index.method">kimber</xsl:param>
<xsl:import href="docbook-xsl/fo/docbook.xsl"/>
<xsl:import href="docbook-xsl/fo/autoidx-kimber.xsl"/>
...
```

   For an HTML customization layer, you would import the corresponding `autoidx-kimber.xsl` file from the `html` or `xhtml` stylesheet directory.

4. During processing with Saxon, you must add the jar file to your CLASSPATH and set a Java property to point to the configuration files.

```
java  \
  -cp "/xml/java/saxon.jar:/xml/java/i18n_support/i18n_support.jar" \
  -Dcom.innodata.i18n.home="/xml/java/i18n_support" \
  com.icl.saxon.StyleSheet \
  -o myfile.fo \
  myfile.xml \
  docbook-xsl/fo/docbook.xsl  \
```

If all the pieces are in place, you should get an index that is generated using the Java extensions. If you had not set a `lang` attribute on your document's root element, or if the value did not match those in the configuration file, then you will see a message like the following:

```
- Failed to find index configuration for language 'xy', trying English.
```

This tells you that the code is working, but the configuration is not quite right. In the location where you unpacked the library, you will find the indexing configuration file `config/botb_index_rules/botb_index_rules.xml` (here *botb* means "back-of-the-book"). That configuration file has an `index_config` element for each locale, containing all the configuration elements for that language. See the white paper mentioned above for details on the configuration elements.

In order for the configuration to work for your language, the `lang` attribute on your document root element must match the value of a `national_language` element in the configuration file. For example, here is the start of the configuration for Czech:

```
<index_config>
  <national_language>cs-CZ</national_language>
  <description> <p>Czech index configuration</p> </description>
  <collation_spec></collation_spec>
  <sort_method>
    <sort_by_members/>
  </sort_method>
  <group_definitions>
    <term_group>
      <group_key>A</group_key>
      <group_members>
        <char_or_seq>a</char_or_seq>
        <char_or_seq>A</char_or_seq>
        <char_or_seq>Á</char_or_seq>
        <char_or_seq>á</char_or_seq>
      </group_members>
    </term_group>
    <term_group>
      <group_key>B</group_key>
      <group_members>
        <char_or_seq>b</char_or_seq>
        <char_or_seq>B</char_or_seq>
        ...
```

A document element should have a `lang="cs-CZ"` in order for this index configuration to be used. Otherwise edit the configuration file's `national_language` element to match your document's `lang` value.

For ideographic languages such as Chinese and Korean, the configuration file can use the `sort_between_keys` sort method, and specify an optional collation rules file, as shown in the following example:

```
<index_config>
  <national_language>ko-KR</national_language>
  <description>
    <p>Index configuration for Korean</p>
  </description>
  <collation_spec>
    <java_collation_spec>
      <include_collation_spec>ko-sort-rules.txt</include_collation_spec>
    </java_collation_spec>
  </collation_spec>
  <sort_method>
    <sort_between_keys/>
  </sort_method>
  <group_definitions>
  <term_group>
    <group_key>&#x3131;</group_key>
    <group_members></group_members>
  </term_group>
```

When `sort_between_keys` is used, all of the index terms are sorted into a stream for processing. As each term is processed, if its first character matches a `group_key` value, that triggers the start of a new index group. All characters in the stream up to the next match are in that group. This method is most suitable for alphabets that have thousands of characters that make group lists impractical. You can also specify your own sort order for the characters by specifying a file containing a Java collation specification. See the white paper described above for more information.

Formatting HTML indexes

The best way to format an HTML index is through CSS styles. Use the `html.stylesheet` parameter to specify the name of an external CSS stylesheet, and then create CSS selectors in it to format your index. Here are the selectors you can use.

Main index title:
`div.index div.titlepage h2.title`

Letter division titles:
`div.indexdiv h3`

Index term:
`div.indexdiv dt`

Reference links:
`div.indexdiv dt a`

If you want to customize how *See* and *See also* index entries format, you will need to customize the templates `<xsl:template match="indexterm" mode="index-see">` or `<xsl:template match="indexterm" mode="index-seealso">`, respectively. Those templates are found in `html/autoidx.xsl` in the stylesheet distribution.

Formatting print indexes

There are several features of print index formatting that you can customize:

• Number of columns.

• Typography of titles.

- Typography of index entries.

- Punctuation of index entries.

- Remove duplicate page numbers using extensions.

Index columns

The stock format for DocBook indexes is two columns with a 12pt column separation. These features are controlled by the `column.count.index` parameter and the `column.gap.index` parameter, respectively. If you set the `column.count.index` parameter to 3, for example, your print index will have three columns per page.

Index titles

The titles in a print index include the main index title, and the titles for the letter subdivisions. The main title is controlled by the titlepage specifications file that generates titlepage templates. See the section called "Title page spec file" (page 184) to learn how to customize the titlepage specs and generate new templates. The main title is controlled by the specifications for `t:element="index"`.

The letter subdivision titles in an index are controlled by the `index.div.title.properties` attribute-set (starting with version 1.68). Attributes defined in that attribute-set are applied to the `fo:block` containing the title, so you can specify the font family, style, and weight, as well as spacing above and below.

Index titles in HTML output can be formatted using CSS styles. Peek in the HTML output to see the `class` attributes that are used, and create CSS selectors to handle them.

Formatting index entries

You can change the way index entries format by using the `index.entry.properties` attribute-set, introduced in version 1.68 of the stylesheets. That attribute-set is applied to the block containing each index entry. By default, this attribute-set is empty. The most common change is to reduce the type size and line spacing so the index uses fewer pages:

```
<xsl:attribute-set name="index.entry.properties">
  <xsl:attribute name="font-size">8pt</xsl:attribute>
  <xsl:attribute name="line-height">8pt</xsl:attribute>
</xsl:attribute-set>
```

Another attribute-set is available to add styles to the page numbers presented in a printed index. Any attributes defined in the `index.page.number.properties` attribute-set (introduced in stylesheet version 1.72) will be added to the `fo:basic-link` element that wraps around each generated page number reference. You can use that to change the color to indicate that the page number is a clickable link in the PDF file.

```
<xsl:attribute-set name="index.page.number.properties">
  <xsl:attribute name="color">blue</xsl:attribute>
</xsl:attribute-set>
```

If you are using XEP, any attributes defined in `index.page.number.properties` are also used in the `xep.index.item.properties` attribute-set, so that they are applied to the page numbers generated in the XEP XSL-FO processor using its indexing extensions.

You can also control the typography of the preferred page number if you use that feature. Preferred page numbers are designated by putting `significance="preferred"` attributes on selected `indexterm` entries in your document. The page numbers for such preferred references are formatted using the `index.preferred.page.properties` attribute-set. By default, that attribute-set changes such page numbers to bold. You can change that to italic by adding this to your customization layer:

```
<xsl:attribute-set name="index.preferred.page.properties">
  <xsl:attribute name="font-weight">normal</xsl:attribute>
  <xsl:attribute name="font-style">italic</xsl:attribute>
</xsl:attribute-set>
```

Index punctuation

You can also control the punctuation used in index entries, if you must meet style requirements or locale conventions. By default the stylesheet automatically inserts the following punctuation:

Description	Default value	Gentext template name	Parameter name
Separator between the end of an index term's text and its first page number.	Comma and space.	term-separator	index.term.separator
Separator between two page numbers.	Comma and space.	number-separator	index.number.separator
Separator between the numbers in a page range.	Dash.	range-separator	index.range.separator

As the last column in the table shows, there are parameters that are available to control the punctuation. However, those exist for convenience and are empty by default in the stylesheet. That's because punctuation differs by language and locale, so a single parameter value would not suffice.

The default values are set using the gentext template names shown in the above table. They are in a `context` element with `name="index"` in each locale's gentext file such as `common/en.xml`. See the section called "Generated text" (page 105) to see how to change the values for different locales.

The parameters shown in the table will override the corresponding gentext value. You can use the parameters for convenience if you are processing documents in a single language that uses one style of punctuation.

XSL-FO processor indexing extensions

There are a few problems in generating page numbers in a print index that an XSL stylesheet cannot solve. The basic problem is that the stylesheet does not know what page number a given index entry will generate, so all it can do is output a page reference for each entry. But if two or more copies of the same index entry happen to land on the same page, then the index will repeat the page numbers. Also, most indexes collapse a consecutive sequence of page numbers for an entry into a page range, but the stylesheet cannot know which page references will be in a sequence.

To solve these problems and improve the quality of printed indexes, most XSL-FO processors provide indexing extensions. These extensions can eliminate duplicate page references in an entry, and collapse a sequence into a range. The DocBook XSL stylesheets use these extensions when the appropriate processor parameter is set.

XSL Formatter from Antenna House supports an index extension attribute to remove duplicate page numbers in an entry. This attribute is output by DocBook XSL when the stylesheet parameter `axf.extensions="1"`:

```
<xsl:attribute name="axf:suppress-duplicate-page-number">true</xsl:attribute>
```

The XEP processor from RenderX takes a more comprehesive approach to indexing. You can activate its extensions in DocBook XSL by setting the stylesheet parameter `xep.extensions="1"`. XEP first defines its own extension attribute (`rx:key`) to use in place of `id` as an index marker. The key value is the text of the `indexterm` element. Then XEP defines two extension elements. The `rx:index-item` is used once for all entries that match, and it uses its `ref-key` attribute to match key values anywhere in the document's output. XEP's other extension element `rx:page-index` is used to specify some formatting properties and to contain the `rx:index-item` element. When processing an `rx:index-item`, the processor locates the page numbers for all the `rx:key` properties that match, and then generates the string of numbers with duplicates removed and sequences collapsed into page ranges. See the XEP documentation for more details.

Customizing indexing templates

The index generating templates in the DocBook stylesheets are among the most complex in the whole set. They use every method and trick to gather, sort, group, and present the output in a usable index. Customizing the index templates requires careful study of the existing templates to learn how they work.

You can learn more about the DocBook indexing templates from a paper published by Jirka Kosek titled *Using XSLT for getting back-of-the-book indexes*[3].

---

[3] http://www.idealliance.org/proceedings/xml04/papers/77/xslindex.html

20

Languages, characters and encoding

Characters in a computer are just numbers. An XML document examined directly in a computer's memory is a long string of numbers. A character set *encoding* is a mapping of those computer numbers to particular characters. For example, in the iso-8859-1 encoding, the number 225 is mapped to á (a acute). Whenever the computer displays the XML document, it uses an encoding to convert the numbers to character glyphs for display. There are many ways to do such mappings, and there are many character sets the numbers can map to. So there are many possible encodings. XML programs use Unicode internally to encode all characters in the computer's memory. However, your DocBook documents do not have to be written in Unicode and your output does not have to be Unicode. But having available a Unicode-aware text editor such as *UniPad*[1] can help resolve many problems with characters and encodings.

If you want more details on encoding in XML, this website *http://skew.org/xml/tutorial/* has an in-depth tutorial.

Document encoding

The creators of the XML specification were well aware that different documents may need different character encodings. So they let you specify the encoding right at the top of each document in the XML declaration:

```
<?xml  version="1.0"  encoding="iso-8859-1"?>
```

In this example, the encoding is specified as iso-8859-1 which is also known as ISO Latin 1. If the encoding is not specified, then UTF-8 encoding is assumed. With the encoding established, an XML program that opens the document knows how to convert the numbers it sees to logical characters, and then convert those characters into the Unicode numbers it uses internally. Of course, the content of the document must actually be encoded with this encoding. That is, you cannot just change the label at the top and think you have a new encoding. The document itself would have to be converted to the new mapping of characters. If the encoding declaration of the document does not match the actual encoding, then you may end up with gibberish.

The following are several common encoding names. Usually either uppercase or lowercase letters are recognized. But do not forget the hyphens.

---

[1] http://www.unipad.org

Table 20.1. Character encodings

UTF-8	The default Unicode encoding.
UTF-16	Another Unicode encoding.
US-ASCII	Basic 128 characters.
ISO-8859-1	Western European languages.
ISO-8859-2	Central European languages.
ISO-8859-4	Baltic languages.
ISO-8859-5	Cyrillic.
ISO-8859-6	Arabic.
ISO-8859-7	Modern Greek.
ISO-8859-8	Hebrew.
ISO-8859-9	Turkish
ISO-8859-15	ISO-8859-1 plus the Euro symbol and other small changes.
Shift_JIS	Japanese on Windows
EUC-JP	Japanese on Unix

What if you need to enter a character that a document's encoding does not include? For example, iso-8859-1 does not include a character for the trademark symbol ™. The solution is to use numerical character references for any characters not in your encoding. The trademark symbol can be entered as ™ in hexadecimal notation, or the equivalent ™ in decimal notation. Of course, having to remember that ™ means trademark is an author's nightmare. Fortunately, the DocBook DTD provides more easily recognized text entities for hundreds of characters you might need. The following is one example from the DTD, this one declared in the iso-num.ent entities file.

```
<!ENTITY trade      "&#x2122;"> <!-- TRADE MARK SIGN -->
```

So you just need to enter ™ in your document, and the DTD converts that to the numerical Unicode character that all XML applications recognize. You can examine the complete set of available character entities by looking in the directory that contains the DocBook DTD. The ent subdirectory contains a number of iso-*something*.ent files, where *something* identifies the set of entity declarations in that file.

It is entirely possible to write a document in any language that is supported by Unicode using only ASCII characters. All characters beyond the basic ASCII character set are written using numerical character references such ÿ for á, and so on. If you want to see examples of such XML files, look at the files containing generated text strings, such as fr.xml in the common directory of the DocBook XSL distribution. Those files for all languages are encoded as ASCII XML files using numerical character references. The raw XML is not very readable, however, unless it is displayed in a program that converts such numerical Unicode references to displayable *glyphs*.

Output encoding

Regardless of what the encoding is for your documents, an XSL engine can convert the output to a different encoding if you need it. When the document is loaded into memory, XML applications such as XSLT engines convert it to Unicode. The XSL engine then uses the stylesheet templates to create a transformed version of the content in memory structures. When it is done, it *serializes* the internal content into a stream of bytes that it feeds to the outside world. During the serialization process, it can convert the internal Unicode to some other encoding for the output.

An XSL stylesheet usually sets the output encoding in an xsl:output element at the top of the stylesheet file. The following shows that element for the html/docbook.xsl stylesheet:

```
<xsl:output method="html"
            encoding="ISO-8859-1"
            indent="no"/>
```

The encoding="ISO-8859-1" attribute means all documents processed with that stylesheet are to be output with the ISO-8859-1 encoding. If a stylesheet's xsl:output element does not have an encoding attribute, then the default output encoding is UTF-8. That is what the fo/docbook.xsl stylesheet for print output does.

When the output method="html", the XSLT processor also adds an HTML META tag that identifies the HTML file's encoding:

```
<meta content="text/html; charset=ISO-8859-1" http-equiv="Content-Type">
```

When a browser opens the HTML file, it reads this tag and knows the bytes it finds in the file map to the ISO-8859-1 character set for display. What if the document contains characters that are not available in the specified output encoding? As with input, the characters are expressed as numerical character references such as ™. It is up to the browser to figure out how to display such characters. Most browsers cover a pretty wide range of character entities, but there are so many that sometimes a browser does not have a way to display a given character.

Most modern graphical browsers can display HTML files encoded with UTF-8, which covers a much wider set of characters than ISO-8859-1. To change the output encoding for the non-chunking docbook.xsl stylesheet, you have to use a stylesheet customization layer. That is because the XML specification does not permit the encoding attribute to be a variable or parameter value. Your stylesheet customization must provide a new <xsl:output> element such as the following:

```
<?xml version='1.0'?>
<xsl:stylesheet  xmlns:xsl="http://www.w3.org/1999/XSL/Transform"
                 version="1.0">

<xsl:import href="/path/to/html/docbook.xsl"/>
<xsl:output method="html"
            encoding="UTF-8"
            indent="no"/>

</xsl:stylesheet>
```

This is a complete stylesheet customization that you can save in a file such as docbook-utf8.xsl and use in place of the stock html/docbook.xsl stylesheet. All it does is import the stock stylesheet and set a new output encoding, in this instance to UTF-8. Any HTML files generated with this stylesheet will have their characters encoded as UTF-8, and the file will include a meta tag like the following:

```
<meta content="text/html; charset=UTF-8" http-equiv="Content-Type">
```

Changing the output encoding of the chunking stylesheet is much easier. It can be done with the chunker.output.encoding parameter, either on the command line or in a customization layer. That's because the chunking stylesheet uses *EXSLT* extensions to generate HTML files. See the section called "Output encoding for chunk HTML" (page 68) for more information.

Saxon output character representation

If you are using the Saxon processor with the chunking stylesheet for non-English HTML output, then you may want to set the stylesheet parameter saxon.character.representation to a value of 'native;decimal'. By default, this parameter (which is defined in html/chunker.xsl) is set to 'entity;decimal'. The default value of entity before the semicolon means that any non-ASCII characters within the encoding are converted to named entity references such as á instead of the numerical character code for that encoding. For example, when using the iso-8859-

1 output encoding, this means one native character is replaced by the 8 ASCII characters that form the named entity reference, which makes your files considerably larger. When `entity` is replaced with `native`, the single character code of the encoding is output. Note that when the output encoding is `UTF-8` and the parameter value uses `native`, then no entity references will be output because there are no XML characters outside of UTF-8.

The value after the semicolon controls how characters that are not in the encoding are output by Saxon. They must be converted to some kind of entity reference, and the value can be `entity` (named entity reference such as `&aacute;` if one exists), `decimal` (decimal numerical character reference such as `&#225;`), or `hex` (hexadecimal numerical character reference such as `&#xE1;`). Saxon outputs named entity references only for characters in ISO-8859-1, not for all DocBook named character entities.

If you are using the chunking stylesheet, then you can use this parameter to set the Saxon output character representation. If you are using the non-chunking stylesheet, then your customization of `xsl:output` as described above needs to be enhanced as follows:

```
<xsl:stylesheet version="1.0"
                xmlns:xsl="http://www.w3.org/1999/XSL/Transform"
                xmlns:saxon="http://icl.com/saxon"
                extension-element-prefixes="saxon">

<xsl:import href="file:///c:/docbook/xsl/html/docbook.xsl"/>

<xsl:output method="html"
            encoding="UTF-8"
            indent="no"
            saxon:character-representation="native;decimal"/>
```

Special characters

XML is based on Unicode, which contains thousands of characters and symbols. A given XML document specifies its encoding, which is a mapping of characters to bytes. But not all encodings include all Unicode characters. Also, your keyboard may not enable you to directly enter all characters in the encoding. Any characters you cannot enter directly are entered as entities, which consists of an ampersand, followed by a name, followed by a semicolon.

There are two kinds of character entities:

numerical character references
> An entity name that consists of a # followed by the Unicode number for the character, such as `&#225;`. The number can be expressed as a decimal number such as `&#431`, or a hexadecimal number (which is indicated using x as a prefix), such as `&#x0022;`.

named character entities
> A readable name such as `&trade;` can be assigned to represent any Unicode character.

The following table shows examples of some characters expressed in both kinds of entities.

Table 20.2. Examples of character references

Character	Decimal character reference	Hexadecimal character reference	Named entity
á	`&#225;`	`&#x00E1;`	`&aacute;`
ß	`&#223;`	`&#x00DF;`	`&szlig;`
©	`&#169;`	`&#x00A9;`	`&copy;`
¥	`&#165;`	`&#x00A5`	`&yen;`
±	`&#177;`	`&#x00B1;`	`&plusmn;`
✓	`&#8658;`	`&#x2713;`	`&check;`

Note:

Leading zeros can be omitted in numerical references. So `&#xE1;` is the same as `&#x00E1;`.

The set of "numerical entities" (character references) is defined as part of the Unicode standard adopted by XML, but the names used for named entities are not standardized. There are several standard named character entity sets defined by ISO, however, and these are incorporated into the DocBook DTD. Among the collection of files in the DocBook XML DTD distribution, there is an `ent` subdirectory that contains a set of files that declare named entities. Each declaration looks like the following:

```
<!ENTITY  plusmn  "&#x00B1;">    <!-- PLUS-MINUS SIGN -->
```

This declaration assigns the numerical character reference `&#x00B1;` to the `plusmn` entity name. Either `&plusmn;` or `&#x00B1;` can be used in your DocBook document to represent the plus-minus sign.

Note:

If you use DocBook named character entities in your document, you must also make sure your document's DOCTYPE properly identifies the DocBook DTD, and the processor must be able to find and load the DTD. If not, then the entities will be considered unresolved and the processing will fail.

Use this reference to look up DocBook entities that you need in your documents:

- *DocBook Character Entity Reference*[2]

If you are a user of the Emacs text editor, then you might want to check out Norm Walsh's Emacs extensions for DocBook, which includes a selector for special characters. See *http://nwalsh.com/emacs/xmlchars/*.

A Unicode reference such as *Unicode Code Charts*[3] can be used to look up numerical character references. Most online references use PDF to display the characters because most browsers cannot display all of Unicode.

Special characters in output

When an XSLT processor reads an entity from the input stream, it tries to resolve the entity. If it is a numerical character reference, it converts it to a Unicode character in memory. If it is a named entity, it checks the list of entity names that were loaded from the DTD. For the DocBook named character entities, these resolve to numerical character references. Then these numerical character references are also converted to Unicode characters in memory. All the characters in the document are handled as Unicode characters in memory during processing.

See the section called "Output encoding" (page 326) for a description of how special characters in memory are converted to output characters.

---

[2] http://www.oasis-open.org/docbook/documentation/reference/html/refchar.html
[3] http://www.unicode.org/charts/

Space characters

The Unicode standard includes several characters that represent spaces that serve different purposes. Below is a table that summarizes most of them.

Table 20.3. Space characters

Unicode name	Character reference	DocBook entity	Description
SPACE	&#x20;		Ordinary space.
NO-BREAK SPACE			Space that may not be broken at the end of a line.
NARROW NO-BREAK SPACE			Thinner than NO-BREAK SPACE.
EN QUAD	&#x2000;		Same as EN SPACE.
EM QUAD	&#x2001;		Same as EM SPACE
EN SPACE			Half an EM SPACE.
EM SPACE			Usually a space equal to the type size in points.
THREE-PER-EM SPACE	&#x2004;		One-third of an EM SPACE, called a thick space.
FOUR-PER-EM-SPACE	&#x2005;		One-fourth of an EM SPACE, called a mid space.
SIX-PER-EM-SPACE	&#x2006;		One-sixth of an EM SPACE, similar to thin space.
FIGURE SPACE			Width of a digit in some fonts.
PUNCTUATION SPACE			Space equal to the narrow punctuation of a font.
THIN SPACE			One-fifth of an EM SPACE, usually.
HAIR SPACE			Thinner than a thin space.
ZERO WIDTH SPACE	&#x200B;		No visible space. Used to allow a line break in a word without generating a hyphen.
ZERO WIDTH NO-BREAK SPACE	&#xFEFF;		No visible space. Used to prevent a line break, as for example, after the hyphen in a word that contains its own hyphen.

Not all of these characters may work in the various output forms. For example, the characters in the Unicode range   to   represent spaces of different widths. However, many print fonts do not support all of the characters in that range. So the print stylesheet uses a set of templates in the stylesheet module `fo/spaces.xsl` to convert them to `fo:leader` elements of different lengths. The length unit used for the leaders is `em`, which scales to the current font size. If you need to customize the width of any of those special space characters, you can change the stylesheet parameters that are defined in that module.

In HTML output, these characters will pass through the stylesheet and be rendered in the output encoding for the HTML file. However, some browsers do not support all of these space characters, and may display a placeholder character instead of the intended space.

Missing characters

When a DocBook document is processed with an XSLT processor, you may find that some or all special characters are missing in the output. There are several possible causes for this problem.

- If only one entity is not resolving, it may simply be entered wrong. If you misspell a named entity, it will not resolve. If you enter a numerical character reference wrong, the number may resolve to a range in Unicode that does not have printable characters. Also, if you intend to enter a hexadecimal value, be sure to include the x prefix or it will be interpreted as a decimal value.

- If you are using named character entities, the DocBook XML DTD must be available to the processor. That's because the named entities are defined in the DTD, and the processor will not know what the names mean unless it can load the DTD. Most XSLT processors do not do full validation, but they do load the entities defined in the DTD. If the DTD is not available, the processor may continue processing the document as a well-formed document, but it will not be able to resolve the named character entities.

- If the output encoding does not include the character, the XSLT processor should convert it to a numerical character entity. Then the downstream viewer or processor must be able to handle such entities. For example, old browsers may not recognize the full range of numerical character references in Unicode.

- The output medium may not have a font loaded that can display a special character. For example, a PDF file that does not contain embedded fonts relies on the system to supply requested fonts. If the font in use does not have a given character, it may not show up in the display or may display as #. If you are using Windows, you can use the Character Map application to investigate whether a given font has a certain Unicode character. With HTML, when a system viewing an HTML file does not have a screen font installed for a given encoding, in may not display all characters.

- If you are doing XSL-FO processing, then the font currently being used may not contain all special characters. See the section called "FO font-family list" (page 331) to configure your output to use the `font-selection-strategy` property to search multiple fonts for a character. If you are using FOP, then this scheme does not work (as of version 0.93) because it does not support the `font-selection-strategy` property. See the section called "Switching to Symbol font" (page 332) for a workaround for this problem.

FO font-family list

A given font has a fixed character set that may not include all special characters. The XSL-FO standard has a `font-selection-strategy` property that lets the processor search through a list of font-families to find a given character. By default, the DocBook XSL stylesheets set `font-selection-strategy="character-by-character"` which enables that feature.

To specify the fonts for the processor to search, a `font-family` attribute in the FO output must contain a comma-separated list of font family names to search. The DocBook FO stylesheet automatically generates a list of fonts wherever the body font is called for. That list is made up of the value of the `body.font.family` parameter and the `symbol.font.family` parameter. So the default list is `serif,Symbol,ZapfDingbats`, and it is stored in the internal `body.fontset` parameter. A similar list is created using the `title.font.family` parameter and stored in the internal `title.fontset` parameter. If a special character is not in the body font, then the Symbol font is searched, and then the ZapfDingbats font. You can expand that list by adding more font names to the `symbol.font.family` parameter, assuming those extra fonts are configured into your processor.

Since XML supports any Unicode character, you may want to add a Unicode font to the list to catch any characters not in any of the others. On Windows, the Lucida Sans Unicode font is available, and the Arial Unicode MS font can be downloaded for free. You can add the font by modifying the `symbol.font.family` as follows:

```
<xsl:param name="symbol.font.family" select="'Symbol,ZapfDingbats,Lucida Sans Unicode'"/>
```

HTML encoding

For a browser to know what encoding an HTML file is written in, it must be told. If a browser is not told, then it may guess wrong and render many characters wrong. The encoding can be communicated to the browser in two ways for HTML files:

- A META tag embedded in the HTML HEAD element of the file:

```
<meta  content="text/html;  charset=UTF-8"  http-equiv="Content-Type">
```

- An encoding instruction in the HTTP header that accompanies the HTML file. The HTTP header is not in the HTML, but is sent by the HTTP server before the file and is hidden from the viewer. It provides information to the browser about the file.

```
Content-type: text/html; charset=UTF-8
```

It is best if both of these methods are used, and of course they must both agree with the actual file encoding. Often you do not have control of the HTTP header, so using the META element is the only option.

For XHTML output, there is a third avenue to convey the encoding. Because the output is XML, it should have an XML declaration, and the declaration should also contain the encoding:

```
<?xml version="1.0"  encoding="UTF-8" ?>
```

Odd characters in HTML output

If you are seeing odd accented characters when you browse your HTML output, then you probably have an encoding problem. You are seeing special characters that are encoded one way being misinterpreted by the browser as a different encoding. For example, if a file is encoded as UTF-8 and the browser thinks it is ISO-8859-1, then a special character such as an em-dash will appear as "â€" in the browser. More commonly, a nonbreaking space character in UTF-8 will appear as a "Â " when viewed as ISO-8859-1.

The previous section describes how to set the encoding in the HTML. But if the HTTP server delivering the HTML gets the encoding wrong, then the browser may use the HTTP header instead of the hints within the HTML. If the odd characters become normal when the HTML file is browsed as a local file, then it is likely an HTTP server issue. For example, an Apache server might have an AddDefaultCharSet directive that sets the default encoding for all files to iso-8859-1. If you cannot fix the Apache server configuration, then you could try adding a .htaccess file to your HTML directory and add your own AddDefaultCharSet directive to it. See the Apache documentation for more details.

Switching to Symbol font

If you are generating PDF output and you find certain special characters are missing, then the problem might be that the body font does not contain the character you need. Many special characters such as math symbols are in the Symbol font, and are not in Times or Helvetica. Your FO processor may not be able to switch to the Symbol font for a single character.

The following is a customization that you can use to coerce a special character into the Symbol font.

```
<xsl:template match="symbol[@role = 'symbolfont']">
  <fo:inline font-family="Symbol">
    <xsl:call-template name="inline.charseq"/>
  </fo:inline>
</xsl:template>
```

With this added to your customization layer, you can mark up a special character such as ≤ (≤, less than or equal to) to be coerced into the Symbol font with <symbol role="symbolfont">≤</symbol>. The customization wraps a fo:inline element around the character to explicitly switch in and out of Symbol font for that character.

Language support

The DocBook XSL stylesheets support documents written in many languages. This support is made easier by the fact that XML itself supports Unicode, which includes characters for most of the world's languages. To write a DocBook document in a given language, you just have to identify a character encoding that expresses the language, and then indicate that character encoding in the XML declaration that must appear at the top of each XML file, such as `<?xml version="1.0" encoding="iso-8859-1"?>`. You write the text of your document using that character encoding, and you use the standard DocBook tags (which have English names) to mark the XML elements. Then you just have to make sure the XSLT processor you use supports your encoding.

- The language support in the DocBook XSL stylesheets is primarily for generated text that the stylesheets produce. For example, an English document should label a chapter with `Chapter 3`, while a German document's chapter should be labeled `Kapitel 3`.

- The XML document encoding does not tell the stylesheets what language the document is written in. You have to supply that information with either a `lang` attribute in the document or a stylesheet parameter at processing time.

- Indexing in DocBook XSL does not sort properly for non-English languages. But there is a customization available that does sort properly. See the section called "Internationalized indexes" (page 314).

Using the lang attribute

The preferred method of indicating language is by adding a `lang` attribute with a language code value, usually on the document root element . This method records the language within the document itself, so it is clear to anyone examining the document. Also, the attribute triggers automatic processing in that language by the stylesheets. That means you do not have to indicate the language on the processing command line.

Since `lang` is one of the common DocBook attributes, it is permissible for all DocBook elements. The attribute applies to the element it is in, and all of that element's descendants. If one of the descendants has a different `lang` attribute, then it overrides the ancestor's value for the scope of that descendant. For example, if a document's root element is book, you can put a `lang` attribute in the book start tag so it applies to the whole document. If one of your chapters is written in a different language, then it can have a `lang` attribute whose value applies only to that chapter. The following example illustrates this usage.

```
<book  lang="de">
  ...
  <chapter>
    <title>Profil verwalten</title>
    ...
  </chapter>
  <chapter  lang="en">
    <title>Special Features</title>
    ...
  </chapter>
  <chapter>
    <title>Junk-E-Mails vermeiden</title>
    ...
  </chapter>
</book>
```

In this example, the document root element sets the lang to de (German) for the document. So the chapters Profil verwalten and Junk-E-Mails vermeiden are processed as German. But the Special Features chapter has its own lang set to en (English). So the second chapter is processed as English. Its label will be Chapter in the chapter title page, the book's table of contents and any cross references to that chapter.

Using language parameters

You can also indicate the language of a document at processing time by using a stylesheet parameter set to a language code. This is useful if you are processing a document that does not have a lang attribute and you cannot edit it to add one, or if you want to override the attribute it does have. There are two stylesheet parameters that can be used to set the processing language:

- The parameterl10n.gentext.language will override any lang attribute set in the document. This parameter is only needed if the document is a single language that is not English, and one of the following conditions.

  —It does not have a lang attribute.

  —The lang attribute it does have is wrong.

  —The lang attribute it does have is not one of those supported by the stylesheets.

- The parameterl10n.gentext.default.language can be used in the same circumstances as the previous parameter, but it will not override any lang attributes in the stylesheet. It will apply only to those elements for which no lang attribute applies. Thus if there is a lang attribute on the document's root element, then the parameter will have no effect.

If you wondering about the names of these parameters, you probably do not recognize the odd abbreviation l10n, which is a lower case L followed by the number 10 and the letter n. This is an abbreviation of "localization" (the first and last letters, and 10 letters in between). It means the gentext strings are adapted to a particular locale in the world. This abbreviation is similar to i18n, which is an abbreviation for "internationalization".

Language codes

As of this writing, DocBook XSL supports 45 languages. That means it has translations for the generated text strings in 45 languages. The translations are stored in XML files named for the language code, such as en.xml, fr.xml, etc. These are stored in the common subdirectory of the stylesheet distribution. So if you want to check if a given language is supported, look in that directory for an XML file of that name. The top of each file looks like the following:

```
<?xml version="1.0" encoding="US-ASCII"?>
<l:l10n xmlns:l="http://docbook.sourceforge.net/xmlns/l10n/1.0"
        language="it"
        english-language-name="Italian">
```

The language attribute identifies the language code. It is this attribute value that the stylesheet uses to match to a lang attribute in a document. The filename just happens to have the same name. The english-language-name attribute gives the language name in English for each language.

Most of the language codes are two-letters, named using the ISO 639 standard. A few have variations to reflect how a given language is used in a different country. For example the pt_br language is for Portuguese as spoken in Brazil. The country codes that are used in the second part of the name are listed in the ISO 3166 alpha-2 standard.

When you specify a language code for your document in an attribute or parameter, you can use upper- or lower-case letters. If it has a country extension, you can use either dash or underscore as the separator. In all these cases the stylesheets will map the code to the supported value.

If you specify a country extension, and there is no translation for that extension, the stylesheet will fall back to using just the two-letter language code. If a two-letter code is not supported, then the stylesheets fall back to English.

Extending the set of languages

In theory, DocBook XSL can support any language that can be expressed in Unicode. In practice, only 45 languages have translated text strings that the stylesheets can access. If you need a language that is not currently available, then you can make the translations and add them to your stylesheets. You should copy the English file `common/en.xml` to a new language code XML file, and then translate the `text` attributes in the file. The translations should use Unicode numerical character references for any non-ASCII characters.

The easiest way to add a new language to the stylesheets is to submit your translation to the DocBook XSL project for integration into the next release. Send email to the project admins at the *DocBook SourceForge*[4] site. Then your new translation will be included in future stylesheet distributions. It also makes it available to other users, who can make contributions to it as well.

If you want to include your translation only in your own stylesheet, you need to do the following:

1. Copy the stylesheet file `common/l10n.xml` to a new filename, such as `common/my-l10n.xml`. It is best to keep it in the same directory because it references all the other language files in that directory.

2. Edit your new file to add a SYSTEM entity declaration to the DOCTYPE and an entity reference to the body of your copied file. Just copy similar lines from the file itself. The entity declaration should point to your new language file location, relative to the `common` directory.

   ```
   <!ENTITY fy SYSTEM "../mystuff/fy.xml">
   ...
   &fy;
   ```

3. Create a stylesheet customization layer if you do not already have one.

4. Add the following line to your customization file:

   ```
   <xsl:param name="l10n.xml"
           select="document('../mystuff/my-l10n.xml')"/>
   ```

   The path to your enhanced `my-l10n.xml` file should be relative to your stylesheet customization file.

The `document()` function loads your customized file into the stylesheet parameter `l10n.xml`. That parameter is searched when looking for a translation.

This arrangement is a bit awkward, and will need to be repeated with each new stylesheet release. It's best to complete the translation and submit it to the DocBook project.

Text direction

Some languages, such as Hebrew and Arabic, read from right to left. When viewing an XML source file, you might think that it reads from left to right, but that view is just an artifact of the viewing device. In fact, an XML file is a linear sequence of bytes, with no particular direction except from beginning to end. The file is in *logical* order, with the beginning of each word appearing earlier in the file than the end of the word, regardless of the language. Any device that interprets the bytes and assigns displayable characters has to choose how to lay out those characters in some readable fashion. For some languages, that presentation is left to right, and for others it is right to left.

There are two principal properties that determine the direction of text:

• Writing mode sets the overall direction for the document.

---

[4] https://sourceforge.net/projects/docbook/

• dir attributes change the direction for specific spans of text.

Note that most right-to-left languages are actually *bidirectional*, because numbers still read from left-to-right, and any words in the Latin alphabet, such as technical terms, still read from left-to-right.

Writing mode

Writing mode is a term from XSL-FO that describes the overall plan for laying out text onto a page. A writing mode is a combination of horizontal direction and vertical direction for text flows. For example, an XSL-FO output with writing-mode="lr-tb" displays inline text that flows from left-to-right (lr), and lines that stack down the page from top-to-bottom (tb). Similarly, in rl-tb the inline text flows from right-to-left, and again the lines stack down the page from top-to-bottom.

If you are conditioned to Latin-based languages that read left-to-right, you may not realize how important the left side is for text layout. Indents that show hierarchy are indented from the left. Numbers in orderedlist and bullets in itemizedlist appear on the left. When outputting a right-to-left language such as Arabic or Hebrew, putting such features on the left does not work. The importance of these formatting features is not that they appear on the left, it is that they appear at the *start of the line*. The XSL-FO standard recognizes this, and uses the term start-indent instead of left-indent.

When writing-mode="rl-tb" (right-to-left), the start-indent property is applied to the right side. Similarly, bullets and numbers appear on the right, at the start of their line. Tables are also reversed, that is, the first table-cell in each row appears on the right.

You can set the writing mode for XSL-FO output by adding an attribute to the root.properties attribute-set:

```
<xsl:attribute-set name="root.properties">
  <xsl:attribute name="writing-mode">rl-tb</xsl:attribute>
</xsl:attribute-set>
```

When you set this property, you will find that your print pages are mirror images of the left-to-right writing mode. Even page headers and footers will be mirrored, because they use tables to lay out the different portions of the headers and footers, and the order of table cells is reversed. You may want to swap your values for the page.margin.inner and page.margin.outer parameters, because the side for binding would change.

> **Note:**
>
> If you set writing-mode="rl-tb" in a document using a Latin-based language, the text does *not* print backwards. Only the layout is mirrored. As described in the next section, the text direction is based on the Unicode character range in use.

For HTML output, a right-to-left writing mode can be established by adding a dir="rtl" attribute to the HTML document element in the output. This currently requires using a customization, which differs if you are doing single-page or chunked output.

Single-page HTML, customize this template from docbook.xsl:

```
<xsl:template match="*" mode="process.root">
  <xsl:variable name="doc" select="self::*"/>

  <xsl:call-template name="user.preroot"/>
  <xsl:call-template name="root.messages"/>

  <html>
    <xsl:variable name="lang">
      <xsl:call-template name="l10n.language"/>
    </xsl:variable>

    <xsl:if test="starts-with($lang, 'he') or
                  starts-with($lang, 'ar')">
      <xsl:attribute name="dir">rtl</xsl:attribute>
    </xsl:if>
  ...
```

Chunked HTML, customize this template from chunk-common.xsl:

```
<xsl:template name="chunk-element-content">
  <xsl:param name="prev"/>
  <xsl:param name="next"/>
  <xsl:param name="nav.context"/>
  <xsl:param name="content">
    <xsl:apply-imports/>
  </xsl:param>

  <xsl:call-template name="user.preroot"/>

  <html>
    <xsl:variable name="lang">
      <xsl:call-template name="l10n.language"/>
    </xsl:variable>

    <xsl:if test="starts-with($lang, 'he') or
                  starts-with($lang, 'ar')">
      <xsl:attribute name="dir">rtl</xsl:attribute>
    </xsl:if>
  ...
```

These customizations call the utility template named l10n.language to get the current document's lang attribute. It then checks to see if it starts with either he (Hebrew) or ar (Arabic) and adds the dir attribute.

dir attribute

When processing content for output, you will find that the inline text direction is mostly handled automatically. That is, if you process an XML document containing Arabic, the formatted output will present the Arabic words from right to left, and any English words from left to right.

How does the formatter know when to switch the direction of presentation? It knows by the range of Unicode characters used in each word. Part of the information in the Unicode standard is the text direction that each range of characters is expected to be presented in. Latin letters are to be presented left to right, and Hebrew characters from right to left. Modern browsers and XSL-FO processors use that information to decide the direction of presentation. In mixed language text, sometimes called *bidirectional* text, the direction can change in mid-sentence. When a formatter encounters a bit of text that should be displayed in the opposite direction, it has to read forward to find the end of such text, print it out character-by-character reading backwards from the end, and then resume normal layout of the text that follows.

There are some combinations of text that make this task harder for the formatter. Punctuation, parentheses, numbers mixed with letters, and other combinations may present ambiguous information to the formatter. In such cases, the author may need to provide some help to the formatter through the XML markup.

The DocBook schemas starting with version 4.3 have supported an attribute named `dir` on almost all elements. The `dir` attribute provides a hint to the formatter for which direction to display the text enclosed by the element with that attribute. There are four possible values:

dir attribute value	Unicode Name	Description
`ltr`	Left-to-Right Embedding	Embed a span of left-to-right characters inside right-to-left text.
`rtl`	Right-to-Left Embedding	Embed a span of right-to-left characters inside left-to-right text.
`lro`	Left-to-Right Override	Force the characters to be treated as strong left-to-right characters.
`rlo`	Right-to-Left Override	Force the characters to be treated as strong right-to-left characters.

You can put a `dir` attribute on any inline element. Use `phrase` if the text is not already inside an inline element. That is particularly useful for problems with parentheses or punctuation. You do not need to write a customization in order for these attribute values to have their effect. They automatically output the correct properties in HTML or XSL-FO for inline text elements. Then it is up to the browser or XSL-FO processor to handle it.

Start and end

When working with a language such as Hebrew or Arabic that reads right to left, you need to pay attention to the XSL-FO `start` and `end` terminology. These designate the two sides of a page, but which side each refers to depends on the writing mode (see the section called "Writing mode" (page 336) for details). The term `start` refers to the side of a page that a sentence starts from. With the default `writing-mode="lr-tb"`, the term `start` refers to the left side. If you set `writing-mode="rl-tb"` (right to left), then `start` means the right side. In each case, `end` means the opposite side, where a sentence ends.

For example, when you set the `body.start.indent` stylesheet parameter to indent paragraphs relative to titles, it inserts a `start-indent` property in the XSL-FO output. That creates an indent on the left by default. But when you use right-to-left writing mode, the indents will be on the right, which is appropriate for those languages.

21

Lists

Lists are an important and useful feature of DocBook. There are several list elements for different purposes. The most often used list elements are these three:

itemizedlist   A list where each item is displayed with a bullet or other symbol, like a ul list in HTML.

orderedlist   A list where each item is numbered sequentially, like a ol list in HTML.

variablelist   A list where each item has a term and an associated description, like a dl list in HTML.

A complete description of all of DocBook's list elements can be found in *DocBook: The Definitive Guide*[1]. This chapter focuses on using parameters and customizations to handle these three primary list types.

List titles

Most DocBook list elements take an optional title element to let you label a list. The title appears before any list items and before any prolog elements that appear at the beginning of a list.

For print output, the title is processed in mode="list.title.mode", with the title as the context node. By default, that mode just calls the template named formal.object.heading with the parent list element as its object parameter. The result is that any list title formats like a figure title (without a number label). But if you want to customize how one kind of list title formats, you can create a template in that mode matching on that list type.

Customizing orderedlist titles for print:
```
<xsl:template match="orderedlist/title" mode="list.title.mode">
  <fo:block font-size="14pt" font-weight="normal"
            xsl:use-attribute-sets="normal.para.spacing">
    <xsl:apply-templates/>
  </fo:block>
</xsl:template>
```

For HTML output, you should copy the formal.object.heading template from html/formal.xsl to your customization layer and modify it as needed. In that template, the context node is the list element, not the title element. You can make the processing conditional on the list type by using an xsl:choose statement as follows:

---

[1] http://docbook.org/tdg/en/html/

```
...
<xsl:choose>
  <xsl:when test="$object/self::orderedlist">
    <!-- processing steps for orderedlist -->
  </xsl:when>
  <xsl:otherwise>
    <!-- processing steps for other formal object headings -->
  </xsl:otherwise>
</xsl:choose>
```

List spacing

The stylesheets provide options for controlling the vertical space before a list and between list items, and for controlling the horizontal spacing of a list and its markers.

List vertical spacing

The spacing between list items in an orderedlist or itemizedlist element can be minimized by the document author by adding a spacing="compact" attribute to the list element. In HTML output, the list will get a compact="compact" attribute on the list start tag to reduce spacing in the browser. In print output, the spacing between items will be determined by the compact.list.item.spacing attribute-set instead of the regular list.item.spacing attribute-set.

In HTML output, to further control vertical spacing, you could create CSS styles such as the following:

Space above a list:
```
div.orderedlist {
  margin-top: 3em;
}
```

Space between list items:
```
div.orderedlist li {
  margin-top: 1em;
}
```

You may want to pay attention to how nested lists are spaced by creating CSS selectors for them as well.

In print output, to control vertical spacing between list items you should customize the attribute-sets named list.item.spacing and compact.list.item.spacing. To customize the vertical space above and below a list, you should customize the attribute-set named list.block.spacing. The latter attribute-set is also used for procedure, substeps, and admonitions such as note.

List horizontal spacing

For HTML output, you can control horizontal spacing for itemizedlist and orderedlist elements using CSS styles. The following are two examples of setting the overall indent for itemizedlists, and the indent of the paragraph relative to the bullet character.

```
div.itemizedlist {
      margin-left: 2em;
}
div.itemizedlist li {
      padding-left: 1em;
}
```

The first style sets the overall left indent of the whole list to 2em. The second style increases the indent of the paragraph relative to the bullet character by 1em.

For print output, you can add a left indent to all lists by adding a `margin-left` attribute to the `list.block.spacing` attribute-set. That indent will be applied to all `itemizedlist`, `orderedlist`, `variablelist`, `procedure`, `substeps`, and admonition elements. If you only want the indent to apply to one type of list, then customize the attribute-set as follows:

```
<xsl:attribute-set name="list.block.spacing">
  <xsl:attribute name="margin-left">
    <xsl:choose>
      <xsl:when test="self::itemizedlist">1in</xsl:when>
      <xsl:otherwise>0pt</xsl:otherwise>
    </xsl:choose>
  </xsl:attribute>
</xsl:attribute-set>
```

When you use this technique, be sure to include an `xsl:otherwise` with some value, or you will generate an empty attribute which will likely produce an error message.

You can also set the indent of the paragraph relative to the bullet or number label. If you want to change the indent globally for all `itemizedlist` elements, then change the stylesheet parameter `itemizedlist.label.width` from its default value of `1.0em`. For `orderedlist` elements, change the `orderedlist.label.width` parameter.

If you want to change an individual list, you can do that using a `dbfo label-width` processing instruction on a list element in your document:

```
<itemizedlist>
<?dbfo label-width="0.25in"?>
  <listitem>
  ...
```

This is useful if you have a very long list and the width of the numbers exceeds the available space. Likewise, when using inherited numbers as described in the section called "Different numbering style" (page 345), you will need more space.

The horizontal spacing of `variablelist` elements is more complex, and is discussed in the section called "variablelist options" (page 347).

itemizedlist options

In addition to controlling the spacing as described in the section called "List spacing" (page 340), you have some control over the bullet character, also known as the mark, as well as print format properties.

Different bullet symbol

The stylesheets provide opportunities for customizing the character sometimes called a bullet used to mark items in an `itemizedlist`. The methods are different for HTML and FO outputs.

If you want to change the mark on any given `itemizedlist`, then set its `mark` attribute to one of the three names that HTML supports. The stylesheets also accept the value `bullet` as equivalent to `disc`, and `box` for `square`. You can change an individual `listitem`'s mark by setting its `override` attribute to one of the names. Unfortunately, HTML does not support the use of arbitrary characters in UL lists.

HTML bullets

In HTML output, the ul element provides the bullet character. When ul lists are nested inside one another, most browsers will change the bullet symbol to indicate nesting. The usual sequence is disc (• solid circle), circle (○ open circle), and square (■ solid square), in that order.

The DocBook HTML stylesheets implement the same sequence for nested lists using the type attribute. The following example shows the output for nested lists:

```
<div class="itemizedlist">
  <ul type="disc">
    <li>
      <p>Level 1</p>
      <div class="itemizedlist">
        <ul type="circle">
          <li>
            <p>Level 2</p>
            <div class="itemizedlist">
              <ul type="square">
                <li>
                  <p>Level 3</p>
                </li>
              </ul>
            </div>
          </li>
        </ul>
      </div>
    </li>
  </ul>
</div>
```

> **Note:**
>
> The HTML attributes described here that control list styles are output only if the stylesheet parameter css.decoration is set to 1 (the default). If it is set to zero, then none of these attributes are output. You may want to do that to control the list styles using a separate CSS stylesheet.

You can change the order of this nesting sequence by customizing a template in common/common.xsl named next.itemsymbol, which looks like the following:

```
<xsl:template name="next.itemsymbol">
  <xsl:param name="itemsymbol" select="'default'"/>
  <xsl:choose>
    <!-- Change this list if you want to change the order of symbols -->
    <xsl:when test="$itemsymbol = 'disc'">circle</xsl:when>
    <xsl:when test="$itemsymbol = 'circle'">square</xsl:when>
    <xsl:otherwise>disc</xsl:otherwise>
  </xsl:choose>
</xsl:template>
```

This template selects the next item symbol name based on the current name in the parameter itemsymbol. The list is circular, so more deeply nested lists repeat the sequence.

You can also manually choose the symbol name for a given list by adding a mark attribute to the list:

```
<itemizedlist mark="square">
```

That will generate a `<ul type="square">` in the HTML output. This will use square bullets for that list, and it will reset the nesting sequence to start on `square` at that point.

You can also override the bullet style for individual list items by adding an `override` attribute:

```
<listitem override="circle">
```

This will override only that list item, and not change the nesting sequence. The HTML output looks like the following:

```
<li style="list-style-type: circle">
```

You may prefer to use CSS to style your lists, rather than put attributes in the HTML. You may want to set the stylesheet parameter `css.decoration` to zero to prevent the hard coded attributes in the HTML. You can use CSS styles as follows:

```
div.itemizedlist ul {
    /* first level */
    list-style-type: square;
}
div.itemizedlist ul div.itemizedlist ul {
    /* second level */
    list-style-type: circle;
}
div.itemizedlist ul div.itemizedlist ul div.itemizedlist ul {
    /* third level */
    list-style-type: disc;
}
```

What about selecting your own bullet character? HTML does not provide a means to do that; it provides only the three named types. But CSS can, if the browsers support newer features of CSS. The following example uses a small graphics image as a list bullet:

```
ul {
    list-style-image: url(bullet.gif);
    list-style-type: disc;
}
```

The `list-style-type` property is included for those browsers that do not support the `list-style-image` property. For a more extensive discussion of CSS and lists, see *CSS Design: Taming Lists*[2].

FO bullets

For print output, the bullet character is the solid black disc, and it is used at all list levels by default. That is because other bullet characters rely on the font having the right glyph, and the XSL-FO processor being able to find the font with that glyph. So the default behavior in FO output is to just indent nested lists and use the same bullet character for all of them.

But you can customize the bullet behavior to use any Unicode character, if your font setup supports it. There are two templates that need to be customized: `next.itemsymbol` and `itemizedlist.label.markup`.

The `next.itemsymbol` template determines which symbol name is used at each nested list level. It is described in the section called "HTML bullets" (page 342). For print output, you can use whatever symbol names you like, as long as they are supported in the second template.

---

[2] http://www.alistapart.com/articles/taminglists/

The `itemizedlist.label.markup` template is what renders each symbol name into FO output. It maps the name to a Unicode character, and if necessary can wrap it in `fo:inline` to select a `font-family` or other property. You can copy the original template from `fo/lists.xsl` to your customization layer and modify it as needed. The following shows what it looks like in version 1.73 of the stylesheets:

```
<xsl:template name="itemizedlist.label.markup">
  <xsl:param name="itemsymbol" select="'disc'"/>
  <xsl:choose>
    <xsl:when test="$itemsymbol='none'"></xsl:when>
    <xsl:when test="$itemsymbol='disc'">&#x2022;</xsl:when>
    <xsl:when test="$itemsymbol='bullet'">&#x2022;</xsl:when>
    <xsl:when test="$itemsymbol='endash'">&#x2013;</xsl:when>
    <xsl:when test="$itemsymbol='emdash'">&#x2014;</xsl:when>
    <!-- Some of these may work in your XSL-FO processor and fonts -->
    <!--
    <xsl:when test="$itemsymbol='square'">&#x25A0;</xsl:when>
    <xsl:when test="$itemsymbol='box'">&#x25A0;</xsl:when>
    <xsl:when test="$itemsymbol='smallblacksquare'">&#x25AA;</xsl:when>
    <xsl:when test="$itemsymbol='circle'">&#x25CB;</xsl:when>
    <xsl:when test="$itemsymbol='opencircle'">&#x25CB;</xsl:when>
    <xsl:when test="$itemsymbol='whitesquare'">&#x25A1;</xsl:when>
    <xsl:when test="$itemsymbol='smallwhitesquare'">&#x25AB;</xsl:when>
    <xsl:when test="$itemsymbol='round'">&#x25CF;</xsl:when>
    <xsl:when test="$itemsymbol='blackcircle'">&#x25CF;</xsl:when>
    <xsl:when test="$itemsymbol='whitebullet'">&#x25E6;</xsl:when>
    <xsl:when test="$itemsymbol='triangle'">&#x2023;</xsl:when>
    <xsl:when test="$itemsymbol='point'">&#x203A;</xsl:when>
    <xsl:when test="$itemsymbol='hand'"><fo:inline
                      font-family="Wingdings 2">A</fo:inline></xsl:when>
    -->
    <xsl:otherwise>&#x2022;</xsl:otherwise>
  </xsl:choose>
</xsl:template>
```

You will notice that most of the choices are commented out by default, because not all systems support all the characters. After you determine which characters work on your system, you can move them out of the comment. Then you can add the symbol name to the `next.itemsymbol` template to use it automatically.

The last example within the comment shows a symbol that requires switching fonts. The character at letter position A in that font is a pointing hand symbol.

Once you have enabled a symbol name in `itemizedlist.label.markup`, you can also use it to set a list style manually using attributes in your document source. The `mark` attribute is used on an `itemizedlist` element to change the bullet for all the items in that list. The `override` attribute is used on a `listitem` element to change the bullet for one item. Examples of both attributes are given in the section called "HTML bullets" (page 342).

Print properties for itemizedlist

For print output, the stylesheet provides a pair of attribute-sets that let you add formatting properties for `itemizedlist` elements.

The `itemizedlist.properties` attribute-set lets you set font properties and side margins for the whole list. It is applied to the `fo:list-block` that contains the output list. As such, its properties do not apply to the optional list title or other child elements before the first `listitem`.

The `itemizedlist.label.properties` attribute-set lets you set font properties for the bullet character. This is useful if you want to change the size or color of the bullet. The attribute-set is applied to each `fo:list-item-label` in the output list.

orderedlist options

In addition to controlling the spacing as described in the section called "List spacing" (page 340), you have control over the list numbering style and starting number, as well as print format properties.

Different numbering style

The stylesheets support list numbering using arabic and roman numerals, as well as uppercase and lowercase letters. If all you want is the numbering style to change for nested `orderedlist` elements, then the stylesheet already handles that. It nests number styles automatically according to the following sequence:

```
1, 2, 3
  a, b, c
    i, ii, iii
      A, B, C
        I, II, III
```

If you want to specify a numbering style for a given `orderedlist`, then add a `numeration` attribute to the list as in the following example:

```
<orderedlist numeration="upperalpha">
  <listitem>
  ...
```

The allowed values for the `numeration` attribute are as follows:

```
arabic
loweralpha
lowerroman
upperalpha
upperroman
arabicindic
```

If you want to change the order in which these styles are used in nested numbered lists, you need to customize the template named `next.numeration` located in `common/common.xsl`. That template takes a `numeration` name as a parameter, and returns the value that should follow at the next level.

The FO stylesheet also supports the `inheritnum="inherit"` attribute on an `orderedlist`. When that attribute is added to an `orderedlist` that is nested inside another `orderedlist`, then the inner list's numbering will inherit the outer `listitem`'s number as a prefix. The following example shows how the attribute is used:

```
<orderedlist>
  <listitem><para>First outer item.</para></listitem>
  <listitem><para>Second outer item.</para>
    <orderedlist inheritnum="inherit">
      <listitem><para>First inner item.</para></listitem>
      <listitem><para>Second inner item.</para></listitem>
      ...
```

This will result in the following print output:

```
1.  First outer item.
2.  Second outer item.
    2.a.  First inner item.
    2.b.  Second inner item.
    ...
```

This inherit feature does *not* work for HTML output, because there is no way to specify such a numbering style in HTML markup. It can be done with CSS, though.

Number continuation

When using orderedlists, there may be situations where you need to continue the numbering from one list to the next, with material intervening between them. The stylesheets support the use of the continuation="continues" attribute on the orderedlist element. When that attribute is added, that list will not start at number 1, but will instead continue from the end of the closest previous orderedlist in the document. The following example shows how to mark up your document:

```
<orderedlist>
  <listitem><para>First item in first list</para></listitem>
  <listitem><para>Second item in first list</para></listitem>
</orderedlist>
(other content)
<orderedlist continuation="continues">
  <listitem><para>First item in continued list</para></listitem>
  <listitem><para>Second item in continued list</para></listitem>
</orderedlist>
```

This will result in the following output:

```
1. First item in first list
2. Second item in first list
(other content)
3. First item in continued list
4. Second item in continued list
```

The continuation feature *does* work in HTML output as well.

List starting number

When using orderedlist, there may be situations where you need to manually set the starting number for a list. You can do that in two different ways:

• With a start processing instruction added inside the orderedlist element, as in the following example:

```
<orderedlist>
  <?dbfo start="8"?><?dbhtml start="8"?>
  <listitem>
    ...
```

If you want consistent numbering in both print and HTML output, you need to add both dbfo and dbhtml processing instructions.

• With an override attribute on the first listitem element, as in the following example:

```
<orderedlist>
  <listitem override="8">
    ...
```

The stylesheet will number the first list item with 8 and continue from there for subsequent list items. This attribute will override a continuation="continues" attribute if there is one on the same list.

Starting in DocBook version 5, the orderedlist element accepts a startingnumber attribute to achieve the same purpose.

Print properties for orderedlist

For print output, the stylesheet provides a pair of attribute-sets that let you add formatting properties to orderedlist elements.

The orderedlist.properties attribute-set lets you set font properties and side margins for the whole list. It is applied to the fo:list-block that contains the output list. As such, its properties do not apply to the optional list title or other child elements before the first listitem.

The orderedlist.label.properties attribute-set lets you set font properties for the item number. This is useful if you want to change the font family, size or color of the number. The attribute-set is applied to each fo:list-item-label in the output list.

variablelist options

The variablelist element is used to present a sequence of terms and their descriptions. Generally, the terms appear on the left, and the descriptions are indented relative to the terms. The amount of indent is the key feature when formatting these lists. The handling of multiple term elements and the methods for print and HTML formatting are described in the next sections.

Multiple term elements

A varlistentry element can contain more than one term element. That's useful when several terms have the same descriptive paragraph. There are two presentation styles to choose from: comma separated terms and stacked terms.

If you want multiple term elements to be set inline and separated by commas, then do nothing because that is the default. The comma and space are actually defined in a stylesheet parameter named variablelist.term.separator. You could customize that parameter if you want to use some other punctuation instead.

If you instead want multiple term elements to stack vertically, then set the stylesheet parameter variablelist.term.break.after to 1 instead of its default value of zero. When set to 1, the stylesheet adds a line break after each term. Unless you want the commas to still show, you should also set the variablelist.term.separator to blank. These parameters apply to both print and HTML output.

Variable list formatting in print

Variable lists present a challenge for formatting because the term hanging out to the left can be of any width. There are several methods for setting the term width, which is effectively the indent width of the listitem paragraphs. Here is the list of methods, with highest priority first.

1. variablelist.as.blocks stylesheet parameter set to nonzero.

2. dbfo list-presentation="blocks" processing instruction in the list.

3. dbfo term-width processing instruction in the list.

4. termlength attribute in the variablelist element.

5. The widths of the `term` elements themselves.

The first two methods put each `varlistentry` into a pair of `fo:blocks` with the term block preceding the list item block. This has the effect of stacking the term above the paragraph, permitting the term to be of any length. The paragraph is indented a small fixed amount. The use of the `variablelist.as.blocks` parameter turns this behavior on globally for all `variablelists`. The processing instruction turns it on for one list. The following is an example.

```
<variablelist>
<?dbfo list-presentation="blocks"?>
  <varlistentry>
    <term>Left button</term>
    <listitem><para>Blah blah</para></listitem>
  </varlistentry>
  ...
</variablelist>
```

Although the `variablelist.as.blocks` parameter is a global setting, you can override it for individual lists with a `<?dbfo list-presentation="list"?>` processing instruction. Then you can also specify a term width.

If the list is not formatted as blocks, then the list is formatted using a `fo:list-block`, which puts the list item text side-by-side with the term. Then the term width can be set by either a processing instruction or an attribute value. Following is an example of that processing instruction.

```
<variablelist>
<?dbfo term-width=".75in"?>
  <varlistentry>
    <term>Left button</term>
    <listitem><para>Blah blah</para></listitem>
  </varlistentry>
  ...
</variablelist>
```

The `term-width` value can be a plain number also, in which case it is assumed to be in em units. The `termlength` attribute of `variablelist` can be set in a similar manner if the processing instruction is not used.

If you do not set a term width with any of the above methods, then the XSL-FO stylesheet counts the characters in all the `term` elements and uses the largest, up to some maximum value. Starting with version 1.62 of the stylesheets, the maximum indent width is controlled by the `variablelist.max.termlength` stylesheet parameter. The default value is 24, roughly 24 character widths. Enter a different integer to change the maximum indent. Any terms that are longer will line wrap. If this default behavior does not produce satisfactory results in a given list, then adjust the indent with one of the methods described above.

Variable list formatting in HTML

Variable lists present a challenge for formatting in HTML because the standard DL list in HTML does not let set the indent width. The DocBook XSL stylesheets support a set of processing instructions (PIs) to enable you to control how a given `variablelist` is formatted in HTML. For HTML output, the list can be put into a two-column HTML TABLE element to control formatting. Following is an annotated example:

```
<variablelist>  ❶
<?dbhtml list-presentation="table"?>  ❷
<?dbhtml term-width="15%"  list-width="85%" ?>   ❸
<?dbhtml term-presentation="bold" ?>   ❹
<?dbhtml term-separator=":" ?>   ❺
<?dbhtml table-summary="mouse buttons described" ?>   ❻
  <varlistentry>
    <term>Left button</term>
    <listitem><para>Blah blah</para></listitem>
  </varlistentry>
  ...
</variablelist>
```

❶ Put the processing instructions somewhere inside the `variablelist` element. You can put them all into one PI, or make separate PIs for each.

❷ This PI enables the formatting PIs to work. It tells the stylesheet to use an HTML `TABLE` instead of a `DL` list for this variable list. If you want to always output tables for variablelists, then you can instead set the stylesheet parameter `variablelist.as.table` to 1. Then you can omit this PI, except when you want to force a particular list to use `DL`, in which case you use `<?dbhtml list-presentation="list" ?>`.

❸ This PI sets the table left column width (`term-width`) and the overall table width (`list-width`). Use percentages for the values. If you omit both, you get the default HTML table formatting.

❹ This PI lets you change the font style for all the terms in a `variablelist`. The choices are `bold`, `italic`, `bold-italic`. In general, such formats should be applied with a CSS stylesheet, but this can be useful for a list that needs different formatting.

❺ This PI lets you add some punctuation or any other text after every term in the list. In this example, each term will be followed by a colon.

❻ You can supply a text string that is put into the HTML table's `summary` attribute.

simplelist options

The `simplelist` element is handy for creating, well, simple lists. It is typically used where you have a collection of one- or two-word items and you just need to list them, such as for a shopping list. The other list types such as `itemizedlist` are too complex for such a simple thing. And a `simplelist` has more options for presentation than the other lists.

A `simplelist` can contain only `member` elements, and a `member` element can contain only text and inline elements. In fact, its content model is identical to the `phrase` element. The following is a short example.

```
<simplelist type="vert" columns="2">
  <member>carrots</member>
  <member>lettuce</member>
  <member>bananas</member>
  <member>potatoes</member>
  <member>cheese</member>
  <member>milk</member>
</simplelist>
```

When you create the `simplelist`, you can specify with the `type` attribute how you want the list presented. The `type` can be:

vert   Format the members in a table, with the sequence running down the columns. The column lengths are balanced to the degree possible. This is the default type if the attribute is not specified. The number of columns can be specified with a `columns` attribute, which defaults to 1. So if you do not set any attributes on the `simplelist` element, you get a single column list.

horiz   Format the members in a table, with the sequence running across the rows. The number of columns can be specified with a `columns` attribute, which defaults to 1. If `columns` is not greater than 1, then each row has a single column and the output reverts to a single-column vertical list.

inline   Format the members inline, in a sequence separated by commas. This type of `simplelist` does not create a line break before and after it, and of all the DocBook list elements, it is the only one that does not. If it appears inside a `para`, then the `simplelist` members flow in the text lines with the other paragraph text. In XSL-FO output, a `simplelist` of this type must be inside a block element or it will generate an error.

Examples of these three types can be seen on the reference page for this element in *DocBook: The Definitive Guide*

http://docbook.org/tdg/en/html/simplelist.html

If you choose one of the tabular layouts, the output table has no additional text formatting, borders between cells, or outer frame. The templates do not provide any parameters or attribute-sets to customize them either. You will have to customize the templates in the `lists.xsl` stylesheet module to change the output. There are separate templates for each of the `type` attribute values.

The default table layout assigns equal proportional column widths to all of the columns in the output table. Proportional columns without an explicit overall table width will expand to take up the full body text measure. If all your entries are short, then they will be widely spread. If you want a narrower listing, you will have to customize the table. This works best if your XSL-FO processor supports `table-layout="auto"`, which lets it measure the widths of cell content to determine the width of columns. The following example works for XEP and Antenna House for `type="vert"`:

Add table-layout="auto" and turn off column settings:
```
<xsl:template match="simplelist[@type='vert']">
  <fo:table table-layout="auto"
            xsl:use-attribute-sets="normal.para.spacing">

    <!-- Remove the call-template name="simplelist.table.columns"
         which sets proportional column widths -->

    <fo:table-body start-indent="0pt" end-indent="0pt">
      <xsl:call-template name="simplelist.vert">
        <xsl:with-param name="cols">
          <xsl:choose>
            <xsl:when test="@columns">
              <xsl:value-of select="@columns"/>
            </xsl:when>
            <xsl:otherwise>1</xsl:otherwise>
          </xsl:choose>
        </xsl:with-param>
      </xsl:call-template>
    </fo:table-body>
  </fo:table>
</xsl:template>
```

Add padding to cells so they do not abutt each other:
```
<xsl:template name="simplelist.vert.row">
  <xsl:param name="cols">1</xsl:param>
  <xsl:param name="rows">1</xsl:param>
  <xsl:param name="cell">1</xsl:param>
  <xsl:param name="members" select="./member"/>
  <xsl:param name="curcol">1</xsl:param>

  <xsl:if test="$curcol &lt;= $cols">
    <fo:table-cell padding-right="8pt" padding-bottom="4pt">
      <fo:block>
        <xsl:if test="$members[position()=$cell]">
          <xsl:apply-templates select="$members[position()=$cell]"/>
        </xsl:if>
      </fo:block>
    </fo:table-cell>
    <xsl:call-template name="simplelist.vert.row">
      <xsl:with-param name="cols" select="$cols"/>
      <xsl:with-param name="rows" select="$rows"/>
      <xsl:with-param name="cell" select="$cell+$rows"/>
      <xsl:with-param name="members" select="$members"/>
      <xsl:with-param name="curcol" select="$curcol+1"/>
    </xsl:call-template>
  </xsl:if>
</xsl:template>
```

This customization will result in all simplelist elements being formatted in closely spaced tabular lists in the output.

If you are using type="inline", then the stylesheet provides one option. You can specify a choice word before the last member to be output. The choice word could be "and" or "or", for example. This indicates to the reader how a choice is to be made, if that is appropriate for the list. You use a processing instruction to set the choice word as follows:

```
<simplelist type="inline">
  <?dbchoice choice="or"?>
  <member>...
```

Whatever text appears in the pseudo attribute value will be output before the last member. As a special case, if the value is "and", it will be automatically translated to the current language because that word is one of the gentext elements already available.

22

Math

DocBook does not have elements to describe mathematics. DocBook does provide two container elements for mathematics: `equation` to format the math as a block (with or without a title), and `inlinequation` to include math within a paragraph or other inline context. You have several alternatives for what you put in the container element:

- Plain text for simple math.

- Capture a representation of the mathematics as a bitmap image.

- Model the mathematics with Scalable Vector Graphics (SVG). This solution is only for output formats that can handle SVG.

- Model the mathematics in TeX if a downstream process can handle TeX.

- Model the mathematics in MathML if a downstream processor can handle MathML.

Plain text math

Some mathematics can be expressed as straight text, using characters from the keyboard and special characters entered as entities. You might think you could put the text in an `inlineequation` element, but its content model does not permit bare text.

Starting with version 4.5 of the DocBook XML DTD, you can use a `mathphrase` element inside an `equation` or `inlineequation` element for plain text math. A `mathphrase` can contain text, `superscript`, `subscript`, and `emphasis`, which is sufficient for simple math expressions. For example:

```
<inlineequation>
  <mathphrase>E = mc<superscript>2</superscript></mathphrase>
</inlineequation>
```

In HTML output, this is output inside a `span class="mathphrase"` container, to which you can assign a CSS style to format it in italics, for example.

In print output, the default behavior does not add any styling to `mathphrase`. If you want it in italics, for example, you could add a customization like the following:

```
<xsl:template match="mathphrase">
   <xsl:call-template name="inline.italicseq"/>
</xsl:template>
```

If you are using DocBook 4.4 or earlier, the only solution seems to be to use `phrase` with a `role="math"` attribute for inline instances. The stylesheets do not apply any special formatting to `phrase` by default, so you would have to create a stylesheet customization if you want special formatting. The following example makes the math italic:

```
<xsl:template match="phrase[@role = 'math']">
  <xsl:call-template name="inline.italicseq"/>
</xsl:template>
```

The math you can display this way is limited to a linear sequence of text and symbols, with `superscript` and `subscript` as the only modifiers.

Graphic math

For complex mathematics that cannot be expressed as linear text, you can use a graphics program to 'draw' the math. You could use bitmap paint application, or a vector graphics application. Then you could save it to one or more graphics file formats for inclusion in a DocBook `mediaobject` element.

The DocBook `equation` element lets you assign a formal `title` to the `mediaobject` it contains. Such formal titles are numbered, and can be included in a List of Equations at the front of a book. The `equation` element also lets you specify an `alt` element, so you can associate a text string with the graphic for sight-impaired readers. The `informalequation` element is similar but does not contain a `title`.

Both `equation` and `informalequation` format the graphic as a separate block. If you need an inline equation, you can use the `inlineequation` element instead. It will embed the graphic equation within a line of text.

The following is an example of a PNG equation file:

```
<equation>
  <title>A Bitmap Equation</title>
  <mediaobject>
    <imageobject>
      <imagedata fileref="math.png" format="PNG"/>
    </imageobject>
  </mediaobject>
</equation>
```

Bitmap files can be used in both HTML and FO output. But small text in bitmap graphics look rough in print. If you drew the math using a vector graphics program, you could save the graphic again to a vector format such as SVG. Since SVG is not supported in all HTML browsers, you may have to include two `imageobject` elements in the `mediaobject` element and use the appropriate one for each output. See Example 18.1, "Multiple graphics in a mediaobject" (page 288).

In HTML output, you can control the spacing and alignment of equations using CSS styles. Each `equation` is wrapped in a `<div class="equation">`, and similarly for `informalequation`, but not for `inlineequation`.

For FO output, the `equation.properties` attribute-set lets you set spacing and alignment on the block that contains an `equation` graphic. There is a similar `informalequation.properties` attribute-set for `informalequation` elements, but no attribute-set for `inlineequation` elements, since they do not need spacing or alignment.

Math in SVG

SVG is another vector graphic format that is gaining support in HTML browsers, and is suitable for print output. See the section called "SVG images" (page 300) for more information. Most XSL-FO processors support SVG and can produce high quality typesetting of mathematics. At this time, though, only a few HTML browsers support SVG directly, but a SVG browser plugin is available. You still may need to provide a bitmap version for those users without the plugin.

MathML

MathML is a W3C markup language for mathematics *http://www.w3.org/Math/*. The DocBook XSL stylesheets cannot format MathML content, but it will pass the markup through so that a downstream processor can format it. For XSL-FO output, the Antenna House XSL Formatter with the optional MathML module can handle MathML markup.

For HTML output, the W3C describes in their document *Putting Mathematics on the Web with MathML*[1] how browsers can handle MathML. For example, the document describes how the W3C makes available an XSL stylesheet that you can attach to an XHTML file that will render MathML markup that is embedded in the XHTML file. This method assumes a browser can apply an XSL stylesheet, and not all do so. Browsers are beginning to add native support for MathML. Mozilla Firefox can format MathML embedded in XHTML files. You might need to use a .xhtml filename extension for the output if you are browsing files locally.

Because not all browsers and XSL-FO processors support MathML yet, some people choose to convert their MathML to graphics format for publication. There are several commercial MathML editors that can generate SVG and other graphics formats. The open source SVGMath software, written in Python, can convert a subset of MathML to SVG. You can download it from *http://www.grigoriev.ru/svgmath/*.

Including MathML in DocBook source files can be tricky because the element names are not in the DocBook DTD. Also, MathML has its own set of character entities such as ⁢ that are defined in the MathML DTD that are not in the DocBook DTD. You can fix these problems by including the MathML DTD into your DocBook DTD. You can use a DTD customization layer for the DocBook DTD to do this, or, as the following example shows, you can do it in the DOCTYPE declaration of each document. Which method you use depends on how much math you use. do not try to do both.

```
<?xml version="1.0" encoding="utf-8"?>
<!DOCTYPE book PUBLIC "-//OASIS//DTD DocBook XML V4.5//EN"
                 "http://www.oasis-open.org/docbook/xml/4.5/docbookx.dtd"
[
<!ENTITY % MATHML.prefixed "INCLUDE">
<!ENTITY % MATHML.prefix "mml">
<!ENTITY % equation.content "(alt?, (graphic+|mediaobject+|mml:math))">
<!ENTITY % inlineequation.content
             "(alt?, (inlinegraphic+|inlinemediaobject+|mml:math))">
<!ENTITY % mathml PUBLIC "-//W3C//DTD MathML 2.0//EN"
        "http://www.w3.org/Math/DTD/mathml2/mathml2.dtd">
%mathml;
]>
<book>
...
```

The above example also shows how you can add MathML elements to the model for the DocBook equation and inlineequation elements by enhancing the equation.content and inlineequation.content parameter entities,

---

respectively, in the DocBook DTD. It copies the parameter entity declarations from the DocBook DTD and extends them. Then you can put your math in DocBook documents like the following:

```
<equation>
<title>My MathML example</title>
<mml:math>
  <mml:mrow>
    <mml:mo>&sum;</mml:mo>
    <mml:mn>4</mml:mn>
    <mml:mo>+</mml:mo>
    <mml:mi>x</mml:mi>
  </mml:mrow>
</mml:math>
</equation>
```

It is important to keep the MathML element names in a separate namespace from the DocBook elements or confusion will reign. When you process a file like this to FO or XHTML, the MathML output elements will still have a namespace prefix on them. If you process to HTML, however, they will not have a namespace prefix. Browsers that do not recognize the MathML elements will ignore the tags and show the characters, but as an unformatted line.

You can also put MathML markup in a separate file. This can help reduce clutter in your DocBook document, since some MathML can be quite long. If you want to be able to validate it, you need to include the MathML DOCTYPE declaration in the separate file:

```
<?xml version="1.0" encoding="utf-8"?>
<!DOCTYPE mml:math PUBLIC "-//W3C//DTD MathML 2.0//EN"
        "http://www.w3.org/Math/DTD/mathml2/mathml2.dtd" [
<!ENTITY % MATHML.prefixed "INCLUDE">
<!ENTITY % MATHML.prefix "mml">
]>
<mml:math xmlns:mml="http://www.w3.org/1998/Math/MathML" id="mymath">
  <mml:mrow>
  ...
  </mml:mrow>
</mml:math>
```

However, once you add a DOCTYPE declaration, you can no longer use a system entity reference to pull in the math content into your DocBook document. Instead, use XInclude, which is described in the section called "Using XInclude" (page 359). You put an XInclude element inside your DocBook document where you want the math to appear:

```
<equation>
  <xi:include href="math.xml" xmlns:xi="http://www.w3.org/2001/XInclude" />
</equation>
```

You'll still need to include the MathML DTD in your DocBook DTD or DOCTYPE declaration, or the document will not validate after the content is pulled in.

Equation numbering

DocBook provides the `equation` element as a wrapper for math if you want to add a title and number to each math example. The default format is similar to numbered tables and figures, as in the following example:

Equation 22.1. Mass Energy Equivalence

$E = mc^2$

You can modify the generated text for the equation number and title by changing the appropriate gentext template. See the section called "Generated text" (page 105) for details on gentext customization. In the English locale file common/en.xml, the equation gentext template looks like the following:

```
<l:context name="title">
  ...
  <l:template name="equation" text="Equation %n. %t"/>
```

Some publications call for a different way of formatting numbered equations, where the title is omitted and the number appears to the left or right of the equation. For example:

$$E = mc^2 \qquad\qquad (3.1)$$

The stylesheets do not have a parameter to select this format, but it can be accomplished with a customization of the stylesheet template for equation. Here is such a customization that works for print output:

```
<xsl:template match="equation">
  <fo:table width="100%" table-layout="fixed">
    <xsl:attribute name="id">
      <xsl:call-template name="object.id"/>
    </xsl:attribute>
    <fo:table-column column-width="90%"/>
    <fo:table-column column-width="10%"/>
    <fo:table-body start-indent="0pt" end-indent="0pt">
      <fo:table-row>
        <fo:table-cell text-align="center">
          <fo:block>
            <xsl:apply-templates/>
          </fo:block>
        </fo:table-cell>
        <fo:table-cell text-align="right" display-align="center">
          <fo:block>
            <xsl:text>(</xsl:text>
            <xsl:apply-templates select="." mode="label.markup"/>
            <xsl:text>)</xsl:text>
          </fo:block>
        </fo:table-cell>
      </fo:table-row>
    </fo:table-body>
  </fo:table>
</xsl:template>
```

It wraps the equation content in a one-row, two-column table, with the content in the left column and the equation number in the right column. The number is generated by processing the equation element in mode="label.markup". You can change the table column order and alignment if you want the number on the left instead. Any title is ignored, although title is optional in the equation element.

23

Modular DocBook files

Modular DocBook means your content collection is broken up into smaller file modules that are recombined for publication. The advantages of modular documentation include:

- Reusable content units.

- Smaller file units to load into an editing program.

- Distributed authoring.

- Finer grain version control.

The best tools for modular documentation are XIncludes and olinks. XIncludes replace the old way of doing modular files using system entities. System entities were always a problem because they cannot have a DOCTYPE declaration, and therefore cannot be valid documents on their own. This creates problems when you try to load a system entity file into a structured editor that expects to be able to validate the document. With the introduction of the XInclude feature of XML, the modular files can be valid mini documents, complete with DOCTYPE declaration. Conveniently, the module's DOCTYPE does not generate an error when its content is pulled in using the XInclude mechanism.

Olinks enable you to form cross references among your modular files. If you try to use xref or link to cross reference to another file module, then your mini document is no longer valid. That is because those elements use an IDREF-type attribute to form the link, and the ID it points to must be in the same document. They will be together when you assemble your modules into a larger document, but the individual mini documents will be incomplete. When you try to open such a module in a structured editor, it will complain that the document is not valid. Olinks get around this problem by not using IDREF attributes to form the cross reference. Olinks are resolved by the stylesheet at runtime, whether you are processing a single module or the assembled document. See Chapter 24, *Olinking between documents* (page 383) for general information about using olinks, and the section called "Modular cross referencing" (page 369) for using olinks with modular files.

Using XInclude

You can divide your content up into many individual valid file modules, and use XInclude to assemble them into larger valid documents. For example, you could put each chapter of a book into a separate chapter document file for writing and editing. Then you can assemble the chapters into a book for processing and publication.

Here is an annotated example of a chapter file, and a book file that includes the chapter file.

Chapter file intro.xml:
```
<?xml version="1.0"?>
<!DOCTYPE chapter PUBLIC "-//OASIS//DTD DocBook XML V4.5//EN"
                  "http://www.oasis-open.org/docbook/xml/4.5/docbookx.dtd"> ❶
<chapter id="intro"> ❷
<title>Getting Started</title>
<section id="Installing">
...
</chapter>
```

Book file:
```
<?xml version="1.0"?>
<!DOCTYPE book PUBLIC "-//OASIS//DTD DocBook XML V4.5//EN"
                  "http://www.oasis-open.org/docbook/xml/4.5/docbookx.dtd"> ❸
<book>
<title>User Guide</title>
<xi:include ❹
    xmlns:xi="http://www.w3.org/2001/XInclude"❺  href="intro.xml"❻ />
...
</book>
```

❶   The chapter file has a complete DOCTYPE declaration that identifies the mini document as a `chapter`.
❷   Unless otherwise specified, an XInclude gets the root element and all of its children.
❸   The book file also has a DOCTYPE declaration, which says this document is a `book`.
❹   The syntax for the inclusion is an empty element whose name is `include`, with the name augmented with a namespace prefix `xi:`.
❺   The namespace declaration for XInclude. The URI in quotes must exactly match this string for it to work. But the namespace prefix `xi:` can be any name, as long as it matches what is used on the `include` element.
❻   The `href` contains a URI that points to the file you want to include. If no `xpointer` attribute is added, then it will pull in the whole file starting with its root element.

When the XInclude is resolved during the processing, the `<xi:include>` element will be replaced by the included `chapter` element and all of its children. It is the author's responsibility to make sure the included content is valid in the location where it is pulled in.

> **Note:**
>
> In one of the draft XInclude standards, the namespace URI was changed to use 2003 instead of 2001 in the name, but it was changed back to 2001 for the final standard. Some XInclude processors may not have caught the change. For example Xerces version 2.6.2 expects the XInclude namespace to use the incorrect 2003 value. Later versions work with 2001 in the namespace.

Here are some other nifty features of XInclude:

- You can nest XIncludes. That means an included file can contain XIncludes to further modularize the content. This might be useful when keeping a collection of section modules that can be assembled into several different versions of a chapter. Then the chapter file is included in the larger book file.

- The `href` value in an XInclude can be an absolute path, a relative path, an HTTP URL that accesses a web server, or any other URI. As such, it can be mapped with XML catalog entries, as described in the section called "XIncludes and XML catalogs" (page 364). A relative path is taken as relative to the document that contains the XInclude element (the including document). That is true for each of any nested includes as well, even when they are in different directories.

- You can select parts of an included document instead of the whole content. See the section called "Selecting part of a file" (page 361) for more information.

- You can include parts of the *including* document in order to repeat part of its content in the same document, if you do it carefully. When you omit the `href` attribute, and add an `xpointer` attribute, then it is interpreted as selecting from the current document. You cannot select the whole document or that part of the document that has the XInclude element, because that would be a circular reference. You also do not want to repeat content that has any `id` attributes, because duplicate id values are invalid.

- A document's root element can be an XInclude element. In that case, there can be only one, since a well-formed document can only have a single root element. Likewise, the included content must resolve to a single element, with its children.

Selecting part of a file

The XInclude standard permits you to select part of a file for inclusion instead of the whole file. That is something that *system entities* were never able to do. In a modular source setup, that means you do not have to break out into a separate file every single piece of text that you want to include somewhere. You can organize your modules into logical units for writing and editing, and the select from within a file if you need just a piece of a module.

The simplest syntax just has an id value in an `xpointer` attribute. The following is an example.

```
<xi:include
      href="intro.xml"
      xpointer="Installing"
      xmlns:xi="http://www.w3.org/2001/XInclude" />
```

If the following chapter file is named `intro.xml`, then this XInclude will select the `section` element because it has `id="Installing"`:

```
<?xml version="1.0"?>
<!DOCTYPE chapter PUBLIC "-//OASIS//DTD DocBook XML V4.5//EN"
                 "http://www.oasis-open.org/docbook/xml/4.5/docbookx.dtd">
<chapter id="intro">
<title>Getting Started</title>
<section id="Installing">
  <title>Running the installation</title>
  ...
</section>
</chapter>
```

For selections based on id, the included document must have a DOCTYPE declaration that correctly points to the DocBook DTD. It is the DTD that declares that `id` attributes are of the ID type (the name `id` is not sufficient). If the file does not have the DOCTYPE or if the DTD cannot be opened, then such references will not resolve.

> **Note:**
>
> Earlier draft versions of the XInclude standard used a URI fragment syntax to select part of a document, as in `href="intro.xml#Installing"`. That syntax is no longer supported. Now the `href` must point to a file, and you must use an `xpointer` attribute to select part of it.

More complex selections can be made using the full XPointer syntax. Several XPointer *schemes* are defined, not all of which are supported by every XInclude processor. Each scheme has a fixed name followed in parentheses by an expression appropriate to that scheme. The following are several examples that are supported by the xsltproc processor.

```
xpointer="element(Installing)"
xpointer="xpointer(id('Installing'))"
```
These two examples of the schemes named `element()` and `xpointer()` are equivalent to `xpointer="Installing"`. They all select a single element with an `id` attribute. Be careful not to confuse the `xpointer` attribute with the `xpointer()` scheme name (see the Note below).

```
xpointer="element(/1/3/2)"
```
This example selects the second child of the third child of the root element of the included document. For example, an included document could consist of a book root element, which contains only `chapter` elements that contain only `section` elements. This inclusion takes the second section of the third chapter of the book. The `element()` scheme always selects a single element for inclusion.

```
xpointer="element(Installing/2)"
```
This example selects the second child of the element that has `id="Installing"` in the included document. With the `element()` scheme, you cannot refer to elements by element name, only by position number or id.

```
xpointer="xpointer(/book/chapter[3]/*)"
```
The `xpointer()` scheme uses a subset of XPath in its expressions. In this case, it selects all of the child elements of the third chapter in the book, but it does not include the `chapter` element itself. The `xpointer()` scheme can select more than one element to be included.

Note:

Not all processors support all XPointer syntax in XIncludes. One confusing aspect of the XInclude standard is the use of the term *xpointer*. The standard specifies an `xpointer` attribute that supports several *schemes* for selecting content. The `element()` scheme shown above is one example. Another scheme is named `xpointer()`, hence the confusion. The `xpointer()` scheme includes a variant on the XPath language for selecting content, but it never went past the Working Draft stage. While all XInclude processors support the `xpointer` attribute, only xsltproc supports part of the `xpointer()` scheme. Check the documentation of your processor to see what parts of XInclude it supports.

Including plain text

You can use XInclude to include plain text files as examples in your DocBook document. The XInclude element permits a `parse="text"` attribute that tells the XInclude processor to treat the incoming content as plain text instead of the default XML. To ensure that it is treated as text, any characters in the included content that are special to XML are converted to their respective entities:

```
&    becomes    &amp;
<    becomes    &lt;
>    becomes    &gt;
"    becomes    &quot;
```

All you need to do is point the `href` attribute to the filename, and add the `parse="text"` attribute:

```
<programlisting><xi:include  href="codesample.c"  parse="text"
     xmlns:xi="http://www.w3.org/2001/XInclude" /></programlisting>
```

If you forget the `parse="text"` attribute, you will get validation errors if the included text has any of the XML special characters.

Since the included text is not XML, you cannot use an `xpointer` attribute with XPointer syntax to select part of it. You can only select the entire file's content.

But you can specify the encoding of the incoming text by adding an `encoding` attribute to the XInclude element. In general a processor cannot detect what encoding is used in a text file, so be sure to indicate the encoding if it is not

UTF-8. The `encoding` attribute is not permitted when `parse="xml"`, because the XML prolog already indicates the encoding of an XML file.

XInclude fallback

An XInclude can contain some fallback content. This permits processing to continue if an include cannot be resolved, maybe because the file does not exist or because of download problems. To use the fallback mechanism, instead of an empty `xi:include` element you put a single `xi:fallback` child element in it. The content of the child is used if the XInclude cannot be resolved at run time.

```
<xi:include  href="intro.xml" xmlns:xi="http://www.w3.org/2001/XInclude">
  <xi:fallback>
    <para><emphasis>FIXME:  MISSING XINCLUDE CONTENT</emphasis></para>
  </xi:fallback>
</xi:include>
```

The fallback content must be equally valid when inserted into the document for it to work. In fact, the `xi:fallback` element can contain another `xi:include`, which the processor will try to resolve as a secondary resource. The secondary include can also contain a secondary fallback, and so on.

Keep in mind that processing of the document does not stop when an XInclude cannot be resolved and it has a fallback child, even if that child is empty. If you want your processing to always continue regardless of how the includes resolve, then add a fallback element to all of your XInclude elements. If, on the other hand, your XIncludes must be resolved, then do not use fallback elements on the innermost includes and let the processing fail.

XIncludes and entities for filenames

Although XIncludes are intended to replace SYSTEM entities, it is still possible to use regular entities with XInclude. You can declare regular entities for filenames in a file's DOCTYPE declaration, and then use an entity reference in the `href` attribute of an XInclude element. That let's you declare all the pathname information at the top of the file, where it can be more easily managed than scattered throughout the file in various includes. The example above could be reworked in the following way:

```
<!DOCTYPE book PUBLIC "-//OASIS//DTD DocBook XML V4.5//EN"
                "http://www.oasis-open.org/docbook/xml/4.5/docbookx.dtd" [
<!ENTITY intro            "part1/intro.xml">
<!ENTITY basics           "part1/getting_started.xml">
<!ENTITY config           "admin/configuring_the_server.xml">
<!ENTITY advanced         "admin/advanced_user_moves.xml">
]>
<book>
<title>User Guide</title>
<para>This guide shows you how to use the software.</para>
<xi:include  href="&intro;"    xmlns:xi="http://www.w3.org/2001/XInclude"/>
<xi:include  href="&basics;"   xmlns:xi="http://www.w3.org/2001/XInclude"/>
<xi:include  href="&config;"   xmlns:xi="http://www.w3.org/2001/XInclude"/>
<xi:include  href="&advanced;" xmlns:xi="http://www.w3.org/2001/XInclude"/>
...
</book>
```

You could also declare all the entities in a central file, and then use a parameter system entity to pull the declarations into all of your documents. See the section called "Shared text entities" (page 373) for an example.

XIncludes and XML catalogs

Since the `href` attribute of an XInclude element contains a URI, it can be remapped with an XML catalog. That setup would let you enter somewhat generic references in your XIncludes, and then let the catalog resolve them to specific locations on a given system. See Chapter 5, *XML catalogs* (page 47) for more information on setting up catalogs.

For example, the following XIncludes use mythical pathnames that do not exist in the file system as they are written.

Example 23.1. XInclude and XML catalog

```
<!DOCTYPE book PUBLIC "-//OASIS//DTD DocBook XML V4.5//EN"
                    "http://www.oasis-open.org/docbook/xml/4.5/docbookx.dtd"
<book>
<title>User Guide</title>
<para>This guide shows you how to use the software.</para>
<xi:include  href="file:///basics/intro.xml"
             xmlns:xi="http://www.w3.org/2001/XInclude" />
<xi:include  href="file:///basics/getting_started.xml"
             xmlns:xi="http://www.w3.org/2001/XInclude" />
<xi:include  href="file:///admin/configuring_the_server.xml"
             "xmlns:xi="http://www.w3.org/2001/XInclude" />
<xi:include  href="file:///user/advanced_user_moves.xml"
             xmlns:xi="http://www.w3.org/2001/XInclude" />
...
</book>
```

This XML catalog can be used to map these mythical pathnames to real file locations on either the local system or a remote system using a URL.

```
<?xml version="1.0"?>
<!DOCTYPE catalog
   PUBLIC "-//OASIS/DTD Entity Resolution XML Catalog V1.0//EN"
   "http://www.oasis-open.org/committees/entity/release/1.0/catalog.dtd">

<catalog xmlns="urn:oasis:names:tc:entity:xmlns:xml:catalog">
  <rewriteURI
    uriStartString="file:///basics/"
    rewritePrefix="file:///usr/share/docsource/modules/IntroMaterial/" />
  <rewriteURI
    uriStartString="file:///admin/"
    rewritePrefix="http://myhost.mydomain.net:1482/library/administration/" />
  <rewriteURI
    uriStartString="file:///user/"
    rewritePrefix="http://myhost.mydomain.net:1482/cgi-bin/getmodule?" />

</catalog>
```

The resource being included could even be the output of a CGI request, as in the last example above. The `href` value would resolve in the catalog to `http://myhost.mydomain.net:1482/cgi-bin/getmodule?advanced_user_moves.xml`. Here `getmodule` could be a CGI script that pulls content from a database or version control system based on the query string submitted. Of course, processing a file that includes such content from the network relies on the resource being available at the time of processing.

XIncludes and directories

Once you break your content up into modules, you may find it desirable to create a hierarchy of directories to organize the modules. You no longer have to organize the source files according to the content flow in a publication. Rather, you are free to organize the modules on your file system in any way that facilitates the management of the content, such as by chapter, subject matter, user level, author, or whatever. Your publications can use XInclude to pick and choose from among your directory hierarchy to assemble the content.

An XIncluded file can contain other XIncludes, which allows you to create a nested hierarchy of XIncludes to build a publication. They can be nested to whatever depth is necessary. The nesting of XIncludes can be completely independent of the nesting of directories. When the master document is assembled by the parser, each sequence of XIncludes is followed through the directory hierarchy to locate the content.

The `href` in an XInclude can be either an absolute URI or a relative URI. Absolute URIs are unambiguous, but not very portable. That is, if you move the content to another machine that has a different base location, all of the addresses will be wrong. But absolute URIs can be made portable by using an XML catalog as described in the previous section. The catalog can map the absolute URIs in the `hrefs` to a different location on the new system.

If you use relative URIs in your XInclude `hrefs`, each path is taken relative to the location of the document that contains the XInclude. So each module only has to keep track of its own XIncludes, and does not have to worry about how it might be used elsewhere in the hierarchy. This means you can process an individual module for testing from its own location, and its XIncludes will work. And it means when you process the module as referenced from another XInclude, its own XIncludes will still work. This is how a modular system should work, and it does.

Relative URIs can use the ".." syntax to indicate a parent or higher directory. The following example will XInclude a file that is located two directory levels up and one level down relative to the current file's location:

```
<xi:include  href="../../userguide/chapter2.xml"
             xmlns:xi="http://www.w3.org/2001/XInclude" />
```

Relative paths work best when they are kept simple. A complicated path like the preceding example indicates how flexible XIncludes can be, but do not get carried away. Remember, you have to maintain these files. If you decide to rearrange your directory hierarchy, you could end up having to fix a lot of XIncludes. You might be better off using an XML catalog with absolute URIs that the catalog can resolve. Then if you rearrange your directories, you just need to rewrite your catalog file.

XIncludes and graphics files

The previous section describes how XIncludes with relative URIs are resolved relative to the current file. The XInclude processor can do that because it fully recognizes each XInclude element from its unique namespace attribute.

But what about relative graphics file references? An XInclude-aware parser does not automatically know that the `fileref` attribute in an `imagedata` element is a path that needs to be resolved relative to the current file's location. It is the stylesheet's responsibility to do that. Fortunately, the XInclude standard helps the stylesheet do that automatically by requiring the XInclude processor to insert `xml:base` attributes when needed.

Here is how it works:

1. When the XInclude processor encounters an XInclude element, it replaces the XInclude element with the content pulled from the other file.

2. As it is copying the root element from the included content, it will add an `xml:base` attribute to that included root element if its directory differs from the location of the current file. The `xml:base` value indicates the location

of the XIncluded file. Any XIncluded file from the same directory as the current file does not need an `xml:base` attribute.

3. When the XSL stylesheet processes the document with all of its XIncludes resolved, the stylesheet uses the `xml:base` attributes to help resolve any relative paths in a graphic element's `fileref`. It does that by scanning back through the graphic's ancestor elements to find an `xml:base` attribute. The stylesheet then prepends that to the `fileref` path.

4. If you have used nested XIncludes in different directories, the stylesheet will continue tracing backwards through the graphic element's ancestors, looking for `xml:base` attributes. The stylesheet combines them into one final path for the `fileref`, which ends up being the path from the master document to the graphics file.

If a `fileref` is an absolute URI, then it is used as it is written, and `xml:base` attributes are not added to it. If for some reason you want all of your `fileref` attributes to be left "as is", then set the stylesheet parameter `keep.relative.image.uris` to 1. The default value is 0 in XSL-FO output, and 1 in HTML output.

To summarize:

- A `fileref` or an `entityref` containing an absolute path is always copied without change.

- An `entityref` containing a relative path is interpreted as relative to the file declaring the entity, without regard to any `xml:base` attributes.

- A relative `fileref` processed without using XInclude is always copied without change.

- A relative `fileref` processed with XInclude and with the parameter `keep.relative.image.uris="0"` is changed to account for any `xml:base` attributes (this is the default setting for print output).

- A relative `fileref` processed with XInclude and with `keep.relative.image.uris="1"` is always copied without change (this is the default setting for HTML output).

XIncludes and external code files

The `xml:base` attributes are also used to resolve relative paths in `fileref` attributes in `textobject` elements. See the section called "External code files" (page 443) for an example.

Entity references in included text

You might be wondering what happens to any entity references that appear in the included content. An entity reference such as `&companyname;` must have an entity declaration in the DTD to be resolved. If your entities are all declared in an extension to the external DocBook DTD, then your main document and the modules that use that DTD will all share the same entity declarations and there is no problem.

But what if you declare an entity in the DOCTYPE of your included file? Does the declaration go along with the included content? The answer is basically yes, with some caveats.

- If your main document has a DOCTYPE declaration at the top, then any entity declarations needed for the included content are copied to that DOCTYPE from the included file.

- If the DOCTYPE in the main document already has an entity declaration for that name, then the declaration in the included file must match it, or else an error will be generated. There is no overriding or substitution of entity values when using XIncludes.

- If there are any entity references in the included content that are not declared in the included file, then the include will fail. In other words, you cannot rely on the entity declarations in the main document to expand entity references in the included text. The text in the included document is parsed before it is included, and any entity references must resolve there.

See the section called "Shared text entities" (page 373) for a good strategy on managing entities in a modular doc setup.

XIncludes in XML editors

XIncludes are a fairly recent addition to the set of XML standards, so XIncludes are not uniformly supported in XML editing software. Certainly any XML editor can create and edit the modular XML files that go into a modular doc set. But an XML editor can go beyond that basic function and help you build those modules into complete documents.

As of early 2007, here is a summary of what some XML editors provide:

- Serna from Syntext, Inc. has extensive support for XIncludes. This graphical editor provides menu options for inserting an XInclude, converting selected content into an XInclude, and converting an XInclude to local content. Even better, it formats and displays the XIncluded content inline in editable form, with the boundaries marked by icons. If you make changes to the content between the icons, the editor writes the changes out to the included file.

- Arbortext Editor from PTC also has extensive support for XIncludes. You can insert an XInclude that will be validated in context, edit the content inline, and save the changes back to the XIncluded file.

- XXE from XMLmind recognizes XIncludes and displays the content inline. The included content is not editable inline, but you can use a menu option to open the included document in another window for editing.

- Oxygen from SyncRO Soft Ltd is an XML code editor that can recognize XIncludes. It supports validation of the master file and also the validation of the individual include files. However, it will not validate the master document with all XIncludes resolved.

- XMetal from JustSystems, Inc. has no direct support for XIncludes, but it has extensive customization features that support modular content reuse.

Validating with XIncludes

The major advantage of XIncludes is that they let you create modular files that can be individually validated. But there is a small problem. The xi:include element itself is not a valid DocBook element, so the master document will not validate. The usual way around this is to resolve the includes before validating. That replaces the nonvalid xi:include with the DocBook content it references, which should be valid when it is inserted. It is also possible to customize the DTD to permit validation before resolution of xincludes.

The **xmllint** utility that is included with the **xsltproc** toolkit can be used to resolve XIncludes and validate XML documents without modifying the DocBook DTD. It has an --xinclude option that resolves XIncludes, and a --postvalid option that validates *after* the includes are resolved. You should also add the --noent ("no entities") option so that all system entities are resolved before validating. So to validate a book document that has XIncludes for its chapters, you could use this command:

```
xmllint --noout --xinclude --postvalid --noent book.xml
```

The effect of this command is to replace each xi:include element with its content, and then validate the result. The validation process never sees the xi:include element, so there is no conflict with the DTD. The --noout option suppresses the normal output of **xmllint**, which is the complete XML content, so that it only reports validation errors. You can omit the --noout option if you want to examine the resolved document.

For Java, the Xerces-J parser (version 2.5.0 and later) will resolve XIncludes. It can validate the including and included files separately, but it cannot validate the merged content in one step. So validation with Xerces requires adding the xi:include element to the DocBook DTD to avoid validation errors, as described in the next section. To validate the assembled document, you will need to resolve the XIncludes into a temporary file, and then validate the temporary file. See the section called "Java processors and XIncludes" (page 375) for information on what is available.

Even if you resolve your XIncludes, you may still run into a problem with xml:base attributes that are inserted into the resolved document in some circumstances. See the section called "Adding xml:base to the DTD" (page 369) for more information.

DTD customizations for XIncludes

There are situations with modular documentation files where you would rather not have to resolve your XIncludes before validating. That is, you would like to be able to validate a file that has an xi:include element. Also, other tools may not resolve XIncludes. For example, if you load the master book document into a validating editor, then it will complain about the xi:include elements.

Adding XInclude to the DTD

You might think you could just add the xi:include element to the DocBook DTD. But declaring the element is not enough. It has to be added into content models of elements as it would appear in documents. But since an XInclude can replace many combinations of elements, trying to cover all possible uses of XInclude would make the content models in the DTD hopelessly complex.

But if you are willing to limit where you put XIncludes in your document, then you can create a DTD customization to support your usage. You have to declare the XInclude elements and then add them to the content models of certain elements. The following is an example that lets you create XIncludes that contain chapters, appendixes, and other immediate children of the book element, a fairly typical use of XIncludes. First you create a system entity (a file) that contains your DTD modifications, such as the following.

Example 23.2. DTD customization for XIncludes

```
<!ELEMENT xi:include (xi:fallback?) >
<!ATTLIST xi:include
    xmlns:xi    CDATA        #FIXED    "http://www.w3.org/2001/XInclude"
    href        CDATA        #IMPLIED
    parse       (xml|text)   "xml"
    xpointer    CDATA        #IMPLIED
    encoding    CDATA        #IMPLIED
    accept      CDATA        #IMPLIED
    accept-language CDATA    #IMPLIED >

<!ELEMENT xi:fallback ANY>
<!ATTLIST xi:fallback
    xmlns:xi    CDATA    #FIXED    "http://www.w3.org/2001/XInclude" >

<!ENTITY % local.chapter.class "| xi:include">
```

All lines but the last declare the xi:include and xi:fallback elements and their attributes. Those declarations make the elements available, but do not put them in any content models. The last line adds the xi:include element to the local.chapter.class parameter entity (be sure to include the pipe symbol). That entity is used in the DocBook DTD to extend the list of elements permitted as children of book. So wherever you could put a chapter element, now you can put an xi:include element that points to a file that contains a chapter. The following shows some other possibilities for placement of XIncludes.

```
<!-- inside chapter or section elements -->
<!ENTITY % local.divcomponent.mix "| xi:include">
<!-- inside para, programlisting, literallayout, etc. -->
<!ENTITY % local.para.char.mix "| xi:include">
<!-- inside bookinfo, chapterinfo, etc. -->
<!ENTITY % local.info.class "| xi:include">
```

Now these DTD extensions need to be made available to your documents. You can do that with a customization layer for the DocBook DTD, or you can add them to the internal DTD subset in each file. For example, if you put the above content in a file named xinclude.mod, you can reference that DTD module as follows:

```
<!DOCTYPE book SYSTEM "docbookx.dtd" [
<!ENTITY % xinclude SYSTEM "xinclude.mod">
%xinclude;
]>
<book>
<title>User's Guide</title>
<xi:include  href="intro.xml" xmlns:xi="http://www.w3.org/2001/XInclude"  />
...
```

This declares a system entity and then references the system entity with %xinclude; in the internal subset of the DTD. With these changes in place, the document can be validated without resolving its XIncludes, as long as they fit the DTD changes you have specified.

Adding xml:base to the DTD

If you are using DocBook DTD version 4.2 or earlier, you may get validation errors *after* resolving your XIncludes, from xml:base attributes. When an included file is in a directory that is different from the including file's directory, the XInclude processor inserts an xml:base attribute in its containing element. This attribute enables any relative file references in the included file to be resolved relative to the included file, rather than relative to the including document. Because xml:base was only added starting in version 4.3 of the DocBook DTD, this generates a validation error for documents written to earlier versions of the DTD. If you use a customized DTD, you could add it yourself to the local.common.attrib parameter entity in the DTD as follows:

```
<!ENTITY % local.common.attrib  "xml:base  CDATA  #IMPLIED">
```

Or you could put this in the DOCTYPE declaration for documents that have this problem:

```
<!DOCTYPE book PUBLIC "-//OASIS//DTD DocBook XML V4.2//EN"
    "http://www.oasis-open.org/docbook/xml/4.2/docbookx.dtd" [
<!ENTITY % local.common.attrib "xml:base  CDATA  #IMPLIED">
]>
```

This DTD extension to version 4.2 permits the xml:base attribute in almost all elements in DocBook, so validation will succeed. This DTD extension will have to be removed when you upgrade to DocBook version 4.3 or later which supports it natively.

Modular cross referencing

Olinks permit you to form cross references among your modules without generating validation errors when you edit or process your modules individually. Olinks are described more completely in Chapter 24, *Olinking between documents* (page 383). This section describes the specifics of using olinks with modular DocBook files.

Without olinks, authors are forced to put all of the content that they want to cross reference among into one huge document, such as a `set`. To avoid validation errors, such authors would always have to edit or process the entire set each time.

With olinks, you have control over the size of the documents you produce from your collection of modules. For example, you may decide that you generally produce books, so you will be cross referencing among your books. Or you might be producing individual articles, and you need to be able to reference other articles.

Keep in mind that while olinks are formed between file modules, they are resolved between produced documents. That's because the resolution of an olink depends on the context in which a module is used. For example, if your modules consist of chapters and you use a chapter module in more than one book, then the chapters might have different chapter numbers in the different books. A cross reference that displays the chapter number needs to get the right number for each book, and that number is not contained in the chapter module itself. Also, resolution in HTML output requires the output filenames and directories for the HTML files to be known.

To use olinks, you need to plan how your content is assembled into documents, and how those documents relate to each other. During processing , each document has a target data set generated for it that records all of the potential cross reference targets in that document. Those data sets are then collected into a target database, which is used to resolve olinks among the documents included in the database.

If you are only producing one set of documents from your collection of modules, then you need only one target database. But you can have more than one target database. That's needed in any of these situations:

* You want to produce two versions of a document with different modules included.

* You want to produce two versions of HTML output for a document, and they use different chunking levels, filenames, or output directories.

* You want to produce different collections of output and control the scope of cross referencing in each collection.

To form an olink, you supply identifiers for the element you are targeting and the document that contains it. The element identifier is its ID attribute value, and it is recorded in the `targetptr` attribute of the olink. This is similar to putting an ID value in a `linkend` attribute of an `xref` element. The document identifier is recorded in the `targetdoc` attribute of the olink. The document identifier is not in the document itself, but is assigned when forming the target database of documents.

How you manage your document identifiers depends somewhat on how you are combining your modules. Keep these points in mind:

* A target database establishes the scope of olink cross referencing. That means it defines what documents can be reached by olinks.

* You can have more than one target database.

* In a given target database, each document identifier must be unique.

* Changing a document identifier may not be easy once it has been in use. The document identifiers are written into the `targetdoc` attribute of olinks in the documents. If you have many of them, changing them all is a nontrivial exercise.

Here are some scenarios to consider when using olinks with modules:

* If you do not reuse your modules, then each document is a unique collection of modules and can have a fixed document identifier. All documents can be in the same target database. And each olink can reliably use one of those document identifiers in its `targetdoc` attribute.

- If you reuse modules in distinctly different documents, then each document can still have a fixed document identifier, and all documents can still be in the same target database. It is ok for an element and its ID to appear more than once in a target database, as long as each is under a different document identifier. Now you have to be more careful in how you write your olinks. They have to point to one finished document or the other, even though they are pointing to the same source module.

- If you reuse modules in different versions of the same document, then you will probably need to create more than one target database. This permits you to use the same document identifier for the different versions, yet they do not conflict in the database. Your olinks can be written with that single document identifier. Which version they resolve to is determined at processing time by which target database is used to resolve olinks.

- If you have a completely free form collection of modules and everything is resolved at processing time, then you can use text entities in your olink `targetdoc` attributes. For example:

```
<olink  targetptr="UsingMouse"  targetdoc="&mousebook;" />
```

In this example, you know you are pointing to the `UsingMouse` ID value on an element in a module. But when you write the olink, you do not know what document that module appears in, because that is not established until processing time. All you know is there had better be some document that contains the mouse information, and you refer to that document identifier in the abstract with a text entity. When you process this olink, the `mousebook` text entity must be assigned a value that resolves to the right document identifier in the target database being used during that processing run. This is very flexible, but also more complex, and more likely to lead to unresolved olinks unless you pay careful attention to details.

- If you are using DocBook 5, then you can use almost any inline element as an olink by using the universal linking attributes available in DocBook 5. See the section called "Universal linking in DocBook 5" (page 35) for more information.

Modular sections

You may find a need to further divide your content into smaller modules such as sections. For example, you might need to produce different versions of a document for beginning and advanced users. Each chapter might share the same title and introduction between versions, but the sections in each chapter may need to be different. This is easy to set up because an XInclude'd document can also be an XInclude'ing document. You can create a `chapter` module that contains the title and introductory material, and then a series of XIncludes for the section modules. Below is what one version of a chapter might look like. Another version of the chapter would use a different selection of XIncludes. Then you can create separate book documents that use XInclude to pull in the different chapter modules, as in the following example.

```
<chapter>
<title>Using a mouse</title>
<para>A mouse is an easy device to use ...</para>
<xi:include  href="rolling.section.xml"
             xmlns:xi="http://www.w3.org/2001/XInclude" />
<xi:include  href="leftclick.section.xml"
             xmlns:xi="http://www.w3.org/2001/XInclude" />
<xi:include  href="rightclick.section.xml"
             xmlns:xi="http://www.w3.org/2001/XInclude" />
...
</chapter>
```

If you want to modularize the introductory material as well, then you need a slightly different XInclude. If you just put the title and introductory paragraphs in a separate file module, then the module would not validate because its content is not contained in a document element. But you can wrap the content in a placeholder `chapter` element, and then use the xpointer() syntax to select only its content, not the chapter element itself. The following example shows how it can be done:

```
<chapter>
<xi:include  href="chapintro.xml"
             xpointer="xpointer(/chapter/*)"
             xmlns:xi="http://www.w3.org/2001/XInclude" />
<xi:include  href="rolling.section.xml"
             xmlns:xi="http://www.w3.org/2001/XInclude" />
<xi:include  href="leftclick.section.xml"
             xmlns:xi="http://www.w3.org/2001/XInclude" />
<xi:include  href="rightclick.section.xml"
             xmlns:xi="http://www.w3.org/2001/XInclude" />

...
</chapter>
```

The xpointer="xpointer(/chapter/*)" attribute is used to locate a selection within the chapintro.xml file. It will select all elements inside the intro chapter element, but not the chapter element itself. It would select the highlighted text in the following example.

```
<chapter>
<title>Using a mouse</title>
<para>A mouse is an easy device to use.</para>
<para>All computers seem to have one now.</para>
</chapter>
```

This enables you to validate the chapintro.xml file module, and still gives you a valid document when its content is included in the chapter itself.

If you decide to modularize your content down to the section level, then you should probably use section tags rather than sect1, sect2, etc. The section element can be included inside other section elements. That lets you assemble content in any arrangement of nesting that makes logical sense, without having to edit tags to get the element nesting right.

The trade off with using section is that you have to be strictly careful about where you place your section elements. Putting a sect1 element inside another sect1 will be flagged as in a validation error But you can put a section element inside another section element; in fact, that is the whole point of that element. Whether you include a section before or after the end tag of another section element changes its section level. The following is an example of using a section XInclude in two different locations:

```
<chapter>
  ...
  <section>                      section level 1
    ...
    <xi:include   href="IDEdrives"
                  xmlns:xi="http://www.w3.org/2001/XInclude" />  section level 2
  </section>
  <xi:include   href="IDEdrives"
                xmlns:xi="http://www.w3.org/2001/XInclude" />  section level 1
</chapter>
```

Either location is valid, and the stylesheets will process either without error. It is up to the author to make sure their sections are nested according to the intended logic of the content.

Shared text entities

Text entities permit you define text strings such as product names or version numbers as variables that can be globally changed by changing the entity declaration. However, using entities with modular files can be a maintenance nightmare if you do not do it properly.

If each module is to be a valid document, it's DOCTYPE declaration must include declarations for any entities that are referenced in the module. You could put the entity declarations that a given module needs at the top of the file in the internal subset of the DTD (included as part of the DOCTYPE declaration). By doing so, however, you prolif-erate declarations with a given entity name, which can lead to inconsistencies and surprises. For example, the xsltproc processor will flag as an error any entities that are declared with the same name but different content in the including and included documents. Also, putting entity declarations in each document file makes them hard to change globally.

Shared text entities are best declared in a separate file that is referenced by each module and master document that assembles modules. An entities file gives you a consistent set of entity declarations across your modules, and lets you change a definition in one place and have it apply to all of your files. You declare and reference the file containing the entity declarations as a parameter entity in the DOCTYPE declaration of all of your modules and document files. The following example shows how it's done.

Example 23.3. Shared text entities

Entities file named myproject.ent:
```
<?xml version="1.0" encoding="iso-8859-1" ?>
<!ENTITY productname "VisionFinder">
<!ENTITY version "3.0.1">
<!ENTITY userguide "Using &productname;">
...
```

Content module using the entities file:
```
<?xml version="1.0"?>
<!DOCTYPE section PUBLIC "-//OASIS//DTD DocBook XML V4.5//EN"
                "http://www.oasis-open.org/docbook/xml/4.5/docbookx.dtd" [
<!ENTITY % myents SYSTEM "myproject.ent" >
%myents;
]>
<section>
<title>Configuring &productname;</title>
...
```

If all of your modules and document files have the same entity declaration and reference, then they will all share the same set of entities. You can use an XML catalog to map the filename to a specific pathname on a system so it can be in a central location. By using a different catalog at runtime, you can map the same filename to a different pathname which might contain different versions of the entities.

> **Note:**
>
> System entities files are assumed to be encoded in UTF-8 character encoding. That's why the example includes an XML declaration (as specified by the XML standard) that indicates that the character encoding for that file should instead be iso-8859-1.

Putting customized entities in the DTD

The above method of sharing entities works fine, but if you have a large number of modular files, then inserting the parameter entity declaration and reference in the DOCTYPE of every file is a tedious process. Fortunately, if you are using a DocBook DTD, you can customize a certain DTD module to contain your entity declarations, and then they are globally available to all file modules that use the DTD.

The DocBook DTD prior to version 5 includes an empty placeholder module named dbgenent.mod that is intended for general entities declared by the user. Here is how it is referenced in the docbookx.dtd file:

```
<!ENTITY % dbgenent PUBLIC
"-//OASIS//ENTITIES DocBook Additional General Entities V4.5//EN"
"dbgenent.mod">
%dbgenent;
```

The DTD declares a parameter entity using both PUBLIC and SYSTEM identifiers, and then it references the entity. In the stock DTD, this effectively does nothing because the dbgenent.mod contains nothing but comments. However, if you populate that file in the DTD directory with your own entity declarations, then they will automatically be incorporated into the DTD and be available for reference in documents.

What if you cannot edit the dbgenent.mod file? That is the case if it is on a shared system or in a read-only directory. One option is to copy the entire DTD to a new location that is writable, edit dbgenent.mod there, and have all your documents reference the DTD in the new location by using an XML catalog.

Another option is to leave the DTD in its original place and use an XML catalog to redirect the lookup of just the dbgenent.mod file. See Chapter 5, *XML catalogs* (page 47) for more information on catalogs. This method works if you are using the Java catalog resolver used in Saxon or Xalan, but not the catalog resolver in xsltproc. Here is how it works:

Using an XML catalog to relocate dbgenent.mod

1. Create your version of dbgenent.mod containing your entity declarations. You can use any filename and directory location.

2. In your XML catalog file, add an entry that matches on the PUBLIC identifier used for dbgenent.mod, but set the uri attribute to locate your new file. Include the prefer="public" on the group wrapper to ensure the public identifier is used before the original system identifier.

   ```
   <group prefer="public">
     <public
         publicId="-//OASIS//ENTITIES DocBook Additional General Entities V4.5//EN"
         uri="mygenent.mod"/>
   </group>
   <nextCatalog catalog="path/to/docbook/catalog.xml"/>
   ```

   The public identifier in the catalog entry must exactly match the one used in your version of the DocBook DTD (this example is for version 4.5). The entry must also appear before the nextCatalog reference to the DocBook catalog file, which would resolve that public identifier to the original empty file.

Then when you process your documents with Saxon or Xalan configured to use your XML catalog, the parser will locate your new entities file and not use the empty version supplied with the DTD.

Note:

Unfortunately, this process does not work with xsltproc, which will skip looking up a file in a catalog if the file's system identifier works. In the case of the DocBook DTD, the original system id does work because the empty file is present, so no catalog lookup takes place. You can force it to use the catalog only by deleting or renaming the empty dbgenent.mod file in the DTD directory.

If you are using DocBook version 5, there is no provision in the DTD or RelaxNG schema to support entity declarations in the schema. You have to put entity declarations, including any named character entities like ™, into an entities file and reference that file in the DOCTYPE declaration, as described in the section called "Shared text entities" (page 373).

Processing your modular documents

You can run XSLT processing on individual modules or on whole documents assembled from modules. If you process whole documents, you will need a processor that can resolve any XIncludes. The following is an example with **xsltproc** and its --xinclude option:

```
xsltproc  \
     --xinclude \
     --stringparam base.dir htmlout/  \
     docbook-xsl/html/chunk.xsl  bookfile.xml
```

DocBook modules with a DOCTYPE declaration are valid mini documents, and they can be processed individually. This is useful for quick unit testing, but will not produce well integrated output. You generally will want to process your content for output using larger master documents that assemble modules. There are several reasons for doing this:

- Numbering of chapters and appendixes depends on the content being processed together in the correct order.

- Complete tables of contents require all the content to be processed together.

- The olink target dataset for a document should be generated for the whole document so all potential olink targets are included and labeled properly.

When a modular file is processed on its own, certain context information is missing. For example, the third chapter in a book does not know it is the third chapter when processed by itself, so its chapter number appears as "1". Likewise, all printed chapters will begin on page 1. In order to process your content in modules and have each bit of output fit into the whole, you would have to create a customization that feeds the processor context information such as chapter number and starting page number.

If you decide to process individual modules for testing, you might want to output the results to a directory separate from where you output the whole document. That way you do not mix up partial builds with complete builds.

Java processors and XIncludes

Some XML parsers used in the Java XSLT processors Saxon and Xalan do not handle XIncludes. Although xsltproc handles XIncludes, you may be required to use Saxon or Xalan to take advantage of some of its extension functions. You have three choices for handling XIncludes with Saxon or Xalan.

- Use the Xerces parser with Saxon or Xalan.

- Use xmllint as a preprocessor to resolve XIncludes.

- Use XIncluder as a preprocessor to resolve XIncludes.

Using Xerces to resolve XIncludes

You can use Xerces-J as the XML parser for your XSLT processing. Support for XInclude was added starting in version 2.5.0, but the later versions have more complete support. Currently Xerces handles inclusions of whole files or selection of a subset using an ID reference or numbered element positions.

The biggest advantage of Xerces is that it integrates completely with Saxon or Xalan. You will need to download the latest Xerces-J from *http://xml.apache.org/xerces2-j/index.html*, add the `xercesImpl.jar` file to your Java CLASSPATH, and add a couple of options to your java command. The following is an example using Saxon:

Example 23.4. XIncludes with Saxon and Xerces

```
java -cp "/xml/saxon653/saxon.jar:/xml/xerces-2_6_2/xercesImpl.jar" \
    -Djavax.xml.parsers.DocumentBuilderFactory=\
      org.apache.xerces.jaxp.DocumentBuilderFactoryImpl \
    -Djavax.xml.parsers.SAXParserFactory=\
      org.apache.xerces.jaxp.SAXParserFactoryImpl \
    -Dorg.apache.xerces.xni.parser.XMLParserConfiguration=\
      org.apache.xerces.parsers.XIncludeParserConfiguration \
    com.icl.saxon.StyleSheet \
    -o bookfile.html \
    bookfile.xml \
    ../docbook-xsl-1.73.1/html/docbook.xsl
```

The first two -D options set up Xerces as the XML parser in Saxon, and the third one turns on the XInclude feature.

If you are also using an XML catalog, you will need to add the catalog resolver options to the command line. They appear *after* `com.icl.saxon.StyleSheet`, because those are options understood by that classname, not the Java interpreter. You must also add to your Java CLASSPATH the `resolver.jar` file and the directory containing the `CatalogManager.properties` file, as described in Chapter 5, *XML catalogs* (page 47). The following example shows the full command line:

Example 23.5. XIncludes and XML catalogs with Saxon and Xerces

```
java -cp "/xml/saxon653/saxon.jar:/xml/xerces-2_6_2/xercesImpl.jar:resolver.jar:." \
    -Djavax.xml.parsers.DocumentBuilderFactory=\
      org.apache.xerces.jaxp.DocumentBuilderFactoryImpl \
    -Djavax.xml.parsers.SAXParserFactory=\
      org.apache.xerces.jaxp.SAXParserFactoryImpl \
    -Dorg.apache.xerces.xni.parser.XMLParserConfiguration=\
      org.apache.xerces.parsers.XIncludeParserConfiguration \
    com.icl.saxon.StyleSheet \
    -x org.apache.xml.resolver.tools.ResolvingXMLReader \
    -y org.apache.xml.resolver.tools.ResolvingXMLReader \
    -r org.apache.xml.resolver.tools.CatalogResolver \
    -o bookfile.html \
    bookfile.xml \
    ../docbook-xsl-1.73.1/html/docbook.xsl
```

To add XInclude processing to Xalan, you only need to use the third -D option, because Xalan already is set up to use the Xerces XML parser. The XInclude version of Xerces has been included since Xalan version 2.6.0. If you are using an older version, you will need at least Xalan-J version 2.5.1 and Xerces 2.5.0. The following is an example command:

Example 23.6. XIncludes with Xalan and Xerces

```
java \
  -Djava.endorsed.dirs="/xml/xerces-2_6_2;/xml/xalan-2_6_0/bin"  \
  -Dorg.apache.xerces.xni.parser.XMLParserConfiguration=\
     org.apache.xerces.parsers.XIncludeParserConfiguration \
  org.apache.xalan.xslt.Process  \
  -out bookfile.html \
  -in bookfile.xml \
  -xsl ../docbook-xsl-1.73.1/html/docbook.xsl
```

This example uses the `java.endorsed.dirs` option to make sure Java uses the newer version of Xalan. See the section called "Bypassing the old Xalan installed with Java" (page 25) for more information. That option identifies the directories that contain the necessary jar files. Put the path to the Xerces directory first so that version of `xercesImpl.jar` will be used instead of the possibly older one that is distributed with Xalan.

Using Xerces-J to validate XIncludes

Starting with version 2.5.0, the Xerces-J XML parser can validate files that have XIncludes. It uses a utility program `sax.Counter` that is included in the `xercesSamples.jar` file that comes with the Xerces-J distribution. The following is an example of how it is used.

Example 23.7. Validating XIncludes with Xerces

```
java \
     -cp "xerces-2_6_2/xercesSamples.jar:xerces-2_6_2/xercesImpl.jar" \
     -Dorg.apache.xerces.xni.parser.XMLParserConfiguration=\
         org.apache.xerces.parsers.XIncludeParserConfiguration \
     sax.Counter -v myfile.xml
```

Here `myfile.xml` contains one or more XIncludes. The file must also validate *before* the XIncludes are resolved, which means the `xi:include` element must be in the DTD. See the section called "DTD customizations for XIncludes" (page 368) for more information.

Using xmllint to resolve XIncludes

You can use **xmllint**'s `--xinclude` option to generate a version of the document with all the XIncludes resolved, and then process the output with Saxon and the DocBook XSL stylesheets. The xmllint tool is included with libxml2 and is available for most platforms. The following example shows how it can be used.

```
xmllint  --xinclude  bookfile.xml  >  resolved.xml

java  com.icl.saxon.StyleSheet  resolved.xml \
     docbook-xsl/html/chunk.xsl  base.dir="htmlout/"
```

The result file `resolved.xml` is a copy of the input file `bookfile.xml` but with the XIncludes resolved. You can validate `resolved.xml` as a second step. The XInclude fallback feature is implemented in xmllint, as is the XPointer syntax that is supported in xsltproc.

Using XIncluder in XOM to resolve XIncludes

If you want a Java tool to preprocess XIncludes, you can try XIncluder written by Elliotte Rusty Harold. An earlier standalone version was available at *ftp://ftp.ibiblio.org/pub/languages/java/javafaq/*, but the latest version is part of his XOM package available at *http://www.ibiblio.org/xml/XOM/*. The package supports the `xpointer` attribute for selecting content, and includes several tools for integrating the engine into applications. But if you just want to resolve a document so you can validate or process it, you can use a command like the following:

Resolve XIncludes:
```
java \
    -cp "xom-1.0b8.jar:xom-samples.jar" \
    nu.xom.samples.XIncludeDriver \
    bookfile.xml  >  resolved.xml
```

Process the resolved file:
```
java  com.icl.saxon.StyleSheet  resolved.xml \
      docbook-xsl/html/chunk.xsl  base.dir="htmlout/"
```

You need to specify the CLASSPATH to include the xom-*version*.jar file from the distribution, as well as the xom-samples.jar file. This example uses the -cp option to specify the CLASSPATH. On Windows systems, replace the colon in the CLASSPATH with a semicolon.

The result file resolved.xml is a copy of the input file bookfile.xml but with the XIncludes resolved. You can validate resolved.xml as a second step. The current version of XIncluder in XOM implements almost all the features of XInclude, including the fallback feature and selection of content using the xpointer attribute (but not the xpointer() scheme within the attribute).

Using an XSL-FO processor with XIncludes

If you are generating print output from your DocBook files, you may be using one of the convenience scripts that are supplied with the XSL-FO processor. These convenience scripts can perform the XSLT transformation to XSL-FO and convert that to PDF in one step. They are described in the section called "Installing an XSL-FO processor" (page 26).

The convenience scripts as they ship are not configured to use an XInclude-aware processor to perform the XSLT transformation to XSL-FO format. Because they do not resolve the XInclude elements before the transformation, the stylesheet will report errors that it has no template to handle xi:include elements.

If the convenience script is in an editable form, and if you understand its scripting language, then you can modify it to use an XInclude-aware XSLT processor in the first step. If you do that, then you will have to remember to repeat the process each time the XSL-FO processor and convenience script is updated. Fortunately, the convenience scripts do not have to perform the XSLT transformation step; they can be used to just convert the XSL-FO to PDF.

The easiest solution is to break the processing into two steps. First use an XInclude-aware processor to generate the XSL-FO file, and then process that file with the convenience script supplied by your XSL-FO processor. That scheme lets you choose any of the XInclude processors described earlier, choosing the one that best meets your needs. It also avoids having to understand and edit the convenience script to splice in an XInclude-aware processor.

For example, if you are using FOP, you can change from single step processing:

```
fop -xml mybook.xml -xsl docbook.xsl -pdf mybook.pdf
```

to two-step processing:

```
xsltproc --xinclude -o mybook.fo docbook.xsl mybook.xml
fop -fo mybook.fo -pdf mybook.pdf
```

Using a module more than once in the same document

You can include the same content in more than one place in a document as long as it is valid. One thing that can make a document invalid is duplicate ID names. If any duplicated content has an ID attribute on any of the elements in it, then you will have duplicate ID names and your document will not be valid. One drastic solution is to eliminate all ID values from modular doc. But that prevents you from forming cross references to that content. If you use IDs to form HTML filenames in your output, then you will not have that feature for such modules and they will have generated filenames.

If you absolutely must have duplicated content with IDs, then you have to figure out how to get different ID values. The following is one example of how XInclude can give you a different ID value if you are using xsltproc.

1. Let's say your modular file has a single section you want to include twice, but it has an ID value.

    ```
    <?xml version="1.0"?>
    <!DOCTYPE section SYSTEM "docbook.dtd">
    <section id="original-id">
     <para>
     blah blah
     </para>
    </section>
    ```

2. Form your first XInclude normally:

    ```
    <xi:include  href="module.xml"
          xmlns:xi="http://www.w3.org/2001/XInclude"/>
    ```

    This pulls in the entire `<section id="original-id">` element, including its children.

3. Put your second XInclude inside its own `section` element with a different ID value. And avoid the original ID value by selecting the children of the `section` element with an XPointer expression. The following is the complete example with both includes.

    ```
    <book>
    <chapter>
      blah blah
      <xi:include href="module.xml"
                xmlns:xi="http://www.w3.org/2001/XInclude"/>
    </chapter>
    <appendix>
      blah blah
      <section id="appendix-id">
        <xi:include  href="module.xml"
                xpointer="xpointer(/section/node())"
                xmlns:xi="http://www.w3.org/2001/XInclude"/>
      </section>
    </appendix>
    </book>
    ```

    When processed with xsltproc, this example results in the second instance being `<section id="appendix-id">`, containing the same set of child elements, comments, and text nodes, and processing instructions (all are selected by the `node()` syntax). Since the new `section` wrapper has a different ID value, it will validate. You can even form a cross reference to either of the instances of the section. Just make sure none of the children have ID values or it will still not validate. Only xsltproc supports the `xpointer()` scheme used in this example. See this **Note** for background on `xpointer()`.

Reusing content at different levels

Sometimes you need to reuse content at a different level from its original source. For example, a chapter in one book might need to be reused as a section in another book. You can reuse content with XInclude, but you cannot always place the same element in a new location. For example, if you are reusing a chapter as a section, you cannot just XInclude a chapter element inside another chapter, as it will not be valid and will not format properly.

The XInclude xpointer() scheme described in the previous section can be used for this purpose. The idea is to create a new container element, and then XInclude all the content of another element into it, without bringing along the other element itself. The section element in the following example does that.

```
<chapter id="container-chap">
  ...
  <section id="chapter-as-section">
    <xi:include  href="userguide.xml"
                 xpointer="xpointer(//chapter[@id = 'intro']/node() )"
                 xmlns:xi="http://www.w3.org/2001/XInclude"/>
 </section>
  ...
</chapter>
```

The path //chapter[@id = 'intro']/node() finds the chapter in userguide.xml whose id attribute is intro, and selects all the content of the element. The node() syntax in the path selects child elements, text nodes, processing instructions, and comments.

The content to be included must fit into its new location. You may have to alter the included chapter a bit to do this. For example, if the title is in a chapterinfo element, then the XSL templates processing the new section will not look for the title there.

Only xsltproc supports the xpointer() scheme used in this example. See this **Note** for background on xpointer()

Using modified id values

Another approach to the problem of duplicate id values on repeated XInclude elements is to modify the id values in the output. You can modify the template named object.id, which is used to assign id values for all *output* elements. It usually just copies an input element's id value, or generates a string if it does not have an id attribute. But you can customize the template to solve this problem.

This solution does not modify the id attributes in the source file, so the file will still be invalid if it has duplicate ids. But if you do not need to validate your resolved files, then this solution will at least let you build output and have functioning tables of contents.

The object.id template is used to generate the output link id references for any element as well as the id attribute itself. As long as it produces consistent output for the same element, your links should work.

In this customization, the template counts the number of preceding elements with the same id value. If the count is greater than zero, then it appends the count to the output id value. The customization also works with DocBook 5 documents that use xml:id.

```
<xsl:template name="object.id">
  <xsl:param name="object" select="."/>

  <xsl:variable name="id" select="@id"/>
  <xsl:variable name="xid" select="@xml:id"/>

  <xsl:variable name="preceding.id"
        select="count(preceding::*[@id = $id])"/>

  <xsl:variable name="preceding.xid"
        select="count(preceding::*[@xml:id = $xid])"/>

  <xsl:choose>
    <xsl:when test="$object/@id and $preceding.id != 0">
      <xsl:value-of select="concat($object/@id, $preceding.id)"/>
    </xsl:when>
    <xsl:when test="$object/@id">
      <xsl:value-of select="$object/@id"/>
    </xsl:when>
    <xsl:when test="$object/@xml:id and $preceding.xid != 0">
      <xsl:value-of select="concat($object/@id, $preceding.xid)"/>
    </xsl:when>
    <xsl:when test="$object/@xml:id">
      <xsl:value-of select="$object/@xml:id"/>
    </xsl:when>
    <xsl:otherwise>
      <xsl:value-of select="generate-id($object)"/>
    </xsl:otherwise>
  </xsl:choose>
</xsl:template>
```

With this template in place, when the id of a repeated element is usage, for example, then the first instance in the output will be usage. But the second instance will instead be usage1, the third instance usage2, etc. This process ensures that each output id is unique.

Note that any instances of xref or link or olink that reference the original id value will not be altered. They will always point to the first instance in the output.

Inserting dynamic content

There may be situations where you need to insert modular content that is generated dynamically. For example, a table might include data from a database, and you want the table to represent the most up-to-date version of the data in the database.

XML and XSLT have no native mechanism for creating content by executing an external process such as database extraction. However, the href attribute of an XInclude can be any URI. If you set up an HTTP server with the capability of generating dynamic content, then your XInclude could use that content generated by the HTTP server. The server could be set up to use a CGI process, *Apache Cocoon*[1], or any other process that can generate DocBook XML. The following is a simple example:

```
<xi:include  href="http://myserver.com/cgi-bin/GetDocBook.pl"
      xmlns:xi="http://www.w3.org/2001/XInclude"/>
```

---

[1] http://cocoon.apache.org/

The `myserver.com` HTTP server must be set up to process the CGI script named `GetDocBook.pl`. That script must return DocBook XML content that is valid for the insertion point in the document. From the point of view of the XML parser handling the document, all it sees is DocBook elements. Of course, the document is dependent on the CGI process each time it is processed. See the section called "XIncludes and XML catalogs" (page 364) for another example of using dynamically generated content.

24
Olinking between documents

When writing technical documentation, it is often necessary to cross reference to other information. When that other information is in the current document, then DocBook provides support with the xref and link elements. But if the information is in another document, you cannot use those elements because their linkend attribute value must point to an id (or xml:id for DocBook 5) attribute value that is in the current document.

The olink element is the equivalent for linking outside the current document. It has an attribute for specifying a document identifier (targetdoc) as well as the id of the target element (targetptr). The combination of those two attributes provides a unique identifier to locate cross references. These attributes on olink are available starting with the DocBook XML DTD version 4.2.

> **Note:**
>
> The olink element has another set of attributes that support an older style of cross referencing using system entities. Those other olink attributes are targetdocent, linkmode, and localinfo. Those attributes are not used in the olink mechanism described here.

But how are external cross references resolved? By contrast, resolving *internal* cross references is easy. When a document is parsed, it is loaded into memory and all of its linkends can be connected to ids within memory. But external documents are not loaded into memory, so there must be another mechanism for resolving olinks. The simplest mechanism would be to open each external document, find the target id, and resolve the cross reference. But such a mechanism would not scale well. It would require parsing a potentially large document to find one target, and then repeating that for as many olinks as you have. A more efficient mechanism would parse each document once and save the cross reference target information in a separate target database that can be loaded into memory for quick lookup.

The DocBook XSL stylesheets use such an external cross reference database to resolve olinks. You first process all of your documents in a mode that collects the target information, and then you can process them in the normal mode to produce HTML or print output. The different processing mode is controlled using XSL stylesheet parameters.

How to link between documents

To use olinks to form cross references between documents, you have to spend a little time setting up your files so they can find each other's information. This section describes how to do that. Four of these six steps are performed only once, after which only the last two steps are required to process your documents as needed. This procedure covers olinking for HTML output. A later section describes the differences for linking in PDF output.

Using olink

1. **Identify the documents**

   Decide which documents are to be included in the domain for cross referencing, and assign a document id to each. A document id is a name string that is unique for each document in your collection. Your naming scheme can be as simple or elaborate as your needs require.

   For example, you might be writing mail agent documentation that includes a user's guide, an administrator's guide, and a reference document. These could be assigned simple document ids such as ug, ag, and ref, respectively. But if you expect to also cross reference to other user guides, you might need to be more specific, such as MailUserGuide, MailAdminGuide, and MailReference.

   One simple convention is to use a document's root element id or xml:id attribute value as its document identifier, as long as they are all unique across your set of documents.

   ```
   <book id="MailUserGuide">
   ```

   You can add new documents to a collection at any time. You can also have more than one collection, each of which defines a domain of documents among which you can cross reference. A given document can be in more than one collection.

2. **Add olinks to your documents**

   Insert an olink element where you want to form a cross reference to another document. You supply two attributes in each olink: targetptr is the id or xml:id value of the element you are pointing to, and targetdoc is the document id that contains the element.

   For example, the Mail Administrator's Guide might have a chapter on user accounts like the following:

   ```
   <chapter id="user_accounts">
   <title>Administering User Accounts</title>
   <para>blah blah</para>
   ...
   ```

   You can form a cross reference to that chapter in the Admin Guide by adding an olink in the User's Guide like the following:

   ```
   You may need to update your
   <olink targetdoc="MailAdminGuide" targetptr="user_accounts">user accounts
   </olink>
   when you get a new machine.
   ```

   When the User's Guide is processed into HTML, the text user accounts will become a hot spot that links to the Admin Guide.

   If instead you create an empty olink element with the same attributes, then the hot text will be generated by the stylesheet from the title in the other document. In this example, the hot text would be Administering User Accounts. This has the advantage of being automatically updated when the title in the Admin Guide is updated.

3. **Decide on your HTML output hierarchy**

   To form cross references between documents in HTML, their relative locations must be known. Generally, the HTML files for multiple documents are output to different directories, particularly if chunking is used. So before going any further, you must decide on the names and arrangement of the HTML output directories for all the documents in your collection.

Here are the output directories for our example docs:

```
documentation
    |
    |-- guides
    |        |-- mailuser        contains MailUserGuide files
    |        |-- mailadmin       contains MailAdminGuide files
    |
    |-- reference
             |-- mailref         contains MailReference files
```

It is only the relative location that counts; the top level name is not used. The stylesheet will compute the relative path for cross reference URLs using the relative locations.

4. **Create the target database document**

Each collection of documents has a master target database document that is used to resolve all olinks in that collection. The target database document is an XML file that is created once, by hand. It provides a framework that pulls in the target data for each of the documents in the collection. Since all the document data is pulled in dynamically, the database document itself is static, except for changes to the collection.

The following is an example target database document named olinkdb.xml. It structures the documents in the collection into a sitemap element that provides the relative locations of the outputs for HTML. Then it pulls in the individual target data using system entity references to the files generated in step 5 below.

Example 24.1. Target database document

```
<?xml version="1.0" encoding="utf-8"?> ❶
<!DOCTYPE targetset
        SYSTEM "file:///tools/docbook-xsl/common/targetdatabase.dtd" [
<!ENTITY ugtargets SYSTEM "file:///doc/userguide/target.db"> ❷
<!ENTITY agtargets SYSTEM "file:///doc/adminguide/target.db">
<!ENTITY reftargets SYSTEM "file:///doc/man/target.db">
]>
<targetset> ❸
  <targetsetinfo> ❹
    Description of this target database document,
    which is for the examples in olink doc.
  </targetsetinfo>

  <!-- Site map for generating relative paths between documents -->
  <sitemap> ❺
    <dir name="documentation"> ❻
      <dir name="guides"> ❼
        <dir name="mailuser"> ❽
          <document targetdoc="MailUserGuide" ❾
                    baseuri="userguide.html"> ❿
            &ugtargets; ⓫
          </document>
        </dir>
        <dir name="mailadmin">
          <document targetdoc="MailAdminGuide">
            &agtargets;
          </document>
        </dir>
      </dir>
      <dir name="reference">
        <dir name="mailref">
          <document targetdoc="MailReference">
            &reftargets;
          </document>
        </dir>
      </dir>
    </dir>
  </sitemap>
</targetset>
```

❶ Set the database encoding to utf-8 for the database, regardless of what encoding your documents are written in. The individual data files are written out in utf-8 so a database can have mixed languages and not have mixed encodings.

❷ Declare a system entity for each document target data file. This assigns a path to the target.db file for each document in the collection.

❸ Root element for the database is targetset.

❹ The targetsetinfo element is optional, and contains a description of the collection.

❺ The sitemap element contains the framework for the hierarchy of HTML output directories.

❻ Directory that contains all the HTML output directories.

❼ Directory that contains only other directories, not documents.

❽ Directory that contains one or more document output.

❾   The document element has the document identifier in its `targetdoc` attribute.

❿   For documents processed without chunking, the output filename must be provided in the `baseuri` attribute since that name is not generated by the document itself. Then cross references can be resolved using the form *filename.html#targetptr*. An alternative process is to leave off the `baseuri` attribute and instead set the `olink.base.uri` parameter to the HTML filename when you generate its `target.db` file. That writes the HTML name into each `href` attribute in the target data. That lets you set the filename at runtime.

⓫   The system entity reference pulls in the target data for this document.

When this document is processed, the content of the `target.db` file is pulled into its proper location in the hierarchy using its system entity reference, thus forming the complete cross reference database. That makes all the information available to the XSL stylesheets to look up olink references and resolve them using the information in the database.

The use of system entities permits the individual target.db data files for each document to be updated as needed, and the database automatically gets the update the next time it is processed.

System entities also permit the use of XML catalogs to resolve the location of the various data files.

5.   **Generate target data files**

For each document in your collection, you generate a data file that contains all the potential cross reference targets. You do that by processing the document using your regular DocBook XSL stylesheet but with an additional `collect.xref.targets` parameter. The following is an example command.

```
xsltproc  \
    --stringparam  collect.xref.targets  "only"  \
    docbook.xsl  \
    userguide.xml
```

This command should generate in the current directory a target data file, named `target.db` by default. You can change the filename or location by setting the parameter `targets.filename`. The generated file is an XML file that contains only the information needed to form cross references to each element in the document.

The DocBook XSL stylesheets contain the code needed to generate the target data file. The parameter `collect.xref.targets` controls when that code is applied, and has three possible values.

no   do not generate the target data file (this is the default). Use this setting when you want to process just your document for output without first regenerating the target data file. This is the default because any documents without olinks do not need to do this extra processing step.

yes   Generate the target data file, and then process the document for output. Use this setting when you change your document and want to regenerate both the target data file and the output.

only   Generate the target data file, but do not process the document for output. Use this setting when you want to update the target data file for use by other documents, or when you set things up for the first time.

In the command examples above, *docbook.xsl* should be the pathname to the DocBook stylesheet file you normally use to process your document for HTML output. For example, that might be:

```
../html/docbook.xsl
```

If you use the DocBook chunking feature, then it would be the path to `chunk.xsl` instead. If you use a DocBook XSL customization file, then it should be pathname to that file. It will work if your customization file imports either `docbook.xsl` or `chunk.xsl`, and it will pick up whatever customizations you have for cross reference text. If you use different stylesheet variations for different documents, be sure to use the right one for each document.

For example, you might use chunking on some long documents, but not on short documents. Use Makefiles or batch files to keep it all consistent.

If you are processing your document for print, then generate the `targets.db` file using the HTML stylesheet, and then process your document with the FO stylesheet.

6. **Process each document for output**

    Now all that remains is to process each document to generate its output. That's done using the normal XSL DocBook stylesheet with an additional parameter, the database filename. The DocBook XSL stylesheets know how to resolve olinks using the target database.

    The following are command examples for three XSL processors:

    xsltproc:
    ```
    xsltproc  --output /http/guides/mailuser/userguide.html \
       --stringparam target.database.document "olinkdb.xml" \
       --stringparam current.docid "MailUserGuide" \
       docbook.xsl  userguide.xml
    ```

    Saxon:
    ```
    java com.icl.saxon.StyleSheet -o /http/guides/mailuser/userguide.html \
            userguide.xml  docbook.xsl \
            target.database.document="/projects/mail/olinkdb.xml" \
            current.docid="MailUserGuide"
    ```

    Xalan:
    ```
    java org.apache.xalan.xslt.Process \
            -OUT /http/guides/mailuser/userguide.html  \
            -IN userguide.xml \
            -XSL  docbook.xsl \
            -PARAM target.database.document "/projects/mail/olinkdb.xml" \
            -PARAM current.docid "MailUserGuide"
    ```

    The only difference from the normal document processing is the addition of the two parameters. The `target.data-base.document` parameter provides the location of the master target database file. As your document is processed, when the stylesheet encounters an olink that has `targetdoc` and `targetptr` attributes, it looks up the values in the target database and resolves the reference. If it cannot open the database or find a particular olink reference, then it reports an error.

    Note:

    If you specify a *relative* path in the `target.database.document` parameter, it is taken as relative to the document you are processing. You can also use a full path or an XML catalog to locate the file.

    The other parameter `current.docid` informs the processor of the current document's `targetdoc` identifier. That lets the stylesheet compute relative pathname references based on the sitemap in the master database document. The current document's identifier is not recorded in the document itself, so the processor must be told of it by using this parameter.

Tip:

If you assign the `targetdoc` value that you create for each document to the `id` attribute of the document's root element, then your processor can identify each document. Then the `current.docid` parameter can be automatically set by adding this to your customization layer:

```
<xsl:param name="current.docid" select="/*/@id"/>
```

During processing, this will set the `current.docid` parameter to the value of the `id` attribute of the current document's root element. Then you do not have to set the parameter on each command line. You can still override it on the command line if you ever need to. Just make sure all your document `id` attributes are unique. For DocBook 5, use `xml:id` instead.

Example of target data

The following is an example of target data collected for a short document. The document it was extracted from consists of a `chapter` that contains just a `table` and one `sect1`.

Example 24.2. Olink target data

```
<?xml version="1.0" ?> ❶
<div element="chapter" href="#publish" number="1" targetptr="publish"> ❷
  <ttl>Publishing DocBook Documents</ttl> ❸
  <xreftext>Chapter 1</xreftext> ❹
  <obj element="table" href="xsl-processors" number="1.1"
       targetptr="xsl-processors"> ❺
    <ttl>XSL Processors</ttl>
    <xreftext>Table 1.1</xreftext>
  </obj>
  <div element="sect1" href="#xsl-arch" number="" targetptr="xsl-arch">
    <ttl>DocBook XSL Architecture</ttl>
    <xreftext>the section called "DocBook XSL Architecture"</xreftext>
  </div>
</div>
```

❶ It is a well-formed XML fragment that follows the `targetdatabase.dtd` DTD. However, because the file may be used as a system entity, it should not have a DOCTYPE declaration.

❷ DocBook structure elements are recorded in `div` tags. Some information is stored in attributes and other information in child elements. Attributes record the element's name, generated number, `id` or `xml:id` value (as `targetptr`), and potential href fragment.

❸ The `ttl` tag records the object's title.

❹ The `xreftext` tag records the generated text that would be output if an `xref` pointed to that element. This field uses the gentext strings of the stylesheet that generates the target data file. The exception is when a target element includes an `xreflabel` attribute, which overrides the gentext string as it would for an `xref`.

❺ Non-structural elements like tables and figures are recorded in `obj` (object) tags. The `div` elements can nest, but the `obj` elements do not.

Similar data files are generated for other documents in your collection. These separate data files are assembled into one large target database by pulling them in as system entities to a master database document. See Example 24.1, "Target database document" (page 386) to see how these data files are inserted into `document` elements within the master file. Keeping them as separate system entities means they can be individually updated as needed. Yet they are all accessible from a single master document.

For the database to work, all of the system entities referenced in it must be available when processing takes place. A missing data file will be reported as an error, and any olinks to that document will not resolve. If a set of linked documents has a definite publishing date, you can freeze a copy of the database as a snapshot of the released documents for future documents to reference. If you replace the system entity references with the actual data for each document, you can save it as one big file.

Universal olinking in DocBook 5

If you are using DocBook version 5 or later, then you can use other inline elements as olinks. DocBook 5 supports universal linking, which means it permits `xlink:href` attributes on most elements to create a link from the current element to some target. See the section called "Universal linking in DocBook 5" (page 35) for background information.

The link can be made into an olink if you add a special `xlink:role` attribute, and use slightly different syntax in the link. The following example shows how to use a `command` element as an olink:

```
<para>Use the <command xlink:role="http://docbook.org/xlink/role/olink"
xlink:href="refguide#preview">preview</command>
...
```

Two features make this example an olink:

- The added `xlink:role` attribute identifies this XLink as an olink in this application. That informs the processor so it can interpret the special `xlink:href` syntax. You must use exactly that string in the `xlink:role` attribute for it to work.

- The `xlink:href` attribute has special syntax, with the equivalent of `targetdoc` before the # mark, and the equivalent of `targetptr` after the # mark.

So instead of separate attributes for `targetdoc` and `targetptr`, the values are combined with a # separator in a single attribute. In this example, the content of the element will be formatted as a `command`, and that formatted text will be made into a hot link. The link connects to the output whose document identifier is `refguide`. As for all olink document identifiers, that value must appear in a `targetdoc` attribute in a `document` element in the database. The `#preview` part of the link targets the `xml:id` of a specific element in that document. Remember that DocBook 5 uses `xml:id` instead of `id`.

When these two XLink attributes are used on DocBook inline elements, the content of the element is formatted as usual and converted into the hot link text. No text will be generated from the target, as is done for an empty `olink` element. However, the processor will still add the optional page reference for internal links, or the optional document title for external links, if those are configured for other olinks.

You can also use these two XLink attributes in the `olink` element itself, instead of the traditional `targetdoc` and `targetptr` attributes. They will be processed identically in the stylesheets. See Table 4.1, "DocBook 5 linking examples" (page 37) for a list of all the choices for olink syntax.

Details to watch out for

Olinks provide the tremendous power of cross referencing between documents, but they have a price. Olinks introduce dependencies between documents that are not an issue with standalone documents. The documents in a collection must "play together", and so they must follow a few rules.

- If you change a document, you should always regenerate its `target.db` data file. Once a collection is set up, this step is most easily done by processing a modified document with the parameter `collect.xref.targets` set to the value `yes`. That will make two passes through the document, the first to regenerate the target data file and the second to generate the normal output.

- It is a good idea to enter `id` attributes (use `xml:id` in DocBook 5) on any element you might want to link to. . Without an `id` attribute, the stylesheet will generate a value, but it will not necessarily be the same value in each process. For a stable target value, you must enter an `id` attribute. In HTML processing, if you set the stylesheet parameter `id.warnings` to 1, then you will get a warning about any titled elements that do not have an `id` attribute.

- If you change a document, then you may need to reprocess other documents that make cross references to that data file. Such dependencies are most easily tracked using Makefiles or Ant tasks, so the update process can be automated.

- The output locations specified in the `sitemap` element in the target database document must match where the HTML or PDF output actually lands. If they do not match, then the hot links you generate between documents will not reach the actual documents.

- Whatever DocBook stylesheet (standard or customized) that you use to process a document for output should also be used to process the document for extracting the target data. Only then can you be sure that the style and content of the cross references will match the document.

- If you use profiling (conditional text), you need to keep your target data separate for the different profiles. See the section called "Olinks with profiling (conditional text)" (page 403) for how to do that.

- If you are generating XHTML with the Saxon processor, then you may have a problem with your `target.db` data files. That processor always adds a DOCTYPE declaration to the data files, and a system entity cannot contain a DOCTYPE. If you use system entities in your main target database to load the data files, then it will fail when using Saxon. You can use xsltproc instead, or use XIncludes instead of system entities in your target database. See the section called "Using XInclude in the database document" (page 401) for more details on the latter option.

Target database location

The location of the olink targets database is specified by the stylesheet parameter `target.database.document`. Note these features:

- The `target.database.document` parameter has no default value, so you must always set this parameter if you are using olinks.

- The parameter value can be a full path, but then it should be expressed using URI syntax since that is what the XSLT `document()` function expects. For example:

```
<xsl:param name="target.database.document">file:///c:/xml/tools/olinkdb.xml</xsl:Param>
```

- The parameter value can be a relative path, in which case it is taken as relative to the directory containing the document being processed. Since the parameter takes URI syntax, you can use forward slashes even on Windows. You can include `../` in the path to access directory levels above the current document.

- You cannot use a relative path if you are using `profile-docbook.xsl` or `profile-chunk.xsl`. Those stylesheets create an in-memory copy of your document that does not have a base directory. Use a full path, or use two-pass profiling (see the section called "Two-pass processing" (page 431)).

- An XML catalog entry can be used to map the parameter value to a specific location in a filesystem. Note that when using a Java processor, the parameter value must be a full path expression in order for the catalog entry to work, because Java will replace any relative path with an absolute path before the catalog resolver sees it.

If you are sharing a target database among several documents, as is common with olinking, you should put it in a path that is accessible to all documents in the collection. If the relative path from all your documents to the database is the same, then you can just put that path in the parameter. If the relative paths to the shared database are not the same, you have some choices:

- Set the `target.database.document` parameter in the build script for each document directory, using an appropriate relative path for documents in that directory.

- Set the parameter to a fixed full path to the database file.

- Use a phony full path that is mapped to the actual location using an XML catalog file. See the section called "Relative SYSTEM identifiers may not work" (page 50) for more information on this trick.

Using a sitemap

One of the most powerful features of the olink system is the `sitemap` in the target database document. The sitemap is an XML structure that parallels the directory structure of your HTML or PDF output tree. By recording the output locations for all the documents in your olink database, the stylesheet can compute relative links between any two documents. The stylesheets compute the correct number of `../` steps to move up, and the right sequence of directory names to move down to locate a file. Relative links make your HTML highly portable, as long as you keep the same directory structure when you move the files.

If you put all your output in one directory, then you do not need to use a sitemap. You can omit the `sitemap` and `dir` elements, and just create a flat list of `document` elements as children of the `targetset` element in the database file. For PDF output or non-chunked HTML output, the `baseuri` attribute of each `document` element must still contain the filename of its PDF or HTML output file, because that name is not available to the stylesheet.

Keep in mind that the sitemap records the HTML or PDF *output* hierarchy, not the XML source hierarchy. The location of your XML documents does not matter. Creating an output sitemap requires advanced planning for your document collection. You need to decide the name and location of each directory containing output. If you change where you put your HTML or PDF files, be sure to update your sitemap as well.

For the sitemap to work, you have to set the `current.docid` parameter for each document you process. You set the parameter value to the `targetdoc` identifier for the current document. That informs the stylesheet of the starting point for computing relative references, since that information is not recorded in the document itself.

Here are some guidelines for understanding the sitemap feature. See Example 24.1, "Target database document" (page 386) for examples.

- The `sitemap` element itself must contain just a single top-level `dir` element that serves as a container for the other `dir` elements. The top-level `name` attribute is irrelevant, since it is never used in `hrefs` (it is always represented by `../`).

- The output directory hierarchy is represented by nested `dir` elements under the top level `dir` in the sitemap. Each `dir` element's `name` attribute must match the name of its output directory. Thus a sequence of `dir` descendants can represent part of a pathname.

- A `dir` element can also contain one or more `document` elements. A typical setup will have terminal `dir`s containing a single `document` element, especially if that document is chunked. But a `dir` element can contain a `document` element and other `dir` elements, if that is your directory structure.

- Each `document` element's `targetdoc` attribute value is the same document identifier used for olinking to that document. This identifier keys the stylesheet to the current document's location in the sitemap so it can compute relative paths from there to other documents.

- The content of each `document` element is the set of target data collected for that document. This is usually inserted as a system entity reference, although XInclude can be used as well (see the section called "Using XInclude in the database document" (page 401)).

- Non-chunked documents may need a `baseuri` attribute on their `document` element to indicate the HTML filename. This is necessary if the `olink.base.uri` parameter was not used to write the same filename into each `href` in the target data.when collecting the document's target data. do not use both the parameter and the attribute, or both will appear in the generated hrefs.

- A directory can contain the output for more than one document. Expressed in the sitemap, this means a `dir` element can contain more than one `document` element. This feature is most useful for putting together several non-chunked documents. Chunked documents run the risk of duplicate filenames that would overwrite each other.

Olinking in print output

You can use `olink` to form active hotlinks between PDF documents. In stylesheet versions prior to 1.66, the olink text would be generated, but the links would only be active if they were to a destination within the same document. Now an olink can open another PDF file, and, under the right circumstances, can scroll to the exact location in the external document.

Scrolling to the exact location means that the *fragment identifier* that the stylesheet adds to a PDF reference is resolved:

```
myotherbook.pdf#intro
```

This should open the PDF file named `myotherbook.pdf` and scroll to the point in the document where the `intro` id is located.

The use of fragment identifiers is currently somewhat limited because of the inconsistent behavior of XSL-FO processors and PDF browsers. Only the XEP and Antenna House XSL-FO processors add the correct ID information to the PDF document for it to work. Neither FOP nor Xml2PDF write ihe original ID values from the XSLT process to the PDF file. So although a link with a fragment identifier is properly formed, the ID value it points to does not exist in the destination PDF.

If you are using XEP, you may find that some external olinks work and others do not, even though they should. This could be because some of the `id` or `xml:id` attributes from the source document were not copied to the PDF file. By default, XEP only writes `id` values that are internally referenced. There is a special XEP processing instruction that enables all `id` values, but it first appeared in version 1.68 of the DocBook stylesheets. If you are using a stylesheet version prior to that, you need to add this option to your XEP command:

```
-DDROP_UNUSED_DESTINATIONS=false
```

See your XEP documentation for more information.

Also some browsers do not properly interpret PDF fragment identifiers. Adobe Reader seems to work, but Adobe Reader used as a PDF plugin inside Internet Explorer does not. Another factor is whether the PDF file is accessed as a local file or from an HTTP server. In some cases, the hot link will open the other PDF file but will not scroll to the exact location. In other cases, the browser will complain that it cannot open the other document at all because it is misinterpreting the fragment identifier as part of the filename.

Because the fragment identifiers in PDF olinks can cause such problems, the FO stylesheet turns them off by default. Without the fragment identifiers, an olink to another PDF document will open the document and display its first page. You can turn fragment identifiers on if your situation permits by setting the stylesheet parameter `insert.olink.pdf.frag` to 1.

Setting up PDF olinking

Since the FO stylesheet now supports olinks, it can also be used to generate a document's olink data file (whose default name is `target.db`). In previous versions you had to use the HTML stylesheet to generate the data file. Now you can set the `collect.xref.targets` parameter when using the FO stylesheet.

You may need to maintain separate olink data files for HTML and FO processing. If you do not customize the text that is generated for cross references, then you can use one olink data file. Or if you customize the generated text but do it the same for both HTML and FO output, then you can still use one olink data file. But if your generated text differs between HTML and FO output, then you will need to maintain separate target data files. That's because those files store copies of the generated text for each target. Use the `targets.filename` parameter to change the default data filename from `target.db` to something else. Or specify the same filename but in a different directory, since the parameter accepts a pathname.

Regardless of whether you need to create separate target data files for each document, you *will* need to create separate master olink database files (identified by the `target.database.document` parameter) for HTML and FO output. That's because the `baseuri` attributes on the `document` element in the database must differ.

For HTML output, the `baseuri` would be either the HTML filename (for nonchunked output), or a directory name (for chunked output). For FO output, the `baseuri` must point to the PDF file. If you are using XEP, local file access requires using a `file:` protocol, so it should be `file:myfile.pdf`. For other XSL-FO processors the `baseuri` should be just `myfile.pdf`. If you are olinking to a PDF document on a web server, then the `baseuri` should be the URI of the PDF file, such as `http://mysite.com/myfile.pdf`.

If you are olinking among a collection of PDF document located in different directories, you can use the `sitemap` feature of the olink database to indicate their relative locations. Then the processor can compute a relative path between documents to form the link. See the section called "Using a sitemap" (page 392) for more information.

Open target in new window

When you click on an olink, the usual behavior is to close the current document and open the target document. If you want to keep the current document open, and open the target document in a new window, you can customize the `olink.properties` attribute-set as follows:

```
<xsl:attribute-set name="olink.properties">
  <xsl:attribute name="show-destination">new</xsl:attribute>
</xsl:attribute-set>
```

The `olink.properties` attribute-set is applied to the `fo:basic-link` element for the link. Adding a `show-destination="new"` property causes the link to open in a new window. This only works for stylesheet version 1.73 and later, because the `show-destination` property was hardwired into the template before that version.

Linking between HTML and PDF documents

It is possible to form olinks between HTML and PDF documents. In the olink database file (identified by the `target.database.document` parameter), an HTML document can have an HTML `baseuri`, and another document in PDF form can have a PDF `baseuri`. But you cannot do both formats for one document in the same database because each `targetdoc` attribute must be unique within each language. So when you set up the olink database file, you have to decide if you are targeting the HTML or PDF version of a given document.

Whether your links work at runtime will depend on your browser setup. An HTML browser needs to detect that the link is a PDF file, and load it into a PDF viewer. Going in the other direction, a PDF viewer needs to detect that the link is an HTML file, and pass the URI off to an HTML browser.

Page references in olinks

There are two situations for generating page numbers for olinks: internal and external olinks. Internal olinks are used within a document when its text is divided among multiple separate file modules. As described in the section called "Modular cross referencing" (page 369), olinks are used to form cross references between modules so that each module can be validated. The stylesheet recognizes when an olink is to a location within the same document when the `current.docid` parameter is set and its value matches the `targetdoc` attribute in an olink. Such olinks will be treated as if they were internal `xref` links, and they will get a page reference if that feature is turned on for internal links.

For olinks to external documents, the situation is different. The olink mechanism includes partial support for page number references to external documents. That means you could refer someone to an actual page number in the other document. In the olink data set for document, the page number for each target can be stored in a `page` attribute on each `div` or `obj` element. If an olink style calls for a page number, and if the data is there, it will be output.

But there is currently no standard way of populating the `page` attribute in the olink data. Since page numbers are only available in the XSL-FO processor and not the stylesheet, some sort of postprocessing would be needed to extract the page numbers for each element. The collecting of page numbers is not part of the stylesheets at this time.

Generating olink text

Olinks that do not contain any text must have the content generated by the stylesheet. If the `olink` element contains text content (is not empty), then that text will always be used as the olink text, and no other text is added. All the features described in this section are for empty olinks.

You have several options for the text that is generated for an empty olink:

- Use the default olink text.

- Add the document title.

- Use local cross reference styles.

- Use xrefstyle attributes.

- Customizing the olink template.

Default olink text

By default, the text that is generated for an `olink` is the same text that would be generated for an `xref` in the other document pointing to an internal target. For example, an internal `xref` to a chapter might generate text like the following:

```
Chapter 3: "Using a Mouse"
```

This is the same text that another document will get if it forms an olink to the chapter. That's because the olink data file contains a copy of the `xref` text for every element with an `id` or `xml:id` attribute in the document. The default olink text is that preformed cross reference text.

The olink data file also contains the individual pieces of cross reference information, such as title, number, and element type. These can be used to assemble alternate text for an olink, as described in the sections that follow.

Adding the document title

You may want to make it obvious that olinks are refering to another document rather than the current document. For example, if the reference just says `Chapter 3: "Using a Mouse"`, the reader might think it was referring to Chapter 3 in the current book. To solve that problem, you can set the parameter `olink.doctitle` to `yes`, then the stylesheet will append the other document's title to the reference. The title is taken from the `title` child element of the root element in the external document. So if the other document is a `book`, then it will be the book's title.

See the section called "Using xrefstyle attributes" (page 396) for more options you can use in adding the target document's title.

Using local styles

The target data file for each document contains both the generated text and the pieces of text for each target. That is, it contains the fully formed cross reference text, as well as separate fields for the title, subtitle, element type, and number. That permits you to use the default preformed text, or to assemble the generated text in a different way.

The preformed text is based on the *gentext templates* in each language file in the `common` directory, using the gentext for resolving `xref` elements. For example, if you look in the file `common/en.xml` in the `context` element with attribute `name="xref-number-and-title"`, you will find the gentext templates used to form `xref` text to target elements that have a number and title. The following is the gentext template for chapter, where `%n` refers to its number and `%t` refers to its title:

```
<l:template name="chapter" text="Chapter %n, %t"/>
```

Although these gentext templates were written for `xref` elements, they are also used for olinks. But what if you have customized these gentext templates? How does that change the generated text for olinks?

The answer depends on which stylesheet was used to generate the target data file for a document. That is the stylesheet that determines how the preformed olink text will look. If that stylesheet was customized, then the stored olink text will have those customizations. If another document olinks to that data, they get the customized version.

But what if you prefer that all your olinks use the cross reference styles of the current stylesheet? You can do that by setting the parameter `use.local.olink.style` to a value of 1 instead of the default zero. Then instead of using the preformed text from the target data file, the current stylesheet extracts the element name, title, and number from the target data, and forms the text using the current stylesheet's gentext templates.

So this parameter is useful only if you are processing a document with a stylesheet whose cross references are styled differently from the stylesheet that generated the target data file.

Using xrefstyle attributes

There are many situations where the default preformed text does not look right. For example, you might create a list of section title references. The default formatting would put each title in quotes, but the list would look more inviting without the quotes. What you need is a way to specify how you want an individual olink to look. You can do that with the `xrefstyle` attribute.

Olinks support the `xrefstyle` attribute that was introduced in version 4.3 of the DocBook DTD. The `xrefstyle` attribute on an `xref` or `olink` element is used to pass hints to the XSL stylesheet about how to generate the text for the current cross reference instance. You can specify a named style, a select list of keywords, or a gentext template. Starting with version 1.66 of the stylesheets, olinks support the same features of `xrefstyle` as for the `xref` element. See the section called "Customizing with an xrefstyle attribute" (page 262) for a complete description of using `xrefstyle`.

In the `select:` type of `xrefstyle`, you use keywords to specify what text pieces to include. Two new keywords were added for olinks. The `docname` keyword will generate the title of the other document, and the `docnamelong` keyword can be used to generate a longer reference to the title. These keywords are resolved using the following gentext templates for English:

```
<l:template name="docname" text=" in %o"/>
<l:template name="docnamelong" text=" in the document titled %o"/>
```

The `%o` placeholder is filled in with the other document's title. It is taken from the title associated with the root element of the other document in the olink database. You can customize the wording of these two gentext templates to suit your needs, and translate them for other languages. You can also use the `%o` in named xrefstyles in the gentext templates as well.

You can also use the `%o` placeholder in a `template:` type of xrefstyle. That syntax lets you word a cross reference instance as you like and include the other document's title.

You can also globally control the addition of the other document's title using the `olink.doctitle` stylesheet parameter. There are three possible values for this parameter:

yes   If it is set to `yes`, then the stylesheet will append the other document's title for every external olink. However, if the target of the olink is the root element of the other document, then the extra title is omitted so it does not repeat the title. If you need to turn off the generated document title for a particular olink, you can use `select: nodocname` in its `xrefstyle` attribute.

        To generate the title, the stylesheet uses the gentext template with `name="docname"` in the current language's locale file in the `common` directory of the distribution (such as `common/en.xml`). Such gentext templates can be customized to alter the punctuation or connecting words.

maybe   If the parameter is set to `maybe`, then you will get a title only if the `xrefstyle` attribute contains `docname` or `docnamelong`.

no   If you set the parameter to `no`, then no olinks will get a document title, even if the `xrefstyle` attribute calls for it. This setting lets you turn off the feature for all olinks. The default value of the parameter is `no`.

You can also use the `%p` placeholder to generate a page number reference for an olink. If it is an internal olink, then it will be handled like an `xref`. If it is an external olink, this requires your olink database to have `page` attribute values on the `div` and `obj` elements, something that the stylesheet currently cannot generate. But if you find a way to collect such page number information, the olink template will use the data to generate a page number reference.

If you have set up page number processing for external olinks, then you can also turn them on or off globally using the `insert.olink.page.number` parameter. The values and behavior of this parameter are like that of `olink.doctitle`. If `insert.olink.page.number` is set to `yes`, then the stylesheet will try to append a page reference to each external olink. It will use the gentext template named `olink.page.citation` to generate the text, so you can customize that. If the page data for an olink is empty, then no text is generated. If you set the parameter to `maybe`, then you will get a page reference only if the xrefstyle calls for it. If you set the parameter to `no`, then no external olinks will get a page reference, even if the xrefstyle calls for it. The `no` setting lets you turn off the feature for all external olinks. The default value of `insert.olink.page.number` is `no`.

Customizing the olink template

If you need to customize the generated text for olinks beyond what the previous options can do, you can always customize the template with `match="olink"` in the stylesheet module `xref.xsl`. For example, some languages may require a different arrangement of the components of a link, such as putting the page reference first. You can copy the template to your customization layer and make any changes you need.

The first part of the olink template establishes the olink database, gets the data record for the current olink request, and puts the information into a set of variables. The olink template calls several utility templates to perform these functions. Most of the utility templates are located in the stylesheet module common/olink.xsl. You may need to customize one of those templates, depending on your changes. See the section called "Customizing olink XSL templates" (page 404) for a description of those templates.

The second part of the olink template assembles the information into a link written to the output. For example, in XSL-FO output:

```
...
<fo:basic-link external-destination="url({$href})"
               xsl:use-attribute-sets="olink.properties">
  <xsl:copy-of select="$hottext"/>
</fo:basic-link>
<xsl:copy-of select="$olink.page.citation"/>
<xsl:copy-of select="$olink.docname.citation"/>
...
```

If you are customizing the olink template, here you can rearrange the elements, or add text or punctuation.

Formatting olinks

In print, if you want to apply formatting styles to olinks, you can use the olink.properties attribute-set, introduced in version 1.66 of the stylesheet. See the section called "Attribute sets" (page 103) for general information on using attribute-sets.

Any attributes defined in this attribute-set are added to the fo:basic-link element in the output. Typically font changes and color changes are applied in this way. The optional document title and page citation information are not included inside the fo:basic-link, and so are not affected by the style attributes.

If you need a property value to be conditional, then you can add an xsl:choose statement to an attribute body. For example:

```
<xsl:attribute-set name="olink.properties">
  <xsl:attribute name="color">
    <xsl:choose>
      <xsl:when test="@xrefstyle = 'MainLink'">red</xsl:when>
      <xsl:otherwise>inherit</xsl:otherwise>
    </xsl:choose>
  </xsl:attribute>
</xsl:attribute-set>
```

In this example, if an olink has a named xrefstyle="MainLink", then it will appear in red. Be sure to include an xsl:otherwise clause so you do not create an empty property.

For HTML, each olink in the output has a class="olink" attribute on the anchor tag. That permits a CSS stylesheet to apply format styles to olinks.

Options for resolving olinks

The stylesheets have a few options for locating the target of an olink.

If you want to point to the top of another document, you can omit the targetptr attribute on the olink element. The stylesheet will use the targetdoc attribute to locate the data file for the document, and will use the targetptr of the root element in the target data to resolve the link.

In one special circumstance you can omit the `targetdoc` attribute from your olinks. You can do this only if you include a `targetptr` attribute, and there is a single document in the olink database. When is that useful? When you are using olinks only within a modular document that is assembled by XInclude. Using `olink` instead of `xref` for modular documents is described in the section called "Modular cross referencing" (page 369). When you process the document, the olinks must have an olink database to resolve such olinks. If you are not using olinks for external cross references, then the olink database just needs to include the single document.

Another feature to support modular source files is the `prefer.internal.olink` stylesheet parameter. This is useful when you reuse a content module in more than one document. If you cross reference to such a module, you do not want to open another document if the content exists in the current document. Setting `prefer.internal.olink` to 1 causes the stylesheet to first test the current document's olink data to see if it has the `id` or `xml:id` value of the `targetptr`. If it does not, then the stylesheet falls back to the requested `targetdoc` data set.

Language fallback option

Olinks will try to resolve to a document in the same language as the source document. If that fails, then the stylesheet can fall back through a sequence of languages that you specify in the `olink.lang.fallback.sequence` parameter. This is similar to the language negotiation performed by an HTTP browser and server.

This means olinks can work within a collection in which only some of the documents are currently translated. In general you want an olink to resolve to a target document in the same language. This means the olink database should include the data for all translated versions of a document. You can do this by including multiple `document` elements in the database and setting the `lang` attribute in each to different values. You can have `document` elements with duplicate `targetdoc` attributes only if their `lang` attributes differ.

During processing, an olink's source language is determined by the closest ancestor `lang` attribute in the source document. The stylesheet looks for the olink's `targetdoc` in that language first. That is, it looks in the olink database for a `document` element that has both of the matching `targetdoc` and `lang` attributes. If that fails, then it tries the first language in the fallback sequence. If that fails, it goes on to the next, etc.

For example, if you set the `olink.lang.fallback.sequence` parameter to `de en`, and the olink's closest ancestor lang attribute in the source document is `fr`, then the stylesheet first looks in the olink database for a `document` element with a matching `targetdoc` and with `lang="fr"`. If that combination is not found, then stylesheet looks for the same `targetdoc` with `lang="de"`, and finally `lang="en"`.

Debugging olinks

Because olink resolution is more complex now, a new stylesheet parameter `olink.debug` was added. When set to 1, the stylesheet will output messages on how each olink is being resolved. The messages are verbose, and you will likely need to study the XSL templates that generate the messages to understand them fully.

Processing options

The system of processing documents with olinks has some flexibility to adapt to your particular needs. These are some options that might be useful.

- Naming your data files.

- Using Makefiles.

- Using XInclude in the database.

- Profiling with olinks.

- Catalog files.

- Remote olinks.

Naming your data files

You can specify the filename and directory of the generated target data file for a document by using the `targets.fi-lename` parameter. This is useful when you have more than one XML document in the same directory and you need to give them separate data files, or you want to put them in a shared directory.

Using the Saxon example:

```
java com.icl.saxon.StyleSheet  userguide.xml  docbook.xsl \
    collect.xref.targets="only" \
    targets.filename="../shared/mytargetfile"
```

Be sure to specify the same filename for that data file when you create your master target database document.

Likewise, you can choose your own filename and location for the master database file using the `target.database.doc-ument` parameter (`olinkdb.xml` is just a suggested name). This name is used when you want to resolve olinks, so you pass the name to the processor as a command line parameter:

```
xsltproc  --stringparam  target.database.document  "../shared/olinkdb.xml" \
  docbook.xsl  userguide.xml
```

A relative path here is taken as relative to the document being processed.

Using Makefiles with olinking

Olinks create dependencies between documents, and Makefiles are good at tracking dependencies. The following is a simple Makefile for one example document. Other documents would have similar Makefiles.

```
SINGLESTYLE = /tools/xsl/docbook-xsl/docbook.xsl
CHUNKSTYLE = /tools/xsl/docbook-xsl/chunk.xsl

UGOUTPUT = /http/guides/mailuser
AGOUTPUT = /http/guides/mailadmin
REFOUTPUT = /http/reference/mailref

AdminTargets = ../adminguide/target.db
RefTargets = ../man/target.db

html:  $(UGOUTPUT)/userguide.html

$(UGOUTPUT)/userguide.html : userguide.xml target.db  \
                          $(AdminTargets) $(RefTargets)
      java com.icl.saxon.StyleSheet -o $(UGOUTPUT)/userguide.html \
          userguide.xml $(SINGLESTYLE) \
          target.database.document="/projects/mail/olinkdb.xml"

target.db : userguide.xml
      java com.icl.saxon.StyleSheet userguide.xml $(SINGLESTYLE) \
          collect.xref.targets="only" \
          targets.filename="target.tmp"
      if ! diff target.db target.tmp > /dev/null 2>&1 ; \
          then cp target.tmp target.db; fi
      rm target.tmp
```

In the `target.db` rule, the target data is saved to a temporary file first. If it differs from the existing `target.db` file, then it overwrites it. If it does not differ, then the file is not overwritten and its timestamp is left unchanged. Any document changes that do not affect cross reference targets would thus not update the data file. That would prevent unnecessary processing of other documents that have a dependency on its cross reference data.

An alternative to Makefiles is Apache Ant, which is written in Java so it runs on all platforms. It is described at *http://ant.apache.org/*. For help in using Ant with DocBook, see Dave Pawson's article *Docbook and Ant*[1].

Using XInclude in the database document

You can use XInclude instead of system entities in the `olinkdb.xml` database file. That has the advantage of not needing to declare system entities. An XInclude can just specify a path directly to a data file. You also would not need the DOCTYPE document type declaration and the DTD. But you would need an XSL processor that handles XIncludes. See the section called "Processing your modular documents" (page 375) for more information.

The following is a portion of the example database using XInclude:

---

[1] http://www.dpawson.co.uk/docbook/ant.html

```
<?xml version="1.0"?>
<targetset>
  <targetsetinfo>
    Description of this target database document,
    which is for the examples in olink doc.
  </targetsetinfo>

  <!-- Site map for generating relative paths between documents -->
  <sitemap>
    <dir name="documentation">
      <dir name="guides">
        <dir name="mailuser">
          <document targetdoc="MailUserGuide" baseuri="userguide.html">
            <xi:include href="/doc/userguide/target.db"
                        xmlns:xi="http://www.w3.org/2001/XInclude"/>
          </document>
        </dir>
        ...
```

The path to the data file is in the href attribute. You must also declare the XInclude namespace in each include element.

Using catalogs for olink data

You can use catalog files to find your target data files. Catalog files let you map logical names to actual pathnames on a filesystem. That provides greater flexibility, reduces maintenance, and makes your system more portable, since you can just edit catalog files to make changes in locations. These features become more important when you have cross references between documents because the cross reference data files have to be found by the processor at runtime.

If you use system entities in your target database, then you can simplify that file and let the catalog resolve the actual paths to the target data files. The following is what the top of an olink database might look like:

/projects/mail/olinkdb.xml:
```
<?xml version="1.0"?>
<!DOCTYPE targetset SYSTEM "targetdatabase.dtd" [
<!ENTITY ugtargets SYSTEM "ugtargets.ent">
<!ENTITY agtargets SYSTEM "agtargets.ent">
<!ENTITY reftargets SYSTEM "reftargets.ent">
]>
```

The XML catalog file that could resolve those entity paths into actual file pathnames could look like the following:

/tools/catalog.xml:
```
<?xml version="1.0"?>
<!DOCTYPE catalog
    PUBLIC "-//OASIS/DTD Entity Resolution XML Catalog V1.0//EN"
    "http://www.oasis-open.org/committees/entity/release/1.0/catalog.dtd">
<catalog xmlns="urn:oasis:names:tc:entity:xmlns:xml:catalog">
  <system systemId="targetdatabase.dtd"
          uri="file:///tools/docbook-xsl-1.73.1/common/targetdatabase.dtd" />
  <system systemId="ugtargets.ent"
          uri="file:///doc/userguide/target.db" />
  <system systemId="agtargets.ent"
          uri="file:///doc/adminguide/target.db" />
  <system systemId="reftargets.ent"
          uri="file:///doc/man/target.db" />
</catalog>
```

When the processor reads the `olinkdb.xml` file, it will use the catalog to resolve the locations of the system entities for each of the target data files. See Chapter 5, *XML catalogs* (page 47) for more information about using XML catalog files.

Olinks with profiling (conditional text)

If you use profiling (conditional text), then you must separate your data for the different profiles. You do not want target data in a data file for elements that may be excluded from the current profile. That would lead to olinks that seem to resolve, but that do not actually work in the HTML output.

You need to create a separate data file for each profile a document can be rendered in. You do that by running the collection process with the profile parameters set, and saving the output to a different name by setting the `targets.filename` parameter. Because the target collection process uses the same stylesheet settings as when you process the document in a given profile, the data will include only elements in that profile. The following is an example of collecting targets while processing for output with a profile:

```
xsltproc --output unixbook.html \
    --stringparam profile.os "unix" \
    --stringparam targets.filename  "unix.profile.db" \
    --stringparam collect.xref.targets "yes" \
    .../html/profile-docbook.xsl  mybook.xml
```

This will generate the `unixbook.html` output and the target data file named `unix.profile.db`. When you process other documents with olinks for that profile, you need to use this data file to resolve them.

To use profiled data files, you can do it in either of two ways.

- Set up multiple master database documents, one for each profile. Then you can reference the appropriate profiled data filenames in each database. When you process your documents with olinks, you specify the profiled database with the `target.database.document` parameter at runtime.

- Use a single master database document, but remap its references using an XML catalog. You set up a catalog for each profile, and then specify at runtime the correct catalog for a given profile. Each catalog maps whatever the identifier is for a given document in the master database to its appropriate profiled data file. For example, the following entry in a master database:

```
<!ENTITY ugtargets SYSTEM "/doc/userguide/target.db">
```

could be remapped with this entry in a "unix profile" XML catalog:

```
<system
   id="/doc/userguide/target.db"
   uri="file:///doc/userguide/unix.profile.db" />
```

If you have multiple independent profile selectors, it is quite possible the number of permutations is too complex for olinks. You might establish the writing convention that olinks are not to be pointed at targets that have conditional attributes. Point to a higher level container without conditional attributes instead.

Remote olink targets

You can use olinks to link to documents that are available on a website. The only requirement is that you be able to obtain the olink target data for such documents. Then you can set the `baseuri` attribute to a full path URI that points to the document's path on the website. You can mix remote documents with local documents as well, as this example illustrates:

```
<document targetdoc="moduleA" baseuri="../doc">
  <xi:include href="moduleA/target.db" ...>
</document>
<document targetdoc="moduleG" baseuri="http://my.website.net/modules">
  <xi:include href="moduleG/target.db" ...>
</document>
```

When an olink points to `targetdoc="moduleA"`, it will form a local link. When an olink points to `targetdoc="moduleG"`, then it will form a full URL to the website.

Customizing olink XSL templates

The XSL templates for generating olinks were modularized in version 1.66 to permit easier customization. These are the templates that can be customized to change the behavior of olinking.

`select.target.database`	This template is called for each olink to select the olink target database filename. By default, it selects the value of the `target.database.document` parameter. If you customize this template, then you could use more than one olink database when processing a document.
`select.olink.key`	This template is called for each olink to select the data for the olink. The key here is the combination of `targetdoc/targetptr/lang` that will actually be used for this olink. Currently this template recurses through the languages to find the best match. It also handles the cases of a missing `targetdoc` or `targetptr` attribute, and the `prefer.internal.olink` parameter.
`make.olink.href`	This template assembles the complete URI for each olink. This is output as the `href` for an HTML link, or as the `external-destination` attribute for an FO link.
`olink.hottext`	This template assembles the generated text for an olink, except for the optional document title or page citation.
`olink.docname.citation`	This template generates the optional title of the target document. You may not need to customize this template if you customize the associated gentext template instead.

olink.page.citation
This template generates the optional page number citation for an olink. You may not need to customize this template if you customize the associated gentext template instead.

insert.olink.docname.markup mode
This is a mode that handles wrapping format styles around the optional document title generated for a olink. This permits you to make the other document's title italic or some other format.

See the section called "Replacing templates" (page 107) for a general discussion of customizing DocBook XSL templates.

Target database additional uses

You may find additional uses for the target database that keeps track of potential olink targets. The database contains structured information about a collection of documents. The information includes the hierarchy of division and section elements, with enough information to form links to them. You could, for example, generate a master table of contents for all of your documents. Or you could parse the XML data into a relational database that can be used to manage your modules and their content.

25

Other output forms

The DocBook XSL stylesheets have a flexible design that permit them to be customized for specific applications. These customizations are included with the DocBook XSL distribution or are available from the DocBook SourceForge website at *http://sourceforge.net/projects/docbook/*.

XHTML	For generating XHTML (*Extensible HyperText Markup Language*) from DocBook XML files.
HTML Help	For generating HTML files suitable for use in the Microsoft HTML Help online documentation system.
JavaHelp	For generating HTML files suitable for use in Sun Microsystem's JavaHelp™ online documentation system.
Eclipse Platform help system	For generating HTML files suitable for use in the Eclipse Platform help system.
Formatted plain text	A method, not a stylesheet, for generating formatted plain text output.
Unix man pages	For generating manual pages in troff markup from `refentry` elements.
Microsoft Word	For generating a WordML that can be loaded into Microsoft Word. You can also create Word files that can be converted DocBook.

XHTML

XHTML is HTML reformulated in XML. XHTML is a W3C Recommendation, and is described in *XHTML™ 1.0 The Extensible HyperText Markup Language (Second Edition)*[1]. One of the goals of the reformulation was to move all formatting out of the HTML and into the CSS stylesheet, thus separating content from style. But the authors also recognized the need to transition from existing HTML, so there are actually three DTDs for XHTML 1.0:

Strict (xhtml1-strict.dtd)
The strictest version of XHTML, with no formatting elements or attributes.

---

[1] http://www.w3.org/TR/xhtml1/

Transitional (xhtml1-transitional.dtd)
> Retains most HTML formatting elements of HTML 4.

Frameset (xhtml1-frameset.dtd)
> Same as Transitional buts adds HTML frameset elements.

XHTML uses XML syntax, so it differs from HTML. The original HTML was written in SGML, and uses features that are only in SGML and not XML:

- Omission of end tags is permitted in HTML, so you will often see a `<P>` tag without its closing `</P>` tag. Such omissions are not allowed in XML, so all start tags in XHTML must have a closing tag (except empty elements).

- Empty elements in HTML do not use the trailing slash character. Thus HTML uses `<HR>` while XHTML uses `<HR/>`, or sometimes `<HR />`. The extra space is often included for backwards compatibility with browsers that are not XHTML-aware.

There are several other differences between HTML and Transitional XHTML. The W3C included *HTML Compatibility Guidelines*[2] in the XHTML specification to help create XHTML that is compatible with existing HTML browsers.

Strict XHTML is very different from HTML. It permits no elements or attributes that are intended for formatting, on the assumption that a CSS stylesheet will be handling all formatting. So attributes such as `type` on an `ol` list are not permitted (indicates number format for numbered list), or `width` on a table cell.

Generating XHTML

The DocBook XSL stylesheet distribution includes a set of stylesheets that generate XHTML. These stylesheets are in the `xhtml` subdirectory of the distribution, and include versions of `docbook.xsl` for single-file output and `chunk.xsl` for chunked output. These stylesheets are derived from the HTML stylesheets, so they have all the same features and parameters.

Keep in mind that not all browsers support XHTML. Some people are still using web browers that predate XHTML. If you want the highest number of people to be able to read your output without problems, then you will have to use HTML for awhile yet.

XHTML using xsltproc

To generate XHTML output using xsltproc, you can use commands such as these:

Single file XHTML:
```
xsltproc  \
    --output  myfile.xhtml  \
   xhtml/docbook.xsl  myfile.xml
```

Chunked XHTML:
```
xsltproc  \
   --stringparam chunker.output.doctype-public \    For versions 1.61 and earlier
           "-//W3C//DTD XHTML 1.0 Transitional//EN" \
   --stringparam chunker.output.doctype-system \    For versions 1.61 and earlier
           "http://www.w3.org/TR/xhtml1/DTD/xhtml1-transitional.dtd" \
   xhtml/chunk.xsl  myfile.xml
```

---

[2] http://www.w3.org/TR/xhtml1/#guidelines

Prior to version 1.62 of the stylesheets, the chunking stylesheet did not output a DOCTYPE declaration, so you had to specify the extra parameters as shown here. Since version 1.62, the Transitional DOCTYPE is output automatically so you do not need those parameters.

If you examine the output, you will notice some differences from the HTML version of the output:

- The top of the output file has an XML declaration and a reference to the XHTML DTD in its DOCTYPE:

```
<?xml version="1.0" encoding="UTF-8"?>
<!DOCTYPE html PUBLIC "-//W3C//DTD XHTML 1.0 Transitional//EN"
    "http://www.w3.org/TR/xhtml1/DTD/xhtml1-transitional.dtd">
```

- The output encoding is UTF-8, the default XML encoding.

- The head element includes an XHTML namespace declaration:

```
<html  xmlns="http://www.w3.org/1999/xhtml">
```

Since this declaration appears in the document's root element, its scope is the whole document. The declaration does not include a namespace prefix, which means it is the default namespace, so all tags without a prefix are in that namespace. That permits content in other namespaces (such as MathML) to be mixed in as long as its elements use their own namespace prefix.

- The body element has no attributes, which are not permitted in XHTML Strict.

- Anchor name attributes are replaced with id attributes.

The nice thing about using xsltproc is that it detects that the DOCTYPE is XHTML and adjusts the serialization of the output so it follows most of the HTML compatibility guidelines. This enables more browsers to be able the read the XHTML.

XHTML using Saxon

To generate XHTML using Saxon, you use commands similar to those of xsltproc. However, Saxon does not automatically detect that it is outputting XHTML. Fortunately, you can use a Saxon extension that causes Saxon to adjust its output to satisfy the HTML compatibility guidelines. You must set up the extension in a customization layer. Here are the steps.

1. Create a customization layer for XHTML processing. It is like other DocBook customization files, except in the xsl:import statement you import one of the XHTML stylesheets, xhtml/docbook.xsl or xhtml/chunk.xsl.

2. Make the following changes, highlighted in boldface, to the customization layer:

```
<xsl:stylesheet xmlns:xsl="http://www.w3.org/1999/XSL/Transform"
        xmlns:saxon="http://icl.com/saxon"
        version="1.0">
<xsl:import href="../docbook-xsl/xhtml/chunk.xsl"/>
<xsl:output method="saxon:xhtml" />
```

These changes add the saxon namespace to the stylesheet's root element, and then use that namespace to declare a Saxon extension output method.

3. Use a standard Saxon command to process your documents with your customization layer:

Single file XHTML:
```
java com.icl.saxon.StyleSheet \
    -o myfile.html  myfile.xml  \
    custom-xhtml-docbook.xsl
```

Chunked XHTML:
```
java com.icl.saxon.StyleSheet \
    myfile.xml  \
    custom-xhtml-chunk.xsl
```

Notice that you do not have to use the chunker.output.doctype parameters to get the XHTML DOCTYPE in chunked output. Saxon does that automatically. You can, however, add other stylesheet parameters as needed.

Generating Strict XHTML

By default, the DocBook XSL stylesheets generate Transitional XHTML. There is no option or parameter for turning on Strict XHTML processing. By following certain Strict XHTML guidelines, you can produce output that would validate with the Strict DTD. However, the DOCTYPE declaration in the output will still refer to the Transitional XHTML DTD. Here is how you insert a reference to the Strict XHTML DTD instead.

If you are using the docbook.xsl stylesheet , then you need a stylesheet customization layer to change the xsl:output element to specify a different DTD. This is how it should appear in your customization file:

```
<xsl:output method="xml"
    encoding="UTF-8"
    indent="no"
    doctype-public="-//W3C//DTD XHTML 1.0 Strict//EN"
    doctype-system="http://www.w3.org/TR/xhtml1/DTD/xhtml1-strict.dtd"/>
```

If you are using the chunk.xsl stylesheet, you can change it with two parameters. You can set the parameters in a customization layer, or on the command line as shown here:

```
xsltproc \
    --stringparam chunker.output.doctype-public \
        "-//W3C//DTD XHTML 1.0 Strict//EN" \
    --stringparam chunker.output.doctype-system \
        "http://www.w3.org/TR/xhtml1/DTD/xhtml1-strict.dtd" \
    xhtml/chunk.xsl  myfile.xml
```

You can also use these parameters for single file output if you use the xhtml/onechunk.xsl stylesheet instead of xhtml/docbook.xsl. See the section called "Single file options with onechunk" (page 69) for more information on using onechunk.xsl.

Validating XHTML

The DocBook XSL stylesheets are capable of producing XHTML that can be validated with either the Transitional or Strict XHTML 1.0 DTDs (the Frameset DTD is not considered because DocBook does not output frameset elements). But it is also possible to produce XHTML that will *not* validate with either of them.

If your goal is to produce valid XHTML, you need to keep some guidelines in mind when creating your DocBook XML source files and selecting your processing options.

Transitional XHTML guidelines

By default, the DocBook XSL xhtml stylesheets output Transitional XHTML. However, there are still some things you need to do to satisfy the requirements of the DTD.

- In XHTML, all `img` elements are required to have an `alt` attribute. See the section called "Alt text" (page 294) for more information on outputting `alt` attributes.

Strict XHTML guidelines

To validate with the Strict XHTML DTD, you need to follow the Transitional XHTML guidelines as well as the following Strict guidelines:

- Process your documents with the `css.decoration` parameter set to zero. That will avoid the use of style attributes in XHTML elements where they are not permitted.

- Your images in `mediaobject` elements cannot make use of a *viewport*. To create a viewport in HTML, the stylesheets use a table and set the row height. Unfortunately, a `height` attribute is not permitted on an XHTML Strict `tr` element.

- In your `imagedata` elements, avoid the use of alignment attributes `align` and `valign`.

- If you have `textobjects` that will generate `longdesc` attributes in images, then you need to turn that feature off because it includes an alignment attribute in the `div` element. You can turn it of by setting the `html.longdesc` parameter to zero.

- Set parameter `ulink.target` to null because the `target` attribute is not permitted on a anchor elements.

- Table data element `td` does not take a `width` attribute.

- `ol` does not take a `type` attribute.

- Set parameter `use.viewport` to zero so that `img` does not get a `border="0"` attribute.

- Footnotes generate an `hr` element with `align="left"` and `width="100%"`, neither of which are permitted.

Customizing XHTML

The XHTML stylesheets can be customized in a manner very similar to the HTML stylesheets. You create a customization layer that imports the XHTML stylesheet, and then sets parameters and customizes templates. The following example shows how to get started.

```
<?xml version="1.0"?>
<xsl:stylesheet xmlns:xsl="http://www.w3.org/1999/XSL/Transform"
        version='1.0'>

<xsl:import href="/path/to/docbook-xsl/xhtml/docbook.xsl"/>
```

Your customizations go here.

```
</xsl:stylesheet>
```

Keep these differences in mind:

- The output method is XML, not HTML.

  ```
  <xsl:output  method="xml"/>
  ```

- All literal output elements need to be in the XHTML namespace. The easiest way to do that is to make it the default namespace for your stylesheet customization layer. You can do that by including the namespace attribute in the root element of your stylesheet customization file:

```
<xsl:stylesheet xmlns:xsl="http://www.w3.org/1999/XSL/Transform"
                xmlns="http://www.w3.org/1999/xhtml"
                version="1.0">
```

If you do not include the namespace attribute in the stylesheet, then you will get namespace attributes in your XHTML output as an element switches out of the default XHTML namespace.

HTML Help

HTML Help is a version of HTML suitable for generating help documents for Microsoft Windows. You can write your help information in DocBook XML, and generate HTML Help files using a customized DocBook XSL stylesheet that is included with the distribution.

Generating HTML Help

Creating HTML Help is a two-step process:

1. Process your DocBook XML document with the DocBook `htmlhelp.xsl` stylesheet.

2. Compile the resulting files with a HTML Help compiler, either from Microsoft or a third party.

In the first step, you process your DocBook help document like you would for chunked HTML, but with a customized version of the chunking stylesheet. The customized stylesheets are located in the `htmlhelp` subdirectory of the stylesheet distribution. You use one of these stylesheets with your favorite XSLT processor:

`htmlhelp.xsl`   The main stylesheet file for generating HTML Help output.

`profile-htmlhelp.xsl`   A further customization that supports profiling to filter your DocBook XSL files before generating output.

For example:

```
xsltproc \
    ../docbook-xsl/htmlhelp/htmlhelp.xsl \
    myhelpdoc.xml
```

The output of this process is a collection of HTML files and some non-HTML files. The HTML files are chunked HTML files with the navigational headers and footers removed. In fact, you can use all of the stylesheet parameters and customizations you would normally use when generating chunked HTML.

The non-HTML files provide information to the HTML Help compiler. These files include:

`htmlhelp.hhp`   The HTML Help project file lists compile options, the size and location of the help window, and a list of HTML files to be included.

`toc.hhc`   The contents file provides the information for creating the left pane table of contents in HTML Help. It uses nested UL lists to indicate structure, and includes the section titles and HTML file-names so links will work.

index.hhk
: The HTML Help index file. This file will contain index entries if your document contains DocBook indexterm elements and you set the htmlhelp.use.hhk parameter to 1. See the section called "Generating an index" (page 416) for more information.

alias.h
context.h
: Optional files, generated if you are doing context sensitive help. See the section called "Context-sensitive help" (page 418) for more information.

The filenames can be changed with stylesheet parameters, as described in the section called "Filenames and locations" (page 416). Once you have generated the set of files, you can compile them into HTML Help. There are several options for that:

- Start Microsoft's HTML Help Workshop application, and use the File menu to open the htmlhelp.hhp project file. It should list the contents, and provide you with an option to compile it. If you do not have Microsoft's HTML Help Workshop, you can download it for free from *http://msdn.microsoft.com/*.

- Use Microsoft's command line compiler hhc.exe with the project file as its first argument. The compiler is included with Microsoft's HTML Help Workshop.

- Use a third-party HTML Help compiler.

Processing options

The DocBook HTML Help stylesheets let you control various options by setting stylesheet parameters. Each parameter has a reference page that is included with the distribution documentation, and can also be reached online at *http://docbook.sourceforge.net/release/xsl/current/doc/html/* in the HTML Help section.

Display options

With stylesheet parameters, you can control:

- The help window title, size and position.

- Whether the help menu appears.

- Which standard toolbar buttons are displayed.

- Adding custom toolbar buttons.

Here are the parameters that control these features.

Window options

htmlhelp.title
: The Help application title to display in the window's title bar.

htmlhelp.window.geometry
: Set the size and position of the HTML Help window when it opens. Its value looks like the following:

```
[160,64,992,704]
```

The first two numbers indicate the position of the upper-left corner of the window, and the second two numbers the position of the lower-right corner. All numbers are in pixels, measured from the upper-left corner of the screen. So this example creates a window that is 832 pixels wide (992 - 160) and 640 pixels tall, positioned 160 pixels from the left edge and 64 pixels down from the top.

`htmlhelp.remember.window.position`
> If set to 1, the Help window will restore its last size and position when it starts again.

`htmlhelp.hhp.windows`
`htmlhelp.hhp.window`
> These two parameters help you create additional windows for your HTML Help application. The first parameter lets you create additional windows for the Help application. For example:

```
<xsl:param name="htmlhelp.hhp.windows">secondWindow=,"Another Help Window",,\
    "furtherHelp.html",,,,,,0x20,,0x4c,[100,200,422,394],,,,,,,0</xsl:param>
```

> The content of the parameter is appended to the [Windows] section of the generated project file. The second parameter tells the application which is the default window to use when opening. It should be a window name as defined in the project file. To put content or links into the secondary windows, you need to customize the XSL stylesheet to insert script code in the HTML files. See the Microsoft's HTML Help documentation to see what code to insert. See the section called "Inserting external HTML code" (page 152) for an example of inserting code in DocBook-generated HTML.

Display the menu

`htmlhelp.show.menu`
> If set to 1, the Help application will have the standard menus at the top. Otherwise, there is no menu and navigation is done by buttons only.

Display standard buttons and tabs

You can select which toolbar buttons are displayed in your Help application. Each parameter controls one button. Set its value to 1 to display the button, or to zero to hide it. The following table lists the button parameters.

Standard button name	Parameter
Hide/Show	`htmlhelp.button.hideshow`
Back	`htmlhelp.button.back`
Forward	`htmlhelp.button.forward`
Stop	`htmlhelp.button.stop`
Refresh	`htmlhelp.button.refresh`
Home	`htmlhelp.button.home`
Options	`htmlhelp.button.options`
Print	`htmlhelp.button.print`
Locate	`htmlhelp.button.locate`
Next	`htmlhelp.button.next`
Previous	`htmlhelp.button.previous`
Zoom	`htmlhelp.button.zoom`

Another parameter, `htmlhelp.show.toolbar.text`, turns on or off the text labels that appear below the buttons.

Create custom buttons

You can add one or two buttons that link to HTML pages outside of the Help application. These buttons are called jump buttons, and each one has three parameters: to display the button, to label the button, and to identify the link for the button. The following table lists the parameters that control the custom buttons.

Custom button	Parameters	Description
Custom button 1	`htmlhelp.button.jump1`	When set to 1, display this button.
	`htmlhelp.button.jump1.title`	Specify the text to show below the button.
	`htmlhelp.button.jump1.url`	Jump to this URL when pressed.
Custom button 2	`htmlhelp.button.jump2`	When set to 1, display this button.
	`htmlhelp.button.jump2.title`	Specify the text to show below the button.
	`htmlhelp.button.jump2.url`	Jump to this URL when pressed.

Table of contents pane

The following parameters let you control various aspects of the table of contents window pane that appears to the left of the Help text. That pane shows an expandable table of contents for the Help content.

`htmlhelp.hhc.show.root`
> If set to 1 (the default), then the top level of the TOC list is the book title. Since this single entry at this level is often redundant with the window frame title, it is frequently set to zero, which shows a longer list of topics to choose from.

`htmlhelp.hhc.width`
> Specifies the width of the TOC pane, in pixels. If not set, then you get the default width.

`htmlhelp.autolabel`
> If set to 1, displays numbering of chapters and sections in the TOC pane if they are numbered in the content. This feature is off by default.

`htmlhelp.hhc.section.depth`
> Specifies how many levels of nested sections to include in the TOC pane. Set to 5 by default, which means all section levels are included.

`htmlhelp.default.topic`
> Specifies the HTML chunk filename to be displayed in the right-hand pane when the Help window opens. If not specified, then it takes the chunk generated by the root element of the document, which is usually `index.html`. Since this chunk usually repeats the table of contents that is already being shown in the left pane, it is not uncommon to choose the first real content chunk for this parameter.
>
> To get a stable chunk filename to point to, add an `id` attribute (or `xml:id` for DocBook 5) to the topic's element in your DocBook file, and set the stylesheet parameter `use.id.as.filename` to 1. Then the `id` or `xml:id` value will be used as the filename.

`htmlhelp.show.favorites`
> If set to 1, then a Favorites tab is added to the top of the TOC pane. The Favorites pane lets the reader save bookmarks into the Help file. The default is zero.

`htmlhelp.show.advanced.search`
> If set to 1, then the Search pane has more advanced search options. If set to zero (the default), then the Search pane has just basic search options.

`htmlhelp.hhc.folders.instead.books`
> If set to 1 (the default), then the TOC list displays icons that look like folders instead of books. Note that this parameter has no effect if the `htmlhelp.hhc.binary` is set to 1.

`htmlhelp.hhc.binary`
> If set to 1 (the default), it compiles the TOC into a binary form to improve performance. This setting also enables the Next and Previous buttons.

Generating an index

When you generate your HTML Help using DocBook XSL, your Help file will have an Index tab in the TOC pane that contains all the titles in your document. That is the minimum index that can be generated. They appear because the stylesheet embeds code like the following in the HTML output for each title:

```
<OBJECT type="application/x-oleobject"
        classid="clsid:1e2a7bd0-dab9-11d0-b93a-00c04fc99f9e">
  <param name="Keyword" value="My Title"/>
</OBJECT>
```

If your DocBook document contains `indexterm` elements, then those will also automatically be converted to entries in the Help index.

The `htmlhelp.use.hhk` parameter controls how your `indexterm` elements are converted to index entries. If `htmlhelp.use.hhk` is set to zero, then the stylesheet inserts an `OBJECT` element similar to the above example into the HTML output for each `indexterm`. If the parameter is set to 1, then the terms are instead put into the `index.hhk` file. You will still get a `index.hhk` file if the parameter is set to zero, but it will be almost empty. You can ignore the warning issued by the compiler about the empty file.

The advantage of putting the index entries in the separate `index.hhk` file is that the links to the index terms will go to the exact location in the HTML file, instead of to the top of the topic. Unfortunately, if there are multiple occurances of the same index term, the index list will display the term instead of the topic titles (this is a bug in HTML Help). There is no known workaround for this problem, except to leave the parameter value at zero and accept links going to the top of the topic.

Filenames and locations

Each of the non-HTML files that are generated by the stylesheet can have its filename changed by its own parameter.

`htmlhelp.hhp`
> Change the filename of the project file from the default `htmlhelp.hhp`. You should retain the `.hhp` suffix so the compiler can recognize the file type.

`htmlhelp.hhc`
> Change the filename of the table of contents file from the default `toc.hhc`.

`htmlhelp.hhk`
> Change the filename of the help index file from the default `index.hhk`.

`htmlhelp.chm`
> Change the filename of the compiled Help file from the default `htmlhelp.chm`. This file is generated by the compiler, but its name is specified in the project file.

`htmlhelp.map.file`
> Change the filename of the optional context-sensitive help map file from the default `context.h`.

`htmlhelp.alias.file`
> Change the filename of the optional context-sensitive help alias file from the default `alias.h`.

In addition to specifying the filenames, two more parameters control where the HTML files are generated.

base.dir
> This standard chunking parameter lets you add a directory prefix to all the HTML files generated by the chunking process.

manifest.in.base.dir
> If this parameter is set to 1, then the non-HTML Help files such as htmlhelp.hhp are also placed in the directory specified by the base.dir parameter.

If manifest.in.base.dir is set to 1, then all your files end up in the same directory, the one specified by the base.dir parameter. Also, all references to the files from the htmlhelp.hpp project file will have no path prefix. Because they are in the same directory as the project file, the Help compiler will find them.

If manifest.in.base.dir is set to 0 (the default), then your non-HTML files end up in the current directory. All references to HTML files from the htmlhelp.hpp project file will have the base.dir path prefix added to them so the compiler can find them. The Help file will build with either configuration, so it is mostly a matter of your preference for managing files.

If you use a CSS stylesheet to style your HTML, you will have to copy it manually to the directory specified by the base.dir parameter. The same is true for any image files.

Language and encoding

If you are processing non-English files, there are two features of the stylesheets you need to consider.

- The language code for the Help file.

- The character encoding of the HTML files.

Even if you are processing English files, you need to consider the encoding in order to get all the special characters you might be using in your document.

HTML Help language

The Help compiler needs to know what language the project files are in, because they do not have any encoding identifiers like the HTML files do. That information is supplied by a Language property in the htmlhelp.hhp project file, as for example:

Language=0x0409 English (UNITED STATES)

That property is inserted into the project file by the stylesheet based on the root element's lang attribute in your DocBook document. If there is no lang attribute on the root element, then en is used. The actual text string is taken from the gentext file for that language, such as common/en.xml:

```
<l:context name="htmlhelp">
   <l:template name="langcode" text="0x0409 English (UNITED STATES)"/>
</l:context>
```

If the wrong value is inserted, then you will likely get mangled output. If for some reason you need a language string that is different from the one supplied by the stylesheet for your language, you can customize the gentext template, using the process described in the section called "Customizing generated text" (page 106).

HTML Help encoding

You must also consider the character encoding of the HTML files that are generated by the stylesheet. For a general discussion of encoding, see Chapter 20, *Languages, characters and encoding* (page 325).

The encoding of the HTML output has to be one that your Help compiler recognizes. The UTF-8 encoding covers most languages and special characters. Unfortunately, the Microsoft Help compiler does not recognize UTF-8 encoding. Some of the third-party Help compilers do support UTF-8. If you are using the Microsoft compiler, two encodings that are often used are iso-8859-1 and windows-1252.

You can establish the output encoding of the stylesheet using the htmlhelp.encoding parameter, which is set to iso-8859-1 by default. That encoding covers the basic European languages, but does not contain some special characters such as longer dashes, typographical quotes, or the ™ or Euro symbols. The windows-1252 encoding is identical to iso-8859-1 over most of its range, but includes more special characters, including trademark and euro.

If you want to use windows-1252 as your output encoding, you have to consider what XSLT processor you are using. The xsltproc processor can output windows-1252, as can any XSLT processor that implements the *EXSLT* document() extension function. On the other hand, Xalan does not support changing the output encoding for chunked files, so it cannot output windows-1252.

Saxon 6.5.5 can output the windows-1252 encoding under the right conditions. You must use the DocBook Saxon extension file from version 1.67 or later of the stylesheets. To do that, you add the extensions/saxon653.jar file from the stylesheet distribution to your CLASSPATH. You must also set three stylesheet parameters and a Java property for it to work:

```
java
    -Dencoding.windows-1252=com.nwalsh.saxon.Windows1252 \
    com.icl.saxon.StyleSheet  \
    myhelpfile.xml  \
    docbook-xsl/htmlhelp/htmlhelp.xsl  \
    htmlhelp.encoding=windows-1252 \
    chunker.output.encoding=windows-1252 \
    saxon.character.representation=native
```

These complications are necessary because Saxon 6.5.5 does not itself support that encoding. It is written as a Saxon extension and included with the DocBook XSL distribution.

Context-sensitive help

If you intend for your Help file to be used for context-sensitive help with an application, you must provide additional information in your DocBook document. The additional information provides the connections between points in your application and points in your document, so that help requests return context-sensitive help.

The extra information is added in the form of processing instructions. For example:

```
<chapter id="install">
  <?dbhh topicname="IDH_opt_installation" topicid ="1234"?>
  <title>Installing optional components</title>
  ...
```

The IDH_opt_installation is a unique identifier string for this help topic, and the 1234 topicid is a unique number that can be added to your application to find that topic.

When you process your document with htmlhelp.xsl, you will find two new non-HTML files generated, context.h and alias.h. They will contain lists of the information you provided in the processing instructions:

In context.h:
```
#define IDH_opt_installation  1234
```

In alias.h:
```
IDH_opt_installation=install.html
```

These two files are identified in the `htmlhelp.hhp` project file properties in the `[MAP]` section and the `[ALIAS]` section, respectively. See the Microsoft HTML Help API reference for more information about using context-sensitive help topics in your application.

You do not have to embed processing instructions in your document to do context-sensitive help. The `context.h` and `alias.h` files can be written by hand, perhaps based on information provided by the software application developer. You can then set the `htmlhelp.force.map.and.alias` parameter to 1 so these files will still listed in the project file.

Build options

There are a few stylesheet parameters that control features of the build process.

`htmlhelp.htmlhelp.only`
> If set to 1, then the stylesheet builds only the non-HTML files. This is useful when you are not changing the DocBook document, only the parameters used to configure the Help files. The default value is 0.

`htmlhelp.display.progress`
> If set to 1 (the default), then the compile displays its progress as it goes.

`htmlhelp.hhp.tail`
> If you have special content you need to add to the end of your project file, then put that content into this parameter. Whatever is there will be appended to the `htmlhelp.hpp` file each time the stylesheet is used.

`htmlhelp.enhanced.decompilation`
> When set to 1, allows for enhanced decompilation for your `.chm` help file. The default is zero.

`htmlhelp.enumerate.images`
> If set to 1, then the pathnames of all the images used in the document are added to the project file's `[FILES]` section. This is not necessary if your images all use relative `fileref` attributes in your DocBook file to find them, and they are located in the same directory or a subdirectory of the project file location. But if they use absolute paths, are located outside the project directory tree, or if they use `entityref` in the DocBook file, then you should turn on this parameter to help the compiler find the files. The default value is 0.

`htmlhelp.force.map.and.alias`
> If set to 1, then the stylesheet will add the following lines to the project file, even if you have no `dbhh` processing instructions in your document.
>
> ```
> [ALIAS]
> #include alias.h
> [MAP]
> #include context.h
> ```
>
> These files are used for context-sensitive help. Set this parameter to 1 when you will be creating or enhancing these files manually.

Formatting options

The primary areas of controlling formatting for HTML Help are:

- Chunking control.

- Tables of contents.

- Section numbering.

- CSS styles.

- Headers and footers.

These are described in the sections that follow.

Chunking control

Online help is usually presented in small chunks of content rather than long scrolling files. You should consider to what level of section depth you should chunk your content, in order to keep the chunks small but not so small that they contain too little information.

Because the `htmlhelp.xsl` stylesheet is a customization of the `chunk.xsl` stylesheet, you can use all of that stylesheet's parameters to configure the chunking behavior.

`chunk.section.depth`
> The maximum section depth that will become a chunk. If set to 1 (the default), then all sections at level 1 become a chunk, and any sections at higher levels are contains as subsections within their chunk. If set to 2, then all sections at levels 1 and 2 become chunks, and so on.

`chunk.first.sections`
> If set to 1, then the first section in each chapter becomes a chunk. If set to zero (the default), then the first section is part of the beginning-of-chapter chunk.

`root.filename`
> Determines the name of the top-level chunk filename (without the suffix). It is `index` by default.

`use.id.as.filename`
> If set to 1, then the HTML filename uses the element's `id` or `xml:id` attribute as the first part of the filename. The default is zero.

`html.ext`
> Determines the filename suffix for each generated HTML file. The default is `.html` (include the dot).

`chunk.tocs.and.lots`
> If set to 1, then the top level table of contents and any lists of titles (such as List of Figures) are put into a separate chunk. The default is zero.

`chunk.separate.lots`
> If set to 1, then each list of titles (such as List of Figures, List of Tables, etc.) is put into its own chunk, and a link to each is added under the table of contents. The default is zero.

`chunk.tocs.and.lots.has.title`
> If set to 1, then the top level table of contents chunk displays a repeat of the top level title. The default is zero.

Tables of contents

You may want to turn off all tables of contents in the HTML content, because the Help TOC frame on the left provides that information. If you turn off TOCs in the content, then that information is not repeated in the content pane on the right. The easiest way to turn off all TOCs in content is to set the `generate.toc` parameter to an empty string.

If instead you want to customize how TOCs are rendered in content, then see the section called "Tables of contents (TOC)" (page 125).

Section numbering

You can turn on chapter or section numbering using standard DocBook stylesheet parameters, as described in the section called "Chapter and section numbering" (page 74). By default, the chapter and section numbers that appear in the right content pane do not appear in the left TOC pane in the Help viewer. This parameter turns them on:

`htmlhelp.autolabel`
> If set to 1, includes the numbers of chapters and sections in the TOC pane. This feature is off by default. It will only display numbers of items are numbered in the content.

CSS styles

HTML Help supports using a CSS stylesheet for controlling formatting of the displayed content. The CSS code must be compatible with the Internet Explorer browser that will be used to read the help file. The basic process of writing and using a CSS stylesheet with DocBook is described in the section called "Using CSS to style HTML" (page 71). To ensure that your stylesheet is included in the Help file, you must set the `html.stylesheet` parameter to the name of the file. That will put a `LINK` element in each HTML file, and the compiler will include the referenced stylesheet in the compiled Help file.

If your CSS file references other files, such as graphical icons, then those are not automatically detected, and will need to be added to the project's file list. That can be done with the `htmlhelp.hhp.tail` parameter that can contain another `[Files]` section to be added to the end of the project file.

Headers and footers

The HTML Help customization turns off the regular chunk headers and footers in the output. Those headers and footer provide navigation links that are instead provided by the Help interface. However, you can turn them back on, or you can substitute your own through parameters and customization.

* To restore the normal chunk headers and footers, then set the `suppress.navigation` parameter to zero. It is set to 1 by default to turn them off in HTML Help.

* To create customized headers and footers, see the section called "HTML headers and footers" (page 148).

Additional resources

Here are some additional resources when working with DocBook HTML Help:

* Dave Pawson's *HTML Help FAQ*[3].

* Microsoft's help files for HTML Help Workshop. You can sometimes make a change to a project using the Workshop interface, and then examine the project file to see what changed. You could then incorporate those changes into a parameter or customization of the XSL stylesheet.

* The `docbook-apps` mailing list, which has many active users of DocBook HTML Help who can answer questions.

JavaHelp

Sun Microsystem's JavaHelp™ online documentation system can be used to provide help for Java-based applications. The best source of information on JavaHelp is Sun's website *http://java.sun.com/products/javahelp/*. They offer a JavaHelp User's Guide, a FAQ, and other documentation.

---

[3] http://www.dpawson.co.uk/docbook/styling/htmlhelp.html

The standard DocBook XSL distribution includes customized stylesheets that can generate JavaHelp files from DocBook XML documents. The stylesheets are located in the `javahelp` subdirectory of the distribution. You can use one of the following stylesheet files with your favorite XSLT processor:

`javahelp.xsl`   The main stylesheet file for generating JavaHelp output.

`profile-javahelp.xsl`   A further customization that supports profiling to filter your DocBook XSL files before generating output.

You use these stylesheets as you would the regular chunking DocBook XSL stylesheets. For example:

```
xsltproc \
    --stringparam  base.dir  helpfiles/  \
    --stringparam  use.id.as.filename  1 \
    javahelp/javahelp.xsl \
    myfile.xml
```

Since `javahelp.xsl` is based on `chunk.xsl`, it has all the same default settings, and accepts all the same parameters for changing those defaults. Since the preceding command example does not change the chunking level, it chunks on `sect1` (and equivalent first-level `section`), but not the first one in each chapter.

The `javahelp.xsl` stylesheet also generates the support files needed for JavaHelp:

`jhelpset.hs`   HelpSet file that defines the components of your help application.

`jhelptoc.xml`   JavaHelp table of contents file.

`jhelpmap.jhm`   JavaHelp Map file that maps `id` values to HTML files.

`jhelpidx.xml`   A JavaHelp index,. The index is empty unless your document has `indexterm` elements.

Eclipse Platform help system

The *Eclipse Platform*[4] is an open-source integrated development environment (IDE) for programmers. Its open architecture permits new modules to be added to the platform as plugins by anyone. To provide online help for any new modules, Eclipse Platform includes a help system that is based on HTML. When you install your help files, also as a plugin, then your help content will appear in the Eclipse Platform help table of contents.

Starting with version 1.62.0, the DocBook XSL distribution included a stylesheet for generating Eclipse Platform help files. The stylesheet, authored by Jirka Kosek, is located at `eclipse/eclipse.xsl` in the DocBook XSL distribution.

The `eclipse.xsl` stylesheet is a customization of the chunking stylesheet for HTML output. You can apply it to your DocBook XML help document with your favorite XSLT processor, just as you would with the chunking stylesheet. In addition to generating a set of chunked HTML files, the `eclipse.xsl` stylesheet generates these two extra files:

`plugin.xml`   The manifest file that tells Eclipse Platform how to integrate your help files into the Eclipse help system.

`toc.xml`   The table of contents of your document prepared as an XML file for the Eclipse Platform.

---

[4] http://www.eclipse.org/

You will need to set three stylesheet parameters, either on the XSLT processor command line or in a stylesheet customization layer. These parameters pass information to the `plugin.xml` manifest file to properly configure your content for the Eclipse Platform.

`eclipse.plugin.name`	The title of the help content. This will be displayed in the Eclipse Platform help list.
`eclipse.plugin.id`	A unique identifier for this plugin, such as `org.eclipse.help.example.ex1`. This is also the directory name of your help plugin in the Eclipse `plugin` directory.
`eclipse.plugin.provider`	Your name, company name, or organization name.

1. Process your DocBook XML file with the `eclipse.xsl` stylesheet with the three stylesheet parameters set.

2. Put the resulting html files, `toc.xml` file, and `plugin.xml` file into a directory named for your `eclipse.plugin.id`.

3. Install that directory in the Eclipse Platform's `plugins` directory on the systems that need to use the help content.

The next time the user starts the Eclipse Platform, the new help content should be available in the Help Contents.

For additional information on the Eclipse Platform help system, see the article *DocBook for Eclipse: Reusing DocBook's Stylesheets*[5] by Jirka Kosek, and the *Online Help Sample* in the Eclipse Platform help contents after you install Eclipse.

Formatted plain text

Sometimes it is useful to be able to generate output that is simply plain text. For example, you may need plain text for a README file. It would be fairly simple to delete all the markup tags from a DocBook document, but the result would not be very satisfactory. Paragraphs might be readable, but tables would not be. Also, there would be no generated text such as number labels and xref text.

What you want is text that is processed by a DocBook stylesheet and formatted sufficiently to be meaningful. Unfortunately, there is no DocBook XSL stylesheet dedicated to generating formatted plain text. Most people who need formatted text use a two-step process:

1. Process the DocBook into HTML output.

2. Use a text-based web browser to convert the HTML to formatted plain text.

There are at least three nongraphical text-based web browsers that you can choose from to format HTML as plain text:

Lynx   The original text-based web browser, still used by many people. The latest version handles simple tables. Lynx is available from *http://lynx.browser.org/* for most platforms. You can use its `-dump` option to save the formatted text to a file:

```
lynx -dump myfile.html > myfile.txt
```

ELinks   An enhanced version of the Links (no relation to Lynx) character browser. It handles tables better than Lynx. ELinks is available from *http://www.elinks.or.cz/*. It also has a `-dump` option:

```
elinks -dump myfile.html > myfile.txt
```

---

[5] http://www.xml.com/pub/a/2003/08/13/docbook-eclipse.html

W3M   A text-based browser developed in Japan that can handle tables. It is available from
http://w3m.sourceforge.net/. W3m also has a -dump option:

```
w3m -dump myfile.html > myfile.txt
```

Conversion of HTML generated by DocBook works quite well with these browsers. That's because the HTML is
pretty clean. DocBook's HTML output does not use frames, layout tables or Javascript, all features that are hard for
text-only browsers to handle. Any CSS styling you apply will be lost, of course.

Refentry to man

If you work in a Unix or Linux environment, then you are probably familiar with reference manual pages, or "man
pages". A man page typically documents a single command in great detail. It is divided into several standard subsections, such as Name, Synopsis, and Description, among others. The DocBook refentry element was originally
modeled on the man page structure. The format of a man page consists of text interspersed with nroff markup using
the man macro set. The Unix or Linux **man** command converts such markup into a formatted page on demand.

You may be called upon to convert DocBook refentry elements to standard man page format for distribution with
a product. Fortunately, there is a stylesheet available to do just that. It is also named docbook.xsl, and it is included
in the DocBook XSL distribution in the manpages subdirectory. This stylesheet is different from the other stylesheets
in that it outputs plain text rather than HTML or XML. This is triggered by this xsl:output stylesheet element:

```
<xsl:output method="text"
        encoding="ISO-8859-1"
        indent="no"/>
```

This stylesheet only knows how to convert refentry elements to man page files. If you process a DocBook document
that contains refentry elements, it will generate one man page file for each refentry element. It will ignore the
other parts of the document.

The filename for each man page is generated from refentry content elements. The filename prefix is the refname,
and the suffix is the manvolnum from within the refmeta element. A typical filename might be myfunction.3. If there
is more than one refname in a refentry, then only the first one is used for the filename.

> **Caution:**
>
> If you are processing many refentrys from the same document, make sure they will all produce unique filenames, or else any
> duplicates will overwrite each other.

To generate a set of man pages from a DocBook document, you can use a command like the following:

```
xsltproc  manpages/docbook.xsl  myfile.xml
```

You do not have to specify an output file because the names are generated by the stylesheet. The stylesheet will list
each file as it is produced.

Man to refentry

You may be faced with the opposite problem: you have man pages but you need to convert them to DocBook
refentry elements. In that case, you want to use the free **doclifter** utility written by Eric Raymond. It is designed
to convert troff markup into DocBook files. You can download the utility from *http://www.catb.org/~esr/doclifter/*. The
documentation provides the syntax and options. You may need to clean up some parts of the conversion, because
man pages are quite varied in their use of troff macros.

Microsoft Word

Sometimes it is necessary to deliver DocBook content in a file format that is compatible with Microsoft® Word. There are several approaches that use different input files that Word understands.

- Use the DocBook XSL-FO stylesheet to convert your file to XSL-FO, and then use XMLmind's XFC product to convert the FO to RTF, which Microsoft can load. XMLmind's XFC is an XML conversion engine, with one output being RTF. It comes in a free Personal edition, and a Professional edition that is not free. See the *XMLmind website*[6] for more information.

- If you are willing to author your DocBook using a subset of its elements, then you can use the stylesheets that are included in the `roundtrip` directory in the DocBook XSL distribution (these stylesheets were created by Steve Ball and were in the `wordml` directory prior to version 1.72 of the stylesheets). These stylesheets can convert a subset of DocBook elements to WordML, which is an XML vocabulary that Word understands. You can also export from Word to WordML, and convert that to Docbook using other stylesheets in the same directory. See the file named `supported.xml` in the `roundtrip` directory for a list of supported DocBook elements. See Steve Ball's website *http://www.explain.com.au/oss/docbook/* for documentation.

- Jfor is an XSL-FO to RTF converter that is maintained on SourceForge, but it appears to no longer be an active project.

---

[6] http://www.xmlmind.com/foconverter/what_is_xfc.html

26
Profiling (conditional text)

Profiling is the term used in DocBook to describe conditional text. Conditional text means you can create a single XML document with some elements marked as conditional. When you process such a document, you can specify which conditions apply for that version of output, and the stylesheet will include or exclude the marked text to satisfy the conditions. This feature is useful when you need to produce more than one version of a document, and the versions differ in minor ways. Then you do not have to maintain separate documents that are nearly but not quite the same, and thereby run the risk of the separate documents getting out of synchronization as you make changes. With conditional text, you keep all the variations in the same document and select the ones you want at production time.

This feature is typically used to create different versions of a document for different audiences. That's where the term profiling comes in. You can create a document profiled for a particular audience. For example, software that runs on different platforms might need different installation instructions for each platform, but might otherwise be the same. You can create one version profiled for Linux customers and another profiled for Windows customers.

Marking conditional text

To mark text for inclusion or exclusion, the DocBook DTD provides several appropriate attributes that are common to most elements. You need to select one or more attributes and assign key words based on the conditions you want to apply. For example, the os attribute is used to specify a software operating system. You can assign the keywords linux or win to mark an element as conditional for Linux or Windows, respectively. It is up to you to pick the key words, and you must be consistent in their usage.

The following table summarizes the common attributes that can be used to conditionalize elements. The table also shows the profiling parameter used to select content marked with each attribute, as described in the section called "Processing profiled versions" (page 430).

Table 26.1. Profiling attributes

Attribute Name	Description	Profiling parameter
arch	Computer or chip architecture, such as i386.	profile.arch
audience	Intended audience of the content, such as instructor. Added in DocBook version 5.0.	profile.audience
condition	General purpose conditional attribute, with no preassigned semantics.	profile.condition
conformance	Standards conformance, such as lsb (Linux Standards Base).	profile.conformance
lang	Language code, such as de_DE.	profile.lang
os	Operating system.	profile.os
revision	Editorial revision, such as v2.1.	profile.revision
revisionflag	Revision status of the element, such as changed. This attribute has a fixed set of values to choose from.	profile.revisionflag
role	General purpose attribute, with no preassigned semantics. Use with caution for profiling.	profile.role
security	Security level, such as high.	profile.security
status	Editorial or publication status, such as InDevelopment or draft.	profile.status
userlevel	Level of user experience, such as beginner.	profile.userlevel
vendor	Product vendor, such as apache.	profile.vendor
wordsize	Word size (width in bits) of the computer architecture, such as 64bit. Added in DocBook version 4.4.	profile.wordsize

You can also designate any attribute name as a profiling attribute by setting a couple of stylesheet parameters. This is most useful when you have extended the DTD to add custom attributes. See the section called "Custom profiling attribute" (page 433) for more information.

Caution:

The only profiling attribute that requires particular care is role, which might be used for other purposes besides marking conditional text. See the section called "Using the role attribute for profiling" (page 436) for more information. If the condition key words you want to use do not seem to fit any of the other profiling attribute descriptions, then use the general purpose condition attribute since it is made for that purpose.

The following is an example of how one of these attributes might be used.

```
<sect1 os="win">
  <title>Installation on Windows</title>
  ...
</sect1>
<sect1 os="linux">
  <title>Installation on Linux</title>
  ...
</sect1>
```

This example has two parallel sect1 elements with different values for the os attribute, one for the Windows version and one for the Linux version. In general you only want one of these sections to appear in the output for a particular version.

A conditional attribute applies to the element and its children, so each entire section is conditionalized by adding the attribute to the `sect1` start tag. You can use these common attributes on almost any element, from high level elements like `chapter` down to low-level elements like `para` or even inline elements within a paragraph.

Marking small bits of text

If you want to conditionalize just part of the text of an element, you can use the `phrase` element to mark the text. For example, if the only difference is one sentence within a paragraph, you can mark it this way:

```
<para>To open a file, select File Open. <phrase os="win">The default
configuration lists share drives such as E: as well as the C: hard
drive.</phrase>
<phrase os="linux">The default configuration lists NFS-mounted filesystems
as well as local filesystems.</phrase> Choose the file from the list.</para>
```

Note these features of using `phrase`:

- A `phrase` element is permitted in most places that general text can be used, including within `para`, `title`, and `literallayout`, among others. The DocBook DTD is the final authority for where `phrase` can be used.

- It can contain any text from a single word up to many sentences, and can include inline markup including index terms. However, `phrase` cannot contain block elements like `para` and such.

- It is especially useful within a `title` element, since the DTD permits only one title child element per parent. Instead of trying to conditionalize two title elements, put two conditionalized `phrase` elements within a single `title` element.

Multiple profiling conditions

Your profiling needs may be more complex and require you to use more than one category of profiling. For example, you might have conditions for `userlevel` and `os`.

Note these features of multiple profiling conditions:

- You can use more than one profiling attribute in a document, and even on the same element. For example:

  ```
  <para  os="win"  userlevel="beginner">
  ...
  </para>
  ```

  Both conditions must be matched at processing time for the element to be included.

- Whichever profiling attributes are used in your documents must be accounted for when you process the documents. If you are using three different profiling attributes, you will need to set three conditions at processing time.

- You can assign more than one key word to a profiling attribute by separating them with semicolons. For example, if you profile on `os` with the key words `linux`, `unix`, or `win`, then an element that applies to both `linux` and `unix` should have the attribute `os="linux;unix"`. Then it will be selected if either of `linux` or `unix` is specified at processing time.

- If you need AND logic on a profile parameter, you can use two profiling passes. For example, normally an element with `os="linux;unix` is selected if either `linux` OR `unix` is specified at runtime. If you need this to mean `linux` AND `unix`, and exclude the single values `os="linux"` and `os="unix"`, then perform two profiling passes. In the first pass, set `profile.os="linux"` to exclude `os="unix"`, and in the second pass select `profile.os="unix"` to exclude `os="linux"`. Only those with `os="linux;unix"` will survive.

- Take special care if you need to nest conditionalized elements. A condition applies to an element and all of its content. If the container element is not selected during processing, then the interior elements are never even considered.

Processing profiled versions

After you have marked your conditional content with profiling attributes, you select which content to include at runtime by setting certain profiling parameters. For example, if you set the stylesheet parameter `profile.userlevel` to the value advanced, then the stylesheet will include all elements with a userlevel="advanced" attribute, and exclude all elements that have a userlevel attribute with some other value. All the profiling parameters are listed in Table 26.1, "Profiling attributes" (page 428).

There are actually two methods for running the profiling process to select content:

- *Single-pass processing*, in which the profiling stylesheet first selects the profiled content, stores it in an internal node-set, and then generates the output from that internal node-set. This is all done with a single XSLT process.

- *Two-pass processing*, in which you use a separate stylesheet that generates a profiled version into a temporary file, and then you process that temporary file with the standard DocBook stylesheet or customization. This requires two separate XSLT processes run in sequence.

Which method you use depends on these factors:

- If your document contains xref or link cross references, then you may need to use the two-pass method. That is because ID lookups are not standardized for internal node-sets, so not all processors can resolve them. Saxon and Xalan work, but xsltproc does not. Switching all cross references to use olink would permit you to use single-pass processing.

- If your XSLT processor does not support the *EXSLT*[1] node-set() function, then you must use the two-pass method. Saxon, Xalan, and xsltproc support it, but MSXSL does not, for example.

- If you want to be able to examine the effects of profiling on your XML content, then use two-pass processing and examine the temporary profiled version.

Single-pass processing

In the current implementation, single-pass profiling is handled with customized versions of the DocBook stylesheets. This was done to avoid the overhead of profiling for those who do not use the feature. The profiling stylesheets perform the normal DocBook XSL processing after doing the profiling step to select the content to process. These stylesheets are included with the DocBook XSL distribution.

Table 26.2. Profiling stylesheets

For generating this output:	Instead of this standard stylesheet:	Use this profiling stylesheet:
Single HTML file	`html/docbook.xsl`	`html/profile-docbook.xsl`
Multiple chunked HTML files	`html/chunk.xsl`	`html/profile-chunk.xsl`
XSL-FO file	`fo/docbook.xsl`	`fo/profile-docbook.xsl`

---

[1] http://www.exslt.org

These stylesheets can be used by any XSLT processor that supports the *EXSLT*[2] `node-set()` function. That includes Saxon, Xalan, and xsltproc. It does not include MSXSL, however. For that processor and others that do not support EXSLT `node-set()`, you need to perform a separate profiling step as described in the section called "Two-pass processing" (page 431).

By default, the profiling stylesheets will output all elements, whether they are marked with profiling attributes or not. That is probably not what you want. You set the conditions for selecting marked elements by passing stylesheet parameters to the XSLT processor. For example, if you want to select elements whose profiling attribute os has the value `linux`, you would set the stylesheet parameter `profile.os` to `linux`. Here are some command examples.

Using xsltproc:
```
xsltproc  --output  myfile.linux.html  \
    --stringparam  profile.os  "linux" \
    html/profile-docbook.xsl  \
    myfile.xml
```

Using Saxon:
```
java  -cp  "../saxon653/saxon.jar" \
    com.icl.saxon.StyleSheet \
    myfile.xml \
    html/profile-chunk.xsl \
    profile.os="linux" \
    base.dir="html/"
```

Using Xalan:
```
java  org.apache.xalan.xslt.Process \
    -out  myfile.linux.html \
    -in  myfile.xml \
    -param  profile.os  linux \
    -xsl  html/profile-docbook.xsl
```

When the `profile.os` parameter is set to a non-blank value like `linux`, then all instances of the os attribute in the document are examined and only those elements with the `linux` value are included in the output. Any other elements that have an os attribute whose value does not match `linux` are ignored. And of course any elements that do not have an os attribute at all are included in the output as well.

Similar stylesheet parameters are available for the other profiling attributes. If you are profiling on the `condition` attribute, then you would set the `profile.condition` stylesheet parameter to the selected value, and so on.

If you are using more than one profiling attribute, you will need to set a parameter for each one. Any for which you do not will have all versions included in the output, which is probably not what you want.

If you need to specify two or more key words for one profiling attribute, you can put them in the parameter separated by semicolons (but no spaces). For example, if you want to select all elements whose arch attribute value is `i386`, `i486`, or `i586`, then specify the `profile.arch` parameter as `i386;i486;i586`.

Two-pass processing

A separate stylesheet is available to perform just the profiling step, without also applying the DocBook style templates. The output is a filtered version of your original XML document, with the profiling conditions applied so that some elements are excluded. That profiling-only stylesheet is useful when your document contains xref or link which

---

[2] http://www.exslt.org

cannot be resolved with the single-pass processing, or if you are using an XSLT processor that does not support the EXSLT `node-set()` function.

The profiling-only stylesheet can be found at `profiling/profile.xsl`, a separate directory in the DocBook XSL distribution. It accepts the same profiling parameters as the single-pass profiling stylesheets. The following is an example of how to use it.

Generate profiled XML file:
```
xsltproc  --output  myfile.linux.xml  \
    --stringparam  profile.os  "linux" \
   profiling/profile.xsl \
   myfile.xml
```

Generate output:
```
xsltproc
    --output myfile.linux.html \
   html/docbook.xsl \
   myfile.linux.xml
```

The result of the first command is a file named `myfile.linux.xml`, which is your original document but with the non-linux elements removed. It is then processed with the stock DocBook XSL stylesheet.

Customization and profiling

If you are using a stylesheet customization layer, you can still do profiling with it. Two methods are available:

- Import the profiling stylesheet instead of the stock DocBook stylesheet into your customization layer. For example:

  ```
  <xsl:import  href="../html/profile-docbook.xsl"/>
  ```

  You might want to create separate profiled customization files, one for each profiling stylesheet you need.

- Or use two-pass processing. Use the profile-only stylesheet to create a profiled DocBook document, and then process it with your customized stylesheet.

Validation and profiling

If you use profiling, you will want to make sure that your documents are valid both before and after the profiling step. You will want them to be valid before profiling so that you can use a validating authoring tool to help you write the files. And the profiled versions should also be valid because the DocBook XSL stylesheets assume the document being processed is valid DocBook. You may get strange results if it is not valid. The profiling step could make a valid document invalid, and most XSLT processors do not take the time to validate the input XML.

Here are some of the areas to watch out for:

- When you add a profiling attribute to an element, consider whether the document will still be valid if the element is deselected during profiling. Even if it is valid, make sure the document will still make sense if it is profiled out.

- do not try to use multiple `title` elements at the same location. The DTD permits only a single `title` in any element. Instead, use multiple `phrase` elements within the single `title` element, and put the profiling attributes on the `phrase` elements.

Alternatively, you could exploit the fact that DocBook info elements such as `chapterinfo` permit multiple `title` elements. You could put multiple profiled titles inside the element's info element. In either case, make sure only one of the titles is selected during processing.

- You cannot have duplicate `id` or `xml:id` attributes in a document. If you need to put an `id` or `xml:id` on a chapter, section, or figure for cross referencing, then you cannot have multiple versions of that element with the same id value. You'll have to create a single element with the id and make the content of the element conditional. It helps if only part of the content needs to be conditional.

- Nesting conditional elements adds significant complexity to your document. You have to consider each combination of profiling values to see if it will be valid and make sense.

To ensure that your profiled documents are valid, you might want to apply the profiling-only stylesheet described in the section called "Two-pass processing" (page 431). You will want to perform just the first step to generate the profiled DocBook document, and then run a DTD validation check on that temporary document. However, by default the profiled output does not include a DOCTYPE declaration, and so a validator does not know what DTD to validate the document against.

To validate a profiled document, you could use `xmllint` with the `--dtdvalid` option, which can apply an external DTD that is designated on the command line. The `xmllint` program is included in the `libxml2` distribution necessary for xsltproc. For example:

```
xmllint --dtdvalid /path/to/docbookx.dtd --noout myfile.xml
```

You could also create a customization layer for the profiling stylesheet which inserts a DOCTYPE declaration in the profiled output. The `xsl:output` element lets you specify both the PUBLIC and SYSTEM identifiers for a DOCTYPE. The profiling stylesheet does not do that by default because it does not know what version of the DTD you want to validate against. The following customization layer will generate a DOCTYPE for version 4.5 of the DocBook DTD:

```
<?xml version="1.0"?>
<xsl:stylesheet xmlns:xsl="http://www.w3.org/1999/XSL/Transform"
                version='1.0'>

<xsl:import href="../docbook-xsl/profiling/profile.xsl"/>

<xsl:output method="xml"
   doctype-public="-//OASIS//DTD DocBook XML V4.5//EN"
   doctype-system="http://www.oasis-open.org/docbook/xml/4.5/docbookx.dtd"/>
</xsl:stylesheet>
```

This will result in a profiled document that includes a DOCTYPE:

```
<?xml version="1.0"?>
<!DOCTYPE book PUBLIC "-//OASIS//DTD DocBook XML V4.5//EN"
      "http://www.oasis-open.org/docbook/xml/4.5/docbookx.dtd">
<book>
...
```

With this DOCTYPE in place, you can validate the profiled output against the standard DocBook DTD.

Custom profiling attribute

The profiling stylesheets let you designate any attribute name as a profiling attribute by setting a couple of parameters. This is most useful when you want to profile on an attribute that is not normally used for such. See the next section if you want to create entirely new attributes for profiling.

As an example of using an existing attribute for profiling, you may be preparing a new draft of a document at the same time you are producing the current released version. You could mark those elements that are scheduled to be deleted with the attribute `revisionflag="deleted"`, and then use the `revisionflag` attribute as the profiling attribute.

First set the `profile.attribute` stylesheet parameter to the value `revisionflag` to indicate the attribute name to profile on.

When you want to produce a version that omits the elements marked for deletion, then set the `profile.value` parameter to the value `changed;added;off`. Since `revisionflag` in an enumerated attribute, these are all the allowed values except `deleted`. The profile process will include all content marked with `revisionflag` set to anything but `deleted`, as well as any content without a `revisionflag` attribute.

Adding new profiling attributes

Your need for profiling conditions may go beyond those provided by the standard DocBook profiling attributes, most of which are computer related (`os`, `arch`, etc.). What if you want to profile on model number, or OEM business name, or some other property for which there is no suitable attribute in DocBook?

If you want to add custom attributes to DocBook and use them for profiling, you need to take two steps:

1. Add the attribute declarations to the DocBook DTD (DocBook version 4) or RelaxNG (DocBook version 5).

2. Add support for your new attributes in the stylesheets.

Adding attributes to the DTD

Adding new profiling attributes to the DocBook 4 DTD is pretty easy because the DocBook DTD has hooks for customization in the form of empty parameter entities. A parameter entity is an entity that is used only in the DTD. If you declare such an entity before the empty declaration, then your entity's content will take precedence and be merged into the DTD.

The DocBook 4 DTD has a set of common attributes that are available on almost all elements. A subset of those common attributes are the profiling attributes, and they are declared in a parameter entity named `effectivity.attrib`. There is another parameter entity named `local.effectivity.attrib` that can be used to add new attributes.

You can extend the DTD in the internal or external subset of the DTD. The internal DTD subset is declared in the DOCTYPE inside your documents. The following example declares two new profiling attributes:

```
<!DOCTYPE book PUBLIC "-//OASIS//DTD DocBook XML V4.5//EN" "docbookx.dtd" [
<!ENTITY % local.effectivity.attrib
   "model  CDATA  #IMPLIED
    oem  CDATA  #IMPLIED">
]>
<book>
...
```

If you have a lot files, adding declarations to the internal subset can be a tedious process. In such cases, it is usually easier to add to the external DTD subset, which is in the DTD files stored outside the documents. For DocBook, you can create a custom DTD file that contains your custom parameter entity declarations and then imports the standard DTD.

```
<!ENTITY % local.effectivity.attrib
    "model  CDATA  #IMPLIED
    oem  CDATA  #IMPLIED">

<!ENTITY % DocBookDTD PUBLIC "-//OASIS//DTD DocBook XML V4.5//EN"
                "docbookx.dtd">
%DocBookDTD;
```

This example assumes you are putting the custom DTD in the same directory as docbookx.dtd. You can use a relative path, an absolute path, or a catalog entry to resolve the path. Then the DOCTYPEs in your documents just need to reference your custom DTD file instead of the standard DTD. You can avoid that editing chore by using an XML catalog file to redirect your existing PUBLIC or SYSTEM identifier to your new file.

Once you have added the new attribute declarations, you can use your new attributes in your documents for profiling. For example:

```
<para oem="acme">The Acme Company ...</para>
<para oem="bingham">The Bingham Company ...</para>
```

Adding attributes to RelaxNG

If you are using DocBook version 5, then the standard schema for it is written in RelaxNG. The schema is written using the compact syntax of RelaxNG, and it is structured to make it easy to add attributes in a customization of the schema. The flexibile parameter entity structure used in DocBook 4 is replaced with an even more flexible named pattern system in DocBook 5's RelaxNG. Although there is a DTD version of DocBook 5 available, but it is not structured with parameter entities as in DocBook 4, so it is harder to customize.

To add an attribute to the RelaxNG schema in the compact syntax, you create a new file that imports the stock schema and then adds any changes. To add an attribute, you must first find the named pattern in the schema that would best hold your new attributes and then use the RelaxNG append syntax. Here is an example similar to the one in the previous section.

```
namespace db = "http://docbook.org/ns/docbook"

include "docbook.rnc" inherit = db

db.effectivity.attributes &=
    attribute model { text }?
    & attribute oem { text }?
```

The &= syntax means to append these new attributes to the existing pattern named db.effectivity.attributes. That pattern contains the other profiling attribute declarations, and is part of the common attributes used by most elements.

Profiling with new attributes

Once you have created your new attributes, you need to customize the stylesheets to recognize and respond to them for profiling. This can be done by copying and customizing one big template from the stylesheet module profiling/profile-module.xsl. This needs to be done in a customization of a profiling stylesheet, as described in the section called "Customization and profiling" (page 432).

```
<xsl:template match="*" mode="profile">  ❶

  <xsl:variable name="arch.content">  ❷
    <xsl:if test="@arch">
      <xsl:call-template name="cross.compare">
        <xsl:with-param name="a" select="$profile.arch"/>
        <xsl:with-param name="b" select="@arch"/>
      </xsl:call-template>
    </xsl:if>
  </xsl:variable>
  <xsl:variable name="arch.ok" select="not(@arch) or not($profile.arch) or
                                       $arch.content != '' or @arch = ''"/>

  <xsl:variable name="oem.content">  ❸
    <xsl:if test="@oem">
      <xsl:call-template name="cross.compare">
        <xsl:with-param name="a" select="$profile.oem"/>
        <xsl:with-param name="b" select="@oem"/>
      </xsl:call-template>
    </xsl:if>
  </xsl:variable>
  <xsl:variable name="oem.ok"  ❹
                select="not(@oem) or not($profile.oem) or
                        $oem.content != '' or @oem = ''"/>
...

  <xsl:if test="$arch.ok and $oem.ok and $condition.ok and  ❺
      $conformance.ok and $lang.ok and $os.ok and
      $revision.ok and $revisionflag.ok and $role.ok and
      $security.ok and $status.ok and $userlevel.ok and
      $vendor.ok and $attribute.ok">
    <xsl:copy>  ❻
```

❶ This is the main template for selecting profiled content. It matches on all elements.

❷ This variable is an example of how an existing profile attribute such as arch is handled. You should copy these lines and change the name for your new attribute.

❸ New variables created for a new profile attribute, modeled after an existing profile attribute.

❹ This variable determines if the new attribute is to be selected during profiling.

❺ Include the oem.ok variable in the final test where all conditions are applied.

❻ If the profiling attributes permit, then copy the current element to the output. Thus this element is selected for inclusion during profiling.

Using the role attribute for profiling

It generally is not a good idea to use role as your profiling attribute. That's because role can be used for other purposes in a document, with other key words to express those purposes. If you use role for profiling, and if you do not add those other key words in your selection parameter, then you may exclude text unintentionally.

As an example, you might use role="strong" in an emphasis element that is to be rendered in boldface in print. You might also use role="linux" to mark conditional text, and then process the file with the parameter profile.role="linux" to select that text. But remember that every instance of the profiling attribute is examined, so every <emphasis role="strong"> element will simply disappear from your profiled output because strong does not match linux.

If you insist on using `role` as your profiling attribute, then you can compensate by using multiple keywords in the parameter, separated by semicolons. You need to include all other possible values of `role` that are not to be treated as conditional text. In this simple case, you would set the parameter to `profile.role="linux;strong"`.

27

Program listings

Technical documentation often requires presentation of examples of program code. The examples must preserve the line breaks and indents in order to be understood. The preferred element to contain such examples is `programlisting`, although `screen` or `literallayout` may also be used. If you use `literallayout`, you should set its `class` attribute to the value of `monospaced` to ensure presentation in a monospaced font by the stylesheets. The `programlisting` and `screen` elements are always presented in a monospaced font. Any of these elements can also be wrapped in `example` or `figure` elements if you want to add a title. This chapter focuses on `programlisting`, but most of the features apply to the other display elements as well.

You can type your text directly in a `programlisting` element, and its indents and line breaks will be preserved. Use multiple spaces instead of tab characters for indents. Tab characters are not defined in the XSL-FO spec, so they will likely be converted to single spaces and ruin your indent alignments. See the section called "Tab expansion" (page 440) for solutions if you need to use tab characters.

A `programlisting` element permits some child elements that you can use to highlight certain text, including `replaceable`, `emphasis`, and `parameter` among others. You can also use character entities such as `&trade;` or math symbols. In fact, you must use character entities `&lt;`, `&gt;`, and `&amp;` for the XML special characters <, >, and &, which would otherwise be interpreted as XML markup. Keep in mind that element tags and entities take up more space in the raw XML than in the output, so you have to take that into account while editing for alignment.

You can turn off interpretation of characters that would be recognized as XML markup by enclosing the text in a CDATA section, as in the following example:

Example 27.1. CDATA example

```
<programlisting><![CDATA[          Start of CDATA section
# Shell redirection and background processing
sort -o sorted  < unsorted  &
]]>                                       End of CDATA section
</programlisting>
```

Without the CDATA markup, the < and & characters would be interpreted as start-of-element and start-of-entity characters, respectively. Within the CDATA markup, they are treated as ordinary characters. In fact, the only markup recognized within CDATA is the sequence]]> to terminate the CDATA section. That means you cannot use DocBook elements like <emphasis> or entities like ™ within a CDATA section.

Formatting listings

Formatting a program listing for HTML output is best handled by CSS. Read the `class` attributes generated by the HTML stylesheet and write CSS selectors to apply styles. See the section called "Styling displays with CSS" (page 72) for an example.

For print output, there are a few parameters and attribute sets that can alter the style of displays. The `monospace.verbatim.properties` attribute-set applies attributes to the `fo:block` that contains the listing. In it you can set the `font-family`, `font-size`, `line-height`, and other formatting properties to match your design. For example:

```
<xsl:attribute-set name="monospace.verbatim.properties">
  <xsl:attribute name="font-family">Lucida Sans Typewriter</xsl:attribute>
  <xsl:attribute name="font-size">9pt</xsl:attribute>
  <xsl:attribute name="keep-together.within-column">always</xsl:attribute>
</xsl:attribute-set>
```

The `keep-together` property will try to keep each listing together on a page. That works well if your listings are short. If they are long, though, you may get large white spaces in your output, if a long listing that might start in the middle of a page is instead bumped to start on the next page. If you have a mix of lengths, see the section called "Keep-together processing instruction" (page 89) for how to use a processing instruction for some of them.

You can add background shading to listings by setting the `shade.verbatim` stylesheet parameter to 1. When you do that, another attribute-set named `shade.verbatim.style` is applied to the block. The following example customization sets a background color and draws a border (with a little padding) around each listing.

```
<xsl:param name="shade.verbatim" select="1"/>

<xsl:attribute-set name="shade.verbatim.style">
  <xsl:attribute name="background-color">#E0E0E0</xsl:attribute>
  <xsl:attribute name="border-width">0.5pt</xsl:attribute>
  <xsl:attribute name="border-style">solid</xsl:attribute>
  <xsl:attribute name="border-color">#575757</xsl:attribute>
  <xsl:attribute name="padding">3pt</xsl:attribute>
</xsl:attribute-set>
```

> **Tip:**
>
> When you turn on shading, and especially if you turn on borders, you will find that extra blank lines at the beginning or end of a `programlisting` element become quite obvious. You will want to edit those out.

Tab expansion

Often a program listing will include tab characters to indent lines of code. When such a listing is imported to DocBook XML and formatted, the tab characters are not expanded as they are in the program editor. That's because in XSL-FO and HTML, tab stops and tab expansion are not described in either HTML or XSL-FO standards. By default, an XSL-FO processor treats a tab character as a single space, which leads to unsatisfactory results.

One solution is to prepare each such program listing by converting each tab character to a suitable number of space characters. The algorithm is not quite as simple as replacing each tab with a fixed number of spaces, because tab stops are at fixed locations and not fixed space widths. If you only have a few listings and you do not have to update them in the future, this is a feasible solution. If you are importing many such program listings, or they need to be updated on a regular basis, then converting the tabs ahead of processing is a tedious chore.

There is an extension function written in Java for the Saxon XSL processor that will expand tab characters so they appear formatted as in a program editor. The extension was written by Tomas Hajek and is available for download from *http://www.tomashajek.net/*. Here are the steps for using this extension with the Saxon processor.

1. Download the `saxon.tomashajek.net1.0.jar` file from his website, install it in a convenient location, and add it to your Java CLASSPATH.

2. In your customization layer, add the following to your stylesheet root element:

```
<xsl:stylesheet
    xmlns:hajek="http://net.tomashajek.saxon.Tabify"
    exclude-result-prefixes="hajek"
    ...
```

If your stylesheet already has an `exclude-result-prefixes` attribute, then just add the `hajek` prefix name to the list.

3. Add the following template that executes the extension function if it is available:

```
<xsl:template match="text()">
  <xsl:choose>
    <xsl:when test="function-available('hajek:tabify')">
      <xsl:value-of select="hajek:tabify(.,8)"/>
    </xsl:when>
    <xsl:otherwise>
      <xsl:value-of select="."/>
    </xsl:otherwise>
  </xsl:choose>
</xsl:template>
```

The second argument to the `tabify()` function (8, in this case) indicates the spacing of tab stops.

Once this is set up, you should be able to process program listings that include tab characters and they should expand. If they do not expand, it is most likely because the command is not finding the function due to problems with the Java CLASSPATH.

Fitting text

Some code examples may have lines that are too long or too deeply indented to fit on a printed page. Long lines are not a problem in HTML output, because a browser window can be scrolled to view long lines. But printed text should not exceed the established margins. Three possible solutions are full-page width, reducing the font size, or breaking long lines.

Full-width examples

If your body text is normally indented on the printed page, you might want to take advantage of the extra space for wide listings and other wide examples.

If you put your `programlisting` element inside an `example` (with title) or `informalexample` (no title), then you can add a processing instruction to force full-page width. The following is an example:

```
<informalexample>
  <?dbfo pgwide="1"?>
  <programlisting>Wide listing that needs full-page width ...
  ...
```

This processing instruction will cause the stylesheet to apply the attribute-set named `pgwide.properties`, which sets the `start-indent` property to 0pt. You can customize that attribute-set to change the properties.

Reducing font size

One solution is to reduce the font size for such listings. You can set the font size for all listings by adding a `font-size` attribute to the `monospace.verbatim.properties` attribute-set.

But you may only want to reduce the font size for certain `programlisting` elements that have this problem. If so, you can use a combination of a processing instruction and a conditional attribute value. The processing instruction could look like the following:

```
<programlisting><?db-font-size 75% ?># A long line listing
  ...
```

The name of the PI is your choice. Then make the attribute value conditional on this PI by adding the following to your print customization layer:

```
<xsl:attribute-set name="monospace.verbatim.properties">
  <xsl:attribute name="font-size">
    <xsl:choose>
      <xsl:when test="processing-instruction('db-font-size')"><xsl:value-of
          select="processing-instruction('db-font-size')"/></xsl:when>
      <xsl:otherwise>inherit</xsl:otherwise>
    </xsl:choose>
  </xsl:attribute>
</xsl:attribute-set>
```

The `xsl:attribute` element will be evaluated for each `programlisting`. If it contains a PI with matching name, it takes its value to be the font-size. The value can be a percentage as in this example, or a fixed value such as 7pt. Be sure to include the `xsl:otherwise` clause to avoid generating an empty attribute value.

Reducing font size will work when the lines are close to fitting. But when lines are very long, you would have to reduce the font size so much that the text becomes hard to read. Those lines require some means of breaking the lines.

Breaking long lines

Another solution for fitting text in a `programlisting` is to break each long line into two lines. The best results will be had from manually breaking any long lines after you see which ones do not fit on a page. Manual line breaking permits you to match the appropriate indent level of the text, or break at appropriate points in the syntax. But this manual solution may not be practical for documents with many listings.

You can create automatic line breaks by permitting the lines to wrap inside the program listing. You can do that by setting the `wrap-option` attribute in the `monospace.verbatim.properties` attribute-set:

```
<xsl:attribute-set name="monospace.verbatim.properties">
    <xsl:attribute name="wrap-option">wrap</xsl:attribute>
</xsl:attribute-set>
```

This will break a long line on a space between words, but it leaves no indication that the first line should logically be continued with the second line. It would be better if the line break inserted a character at the end of the first line that indicated the line break. You can do that by setting the `hyphenate.verbatim` parameter to 1. You also need to add another attribute to the attribute set:

```
<xsl:attribute-set name="monospace.verbatim.properties">
    <xsl:attribute name="wrap-option">wrap</xsl:attribute>
    <xsl:attribute name="hyphenation-character">\</xsl:attribute>
</xsl:attribute-set>
```

The second attribute `hyphenation-character` identifies the character to use when the line is broken, in this case a backslash. You could use any Unicode character you like, but the character has to be available to the XSL-FO processor at that point. Note that FOP does not support the `hyphenate.verbatim` feature at all.

External code files

You may want to insert external program files into your DocBook documents to use as examples. That way you do not have to type them into your document and maintain them there. It would also be nice if you did not have to escape the special XML characters such as < and & which are used in programming languages.

This can be done in two ways: with an XSLT extension in Saxon or Xalan, or with XInclude for xsltproc.

The stylesheets come with an XSLT extension function to insert text from a file and escape the XML markup characters. Such extension functions are available for Saxon and Xalan, but not currently for xsltproc. To enable this extension, you have to set two parameters, either in your customization layer or on the command line. The parameters are `use.extensions=1` and `textinsert.extension=1`. Both must be set for it to work. You must also make sure the appropriate DocBook extensions file is included in your Java CLASSPATH. See the Saxon or Xalan section in the section called "Installing an XSLT processor" (page 15) for more on setting the CLASSPATH.

Once the parameters and CLASSPATH are properly set, then you can use markup like the following to insert an external text file:

```
<example><title>My program listing</title>
  <programlisting><textobject><textdata
    fileref="mycode.c" /></textobject></programlisting>
</example>
```

You can also use `entityref` instead of `fileref` so that you are referencing a system entity instead of a file pathname. Using a system entity provides one level of indirection, enabling you to change the declaration of the system entity in the DTD without having to edit the reference to it in the document. The system entity declaration must indicate the NDATA type as `linespecific` (which is declared in the DTD), so the processor knows it is a text file. The following is an example of declaring a system entity and then referencing it.

```
<!DOCTYPE book SYSTEM "docbook.dtd" [
<!ENTITY code3 SYSTEM "codesamples/mycode.c" NDATA linespecific>
]>
<book>
...
<example><title>My program listing</title>
  <programlisting><textobject><textdata
    entityref="code3" /></textobject></programlisting>
</example>
```

If for some reason the entity reference does not resolve, then your `programlisting` will be blank.

Note:

> If your DTD is earlier than version 4.2, then you cannot put a `textobject` directly inside a `programlisting`. You have to use an `imageobject` element inside a `inlinemediaobject` element. And you must add a `format="linespecific"` attribute to its `imagedata` element, as in the following example.
>
> *For DocBook 4.1.2 DTD and earlier:*
> ```
> <programlisting><inlinemediaobject><imageobject><imagedata
>     fileref="mycode.c"
>     format="linespecific"/></imageobject></inlinemediaobject>
> <programlisting>
> ```

Notice that the elements inside these `programlisting` examples have no space or line breaks between elements, only between attributes. That's because spaces and line breaks between elements are always preserved inside `programlisting`, so this style avoids introducing extraneous spaces in the output. You can break a line between attributes within an element's start tag.

Missing text

If your output does not have the included text, then you need to check for these problems:

- If instead of the code text you get an element with `xlink:href` and other XLink attributes in your output, then the two extension parameters described above have not been properly set.

- If the two parameters are properly set, and you get a message about "No insertfile extension available.", then either you need to use Saxon or Xalan, or the CLASSPATH does not include the Saxon or Xalan extension file.

- If you get a message "Cannot read file:...", then the textinsert extension is working, but the pathname is not resolving, or the file is unreadable by the process.

Using XInclude for text inclusions

If you are using an XInclude-enabled processor such as xsltproc, then you can use an XInclude element instead of a `textobject` element. The following is an example that accomplishes the same as the previous example:

```
<example><title>My program listing</title>
  <programlisting><xi:include  href="mycode.c"  parse="text"
      xmlns:xi="http://www.w3.org/2001/XInclude"/></programlisting>
</example>
```

The `parse="text"` attribute ensures that any characters that might be misinterpreted as XML are properly escaped when the text is included. But using `parse="text"` also means you cannot select part of the external file with XPointer syntax, because the file is not treated as XML (even if it happens to be XML).

Since the `xi:include` element is not part of the standard DocBook DTD, you will get validation errors when you try to validate a document with such a `programlisting`. However, you can add `xi:include` to the DTD, as described in the section called "DTD customizations for XIncludes" (page 368), to avoid such errors.

Annotating program listings

It is often the case that you need to comment on lines of code to explain it. There are three mechanisms you can use for that purpose.

- Line annotations.

- Line numbering.

- Callouts.

Line annotations

You can mix `lineannotation` elements in with your code to explain something directly in the text. For example:

```
<programlisting># constructor
sub new {
    my ($file, $output) = @_; <lineannotation>Store args</lineannotation>
    my $dir = basename $file; <lineannotation>Get dir name</lineannotation>
}
</programlisting>
```

Lineannotations in the stock stylesheet print as italic, but they inherit the monospace font family of the `programlisting`. You may want them to appear in the italic version of the body font to make them stand out more. The following is such a customization for a print customization layer:

```
FO template customization:
<xsl:template match="lineannotation">
  <fo:inline font-family="{$body.font.family}"
             font-style="italic">
    <xsl:call-template name="inline.charseq"/>
  </fo:inline>
</xsl:template>
```

For HTML output, you can let the CSS stylesheet handle the formatting:

```
HTML CSS stylesheet:
span.lineannotation {
    font-family: serif;
    font-style:  italic;
}
```

Line annotations cannot be added in files inserted using `textobject` or `<xi:include parse="text">` because the "<" character that starts the element will be escaped as `&lt;` when it is brought in. You can use lineannotations in files brought in with `<xi:include parse="xml">`, but then you have to be careful to escape other XML characters in your program file. Line annotations also cannot be used with examples marked as CDATA, because any `lineannotation` element will not be recognized as an XML element.

Line numbering

You can add line numbers to the listing, and then your paragraphs can refer to the line numbers. Currently line numbering is only available with the Java processors Saxon and Xalan, not xsltproc, because it is done with an extension function.

Line numbers are turned on by a `linenumbering` attribute on each `programlisting` element that needs line numbering. By default, the numbering starts at 1, but you can assign your own starting number with the optional `startinglinenumber` attribute. You can also continue the numbering from the most recent `programlisting` that had line numbering by adding a `continuation="continues"` attribute to the current element. The following is an example with `startinglinenumber`:

```
<programlisting linenumbering="numbered" startinglinenumber="12">
...
```

You have to enable the line numbering feature by setting a couple of stylesheet parameters. The parameters are `use.extensions=1` and `linenumbering.extension=1`. Both must be set for it to work.

Once your lines are numbered, you can refer to the line numbers in the paragraphs. The problem with line numbers, though, is you cannot see them until the text is formatted at least once. Also, if you edit the code, the line numbers may change and you will need to adjust your number references. It is useful for stable code examples, though.

The formatting of line numbers can be controlled using a set of line numbering parameters for all program listings (and `screen` and `cmdsynopsis` elements). You can also override the formatting for a single program listing using special processing instructions. The line numbering parameters are:

`linenumbering.everyNth`	By default, every 5th line of the programlisting displays its number, so the visible numbers are 5, 10, 15, etc. If you set this parameter to 3, for example, then every third line shows its number. Setting it to 1 numbers all lines.
`linenumbering.width`	This is the number of spaces at the beginning of each line reserved for the line numbers. The default value is three, so numbers up to 999 will fit. You can set this parameter to a different integer to save fewer or more spaces for the line numbers. The numbers are right-aligned within this space so the digits line up properly.
`linenumbering.separator`	The literal content of this parameter is printed after the line number and before the program listing text. The default value is a single space, but it could be changed to any text.

To control the line number formatting for an individual program listing, you can use equivalent processing instructions. The processing instructions begin with `<?dbhtml` for HTML output, or `<?dbfo` for print output. The following is an example.

```
<programlisting
    linenumbering="numbered" ❶><?dbhtml linenumbering.everyNth="2"
    linenumbering.separator=" &gt;" linenumbering.width="2" ❷
?><?dbfo linenumbering.everyNth="2"
    linenumbering.separator=" &gt;" linenumbering.width="2" ❸
?><textobject><textdata fileref="mycode.c" /></textobject>
</programlisting>
```

❶ Put the processing instructions somewhere inside the `programlisting` element. Be sure to not introduce spaces and line breaks between them and any elements, since such white space is preserved in a `programlisting` and appears in the output. You can put line breaks within a processing instruction, however.

❷ This PI sets the three values for HTML output.

❸ This PI sets the three values for print output.

When processed, this particular program listing will have a number appearing on every other line, with two spaces allocated for the numbers, and with a literal > character (`&gt;`) separating the number from the line of code.

Callouts

You can use callouts to mark specific locations in a program listing and link explanatory text to the marks. To see how callouts look in output, see the example below. In DocBook, the `callout` element contains the explanatory text. The mark, which is called a *callout bug*, is most easily placed using the `co` element. Those two elements can be linked to each other to allow the reader to move back and forth between them.

The callout bug is usually rendered as a white number in a black circle. To see other options for rendering the callout bugs, see the section called "Callout icons" (page 78).

The following is an annotated example of how callouts are written, using actual callouts to identify the important points.

```
<programlisting>
#ifndef _My_Parser_h_   <co❶  id="condition-co"❷  linkends="condition"❸ />
#define _My_Parser_h_
#include "MyFetch.h"   <co id="headerfile-co" linkends="headerfile" />
class My_Parser  <co id="classdef-co" linkends="classdef" />
{
public:
        //
        // Construction/Destruction
        //
        My_Parser();  <coref  linkend="classdef-co"/>  ❹
        virtual      ~My_Parser() = 0;
        virtual int  parse(MyFetch &amp;fetcher) = 0;
};
#endif
</programlisting>

<calloutlist>❺
  <callout❻ arearefs="condition-co"❼  id="condition"❽ >
    <para>Make this conditional.</para>
  </callout>
  <callout arearefs="headerfile-co" id="headerfile">
    <para>Load necessary constants.</para>
  </callout>
  <callout arearefs="classdef-co" id="classdef">
    <para>Define new class</para>
  </callout>
</calloutlist>
```

❶ Use a co element to place a callout bug in your code sample. The element is empty, with all the information in attributes.

❷ Give the co an id or xml:id value so the callout text can be linked directly to the callout bug location.

❸ Its linkend attribute value (condition) should match the id or xml:id value of its callout element (see callout #8). That forms a link from the callout bug to the text.

❹ Use a coref instead of a co when you want to create a duplicate bug number. That is, when you have more than one location in your code that needs to refer to the same callout paragraph, use a coref for any but the first location. The linkend of the coref must point to the id of the master co element. The duplicate callout icons will all hotlink to the same callout paragraph. But the icon next to the callout paragraph will link back only to the master co element.

❺ A calloutlist contains a set of callout elements, and formats them as a list.

❻ Each callout element is paired up with a co element. The numbering order is based on the co order, so you should keep the callout elements in the same order.

❼ The arearefs attribute value (condition-co) matches the id value of its co callout bug (see callout #2). That forms a link from the callout text to the callout bug.

❽ Give the callout an id value so the callout bug can link directly to its callout text.

It helps to establish a naming scheme for the ids to track the two-ended links. This example uses the same name on both ends except the one on the co element adds a -co suffix. If you have to edit the code sample and move lines around, be sure to move any co elements with them. Also, remember when cutting and pasting to not duplicate any id values, which will produce a validation error.

A callout number sequence normally starts and ends within a display element that contains a group of co elements. The following template in fo/callouts.xsl generates each callout and determines its number using xsl:number:

```
<xsl:template match="co" mode="callout-bug">
  <xsl:call-template name="callout-bug">
    <xsl:with-param name="conum">
      <xsl:number count="co"
                  level="any"
                  from="programlisting|screen|literallayout|synopsis"
                  format="1"/>
    </xsl:with-param>
  </xsl:call-template>
</xsl:template>
```

The from attribute of the xsl:number contains a list of element names that are to restart the number sequence at 1. If you use co inside other elements (such as table, for example), you may need to customize this template to restart numbering as you want it.

Callouts on imported text

Can you put callouts on code imported from an external file? Yes, but it is not easy, since you have to place the callout bugs by coordinates rather than literally in the code. This feature lets you use unmodified code files, though. Just do not try it with code samples that change with any frequency, because you will have to remap the coordinates.

You have to wrap your programlisting and calloutlist in a programlistingco element, because it supports the use of an areaspec to provide the coordinates. You also must use either Saxon or Xalan to process the files, because placing the callouts at the coordinates takes an XSLT extension function that is not available in xsltproc. To enable this function in Saxon or Xalan, you must set the stylesheet parameters use.extensions=1 and callouts.extension=1. Both must be set for it to work. do not forget to include the appropriate DocBook XSL extensions jar file in your CLASSPATH as well.

To place a callout bug, you use an area element inside of a separate areaspec element, instead of a co element inside the code sample. Placing the bugs is the tedious part, because you must count lines and columns for each one.

You specify where the bug goes in the area element's coords attribute. Although the DTD allows you to specify a variety of units to use as coordinates, the DocBook XSL extension functions only support linecolumn and linerange unit types. The units attribute can be specified in the areaspec for all included areas, or in each individual area. If no units are specified, then linecolumn is assumed. With linecolumn, the coords attribute specifies a line number and column number, separated by a space. If the second number is absent, then the value of the stylesheet parameter callout.defaultcolumn is used, which is 60 by default. With linerange, the two numbers specify beginning and ending line numbers.

The following is an example that produces results like the previous one, but using an external file to hold the code sample. Note that the textobject does not have a line break before it, which would throw off the line counting co-ordinates.

Example 27.2. programlistingco with areaspec

```
<programlistingco>
  <areaspec units="linecolumn">
    <area id="condition-co" linkends="condition" coords="1 23"/>
    <area id="headerfile-co" linkends="headerfile" coords="3 23"/>
    <area id="classdef-co" linkends="classdef" coords="4 18"/>
  </areaspec>

  <programlisting><textobject>
      <textdata  fileref="mycode.c" />
    </textobject>
  </programlisting>

  <calloutlist>
    <callout arearefs="condition-co"  id="condition" >
      <para>Make this conditional.</para>
    </callout>
    <callout arearefs="headerfile-co" id="headerfile">
      <para>Load necessary constants.</para>
    </callout>
    <callout arearefs="classdef-co" id="classdef">
      <para>Define new class</para>
    </callout>
  </calloutlist>

</programlistingco>
```

The following is an example command to process this file with Saxon:

```
CLASSPATH=../saxon653/saxon.jar:../docbook-xsl/extensions/saxon653.jar \
 java  com.icl.saxon.StyleSheet \
        -o outputfile.html \
        myfile.xml \
        ../docbook-xsl/html/docbook.xsl \
        use.extensions=1 \
        callouts.extension=1 \
        textinsert.extension=1
```

Callouts on graphics

The DocBook DTD has a mediaobjectco element that is designed to associate callouts with a graphical image. Unfortunately, this feature is currently not implemented in the DocBook XSL stylesheets.

Syntax highlighting

It is sometimes desirable to add syntax highlighting to code listings. Syntax highlighting adds formatting attributes to keywords and punctuation in a way that makes it easier for the reader to separate code from text.

The DocBook XSL stylesheets provide support for syntax highlighting if you are using the Saxon XSLT processor. Some of the support is integrated into the stylesheets (starting with version 1.71.1), but most of the work is performed by the separate XSLTHL package written in Java that you download and install on your system.

Here are the steps to get syntax highlighting working on your system:

1. Download and copy to some convenient location the `xslthl.jar` file from the XSLTHL project's SourceForge
    page at *http://sourceforge.net/projects/xslthl*.

2. In your `programlisting` elements, add a `language` attribute to indicate the programming language. For example:

    ```
    <programlisting language="java">
    ...
    ```

    See the configuration files in the DocBook XSL `highlighting` subdirectory to see what languages are currently
    supported.

3. In your stylesheet customization layer or processing command line, set the stylesheet parameter `high-
    light.source` to 1.

    ```
    <xsl:param name="highlight.source" select="1"/>
    ```

4. Process your documents with Saxon, configured to include the `xslthl.jar` file in your CLASSPATH and the
    XSLTHL configuration file specified as a resource. For example:

    ```
    java -cp "c:/java/saxon.jar;c:/java/xslthl.jar" \
        -Dxslthl.config="file:///c:/docbook-xsl/highlighting/xslthl-config.xml" \
        com.icl.saxon.StyleSheet   \
        -o myfile.fo   \
        myfile.xml   \
        docbook-xsl/fo/docbook.xsl
    ```

    The configuration file `xslthl-config.xml` is included with the DocBook XSL distribution in the `highlighting`
    subdirectory.

Note these features of the highlighting extension:

*   Highlighting works in XSL-FO and HTML output formats.

*   Highlighting works with `programlisting`, `screen`, and `synopsis` elements that have a `language` attribute.

*   Highlighting works with any of the external code inclusion methods described in the section called "External
    code files" (page 443).

*   Highlighting works with the line numbering extension described in the section called "Line numbering" (page
    445)

If you want to customize the highlighting properties, then you will need to customize copies of the templates in the
`highlight.xsl` stylesheet module from either the `fo` or `html` directories. In your customization layer, you will also
need to add the the namespace declaration for the `xslthl` prefix. For example, this customization adds blue color
to keywords and grey color to comments for print output.

```
<?xml version='1.0'?>
<xsl:stylesheet xmlns:xsl="http://www.w3.org/1999/XSL/Transform"
                xmlns:fo="http://www.w3.org/1999/XSL/Format"
                xmlns:xslthl="http://xslthl.sf.net"
                exclude-result-prefixes="xslthl"
                version='1.0'>

<xsl:template match='xslthl:keyword'>
  <fo:inline font-weight="bold" color="blue"><xsl:apply-templates/></fo:inline>
</xsl:template>

<xsl:template match='xslthl:comment'>
  <fo:inline font-style="italic" color="grey"><xsl:apply-templates/></fo:inline>
</xsl:template>
...
```

For XSL-FO output, be sure to set xsl:output indent="no" to make sure the highlighting templates do not accidentally insert unwanted whitespace in the code listing.

28

Q and A sets

The Question and Answer feature of DocBook is often used to generate Frequently Asked Question (FAQ) documents. It consists of a set of qandaentry elements contained in a qandaset. The set can be further subdivided with qandadiv containers. The following short example shows how to create a Q&A in your document.

```
<qandaset>
  <title>Frequently Asked Questions (FAQ)</title>
  <qandadiv>
    <title>Questions about Networking</title>
    <qandaentry>
      <question>
        <para>How do I get an IP address?</para>
      </question>
      <answer>
        <para>Ask your system administrator.</para>
      </answer>
    </qandaentry>
    <qandaentry>
      ...
    </qandaentry>
    ...
  </qandadiv>
</qandaset>
```

Starting with version 1.70.1 of the stylesheets, a qandaset can be the root element of a document. In that case, the stylesheet creates a page-sequence for the qandaset. Otherwise, the qandaset is output within its parent element's page-sequence.

The stylesheets let you control the following features of qandaset elements:

• Labels and formatting for questions and answers.

• Lists of questions.

• Cross referencing to questions.

Q and A labeling

By default, the questions in a qandaset are numbered, and the number will be prefixed with the chapter or section number:

```
1.1 First question in chapter 1.
    First answer.
1.2 Second question in chapter 1.
    Second answer.
...
2.1 First question in chapter 2.
    This answer.
2.2 Second question in chapter 2.
    That answer.
```

This behavior comes from the default values of the qanda.defaultlabel parameter, which is set to number by default, and the qanda.inherit.numeration parameter, which is set to 1 by default. Here *inherit* means the label inherits the chapter or section number as its prefix.

If you would rather have them all labeled with letters, then set the qanda.defaultlabel parameter to qanda. The results look like the following:

```
Q:  First question in chapter 1.
A:  First answer.
Q:  Second question in chapter 1.
A:  Second answer.
```

For other languages, it will use appropriate labels defined in the gentext files. You can also set the qanda.default-label parameter to the literal none to get no labels at all.

If you want to number your questions without the chapter or section number prefix, then set the qanda.inherit.numeration parameter to zero. Then every chapter's questions will start over with numbering. The results look like the following:

```
1.  First question in chapter 1.
    First answer.
2.  Second question in chapter 1.
    Second answer.
...
1.  First question in chapter 2.
    This answer.
2.  Second question in chapter 2.
    That answer.
```

If you want to override the label style for a particular qandaset element in your document, then add a defaultlabel attribute to that qandaset in your document. You can set it to any of the allowed values, which are number, qanda, or none. This attribute will override the global qanda.defaultlabel for that qandaset only. The following example shows how it is used:

```
<qandaset defaultlabel="qanda">
  <title>Frequently Asked Questions (FAQ)</title>
  ...
</qandaset>
```

You can also control the label on any or all individual questions or answers by including a label element in each question or answer element. For example:

```
<qandaentry>
  <question>
    <label>Important Question:</label>
    <para>What is the meaning of life?</para>
  </question>
  <answer>
    <label>Typical Answer:</label>
    <para>No one knows!</para>
  </answer>
</qandaentry>
```

The `label` element overrides any of the generated labels. The indent will be automatically adjusted to accommodate the label width.

If you want to do further customization of the labeling of QandA sets, then you'll probably need to customize a template. You should copy to your customization layer the template that starts with the following line, from common/labels.xsl:

```
<xsl:template match="question|answer" mode="label.markup">
...
```

The template generates whatever label is applied to questions and answers. By customizing it, you can alter how the label options are handled, or you can simplify it by removing most of the options and just enacting what your style is.

For example, if you wanted to number all of the questions throughout the document with Q1, Q2, Q3, etc., using consecutive numbers that do not restart at all, you could add this template to your customization layer to override the default template:

```
<xsl:template match="question" mode="label.markup">
    <xsl:text>Q</xsl:text>
    <xsl:number level="any" count="qandaentry" format="1"/>
</xsl:template>
```

The `level="any"` attribute causes the `xsl:number` counter to count all `qandaentry` elements at any level with one sequence of numbers.

Q and A formatting

For HTML output, the stylesheets use an HTML TABLE element to lay out the question and answer text and their labels. Each `qandaentry` takes up two rows, one for the question and one for the answer. It is a two-column table with the labels in the left column and the question and answer text in the right column.

HTML tables do a good job of automatically adjusting their column widths to fit their text, but you may want finer control. There are certain features of the Q and A table formatting that you can control using processing instructions embedded in your document. For example:

```
<qandaset>   ❶
<?dbhtml label-width="10%" ?>   ❷
<?dbhtml toc="1" ?>   ❸
<?dbhtml cellspacing="3px" cellpadding="3px" ?>   ❹
  <qandaentry>
    <question>Left button</question>
    <answer><para>Blah blah</para></answer>
  </qandaentry>
  ...
</qandaset>
```

❶ Put the processing instructions somewhere inside the `qandaset` element. You can put them all into one PI, or make separate PIs for each.

❷ This PI sets the table left column minimum width, which is the space used for the labels. Use percentages for the values. The default is 1%, but the HTML browser will widen that to fit the labels used in the table.

❸ You can generate a table of contents for this `qandaset` by setting `toc` to nonzero in the processing instruction. This produces a list of questions that appears before the first question.

❹ You can adjust the HTML table cell spacing and padding with these values.

If you need more control in HTML output, then you can customize the template named `process.qandaset` in `html/qandaset.xsl`. That template creates the layout table and generates the rows.

For FO output, a `qandaset` is processed as an `fo:list-block` in a manner similar to a `variablelist`. The labels are processed into `fo:list-item-label` elements, and the question and answer text as `list-item-body` elements. The width allocated for the labels is automatically calculated by the stylesheet. Or you can use a dbfo `label-width` processing instruction to manually adjust the width for a given `qandaset`. Use it like the dbhtml processing instruction described above.

For print output, the stylesheets provide the following attribute-sets for customizing titles in `qandaset` and `qandadiv` elements.

`qanda.title.properties`	*General properties for all levels*
`qanda.title.level1.properties`	*Properties specific to each level*
`qanda.title.level2.properties`	
`qanda.title.level3.properties`	
`qanda.title.level4.properties`	
`qanda.title.level5.properties`	

These attribute sets are nearly identical to the `section.title.properties` attribute-sets. See the section called "Section titles" (page 176) for examples of how to customize such attribute-sets. The main difference with these attribute-sets is that the level is used somewhat differently. A `qandaset` is contained within a section, so its title level is considered one below its container section level in the hierarchy. So a `qandaset` within a `sect1` would be treated as level 2 for its title. Any `qandadiv` elements inside it would have their titles treated as level 3. If you prefer that all your `qandaset` titles be the same size regardless of their location within a section hierarchy, then you need to set that font size in each of attribute-sets with `level` in their name.

By default, `qandadiv` elements have numbered titles. You can set the `qandadiv.autolabel` parameter to zero to turn off the numbering of the `qandadiv` titles.

Q and A list of questions

Each `qandaset` can have its own local table of contents (TOC) that lists the questions in the set. You can globally turn the lists on or off, and then locally turn an individual list on or off.

The `generate.toc` parameter is used to globally control all TOCs, including all `qandaset` elements in the document. To turn them on, the stylesheet parameter `generate.toc` must include the line:

```
qandaset  toc
```

This line is included by default in the stylesheets. To turn them all off, the line should be omitted or replaced with this line:

```
qandaset  nop
```

See the section called "Which components have a TOC" (page 125) for more on the `generate.toc` parameter.

Once you have established the global pattern with `generate.toc`, you can use a processing instruction to turn the list on or off for an individual `qandaset`. The example below shows the use of the processing instruction that turns on the TOC for a single `qandaset` when they are turned off globally:

```
<qandaset><?dbhtml toc="1" ?>
  <qandaentry>
  . . .
```

Likewise, the following PI can be used to turn off the TOC for a single `qandaset` when they are turned on globally:

```
<qandaset><?dbhtml toc="0" ?>
  . . .
```

The combination of the two mechanisms gives you complete control over the question lists.

There is one other stylesheet parameter that affects the list of questions. The DocBook DTD permits an answer element to include nested `qandaentry` elements. By default, the nested elements are not included in the list of questions. If you want them included, then set the stylesheet parameter `qanda.nested.in.toc` to 1.

You may have a requirement to customize the template that generates the list of questions. For print output, customize the template named `qandaset.toc` found in the stylesheet module `fo/autotoc.xsl`. For HTML output, customize the template named `process.qanda.toc` in the stylesheet module `html/qandaset.xsl`.

Hiding the answers

If you are using a `qandaset` for student exercises, then you may want to produce two versions of your document: one with answers for the teacher, and one without answers for the students. The general process of producing a different document for different audiences is called *profiling* in DocBook. It is described in Chapter 26, *Profiling (conditional text)* (page 427).

Normally in profiling you add profiling attributes to DocBook elements you want to make conditional in your document. Then you process the document with the profiling stylesheet, while setting parameters that identify which profiling values to accept and which to reject. For example, you might put a `userlevel="teacher"` attribute on each answer element in your document. To generate the output version with the answers, you process your document with the parameter `profile.userlevel` set to `teacher`. Since that value matches the attribute value, the answers are included in the output. When you process the document with the parameter `profile.userlevel` set to `student`, the value does not match and the answers are left out.

This process is a bit cumbersome if you have many questions, because you have to add the `userlevel="teacher"` attribute to every answer element. You also have to use the profiling stylesheet. You can avoid both problems by using a stylesheet customization instead.

This stylesheet customization will turn off all the answers when the parameter `profile.userlevel` is set to `student`, without having to put a profiling attribute on every answer, and without having to use the profiling stylesheet.

```
<xsl:template match="answer">
    <xsl:if test="$profile.userlevel = 'teacher'">
        <xsl:apply-imports/>
    </xsl:if>
</xsl:template>
```

Since this template is in your customization layer, it has a higher import precedence than the stock template that matches on answer. When this template is applied, it first tests to see if the parameter profile.userlevel is set to teacher. If so, then it calls xsl:apply-imports, which applies the original match="answer" template to generate the answer in the output. If the parameter is any other value, then this template does nothing, so the answer is not output.

Q and A cross references

Cross referencing to Q and A elements is similar to other cross references. You put an id (or xml:id in DocBook 5) attribute on the element you want to reference, and then you use xref, link, or olink to cross reference to it. When referencing a specific question, reference the id on the qandaentry rather than the question element.

The generated text for a qandaset or qandadiv comes from the title element, so be sure your elements have a title (it is optional on those elements).

The generated text for a qandaentry depends on your parameter settings. The default behavior is to output a Q: and the question number. The following are some examples:

Parameters	Example xref

`<xsl:param name="qanda.defaultlabel">number</xsl:param>`
`<xsl:param name="qanda.inherit.numeration" select="1"/>`
`<xsl:param name="qandadiv.autolabel" select="1"/>`
	Q: 2.1.3
	
	where the question has a number label of 2.1.2, with 2.1 from the division number and .3 from the third question in that division.

`<xsl:param name="qanda.defaultlabel">number</xsl:param>` `<xsl:param name="qandadiv.autolabel" select="0"/>`	Q: 3 for the third question in any division.
`<xsl:param name="qanda.defaultlabel">qanda</xsl:param>`	Q:

In the second two examples, the information provided in the cross reference text is not particularly helpful. The links will work, but they do not provide the reader with much context. It is particularly bad when numbering is not used for questions, as in the last example.

You might be wondering why the stylesheet does not use the question text for the cross reference? A question element can be long and complex, because its schema content model permits tables, figures, lists, etc. Copying such text as cross reference text would be very confusing to the reader, so the stylesheet does not do that by default.

But if you can write your questions with cross references in mind, you can create a customization that could work with questions. The following customization uses the first para element for the cross reference text. Just keep the first para in all your question elements short.

```
<xsl:template match="question" mode="object.xref.markup">
  <xsl:call-template name="gentext">
    <xsl:with-param name="key" select="'question'"/>
  </xsl:call-template>
  <xsl:text> </xsl:text>
  <xsl:call-template name="gentext.startquote"/>
  <xsl:apply-templates select="para[1]/node()"/>
  <xsl:call-template name="gentext.endquote"/>
</xsl:template>
```

Although your xref is referencing a qandaentry, the stylesheet generates the cross reference text by processing its question child element in mode="object.xref.markup". Normally that mode uses a gentext template for the current locale and fills in the question number.

In this customization, it instead outputs the Q: label for the current locale, and puts the text of the first para element in quotes. The select="para[1]/node()" selects the content of the para element, not the para itself, which would generate a block instead of an inline. If you want to change the Q: part, then customize the gentext template for question, as described in the section called "Generated text" (page 105).

Another method to reference a question that does not require a stylesheet customization is to use an endterm attribute as described in the section called "Use another element's text for an xref" (page 259).

Chunking Q and A

If you publish a large FAQ (frequently asked questions) document to HTML, you might want to group related questions together and chunk each group into a separate HTML file. The qandadiv element is designed to group together questions, but it is not suitable for chunking. That's because it is a block-type element, not a section-type element, so the chunking stylesheets will not create a chunk with it. Also, a qandadiv title does not normally appear in the table of contents.

The best approach to chunking a large Q and A is to break it into DocBook section elements (or the equivalent sect1, sect2, etc). Each section contains a qandaset that holds that group of qandaentrys. The section element provides the hook for chunking, and a title that shows up in the table of contents. You can also nest them to form hierarchies of questions.

```
<section id="group1">
 <title>First group of questions</title>
 <qandaset>
   <qandaentry id="group1_1">
      <question>
          <para>...</para>
      </question>
      <answer>
          <para>...</para>
       </answer>
   </qandaentry>
   ...
 </qandaset>
</section>
```

See the section called "Controlling what gets chunked" (page 67) to control what sections become chunks in the HTML output.

Q and A in table of contents

In a FAQ (Frequently Asked Questions) document, the questions and answers form the bulk of the content. When a FAQ grows large, perhaps with several divisions, it needs a table of contents to help the reader locate the question they need an answer to. In such cases, it should be part of the main table of contents at the front of the document. The list of questions described in the section called "Q and A list of questions" (page 456) appears only within a qandaset and is probably not sufficient.

The DocBook stylesheets provide an option to include Q and A information in a document's table of contents. If you set the stylesheet parameter qanda.in.toc to 1, then qandaset titles, qandadiv titles, and qandaentry question elements are included in the document's table of contents. This feature was added starting in version 1.73 of the stylesheets.

Including this information in a TOC is unusual for DocBook, because the TOC normally contains only titles of hierarchical elements, and the Q and A elements are block elements. Mixing the two types of elements in a TOC might lead to odd combinations or sequences, depending on your content. For example, if your sections are numbered, and you set qanda.defaultlabel to number to number your questions, then your TOC may become a bit confusing. The same number may be used for both a section title and a question, and it is not obvious to the reader that they are different elements. You might need to change your style or do further customization to make the TOC more clear.

29

Revision control

DocBook is often used in situations where content is published periodically or on a continuous basis, with revisions and updates incorporated into each new release. It is often necessary to keep track of changes and be able to identify changed documents or elements, for reasons such as:

- You want to be able to produce multiple states of a document, such as the most recently released version and the current draft version under development, from the same source files.

- Reviewers only want to review what has changed, not an entire document.

- You want to be able to print a list in a preface or appendix what has changed in the current version.

- The documents are translated into other languages, and you only want to pay for retranslation of content that has changed.

The DocBook DTD provides several elements and attributes that are useful for tracking changes, and the DocBook XSL stylesheets provides support for rendering those elements and attributes in useful ways for readers. These tools can be used in conjunction with revision control software that stores multiple versions of a document.

Revision elements and attributes

The following is a summary of the elements and attributes that can be used to record changes and release information for documents and elements.

Table 29.1. Revision elements and attributes

Name	Type	Description
revhistory	Element	Contains a record of changes for an element, each change recorded in a revision element. It can appear at many document levels inside any of the info elements, as well as in qandaentry and glossentry.
revision	Element	Records a single change in a revhistory, using a revision number, date, and description.
releaseinfo	Element	Typically used to indicate a version number or name for a released document. Can be used in any of the info elements.
edition	Element	Typically used to indicate a document edition number.
pubdate	Element	Typically used to indicate a publication release date.
printhistory	Element	Can contain a sequence of para elements describing a publication history.
revisionflag	Attribute	Can be used to indicate that the element has changed. This common attribute is available on all elements, with enumerated values added, deleted, changed, or off.
revision	Attribute	Can be used to indicate revision information on an element. This common attribute is available on all elements, and can take any text value.
status	Attribute	Can be used to indicate the status of an element, such as its current production status. Available on all division and component elements, and can take any text value.

If you want to record the history of revisions in a document, you can use the revhistory element which contains a sequence of revision elements to record each change. The stylesheets do not output revhistory by default, but it can be output as described in the section called "Formatting revhistory" (page 463).

The releaseinfo, edition, and pubdate elements are usually updated just prior to publication to identify a particular release of a document. They are typically printed on a title page, if at all. See Chapter 11, *Title page customization* (page 141).

The three attributes revisionflag, revision, and status can be used to track changes at the level of each element. The revisionflag element can indicate only that an element has changed, while revision can take any text value to describe a revision.

> **Tip:**
>
> If you use a content management system such as CVS, you can store revision keywords in a revision attribute in your document. The keywords will be expanded during checkout, so the attribute will contain the latest CVS information for the document. For example:
>
> *Enter a revision attribute:*
> ```
> <article revision="$Id: dbxsl.xml,v 1.131 2007/10/06 05:56:46 bobs Exp $">
> ...
> ```
>
> *After checkout:*
> ```
> <article revision="$Id: dbxsl.xml,v 1.131 2007/10/06 05:56:46 bobs Exp $">
> ...
> ```

If you manually enter revisionflag attributes, keep in mind that they can quickly become out of date. For example, a section marked as added in one release should not be so marked for the following release, or even the next review cycle. After a release or review, you may need to go back and clear all revisionflag attributes to start the next cycle.

The revisionflag attribute is most useful when it is generated in a temporary document created by comparing two versions. See the section called "Highlighting changes" (page 467) for more information.

The status attribute only appears on elements that make up the hierarchy of a document, and is typically used for tracking the production status such as draft, edited, final, etc. It can take any text value, so you might want to decide on a few enumerated values for your authors to use in order to maintain consistency. You can use status in profiling to select content for output, or add a customization to highlight elements with different status using color or some other effect. See the section called "Using the status attribute" (page 465) for more information.

Formatting revhistory

If you use a revhistory element, you will find that the information is output by default on the title page of every element except book. If you want to output revhistory for book, or not output it for other elements, then you can customize the title page specifications file and regenerate the title page stylesheet module, as described in Chapter 11, *Title page customization* (page 141).

> **Tip:**
>
> A quick way to turn off revhistory from output is to define an empty template for it in a customization layer. The following example will turn it off for all elements that contain a revhistory:
>
> ```
> <xsl:template match="revhistory" mode="titlepage.mode"/>
> ```

When it is output, a revhistory is formatted as a table, with each revision displayed with revnumber, revdate, and revauthor in one row, and revremark in a second row spanned across all columns. The default table format is rather plain looking, though.

XSL-FO output for revhistory

For print output, you can customize the look of a revhistory table using these attribute-sets:

revhistory attribute-set	Description
revhistory.title.properties	Properties applied to the table title, which is generated from the stylesheet gentext file, using the template with key="RevHistory". Use this attribute-set for the font properties, alignment, and space above the table.
revhistory.table.properties	Properties applied to the fo:table containing the history. Use this attribute-set for a table border, width, or background color
revhistory.table.cell.properties	Properties applied to each fo:table-cell. Use this attribute-set for cell borders, and font properties of revision entries.

The following example customizes a revision history to make the title bold and centered, add borders and background colors, and set the font size:

```
<xsl:attribute-set name="revhistory.title.properties">
  <xsl:attribute name="font-size">12pt</xsl:attribute>
  <xsl:attribute name="font-weight">bold</xsl:attribute>
  <xsl:attribute name="text-align">center</xsl:attribute>
</xsl:attribute-set>

<xsl:attribute-set name="revhistory.table.properties">
  <xsl:attribute name="border">0.5pt solid black</xsl:attribute>
  <xsl:attribute name="background-color">#EEEEEE</xsl:attribute>
  <xsl:attribute name="width">50%</xsl:attribute>
</xsl:attribute-set>

<xsl:attribute-set name="revhistory.table.cell.properties">
  <xsl:attribute name="border">0.5pt solid black</xsl:attribute>
  <xsl:attribute name="font-size">9pt</xsl:attribute>
  <xsl:attribute name="padding">4pt</xsl:attribute>
</xsl:attribute-set>
```

If you want to further customize the revhistory table, for example to adjust column widths or create single-row entries, then customize the templates in fo/titlepage.xsl that start with:

```
<xsl:template match="revhistory" mode="titlepage.mode">
...
<xsl:template match="revhistory/revision" mode="titlepage.mode">
...
```

HTML output for revhistory

For HTML output, the DocBook XSL stylesheets do not provide much help with easy customization. The revhistory is still output as a table, and borders are included by default. The only class attribute is on the div class="revhistory" that contains the whole table.

If you need to customize HTML output, you probably will need to customize the templates in html/titlepage.xsl that start with:

```
<xsl:template match="revhistory" mode="titlepage.mode">
...
<xsl:template match="revhistory/revision" mode="titlepage.mode">
...
```

The one option that the stylesheet does provide for HTML output of revhistory is putting it in a separately chunked file. Instead of displaying it on the main titlepage, it displays only a link that connects to the separate HTML file. Set the stylesheet parameter generate.revhistory.link to 1 to get this effect. It works with either the chunking or non-chunking stylesheet.

Draft mode

When you want to print a document that is marked as draft, you can set the draft.mode parameter as described below. When it is turned on, the default output prints "Draft" in the header for print output.

The draft.mode parameter has three possible values:

yes   Turn on draft printing for the whole document.

no   Turn off draft printing for the whole document.

maybe   Draft printing is off unless the element (or one of its ancestors) generating the current page has a `status="draft"` attribute. Putting this attribute in a book element turns on draft mode for the whole book, while putting it in a chapter element only turns it on for that chapter.

Draft mode will also print a faint background image across the page that indicates draft status. This works for both print and HTML output. The pathname for the image file `draft.png` is contained in the `draft.watermark.image` parameter, which by default is set to a web address, so you might want to set it to a local file. Or you could use an XML catalog entry to redirect the parameter's URL value to a local file.

For HTML output, be sure to copy the image to the HTML output directory where it will be expected. The background image placement is handled by CSS.

To turn off the draft watermark image, set the `draft.watermark.image` parameter to a blank string.

Using the status attribute

The `status` attribute is available on all hierarchical elements, from set and book down to section and refentry. It is generally used to indicate the current status of production for an element, such as whether it is in draft, edited, or final state. But you can use it for any kind of status that you want. This attribute can take any text value, so you might want to decide on a few enumerated values and use those consistently. You could also customize the DTD to change the attribute declaration to your set of enumerated values.

You can use the `status` attribute in several ways:

- Profile a document on the `status` attribute. See the section called "Profiling on status" (page 465).

- Highlight parts of a document. See the section called "Highlighting status" (page 465).

- Control the draft page markings, as described in the the section called "Draft mode" (page 464).

Keep in mind that `status` attributes can get out of date, so if you use them, be prepared to spend the time to maintain them.

Profiling on status

The `status` attribute is one that the DocBook stylesheets support for profiling (conditional text). You might need to do such profiling to produce different versions of a document. For example, while a document is under development, you may want to include unfinished sections for reviewers, but exclude them for customers. If the unfinished sections all have a `status="draft"` attribute, then you can profile them out for the customer version.

To include all content marked with `status="draft"`, run the profiling process while setting the stylesheet parameter `profile.status` to draft. That will include any elements with `status="draft"` or no `status` attribute, and exclude those elements with any other value of `status`.

You might also set the `draft.mode` parameter to maybe, which will mark as draft only those sections with the draft attribute. See the section called "Draft mode" (page 464) for more information.

When you want to exclude draft sections to produce the non-draft version, then set the `profile.status` parameter to any other value (except blank). That will deselect all the content marked with `status="draft"`.

Highlighting status

Although setting the `draft.mode` parameter to maybe will print a background image, this method has limitations. For print output, it puts the background image on the body region of the page-master, which means all the pages in a page-sequence will have the background image. Also, it only works for a value of status="draft", not other attribute values.

For finer control, more attribute values, and different presentation, you can customize the stylesheets. For example, you may want to show elements in different colors for different status values. The following customization works in print output:

Example 29.1. Highlighting status attributes with color

```
<xsl:param name="enable.status.coloring">1</xsl:param>  ❶

<xsl:template name="set.status.color">  ❷
  <xsl:param name="node" select="."/>
  <xsl:choose>
    <xsl:when test="$enable.status.coloring = 0">inherit</xsl:when>   ❸
    <xsl:when test="$node/@status = 'deleted'">#EEEEEE</xsl:when>   ❹
    <xsl:when test="$node/@status = 'reviewed'">green</xsl:when>
    <xsl:when test="$node/@status = 'draft'">blue</xsl:when>
    <xsl:otherwise>inherit</xsl:otherwise>   ❺
  </xsl:choose>
</xsl:template>

<xsl:attribute-set name="section.properties">   ❻
  <xsl:attribute name="color">
    <xsl:call-template name="set.status.color"/>   ❼
  </xsl:attribute>
</xsl:attribute-set>

<xsl:template name="set.flow.properties">   ❽
  <xsl:param name="element" select="local-name(.)"/>
  <xsl:param name="master-reference" select="''"/>

  <xsl:attribute name="color">
    <xsl:call-template name="set.status.color"/>
  </xsl:attribute>
  ...
```

❶   Create a new stylesheet parameter so you can turn the status coloring on and off from the command line.
❷   Create a template that returns a color value based on the value of the status attribute.
❸   Skip the color choices if the coloring parameter is turned off.
❹   Select a color based on the value of the status attribute.
❺   Be sure to include inherit as a default value to avoid empty attribute errors.
❻   Add a color attribute in the section.properties attribute-set, which is used by sections at all levels.
❼   Call the color choice template. The attribute-set is processed each time it is used, so the template will be called for each section element.
❽   The set.flow.properties template can set a property on an entire page-sequence, such as for chapter, appendix, or other components.

For HTML output, a different approach using CSS works best. You can create a customization of templates using mode="class.value" to create new class values for different values of status (this mode is first available in version 1.72 of the stylesheets).

The following example customizes the original template in html/html.xsl to append the status value to the element name to form a class value:

```
<xsl:template match="*" mode="class.value">
  <xsl:param name="class" select="local-name(.)"/>
  <!-- permit customization of class value only -->
  <!-- Use element name by default -->
  <xsl:value-of select="$class"/>
  <xsl:if test="@status">
    <xsl:value-of select="concat('-', @status)"/>
  </xsl:if>
</xsl:template>
```

For each `section` element with `status="deleted"`, this will generate a `class="section-deleted"` attribute on its div element. Then you can add a CSS selector to your CSS stylesheet to color the element:

```
div.section-deleted {
  color: #EEEEEE;
}
```

You can add other CSS selectors and properties for other combinations of element name and status value. Since this is a mode, you can also create custom templates that match on specific elements to customize the class value per element.

Highlighting changes

Change bars are a traditional way of showing where a document has changed so that reviewers can quickly review only the changes without having to read the entire document. A change bar feature typically prints a vertical bar in the margin next to any text that has changed.

The formatter may also highlight changed text in other ways. For example, deleted text may be displayed but overstruck, while new text may be underlined. Color can also be used, but keep in mind that not everyone can distinguish all colors, and many document printers are monochrome.

Change highlighting requires two steps:

1. Add markup to the XML files to indicate where content has changed.

2. Apply a special change highlighting stylesheet to format the changes.

Change markup

In order for a formatter to show changes, there must be some markup in the XML file to indicate which content has changed.

In DocBook, the `revisionflag` attribute can be added to any element, using any of the attribute's enumerated values `added`, `deleted`, `changed`, or `off`. You might wonder what the `off` value is for. It can be used to indicate that a change marked on a containing element does not apply to the current element.

Adding `revisionflag` attributes by hand is a tedious process. You not only have to find the differences, you have to make sure you add the attributes to the right elements. And then, once you have produced a highlighted version, you will probably have to go through the document and remove all the `revisionflag` attributes to start the next cycle of revision.

Fortunately, if you maintain copies of your revisions, you can use a program named `DiffMk` to compare two versions and generate a temporary version with `revisionflag` markup. A revision control system such as CVS or SVN can easily store and retrieve versions for comparison.

Using DiffMk

The DiffMk program written by Norman Walsh takes as input two versions of a document, compares them, and adds change markup that can be used by a formatter. It is written in Java and is available free for download from the DiffMk SourceForge project. (An earlier version written in Perl is available as a perl-diffmk package available from some Perl distribution centers. It is not covered here.)

Here is how you set up and use the Java version of DiffMk:

1. Download and unpack the DiffMk distribution from the SourceForge project at *http://sourceforge.net/projects/diffmk/*.

2. Locate the diffmk.xml file in the distribution (in the config subdirectory). It is required for configuring the program.

3. Locate the DiffMk.properties file in the distribution (it originates in the config subdirectory). Copy or edit that file to make sure the config property value is a relative path to the diffmk.xml configuration file.

4. You will also need the Java resolver.jar file that is used for XML catalogs. DiffMk is dependent on it, even if you do not use an XML catalog file. See the section called "Using catalogs with Saxon" (page 54) for information on getting and using resolver.jar.

5. Extract two versions of a DocBook document from a revision conrol system for comparison.

6. Set up a Java CLASSPATH that includes the following:

    *   bin/diffmk.jar from the DiffMk distribution.

    *   The directory containing the DiffMk.properties file.

    *   resolver.jar

    *   The directory containing your CatalogManager.properties file, which is used by resolver.jar.

7. Process your two document versions with a Java command like the following (assuming the CLASSPATH is set):

```
java \
        net.sf.diffmk.DiffMk \
        --output diffs.xml \
        --words \
        old-version.xml \
        new-version.xml
```

The output file diffs.xml will contain a version of the document with revisionflag attributes added.

The --words option compares at the word level to provide more detail. It will insert phrase elements as needed to hold the revisionflag attributes. By showing deleted text as well as added text, it sometimes makes the change document hard to read. If you just want reviewers to read changed parts, then you can leave out the --words option.

You can set options for DiffMk in the DiffMk.properties file, or on the command line. Also, the program's configuration file diffmk.xml specifies the attribute and its values to be used for change markup. It allows the program to be used with other grammars besides DocBook.

HTML change output

Once you have generated a version of a document with change markup using DiffMk, you can apply a stylesheet to format it to display the changes.

For HTML output, change bars displayed in the margin are not a supported feature of the HTML standards nor of browsers. Color can be used, as can underline and overstrike at the word level. These would typically be applied with a CSS stylesheet to HTML `class` attributes generated by the stylesheet.

The DocBook XSL distribution comes with a stylesheet to do just that. If you apply the `html/changebar.xsl` stylesheet to a change version generated by DiffMk, then the resulting HTML file will apply the following styles:

- `class="added"` has `text-decoration: underline`; and a yellow background color (#FFFF99).

- `class="deleted"` has `text-decoration: line-through`; a pink background color (#FF7F7F).

- `class="changed"` has a green background color (#99FF99).

The `changebars.xsl` stylesheet imports the stock `docbook.xsl` stylesheet and adds some customizations to insert the CSS `style` element and convert the `revisionflag` attributes into `class` attributes in the output. By including the CSS styles in the file, it is more portable because it does not require a separate CSS stylesheet file.

If you have a customization of the HTML stylesheet that you would rather use to format the results, then copy the `changebars.xsl` stylesheet and change the `xsl:import` statement to import your stylesheet instead of the stock `docbook.xsl`. It will work with chunking or nonchunking customizations.

You change the colors and styles of the change markup by customizing the template named `system.head.content` from the `changebars.xsl` file.

XSL-FO change output

For print output, actual change bars are possible, in addition to other highlighting. Change bars were not part of the XSL-FO 1.0 specification, but they are included in the 1.1 specification, which reached final W3C Recommendation stage in December 2006. So XSL-FO processor vendors are adding change bar support to adhere to the new standard.

XSL-FO 1.1 introduces the `fo:change-bar-begin` and `fo:change-bar-end` formatting objects. These are empty elements, and are used to bracket the start and end of a change area. This method allows the change area to cross element boundaries. The formatting properties let you control the color, offset, width, placement and style of the generated change bars.

Currently three XSL-FO processors are known to support change bars: Antenna House's XSL Formatter (version 4), PTC's Arbortext, and RenderX's XEP.

There is not yet a stylesheet in the DocBook XSL distribution for XSL-FO change output like there is for HTML output. However, there is a freely downloadable stylesheet `changebars.xsl` from DeltaXML Ltd. at *http://www.deltaxml.com/library/how-to-compare-docbook.html*. The company sells the DeltaXML difference engine, and provides a free comparison service to try it out. The stylesheet works with their DocBook change output, as well as the output from DiffMk.

The DeltaXML `changebars.xsl` stylesheet imports the stock `fo/docbook.xsl` stylesheet. You may need to edit the `changebars.xsl` file to change the relative path in the `xsl:import` statement to find your local copy of the DocBook stylesheets.

30

Tables

DocBook tables are written using either *CALS* table elements or HTML table elements. CALS is an SGML standard developed by the U.S. military, and their set of table tags was one of the first to be developed that included complex features for tables. DocBook adopted the CALS table model because it was already developed.

Later, because of widespread familiarity with HTML tables, DocBook added HTML table elements, starting with version 4.3 of the DocBook DTD. Now you can use `tr` and `td` instead of `row` and `entry` in a table. You cannot mix them in one table, however. Also, the content of each table cell has to be valid DocBook, so you cannot usually just cut and paste an HTML table into your DocBook document. But the DTD does permit a document to contain both CALS tables and HTML tables. The `tgroup` element is the distinguishing characteristic between them. A CALS table requires a `tgroup`, and an HTML table does not permit one.

There are many similarities between DocBook (CALS) tables and HTML tables, as the following table shows. But you cannot cut and paste between them.

Table 30.1. Comparison of CALS and HTML tables

Purpose	HTML Element	CALS Element	Comments
Container for table elements.	table, informaltable	table, informaltable	The CALS table element requires a title, an HTML table element requires a caption. An informaltable accepts neither.
Table title	caption	title	Use informaltable for an HTML table without a caption.
Wrapper for table section	Not available	tgroup	HTML tables do not support subsections of a table with different column specifications. CALS requires at least one tgroup.
Column specifications	col, colgroup	colspec, spanspec	The CALS spanspec element specifies horizontal spanning (joining) of cells.
Wrapper for header rows	thead	thead	
Wrapper for body rows	tbody	tbody	
Wrapper for footer rows	tfoot	tfoot	In both HTML and CALS, tfoot must appear before tbody.
Row	tr	row	All open tr tags must have a closing tag.
Cell	td, th	entry	All open td tags must have a closing tag.
Nested table	informaltable inside a td	entrytbl inside a row	Nested HTML tables permitted since version 4.4 of the DTD.

To learn how to write table elements, you should consult the reference page for table in *DocBook: The Definitive Guide*[1]. It has an example table that uses most of the table elements and features.

Formatting of tables is controlled through a combination of elements, attributes, and processing instructions for the stylesheet. The following sections provide detailed information for CALS table formatting. Because DocBook tables created with HTML table elements use different elements and attributes, there is a separate section for DocBook HTML tables. See the section called " HTML table elements" (page 497) for more information.

Table width

The overall table width can be controlled in two ways: a parameter or a processing instruction. It can be set globally for all tables in the document by setting the default.table.width stylesheet parameter to a width measurement or a percentage. A percentage is taken to be of the available width. This parameter has no default value and so has no effect unless you set it to some value.

The width of a single table using HTML markup can be set using the width attribute. However, that attribute is not supported on tables using CALS table elements. The width of a single CALS table can be specified with a processing instruction. The processing instruction is named dbhtml for HTML output, or dbfo for FO output. If you want to control the width for both outputs, you will need to provide both processing instructions. These processing instructions will override the default global width if one is specified. The following is an example.

---

[1] http://docbook.org/tdg/en/html/table.html

```
<table><title>My table</title>
<?dbhtml table-width="75%" ?>
<?dbfo table-width="75%" ?>
<tgroup>
...
```

For FO output, the stylesheet has an internal default value as well. This is used if neither the parameter nor the processing instruction or attribute establish a table width. For most processors the internal default value for table width is `auto`, which triggers automatic table layout. But some XSL-FO processors, such as FOP, have not implemented automatic table layout. So if `fop.extensions` or `fop1.extensions` parameter is set to 1, the internal default value is 100%. Either of these values can be overridden for all tables by setting the `default.table.width` parameter, or for an individual table with the PI or attribute.

The automatic table layout algorithm in XSL-FO is borrowed from the *CSS2 specification*[2]. It combines any column width specs with the measured width of the text in the table cells to arrive at a total table width. Each cell has a minimum and maximum width. The minimum assumes line breaks between all words. The maximum assumes no line breaks except those that are explicit in the data. The processor then computes a width for each column and lays out the table for the best fit.

Table alignment

Tables that are less that the full page width are generally left-aligned. If you want a different alignment for tables in HTML output, then you can use CSS. For example, the following CSS fragment will center all `table` and `informaltable` elements:

```
div.table {
    text-align: center;
}
div.informaltable {
    text-align: center;
}
```

This works because the HTML stylesheets add these `class` attributes to the HTML `div` elements containing a table.

Centering tables in XSL-FO is a different matter. What should work (but does not) is setting the `text-align` attribute to `center` in the attribute-set named `table.table.properties`. That attribute-set adds properties to the `fo:table` element in the output. Oddly enough, the `text-align` property is not allowed on `fo:table`, so that is why the attribute-set approach does not work to center tables.

The `text-align` property is allowed on `fo:table-and-caption`. However, the DocBook XSL stylesheet does not output a `fo:table-and-caption` element for this purpose because FOP does not support `fo:table-and-caption`, and XEP does not support the `text-align` property on it. Only Antenna House's XSL Formatter works to center a table inside a table-and-caption element.

There is a workaround in XSL-FO for centering tables, which involves creating an outer one-row table with your table contained in the center cell. But the DocBook stylesheets do not do that because of inconsistent behavior among the XSL-FO processors. See the XEP website at *http://www.renderx.net/lists/xep-support/1444.html* if you want to customize tables for centering.

The following customization will center tables in XEP output:

---

[2] http://www.w3.org/TR/REC-CSS2/tables.html#auto-table-layout

```
<xsl:template name="table.layout">
  <xsl:param name="table.content"/>

  <fo:table width="100%">
    <fo:table-column column-width="proportional-column-width(1)"/>
    <fo:table-column/>
    <fo:table-column column-width="proportional-column-width(1)"/>
    <fo:table-body start-indent="0pt">
      <fo:table-row>
        <fo:table-cell/>
        <fo:table-cell>

          <fo:table>
            <fo:table-body start-indent="0pt">
              <fo:table-row><fo:table-cell><fo:block>
                <xsl:copy-of select="$table.content"/>
              </fo:block></fo:table-cell></fo:table-row>
            </fo:table-body>
          </fo:table>

        </fo:table-cell>
        <fo:table-cell/>
      </fo:table-row>
    </fo:table-body>
  </fo:table>
</xsl:template>
```

This customization takes advantage of a placholder template named `table.layout` in the DocBook stylesheet. The `table.content` parameter passed to the template is the entire table, and this template wraps that in another `fo:table` for layout purposes. In this case, it defines proportional columns on either side of the second column, and those effectively center the middle column.

Full-width tables

Wide tables in print output may need more space than is available in the standard body text width. Indents that are often used for content formatting can shorten the available width for a given table. For example, the default layout in the print stylesheet indents body text relative to section headings. Also, a table inside a list is indented further. If a table in that context happens to need more columns and width than is available, then the table width needs to be expanded into the indent space.

The `table` and `informaltable` elements have an attribute named `pgwide` that can be used to indicate that a given table needs to expand to the full page width between the margins. When a table has `pgwide="1"`, then the print stylesheet sets the `start-indent` property to `0pt`, which removes all indents on the table, bringing its left edge out to the left page margin. This property is actually set by an attribute-set named `pgwide.properties` if you need to customize it.

The `pgwide="1"` attribute can also cause a table in a multi-column layout to span all columns by setting `span="all"` on the output table. However, this may not work in all XSL-FO processors because the span property is not on a block that is the direct child of the `fo:flow` element. For this reason, the `span` attribute is not automatically set in the `pgwide.properties` attribute-set, so you have to add it to a customization of that attribute-set. See the section called "Attribute sets" (page 103) for more information.

If you are using `tabstyle` attributes to select different table styles, then you can also customize the stylesheet to respond to such style names. For example, if you have a table style named `smallfont-wide`, then you could customize the `table.properties` attribute-set to use a smaller font and no indent.

```
<xsl:attribute-set name="table.properties">
  <xsl:attribute name="start-indent">
    <xsl:choose>
      <xsl:when test="@tabstyle = 'smallfont-wide'">0pt</xsl:when>
      <xsl:otherwise>inherit</xsl:otherwise>
    </xsl:choose>
  </xsl:attribute>
  <xsl:attribute name="font-size">
    <xsl:choose>
      <xsl:when test="@tabstyle = 'smallfont-wide'">8pt</xsl:when>
      <xsl:otherwise>inherit</xsl:otherwise>
    </xsl:choose>
  </xsl:attribute>
</xsl:attribute-set>
```

Each `xsl:attribute` element contains an `xsl:choose` statement to set its value. The choice is processed each time the attribute-set is used, so the context for `@tabstyle` is the current table. You could have additional `xsl:when` clauses for other table styles. Be sure to include the `xsl:otherwise` to provide the `inherit` value as a default so you do not end up with an empty attribute in the FO output.

Column widths

Table column widths in CALS tables can be controlled by setting a `colwidth` attribute in a `colspec` element for each column inside the `tgroup` element. You also assign each column a number (`colnum` attribute) and an optional name (`colname` attribute). The name can be used in other specifications in the table, such as spans. It is recommended that you provide `colspec` elements for each column to make it easier for the processor to format the table.

The DocBook XSL stylesheets provide XSL extension functions to assist in the adjustment of table columns. These extension functions are only available for the Saxon and Xalan processors. They are enabled by setting both the `use.extensions` parameter and the `tablecolumns.extension` parameter to 1. If you turn on these parameters for other processors, then you will get an error message about `No adjustColumnWidths function available` at the first table.

For HTML output, the extension functions are required if you want to manually set column widths with the `colwidth` attribute. That is because CALS tables permit widths to be specified in ways that cannot be translated by XSLT to HTML table values. The result of this requirement is if the two parameters are not set, then any `colwidth` attributes are ignored. In general, the table columns extension is more important for HTML output than FO output, since the major XSL-FO processors handle table column widths without it. If you use these extensions, do not forget to include the extensions jar file in your Java CLASSPATH.

The following is an example for a four column table:

```
<table><title>My table</title>
<tgroup cols="4" >
<colspec colnum="1" colname="col1" colwidth="1*"/>
<colspec colnum="2" colname="col2" colwidth="2*"/>
<colspec colnum="3" colname="col3" colwidth="1.5*"/>
<colspec colnum="4" colname="col4" colwidth="1*"/>
<thead>
...
```

Here is how you specify column width values:

> colwidth specifies the desired width of the relevant column. It can be either a fixed measure using one of the CALS units (36pt, 10pc, etc.) or a proportional measure. Proportional measures have the form "number*", meaning this column should be number times wider than a column with the measure "1*" (or just "*"). These two forms can be mixed, as in "3*+1pc".
>
> —DocBook: The Definitive Guide

In this example, the first and fourth columns have the same proportion, the second column is twice as wide, and third is 1.5 times as wide. The widths could also have been specified with measurement units, but then they do not adjust to the overall table width.

Cell spacing and cell padding

The stylesheets provide some control over cell spacing (extra space between table cells, visible as space between cell borders if they are turned on), and cell padding (extra space between the cell border and cell content).

For HTML output, you can specify values for the HTML attributes cellspacing (space between cell borders) and cellpadding (space between cell content and cell border) in two ways. You can set values for these globally for all tables in the document by setting the html.cellspacing and html.cellpadding stylesheet parameters, respectively.

To set values for an individual table in HTML output, you use processing instructions inside the tgroup element. For example:

```
<table><title>My table</title>
<tgroup>
<?dbhtml cellspacing="0" ?>
<?dbhtml cellpadding="2" ?>
...
```

This example makes sure the cellspacing is zero and the cellpadding is 2 pixels for this table, possibly overriding the global values set by the parameters. In HTML, cell padding applies to both the top and bottom as well as the left and right of the cell.

For FO output, you can specify the cell padding but not the cell spacing. But you can specify the cell padding for each direction in the cell. If you want to set cell padding values globally for all tables in the document, then copy the attribute-set named table.cell.padding from fo/param.xsl to your customization layer and change the values. The following is an example showing the default values for FO output.

```
<xsl:attribute-set name="table.cell.padding">
  <xsl:attribute name="padding-left">2pt</xsl:attribute>
  <xsl:attribute name="padding-right">2pt</xsl:attribute>
  <xsl:attribute name="padding-top">2pt</xsl:attribute>
  <xsl:attribute name="padding-bottom">2pt</xsl:attribute>
</xsl:attribute-set>
```

As you can see, you specify separate values for top, bottom, left, and right padding in the cell. At this time, you cannot set the padding values for individual tables for FO output.

Row height

You can control the vertical height of any row by putting a processing instructions in that row. Currently this only works for HTML output. The following is an example that sets a row height to 20 pixels.

```
<row><?dbhtml row-height="20" ?>
  <entry>...</entry>
  <entry>...</entry>
</row>
```

Cell alignment

In DocBook tables, you can control the horizontal and vertical positioning of content with a cell by using the `align` and `valign` attributes, respectively. The scope of entries affected by the attribute depends on which table element has the attribute.

Horizontal alignment

You can set horizontal alignment of cell content by setting the `align` attribute to any of these values:

```
left
center
right
char
justify
```

A value of `char` means the content should line up according to a certain character in the cell data, typically a decimal character. Then a column of numbers with decimals will have the decimals lined up. If you set `align="char"` for a column, you need to specify a `char="."` attribute (or other character) as well to tell the processor on what character to line up the entries.

The `align` attribute can be set on any of the following elements, so it applies to the scope of that element:

```
tgroup
colspec
spanspec
entry
```

For example, you could set `align="left"` in `tgroup` for the whole table (if you have one tgroup). Then you can set `align="center"` in one `colspec` to center all entries in that column. The following is an example.

```
<table><title>My table</title>
<tgroup cols="4" align="left">
<colspec colnum="1" colname="col1" colwidth="1*" />
<colspec colnum="2" colname="col2" colwidth="2*" align="center" />
<colspec colnum="3" colname="col3" colwidth="1.5*"/>
<colspec colnum="4" colname="col4" colwidth="1*" align="char" char="."/>
<thead>
...
```

In this example, the `tgroup` element sets the default alignment for the table to `left`. Entries in column 2 will instead be centered, and entries in column 4 are to be aligned on the decimal character in the cell data.

Vertical alignment

You can set vertical alignment of cell content by setting the `valign` attribute to any of these values:

```
top
middle
bottom
```

The `valign` attribute can be set on any of the following elements so it applies to the scope of that element:

```
thead
tbody
tfoot
row
entry
```

For example, you could set `valign="top"` in tbody for the whole table. Then you can set `valign="middle"` in one row to middle-align all cells in that row, or on a single `entry` to middle-align only that cell. The following is an example.

```
<table><title>My table</title>
<tgroup cols="4" >
...
<thead valign="bottom">
...
<tbody valign="top">
  <row valign="middle">
    <entry>...</entry>
    <entry valign="top">...</entry>
...
```

In this example, the row alignment overrides the tbody alignment, and then the entry alignment overrides the row alignment.

Cell rotation

The CALS `rotate` attribute on the `entry` element is not supported in the DocBook XSL stylesheets. However, it is possible to rotate the contents of individual table cells by 90 degree increments using special DocBook processing instructions. This can be useful when you have many narrow data columns that have long column headings. Rotating the column headings by 90 degrees can provide room for more columns.

This only works for printed output, and not all XSL-FO processors support such rotations. The processor must be able to support the `fo:block-container` element inside the `fo:table-cell`. The following is an example of a rotated table entry:

```
<entry><?dbfo orientation="90"?>
<?dbfo rotated-width="1in"?>Cell rotated left
</entry>
```

You have to provide two processing instructions to make this work. The `<?dbfo orientation="90"?>` processing instruction tells the processor to rotate the text 90 degrees counter-clockwise. The `<?dbfo rotated-width="1in"?>` processing instruction informs the processor of how wide the text was before it was rotated. That enables it to adjust the row-height to fit the length of the rotated text.

Cell spanning

Cell spanning means joining cells together to make a larger cell. You can join cells horizontally, vertically, or both.

Horizontal spans

To join cells horizontally, you must specify `colname` attributes in your `colspec` elements in your table. Then you use those names in an `entry` element to indicate the starting and ending columns for the horizontal span. You use `namest` to indicate the starting column name, and `nameend` to indicate the ending column name. The following example shows how to use them.

```
<table><title>Horizontal span</title>
<tgroup cols="4" >
<colspec colnum="1" colname="col1" colwidth="1*"/>
<colspec colnum="2" colname="col2" colwidth="2*"/>
<colspec colnum="3" colname="col3" colwidth="1.5*"/>
<colspec colnum="4" colname="col4" colwidth="1*"/>
<thead>
  <row>
    <entry>First column</entry>
    <entry namest="col2" nameend="col3" align="center">Span columns 2 and 3</entry>
    <entry colname="col4">Fourth column</entry>
  </row>
</thead>
<tbody>
  <row>
    <entry>Body first</entry>
    <entry>Body second</entry>
    <entry>Body third</entry>
    <entry>Body fourth</entry>
  </row>
...
```

Example 30.1. Horizontal span in table

First column	Span columns 2 and 3		Fourth column
Body first	Body second	Body third	Body fourth
...	...	...	...

The second `entry` creates a horizontal span that starts in column 2 and stops in column 3. The third `entry` includes a `colname="col4"` attribute, a good practice to remind the editor that although it is the third entry, it will appear in the fourth column because of the span.

If you repeatedly use the same span in a table, you can specify a named `spanspec` element in `tgroup` to pre declare the start and end column names. Then an entry can just refer to the named `spanspec`, using one attribute instead of two (and reducing the possibility of error). The following is the previous example expressed with a `spanspec`.

```
<table><title>My table</title>
<tgroup cols="4" >
<colspec colnum="1" colname="col1" colwidth="1*"/>
<colspec colnum="2" colname="col2" colwidth="2*"/>
<colspec colnum="3" colname="col3" colwidth="1.5*"/>
<colspec colnum="4" colname="col4" colwidth="1*"/>
<spanspec spanname="twothree" namest="col2" nameend="col3"/>
<thead>
  <row>
    <entry>First column</entry>
    <entry spanname="twothree">Span columns 2 and 3</entry>
    <entry colname="col4">Fourth column</entry>
  </row>
</thead>
...
```

Like colspec, a spanspec element can also have an align attribute.

Vertical spans

To join cells vertically, you add a morerows attribute to an entry element. That attribute is an integer that indicates how many more rows to add to the current row for this element. The following example uses morerows:

```
<table><title>Vertical span</title>
<tgroup cols="4" >
<colspec colnum="1" colname="col1" colwidth="1*"/>
<colspec colnum="2" colname="col2" colwidth="2*"/>
<colspec colnum="3" colname="col3" colwidth="1.5*"/>
<colspec colnum="4" colname="col4" colwidth="1*"/>
<tbody>
  <row>
    <entry>First column</entry>
    <entry morerows="1" valign="middle">Second column</entry>
    <entry>Third column</entry>
    <entry >Fourth column</entry>
  </row>
  <row>
    <entry>Another first</entry>
    <entry colname="col3">Another third</entry>
    <entry colname="col4">Another fourth</entry>
  </row>
...
```

Example 30.2. Vertical span in table

First column	Second column	Third column	Fourth column
Another first		Another third	Another fourth
...	...	...	...

In this example, the second entry in the first row spans downward one additional row. So the second row contains only three entry elements. The second and third entries will appear in columns 3 and 4 because the vertical span from the row above is taking up column 2. It is a good idea to tag the last two entries with `colname` so it is clear that the second `entry` in that row will appear in the third column, and so on.

You can put attributes for both horizontal and vertical span in the same `entry` element, and it will span in both directions. Then tagging of column names in the surrounding entries becomes even more important to prevent errors in editing.

Borders

In DocBook tables, the box around a table and the grid lines separating table cells are controlled by different attributes. For the table frame, you can indicate which sides are to have rule lines. For cell separators, you can indicate which columns and rows are to have separators, or you can set it for the whole table. For HTML output, controlling individual cell borders requires turning on the `table.borders.with.css` stylesheet parameter.

Table border

The border around a given table is turned on by adding a `frame` attribute to the `table` element. You must select one of the following values, which indicate which sides of the table are to have a border.

```
all
bottom
none
sides
top
topbot
```

If you want a box around your table, then set `frame="all"`. If you just want horizontal lines at the top and bottom of the table, set `frame="topbot"`.

If you want all your tables to have the same frame style without adding `frame` attributes to them all, then set the stylesheet parameter `default.table.frame` to one of the above values. You can still override the parameter setting by using a `frame` attribute on a given table. This parameter was added in version 1.73 of the stylesheets, and works with both print and HTML output.

In printed output, when a long table breaks across a page boundary, the bottom table border is not normally displayed at the break, nor is the top border after the page break. To some readers, this feature indicates that the table is continuing to the next page. To others, it looks odd. If you want the bottom and top table borders to display at the page breaks, then add this to your customization layer:

```
<xsl:attribute-set name="table.table.properties">
  <xsl:attribute name="border-after-width.conditionality">retain</xsl:attribute>
  <xsl:attribute name="border-before-width.conditionality">retain</xsl:attribute>
</xsl:attribute-set>
```

You might think you can turn borders on and off with the `table.table.properties` attribute-set, but that does not work. That's because a template named `table.frame` is called to apply borders after the attribute-set is applied. Any border properties set by the template override the same property in the attribute-set.

To customize table borders in print output, perhaps responding to a `tabstyle` attribute on a table, you need to customize the `table.frame` template in `fo/table.xsl`. That template outputs border attributes for the various `frame` attribute values.

To customize table borders in HTML output, you need to set the stylesheet parameter `table.borders.with.css` to 1 and customize the template named `border` in `html/table.xsl`.

Row borders

Horizontal grid lines drawn below rows are turned on by setting the attribute `rowsep="1"`. You can turn it off by setting `rowsep="0"`. This attribute can be set on any of the following elements so it applies to the scope of that element.

```
table
tgroup
colspec
spanspec
row
entry
```

So you can turn it on for all rows by setting the value to 1 in `table`, and then turn it off for specific rows by setting it to 0 in those rows. In `colspec` or `spanspec`, it applies on to the cells in that column or span. When cells are spanned vertically, no lines are drawn within the range of the span, only at the bottom of the span. Any `rowsep` value for the last row is ignored, because the table's `frame` attribute controls the bottom border.

Column borders

Vertical grid lines drawn to the right of each table cell are turned on by setting the attribute `colsep="1"`. You can turn it off by setting `colsep="0"`. This attribute can be set on any of the following elements so it applies to the scope of that element.

```
table
tgroup
colspec
spanspec
entry
```

So you can turn it on for all columns by setting the value to 1 in `table`, and then turn it off for specific columns by setting it to 0 in those `colspec` elements. When cells are spanned horizontally, no lines are drawn within the range of the span, only at the end of the span. Any `colsep` value for the last column is ignored, because the table's `frame` attribute controls the right border. The following example turns grid lines on and off.

```
<table frame="topbot" colsep="1" rowsep="1">
<title>Table borders</title>
<tgroup cols="4">
<colspec colnum="1" colname="col1" colwidth="1*"/>
<colspec colnum="2" colname="col2" colwidth="1*" colsep="0"/>
<colspec colnum="3" colname="col3" colwidth="1*"/>
<colspec colnum="4" colname="col4" colwidth="1*"/>
<thead>
<row>
<entry>Column 1 heading</entry>
<entry>Column 2 heading</entry>
<entry>Column 3 heading</entry>
<entry>Column 4 heading</entry>
</row>
</thead>
<tbody>
<row>
<entry>Entry 1.1</entry>
<entry>Entry 2.1</entry>
<entry>Entry 3.1</entry>
<entry>Entry 4.1</entry>
</row>
<row rowsep="0">
<entry>Entry 1.2</entry>
<entry rowsep="1" colsep="1">Entry 2.2</entry>
<entry>Entry 3.2</entry>
<entry>Entry 4.2</entry>
</row>
<row>
<entry>Entry 1.3</entry>
<entry>Entry 2.3</entry>
<entry>Entry 3.3</entry>
<entry rowsep="0">Entry 4.3</entry>
</row>
</tbody>
</tgroup>
</table>
```

Example 30.3. Table borders

Column 1 heading	Column 2 heading	Column 3 heading	Column 4 heading
Entry 1.1	Entry 2.1	Entry 3.1	Entry 4.1
Entry 1.2	Entry 2.2	Entry 3.2	Entry 4.2
Entry 1.3	Entry 2.3	Entry 3.3	Entry 4.3

Note these features of this example:

- The table frame attribute creates borders at the top and bottom of the table.

- The table attributes also turn on row and column lines for the whole table.

- The colspec for column 2 turns off the vertical line to the right of column 2.

- The row element for the second row turns off the horizontal line below that row.

- Entry 2.2 turns on the vertical line to the right of and the horizontal line below that cell, overriding the removed lines.

- The rowsep="0" in Entry 4.3 has no effect because the bottom rule comes from the table frame attribute.

Border styles

The DocBook stylesheets provide parameters for controlling table border styles. You can control the color, thickness, and style of borders, and control them separately for table frame and cell borders. You can set these parameters on the command line or in a stylesheet customization layer. Because these are stylesheet parameters, they apply to all tables in a document.

Example 30.4. Table border properties

Property	Parameters	Possible Values
Border color	table.frame.border.color table.cell.border.color	**Color keywords:** aqua, black, blue, fuchsia, gray, green, lime, maroon, navy, olive, purple, red, silver, teal, white, yellow.
		RGB color: #2D33FF, #001A3D, etc.
Border thickness	table.frame.border.thickness table.cell.border.thickness	**Thickness keyword:** thin, medium, thick.
		Thickness length: 0.5pt, 3px, 2mm, etc.
Border style	table.frame.border.style table.cell.border.style	**Style keywords:** none, dotted, dashed, solid, double, groove, ridge, inset, outset

Some of these properties may not be completely supported in all output formats or by all HTML browsers.

Background color

You can insert a background color for individual table cells by using a processing instruction, or whole rows with a customization. Currently the row customization only works for HTML output.

Cell background color

You can use a dbhtml or dbfo processing instruction to set the background color for an individual table cell. The processing instructions can appear anywhere within the entry element. The following is an example.

```
<table>
<title>Background color</title>
<tgroup cols="4">
<colspec colnum="1" colname="col1" colwidth="1*"/>
<colspec colnum="2" colname="col2" colwidth="1*"/>
<colspec colnum="3" colname="col3" colwidth="1*"/>
<colspec colnum="4" colname="col4" colwidth="1*"/>
<thead>
<row>
<entry>Column 1 heading
<?dbhtml bgcolor="#EEEEEE" ?><?dbfo bgcolor="#EEEEEE" ?></entry>
<entry>Column 2 heading</entry>
<entry>Column 3 heading
<?dbhtml bgcolor="#EEEEEE" ?><?dbfo bgcolor="#EEEEEE" ?></entry>
<entry>Column 4 heading</entry>
</row>
</thead>
<tbody>
<row>
<entry>Entry 1.1</entry>
<entry>Entry 2.1</entry>j
<entry>Entry 3.1</entry>
<entry>Entry 4.1</entry>
</row>
...
```

This example puts a light gray background behind two of the table headings. You need to use both processing instructions if you want the background color in both HTML and print.

Row background color

You can also use the bgcolor processing instructions to turns on background color for a whole row. To associate the PI with the row, it has to be inside the row element but not inside any entry element. So place the PI between the start tag of the row element and the start tag of the first entry element.

```
<row>
<?dbhtml bgcolor="#EEEEEE" ?><?dbfo bgcolor="#EEEEEE" ?>
<entry>Column 1 heading</entry>
<entry>Column 2 heading</entry>
<entry>Column 3 heading</entry>
<entry>Column 4 heading</entry>
</row>
```

You can still override the row color for specific cells by adding a PI in each individual entry element within the row.

What if you want a table that put a background color on alternating rows? You could put the same bgcolor processing instruction on each row, but that can become tedious.

The alternative is to create a stylesheet customization that allows you to apply styles to rows based on either a role attribute or a row count. The HTML stylesheet provides an empty template named tr.attributes that can be customized for such purposes. The following is an example that puts a class="oddrow" attribute on every other row if the table's tabstyle attribute is set to striped. Then you supply a CSS stylesheet that applies a background color to the TR rows with a class="oddrow" attribute.

```
<xsl:template name="tr.attributes">
  <xsl:param name="row" select="."/>
  <xsl:param name="rownum" select="0"/>

  <xsl:if test="ancestor::table/@tabstyle = 'striped'">
    <xsl:if test="$rownum mod 2 = 0">
      <xsl:attribute name="class">oddrow</xsl:attribute>
    </xsl:if>
  </xsl:if>

</xsl:template>
```

This template could also respond to other `tabstyle` attribute values to produce different styles. For example, if you turn on the background color for all rows, then effectively the whole table has a background color.

To get alternating color rows for print output, you can customize the `table.row.properties` template. See the section called "table.row.properties template" (page 489) for examples of such customizations.

Long tables

Long tables are generally not a problem in DocBook XSL. In HTML output, in which web pages have no limit in length, long tables are presented without interruption. In print output, however, long tables have to span more than one page.

The XSL-FO standard accomodates long tables in the headers and footers for print output:

- Table header rows (those contained in `thead`) are repeated on all pages containing the table. So if a table breaks across a page boundary, the table header rows are repeated at the top of the next page.

- Likewise, table footer rows (those contained in `tfoot`) are repeated before each page break, not just at the end of the table.

In the case of a `table` element with `title`, there is no provision in XSL-FO 1.0 for repeating the title (perhaps with the word "continued") after each page break. This problem is addressed in XSL-FO 1.1 with table markers, but DocBook XSL does not yet support that. Some XSL-FO processors have extension mechanisms to provide a "continued" title. See the section called "Table "continued" label" (page 499) for an example using XEP.

If you have exceptionally long tables (several hundred rows), then you may run into problems with processor memory. In particular, Java processors such as Saxon and Xalan may run out of stack space. This happens because of the way the DocBook XSL stylesheets compute row spans. Since any entry may be affected by row spans above it, the stylesheet recursively processes the rows above to find such spans. Recursive templates use up stack space, and if there are hundreds of rows you might run out of stack space. One solution is to break the table into multiple smaller `tgroup` elements, each specifying the same fixed column widths. If you are using Java 6 or higher, you can simply increase the Java thread stack space with a command line option such as the following:

```
java -Xss2m ...
```

Earlier versions of Java do not support this option.

Table styles in print output

The stylesheets provide several attribute-sets and templates for controlling table styles at different levels in a table. Here is a summary of them, and each is further described in the following sections.

Table 30.2. Table styles for print output

Name	XSL element	Properties are applied to:
table.properties	attribute-set	The outer `fo:block` that wraps the table and its title.
formal.title.properties (page 487)	attribute-set	The `fo:block` containing the table title. Applies also to example, figure, and equation titles.
informaltable.properties	attribute-set	The `fo:block` containing the informaltable.
table.table.properties	attribute-set	The `fo:table` element, for both table and informaltable.
tabstyle	template	Utility template that returns the value of the current table's `tabstyle` attribute from within any table element context.
table.frame	template	The `fo:table` element, computing `border` properties.
table.row.properties	template	Each `fo:table-row` element.
table.cell.properties	template	Each `fo:table-cell` element.
table.cell.block.properties	template	The `fo:block` element inside each `fo:table-cell`.

Many publications define certain styles that are to be used for all tables within a publication. With DocBook XSL, you can define a set of table style names, each of which is associated with a particular table style. Then your authors can select which style to use by specifying the style name in a `tabstyle` attribute on a given table. This system lets the designer control the overall styles for tables, and makes it easy for an author to select a style that suitable for a particular table. If necessary, the author can override certain features of a table style, depending on how the customization is written.

table.properties attribute-set

Use the `table.properties` attribute-set to set styles for the `fo:block` that contains a `table` and its title (but not an `informaltable`). By default, this attribute-set just uses the attributes from the `formal.object.properties` attribute-set:

```
<xsl:attribute-set name="formal.object.properties">
  <xsl:attribute name="space-before.minimum">0.5em</xsl:attribute>
  <xsl:attribute name="space-before.optimum">1em</xsl:attribute>
  <xsl:attribute name="space-before.maximum">2em</xsl:attribute>
  <xsl:attribute name="space-after.minimum">0.5em</xsl:attribute>
  <xsl:attribute name="space-after.optimum">1em</xsl:attribute>
  <xsl:attribute name="space-after.maximum">2em</xsl:attribute>
  <xsl:attribute name="keep-together.within-column">always</xsl:attribute>
</xsl:attribute-set>
```

By setting any or all of these attributes in the `table.properties` attribute-set, you override the values copied from `formal.object.properties`. You can also add new properties. Whatever properties you use must be applicable to `fo:block` elements. If they are inheritable, they will be inherited by all blocks in the table, including the table title. You can use the `formal.title.properties` attribute-set to apply properties to just the number and title, although those properties will also be applied to example, figure, and equation titles.

Note in particular that the last attribute inherited from `formal.object.properties` adds a *keep* to the table block. This keeps the table title with the table, but it also means the table will be forced to a new page if the whole table does not fit on the current page. That may be inappropriate for long tables that could start on the current page. For individual tables, you can use a processing instruction to allow a table to break, as described in the section called "Keep-together processing instruction" (page 89). Or you can change the attribute value to `auto` to turn off the keep for all tables, and use the PI in individual tables to keep them together. This change can be made in the `table.properties` attribute-set. You do not have to worry about keeping a table's title together with the table, because the title block itself has a `keep-with-next` property.

The following example adjusts the space-before and adds a background shading to all tables. Because the background-color property is on the block, it encompasses the table and its title.

```
<xsl:attribute-set name="table.properties">
  <xsl:attribute name="space-before.optimum">12pt</xsl:attribute>
  <xsl:attribute name="background-color">#EEEEEE</xsl:attribute>
</xsl:attribute-set>
```

If you want a property's value in this attribute-set to be dependent on a table's `tabstyle` attribute, then you can make the value conditional using `xsl:choose`. In the next example, when `tabstyle="shaded"` the block containing the table and its title will have a background color.

```
<xsl:attribute-set name="table.properties">
  <xsl:attribute name="background-color">
    <xsl:choose>
      <xsl:when test="@tabstyle='shaded'">#EEEEEE</xsl:when>
      <xsl:otherwise>inherit</xsl:otherwise>
    </xsl:choose>
  </xsl:attribute>
</xsl:attribute-set>
```

Since the context in which `table.properties` is applied is the `table` element, the attribute can simply test for its `@tabstyle` attribute value. The test is executed each time the attribute-set is applied.

informaltable.properties attribute-set

If you use an `informaltable` element (a table without a number and title), then you will find that the attributes in `table.properties` do not apply. The `informaltable.properties` attribute-set is used for `informaltable` elements. So if you want a property to apply to both, you have to add the attribute to both attribute-sets. Or you can have one attribute-set use the other:

```
<xsl:attribute-set name="informaltable.properties"
                   xsl:use-attribute-sets="table.properties"/>
```

Just as `table.properties` uses all the attributes from `formal.object.properties` attribute-set, so does `informaltable.properties` use all the attributes from `informal.object.properties`.

See the section called "table.properties attribute-set" (page 487) for tips on using these attribute-sets.

table.table.properties attribute-set

While the `table.properties` attribute set can be used to add properties to the `fo:block` containing a table, you can use the `table.table.properties` attribute-set to add properties to the `fo:table` element itself. Table-specific properties such as `table-layout` or `table-omit-header-at-break` must be applied this way. The default attributes in this set are used for managing borders:

```
<xsl:attribute-set name="table.table.properties">
  <xsl:attribute name="border-before-width.conditionality">retain</xsl:attribute>
  <xsl:attribute name="border-collapse">collapse</xsl:attribute>
</xsl:attribute-set>
```

If you want a property's value in this attribute-set to be dependent on a table's `tabstyle` attribute, then you can make the value conditional using `xsl:choose`. In the next example, when `tabstyle="shaded"` the table will have a background color. It differs from the similar example in the section called "table.properties attribute-set" (page 487) in that the area behind a table's title is not shaded.

```
<xsl:attribute-set name="table.table.properties">
  <xsl:attribute name="background-color">
    <xsl:choose>
      <xsl:when test="ancestor-or-self::table[1]/@tabstyle='shaded' or
        ancestor-or-self::informaltable[1]/@tabstyle='shaded'">#EEEEEE</xsl:when>
      <xsl:otherwise>inherit</xsl:otherwise>
    </xsl:choose>
  </xsl:attribute>
</xsl:attribute-set>
```

Since the context in which `table.table.properties` is applied is the `tgroup` element, the attribute must test for the `@tabstyle` attribute on the ancestor table element. In the case of HTML markup tables (permitted in DocBook since version 4.3), the `tgroup` element is not used so the test must include `ancestor-or-self`. The test is executed each time the attribute-set is applied.

Properties such as `background-color` that are are set on the `fo:table` can be overridden in the table rows or cells by local attributes or processing instructions.

tabstyle template

The `tabstyle` named template is a utility template that can be used by any table element's template to determine the current `tabstyle` attribute value. A table formatting property may be implemented at any of several levels in a table, such as at the table, row, or cell levels. Any table element template can call the `tabstyle` template, which returns the value of the current table's `tabstyle` attribute. Using such a utility template makes it easy for all levels to work with the same value.

> **Note:**
>
> If a table element (`table` or `informaltable`) does not have a `tabstyle` attribute, the template also checks for a `tgroupstyle` attribute on the `tgroup` element. That attribute would only be needed if a table uses more than one `tgroup` and they need different styles.

Generally a template handling a table element calls the `tabstyle` template and saves the result in a variable. Then it can use the variable in an `xsl:choose` statement to implement different properties at that level for different table styles. See Example 30.6, "Customized table.cell.properties" (page 492) for an example of such usage. The `tabstyle` template was added to the stylesheets starting with version 1.72.

table.row.properties template

The template named `table.row.properties` applies properties to each `fo:table-row` in a table. Note that this is a named *template*, not an attribute-set. By making it a template, it is easier to customize for multiple properties on each row. This template is called just after the `fo:table-row` opening tag in the output. The template should output one or more `xsl:attribute` elements, which are applied to the table row just opened. The template must not output anything else, or it will generate errors in the table processing.

By default, the template processes any `dbfo` processing instructions for background color and adds that property to the current row. See the section called "Row background color" (page 485) for more information on that processing instruction.

The following is an example of a customization that applies a background color to alternating rows of a table when its tabstyle attribute is set to striped.

```
<xsl:template name="table.row.properties">

  <xsl:variable name="tabstyle">
    <xsl:call-template name="tabstyle"/>
  </xsl:variable>

  <xsl:variable name="bgcolor">
    <xsl:call-template name="dbfo-attribute">
      <xsl:with-param name="pis" select="processing-instruction('dbfo')"/>
      <xsl:with-param name="attribute" select="'bgcolor'"/>
    </xsl:call-template>
  </xsl:variable>

  <xsl:variable name="rownum">
    <xsl:number from="tgroup" count="row"/>
  </xsl:variable>

  <xsl:choose>
    <xsl:when test="$bgcolor != ''">
      <xsl:attribute name="background-color">
        <xsl:value-of select="$bgcolor"/>
      </xsl:attribute>
    </xsl:when>
    <xsl:when test="$tabstyle = 'striped'">
      <xsl:if test="$rownum mod 2 = 0">
        <xsl:attribute name="background-color">#EEEEEE</xsl:attribute>
      </xsl:if>
    </xsl:when>
  </xsl:choose>
</xsl:template>
```

table.cell.properties template

The table.cell.properties named template applies properties to each fo:table-cell in a table. Note that this is a named *template*, not an attribute-set. By making it a template, it is easier to customize for multiple properties on each cell. This template is called just after the fo:table-cell opening tag in the output. The template should output one or more xsl:attribute elements, which are applied to the table cell just opened. The template must not output anything else, or it will generate errors in the table processing.

By default, the table.cell.properties template outputs properties that are passed to it as template parameters. These parameters deliver the values of properties set on that DocBook entry element, or properties that were inherited from one of its table ancestor elements. For a discussion of how table properties such as align can be inherited, see the section called "Cell alignment" (page 477). The following annotated example shows the first part of the template before any customization:

Example 30.5. Default table.cell.properties template

```
<xsl:template name="table.cell.properties"> ❶
  <xsl:param name="bgcolor.pi" select="''"/> ❷
  <xsl:param name="rowsep.inherit" select="1"/> ❸
  <xsl:param name="colsep.inherit" select="1"/> ❹
  <xsl:param name="valign.inherit" select="''"/> ❺
  <xsl:param name="align.inherit" select="''"/> ❻
  <xsl:param name="char.inherit" select="''"/> ❼

  <xsl:if test="$bgcolor.pi != ''"> ❽
    <xsl:attribute name="background-color">
      <xsl:value-of select="$bgcolor.pi"/>
    </xsl:attribute>
  </xsl:if>

  <xsl:if test="$rowsep.inherit &gt; 0">
    <xsl:call-template name="border">
      <xsl:with-param name="side" select="'bottom'"/>
    </xsl:call-template>
  </xsl:if>

  <xsl:if test="$colsep.inherit &gt; 0 and
                     $col &lt; ancestor::tgroup/@cols">
    <xsl:call-template name="border">
      <xsl:with-param name="side" select="'right'"/>
    </xsl:call-template>
  </xsl:if>

  ...
```

❶ This mechanism uses a named *template*, not an attribute-set.
❷ The inherited background color, based on the dbfo bgcolor processing instruction in either the row or the entry element.
❸ The inherited rowsep value, which controls the border below the cell.
❹ The inherited colsep value, which controls the border to the right of the cell.
❺ The inherited vertical alignment value.
❻ The inherited horizontal alignment value.
❼ The inherited value of the char attribute, which specifies a character on which to align the entry.
❽ The bit of logic that determines whether a background-color property is output using xsl:attribute. By default, it outputs the property only if it is passed an inherited value.

The table.cell.properties template provides the opportunity to customize how cell properties are added to the output. Instead of just outputting the inherited value, the template can use whatever logic you want. For example, you can check the table's tabstyle attribute value, and output the properties that are appropriate for a given named table style.

The following example shows how you can customize background color for a table with a tabstyle="styleA" attribute:

Example 30.6. Customized table.cell.properties

```
<xsl:template name="table.cell.properties">
  <xsl:param name="bgcolor.pi" select="''"/>
  ...
  <xsl:variable name="tabstyle">
    <xsl:call-template name="tabstyle"/>   ❶
  </xsl:variable>

  <xsl:variable name="bgcolor"> ❷
    <xsl:choose>
      <xsl:when test="$tabstyle = 'styleA'
                      and ancestor::thead">#BBBBBB</xsl:when>   ❸
      <xsl:when test="$tabstyle = 'styleA'">#DDDDDD</xsl:when>  ❹
      <xsl:when test="$bgcolor.pi != ''"> ❺
        <xsl:value-of select="$bgcolor.pi"/>
      </xsl:when>
    </xsl:choose>
  </xsl:variable>

  <xsl:if test="$bgcolor != ''"> ❻
    <xsl:attribute name="background-color">
      <xsl:value-of select="$bgcolor"/>
    </xsl:attribute>
  </xsl:if>
  ...
```

❶ Get the tabstyle attribute value for the containing table into a variable by calling the tabstyle named template.
❷ Put the resolved color value into another variable.
❸ Use color #DDDDDD if the table has tabstyle="styleA" and the current cell is inside a table header row.
❹ Use color #BBBBBB if the table has tabstyle="styleA" and the current cell is *not* in a header row.
❺ If no tabstyle match, then fall back on the inherited value if there is one.
❻ Finally output a background-color attribute if one of the options provided a value.

Here is some useful information about using this template:

• The context for the template call is the current entry element.

• You can use xsl:number to get the current entry's position in the table. For example:

```
<xsl:variable name="rownumber">
  <xsl:number count="row" from="tbody"/>
</xsl:variable>
<xsl:variable name="cellnumber">
  <xsl:number count="entry" from="row"/>
</xsl:variable>
```

The $rownumber and $cellnumber variables can be used in expressions to determine property values.

• You can implement as many tabstyle names as you need, and you can have them generate as many properties as you need.

• Each property must be permitted on an fo:table-cell. You can use font properties, and they will be inherited by any block elements in the cell.

- You can decide if an inherited value should override a `tabstyle` value, or vice versa.

table.cell.block.properties template

The `table.cell.block.properties` named template applies properties to the `fo:block` that is inside each `fo:table-cell` in the output of a table. Note that this is a named *template*, not an attribute-set. By making it a template, it is easier to customize for multiple properties.

This template is called just after the `fo:block` opening tag that appears at the beginning of each `fo:table-cell` in the output. The template should output one or more `xsl:attribute` elements, which are applied to the block just opened.

This template is used mainly to set font properties on the content of table cells. This template, because its output block is nested inside the `fo:table-cell`, will override any properties set by the `table.cell.properties` template.

By default, the `table.cell.block.properties` template just makes table header cells bold. The following is the template before any customization:

```
<xsl:template name="table.cell.block.properties">
  <xsl:if test="ancestor::thead">
    <xsl:attribute name="font-weight">bold</xsl:attribute>
  </xsl:if>
</xsl:template>
```

See the section called "table.cell.properties template" (page 490) for details of how to customize setting properties in table cells.

Table page breaking

The default behavior for the print stylesheet is to try to keep each table together on a page. For short tables, this is usually desirable. But for larger tables, it can lead to awkward page breaks that leave large empty spaces on a page.

You can control how tables break across pages in the following ways:

- You can turn on or off the `keep-together` property for all tables by changing the property value in the `table.properties` and `informaltable.properties` attribute-sets. See the section called "table.properties attribute-set" (page 487) for more information.

- For individual tables, you can use a processing instruction to control the `keep-together` property. See the section called "Keep-together processing instruction" (page 89) for more information.

- You can keep each row together by adding the `keep-together` property to `table.cell.properties` template. Since it is applied to each cell, it will as a side effect keep each row together. Vertically spanned cells will bring along cells in other rows.

Landscape tables

Some tables are too wide to fit on a normal portrait page. Such tables may fit if the table is rotated 90 degrees and presented in landscape mode.

You can make a table print in landscape mode by putting a `orient="land"` attribute on the `table` or `informaltable` element. That will rotate the table 90 degrees counter-clockwise, including any table title. This assumes your XSL-FO processor is capable of rotating the content of a `fo:block-container` element. XEP, Antenna House, and Xml2PDF can, but the current FOP cannot.

Depending on the width of the table content, you may also want to set the width of the table. You can use a processing instruction as described in the section called "Table width" (page 472).

There is one pretty big caveat for a landscape table: it must have few enough rows to fit onto one page. The current XSL-FO standard does not support carrying over content in a block-container to more than one page. The last rows of your table will simply not appear in the printed output if you try.

There is a workaround for this problem, though. G. Ken Holman of *Crane Softwrights Ltd.*[3] has published a method for creating multipage landscape tables in XSL-FO. His Page Sequence Master Interleave (PSMI) method uses two passes to rearrange the pages in an FO file. PSMI is described at *http://www.cranesoftwrights.com/resources/psmi/index.htm*.

Table title formatting

The main stylesheet feature that is used to format table titles for print output is the `formal.title.properties` attribute-set. The following is the default definition of the attribute-set:

```
<xsl:attribute-set name="formal.title.properties"
                   use-attribute-sets="normal.para.spacing">
  <xsl:attribute name="font-weight">bold</xsl:attribute>
  <xsl:attribute name="font-size">
    <xsl:value-of select="$body.font.master * 1.2"/>
    <xsl:text>pt</xsl:text>
  </xsl:attribute>
  <xsl:attribute name="hyphenate">false</xsl:attribute>
  <xsl:attribute name="space-after.minimum">0.4em</xsl:attribute>
  <xsl:attribute name="space-after.optimum">0.6em</xsl:attribute>
  <xsl:attribute name="space-after.maximum">0.8em</xsl:attribute>
</xsl:attribute-set>
```

That attribute-set is used for titles of tables, figures, examples, equations, blockquotes, and procedures. If you make a change to the attribute-set, then it will be reflected in the titles of all of those elements.

However, it is possible to make a property value conditional when setting an attribute. The following is a customization that centers table titles, but not any of the other titles. All other properties are left as they were:

```
<xsl:attribute-set name="formal.title.properties">
  <xsl:attribute name="text-align">
    <xsl:choose>
      <xsl:when test="self::table">center</xsl:when>
      <xsl:otherwise>left</xsl:otherwise>
    </xsl:choose>
  </xsl:attribute>
</xsl:attribute-set>
```

The body of the `xsl:attribute` whose name is `text-align` has an `xsl:choose` statement that checks to see if the current element in context is a `table`. If it is, then set the value of `text-align` to `center`. Otherwise, set it to `left`. This works because the `xsl:attribute` is evaluated each time it is referenced in the `attribute-set`.

Table titles without number labels

What if you want to print all your table titles without the number label such as `Table 3.2`? There is no stylesheet parameter that will turn them off. In order to eliminate table numbers from the table titles, any "table of tables",

---

[3] http://www.cranesoftwrights.com

and any cross references to tables, the following customization is necessary. A similar customization could be used for figures, examples, or equations.

```
<xsl:param name="local.l10n.xml" select="document('')"/>
<l:i18n xmlns:l="http://docbook.sourceforge.net/xmlns/l10n/1.0">
  <l:l10n language="en">
    <l:context name="title">
      <l:template name="table" text="%t"/>
    </l:context>
    <l:context name="xref-number-and-title">
      <l:template name="table" text="the table titled &#8220;%t&#8221;"/>
    </l:context>
  </l:l10n>
</l:i18n>

<xsl:template match="table" mode="label.markup"/>
```

The local.l10n.xml parameter is used to alter the generated text. In this case, you are changing the gentext templates for the table element in the contexts of title and xref-number-and-title, which are the contexts that all the formal objects use. The changes eliminate the use of the word Table and the %n placeholder that generates the number. You can reword the cross reference text any way you like. Repeat the process for all the languages you are using.

The last line of the customization makes empty the template that matches on table in mode label.markup. That mode generates the number for an element. It is used in the table of contents when a table of tables is generated.

Table styles in HTML output

When outputting HTML, the stylesheets assume that most styling will be handled by an external CSS stylesheet. For that reason, there are no XSL attribute-sets to add properties to the HTML table cells as there are with FO tables.

If your DocBook table has a tabstyle attribute, then its value it passed to the HTML output table as a class attribute. For example, if you have a DocBook table with a tabstyle="styleA" attribute, then you can use a CSS selector such as table.styleA to apply styles to it.

DocBook XSL has another feature that lets you apply HTML styles to individual table cells. You can add a role attribute value to any entry element in your DocBook table. The role value will be transferred to a class attribute on the corresponding HTML TD table cell. Then you can write a CSS stylesheet that includes a selector for such elements that can apply any of the HTML styles to the cell. You can create any number of role values and assign styles to them. The following is an example that marks entries in the first column with a role attribute so they can be styled in bold, as for when you need a row heading.

```
<table>
<title>HTML styles</title>
<tgroup cols="4">
...
<tbody>
<row>
  <entry role="rowhead">Row heading 1.1</entry>
  <entry>Entry 2.1</entry>
  <entry>Entry 3.1</entry>
  <entry>Entry 4.1</entry>
</row>
<row>
  <entry role="rowhead">Row heading 1.2</entry>
  <entry>Entry 2.2</entry>
  <entry>Entry 3.2</entry>
  <entry>Entry 4.2</entry>
</row>
...
```

The following CSS stylesheet entry will apply the bold style to those table cells:

```
TD.rowhead { font-weight: bold ; }
```

You can turn this feature off if you do not want `entry` role values output as `class` attributes. Just set the stylesheet parameter `entry.propagates.style` to zero (its default value is 1).

Another feature of the HTML stylesheets permits you to add a `class` attribute to individual table rows. This is useful when certain rows act as subdivision labels in a table.

To add a `class` attribute to a table row, add a `dbhtml` `class` processing instruction to the `row` element:

```
<row><?dbhtml class="subhead"?>
<entry>...
```

When processed, this will result in `<tr class="subhead">`. That `class` value can then be used in a CSS selector to style the subdivider rows.

Table summary text

For HTML output, you can add a table summary to each table. A table summary is output as a `summary` attribute on the HTML `TABLE` element. You have two options for providing a table summary. If you do not use either option, then the table's title (if it has one) will be used as the summary.

- If your DocBook `table` element has a `textobject` element that contains a `phrase` element, then that text will be used in the summary. The DTD permits `table` to have a `textobject` element between the `title` and the `tgroup` elements.

  ```
  <table>
  <title>Mouse buttons</title>
  <textobject>
    <phrase>Summarizes the click sequences for mouse buttons</phrase>
  </textobject>
  <tgroup>
  ...
  ```

- You can add a processing instruction for a table summary. It must appear inside the `tgroup` element to work.

```
<table>
<title>Mouse buttons</title>
<tgroup>
<?dbhtml table-summary="Summarizes the sequences for mouse buttons" ?>
<row>
...
```

HTML table elements

DocBook added HTML table elements beginning with version 4.3 of the DocBook DTD. This means authors who are already familiar with HTML table markup can use `tr`, `th`, `td`, and other HTML table elements inside `table` or `informaltable` elements within DocBook documents. See Table 30.1, "Comparison of CALS and HTML tables" (page 472) for a comparison of CALS and HTML table markup.

> **Note:**
>
> Since the DocBook `table` element means a table with a title, you must add a `caption` element instead of a `title` element when using HTML markup in a `table` element. The stylesheets will use the `caption` for the numbered title, as well as in cross references and any list of tables in the front of a book. If you want a table without a title, then use `informaltable` with the HTML markup instead.

The stylesheets process tables with HTML markup using templates separate from the CALS table templates. When the stylesheets encounter a `table` or `informaltable` element, they check to see if it contains a `tgroup` element. If so, then it is processed as a CALS table, which requires that element. HTML tables do not permit a `tgroup` element. If the table contains `tgroup`, then it must use `row` and `entry`. If it does not contain `tgroup`, then it must use `tr`, `th`, and `td`.

The templates for print output from HTML table markup share some of the templates and attribute-sets used for CALS tables, beginning with version 1.68 of the stylesheets. See Table 30.2, "Table styles for print output" (page 487) for a list. For example, when you have customize the `table.cell.properties` and `table.cell.block.properties` templates to respond to `tabstyle` attributes in CALS tables, then those customizations are also applied to HTML markup tables that use `tabstyle` attributes.

One advantage of using HTML table markup shows up when generating HTML output. Many elements are simply copied from the source document to the output, along with any attributes. It is a shallow copy, meaning child elements are not necessarily copied. Of course, the content of `td` or `th` is processed, not just copied, because it is not HTML markup. The complete list of elements that are copied to HTML output are:

```
table
colgroup
col
caption
thead
tbody
tr
th
td
```

This feature lets you use HTML specific attributes such as `cellpadding` or `onmouseover` and they are copied to the output. Any HTML-specific attributes that are not supported in FO output will be ignored by the print stylesheet.

Table template customization for printed output

The templates that generate tables in printed output are highly structured in DocBook XSL to facilitate customization. In addition to separate templates handling each table element, there are separate templates to handle different levels of processing for the table itself. These extra layers enable such features a floats, landscape tables, and table titles that are repeated after a page break with a (continued) label.

Table 30.3, "Print table templates" (page 498) lists the principal templates used for format tables for printed output. The descriptions should help you decide at what level you might apply a customization. These descriptions apply to version 1.70.1 and later of the stylesheets.

Table 30.3. Print table templates

Stylesheet template	Location	Description
match="table|informaltable"	fo/formal.xsl	Top-level template that starts table processing. It calls a template named make.table.content and stores the result in a variable named table.content. It manages the subsequent layers of table processing, and finally outputs the table either directly or as a float.
name="make.table.content"	fo/table.xsl	A short template that determines the table markup type (CALS or HTML markup). If it is a CALS table, it calls a template named calsTable. If the table uses HTML table markup, it applies templates in mode="htmlTable". The result of make.table.content is an fo:table element with all its children processed as the table content, but does not include the table title, footnotes, or other processing.
name="calsTable"	fo/table.xsl	This template processes each tgroup element into an fo:table element containing rows and columns, but not the title, footnotes, or other processing. It applies the table.table.properties attribute-set to the fo:table element.
mode="htmlTable"	fo/htmltbl.xsl	This template processes the content of the table into an fo:table element, to which it applies the table.table.properties attribute-set. It does not include the title, footnotes, or other processing.
name="table.layout"	fo/table.xsl	This template processes the result of make.table.content. It is a placeholder template that provides an opportunity for customization. It enables wrapping an fo:table in another table for purposes of layout (such as centering) or applying extensions such as XEP table-omit-initial-header to create "continued" titles after page breaks. By default, this template just copies the table content for the next stage.
name="table.block"	fo/table.xsl	This template processes the result of table.layout. It does the following. • It creates an fo:block to contain the table title (if it has one), layout table, and table footnotes (if any). • It applies the table.properties attribute to the fo:block. • A table title is generated by formal.object.heading using the title element in a CALS table or the caption element in an HTML table. • It copies the table layout from the previous stage. • It calls table.footnote.block to handle any footnotes.

Stylesheet template	Location	Description
name="table.contain-er"	fo/table.xsl	This template processes the result of table.block. It adjusts the placement of the entire table block on the page. • If orient="land", it puts the table block in an fo:block-container rotated by 90 degrees. • If pgwide="1", it puts the table block in another fo:block that spans all columns and sets start-indent to zero. • If neither of those attributes are present, then it copies the table block through.
match="table|inform-altable"	fo/formal.xsl	The end of this template processes the result of table.container. If the table as a floatstyle attribute, it wraps the table container in an fo:float and outputs that. If the table has no floatstyle attribute, it just copies the table container to the output.

While this sequence of templates may seem complicated, its purpose is to separate the various processing functions so they do not interfere with each other. The various layers of table processing are built up from the inside out, with each stage processing the result of the previous stage. This modular style makes for smaller templates that are easier to customize, and makes it easier to find where to apply a customization. The following section provides an example of table customization.

Table "continued" label

When a long table breaks across a page, it helps the reader if the table title is repeated at the top of the new page. But it helps even more if the title is labeled as "continued" so the reader knows the table is not starting there.

A "continued" label for long tables is not a standard feature of XSL-FO 1.0. It is supported in XSL-FO 1.1 using the retrieve-table-marker property. Since version 1.1 became a standard only in December 2006, support for its features is gradually being added to XSL-FO processors. You might check your XSL-FO processor documentation to see if that property is supported. If so, then a different customization is needed than the one described here. The DocBook XSL stylesheets will output 1.1 features when more processors support them.

However, if you are using the XEP processor from RenderX, then you can use an extension long provided by that processor. The extension is in the form of an attribute rx:table-omit-initial-header="true" that is applied to a layout table that wraps around the table content, but is inside the fo:block that contains the table title too.

This strangely-named attribute's function is to prevent a table header row from appearing on the first page of a table, and allowing it to appear on any subsequent pages if the table is long enough to break across a page boundary. You do not use it on the table's column headings, but rather on a special table header that repeats the table title along with the "continued" label. By omitting it on the first page of the table, you get the behavior you want.

The additional table header is not in the original fo:table, but in a wrapper table around it. The wrapper table has one column, the width of the entire table, one header cell for the continued title, and one body cell to contain the original fo:table. When such a table breaks across the page, the new page will display the continued title, a repeat of the original table column headings, and then continue the table rows.

This feature is applied using a customization of the template named table.layout described in the previous section.

Example 30.7. Table "continued" customization for XEP

```
<xsl:template name="table.layout">  ❶
  <xsl:param name="table.content"/>  ❷

  <xsl:choose>
    <xsl:when test="$xep.extensions = 0 or self::informaltable">  ❸
      <xsl:copy-of select="$table.content"/>
    </xsl:when>
    <xsl:otherwise>
      <fo:table rx:table-omit-initial-header="true">  ❹
        <fo:table-header start-indent="0pt">
          <fo:table-row>
            <fo:table-cell>
              <fo:block xsl:use-attribute-sets="formal.title.properties">  ❺
                <xsl:apply-templates select="." mode="object.title.markup"/>
                <fo:inline font-style="italic">
                  <xsl:text> (continued) </xsl:text>  ❻
                </fo:inline>
              </fo:block>
            </fo:table-cell>
          </fo:table-row>
        </fo:table-header>
        <fo:table-body start-indent="0pt">
          <fo:table-row>
            <fo:table-cell>
              <xsl:copy-of select="$table.content"/>  ❼
            </fo:table-cell>
          </fo:table-row>
        </fo:table-body>
      </fo:table>
    </xsl:otherwise>
  </xsl:choose>
</xsl:template>

<xsl:attribute-set name="table.properties">
  <xsl:attribute name="keep-together.within-column">auto</xsl:attribute> ❽
</xsl:attribute-set>
```

❶ Customize the placeholder template named `table.layout` from fo/table.xsl.

❷ The already-processed table is passed in to the template as the `table.content` template parameter. This template forms a wrapper around that content.

❸ If you are not using XEP, or if this is an `informaltable` (no title), then just copy the table content.

❹ Start the wrapper table and add the extension attribute that is highlighted. Be sure to add the `xmlns:rx` namespace declaration to the top of your customization layer or the extension attribute will generate an error.

❺ Create an `fo:block` to contain the title and continued label, using the `formal.title.properties` to format the block. The title is generated by processing the current table in `mode="object.title.markup`, which will include the number label and title.

❻ Add a "continued" label, in this case formatting it with italic.

❼ Copy the original table content into the single body cell of the wrapper table.

❽ For long tables, you might want to set the `keep-together.within-column` property to `auto` to permit tables to break. If you do not make that change, then tables inherit the keep value of `always` from the `formal.object.prop-erties` attribute-set. Trying to keep long tables together usually results in large white gaps on pages where a table might have started but it did not entirely fit.

31
Website

The DocBook Website package is a customization of the DocBook XSL stylesheets that can be used to generate a set of webpages that make up a website. You write the webpages in XML and use the Website stylesheets to convert them to HTML. Here are some of its features:

- You can create a hierarchy of webpages that descend from the home page.

- You can display a table of contents on the left side of each generated page that shows the content of the whole website. The table of contents is repeated on all generated pages, with the current page marked with an arrow graphic.

- The table of contents list can expand and collapse to expose or hide the hierarchy of content.

- You can incorporate references to other HTML content, using website to organize and present the content.

  Note:

  Website is not meant to be used to dynamically generate webpages on request by a browser. Rather, it is used to produce a set of relatively static pages from XML source.

The overall process of using Website can be summarized in these steps:

1. For each individual webpage that you want to generate, create an XML file using the webpage element .

2. Structure your hierarchy of webpages by creating a layout.xml file that has references to your webpage XML files.

3. Process your layout.xml file with the autolayout.xsl Website stylesheet to generate the autolayout.xml file.

4. Process the autolayout.xml file with one of the Website stylesheet to generate HTML webpages in the location specified by the output-root parameter.

This document does not cover all the details and options for using Website. See the Website documentation at *http://docbook.sourceforge.net/release/website/example/index.html* for more information.

Also, there is available an extended version of DocBook Website. See the section called "SilkPage: enhanced Website" (page 520).

Creating a webpage XML file

Each webpage is written using DocBook XML elements and some additional Website elements. The document root element of each webpage file must be webpage, followed by any optional config elements, a required head element, and then the content of the page marked up with DocBook elements. The following is the top of the home page example file that is included with the Website distribution:

Example 31.1. Sample webpage XML file

```
<?xml version="1.0"?>
<!DOCTYPE  webpage ... >
<webpage id="home">  ❶

  <config param="desc" value="The Test Home Page"/>  ❷
  <config param="rcsdate" value="$Date: 2007/10/06 05:56:46 $"/>
  <config param="footer" value="about.html" altval="About..."/>

  <head>  ❸
    <title>Welcome to Website</title>  ❹
    <summary>Introduction</summary>  ❺
    <keywords>Norman Walsh, DSSSL, SGML, XML, DocBook, Website</keywords>
  </head>

<para>This small, somewhat contrived website demonstrates the  ❻
Website document type. Website provides a system for building static
Websites from XML content.</para>
...

</webpage>
```

❶   The document root element is webpage with a required id attribute. Each id value must be unique across all of your webpages in the website.
❷   Optional config elements provide metadata for this page.
❸   Required head element.
❹   Required title element, which appears in the HTML TITLE element in the HTML HEAD element. It also appears at the top of the HTML page, except for the home page.
❺   Optional summary is used in the title attribute in HTML links, and in any webtoc that is generated.
❻   The content to be displayed on this webpage, marked up with DocBook elements.

Allowed DocBook elements

Not all DocBook elements are available to be used within a webpage element. That's because the hierarchical relationship of the pages is expressed in a separate website layout file.

The allowed elements are determined by the DOCTYPE in each webpage file. There are two Website DTDs to choose from.

website.dtd   A subset of the Simplified DocBook DTD. The *Simplified DocBook DTD*[1] is itself a subset of the Docbook DTD, and was designed for cases where the full DTD is not needed. There are approximately 150 elements in the website.dtd.

---

[1] http://www.oasis-open.org/docbook/xml/simple/

website-full.dtd   A subset of the full DocBook DTD. There are approximately 400 elements in the website-full.dtd

Although the website-full.dtd is much bigger, most of the extra elements are not usable within a webpage element. For example, none of the elements set, book, chapter, article, or index can be used, although they are included in the website-full.dtd. It helps to think of each webpage as roughly equivalent to a section element, with a title, various block elements like paragraphs and lists, and possibly subsections. The website-full.dtd has a somewhat richer selection of elements that can appear on a webpage.

The following is a list of elements that can be used with either DTD:

Example 31.2. Elements common to website.dtd and website-full.dtd

abbrev	computeroutput	imagedata	personblurb	subject
abstract	config	imageobject	personname	subjectset
acronym	copyright	informaltable	phrase	subjectterm
affiliation	coref	inlinemediaobject	programlisting	subtitle
answer	corpauthor	issuenum	pubdate	summary
appendix	date	itemizedlist	publishername	surname
attribution	edition	jobtitle	qandadiv	systemitem
audiodata	editor	keyword	qandaentry	table
audioobject	email	keywords	qandaset	tbody
author	emphasis	keywordset	question	term
authorblurb	entry	label	quote	textdata
authorgroup	entrytbl	legalnotice	rddl:resource	textobject
authorinitials	epigraph	lineage	refsectioninfo	tfoot
base	errortext	lineannotation	releaseinfo	tgroup
bibliocoverage	example	link	replaceable	thead
bibliodiv	figure	listitem	revdescription	title
bibliography	filename	literal	revhistory	titleabbrev
biblioid	firstname	literallayout	revision	trademark
bibliomisc	footnote	mediaobject	revnumber	ulink
bibliomixed	footnoteref	member	revremark	userinput
bibliomset	head	meta	row	variablelist
bibliorelation	holder	note	rss	varlistentry
bibliosource	honorific	objectinfo	script	videodata
blockinfo	html:button	olink	section	videoobject
blockquote	html:form	option	sectioninfo	volumenum
caption	html:input	orderedlist	sgmltag	webpage
citebiblioid	html:label	orgname	sidebar	webtoc
citetitle	html:option	othercredit	simplelist	xref
colspec	html:select	othername	spanspec	year
command	html:textarea	para	style	

The only additions beyond the standard DocBook elements are the handful with the html: namespace for inserting HTML form elements.

The following is a list of additional elements in website-full.dtd that can be used within a webpage element.

Example 31.3. Additional elements in website-full.dtd

address	glossary	informalequation	refentry	simplelist
anchor	glosslist	informalexample	remark	simplesect
bridgehead	graphic	informalfigure	screen	synopsis
calloutlist	graphicco	mediaobjectco	screenco	tip
caution	highlights	msgset	screenshot	warning
classsynopsis, etc.	important	procedure	sect1, sect2, etc.	
equation	index	programlistingco	segmentedlist	
formalpara	indexterm	qandaset	simpara	

The choice of DTD is specified in the DOCTYPE declaration in each webpage XML file. You would use one of these:

```
<!DOCTYPE webpage PUBLIC "-//Norman Walsh//DTD Website V2.5.0//EN"
         "website.dtd" >
```
or
```
<!DOCTYPE webpage PUBLIC "-//Norman Walsh//DTD Website Full V2.5.0//EN"
         "website-full.dtd">
```

For each file you can choose the appropriate DTD; you do not have to be consistent among your webpage files. In general, you should use the smaller `website.dtd` unless you need one of the elements from the larger set in `website-full.dtd`.

When you process your files, the processor will need to resolve the DTD location. You might want to use the XML catalog file that comes with the Website distribution to resolve the PUBLIC identifiers in the DOCTYPE to the actual file locations on your system. This is most easily done by adding an entry like the following to your existing `catalog.xml` file:

```
<nextCatalog catalog="catalog.xml"
       xml:base="file:///usr/share/xml/website/website-2.5.0/" />
```

See Chapter 5, *XML catalogs* (page 47) for more information.

Structuring your webpages

You create the content and logical structure for your website by writing a `layout.xml` file. You can name the file whatever you like. For each webpage XML file, you add a `tocentry` element to `layout.xml` to indicate its location in the logical hierarchy. Think of it as writing a table of contents. By nesting `tocentry` elements, you create nested heading levels in the your table of contents similar to chapter, sect1, sect2, etc. in a book's table of contents. You can also put various `config` elements in the file to provide configuration parameters for your website.

The following shows the first part of the example `layout.xml` file included with the Website distribution:

Example 31.4. Example layout.xml file

```
<?xml version="1.0"?>
<!DOCTYPE layout PUBLIC "-//Norman Walsh//DTD Website Layout V2.5.0//EN"
      "http://docbook.sourceforge.net/release/website/2.5.0/layout.dtd"> ❶
<layout>  ❷
  <config param="text-prefix" value="txt"/>

  <config param="homebanner-tabular" value="graphics/homebanner.png"  ❸
          altval="Home Banner"/>
  <config param="banner-tabular"      value="graphics/banner.png"
          altval="Banner"/>

  <config param="homebanner" value="graphics/homebanner.png"
          altval="Home Banner"/>
  <config param="banner"      value="graphics/icons/iconhome.gif"
          altval="Banner"/>

  <copyright>  ❹
    <year>1999</year><year>2000</year><year>2001</year>
    <holder role="http://nwalsh.com/~ndw/">Norman Walsh</holder>
  </copyright>

  <style src="example.css" type="text/css"/>  ❺

  <toc page="website.xml"
       filename="index.html">  ❻
    <tocentry page="wslayout.xml"
              revisionflag="changed"
              filename="layout.html"/>  ❼
    <tocentry page="olink.xml"
              filename="linking.html"/>
    <tocentry page="custom.xml"
              filename="custom.html"/>
    <tocentry page="building.xml"
              filename="building.html"
              tocskip='1'>  ❽
      <tocentry page="build-make.xml"
                filename="buildmake.html"
                dir="build"/>  ❾
      <tocentry page="build-ext.xml"
                filename="buildext.html"
                dir="build"/>  ❿
      <tocentry page="build-textonly.xml"
                filename="textonly.html"
                dir="build"/>
    </tocentry>
    <tocentry page="test2.xml"
              filename="formtest.html"/>
    ...

  </toc>
</layout>
```

❶ The DTD is a separate layout.dtd. You may want to utilize an XML catalog to resolve the DTD location.

❷ The root element must be layout.

❸ Optional config elements specify configuration information for the whole site. The param attribute specifies the name of the parameter, and the value attribute holds the value for that parameter. This example specifies a graphics filename to be displayed at the top of the home page when the tabular presentation is used.

❹ The copyright element prints copyright information in the footer of each webpage.

❺ The style element specifies a CSS stylesheet name that each generated HTML file should reference. HTML files output to subdirectories will have proper relative pathnames generated for them so only a single stylesheet location need be specified. You will have to copy that stylesheet file into place, however.

❻ The site starts with a single top-level toc element. That specifies the site's home page. It does not appear in the table of contents listing

❼ Each tocentry element adds a line to the site's table of contents. The page attribute specifies the webpage XML file used to create the HTML file whose name is specified in the filename attribute. do not put subdirectory paths in filename. Instead use the dir attribute.

❽ This tocentry contains three others, which become its subheadings in the table of contents. The tocskip attribute is set when you want the container link to skip directly to the first subpage.

❾ These nested tocentry elements appear under the container element.

❿ An optional dir attribute puts the generated HTML page in a subdirectory of that name. Such subdirectories nest if the tocentry elements nest, unless an absolute path is specified. You must create any subdirectories by hand since XSL stylesheets cannot create directories.

Note these features while creating the layout.xml file:

- Your XML webpage files do not have to be stored in one directory, nor do their locations have to reflect the website's logical hierarchy. You can place them individually in any locations that the stylesheets can reach from the current location.

- The HTML output hierarchy also does not have to reflect the website's logical hierarchy. You can use dir attributes to create any convenient set of subdirectories for the HTML output.

- All HTML output will be placed below a location specified by the output-root parameter, whose default value is "." (current directory). It can be a relative or absolute path.

- If you specify a relative path in a dir attribute, it is taken as relative to the dir value of any ancestor tocentry elements. That way you do not have to specify complete pathnames. This is useful if you want the HTML output tree to reflect the website's logical hierarchy.

- If you specify an absolute path (starting with "/") in a dir attribute, it is taken as relative to the output-root.

Generating your webpages

The process of generating your HTML webpages is basically two steps:

1. Process your layout.xml file with the autolayout.xsl stylesheet to produce an intermediate file named autolayout.xml.

2. Use the intermediate file to manage the processing of your XML webpage files with one of the Website stylesheets to produce your HTML output files. The stylesheet you use depends on the output style and the processing method you choose.

Choose an output style

Tabular pages   In the tabular style of website output, each generated HTML page has a table of contents on the left. The table of contents is an expandable and collapsible list of all the pages in the website. The same list appears on each page, but it may appear somewhat different depending on what is expanded. Also, the current page is marked with an arrow pointing to its title. This list makes it very easy to navigate through the website.

This style is called *tabular* because a two-column HTML TABLE element is used to form the layout. Unfortunately, webpages that are laid out with a table are difficult for text-only or audio browsers, both important considerations for website access.

Non-tabular pages   In the non-tabular style, no HTML table is used to lay out the page. That enables it to be more easily browsed with a text-only or audio browser. In this style, the navigational links are placed horizontally at the top of each page. For those pages that contain a hierarchy of `tocentry` elements in your `layout.xml` file, you can put an optional empty `webtoc` element somewhere in your `webpage` source. This will generate and display the list of subpages at that point.

There are also two processing methods. Both methods attempt to track the dependencies between the input XML and the output HTML. That way if only one XML file changes, you only have to regenerate one HTML file rather than the whole website. Here are the two methods.

Choose a processing method

Use XSLT only   You let an XSL extension function determine which XML files need processing. It executes a single XSLT process to select the files and apply the stylesheet. It uses parts of the DocBook XSL chunking stylesheets to output multiple HTML files from one XSLT process, although it does not actually chunk sections into separate files. This method is easier to use because you do not have to write a `Makefile`. It uses an XSL extension function to determine which XML files have changed and need reprocessing. That extension function is currently only available for the Saxon and Xalan processors. You can still use other processors such as xsltproc, but it will have to process all the files each time since it cannot determine which files have changed.

Use a make utility with XSLT   You create a `Makefile` to apply the stylesheet only to changed XML files. In this method, a separate XSLT process is executed for each XML file that needs processing. This method requires knowledge of writing and using a `Makefile`, but it is more flexible and works with any XSLT processor.

There are four Website stylesheets that cover the combinations of these four options. Use this table to select your stylesheet.

Table 31.1. Website stylesheets

	Using XSLT only	**Using make with XSLT**
Tabular output style	chunk-tabular.xsl	tabular.xsl
Non-tabular output style	chunk-website.xsl	website.xsl

do not be misled by the word *chunk* in the filenames. Those stylesheets will not chunk a single XML `webpage` file into multiple HTML files. Rather, some of the DocBook chunking templates are borrowed to output multiple HTML files from a single XSLT process that is reading in all the XML `webpage` files.

The most popular stylesheet is probably `chunk-tabular.xsl` because it uses the easier processing method and produces nicer looking output.

Build with XSLT only

With this method, you process your Website in two steps:

1. **Generate autolayout.xml**

   Generate the intermediate file `autolayout.xml` from your `layout.xml` file. For example:

   With Saxon:
   ```
   java \
     -cp "/xml/saxon653/saxon.jar" \
     com.icl.saxon.StyleSheet \
     -o autolayout.xml \
     layout.xml \
     ../website/xsl/autolayout.xsl
   ```

   With xsltproc:
   ```
   XML_CATALOG_FILES=../website/catalog.xml \
     xsltproc \
     --output autolayout.xml \
     ../website/xsl/autolayout.xsl \
     layout.xml
   ```

   In either command, substitute the actual path to the `autolayout.xsl` stylesheet file located in the `xsl` subdirectory of the Website distribution. This example includes a reference to the Website catalog file to help resolve addresses.

   During the process, a message will indicate each XML webpage filename and its corresponding HTML output filename. Any XML `webpage` without an `id` attribute will cause the process to fail. Likewise with any `tocentry` elements that are missing required attributes.

2. **Create output subdirectories**

   If you specified `dir` attributes in your `layout.xml` file, you will need to create the output directories by hand. An XSL processor cannot create new directories. This step only needs to be done once.

3. **Generate HTML output**

   Process your intermediate `autolayout.xml` file with your chosen stylesheet, using a command similar to one of the following:

   With Saxon:
   ```
   java \
     -cp "/xml/saxon653/saxon.jar:../website/extensions/saxon653.jar" \
     com.icl.saxon.StyleSheet \
     autolayout.xml \
     ../website/xsl/chunk-tabular.xsl \
     output-root=htdocs
   ```

   With xsltproc:
   ```
   xsltproc \
     --stringparam output-root htdocs \
     ../website/xsl/chunk-tabular.xsl \
     autolayout.xml
   ```

   • In either command, substitute the actual path to the `chunk-tabular.xsl`stylesheet file. If you want the non-tabular style, replace `chunk-tabular.xsl` with `chunk-website.xsl`.

- Set the `output-root` stylesheet parameter to direct the hierarchy of HTML files to a location other than the current directory.

- Notice that the Saxon command's CLASSPATH option now includes an extensions file that is included with the Website distribution. It contains the extension function the stylesheet uses to tell if an XML webpage file has changed and needs to be reprocessed.

- If you use xsltproc, then all the XML files will be processed every time. That's because that processor lacks such an extension function at this time.

- You may notice that processing is rather slow. If you are not connected to the Internet, it will fail. These problems are caused by the stylesheets including the stock DocBook XSL stylesheet by using a URL over the Internet. See the section called "Website with XML catalogs" (page 514) for help.

4. Add the graphical icons and CSS stylesheet if you want those. You only need to do this the first time you build the output directory.

    - Graphical icons are used for tabular style output. Copy the `example/graphics` directory from the Website distribution to *output-root*/`graphics`. If you are using graphics for your admonitions such as `note`, also copy those icon files to the same directory. All references in the generated HTML files will be made relative to that location.

    - If you have a `style` element in your `layout.xml` file, copy your CSS stylesheet file to your *output-root*. If that element's `src` attribute specifies a path, put the file in that path relative to your *output-root*. All references in the generated HTML files will be made relative to that location. The sample CSS stylesheet in the distribution is `example/example.css`.

    You should now have a complete set of HTML Website files under your *output-root* location. Each file should be in the location specified by the `dir` attribute in its `tocentry` element in `layout.xml`. The navigational features should all work too.

5. If you change any of your XML webpage files or your `layout.xml` file, then you only need to run step 3 again. It will rebuild only those files that need rebuilding.

Build with make

To build with make, you need to write a `Makefile` and the execute **make** commands.

1. Use a text editor to create a `Makefile` similar to the example below, which uses xsltproc as the processor.

2. Create an empty `depends.tabular` file.

3. Execute **make depends** (this only has to be done once manually).

4. Execute **make**. This will build all your Website HTML files.

5. Thereafter, as you edit `layout.xml` or any of your XML webpage files, you only have to execute **make**. The dependencies will be automatic (unless you delete `depends.tabular`, in which case you will have to run **make depends** again).

The following is a complete example for a Website `Makefile`. You enter some of the dependencies, while others are generated for you.

Example 31.5. Website Makefile using xsltproc

```
STYLEDIR=../website/xsl

all:           ❶
        make website

include  depends.tabular  ❷

autolayout.xml: layout.xml  ❸
        xsltproc --output  $@  $(STYLEDIR)/autolayout.xsl  $<
        make  depends

depends: autolayout.xml  ❹
        xsltproc \
          --output  depends.tabular \
          --stringparam  output-root  htdocs  \
          $(STYLEDIR)/makefile-dep.xsl  \
          $<

%.html: autolayout.xml  ❺
        xsltproc \
          --output  $@ \
          --stringparam autolayout-file autolayout.xml \
          --stringparam  output-root  htdocs  \
          $(STYLEDIR)/tabular.xsl \  ❻
          $(filter-out autolayout.xml,$^)

.PHONY : clean
```

The sequence of processing is as follows. Because Makefiles are not processed sequentially, the following paragraphs are shown in *processing* order.

❸   When you execute **make depends**, the autolayout.xml file is generated first, because the depends target has a dependency on it. It processes the layout.xml file with the autolayout.xsl stylesheet to produce autolayout.xml.

❹   Then the depends target itself is processed. It processes the autolayout.xml file with the makefile-dep.xsl stylesheet to produce the depends.tabular file. That file establishes the individual dependency lines between each XML webpage file and its HTML output file, as initially specified in layout.xml. The depends.tabular file also includes the website target, which has dependencies on all the HTML output files.

❶   When you execute **make**, it uses the default target all, which then triggers a **make website** command to recursively load the Makefile.

❷   When **make website** is executed recursively, it executes the include depends.tabular instruction, which this time loads the generated file depends.tabular with its targets for each HTML file. The newly included depends.tabular file has a website target. Its dependencies are all the HTML output files, so each one of those is checked for further dependencies. The included depends.tabular targets has a line for each HTML file that looks like the following:

```
html/productlist.html:  products.xml
```

This says that the HTML file should be regenerated if its XML webpage file is more recent.

❺   Any outdated HTML files trigger the %.html: target.

❻   That target processes the associated XML webpage file with the tabular.xsl stylesheet to produce the selected HTML file (indicated by $@).

The result is that the combination of the `Makefile` and the `depends.tabular` file keep track of the dependencies. Thereafter, you only need to type **make** to update your Website.

Source files in multiple directories

The location of your XML `webpage` files is independent of the layout of your HTML output files. But if you put your XML files in multiple directories, you have to make these changes to your setup and processing.

- In your `layout.xml` file, the `page` attribute in each `tocentry` needs to provide a path to the XML file. Relative or absolute paths will work. The `dir` attribute in `tocentry` is applied to the HTML output file, not the input file.

- When you process with **make**, you need to set the stylesheet parameter `autolayout-file` to the absolute path of your generated `autolayout.xml` file. If you do not, the stylesheet will look for it in the same location as each XML `webpage` file, so it will fail. This parameter is not needed when using the XSLT-only method, because all the files are processed in the same pass after the `autolayout.xml` file is loaded.

Linking between pages

As with any website, you will probably want to create links between your webpages. In a DocBook document, you would use `xref` and `link` to form links between parts of your document. But in Website, each `webpage` is a separate XML document, so you cannot use `xref` or `link` because they only work *within* a document.

To link between your webpages, you can use `olink`. Starting with Website version 2.5, olink became much easier to use. That version adopted the new XSL-based olink mechanism that is described in this book. See Chapter 24, *Olinking between documents* (page 383) for general background information on using olinks. In Website, olinking is even easier than it is for regular DocBook documents. That's because Website maintains information about the separate `webpage` documents in the `layout.xml` file, so it can set up the olink data files automatically. Website can also handle a second olink database to generate links to other documents besides `webpages`.

Olink differs from other linking elements in that it requires two attributes: one to locate the document and one to locate an ID value within that document. The following is an example of an `olink`:

```
<olink targetdoc="home" targetptr="whatsnew"/>
```

- The `targetdoc` attribute identifies the document that contains the target of the link. In Website, the `id` attribute value on the `webpage` element is used as the document identifier since it must exist and it must be unique. Its value should be used in the `targetdoc` attribute of an `olink`.

- The `targetptr` attribute must match an `id` attribute value on an element within that document. If you want to link to the top of the page, then the `targetptr` should have the same value as the `targetdoc` attribute.

- If an `olink` has no content, then the stylesheet generates content in a manner similar to an `xref`. The content comes from a website database document that the stylesheets can create. If an `olink` element does have content, then that is used instead of the generated content.

- Once you enter olinks between your webpages, you need to make sure the `website.database.document` parameter is set to process them. The following sections describe the processing steps for the two build methods in Website.

- You have the option to use a second olink database to form olinks to a collection of documents outside of your `webpage` collection. That database is identified by the `target.database.document` and is discussed fully in Chapter 24, *Olinking between documents* (page 383).

Olinks with XSLT build method

Here is how you process a website with olinks using the XSLT build method.

1. Create your `layout.xml` file the same as before.

2. Process your `layout.xml` file as before with the `autolayout.xsl` stylesheet to create the `autolayout.xml` file.

3. Process your `autolayout.xml` file as before with either the `chunk-tabular.xsl` or `chunk-website.xsl` stylesheet. But set the parameter `collect.xref.targets` to the value "yes".

```
xsltproc \
   --stringparam  collect.xref.targets yes \
   --stringparam  output-root  htdocs \
   ../website/xsl/chunk-tabular.xsl  \
   autolayout.xml
```

That command will generate a database file named `website.database.xml` in the current directory, and use that to resolve olinks.

Olinks with Make method

Here is how you process a website with olinks using the Makefile method.

1. Create your `layout.xml` file the same as before.

2. Do the `autolayout.xml` and `depends` processing steps as before.

3. Generate the website database file by processing your `autolayout.xml` file with the `website-targets.xsl` stylesheet, saving the output to a file named `website.database.xml`.

4. Process your website as you would normally (usually by typing **make website**), but add the `website.database.doc-ument` parameter whose value is the pathname of the generated database file. If you use the default filename `website.database.xml`, then you can omit the parameter on the command line.

The following is a sample `Makefile` using xsltproc and XML catalogs. The extra steps for olinking are highlighted.

```
PROC = XML_CATALOG_FILES=../catalog.xml  xsltproc

all:
        make website

include depends.tabular

autolayout.xml:  layout.xml
        $(PROC) \
        --output  $@ \
        autolayout.xsl  $<

        make depends

depends:  autolayout.xml
        $(PROC) \
        --output depends.tabular \
        --stringparam  output-root  htdocs  \
        makefile-dep.xsl  $<


website.database.xml:  autolayout.xml
        $(PROC) \
        --output $@ \
        website-targets.xsl  $<

%.html: autolayout.xml
        $(PROC) \
        --output $@  \
        --stringparam  website.database.document website.database.xml \
        --stringparam  output-root  htdocs  \
        tabular.xsl  \
        $(filter-out autolayout.xml website.database.xml %xsl,$^)
```

This Makefile proceeds as before, except it also builds a website targets database website.database.xml. It then passes that filename as the website.database.document parameter to the stylesheet when it processes the webpages. These two steps make the target information available to the XSLT processor so it can resolve the olinks in the webpages. Note that website.database.xml was added to the filter-out expression so it is not processed like a normal content file.

Linking to other sites

In your Website table of contents, you might want to point to content from other websites. The tocentry element in your layout.xml file can take an href attribute instead of page and file attributes. Such a tocentry adds a link in your generated table of contents to other content. The href value can be any URL, so it can be used to point to other content on your website, or to other websites. All you need to supply is a URL in the hrefattribute, an id attribute (required), and a title element. The following section has an example.

If you need to link from *within* your webpages to other sites, then you have two choices:

- Use ulink to link to any URL. Such links are not checked during processing, so they require manual maintenance to remain valid.

- Use olink to link to any targets for which you can create a cross reference targets database. Such links are checked during processing, and so may require less maintenance to prevent bad links.

The olink solution requires careful set up, but it can reduce link maintenance time in the long run because the links are resolved from a database of targets. You just have to keep the targets database up to date, a process that can be automated. If, after a database update, one of your olinks no longer resolves, the stylesheet reports the error so you can fix it. Also, olinks can be empty, which causes their link text to be generated from the targets database. That ensures that the link text is kept up to date.

The process of generating and using an olink database is described in the section called "How to link between documents" (page 383). Once you have the targets database, you can pass its pathname to the XSLT processor using the `target.database.document` stylesheet parameter. This database is in addition to (and separate from) the olink database that resolves olinks between webpages in your website. The database of internal olinks is identified with the `website.database.document` parameter. When the processor encounters an olink, it first checks the website database before consulting the offsite database.

Adding other content

If you are creating a website, you probably have some existing content that you want to incorporate into it. You do not need to convert everything to webpage elements. Rather, you can add entries to your website structure that simply point to other documents available at your web address.

As described in the previous section, the tocentry element in your `layout.xml` file can take an href attribute instead of page and file attributes. The href value can point to other documents on your site, using an absolute or relative URL. You just need to add an id attribute and a title element. Following are two examples, one pointing to another website, and the other using a relative reference.

```
<tocentry  id="nwalsh.com"  href="http://nwalsh com">
  <title>Norm Walsh's Website</title>
</tocentry>

<tocentry  id="mybook"  href="../mybook/index.html">
  <title>My Book</title>
</tocentry>
```

Any relative URL is taken as relative to the *output-root* directory for your website (starting with Website version 2.4).

If you want to cross reference from your webpages to the additional content, you can set up your site to use external olinks with the `target.database.document` parameter. See the section called "Linking to other sites" (page 513) for more information.

Website with XML catalogs

XML catalogs can make your website processing easier and faster. An XML catalog can eliminate the slow web access that Website uses by default. It can also eliminate potential errors related to not being able to find a DTD or stylesheet file. See Chapter 5, *XML catalogs* (page 47) for more information on catalogs in general.

Some of the stylesheets that come with the Website distribution import the stock DocBook XSL stylesheets. The `xsl:import` elements use web URLs to fetch the DocBook stylesheets over the Internet. That way it is likely to work upon installation, since there is no way for the files in the distribution to find local copies of the files. But the DocBook XSL stylesheets are big, and downloading them each time slows down the processing considerably.

An XML catalog can be used to redirect the web references to local file locations. For example, the Website stylesheet module `website-common.xsl` used in all of the main stylesheets imports the stock DocBook XSL stylesheet from `http://docbook.sourceforge.net/release/xsl/current/html/docbook.xsl`. An XML catalog entry can redirect this to a local file location such as `/usr/share/xml/docbook-xsl-1.73.1/html/docbook.xsl`. The following example catalog entry does it.

```
<rewriteURI
  uriStartString="http://docbook.sourceforge.net/release/xsl/current/"
  rewritePrefix="file:///usr/share/xml/docbook-xsl-1.73.1/"/>
```

This catalog entry recognizes the first part of the URL and remaps that first part to the value of `rewritePrefix`. By using prefix mapping, you only need one entry to map all the stock DocBook stylesheets.

To put the catalog to use, you have to include XML catalog resolution in your processing commands. See the section called "How to use a catalog file" (page 54) for how to do that.

You can also use an XML catalog to locate the stylesheets and DTDs that are included with the Website distribution. This is most easily done by adding a `nextCatalog` entry to your XML catalog that points to the catalog distributed with Website (starting with version 2.4). For example, add this to your main catalog file:

```
<nextCatalog catalog="/usr/share/xml/website-2.5.1/catalog.xml" />
```

Adjust the path to match where you installed Website. When you process with your main catalog file, the Website catalog will also be loaded. That catalog will resolve references to Website DTDs that your files may contain. It also lets you call one of the Website stylesheets by just specifying its name, rather than the path to the file. For example, you could use a command like the following:

```
XML_CATALOG_FILES=file:///usr/share/xml/catalog.xml \
xsltproc --output autolayout.xml autolayout.xsl layout.xml
```

The reference to `autolayout.xsl` is resolved by your main catalog branching to the Website catalog, where it finds a match on that name.

Website formatting

You have several options for controlling the format of your webpages.

- CSS stylesheet

- Website parameters

- Stylesheet customization.

Using CSS with Website

Since your output is HTML pages, one of the best tools for controlling the formatting of your web pages is with a Cascading Style Sheet (CSS). You may be familiar with the DocBook stylesheet parameter `html.stylesheet` that can be used to specify a CSS stylesheet name. You can use that parameter with Website, but it has the disadvantage that the address of the stylesheet is fixed. That means you must either specify an absolute path, or you must copy the stylesheet file to each directory that gets HTML webpages.

The recommended approach in Website is to add a `style` element to your `layout.xml` file. Then you only need one copy of the stylesheet file for all HTML output. For example, place this element before the `toc` section:

```
<style src="mystyle.css" type="text/css"/>
<toc>
  <tocentry ...>
```

In each generated HTML webpage, the Website stylesheet will compute a relative path to the stylesheet location specified in the `src` attribute, based on which directory the HTML output file is located. That way you can just copy your stylesheet file to one location and all the files can use it. The value in `src` is figured relative to the `output-root` parameter. In this example, if you set `output-root="html"`, then you should copy the stylesheet file to `html/mystyle.css`.

Website config attributes

You can specify several configuration parameters in your website source files using `config` elements. Each `config` element is empty and takes a `param` and `value` attribute. For example:

```
<config  param="navtocwidth"  value="220"/>
```

The `param` attribute specifies the name of the parameter, and the `value` attribute specifies its value.

If you place a `config` element in your `layout.xml` file outside the `toc` element , then the parameter applies to all your webpages. If you place the `config` element as a child of `webpage` in one of your Webpage XML files, then it overrides the global value and applies only to that page. If neither are set, then the stylesheet provides a default stylesheet parameter value for *some* configuration features, as noted in the table below. The default value can be overridden on the processor command line like other stylesheet parameters.

Table 31.2. Website config attributes

Website Feature	param=	value=	Applies to
Background color for navigational list.	navbgcolor[a]	HTML color values such as #4080FF.	Left side of pages generated with tabular.xsl or chunk-tabular.xsl.
Nominal width of navigational list	navtocwidth[b]	HTML width value, such as 220 (pixels).	Left side of pages generated with tabular.xsl or chunk-tabular.xsl
Image for top of left-side navigational list on home page.	homebanner-tabular	Pathname to a graphics file suitable for use in an HTML IMG tag.	Left side of home page generated with tabular.xsl or chunk-tabular.xsl
Image for top of left-side navigational list on non-home pages.	banner-tabular	Pathname to a graphics file suitable for use in an HTML IMG tag.	Left side of pages generated with tabular.xsl or chunk-tabular.xsl
Image for top of non-tabular home page.	homebanner	Pathname to a graphics file suitable for use in an HTML IMG tag.	Top of home page generated by website.xsl or chunk-website.xsl
Image for top of non-tabular page other than home page.	banner	Pathname to a graphics file suitable for use in an HTML IMG tag.	Top of pages generated by website.xsl or chunk-website.xsl

Website Feature	param=	value=	Applies to
Link in footer to a URL.	`footer`	URL value. Also requires an `altval="text string"` attribute.	Center part of footer, shown next to Home link separated by '|' symbol.
Link in footer to another webpage.	`footlink`	ID value of one of your webpages. Also requires an `altval="text string"` attribute.	Center part of footer, shown next to Home link separated by '|' symbol.
Feedback link in footer.	`feedback.href`[c]	URL (typically a `mailto:`).	Left part of footer. Hot text is value of stylesheet parameter `feedback.link.text`. If stylesheet parameter `feedback.with.ids` is nonzero, then current page ID value is appended to each URL.
Date of last revision in footer.	`rcsdate`	Date text string.	Left part of footer.

[a]Value can also be set with `navbgcolor` stylesheet parameter at runtime.

[b]Value can also be set with `navtocwidth` stylesheet parameter at runtime.

[c]Value can also be set with `feedback.href` stylesheet parameter at runtime.

Website stylesheet customization

You can also use the usual methods of stylesheet customization to customize your web pages. Use this method when you want to change how elements are processed or where they are placed on the pages. You can also use a customization layer to record a set of stylesheet parameters so you do not have to enter them on the command line, alter attribute-sets, and fill in placeholder templates used by the stylesheets.

There are many stylesheet parameters that are specific to Website. See the Website file `xsl/param.xsl` for a complete description of the stylesheet parameters. You can also set any stock DocBook stylesheet parameters if they apply to your output.

To start a customization layer for Website, you import the website stylesheet you want to customize rather than the original DocBook stylesheet. The Website stylesheet will then import the parts of DocBook that it needs. See Table 31.1, "Website stylesheets" (page 507) for the list of stylesheets you can import. Then you add any parameter settings and templates that you want to customize. Here is a short example.

```
<?xml version='1.0'?>
<xsl:stylesheet  xmlns:xsl="http://www.w3.org/1999/XSL/Transform"
        version="1.0">

<xsl:import href="chunk-tabular.xsl"/>

<!-- Website stylesheet parameters -->
<xsl:param name="footer.hr" select="0"/>
<xsl:param name="feedback.link.text">Send us feedback</xsl:param>
<xsl:param name="textbgcolor">#C8C8C8</xsl:param>

<!-- DocBook stylesheet parameters -->
<xsl:param name="admon.graphics" select="1"/>

<!-- Template customizations go here -->

</xsl:stylesheet>
```

If you use more than one of the Website stylesheets, you will probably want similar customizations in each. You will need a separate customization file for each stylesheet, because `xsl:import` will not take a parameter value to select the stylesheet. To avoid duplicating your customizations, put them in a separate stylesheet module and use `xsl:include` to include that file in all of your customization layers.

The following table provides starting points for how to customize various features of website.

Table 31.3. Website customizations

Website Feature	Customize this	Applies to
Overall page table properties	The `table.properties` attribute-set in `tabular.xsl`. Takes any HTML TABLE attributes.	Pages generated with `tabular.xsl` or `chunk-tabular.xsl`

Example:	`<xsl:attribute-set name="table.properties">`
	`  <xsl:attribute name="border">1</xsl:attribute>`
	`  <xsl:attribute name="cellpadding">4</xsl:attribute>`
	`</xsl:attribute-set>`	

Navigational list table cell properties	The `table.navigation.cell.properties` attribute-set in `tabular.xsl`. Takes any HTML td attributes.	Left-side list in pages generated with `tabular.xsl` or `chunk-tabular.xsl`

Example:	`<xsl:attribute-set`
	`  name="table.navigation.cell.properties">`
	`  <xsl:attribute name="background">myimage.gif`
	`  </xsl:attribute>`
	`</xsl:attribute-set>`	

Body table cell properties	The `table.body.cell.properties` attribute-set in `tabular.xsl`. Takes any HTML td attributes.	Right-side body area in pages generated with `tabular.xsl` or `chunk-tabular.xsl`

Example:	`<xsl:attribute-set name="table.body.cell.properties">`
	`  <xsl:attribute name="background">myimage.gif`
	`  </xsl:attribute>`
	`</xsl:attribute-set>`	

Website Feature	Customize this	Applies to
Non-tabular page attributes	The `body.attributes` template in `html/doc-book.xsl` in the main DocBook stylesheets. Takes any HTML `BODY` attributes.	Pages generated with any of the Website stylesheets.
Example:	```<xsl:template name="body.attributes"> <xsl:attribute name="bgcolor">blue</xsl:attribute> <xsl:attribute name="text">white</xsl:attribute> <xsl:attribute name="link">#0000FF</xsl:attribute> <xsl:attribute name="vlink">#840084</xsl:attribute> <xsl:attribute name="alink">#0000FF</xsl:attribute> </xsl:template>```	
Banner at top of all pages.	The empty `allpages.banner` template in `web-site-common.xsl`	Pages generated with any of the Website stylesheets. Appears above the page table in tabular pages.
Example:	```<xsl:template name="allpages.banner"> <img src="myimages.gif"> </xsl:template>```	
Top-left header on tabular home page.	The `home.navhead` template in `tabular.xsl`	Body area in pages generated with `tabular.xsl` or `chunk-tabular.xsl`
Example:	```<xsl:template name="home.navhead"> <B><xsl:text>My own left header text</xsl:text></B> </xsl:template>```	
Top-right header on tabular home page.	The `home.navhead.upperright` template in `tabular.xsl`	Body area in pages generated with `tabular.xsl` or `chunk-tabular.xsl`
Example:	```<xsl:template name="home.navhead.upperright"> <B><xsl:text>My own right header text</xsl:text></B> </xsl:template>```	
Horizontal header separator on tabular home page.	The `home.navhead.separator` template in `tabular.xsl`	Body area in pages generated with `tabular.xsl` or `chunk-tabular.xsl`
Example:	```<xsl:template name="home.navhead.upperright"> <hr size="8"/> </xsl:template>```	
Vertical separator between navigational list and body	The empty `hspacer` template in `tabular.xsl`. Takes an HTML `td` element and content.	Pages generated with `tabular.xsl` or `chunk-tabular.xsl`
Example:	```<xsl:template name="hspacer"> <td bgcolor="#333333" width="12"/> </xsl:template>```	
Maximum number of entries displayed in header navigational row.	The `max.toc.width` parameter, set to 7 by default in `website.xsl`	Pages generated with `website.xsl` or `chunk-website.xsl`
Example:	`<xsl:param name="max.toc.width">5</xsl:param>`	

Website Feature	Customize this	Applies to
Turn off header rule.	The `header.hr` parameter, set to 1 by default in `website.xsl`	Pages generated with `website.xsl` or `chunk-website.xsl`
Example:	`<xsl:param name="header.hr">0</xsl:param>`	
Turn off footer rule.	The `footer.hr` parameter, set to 1 by default in `website.xsl`	Pages generated with `website.xsl` or `chunk-website.xsl`
Example:	`<xsl:param name="footer.hr">0</xsl:param>`	
Put allpages.banner after the navigational row.	The `banner.before.navigation` parameter, set to 1 by default in `website.xsl`	Pages generated with `website.xsl` or `chunk-website.xsl`
Example:	`<xsl:param name="banner.before.navigation">0</xsl:param>`	
Turn on `Next` and `Prev` sequence links.	The `sequential.links` parameter, set to 0 by default in `param.xsl`	Pages generated with any of the Website stylesheets.
Example:	`<xsl:param name="sequential.links">1</xsl:param>`	

SilkPage: enhanced Website

A separate open source project named SilkPage has arisen to further develop the ideas and code in DocBook Website. The SilkPage project is based on DocBook Website and adds these features:

- Adds XML based content management.

- Generates Web Standards (WaSP) compliant XHTML output.

- Conforms to main accessibility requirements.

- Separates content from presentation via CSS stylesheets.

- Integrates RSS and RDF.

More information about SilkPage is available from the project website at *http://silkpage.markupware.com/*.

Appendix A. A brief introduction to XSL

XSL is both a transformation language and a formatting language. The XSLT transformation part lets you scan through a document's structure and rearrange its content any way you like. You can write out the content using a different set of XML tags, and generate text as needed. For example, you can scan through a document to locate all headings and then insert a generated table of contents at the beginning of the document, at the same time writing out the content marked up as HTML. XSL is also a rich formatting language, letting you apply typesetting controls to all components of your output. With a good formatting back end, it is capable of producing high quality printed pages.

An XSL stylesheet is written using XML syntax, and is itself a well-formed XML document. That makes the basic syntax familiar, and enables an XML processor to check for basic syntax errors. The stylesheet instructions use special element names, which typically begin with xsl: to distinguish them from any XML tags you want to appear in the output. The XSL namespace is identified at the top of the stylesheet file. As with other XML, any XSL elements that are not empty will require a closing tag. And some XSL elements have specific attributes that control their behavior. It helps to keep a good XSL reference book handy.

The following are examples of a simple XSL stylesheet applied to a simple XML file to generate HTML output.

Example A.1. Simple XML file

```
<?xml version="1.0"?>
<document>
<title>Using a mouse</title>
<para>It's easy to use a mouse. Just roll it
around and click the buttons.</para>
</document>
```

Example A.2. Simple XSL stylesheet

```
<?xml version='1.0'?>
<xsl:stylesheet
           xmlns:xsl="http://www.w3.org/1999/XSL/Transform" version='1.0'>
<xsl:output method="html"/>

<xsl:template match="document">
  <HTML><HEAD><TITLE>
    <xsl:value-of select="./title"/>
  </TITLE>
  </HEAD>
  <BODY>
    <xsl:apply-templates/>
  </BODY>
  </HTML>
</xsl:template>

<xsl:template match="title">
  <H1><xsl:apply-templates/></H1>
</xsl:template>

<xsl:template match="para">
  <P><xsl:apply-templates/></P>
</xsl:template>

</xsl:stylesheet>
```

Example A.3. HTML output

```
<HTML>
<HEAD>
<TITLE>Using a mouse</TITLE>
</HEAD>
<BODY>
<H1>Using a mouse</H1>
<P>It's easy to use a mouse. Just roll it
around and click the buttons.</P>
</BODY>
</HTML>
```

XSL processing model

XSL is a template language, not a procedural language. That means a stylesheet specifies a sample of the output, not a sequence of programming steps to generate it. A stylesheet consists of a mixture of output samples with instructions of what to put in each sample. Each bit of output sample and instructions is called a *template*.

In general, you write a template for each element type in your document. That lets you concentrate on handling just one element at a time, and keeps a stylesheet modular. The power of XSL comes from processing the templates recursively. That is, each template handles the processing of its own element, and then calls other templates to process its children, and so on. Since an XML document is always a single root element at the top level that contains all of the nested descendant elements, the XSL templates also start at the top and work their way down through the hierarchy of elements.

Take the DocBook <para> paragraph element as an example. To convert this to HTML, you want to wrap the paragraph content with the HTML tags <p> and </p>. But a DocBook <para> can contain any number of in-line DocBook elements marking up the text. Fortunately, you can let other templates take care of those elements, so your XSL template for <para> can be quite simple:

```
<xsl:template match="para">
  <p>
    <xsl:apply-templates/>
  </p>
</xsl:template>
```

The <xsl:template> element starts a new template, and its match attribute indicates where to apply the template, in this case to any <para> elements. The template says to output a literal <p> string and then execute the <xsl:apply-templates/> instruction. This tells the XSL processor to look among all the templates in the stylesheet for any that should be applied to the content of the paragraph. If each template in the stylesheet includes an <xsl:apply-templates/> instruction, then all descendants will eventually be processed. When it is through recursively applying templates to the paragraph content, it outputs the </p> closing tag.

Context is important

Since you are not writing a linear procedure to process your document, the context of where and how to apply each modular template is important. The match attribute of <xsl:template> provides that context for most templates. There is an entire expression language, XPath, for identifying what parts of your document should be handled by each template. The simplest context is just an element name, as in the example above. But you can also specify elements as children of other elements, elements with certain attribute values, the first or last elements in a sequence, and so on. The following is how the DocBook <formalpara> element is handled:

```
<xsl:template match="formalpara">
  <p>
    <xsl:apply-templates/>
  </p>
</xsl:template>

<xsl:template match="formalpara/title">
  <b><xsl:apply-templates/></b>
  <xsl:text> </xsl:text>
</xsl:template>

<xsl:template match="formalpara/para">
  <xsl:apply-templates/>
</xsl:template>
```

There are three templates defined, one for the <formalpara> element itself, and one for each of its children elements. The match attribute value formalpara/title in the second template is an XPath expression indicating a <title> element that is an immediate child of a <formalpara> element. This distinguishes such titles from other <title> elements used in DocBook. XPath expressions are the key to controlling how your templates are applied.

In general, the XSL processor has internal rules that apply templates that are more specific before templates that are less specific. That lets you control the details, but also provides a fallback mechanism to a less specific template when you do not supply the full context for every combination of elements. This feature is illustrated by the third template, for formalpara/para. By including this template, the stylesheet processes a <para> within <formalpara> in a special way, in this case by not outputting the HTML <p> tags already output by its parent. If this template had not been included, then the processor would have fallen back to the template specified by match="para" described above, which would have output a second set of <p> tags.

You can also control template context with XSL *modes*, which are used extensively in the DocBook stylesheets. Modes let you process the same input more than once in different ways. A mode attribute in an `<xsl:template>` definition adds a specific mode name to that template. When the same mode name is used in `<xsl:apply-templates/>`, it acts as a filter to narrow the selection of templates to only those selected by the match expression *and* that have that mode name. This lets you define two different templates for the same element match that are applied under different contexts. For example, there are two templates defined for DocBook `<listitem>` elements:

```
<xsl:template match="listitem">
  <li><xsl:apply-templates/></li>
</xsl:template>

<xsl:template match="listitem" mode="xref">
  <xsl:number format="1"/>
</xsl:template>
```

The first template is for the normal list item context where you want to output the HTML `<li>` tags. The second template is called with `<xsl:apply-templates select="$target" mode="xref"/>` in the context of processing `<xref>` elements. In this case the `select` attribute locates the ID of the specific list item and the `mode` attribute selects the second template, whose effect is to output its item number when it is in an ordered list. Because there are many such special needs when processing `<xref>` elements, it is convenient to define a mode name `xref` to handle them all.

Keep in mind that mode settings *not* do automatically get passed down to other templates through `<xsl:apply-templates/>`. You have two choices for processing children while in a template with a mode.

- To continue using that mode, process the children with `<xsl:apply-templates mode="`*mode*`"`, where *mode* is the same mode name. The processor will look for templates with that mode name that match on the child elements. There is no fallback to the templates without mode, so if a child does not have a template match with that mode, it does not get processed. If you want to fall back to the mode-less templates for such children, then include a template like the following:

```
<xsl:template  match="*"  mode="mode">
  <xsl:apply-templates select="." />
</xsl:template>
```

  For any child element that does not have a template in that mode, this template will cause it to be processed with the mode-less templates.

- To use the regular mode-less templates, process the children with `<xsl:apply-templates />`. You can also use named templates, which do not have a mode.

Programming features

Although XSL is template-driven, it also has some features of traditional programming languages. The following are some examples from the DocBook stylesheets.

Assign a value to a variable:
```
<xsl:variable name="refelem" select="name($target)"/>
```

If statement:
```
<xsl:if test="$show.comments">
    <i><xsl:call-template name="inline.charseq"/></i>
</xsl:if>
```

Case statement:
```
<xsl:choose>
    <xsl:when test="@columns">
        <xsl:value-of select="@columns"/>
    </xsl:when>
    <xsl:otherwise>1</xsl:otherwise>
</xsl:choose>
```

Call a template by name like a subroutine, passing parameter values and accepting a return value:
```
<xsl:call-template name="xref.xreflabel">
    <xsl:with-param name="target" select="$target"/>
</xsl:call-template>
```

However, you cannot always use these constructs as you do in other programming languages. Variables in particular have very different behavior.

Using variables and parameters

XSL provides two elements that let you assign a value to a name: <xsl:variable> and <xsl:param>. These share the same name space and syntax for assigning names and values. Both can be referred to using the $name syntax. The main difference between these two elements is that a param's value acts as a default value that can be overridden when a template is called using a <xsl:with-param> element as in the last example above.

The following are two examples from DocBook:

```
<xsl:param name="cols">1</xsl:param>
<xsl:variable name="segnum" select="position()"/>
```

In both elements, the name of the parameter or variable is specified with the name attribute. So the name of the param here is cols and the name of the variable is segnum. The value of either can be supplied in two ways. The value of the first example is the text node "1" and is supplied as the content of the element. The value of the second example is supplied as the result of the expression in its select attribute, and the element itself has no content.

The feature of XSL variables that is odd to new users is that once you assign a value to a variable, you cannot assign a new value within the same scope. Doing so will generate an error. So variables are not used as dynamic storage bins they way they are in other languages. They hold a fixed value within their scope of application, and then disappear when the scope is exited. This feature is a result of the design of XSL, which is template-driven and not procedural. This means there is no definite order of processing, so you cannot rely on the values of changing variables. To use variables in XSL, you need to understand how their scope is defined.

Variables defined outside of all templates are considered global variables, and they are readable within all templates. The value of a global variable is fixed, and its global value cannot be altered from within any template. However, a template can create a local variable of the same name and give it a different value. That local value remains in effect only within the scope of the local variable.

Variables defined within a template remain in effect only within their permitted scope, which is defined as all following siblings and their descendants. To understand such a scope, you have to remember that XSL instructions are true XML elements that are embedded in an XML family hierarchy of XSL elements, often referred to as parents, children, siblings, ancestors and descendants. Taking the family analogy a step further, think of a variable assignment as a piece of advice that you are allowed to give to certain family members. You can give your advice only to your younger siblings (those that follow you) and their descendants. Your older siblings will not listen, neither will your parents or any of your ancestors. To stretch the analogy a bit, it is an error to try to give different advice under the same name to the same group of listeners (in other words, to redefine the variable). Keep in mind that this family is not the elements of your document, but just the XSL instructions in your stylesheet. To help you keep track of such scopes in hand-written stylesheets, it helps to indent nested XSL elements. The following is an edited snippet from the DocBook stylesheet file pi.xsl that illustrates different scopes for two variables:

```
 1 <xsl:template name="dbhtml-attribute">
 2 ...
 3    <xsl:choose>
 4       <xsl:when test="$count>count($pis)">
 5          <!-- not found -->
 6       </xsl:when>
 7       <xsl:otherwise>
 8          <xsl:variable name="pi">
 9             <xsl:value-of select="$pis[$count]"/>
10          </xsl:variable>
11          <xsl:choose>
12             <xsl:when test="contains($pi,concat($attribute, '='))">
13                <xsl:variable name="rest" \
                     select="substring-after($pi,concat($attribute,'='))"/>
14                <xsl:variable name="quote" \
                         select="substring($rest,1,1)"/>
15                <xsl:value-of \
                     select="substring-before(substring($rest,2),$quote)"/>
16             </xsl:when>
17             <xsl:otherwise>
18                ...
19             </xsl:otherwise>
20          </xsl:choose>
21       </xsl:otherwise>
22    </xsl:choose>
23 </xsl:template>
```

The scope of the variable pi begins on line 8 where it is defined in this template, and ends on line 20 when its last sibling ends.[1] The scope of the variable rest begins on line 13 and ends on line 15. Fortunately, line 15 outputs an expression using the value before it goes out of scope.

What happens when an <xsl:apply-templates/> element is used within the scope of a local variable? Do the templates that are applied to the document children get the variable? The answer is no. The templates that are applied are not actually within the scope of the variable. They exist elsewhere in the stylesheet and are not following siblings or their descendants.

To pass a value to another template, you pass a parameter using the <xsl:with-param> element. This parameter passing is usually done with calls to a specific named template using <xsl:call-template>, although it works with <xsl:apply-templates> too. That's because the called template must be expecting the parameter by defining it using a <xsl:param> element with the same parameter name. Any passed parameters whose names are not defined in the called template are ignored.

The following is an example of parameter passing from docbook.xsl:

---

[1]Technically, the scope extends to the end tag of the parent of the <xsl:variable> element. That is effectively the last sibling.

```
<xsl:call-template name="head.content">
   <xsl:with-param name="node" select="$doc"/>
</xsl:call-template>
```

Here a template named `head.content` is being called and passed a parameter named `node` whose content is the value of the `$doc` variable in the current context. The top of that template looks like the following:

```
<xsl:template name="head.content">
   <xsl:param name="node" select="."/>
   ...
```

The template is expecting the parameter because it has a `<xsl:param>` defined with the same name. The value in this definition is the default value. This would be the parameter value used in the template if the template was called without passing that parameter.

Generating HTML output

You generate HTML from your DocBook XML files by applying the HTML version of the stylesheets. This is done by using the HTML driver file `docbook/html/docbook.xsl` as your stylesheet. That is the master stylesheet file that uses `<xsl:include>` to pull in the component files it needs to assemble a complete stylesheet for producing HTML.

The way the DocBook stylesheet generates HTML is to apply templates that output a mix of text content and HTML elements. Starting at the top level in the main file `docbook.xsl`:

```
<xsl:template match="/">
  <xsl:variable name="doc" select="*[1]"/>
  <html>
  <head>
    <xsl:call-template name="head.content">
      <xsl:with-param name="node" select="$doc"/>
    </xsl:call-template>
  </head>
  <body>
    <xsl:apply-templates/>
  </body>
  </html>
</xsl:template>
```

This template matches the root element of your input document, and starts the process of recursively applying templates. It first defines a variable named `doc` and then outputs two literal HTML elements `<html>` and `<head>`. Then it calls a named template `head.content` to process the content of the HTML `<head>`, closes the `<head>` and starts the `<body>`. There it uses `<xsl:apply-templates/>` to recursively process the entire input document. Then it just closes out the HTML file.

Simple HTML elements can be generated as literal elements as shown here. But if the HTML being output depends on the context, you need something more powerful to select the element name and possibly add attributes and their values. The following is a fragment from `sections.xsl` that shows how a heading tag is generated using the `<xsl:element>` and `<xsl:attribute>` elements:

```
1 <xsl:element name="h{$level}">
2   <xsl:attribute name="class">title</xsl:attribute>
3   <xsl:if test="$level<3">
4     <xsl:attribute name="style">clear: all</xsl:attribute>
5   </xsl:if>
6   <a>
7     <xsl:attribute name="name">
8       <xsl:call-template name="object.id"/>
9     </xsl:attribute>
10    <b><xsl:copy-of select="$title"/></b>
11  </a>
12 </xsl:element>
```

This whole example is generating a single HTML heading element. Line 1 begins the HTML element definition by identifying the name of the element. In this case, the name is an expression that includes the variable $level passed as a parameter to this template. Thus a single template can generate <h1>, <h2>, etc. depending on the context in which it is called. Line 2 defines a class="title" attribute that is added to this element. Lines 3 to 5 add a style="clear all" attribute, but only if the heading level is less than 3. Line 6 opens an <a> anchor element. Although this looks like a literal output string, it is actually modified by lines 7 to 9 that insert the name attribute into the <a> element. This illustrates that XSL is managing output elements as active element nodes, not just text strings. Line 10 outputs the text of the heading title, also passed as a parameter to the template, enclosed in HTML boldface tags. Line 11 closes the anchor tag with the literal </a> syntax, while line 12 closes the heading tag by closing the element definition. Since the actual element name is a variable, it could not use the literal syntax.

As you follow the sequence of nested templates processing elements, you might be wondering how the ordinary text of your input document gets to the output. In the file docbook.xsl you will find the following template that handles any text not processed by any other template:

```
<xsl:template match="text()">
  <xsl:value-of select="."/>
</xsl:template>
```

This template's body consists of the "value" of the text node, which is just its text. In general, all XSL processors have some built-in templates to handle any content for which your stylesheet does not supply a matching template. This template serves the same function but appears explicitly in the stylesheet.

Generating formatting objects

You generate formatting objects from your DocBook XML files by applying the fo version of the stylesheets. This is done by using the fo driver file docbook/fo/docbook.xsl as your stylesheet. That is the master stylesheet file that uses <xsl:include> to pull in the component files it needs to assemble a complete stylesheet for producing formatting objects. Generating a formatting objects file is only half the process of producing typeset output. You also need an XSL-FO processor such as FOP.

The DocBook fo stylesheet works in a similar manner to the HTML stylesheet. Instead of outputting HTML tags, it outputs text marked up with <fo:*something*> tags. For example, to indicate that some text should be kept in-line and typeset with a monospace font, it might look like the following:

```
<fo:inline-sequence  font-family="monospace">/usr/man</fo:inline-sequence>
```

The templates in docbook/fo/inline.xsl that produce this output for a DocBook <filename> element look like the following:

```
<xsl:template match="filename">
  <xsl:call-template name="inline.monoseq"/>
</xsl:template>

<xsl:template name="inline.monoseq">
  <xsl:param name="content">
    <xsl:apply-templates/>
  </xsl:param>
  <fo:inline-sequence font-family="monospace">
    <xsl:copy-of select="$content"/>
  </fo:inline-sequence>
</xsl:template>
```

There are dozens of XSL-FO tags and attributes specified in the XSL standard. It is beyond the scope of this document to cover how all of them are used in the DocBook stylesheets. Fortunately, this is only an intermediate format that you probably will not have to deal with very much directly unless you are writing your own stylesheets.

Appendix B. Debugging XSL stylesheets

If you are customizing the stylesheets, there will be times when your changes do not produce the results you expected. To find out what is going wrong, you will need to go through a debugging process. Here are methods you can use.

Inserting messages

The simplest debugging technique is to output debugging messages from specific locations in the templates to tell you what is going on. A message can report the value of a variable or parameter, or list the content of the element currently being processed. That information will help you decide if your code is doing the right thing.

You use the `xsl:message` element to output a debugging message. The content of that element does not go to the standard output where it would mix in with your HTML or FO output. Instead, it goes to the error output (called standard error on Unix). The message can contain plain text, and it can contain XSL elements that generate output. The following is an example that reports the value of a parameter:

```
<xsl:message>In lists.xsl (match="itemizedlist"), the value of the
css.decoration parameter is <xsl:value-of select="$css.decoration"/>
</xsl:message>
```

The text provides the context for the message, and the `xsl:value-of` element outputs the value of the parameter.

Here are some hints for using this method:

- Be sure to include enough context in the message so you know where it is coming from. The order of processing by XSLT is often not intuitive, and may not follow the order of the document. Since the messages are in an output stream separate from the content, it will not be obvious where a message is coming from unless you indicate such. There is no provision in the XSL standard for indicating line numbers of either the input file or the stylesheet.

- If you need to know the name of the current element being processed, then include something like the following:

  ```
  <xsl:value-of select="local-name(.)"/>
  ```

- If you need to know the value of an attribute on the current element, then include something like the following:

  ```
  <xsl:value-of select="@valign"/>
  ```

  If the element currently being processed does not have that attribute, then this will be blank.

- If you want to know the content of the element being processed, you can do this:

  ```
  <xsl:value-of select="."/>
  ```

  When `xsl:value-of` selects an element, you get the text content of the element and its children, without any markup. If the element has no text (such as `imagedata`), then there is no output.

- Any extra whitespace (spaces, tabs, line breaks) in a message is collapsed to single spaces. If you want to insert a line break or indents in your message, use `xsl:text`. In this example, the message will be output on two lines with the second line indented. Since the second line break is after the closing tag of `xsl:text`, it is not preserved as a line break. Note that you cannot include other elements inside `xsl:text`, so it has to end before the `xsl:value-of`.

```
<xsl:message><xsl:text>In lists.xsl (match="itemizedlist"), the value
   of the css.decoration parameter is </xsl:text>
 <xsl:value-of select="$css.decoration"/></xsl:message>
```

- do not insert your messages in the original DocBook stylesheet files. Copy the XSL file you want to modify to a different location and include it in a customization layer. When you have solved the problem you can just delete the modified file, leaving your original stylesheet files intact.

  Note:

  If you are using MSXML 3.0 as your processor, then your messages will be ignored unless you add the optional `terminate="yes"` attribute to your `xsl:message`, which terminates processing.

If you need your message to be inline with your output, then use `xsl:comment` instead of `xsl:message`. That will insert your message into your output, marked as a comment:

```
<!-- This is my message -->
```

Using an XSLT debugger

If you do a lot of stylesheet customization, investing time and money in an XSLT debugger might be worthwhile. Several XSLT debuggers are available that let you trace through your stylesheet processing to quickly find the source of a problem. Here is a sample of what is available.

Komodo[1]	Komodo is a commercial product from ActiveState. It is a multilanguage IDE for Linux or Windows that includes support for XSLT debugging.
oXygen[2]	oXygen is a commercial product from SyncRO Soft Ltd. It is a graphical XML editor and XSLT debugger. It is written in Java, so it runs on all platforms.
Stylus Studio[3]	Stylus Studio is a commercial product from Sonic Software. It is a complete XML authoring environment for Windows, including a graphical XSLT debugger.
WebSphere Studio Application Developer[4]	WebSphere Studio Application Developer is a commercial product from IBM. It is a multilanguage IDE for Linux or Windows that includes support for XSLT debugging.
XMLSpy[5]	XMLSpy is a commercial product from Altova. It is a complete graphical XML development environment that includes an XSLT debugger.
XSLT-process[6]	XSLT-process is a minor mode for GNU Emacs/XEmacs which gives it XSLT processing and debugging capabilities.

Before committing serious money to one of these debuggers, make sure it will work with the DocBook XSL stylesheets. The DocBook stylesheets exercise most of the XSLT spec, so a debugger has to be highly conformant. For example,

---

[1] http://www.activestate.com/Products/Komodo/
[2] http://www.oxygenxml.com/
[3] http://www.stylusstudio.com/
[4] http://www-306.ibm.com/software/awdtools/developer/application/
[5] http://www.xmlspy.com/
[6] http://xslt-process.sourceforge.net/

Stylus Studio's default XSLT processor does not handle DocBook, but you can instead select the Saxon processor in Stylus Studio and it does work.

Also check for support for XSL extensions. DocBook XSL makes use of two kinds: *EXSLT*[7] extensions and Java extensions. For example, the chunk.xsl stylesheet must use an XSL extension function to generate multiple output files from a single input file. Saxon and Xalan each have such a function, and other processors can use the EXSLT document() function. If a debugger does not support one of these extensions, then you cannot debug the chunking process. For example, any debugger based on MSXML will not work for chunking because it does not support Java or EXSLT extensions.

---

[7] http://www-3.ibm.com/software/awdtools/studioappdev/

Glossary

admonition	One of the following DocBook elements: note, important, caution, warning, or tip.
alt text	Brief text associated with an image, to be displayed when the image cannot be displayed. Often stored in the ALT attribute of an HTML img element.
ancestor element	In an XML element hierarchy, any element that contains the current element, with any number of intervening containers.
aspect ratio	The ratio of width to height of an image.
attribute set	A collection of attribute names and values that can be assigned a name and used as a group. See the section called "Attribute sets" (page 103) for more information.
body font	The font used for the ordinary text of a document.
callout	Explanatory text associated with a particular part of an image or text display. Often labeled with *callout bugs* on the image and explanation. See the section called "Callouts" (page 447) for more information.
callout bug	Graphical or numeric marker used to key a particular callout explanation to its associated location in an image or text display.
CALS table	An SGML standard for table element names and structure developed by the U.S. military. The CALS table tags were adopted for use in DocBook.
catalog	A file that provides a mapping of identifiers to actual file locations to be used in the current process. The identifiers could be *PUBLIC* or *SYSTEM identifiers* for DTDs or system entities, as well as URIs for stylesheet files. The file locations being mapped to can be local directory paths or URIs. See Chapter 5, *XML catalogs* (page 47) for more information.
CDATA	Text that is meant to be interpreted as containing no XML markup. All characters are taken literally, which means the < character is not interpreted to indicate the start of an XML element, and the & character is not interpreted as the start of an entity reference.
character entity	An *entity* that represents a single character. A character entity can be expressed with a name such as ™, as a decimal number such as ê, or as a hexadecimal number such as ⍄.
child element	An element contained by the current element, with no intervening containers.
chunking	The process of generating multiple HTML files (chunks) from a single DocBook document. See the section called "Chunking into multiple HTML files" (page 62) for more information.
component	In DocBook, a class of elements that make up the parts of a book. The class includes chapter, appendix, preface, dedication, colophon, article, bibliography, glossary, and index.

CSS	Cascading Stylesheets, a *W3C* standard for HTML stylesheets.
customization layer	An XSL stylesheet that layers customization changes on top of the existing DocBook XSL templates, without altering the original stylesheet files. See the section called "Customization layer" (page 100) for more information.
descendant element	In an XML element hierarchy, any element that is contained by the current element, with any number of intervening containers.
division	In DocBook, a class of elements that make up the highest levels of document hierarchy. The class includes set, book, part, and reference.
DOCTYPE	A declaration at the start of an XML document that identifies the document's *root element* and *DTD*.
document	In DocBook, a well-formed or valid XML document, with a single *root element* that contains the document's content.
DTD	Document Type Definition, which declares a set of XML element names and how they can be used in a document.
encoding	A mapping of numerical codes to visible character glyphs. Examples include UTF-8 and ISO-8859-1 among many others. See the section called "Document encoding" (page 325) for more information.
entity	A declaration that maps a name to some specific bit of information in XML. There are several kinds of entities: character entities, general entities, parameter entities, and system entities. An entity must be declared before it can be referenced.
entity reference	The usage of an *entity* in a document or DTD. An entity reference consists of an ampersand, followed by an entity name, followed by a semicolon, such as `&trade;` for example.
EXSLT	A community initiative to provide extensions to XSLT.
external subset	The parts of a DTD defined in a separate file that is referenced by the PUBLIC and SYSTEM identifiers in a document's `DOCTYPE` declaration.
float	An object such as a graphic or table that can float out of the normal flow of text to a new position on a printed page.
FO	Formatting Objects, the part of the XSL standard used for specifying typesetting instructions. Also known as XSL-FO.
FO processor	See XSL-FO processor.
footer	In DocBook, the text or graphics that appears at the bottom of a printed page or HTML page.
formal	In DocBook, a class of display elements that contain a title and is usually numbered. The class includes figure, table, example, and equation.
fragment identifier	That part of a URL that appears after the # symbol. It points to an internal location within the resource.

general entity | An *entity* that can contain ordinary text, elements, and entity references. Often used to define commonly used strings.

gentext | In DocBook, the system for generating text not present in the document, such as Chapter 3 or Table of Contents. The gentext system supports multiple languages. See the section called "Generated text" (page 105) for more information.

glyph | A displayable character.

hanging indent | A format style that puts a small amount of text hanging out in the left margin, while the main body is indented to make room for it. Used primarily for variablelist elements.

header | In DocBook, the text or graphics that appears at the top of a printed page or HTML page.

i18n | An abbreviation of the word *internationalization* (i, followed by 18 letters, followed by n).

id | In DocBook, the attribute that is used as a unique identifier of an element, for the purpose of cross referencing. This attribute value may also play a role in generating *chunked* HTML filenames.

import precedence | In XSL, the rules governing which of several candidate templates, from the current stylesheet and any imported stylesheets, that could apply is actually used.

informal | In DocBook, a class of display elements that do not have a title and are not numbered. The class includes informaltable, informalfigure, informalexample, and informalequation.

inline element | A DocBook element that can appear within a line of text. An example is an emphasis element used within the text of a para.

internal subset | The parts of a DTD declared within the DOCTYPE declaration at the beginning of an XML document. The rest of the DTD is declared in the *external subset* of the DTD, which is the DTD file referenced by the PUBLIC and SYSTEM identifiers in the DOCTYPE.

internationalization | The process of enabling software to work with multiple languages. It does not necessarily include translation to multiple languages, it just enables such translations.

l10n | An abbreviation for the word *localization* (the letter L, followed by ten letters, followed by n).

keep | A condition added to an XSL-FO file to keep elements together on a page. A keep-together condition keeps all of an element's children together on a page. A keep-with-next keeps the current element with the following element, and a keep-with-previous keeps the current element with the preceding element.

label | In DocBook, the number associated with a numbered item like a chapter or table. Also sometimes refers to the text associated with the number as well, such as Chapter 3.

localization	The process of translating software into another language. This includes translating text, as well as handling the formatting of information such as dates and currency.
mediaobject	An element in DocBook used to contain several `imageobject` elements, only one of which is used for a given output. See Chapter 18, *Graphics* (page 285) for more information.
modular	In DocBook, the splitting of large documents into several smaller document files. Each modular file can be treated as a small document, and they can be merged back together to form larger documents. See Chapter 23, *Modular DocBook files* (page 359) for more information.
namespace	In XML, the means to support elements from different DTDs in the same document. The set of elements from each DTD is said to occupy its own namespace. An element in a given namespace can be identified by assigning a namespace prefix that is attached to element names, as for example `fo:inline`.
namespace name	The URI that identifies a namespace uniquely. For example, `http://docbook.org/ns/docbook`. There is no requirement that any content actually reside at that URI's network address.
namespace prefix	A text string assigned as an element name prefix to a namespace. When an element name is preceded by the prefix and a colon, then that element is in that assigned namespace.
OASIS	Organization for the Advancement of Structured Information Standards, responsible for the development and maintenance of the DocBook DTD.
output encoding	The name of the character encoding used for output files generated by the stylesheet. Examples include utf-8 and iso-8859-1. See Also encoding.
page class	In the DocBook print stylesheets, the name of any of several kinds of page designs. The supported page class names include titlepage, lot, front, body, back, and index.
page master	In XSL-FO, the specifications for a single design for a page. Typically a *page class* will have four page masters for first, odd, even, and blank pages used within the class.
parameter	In XSL, a named value that affects the behavior of the processing. DocBook XSL defines dozens of stylesheet parameters, which can be reset to different values from the command line or a customization layer.
parameter entity	An entity used exclusively within a DTD, never in a document.
parent element	The element containing the current element, with no intervening container elements.
#PCDATA	Ordinary text without any XML element tags.
PDF	Portable Document Format, a file format for electronic documents that can be printed with accurate page fidelity.
PI	Abbreviation for processing instruction.

placeholder

In DocBook XSL, a defined but empty template. Such templates can be redefined in a customization layer, and they are called or applied automatically at the appropriate time.

processing instruction

An XML construct that can be used to embed hidden instructions in a document. Such instructions can provide information to a processor to affect the processor behavior or to apply formatting that cannot be specified with elements or attribute values.

profiling

The act of selecting conditional text in a document to create a version for a given user profile. See Chapter 26, *Profiling (conditional text)* (page 427) for more information.

PUBLIC identifier

A unique identifier for a DTD or system entity. It adheres to the standard for PUBLIC identifier syntax and is usually resolved using a catalog.

recto

The front side of a double-sided printed page. Appears on the right side of an open bound book.

root element

In an XML document, the single element that contains all the content of the document.

run-in title

A title that appears as the first part of a paragraph, with the text of the paragraph starting after the title but on the same line as the title.

SGML

Standard Generalized Markup Language, the predecessor to XML.

side float

A block of content that is positioned out of line to the side of the printed page.

soft page break

A processing instruction that creates a conditional page break. If the conditions are not satisfied, then the page does not break. This differs from a hard page break, which is not conditional.

SourceForge

Website that contains many open source projects, including the DocBook XSL stylesheets.

stylesheet parameter

See parameter.

stylesheet module

A file containing some XSL templates and/or parameters. An XSL stylesheet can be split among several files, and assembled using `xsl:include` and `xsl:import`. Each file is a module of the entire stylesheet.

SVG

Scalable Vector Graphic, a graphic file format written in XML for images that scale smoothly to different sizes. See the section called "SVG images" (page 300) for more information.

system entity

An entity that identifies another file that is to be included when the entity is referenced.

SYSTEM identifier

A URI address for locating a DTD or system identifier.

target database

A database of `id`-related information collected from documents. The information can be used to form cross references between documents using `olink`. See Chapter 24, *Olinking between documents* (page 383) for more information.

template	In DocBook XSL, there are three distinct kinds of templates: XSL, gentext, and titlepage templates. *XSLT* templates perform the main transformation of content. *Gentext* templates define generated text produced by the stylesheets. *Titlepage* templates define what information appears on title pages, and in what order.
TeX	Open-source typesetting system, used in the PassiveTeX FO processor.
text entity	See general entity.
title page	In DocBook, the subsystem that handles the title and other info elements at the beginning of a division or component. In many cases, a title page is not a separate page.
TOC	Table of contents.
Unicode	International encoding standard that provides a superset of many separate encodings.
UTF-8	One of the optional encodings of Unicode. Uses a variable number of bytes in the encoding for different character ranges.
validation	Process that determines if an XML document conforms to its DTD.
vector graphic	Graphical image based on a mathematical specification of geometric elements. Vector graphics scale cleanly to any size.
verso	The back side of a double-sided printed page. Appears on the left side of an open bound book.
viewport	The space in a document presentation that is reserved for an image. The viewport can be larger than the image, leaving extra space around it. Or it can be smaller than the image, clipping the edges. See the section called " Image sizing" (page 290) for more information.
W3C	Worldwide Web Consortium, which develops industry standards for XML and other areas.
Website	In DocBook, the extension of DocBook that can generate a set of HTML pages that make up a website. See Chapter 31, *Website* (page 501) for more information.
well-formed	An XML document that follows all the rules of XML, but has not necessarily been validated against a DTD.
XHTML	A reformulation of HTML to conform to the XML specification.
XInclude	A processing model and syntax for including content from other sources in an XML document. See the section called "Using XInclude" (page 359) for more information.
XLink	A W3C standard for forming links between XML documents.
XPath	A language for addressing parts of an XML document, designed to be used by XSLT.

XSL

Extensible Stylesheet Language, a language for expressing stylesheets in XML syntax. Includes *XSLT* and *XSL-FO*.

XSLT

XSL Transformation, a language for transforming XML documents into other XML documents, HTML, or text.

XSLT processor

Software component that applies an XSL stylesheet to an XML document to produce output in the form of XML, HTML, or text.

XSL-FO

XSL Formatting Objects, a language for expressing formatting semantics using an XML vocabulary.

XSL-FO processor

Software component that converts an XSL-FO document into a formatted document.

Index

Z

Colophon

Production notes:

This book was produced using the tools described herein. The book is written in DocBook XML, version 4.5 of the DTD. The XSL-FO is generated using xsltproc and a stylesheet customization layer that was written using the methods described in this book. The PDF was generated using RenderX's XEP. The book uses Palatino as the body font (except for this page), Tahoma as the title font, and Lucida Sans-Typewriter as the monospace font.

Errata:

An errata sheet for this book is maintained at the publisher's website. You can access the current errata sheet at *http://www.sagehill.net/book-errata.html*.

Feedback welcome:

If you have comments, suggestions, or corrections for this book, please send them by email to `info@sagehill.net`. Sorry, we cannot debug your stylesheet customizations for you. As fun as that is, there are just too many of them out there.

LaVergne, TN USA
17 March 2010
176282LV00005B/6/A